PICASSO & RIVERA

PICASSO

CONVERSATIONS

LOS ANGELES COUNTY MUSEUM OF ART | MUSEO DEL PALACIO DE BELLAS ARTES

DELMONICO BOOKS · PRESTEL
MUNICH · LONDON · NEW YORK

Curated by JUAN RAFAEL CORONEL RIVERA, MICHAEL GOVAN,
DIANA MAGALONI, JAMES OLES, *and* JENNIFER STAGER
with assistance by LILLY CASILLAS

RIVERA ACROSS TIME

Edited by DIANA MAGALONI *and* MICHAEL GOVAN
with contributions by
ÉMILIE BOUVARD, LILLY CASILLAS, JUAN RAFAEL CORONEL RIVERA,
MICHAEL GOVAN, MICHELE GREET, PATRICIA LEIGHTEN,
DIANA MAGALONI, CAMILLE MATHIEU, ITZEL A. RODRÍGUEZ MORTELLARO,
JAMES OLES, *and* JENNIFER STAGER

PICASSO | RIVERA

1881–96

Pablo Ruiz y Picasso is born on October 25, 1881, in Málaga, Spain. His first word is said to be "piz," for *lapiz* (pencil). The family moves to La Coruña in 1891, where his father, Don José Ruiz y Blasco, teaches at the Da Guarda Art School. Talented beyond his years, Picasso enrolls in the school in 1892 and would later boast that "at the age of twelve I drew like Raphael." The family relocates to Barcelona in September 1895 and Picasso enrolls in the School of Fine Arts, known as La Llotja, where his father has accepted a teaching post.

1897–99

Picasso's family encourages him to continue his studies at Spain's most prestigious art academy, the San Fernando Royal Academy in Madrid; he is accepted and moves to Madrid in October 1897. Rebelling against the rigidity of the instruction, he drops out of the academy eight months later. After contracting scarlet fever, he returns to Barcelona; that summer he visits his friend Manuel Pallarès in Horta de Ebro (Horta de San Juan) to recuperate. In February 1899, Picasso returns to Barcelona, becoming a regular at Els Quatre Gats, a central meeting place for the city's bohemians and modernists.

1900–1903

Picasso travels to Paris for the first time with his friend Carlos Casagemas for the Exposition Universelle in October 1900, where his painting *Last Moments* (subsequently painted over) is exhibited at the Spanish Pavilion. During this trip, he meets dealers Berthe Weill and Pedro Mañach. Weill is the first French dealer to sell Picasso's work (she is also the first to exhibit Matisse and will give Diego Rivera his only solo exhibition in Paris). In December, Picasso travels with Casagemas to Barcelona and Málaga, after which Casagemas returns to Paris and Picasso returns to Madrid.

Following Casagemas's suicide in February 1901, Picasso returns to Paris in May (via Barcelona in April). Mañach arranges Picasso's first exhibition at the prestigious Galerie Vollard in June; Ambroise Vollard becomes one of Picasso's main dealers, until Vollard's death in 1939. Picasso paints two works concerning Casagemas's death.

Picasso returns to Barcelona in January 1902 and fully enters his Blue Period, during which he continues to portray the life of the oppressed, including prostitutes, beggars, prisoners, and struggling artists (the latter depicted, for example, in *Portrait of Sebastià Junyer Vidal*, in which his close friend is shown with a prostitute at a café). He exhibits most of his Blue Period works at Berthe Weill's gallery.

1886–1906

Diego Rivera is born on December 8, 1886, to a well-to-do family in Guanajuato, Mexico. The family moves to Mexico City in 1892. In 1897, having already shown a talent for drawing, he enrolls in the prestigious Academy of San Carlos, which follows the European academic model that emphasizes classical art and training.

Although he is a model student, Rivera later recalls feeling repelled by the strict curriculum: "The further I progressed in the academic European forms, the less I liked them and the more I was drawn to the old Mexican art. I particularly detested having to copy engraved replicas and plaster casts." He also recalls visiting the Sala de Monolitos (Hall of Monoliths) at the Museo Nacional in Mexico City, where he first cultivates an admiration for Aztec sculpture.

NOTE TO THE READER

This chronology focuses primarily on the time frame and themes of the exhibition *Picasso and Rivera: Conversations Across Time*. It is not intended as a comprehensive summary of the lives and careers of the artists.

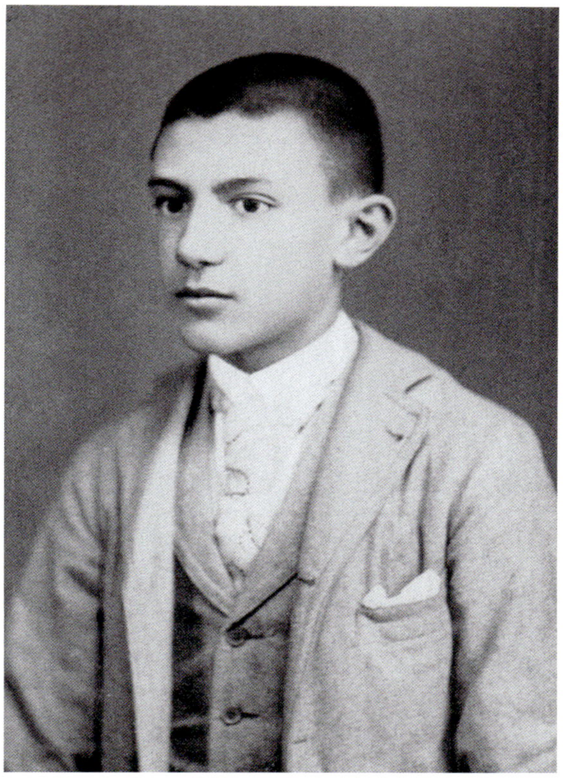

CHRONOLOGY

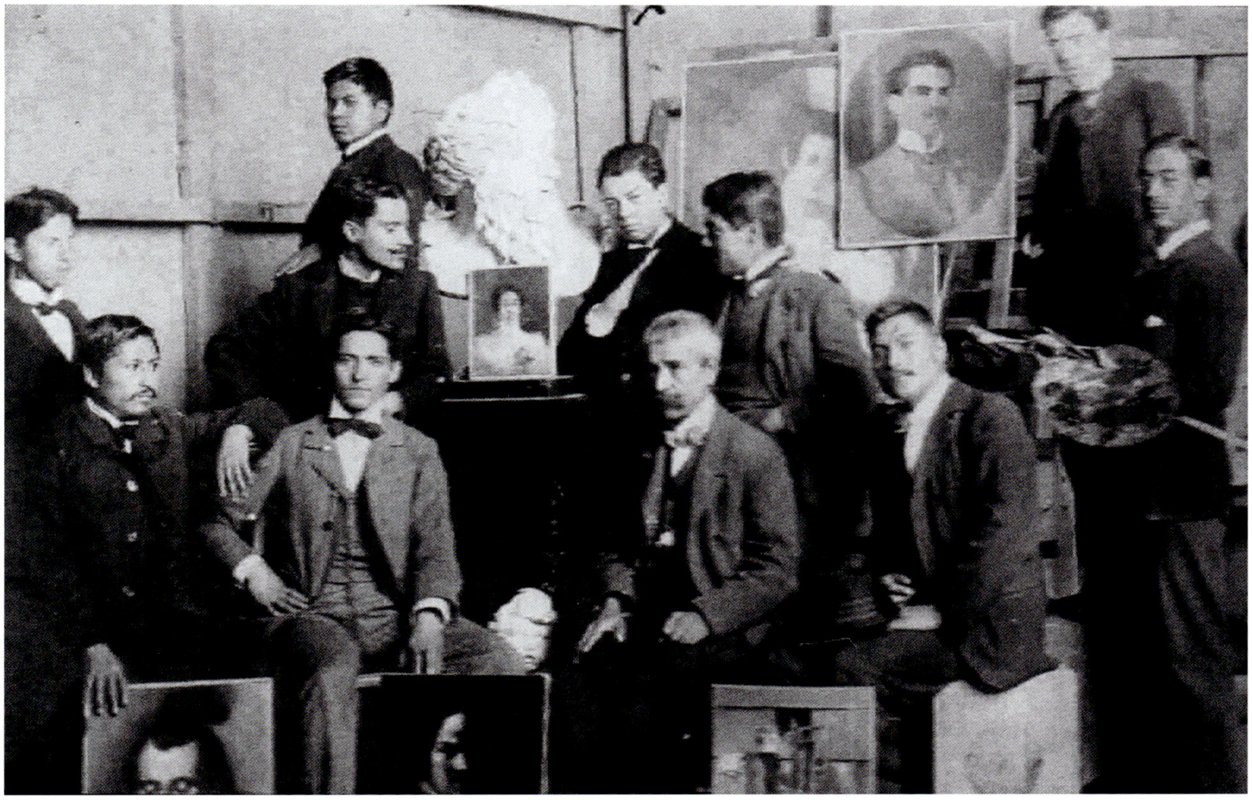

TOP Pablo Picasso, 1896; BOTTOM Diego Rivera (back row, center) at the Academy of San Carlos, 1902

PICASSO

1904–5

Accompanied by Sebastià Junyer Vidal, Picasso settles in Paris permanently. Picasso rents a studio in Montmartre at the Bateau-Lavoir, an apartment building popular with artists and writers. Poet and art critic Guillaume Apollinaire is among Picasso's many neighbors, and the two become close friends. By winter, Picasso's work begins a transition from blue to rose tones.

In 1905, Picasso exhibits his first Rose Period paintings at the Galeries Serrurier. Many of the works feature circus themes and Commedia dell'Arte entertainers, including the harlequin character that will fascinate him for the rest of his life.

1906

At the Louvre, Picasso views ancient Iberian artifacts recently excavated from the Cerro de los Santos and Osuna sites, the latter located near his native Andalucía. He is inspired by these works to explore the sculptural constructions of the head and face, adapting the masklike features for numerous paintings, including self-portraits and *Portrait of Gertrude Stein*.

Picasso spends the summer in Gósol, Catalonia, where he paints a series of works of local peasants in a manner reflecting ancient Iberian sculpture, as in *Woman with Loaves*. After his return from Gósol, Picasso tells Apollinaire that he is ready to create work that will "free art from its shackles."

1907

In March, Picasso purchases two Iberian stone heads from Honoré Joseph Géry Pieret, Apollinaire's secretary, who (unbeknownst to Picasso) had stolen them from the Louvre. During the summer, Picasso visits the Musée d'Ethnographie du Trocadéro to view African sculpture. Inspired by Iberian and African sculptures, Picasso paints his groundbreaking masterpiece, *Les Demoiselles d'Avignon*. In March, he meets Georges Braque.

1908–9

Picasso visits La Rue des Bois in August 1908, returning to Paris by September. His work begins to be influenced by Cézanne. During the winter of 1908–9, Picasso begins working closely with Braque as they both enter their Cubist periods, later reminiscing: "Almost every evening, either I went to Braque's studio or Braque came to mine. Each of us had to see what the other was doing during the day." Returning to Horta de Ebro in the summer of 1909, Picasso's work makes the radical move of "opening" the outlines of forms, increasing the degree of abstraction.

RIVERA

1906–7

Rivera begins exhibiting in group shows in 1906. That same year, he secures a small stipend from Teodoro Dehesa, the governor of Veracruz, and is able to travel to Madrid in early 1907 for an apprenticeship with realist painter Eduardo Chicharro. Once in Madrid, he enrolls in the San Fernando Royal Academy; while studying the old masters, he also yearns to join the avant-garde movement in Paris.

1909

Rivera travels to Paris early in the year with his friend, Spanish novelist Ramón del Valle-Inclán. He revels in Paris, exploring the Louvre, engaging in heated conversations in the cafes of Montparnasse, and painting in the open air by the Seine. In the summer, he visits London, Belgium, and the Netherlands. In Bruges, he meets Russian artist Angelina Beloff; they set up residence in Paris late in the year.

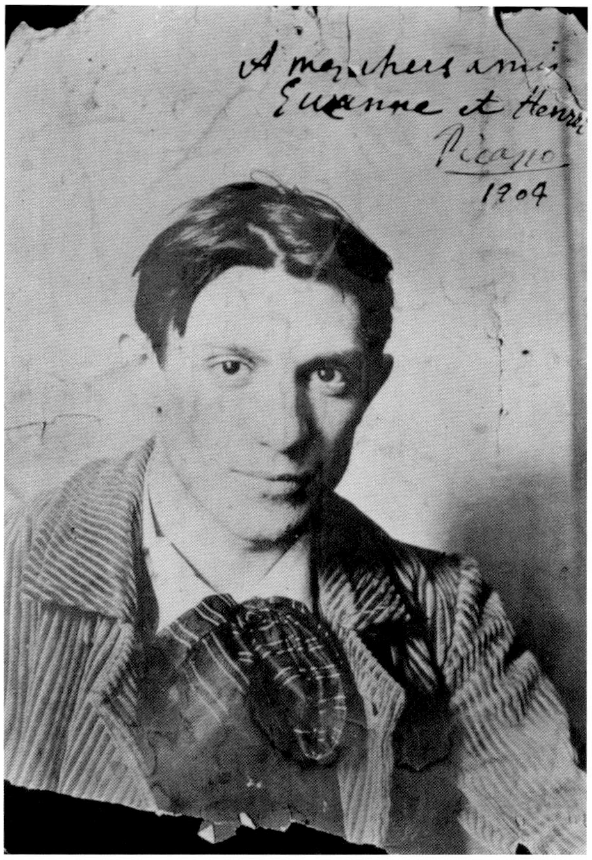

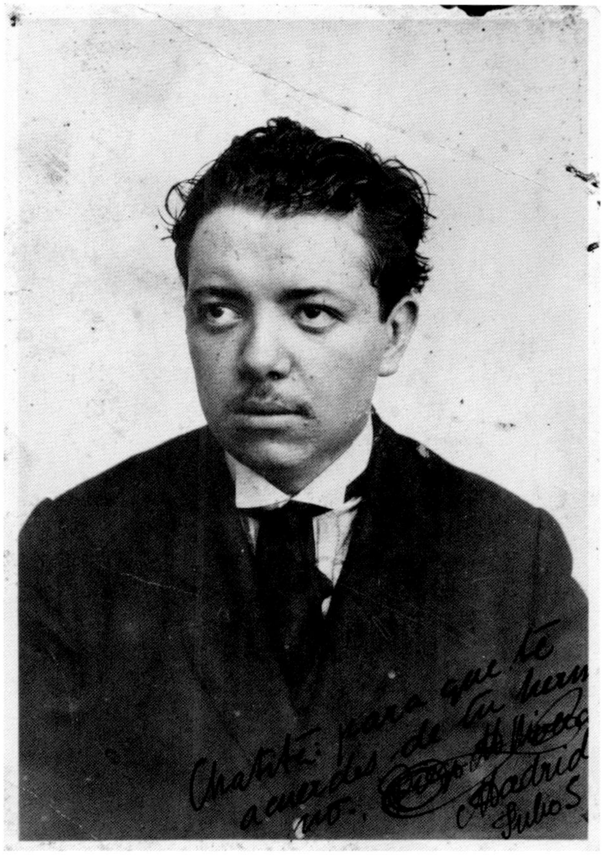

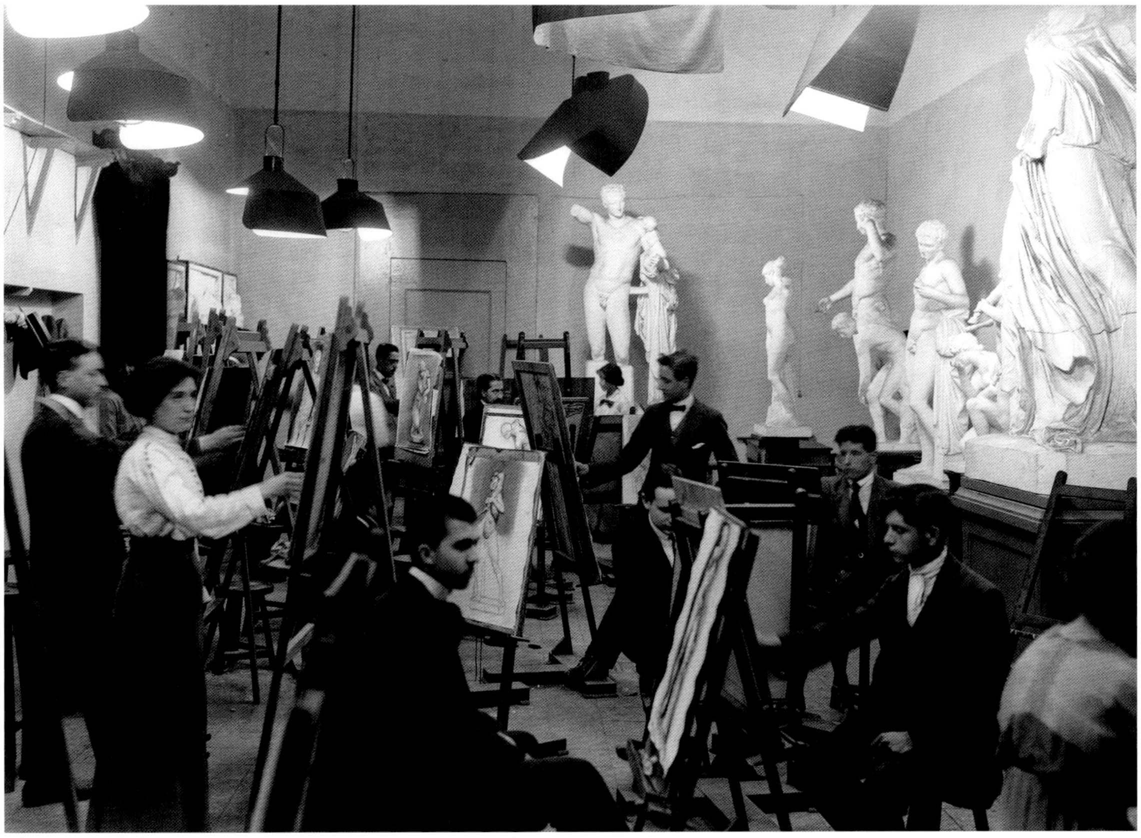

TOP LEFT Pablo Picasso, Paris, 1904 (photo by Ricardo Canals); TOP RIGHT Diego Rivera, c. 1904; BOTTOM Drawing class in La Llotja, Barcelona, Spain, 1914

PICASSO

1910–11

Picasso's work becomes increasingly abstract, with figures that are almost unrecognizable.

In March 1911, Picasso exhibits in the United States for the first time, with a solo show at Alfred Stieglitz's gallery 291 in New York. An article by Mexican gallerist Marius de Zayas, who will later exhibit Rivera in 1916, is published in the exhibition catalogue.

Picasso and Braque spend the summer of 1911 in Céret, in the French Pyrenees, producing paintings that art historian John Golding would later assert are the "culmination and perfection of this particular phase in Cubism."

In August 1911, French newspapers publish news of the theft of the *Mona Lisa* from the Louvre, which Géry Pieret boasts to have stolen. To avoid being implicated in the crime, in September Picasso and Apollinaire, with the help of André Salmon, return the Iberian heads Picasso had purchased from Géry Pieret to the museum.

1912–13

Picasso veers away from total abstraction. His work during this time includes recognizable motifs, letters, words, and numbers, resulting in a new trompe l'oeil aesthetic play in tension with abstraction. In spring 1912, he creates his first collage, and in the fall he and Braque create their first *papiers collés*. Soon thereafter, he reintroduces color and creates his first three-dimensional collage, an innovative sculptural concept called "assemblage." He continues to explore many of these new ideas through 1913.

In December 1912, he signs an exclusive three-year contract with Daniel-Henry Kahnweiler.

1914

In February or March 1914, Picasso and Rivera meet and establish their friendship. Rivera recounts that Picasso saw several of his recently finished Cubist works in this first meeting.

Following the outbreak of war in August 1914, many members of the Parisian avant-garde either volunteer or are conscripted into military service (including Braque, Apollinaire, Raymond Duchamp-Villon, André Derain, and Fernand Léger). Picasso remains in Paris, along with Rivera and fellow Spaniard Juan Gris. During the war years, Picasso and Rivera paint many Cubist works but also create drawings influenced by French Neoclassical painter Jean-Auguste-Dominique Ingres.

RIVERA

1910

In March, Rivera participates in the Sixteenth Exhibition of the Société des Indépendants in Paris.

In October, Rivera makes his first visit back to Mexico City; in November he holds his first solo exhibition at his alma mater, the Academy of San Carlos, as part of the centennial celebration of Mexico's Independence from Spain. That same month a group of dissidents, led by Francisco Madero, revolt against Porfirio Díaz's regime, marking the beginning of the Mexican Revolution.

1911–12

In June 1911, Rivera returns to Paris and moves to Montparnasse with Beloff. He travels frequently between Paris and Toledo, Spain, throughout 1912. In Toledo, he begins to develop an interest in Cubism.

1913

By 1913, Rivera paints his first Cubist work, *The Adoration of the Virgin and Child*, revealing an increasing interest in his engagement with Cézanne, Picasso, and El Greco. He later recalls that by this point, "everything about the [Cubist] movement fascinated and intrigued me."

Rivera exhibits throughout the year. In January, he exhibits work in the Fourth Exhibition of the Free Group at Galerie Bernheim Jeune, a show that is notably reviewed by influential critics Guillaume Apollinaire and Louis Vauxcelles. In March, he participates in the Salon des Indépendants in Paris, and he exhibits work in Munich and Vienna. In the fall, he shows again at the Salon des Indépendants.

1914

In February or March, Rivera and Picasso meet through the Chilean painter Manuel Ortíz de Zárate, marking the beginning of their friendship. In April, Rivera opens his only solo show in Paris at the Galerie Berthe Weill, where Picasso held his first Parisian exhibition years earlier.

World War I breaks out in August. As a foreign national, Rivera does not enlist.

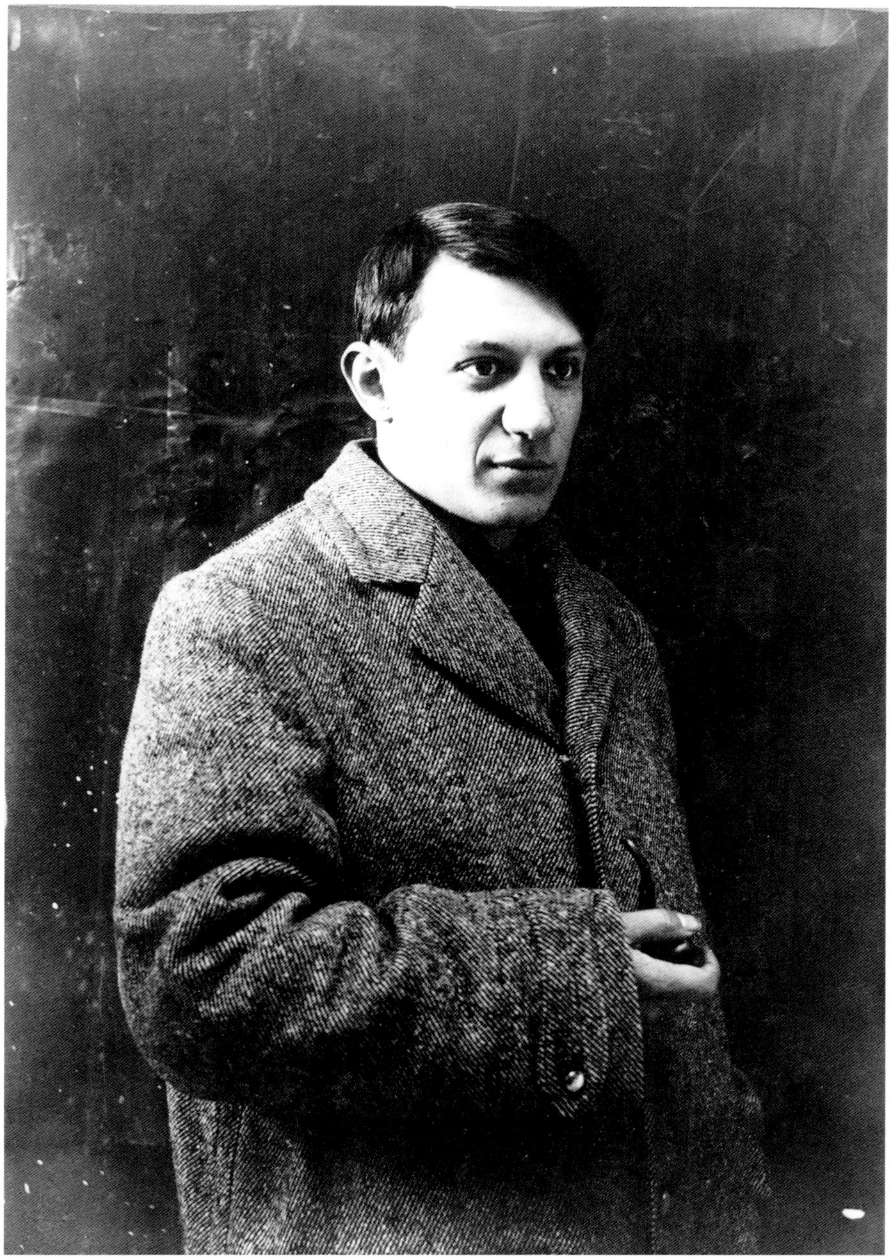

Pablo Picasso, ***Self-Portrait, Paris, Bateau Lavoir***, 1908

PICASSO

1915

In August, Picasso and Rivera quarrel over the authorship of the foliage technique that Rivera uses in *Zapatista Landscape* and that Picasso uses in *Seated Man* (at the time titled *Man Seated in Shrubbery*). Picasso paints over most of the composition that is similar to Rivera's painting, leaving four small rectangular windows into the original shrubbery.

1916–17

Jean Cocteau invites Picasso to work on the set and costumes for Sergei Diaghilev's *Parade* for the Ballets Russes. In February 1917, Picasso travels with the Ballets Russes to Italy to work on developing *Parade*, which opens in Paris in May.

1918

Picasso signs with dealer Paul Rosenberg (Léonce Rosenberg's brother), who will play an important role in bringing Picasso further international recognition.

World War I ends on November 11. Deeply affected by the widespread destruction and human desolation, many avant-garde artists react by setting aside abstraction and Cubism to return to more naturalistic, traditional modes of representation—a period that Jean Cocteau will later term *le rappel à l'ordre* (the return to order).

RIVERA

1915–16

In March 1915, Rivera participates in the first exhibition of Cubist works in Madrid at the Sala de Arte Moderno. He joins other avant-garde artists from Paris, including Robert Delaunay and Jacques Lipchitz, who are seeking refuge from the war.

Rivera returns to Paris and begins one of his most important Cubist works, the painting now called *Zapatista Landscape*. The foliage technique Rivera uses in *Zapatista Landscape* eventually leads to his falling out with Picasso in August.

In February and April 1916, Rivera participates in two group exhibitions at the Modern Gallery in New York, owned by Mexican dealer Marius de Zayas. The Modern Gallery also hosts his solo show in October, when his work is shown alongside ancient Mexican objects for the first time.

In Paris, Rivera signs a two-year contract with Léonce Rosenberg, a leading dealer of the Parisian avant-garde who also represents Picasso.

1917

In March, at a dinner hosted by Rosenberg, a heated argument over the rules of Cubist painting breaks out between Rivera and poet Pierre Reverdy. Known as *l'affaire Rivera*, the conflict ostracizes Rivera from the Cubist milieu.

From April to May, Rivera exhibits two works in the first exhibition by the Society of Independent Artists in New York, where Picasso also exhibits two portraits.

1918

In March, Rivera participates in his last show with the Modern Gallery in New York, along with Picasso, André Derain, Juan Gris, Frank Haviland Burty, and Serge Férat.

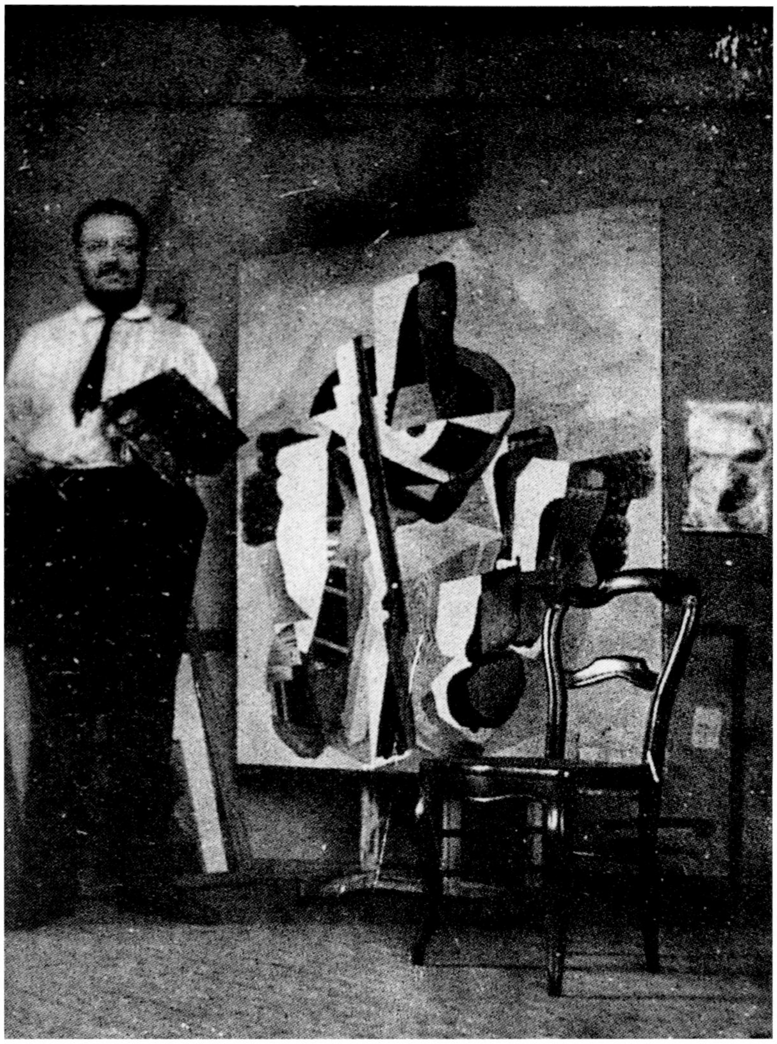

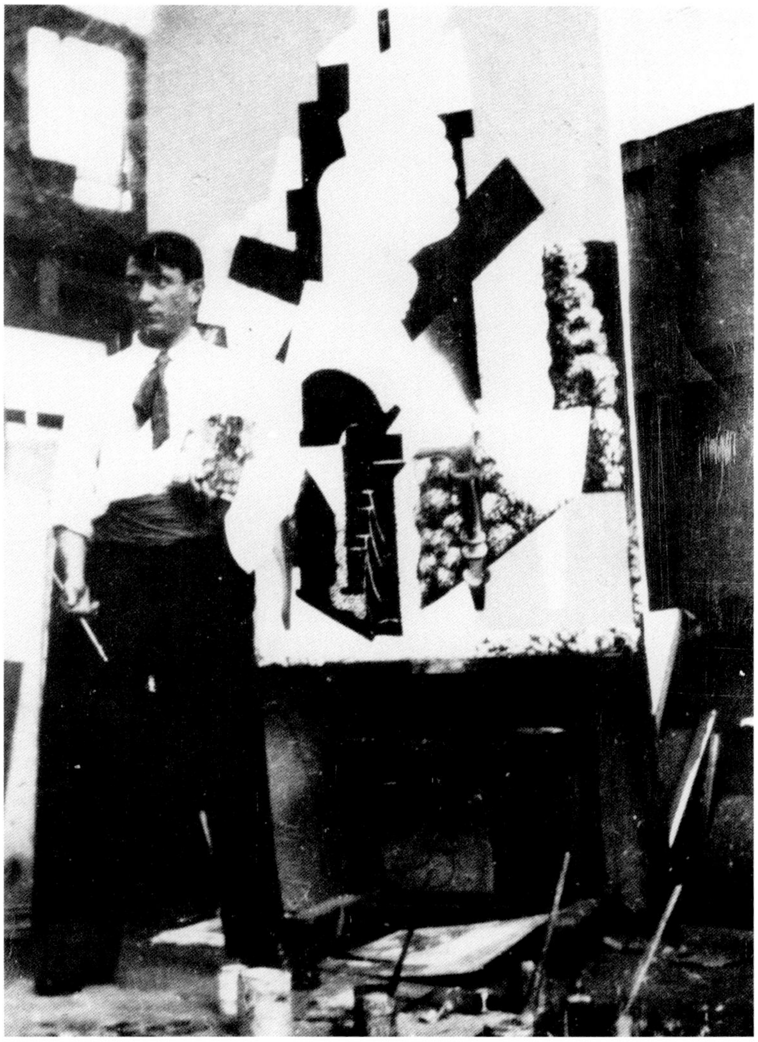

LEFT Diego Rivera in his studio, with ***Zapatista Landscape*** on the easel, 1915; RIGHT Pablo Picasso, ***Self-Portrait with "Seated Man" in Progress***, 1915

PICASSO

1920–23

Picasso explores the power and formal possibilities of recasting classical Greco-Roman sculpture in paintings that transform humble Mediterranean subjects into epic, monumental figures, as in *Three Women at the Spring* (1921) and *La Flûte de Pan* (1923). As he explains to Marius de Zayas in 1923: "To me there is no past or future in art. The art of the Greeks, of the Egyptians, of the great painters who lived in other times, is not an art of the past; perhaps it is more alive today than it ever was."

RIVERA

1920

With a stipend from the Mexican government, Rivera travels to Italy in January to study the great murals of the Renaissance, ultimately staying for seventeen months. He sketches more than three hundred frescoes.

In December he is included in a group exhibition at the Société Anonyme, New York, alongside Picasso, Matisse, Braque, and Juan Gris, among other participants.

Álvaro Obregón is elected president of Mexico on December 1, marking a period of reconstruction after Mexico's bloody civil war.

1921

Rivera returns to Mexico in July. As he later recalls: "My homecoming produced an aesthetic exhilaration which it is impossible to describe. It was as if I were being born anew, born into a new world. All the colors I saw appeared to be heightened; they were clearer, richer, finer and more full of light.... I had the conviction that if I lived a hundred lives I could not exhaust even a fraction of this store of buoyant beauty."

In the fall, José Vasconcelos is appointed minister of public education by President Obregón. Vasconcelos initiates a major, state-sponsored arts program and commissions Rivera's first two murals.

In November, Rivera tours the Maya ruins of Chichén Itzá and Uxmal in the Yucatan Peninsula. That same month, he joins the Mexican Communist Party. He visits the Isthmus of Tehuantepec, Oaxaca, in December.

1922

In an interview with *El Universal*, Rivera states the purpose of his return to his homeland: "I wanted to study popular art and the ruins of our amazing past in order to clarify certain notions of art, certain projects I have; if I can realize them, they will undoubtedly give a broad new sense to my work."

1923

In March, Rivera begins the six-year project of painting his Ministry of Public Education murals. In June, he signs the "Manifesto of Mexican Painters," along with fellow members of the newly formed Revolutionary Union of Technical Workers, Painters and Sculptors. It professes: "We proclaim at this time of social change the creators of beauty must use their best efforts to produce ideological works for the people: Art must no longer be the expression of individual satisfaction, which it is today, but should become a fighting educative art for all."

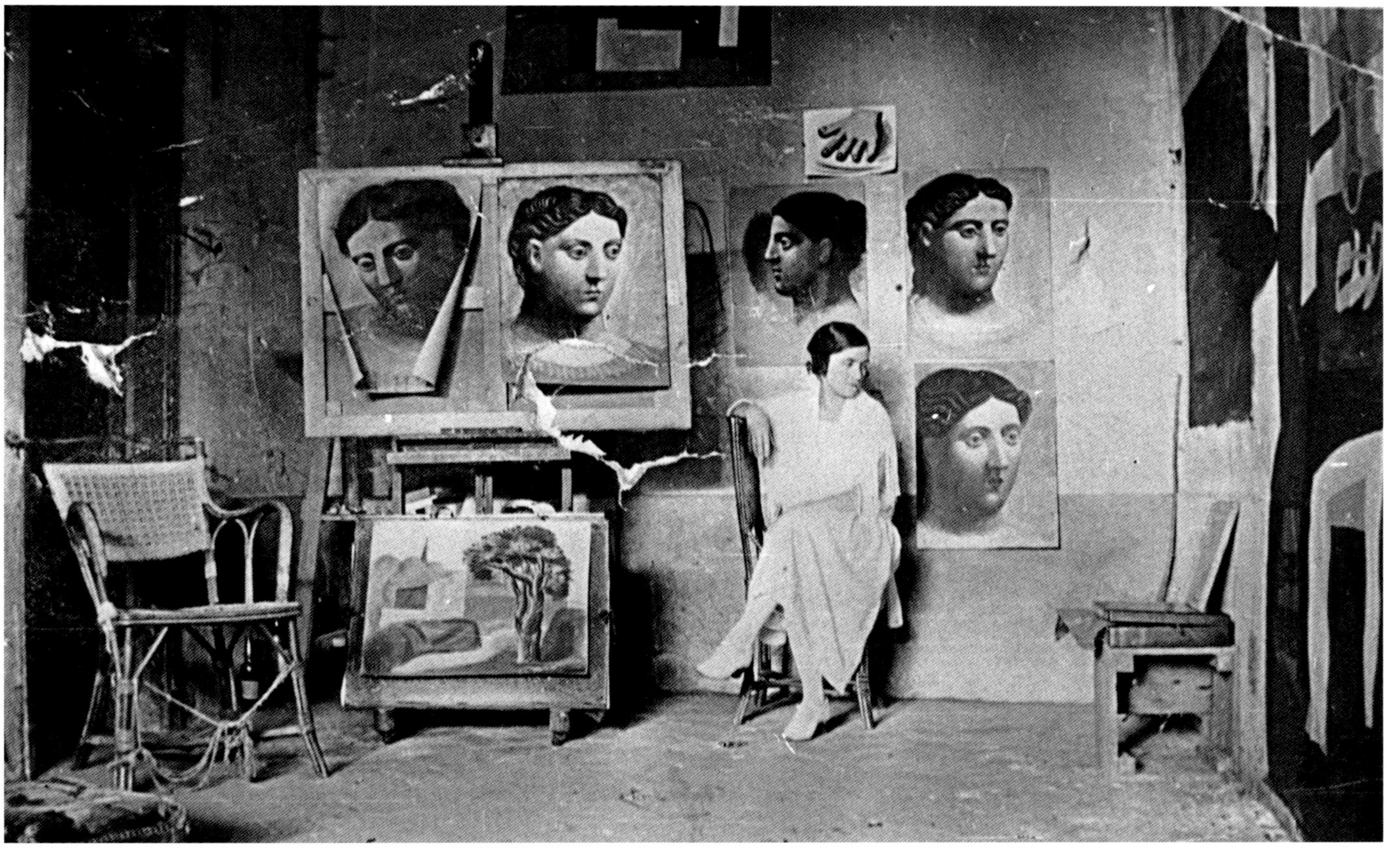

Pablo Picasso, ***Olga Picasso in the Fontainebleau Studio,*** Autumn 1921

PICASSO

1924–27

Picasso is celebrated by André Breton and the Surrealist movement; he is featured in numerous issues of the journal *La Révolution surréaliste* and is included in the first Surrealist group exhibition, *La Peinture Surrealiste*.

1928

Drawing on Greek mythology, Picasso produces his first works on the theme of the Minotaur, which represents a polarity of beauty and monstrosity that he identifies within himself.

1930

Swiss publisher Albert Skira commissions Picasso to illustrate a new edition of Ovid's *Metamorphoses*. The book, comprising thirty etchings, is published in October 1931.

1933

Picasso returns to the Minotaur motif for the cover of issue 1/2 of the Surrealist review *Minotaure*, which also features an article about Picasso by André Breton. Breton's text is first to mention the etchings (including *The Sculptor in His Studio*, *The Artist and His Model*, and *The Blind Minotaur*) that will later be collected as the Vollard Suite.

RIVERA

1925

Rivera's *Flower Day* wins first prize in the First Pan-American Exhibition of Oil Paintings organized by the Los Angeles Museum of History, Science and Art (today the Los Angeles County Museum of Art).

1926

Rivera paints the coat-of-arms for the Quetzalcóatl Rosicrucian Brotherhood, which he joined in 1921. In this painting, he directly references a roof ornament with Tlaloc emblem (p. 112) that was excavated by the Mexican archaeologist Leopoldo Batres and his team in 1905 during the first major excavation of the ancient city of Teotihuacán.

1929

Rivera is expelled from the Mexican Communist Party for his support of Leon Trotsky, who had been forced into exile by the Soviet Union the preceding year.

Rivera marries Frida Kahlo in August.

1931

Rivera creates illustrations for the Popol Vuh, the ancient K'iche' Maya creation myth.

In December, the Museum of Modern Art in New York presents a retrospective of Rivera's work, making him only the second artist to have a solo show there. He paints portable frescoes on Mexican and New York themes.

1933

Rivera finishes his *Detroit Industry* mural at the Detroit Institute of Arts in March (started in 1931). That same month, Rivera begins his *Man at the Crossroads* at Rockefeller Center in New York City; the controversial mural, which includes a positive portrayal of Russian revolutionary leader Vladimir Lenin, will be destroyed before completion.

Rivera returns to Mexico City in December.

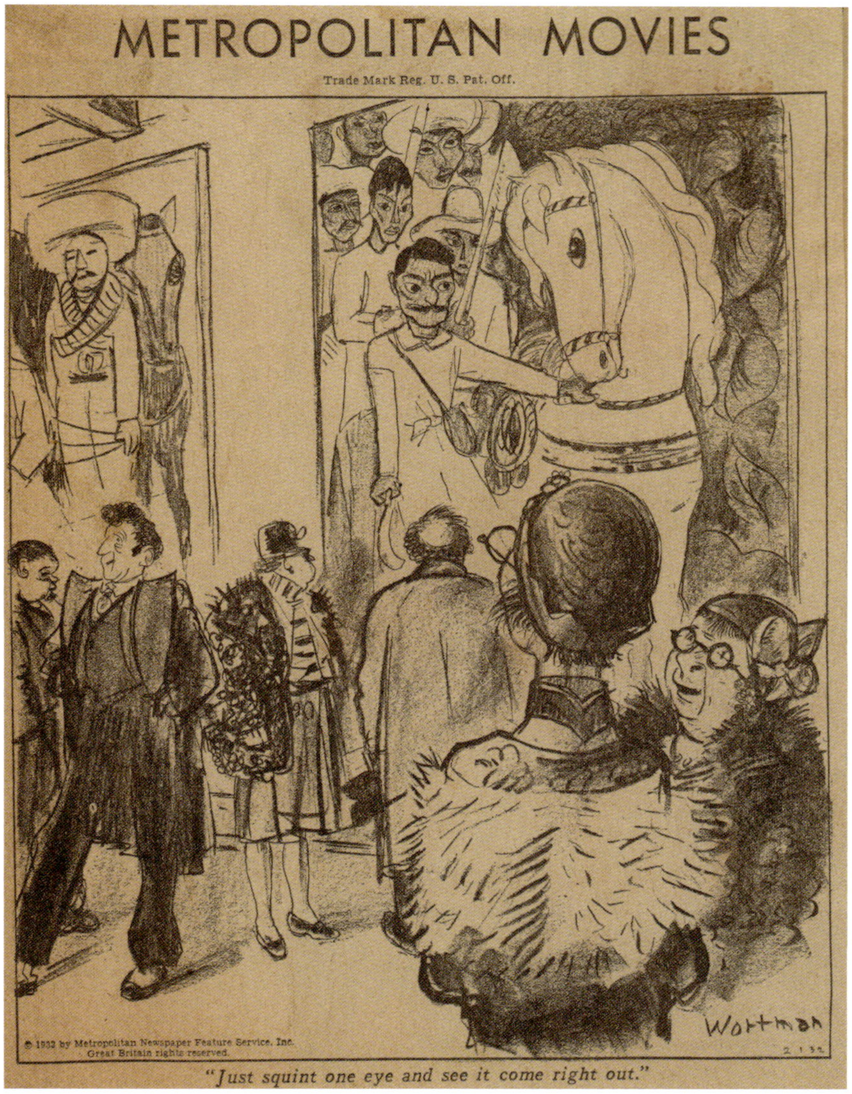

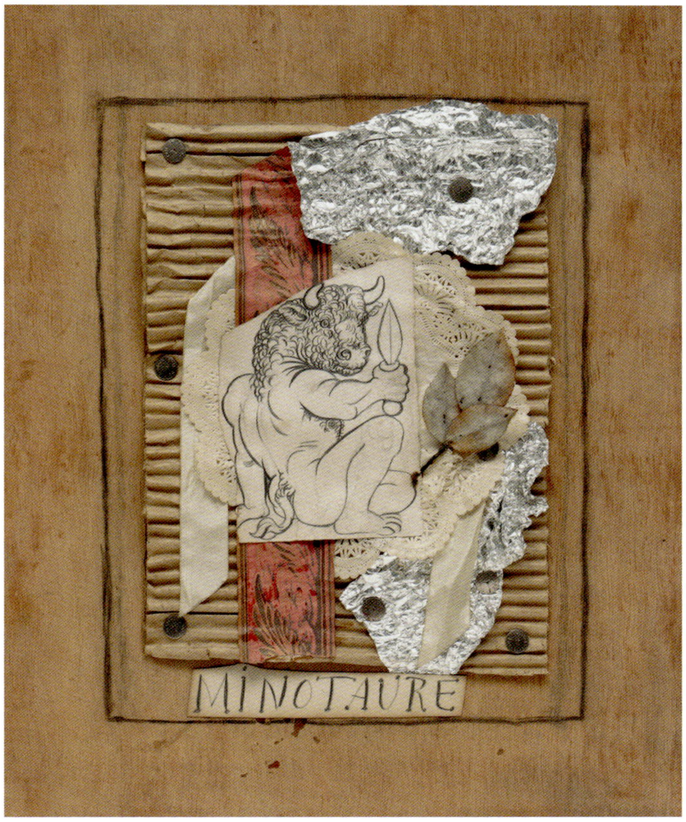

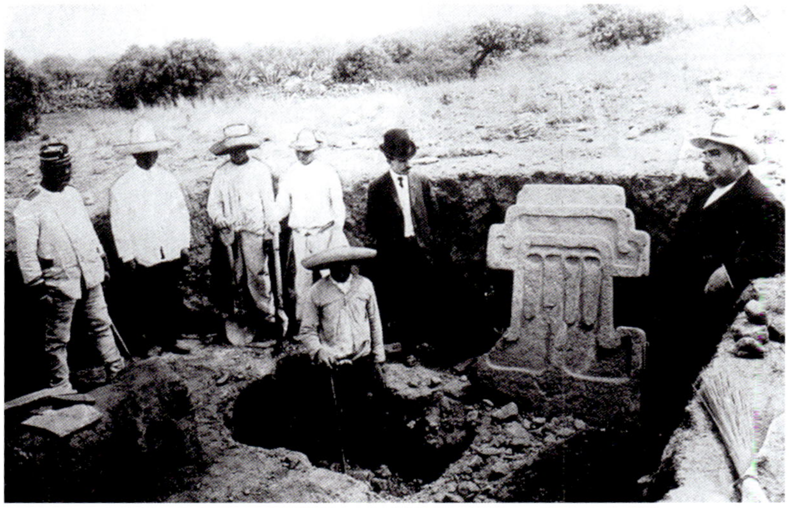

LEFT Pablo Picasso, **Maquette for the cover of the journal *Minotaure***, 1933; mixed media assemblage, 19⅛ × 16⅛ in. (48.5 × 41 cm); The Museum of Modern Art, New York, gift of Mr. and Mrs. Alexandre P. Rosenberg; TOP RIGHT "Metropolitan Movies" cartoon, ***New York World Telegram***, February 1, 1932, depicting Rivera's exhibition at the Museum of Modern Art; ***Liberation of the Peon*** (1931) is on the left and ***Agrarian Leader Zapata*** (1931) is on the right; BOTTOM RIGHT Archaeologist Leopoldo Batres and his team excavating Teotihuacán, 1905

PICASSO

1935

Picasso works on the *Minotauromachy*, one of the most important works on paper of the twentieth century. This etching, rich with iconography, is a key to understanding the symbols that will appear in his later works, including the Minotaur, the bearded man, the bullfight, the dove, and the wounded horse.

1936

The Spanish Civil War begins in July.

1937

In January, Picasso creates the etchings *The Dream and Lie of Franco*, a series of two satirical works and a poem that condemn Spain's dictator, Francisco Franco. That same month, Picasso is commissioned to create a large-scale painting for the Spanish Pavilion at the International Exposition, opening in Paris later in the year.

On April 26, the Basque village of Guernica is bombed by the German air force in support of Franco and against the Spanish Republic. As an intentional airstrike on a civilian population, the bombing generates international shock and condemnation. Picasso responds by abandoning his original project for the Spanish Pavilion and, in May, begins studies for what will become *Guernica*. The work is inaugurated at the Spanish Pavilion on July 12.

RIVERA

1936

Rivera becomes an active member of the Trotskyist Internationalist Communist League and helps facilitate asylum for Leon Trotsky in Mexico.

1938

Surrealist André Breton visits Mexico and meets with Rivera and Trotsky in May. In July, Rivera and Breton sign the Manifesto for an Independent Revolutionary Art, which includes a Surrealist illustration by Rivera. The manifesto is published in Spanish in *Clave: Tribuna Marxista* and in English in the *London Bulletin*.

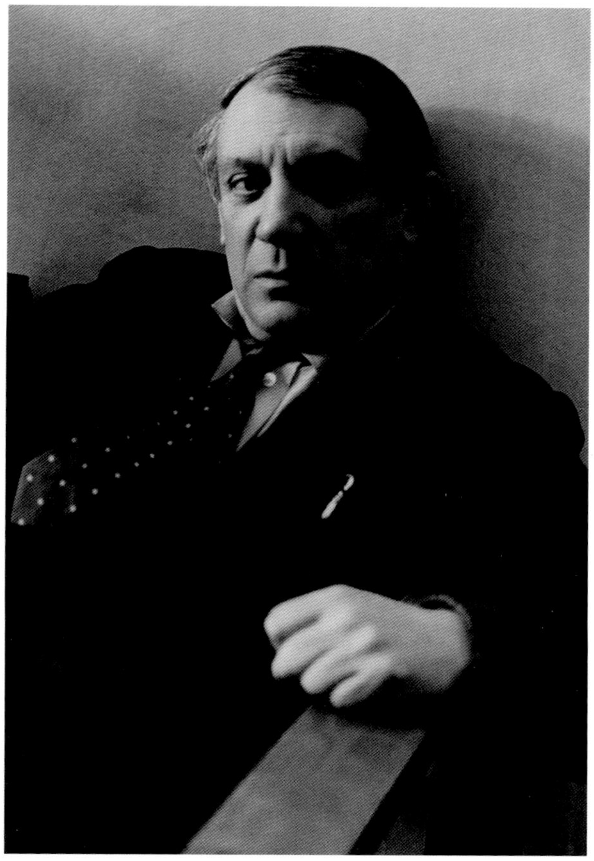

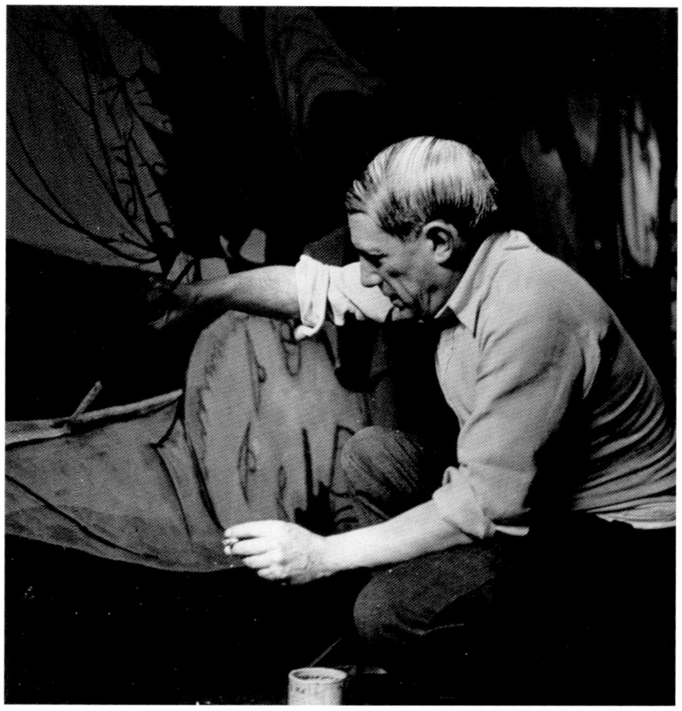

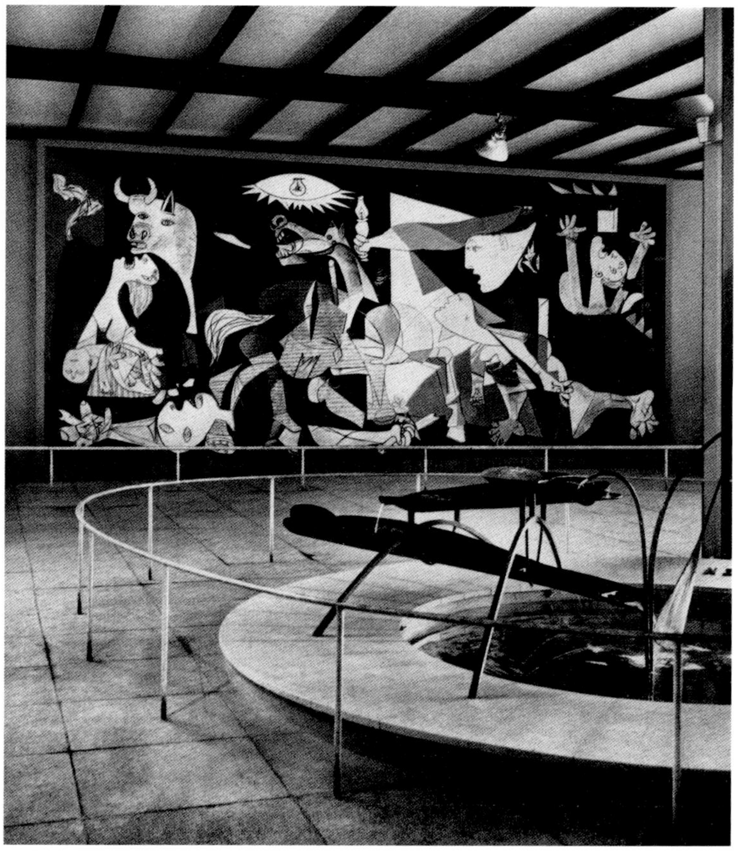

TOP Rogi André (Rozsa Klein), ***Pablo Picasso***, 1935; gelatin silver print, 13 x 9⅜ in. (33 x 23.8 cm); The Museum of Modern Art, New York, gift of Frank Crowninshield (9.1940); BOTTOM LEFT Picasso working on ***Guernica***, 1937 (photo by Dora Maar); BOTTOM RIGHT ***Guernica*** installed at the Spanish Pavilion at the 1937 International Exposition, Paris, with Alexander Calder's ***Mercury Fountain*** in foreground

PICASSO

1939–40

Germany invades Poland on September 1, 1939; two days later, Britain and France declare war on Germany, marking the beginning of World War II. Picasso leaves Paris for Royan, moving between the two locales during the first year of the war.

Germany invades France in May 1940; the Nazi occupation of Paris begins in June. Picasso returns to Paris in August for the remainder of the war.

RIVERA

1939

In March, Rivera participates in the exhibition *Mexique* organized by André Breton at the Galerie Renou et Colle in Paris. In May, Rivera illustrates the back and front covers of the Surrealist journal *Minotaure*, which also includes Breton's article "Souvenir du Mexique."

Rivera and Kahlo divorce in December.

1940

In January, Rivera participates in the Fourth International Surrealist Exhibition in Mexico City with two paintings; he also lends a number of his Pre-Columbian objects. This is the first known exhibition where Rivera's works and his Pre-Columbian collection are exhibited together.

In May, Rivera participates in *Twenty Centuries of Mexican Art* at the Museum of Modern Art in New York. Pre-Columbian and modern art are included in this exhibition but shown on separate floors of the museum.

Rivera is invited to participate in the Art in Action program during the Golden Gate International Exposition in San Francisco. He arrives in San Francisco in June to begin working on the *Pan American Unity* mural, which includes a portrayal of Coatlicue. It opens to the public in December.

In August, Leon Trotsky is assassinated in his home in Coyoacan, Mexico City, by Ramon Mercader. Rivera and Kahlo remarry in December.

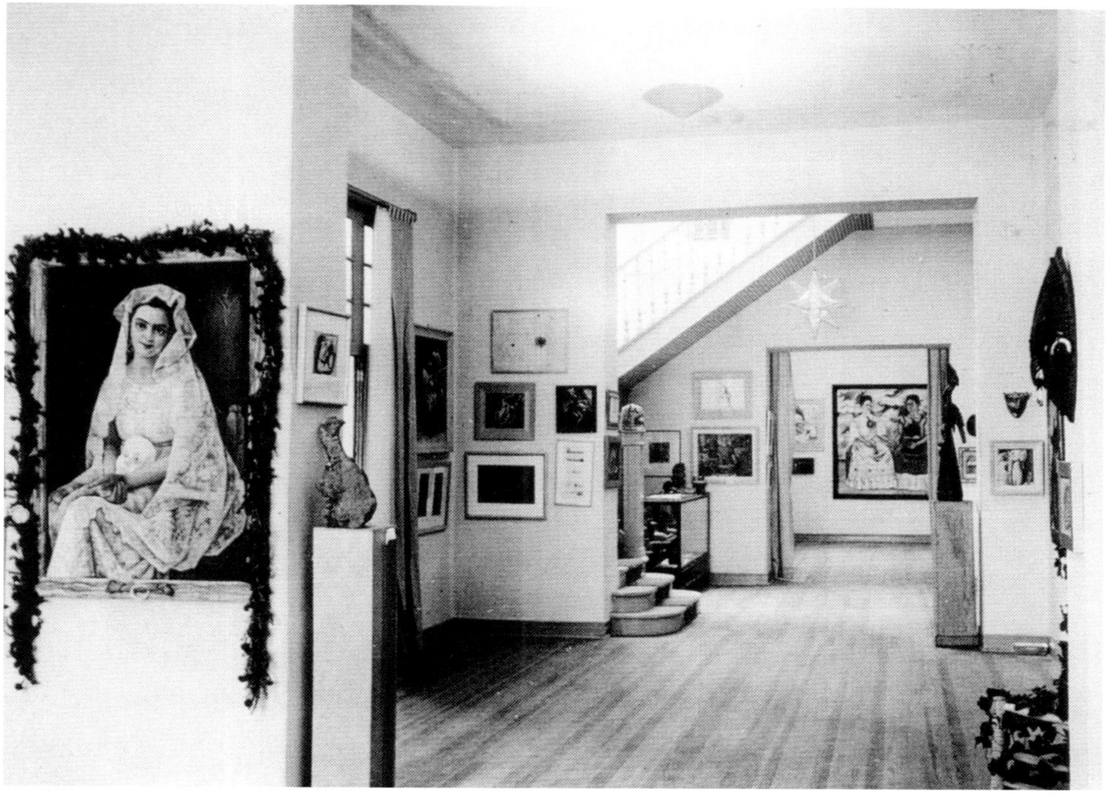

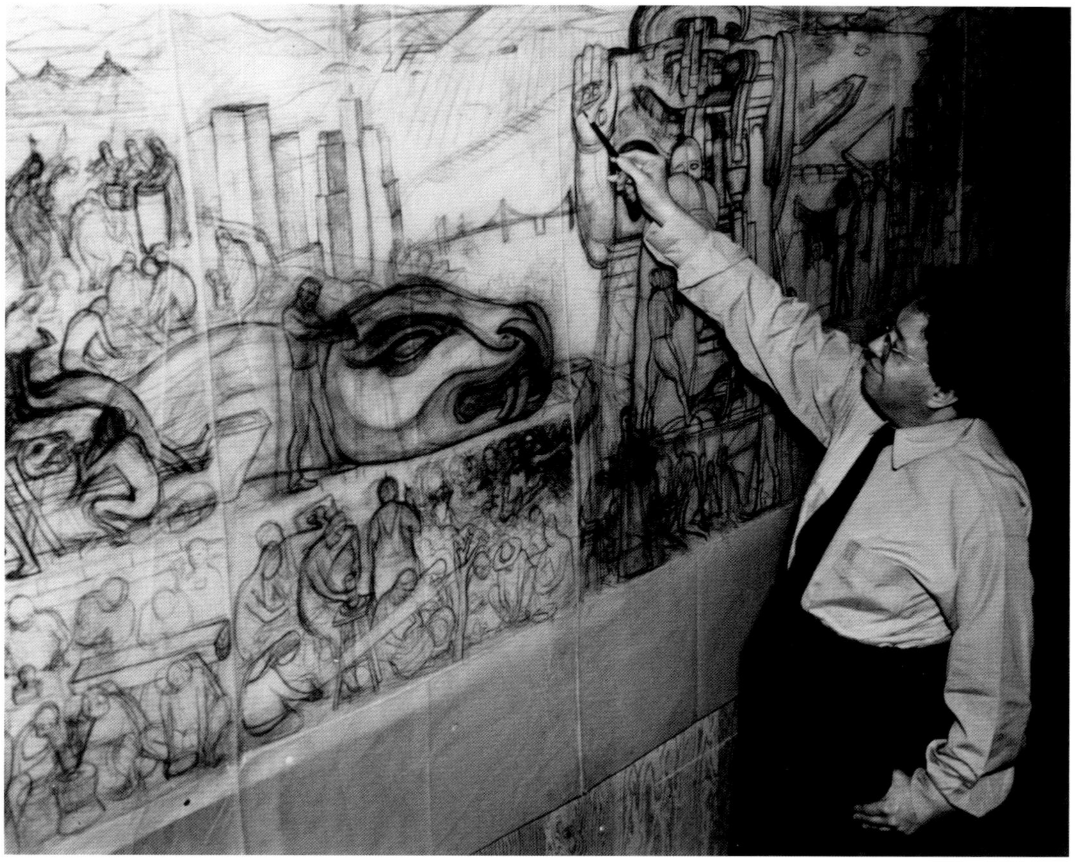

TOP Fourth International Surrealist Exhibition in Mexico City, 1940, with Rivera's ***Mandrake*** at left; BOTTOM Diego Rivera with an early sketch of his ***Pan American Unity*** mural, San Francisco, 1940

PICASSO | RIVERA

1942

Construction begins on the Museo Anahuacalli, designed by Rivera and a team of architects, including Juan O'Gorman.

Rivera begins work on the mural cycle at the Palacío Nacional. It includes an idealized vision of the ancient city of Tenochtitlán and a series of scenes portraying agriculture, trade, and the arts and crafts of Mesoamerican cultures.

1944–45

In August 1944, Paris is liberated from German occupation. Picasso joins the French Communist Party in October, becoming a figurehead of the party. In a statement to the New York newspaper *New Masses* later that month, he asserts: "I have never looked upon painting as an art intended for mere pleasure or amusement: since line and color are my weapons, I have used them in my attempt at gaining a continually greater understanding of the world and of mankind, so that this understanding might give us all a continually greater freedom."

1946–60

In his later years, Picasso continues to explore stories from Greek mythology and depict many of his recurring mythological characters (e.g., the Minotaur, the faun, the satyr) in his work. He also explores the great subjects of the European painting tradition, reinventing masterpieces such as Diego Velázquez's *Las Meninas* in 1957 and Edouard Manet's *Déjenuer sur l'Herbe* in 1960.

1950

Rivera begins working on his *History of Religion* panels, including three panels dedicated to Mesoamerican religion. The imagery is based on the close study of ancient Pre-Columbian painted books and shows Rivera's acquaintance with the iconography and draftsmanship of the ancient painters.

After World War II, Rivera becomes a proponent for an international peace campaign, sending letters to artists around the world and creating a sketch for the poster for the Peace Conference in Stockholm, Sweden.

1953–55

In 1953, Rivera is prominently shown in the exhibition of Mexican and Pre-Columbian art at the Liljevalchs Konsthall in Stockholm and the Tate Gallery, London. Frida Kahlo dies in July 1954. Rivera is readmitted to the Mexican Communist Party that September. Rivera is diagnosed with cancer in July 1955 but continues to work. He marries his art dealer, Emma Hurtado, that same month.

1957

Rivera dies on November 24, 1957, in his Altavista studio in San Ángel, Mexico City.

1973

Picasso dies on April 3, 1973, at his home in Mougins, France.

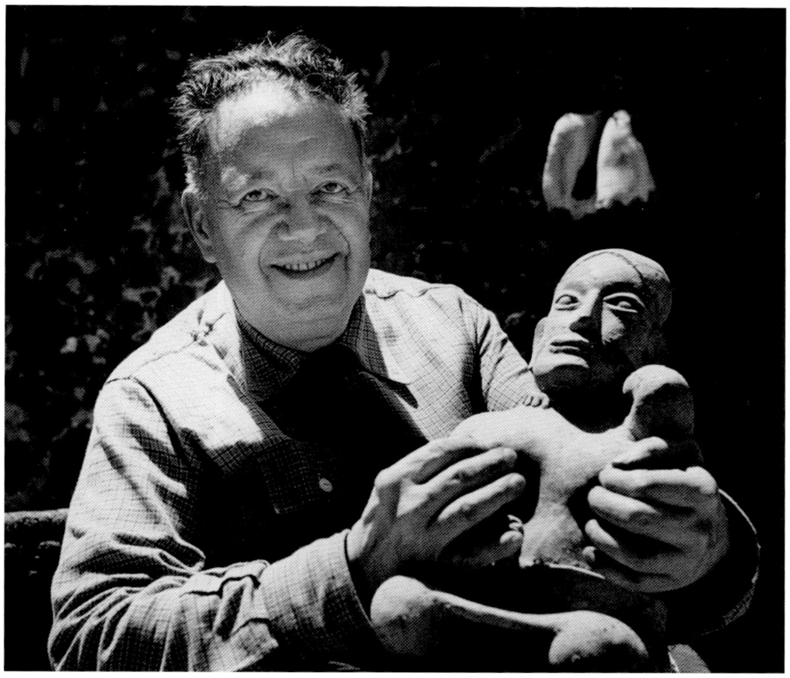

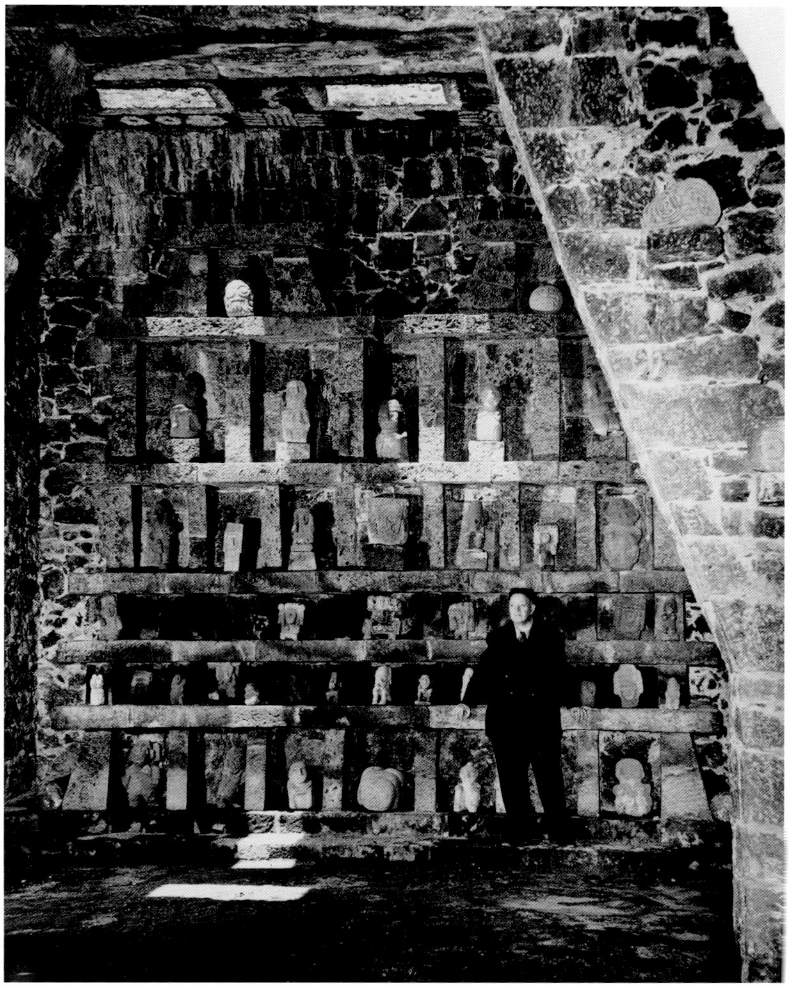

LEFT Diego Rivera, c. 1950s; RIGHT Diego Rivera at the Museo Anahuacalli, Mexico City, c. 1950s

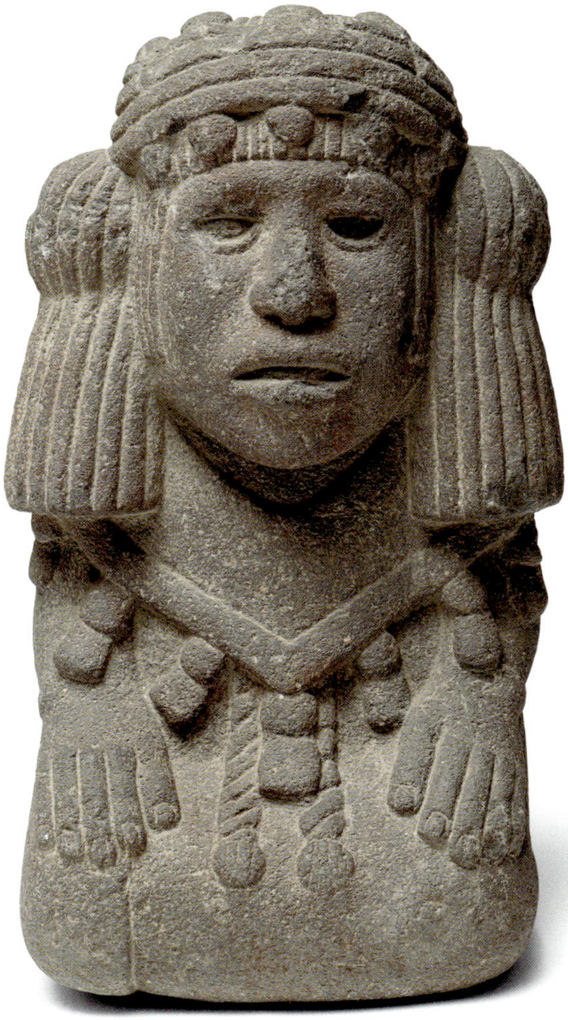

Chalchiuhtlicue (***Water Deity***), Mexico, Aztec, 1200–1521

CONTENTS

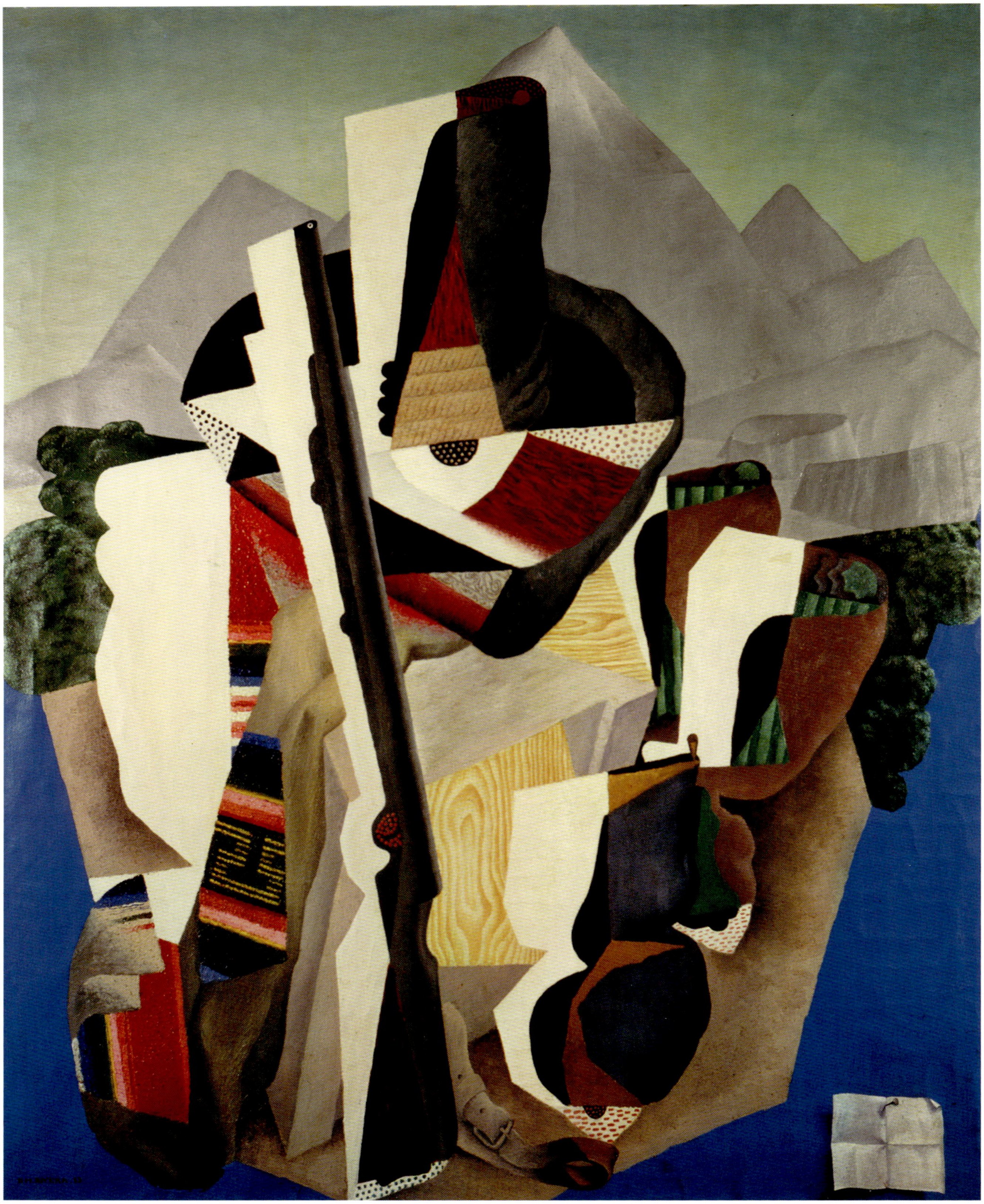

Diego Rivera, ***Zapatista Landscape***, 1915

DIRECTOR'S FOREWORD

My own abiding interest in the ways artists shape relationships with history arose at Williams College, first as a student and then as a curator. There, in 1985, I curated the exhibition *The Minotaur & the Light: Sources for Picasso c. 1935* and published an accompanying essay about Picasso's immersion in classical motifs and Greek mythology in his graphic works of the 1930s, in particular the figure of Minotaur, whom he identified with himself. In 2010, while visiting the Museo Nacional de Antropología in Mexico City, I met Diana Magaloni, the museum's director at the time, who discussed how Diego Rivera similarly drew upon Aztec sculpture in his oeuvre. This exciting conversation led to the inception of *Picasso and Rivera: Conversations Across Time*. When we discovered that the Museo del Palacio de Bellas Artes (MPBA), under the directorship of Miguel Fernández Félix, was researching the connection between Picasso and Rivera concurrent with the development of our exhibition, we decided to seize the opportunity to work together in the spirit of international collaboration.

This exhibition presents for the first time moments of intersection in the formation of modernism in both Europe and Latin America by examining how Pablo Picasso and Diego Rivera related to each other as artists in addition to engaging with their respective ancient Mediterranean and Pre-Columbian histories. Picasso and Rivera followed similar trajectories in the late nineteenth and early twentieth centuries: both trained in the academic tradition, which emphasized drawing casts of classical sculptures; both deployed Cubism—for a time in dialogue with each other—as a means to subvert historical traditions in painting; and both came full circle in returning to a re-examination of ancient art following World War I. Significantly, both artists' return to the art of the past was by no means academic. The deep relationships that they each forged to the arts of antiquity allowed them to challenge the notion of the modern as a definitive break with the ancient, suggesting instead that modernism can flow from continuous metamorphoses of the classical past.

As an encyclopedic museum, the Los Angeles County Museum of Art lends itself to thinking about art history along a continuum. Rather than perpetuating historical or cultural hierarchies, LACMA's programming seeks to create dialogue, particularly given our location in a city full of European tradition that also stands at an international crossroads with both Latin America and the Pacific Rim. In partnership with the MPBA, we have been able to give shape to a original and daring exhibition that could only be possible in the Americas, where our ancient indigenous heritage proposes a novel worldview that can interface with classical Western traditions, bringing both a diversity of points of view and a profound convergence in human and artistic values. This rich mixture can be found in the works of Picasso and Rivera as they reflect our own contemporary multiculturalism.

This exhibition would not have been possible without the invaluable generosity of our lenders and sponsors, including Christie's, The Kenneth T. and Eileen L. Norris Foundation, the Robert Lehman Foundation, and an indemnity from the Federal Council on the Arts and the Humanities. We also thank our colleagues at MPBA, led by Miguel Fernández Félix, for their partnership. Additionally, I wish to express my gratitude to my co-curator, Diana Magaloni. Assisted by Lilly Casillas and in dialogue with a curatorial team that also includes Juan Coronel Rivera, James Oles, and Jennifer Stager, Diana worked tirelessly so that, together, we could tell a new story about two artists whose work helped define the twentieth century even as they reached to the past.

MICHAEL GOVAN
CEO and Wallis Annenberg Director
Los Angeles County Museum of Art

PICASSO AND RIVERA

MODERNISM AND ANCIENT ART

DIANA MAGALONI AND **MICHAEL GOVAN**

As art historian Elizabeth Prettejohn has argued, "we cannot conceive of a modern art without presupposing its ancient alter ego, no more can we envisage an ancient art that is uncontaminated by our own modern perspective."[1] Pablo Picasso (1881–1973) and Diego Rivera (1886–1957) were both originally trained within an academic tradition based in aesthetic values that drew directly on the foundations of classical Greek and Roman art, as well as ideological values that presumed the superiority of European culture as the inheritor of the Greco-Roman tradition. Picasso confronted these ideologies in Europe, where they originated, while Rivera, as a "marginal cosmopolitan," confronted the "vertical nature of the relationship" of Latin America to Europe's cultural centers and its peripheral positioning in the international community.[2] Both Picasso and Rivera found new, creative ways to challenge these values and to propose an alternative canon in which Western and non-Western aesthetic traditions could coexist. *Picasso and Rivera: Conversations Across Time* explores how each artist's search for his own origins led to a dynamic reexamination of the arts of antiquity that profoundly guided their development as modern artists.

Picasso was born in Spain, a primarily rural country that at the time was considered at the periphery of Europe; Rivera was born in Mexico, a former Spanish viceroyalty, where 40 percent of the population spoke an indigenous language before learning Spanish. The experiences that shaped the beginning of their careers can be seen in two self-portraits made by Picasso and Rivera in 1906. In his *Self-Portrait*, young Rivera seems to show his own inner conflicts as a Latin American artist in Europe (p. 28). He presents himself in austere clothing, against a view of his melancholic blue studio. In the background, a large easel stands against the wall, showing only the back of the canvas. In this manner, he portrays himself only tentatively as an artist. Years later, he recalled, "I was slow and timid in translating my inner feelings on canvas…lacking the confidence to express myself directly."[3] The rest of the

1
Elizabeth Prettejohn, *The Modernity of Ancient Sculpture: Greek Sculpture and Modern Art from Winckelmann to Picasso* (London and New York: I. B. Tauris, 2012), 1–2.

2
Natalia Majluf, "'Ce n'est pas le Pérou,' or the Failure of Authenticity: Marginal Cosmopolitans at the Paris Universal Exhibition of 1855," *Critical Inquiry* 23, no. 4 (Summer 1997): 869.

3
Diego Rivera (with Gladys March), *My Art, My Life: An Autobiography* (New York: Citadel Press, 1960), 61.

4
Ibid., 124.

5
James Johnson Sweeney, "Picasso and Iberian Sculpture," *The Art Bulletin* 23, no. 3 (September 1941): 191–92.

6
John Golding, introduction to *Matisse Picasso*, ed. Elizabeth Cowling (London: Tate Publishing, 2002), 14.

7
Patricia Leighten, *Re-Ordering the Universe: Picasso and Anarchism, 1897–1914* (Princeton: Princeton University Press, 1989), 81.

8
David Craven, *Diego Rivera: As Epic Modernist* (New York: G. K. Hall, 1997), 50.

9
Ibid., 49.

background is black, conveying a sense of all that was left unexpressed by Rivera, an unknown world that he would only explore much later upon his return to Mexico in 1921: "My homecoming produced an aesthetic exhilaration.... All the colors I saw appeared to be heightened; they were clearer, richer, finer, and more full of light.... From then on, I worked confidently and contentedly. Gone was the doubt and inner conflict that had tormented me in Europe."[4]

That same year in Paris, Picasso portrayed himself in a confidently modern manner. Both *Self-Portrait* (p. 83) and *Self-Portrait with a Palette* (p. 29) announce him as the inheritor of the artistic lineage of ancient Iberia. These are among the twenty-one self-portraits—seven paintings and fourteen drawings—that he made between the summer and winter of 1906, showing himself with the features of *Man Attacked by a Lion* (p. 82), an Iberian sculpture from Osuna, Spain. These portraits precede his groundbreaking *Les Demoiselles d'Avignon* (p. 131), painted in 1907; as James Sweeney points out, Picasso had become "dissatisfied with the conventional mode of expression" and was searching for an expression that would disregard the "conventional decorum" and "emptiness of the accepted aesthetic canon."[5] He purposefully studied the synthetic, so-called primitive style of the pre-Roman Iberian sculptures at the Louvre to reduce his own style to the essentials, striving to produce art that was devoid of decorative intent, and that would present reality in a new way.

In *Self-Portrait with a Palette*, Picasso created a composite figure of his newly adopted Iberian heritage and his modern persona. He is dressed casually; one hand is tucked into his pocket, while the other holds a palette with fresh paint. His facial features and the shape of his head reproduce the synthetic forms of *Man Attacked by a Lion*. In contrast to Rivera, Picasso presents himself forcefully as an artist rooted in his ancestral heritage; moreover, he "was beginning to exude that sense of universal atavism, which was to brand so large a part of his subsequent production."[6] These new forms challenged the classical European canon and "announced his origins and sympathies as outside of the European tradition."[7]

CUBISM

Picasso, with Georges Braque, helped initiate Cubism in the years following *Les Demoiselles d'Avignon*, audaciously questioning the fundamental conventions in Western art by disallowing hierarchical structures and dissolving perspectival space and figurative references. In this sense, Cubism was a critical exploration of the cultural preconditions of Western representation itself.[8] Furthermore, as Patricia Leighten notes in this volume, "Cubism was also viewed, by both its defenders and detractors, as a 'primitive' expression rooted in the same atavistic impulses that had created cave art and continued in the art of non-Western peoples and folk art" (p. 130). In this way, Cubism became a modernist aesthetic that could accommodate an interplay "between high art and mass culture, between Western and non-Western art,"[9]

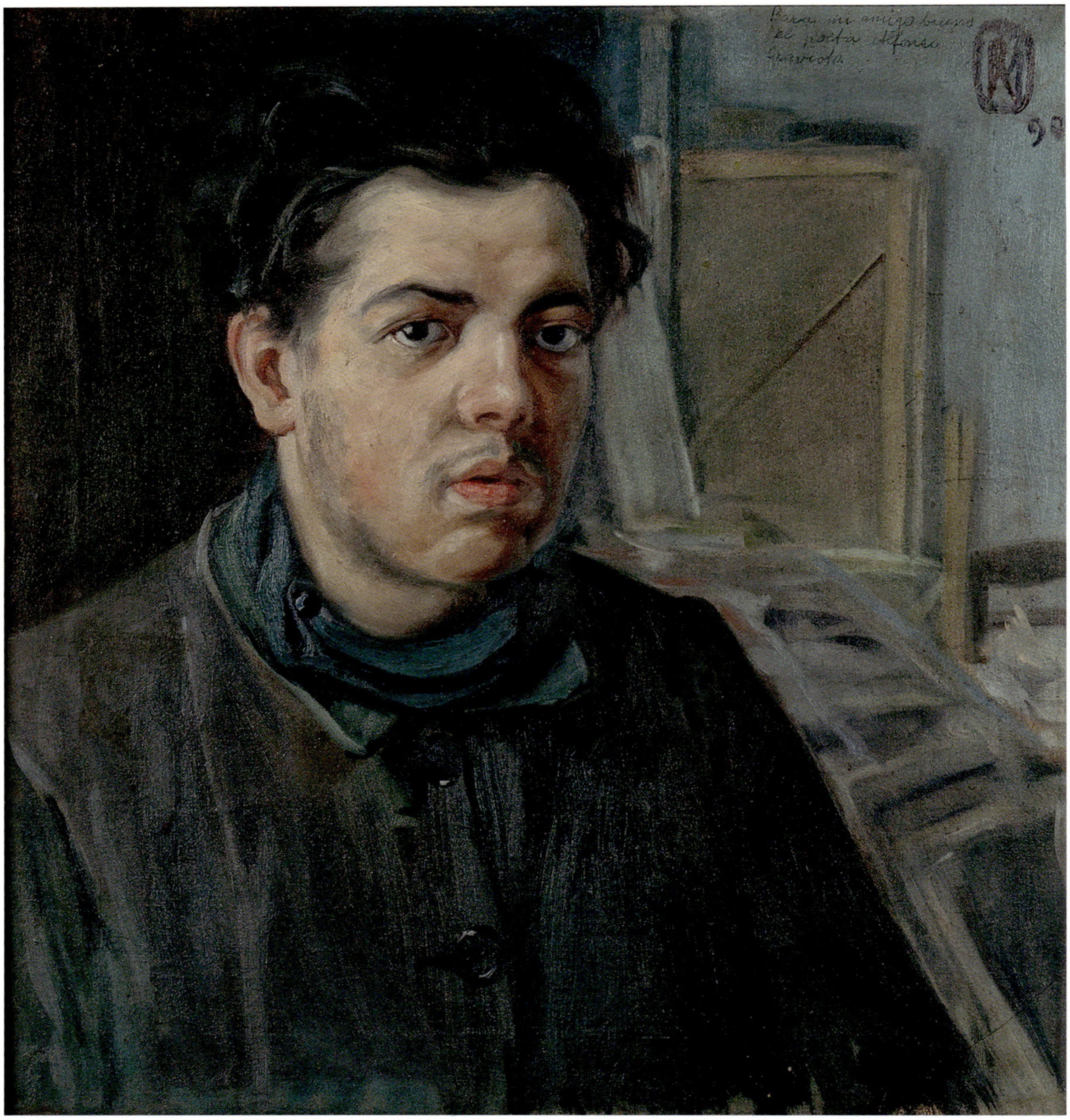

Diego Rivera, ***Self-Portrait***, 1906

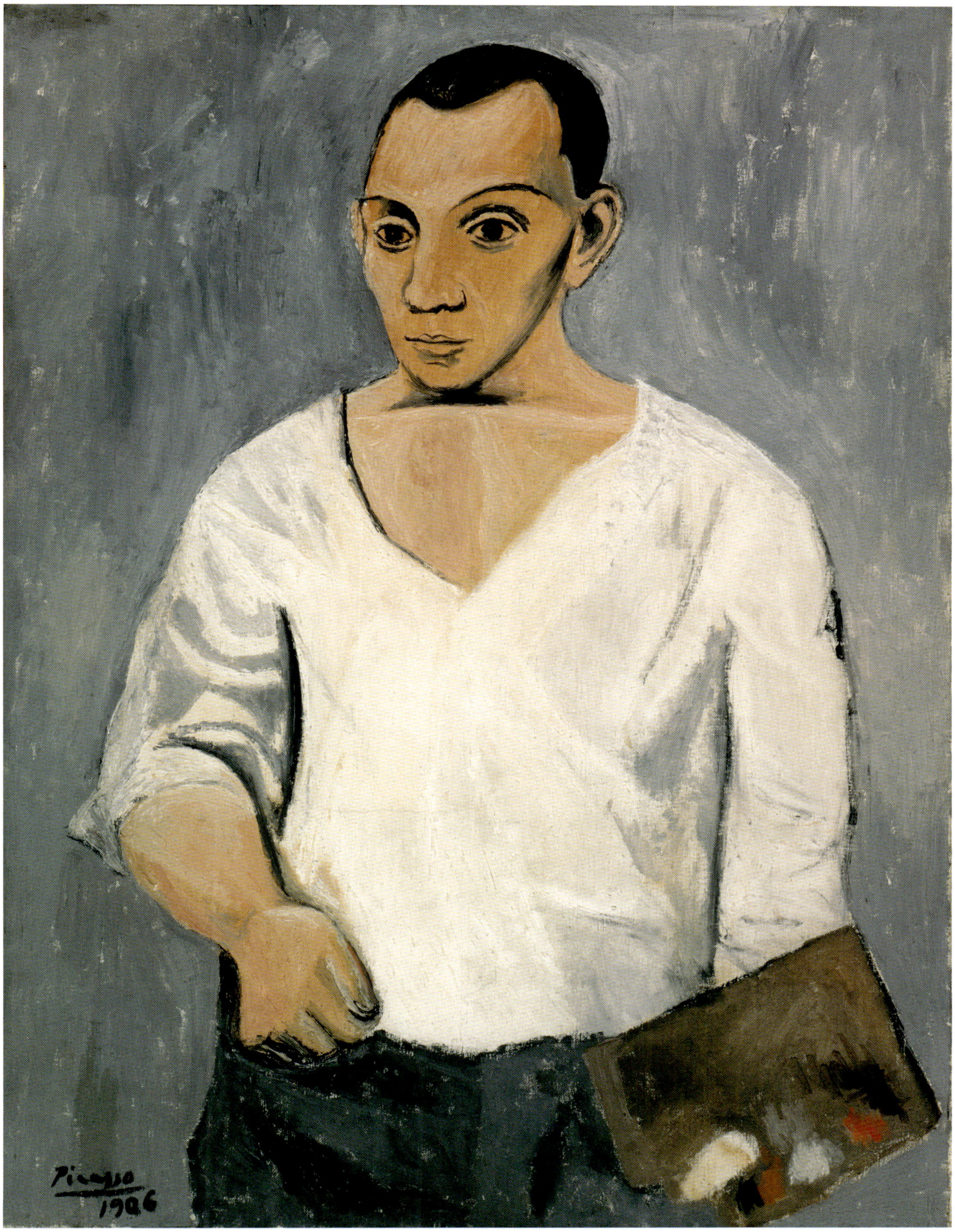

Pablo Picasso, ***Self-Portrait with a Palette***, 1906

10
Rivera, *My Art, My Life*, 17.

11
Ramón Favela, *Diego Rivera: The Cubist Years* (Phoenix, AZ: Phoenix Art Museum, 1984), 70.

12
Ibid., 76.

13
Rivera, *My Art, My Life*, 105.

and the work of both Picasso and Rivera is marked by this intrinsic characteristic of Cubism. Decades later, Rivera would recall Cubism as "a revolutionary movement questioning everything that had previously been said and done in art. It held nothing sacred, as the old world would soon blow itself apart, never to be the same again, so Cubism broke down forms as they had been seen for centuries, and was creating out of the fragments new forms, new objects, new patterns, and ultimately, new worlds."[10]

Rivera's comment reveals how much Cubism reflected the profound shift in the understanding of reality that occurred as a result of the devastation brought on by World War I. As the war had destroyed the precarious social, political, and economic equilibrium of the old world, Cubism proposed painting as a system of relationships where the linearity of time and narrative was replaced by juxtaposition and simultaneity. Rivera's search for this alternative aesthetic in his late Cubist works begins with an exploration of his Mexican heritage, introducing idiosyncratic elements like the fragment of a serape or of a woven straw mat (*petate*), as in *Still Life with Gray Bowl* (p. 111).[11] However, as noted by James Oles in his essay in this volume, the Mexican images of Rivera's late Cubist paintings "were forms of resistance not only to the 'internationalism' of Cubism but also to the charged rhetoric of French nationalism" during the war (p. 149), a period in which both Picasso and Rivera were noncombatant foreigners living in Paris.

In the spring of 1914, Picasso sent his Chilean friend Manuel Ortiz de Zárate to bring Diego Rivera into his studio.[12] This impulse by Picasso has to be considered carefully, for Picasso was firmly established in Paris as one of modernism's leading artists, while Rivera had moved permanently to Montparnasse only in the fall of 1912. As Oles discusses, it is difficult to reconstruct with certainty the story of their friendship; we know about their friendship only through Rivera's writings, which some scholars have considered to be embellished and partial. In an interview with Gladys March, Rivera recounted that during their first meeting he and Picasso almost immediately became good friends, staying up all night talking: "Our theme was Cubism—what it was trying to accomplish, what it had already done, and what future it had as a 'new art form.'"[13] Picasso and Rivera evidently continued to meet and collaborate from this point until their falling out in 1915 over Rivera's accusation that Picasso plagiarized a particular technique of his.

An unpublished document recently located by Juan Coronel Rivera and Lilly Casillas in the Diego Rivera and Frida Kahlo Archive (p. 137) is the only extant evidence of the men's friendship from Picasso's side, and it suggests that their friendship was as close as Rivera remembered. Picasso addressed a photograph of his *Gas-Jet and Guitar* (1913) with a dedication written in both Spanish (their shared mother tongue) and French (the language of the Parisian avant-garde): "A mi querido amigo Diego Rivera, en tout d'accord" [To my dear friend Diego Rivera. We agree on everything]. It is noticeable that Picasso addresses Rivera as *querido amigo* (dear friend) in Spanish and declares his intellectual and artistic affinity (*en tout d'accord*) in French.

14
Lisa Florman, *Myth and Metamorphosis: Picasso's Classical Prints of the 1930s* (Cambridge, MA: MIT Press, 2000), 6.

15
Ibid., 7.

16
See Guillaume Apollinaire, *The Cubist Painters*, trans. Peter Read (1913; Berkeley: University of California Press, 2004).

17
For an in-depth discussion, see Florman, *Myth and Metamorphosis*, 7–13; Prettejohn, *The Modernity of Ancient Sculpture*, 38–103.

18
Florman, *Myth and Metamorphosis*, 11.

19
Stephanie Barron, "New Objectivity: German Realism after Expressionism," in *New Objectivity: Modern German Art in the Weimar Republic, 1919–1933*, ed. Stephanie Barron and Sabine Eckmann, 15–25 (Los Angeles: Los Angeles County Museum of Art; New York: Prestel, 2015), 17.

Rivera kept this photograph as a remembrance of their fruitful conversations, in which, as he recalled, both artists expressed their artistic hopes and convictions. Picasso, too, kept a memento of their friendship: Rivera's *Cubist Composition (Still Life with Bottle of Anis and Inkwell)* (p. 137), which he acquired either as a gift from Rivera or as a purchase from Daniel-Henry Kahnweiler. The painting is still part of the Picasso family collection.

THE MODERNIST CLASSICAL REVIVAL IN FRANCE AND MEXICO

Picasso and Rivera both traveled to Italy (in 1917 and 1920, respectively) and, following the war, embraced a revalorization of the classical tradition. As Michele Greet observes in her contribution, after World War I "artists were seeking an aesthetic model that emphasized continuity over rupture while still expressing their modernity" (p. 237). Art criticism in France during the 1920s revolved around the "relative merits of figuration and abstraction," searching for the commonalities between these two modes of expression in the essential qualities of painting.[14] Picasso's *Études* from 1920 (p. 59), which juxtaposes four classical figures with five Cubist still lifes, clearly indicates that he was thinking about the fundamental bonds—as well as the differences—between the two styles.[15] Poet and critic Guillaume Apollinaire had seen in Cubism a phase of "purification" in which painting would be distilled into its absolute indivisible essence.[16] This painterly essence was coextensive with the core of classicism—that is, with the eternal principles of aesthetics, already characterized in the eighteenth century by art historians Johann Joachim Winckelmann and Gotthold Ephraim Lessing in their analyses of classical Greek sculpture: *Einfalt* (simplicity) and *Still* (tranquility).[17] Lessing had proposed that these essential, paradigmatic qualities of Greek sculpture were the defining qualities of visual art at large. It was precisely the simplicity, the lack of movement that set a painting or a sculpture apart from literature. Essentialism in the 1920s warned against narrative, historic painting, which was thought of as too transient and argued instead for standards of beauty that were the embodiment of the universal: "balance, harmony, wholeness, and unity—that in themselves expressed the atemporality that was considered painting's indivisible essence."[18]

This impulse to return to stable, universal values and traditional aesthetics in the French *rappel à l'ordre* (return to order) also gained traction in Italy with *ritorno al mestiere* (return to craft) and in Germany with *Neue Sachlichkeit* (New Objectivity). As German art historian Gustav Friedrich Hartlaub observed in 1922, New Objectivity was composed of both a conservative right wing (including artists such as George Shrimpf) and a more progressive left wing (including artists such as Otto Dix).[19] All of these movements shared a reactive distrust of novelty (including prewar movements such as Cubism in France, Expressionism in Germany, and Futurism in Italy) and an attraction to the classical past. In Latin American countries with large indigenous populations such as Ecuador and Peru, but particularly in Mexico, the

20
Federico Navarrete Linares, *Las relaciones interétnicas en México* (Mexico City: Universidad Nacional Autónoma de México, 2004), 87–93; Renato González Mello, "Manuel Gamio, Diego Rivera and the Politics of Mexican Anthropology," *RES: Anthropology and Aesthetics* 45 (Spring 2004): 165. (In a sense, the theory of *mestizaje* in Mexico was similar to the idealized conception of the United States as a "melting pot"; paradoxically, both positions tried to deal with the challenges of multiculturalism by creating an ideal of homogeneity.)

21
Kenneth E. Silver, *Chaos & Classicism: Art in France, Italy, and Germany, 1918–1936* (New York: Guggenheim Museum, 2010), 41.

22
González Mello, "Manuel Gamio, Diego Rivera," 161.

23
Craven, *Diego Rivera*, 56.

24
James Oles, *Art and Architecture in Mexico* (London: Thames & Hudson, 2013), 239.

anti-imperialist strategy of the 1920s and 1930s took on the form of *indigenismo*, a complex social and political phenomenon. In Mexico it was created in the 1920s and 1930s through the concerted efforts of anthropologists such as Manuel Gamio and government officials to solve what they perceived as the conundrum of modernity in Mexico: the abrupt cultural, social, and racial disparities between the indigenous population and the educated *criollo* (creole) elites. They looked to solve this problem by creating a racial ideal of the mestizo race, which functioned to broaden the possibility of social inclusion while erasing ethnic and cultural diversity.[20]

Picasso and Rivera's works of this period created an idealized expression that portrayed ordinary people of modern society with the grandeur of the great, ancient cultures, thereby blurring the frontiers between the past and the present, the grand tradition and the vernacular. Picasso's first monumental neoclassical painting, *Three Women at the Spring* (painted in the summer of 1921 in Fontainebleau), represents a refined balance between the classical Greek and archaic sculpture (p. 115). As Kenneth E. Silver notes, "sculpture played an important role in art discourse between the wars as both a symbol of an ancient heritage and the correction for unreliable, contingent, perishable life."[21] The figures here have been reinterpreted with archaic features, their vacant eyes and straight, narrow noses all recalling the expression seen in his 1906 *Self-Portrait* based on the Osuna sculpture. The most striking effect of this endeavor, as noted by Jennifer Stager in her essay in this volume, is that the three women are simultaneously ancient Greek and Iberian goddesses sculpted in stone as well as young women from the contemporary Mediterranean world. In representing the widespread longing for stability during the postwar period in Europe, they become icons of modernity's relationship with the past.

RIVERA'S INDIGENIST CANON

Rivera returned to Mexico in 1921 and was immediately hired by José Vasconcelos, the country's minister of education, to participate in an innovative and revolutionary artistic program that aimed to use mural painting to unify the fragmented nation in the wake of the Mexican Revolution by creating a shared sense of identity as well as to "examine the previously ignored areas of Mexican society: the Indian and the peasant communities."[22] The artistic values behind Rivera's easel and mural paintings of the early 1920s were aligned with David Alfaro Siqueiros's 1923 "Manifesto of the Syndicate of Technical Workers, Painters, and Sculptors," which called for the production of a "universal art" rather than a constricting "national art,"[23] and "privileged public monumental art over bourgeois easel painting and extolled Mexico's popular and indigenous artistic traditions."[24]

In *Flower Day* (p. 89), as Itzel Rodríguez Mortellaro observes in this volume, Rivera seems to have distilled the essential qualities of Aztec sculpture by providing the composition with a geometrized hierarchy through which he turns the chaotic and frenetic energy of the market into an icon—essentially, a still life of a market that conjures the past and the present in one frozen moment. The women seated at the foreground are depicted as the stone sculptures of the ancient goddess Chalchiuhtlicue; the vendor carrying calla lilies on his back looms over the two figures in a respectful position, as though he could see in these simple women of the market the goddess they represent. All of these figures present a powerful paradox: while their bodies are concrete and fleshy, and thus transform the ancient stone sculptures into present-day people, their faces remain abstracted to the point of being anonymous. *Flower Day* by Rivera transforms the aesthetics of the ancient Aztec sculptures into the new classical canon for the Mexican people, and transforms present-day Mexicans into abstracted icons of an idealized past.

Rivera's murals at the Secretaría de Educación Pública (SEP; Ministry of Public Education), painted between 1923 and 1928, show that he was grappling with the same issues that postwar artists from Germany and France were confronting, in particular the relationship between the individual and the group, and the tension between creating portraits versus illustrating phenotypes.[25] For instance, in the *Endowment of Communal Lands* panel, which also includes a representation of revolutionary leader Emiliano Zapata, Rivera has clearly created a typological representation of indigenous *campesinos* (peasants), based in part on the physiological traits of ancient Mexica and Teotihuacán masks (p. 92). The murals in the stairway of the SEP building are probably the most striking representations of the influence that the ideas of Manuel Gamio concerning the greatness of the mestizo race had upon Rivera. As he described, the murals' "allegorical figures personified the ascending stages of the social evolution of the country from the primitive society, through the people's revolutions, to the liberated and fulfilled social order of the future."[26] The primitive stages of society are represented by figures of women rendered in positions and with the drapery characteristic of classical Greek sculptures. They begin their ascending path to social evolution by becoming more and more mixed with the indigenous races, thus transforming themselves into the idealized mestizo women of the utopian Mexico.[27] Rivera's own vision of Mexico's past, present, and future propagates a utopian hybridity, a mestizo world in which the Eurocentric values of classical Greece are supplanted by the great cultural deeds of ancient Mexico.

25
Silver, *Chaos & Classicism*, 40–42.

26
Quoted in Luis-Martín Lozano and Juan Coronel Rivera, *Diego Rivera: The Complete Murals* (Los Angeles: Taschen, 2008).

27
For an elaborate interpretation of this sequence, see Renato González Mello, "Political Vision: Ministry of Public Education, Mexico," in *Diego Rivera: The Complete Murals*, 29.

THE 1930s

With the rise of Mussolini and Hitler in the 1920s and 1930s, an antimodernist view of the classical past became part of the political rhetoric in Europe. "First the Italian fascists, later the German National Socialists, recognized the symbolic power of the classical idea and the real power of violence (its uses and continued threat), which they merged," Kenneth E. Silver has noted.[28] Indeed, fascist art in Germany and Italy would embrace classicism to celebrate race and power by equating classical beauty and values with nationalistic agendas. In Latin America, as different visions of nationalism contributed to institutionalized anthropological and cultural projects designed to promote nativist agendas, "critics accused Indigenism of perpetuating the primitivizing roles that Europeans expected of Latin Americans."[29] While in the 1920s Indigenism was viewed as an avant-garde movement, in the late 1930s it had turned into official government propaganda. Nevertheless, in the 1930s "for many radical artists and intellectuals throughout the world, it was Mexico and not Paris that stood for innovation in the arts."[30] At the onset of World War II, the vanguards' artistic movement evolved into a pan-American phenomenon that included the United States. Rivera and other Mexican muralists such as José Clemente Orozco painted important works in different American cities where the Pre-Columbian informs the modern and creates an alternate view of the past.[31]

During this same period, Picasso delved into Greek literature in order to portray the contradictory human capacities for violence, love, destruction, and creation through a series of works on paper that are as humble in their materiality as they are monumental in their artistic achievement. Picasso's approach to classicism during the 1930s, in particular the Vollard Suite (1930–37) and his illustrations for Ovid's *Metamorphoses* (1931), is complex. Picasso did not search for the classical qualities of "simplicity" and "tranquility" (*Einfalt* and *Still*) that had characterized his painting in the early 1920s, nor did he explore social categories and phenotypes (as did some other modernists in Europe and Mexico at the time); rather, he developed a new narrative approach based on myth and dreams that allowed him to fold in his own personal experiences. Instead of reproducing the essential stability of ancient art in his etchings, he infused his works with the continual capacity of transformation: "Picasso wants us to think of tradition as metamorphosis, as continuity *without* essence, and thus with the potential of thoroughgoing change."[32]

His *Metamorphoses* illustrations, as Jennifer Stager discusses in this volume, are explorations of tragedy that search for answers while seeming to evade any single viewpoint. For instance, in investigating the unspeakable suffering of Philomela's repeated rape by her brother-in-law, Tereus, and his ultimate cruelty of silencing her by cutting out her tongue, Picasso explores all aspects of human nature and positions himself at the crossroads between beauty and monstrosity—a defining trait of classical Greek art. As in his other illustrations for the *Metamorphoses*, Picasso explores the story through multiple studies, depicting the brutality and complexity of Ovid's stories through a simple line style he borrowed from Etruscan mirrors

28
Silver, *Chaos & Classicism*, 160.

29
Michele Greet, *Beyond National Identity: Pictorial Indigenism as a Modernist Strategy in Andean Art*, 1920–1960 (University Park: Pennsylvania State University Press, 2009), 21.

30
Craven, *Diego Rivera*, 53.

31
José Clemente Orozco was the first Mexican artist to complete a mural in the United States in which the past informed the present: *Prometheus* (1930), at Pomona College in Claremont, CA. He also painted *Epic of American Civilization* (1932–34) at Dartmouth College in Hanover, NH. David Alfaro Siqueiros painted *América Tropical* and *Portrait of Present-Day Mexico* in Los Angeles in 1932. After being whitewashed in the late 1930s, *América Tropical* was restored by the Getty Conservation Institute in 2012. *Portrait of Present-Day Mexico* was moved to the Santa Barbara Museum of Art in 2002.

32
Florman, *Myth and Metamorphosis*, 63.

33 Michael Govan, *The Minotaur & the Light: Sources for Picasso c. 1935* (Williamstown, MA: Williams College Museum of Art, 1985), 5–18.

(pp. 198 and 203). The culmination of this narrative classicism came in 1935 with the large etching *Minotauromachy* (p. 217). Here Picasso presents his cast of characters representing symbols of the human experience, extracted from Greek mythology and personal experiences that were developed by him throughout the years when he worked on the Vollard Suite, in which he constructed a world where he becomes part of a mythic tale, transforming himself and his partner, Marie-Thérèse Walter, into the sculptor and his muse, or by depicting himself as Rembrandt, the great master of etching, or as ancient Greek mythological characters, including the Minotaur, the satyr, and Hercules.[33] As Michael Govan notes in his essay in this catalogue, the Vollard Suite's theme of light as a powerful, redemptive symbol is one that Picasso would carry into *Guernica* to denounce the fascist atrocities committed against the citizens of the Spanish town.

CONCLUSION

By placing approximately one hundred paintings, etchings, and watercolors by Picasso and Rivera in dialogue with one another and with dozens of ancient objects—including some known specifically to have influenced the artists—*Picasso and Rivera: Conversations Across Time* aims to advance the understanding of the evolving practice of these revolutionary artists, demonstrating how their contributions to modernism were profoundly influenced by the forms, myths, and structures of the arts of antiquity. This is exemplified in *Man Attacked by a Lion*, which is exhibited for the first time alongside one of Picasso's proto-Cubist self-portraits that it originally inspired in 1906. Similarly, the exhibition allows for the first time an in-depth examination of Picasso's Cubism specifically through Rivera's eyes, indicating how the encounters between the artists allowed Rivera to deploy Cubism as a strategy in developing not only his work but also his own identity as a Mexican artist.

By placing masterworks by Picasso and Rivera alongside Greco-Roman, Etruscan, and Iberian works as well as Pre-Columbian sculptures and ceramic figurines, the exhibition weaves together distant geographies and distant worlds to blur the frontiers of time and space and to view both artists as inventors of a new visual reality in the first decades of the twentieth century. Picasso and Rivera's radical approach to understanding the arts of antiquity was ultimately political: by broadening and diversifying what was considered to be the art historical canon, they reinterpreted the aesthetics of antiquity in order to redefine what was considered "legitimate" art, thereby forging the way for a new and more pluralistic art of the present. As Rivera overcame the weight of European art and history in order to define himself as a Mexican artist, Picasso became a new kind of European artist by freeing both himself and modern art from the shackles of the classical past. They both, in their own ways, embody an epic story of creating a modern sense of self, nation, and identity.

PICASSO AND THE SIMULTANEITY OF TIME

MICHAEL GOVAN

The development of Cubism by Pablo Picasso and Georges Braque was a breakthrough not essentially stylistic, but rather of point of view.[1] The rise of perspective in fifteenth-century European art assembled narrative and space into a coherent simulacrum of three-dimensional vision, away from a medieval two-dimensional mapping out of image and narrative. Some five centuries later, Cubism discarded the primacy of a coherent Euclidean geometry of space and time in favor of the simultaneity of time within a single space. A Cubist portrait or still life presents a physical space from many points of view at once. The destructive aspect of Cubism (destroying the gestalt of a three-dimensional representation of space) is in search of a more complex and expansive assembly of experience over time. Time, more than space, is the object of Cubism.

While Picasso never abandoned Cubism entirely (it continued to form the basis of many of his stylistic advances, particularly in his work in the theater), by 1920 he had mostly returned to a classical figurative style of painting. This shift coincided with both his marriage to Russian ballerina Olga Khokhlova and the general "return to order" impulse in modern art following World War I, as well as his transformation from a bohemian figure of the avant-garde to an internationally successful artist with an increasingly bourgeois lifestyle. As Picasso returned to classical style and form in the 1920s and 1930s, it was the increasing complexity of his personal life—specifically, the deterioration of his marriage to Khokhlova and the beginning of his relationship with Marie-Thérèse Walter—that turned him mostly away from painting for a rare few years, and allowed him to fully indulge the more intimate medium of etching. Occasioned by the commission from publisher Albert Skira to illustrate a new edition of Ovid's *Metamorphoses*, Picasso connected with many cultural sources and influences, from his ancient Iberian ancestors to his art historical mentors such as Rembrandt. In his Cubist compositions Picasso both destroyed and reassembled an experience of the material world by presenting multiple viewpoints simultaneously. This same sensibility allowed him to assemble a multiplicity of historical moments on a static canvas, thereby developing a sort of Cubism of iconography and time—forging a thoroughly modern reconsideration of ancient sources.

It is my proposal that the practice of Cubism ultimately holds within it the mechanism of Picasso's exploration of time and history in his works of the 1930s, culminating in *Guernica* (1937), the grandest public artistic statement of his career. The intimate intaglio prints of this period are among the most poignant works of his prolific oeuvre, and include his illustrations for *Metamorphosis* (1931) as well as Aristophanes' *Lysistrata* (1934), the series of etchings collected in the Vollard Suite (1930–37), and his masterpiece of graphic art, *Minotauromachy* (1935). Mostly figurative line drawings inscribed into etching plates (similar to those inscribed on the backs of ancient Greek bronze mirrors), Picasso's etchings of the 1930s all appear to be set in an ancient Mediterranean landscape, even when they do not specifically illustrate classical texts. But while many of the images emerge from ancient narratives—most notably the Minotaur, an avatar for Picasso himself—many other sources are visible. From Catholic iconography to the Spanish bullfight, both staples of his education and upbringing, to the character of the artist, embodied in many images as a heroic Rembrandt, Picasso's seemingly simple black-and-white etchings are as complex in their fractured and recombined iconography as his Cubist compositions were in depicting a still life, landscape, or portrait from diverse but simultaneous points of view.

1
Of all of Picasso's accomplishments, his pivotal role in developing Cubism remains perhaps his most lasting contribution to art history. Cubism evolved through its adoption by many artists working in Paris and elsewhere, including, as described in this exhibition, Diego Rivera. An innovation discussed with the same importance in Western art as the invention of linear perspective, Cubism helped define modernism and inspired many related movements, including Constructivism, montage, certain forms of Expressionism, and the development of pure abstraction—all of which were most often associated with the rejection of the past in favor of a new order. Many early permutations of abstraction emerged between 1907 and 1917, prefiguring the world-changing tumult of World War I and the Russian Revolution.

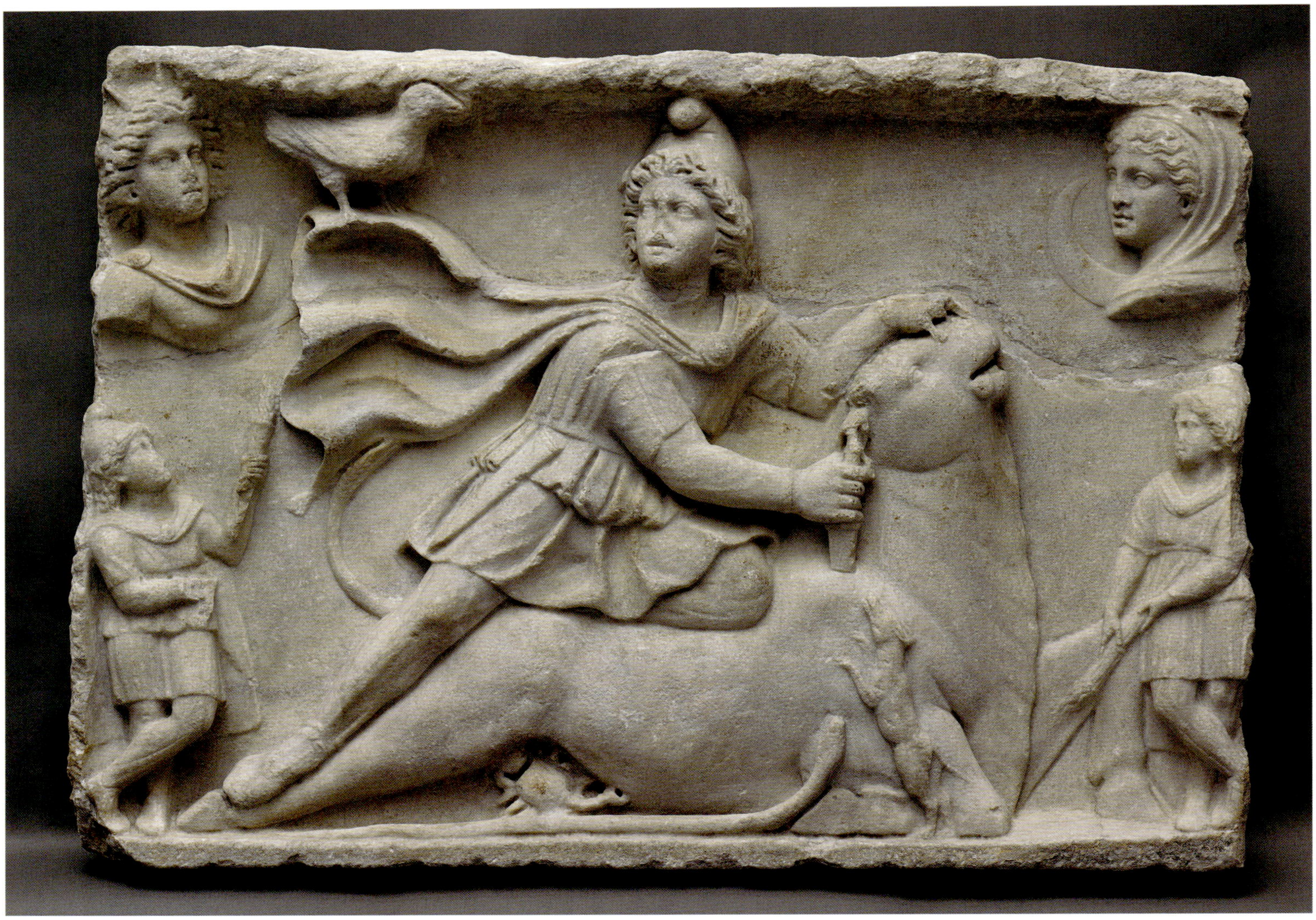

Mithraic Sacrifice Scene, Roman, 2nd century CE

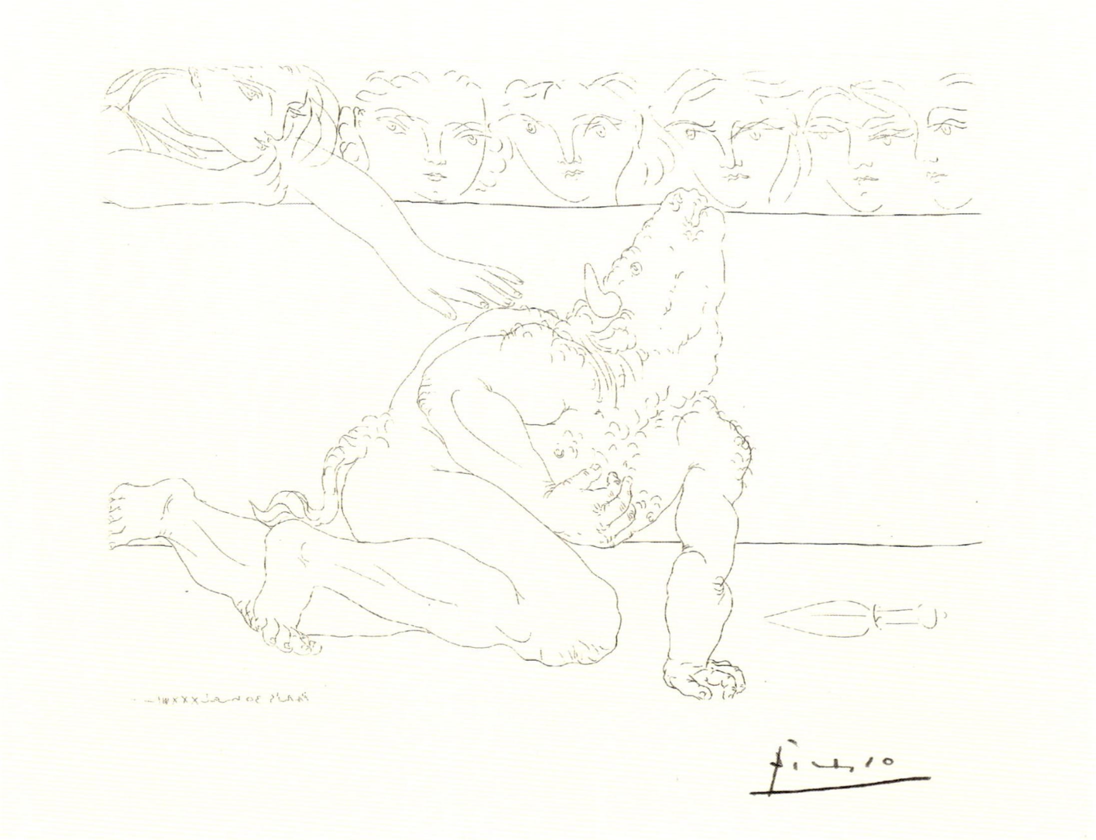

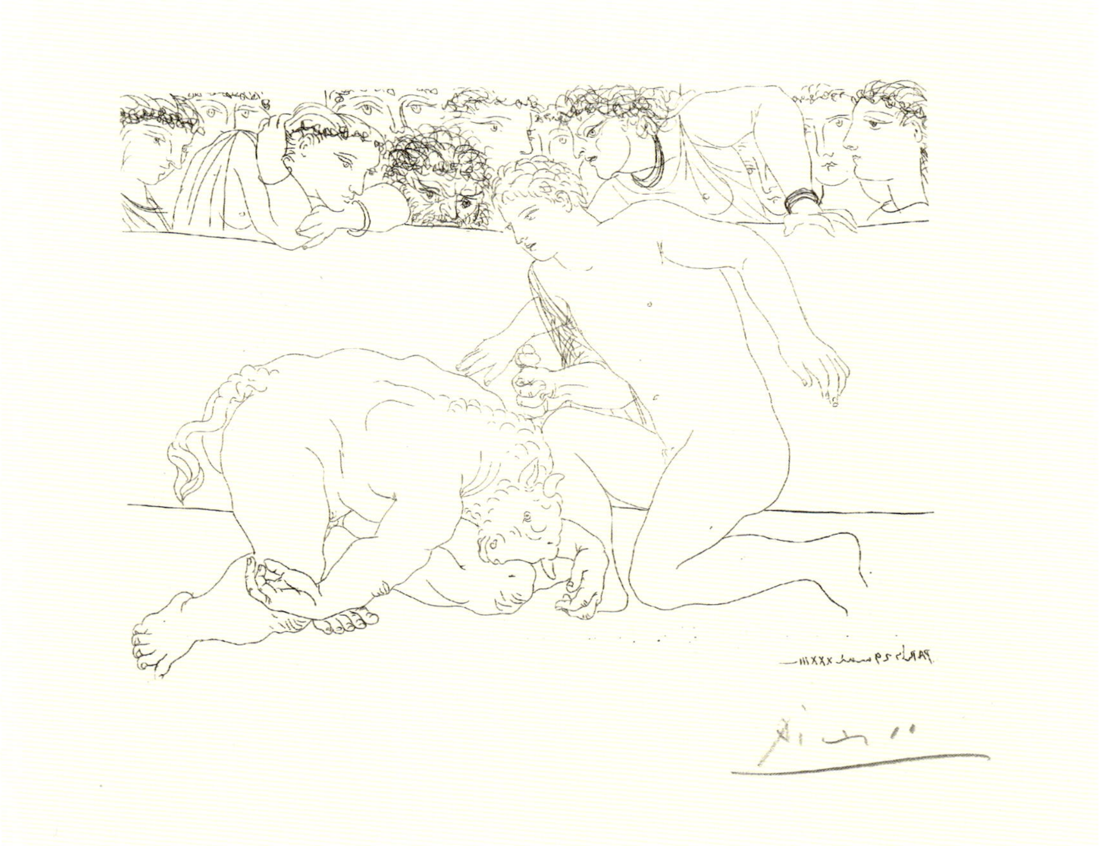

Pablo Picasso, ***Dying Minotaur***, May 30, 1933

Pablo Picasso, ***Vanquished Minotaur***, May 29, 1933

2
Picasso quoted in Lorraine Lévy, *Picasso* (London: Barrie & Jenkins, 1991), 91.
3
Françoise Gilot, *Life with Picasso* (New York: Anchor Books, 1964), 48–49.
4
Ibid., 49.
5
Ibid., 51.
6
Picasso quoted in ibid., 51.

A close analysis of *Minotauromachy* (p. 217), often considered a precursor to *Guernica*, offers insight into Picasso's subtle and complex "cubism of iconography"—his practice of juxtaposing moments from the past to express his present emotional condition within the terms of a larger historical narrative. *Minotauromachy* was made in the spring of 1935, a barren period in the artist's life in terms of the number of paintings he produced, which coincided with the tumult of his personal life. Picasso's relationship with Olga, his wife since 1918, had become unbearable, as Marie-Thérèse, with whom he had been involved since 1927, became pregnant. Olga, along with their fourteen-year-old son, Paulo, moved out of the family's home. Picasso described the end of 1935 as "the worst period of my life."[2]

During these troubled years, the medium of etching became especially important to Picasso. In 1933 and 1934, he not only completed six etchings for Gilbert Selde's adaptation of *Lysistrata* but also produced eighty-two of the one hundred etchings that were later collected as the Vollard Suite. As a whole, these prints allow important insight into the composition of *Minotauromachy*. Most of the prints adhere to a classical motif. They depict emotions of violence, passion, contemplation, and love, and center thematically around the artist, his model, and art. Françoise Gilot, in her book *Life with Picasso*, recalls an episode in 1943 when Picasso showed her the Vollard Suite.[3] Her account of this encounter is one of the most revealing sources of interpretation of the prints. The prints, she observes, are "filled with bearded and clean-shaven men, with Minotaurs, centaurs, faunlike figures, and all kinds of women. Everyone was nude or nearly so and they seemed to be playing out a drama from Greek mythology."[4]

Within the suite can be found the Minotaur, the bullfight, the artist and his model, and Rembrandt. Picasso's lifelong interest in Rembrandt is well documented in his work. In later years, he painted his own versions of Rembrandt's pictures, as he did of Diego Velázquez's. In Picasso's technique, his portraits of Rembrandt, and his compositions such as *Faun Uncovering a Woman* (p. 46), we find striking examples of his encounter with the great master of etching. For Picasso, Rembrandt is a technical source, an emotional source, and a character that the artist used like an intriguing piece of text in his own personal narrative. Gilot quotes Picasso in his usual audacious, yet revealing, tone, pointing to a print in the Vollard Suite of a "darkly bearded Rembrandt-like figure facing a young painter wearing a Phrygian cap."[5] Picasso reflected, "Every painter takes himself for Rembrandt.... Even this one, and you can tell by the cap he flourished at least three thousand years before Rembrandt came along. Everybody has the same delusions."[6]

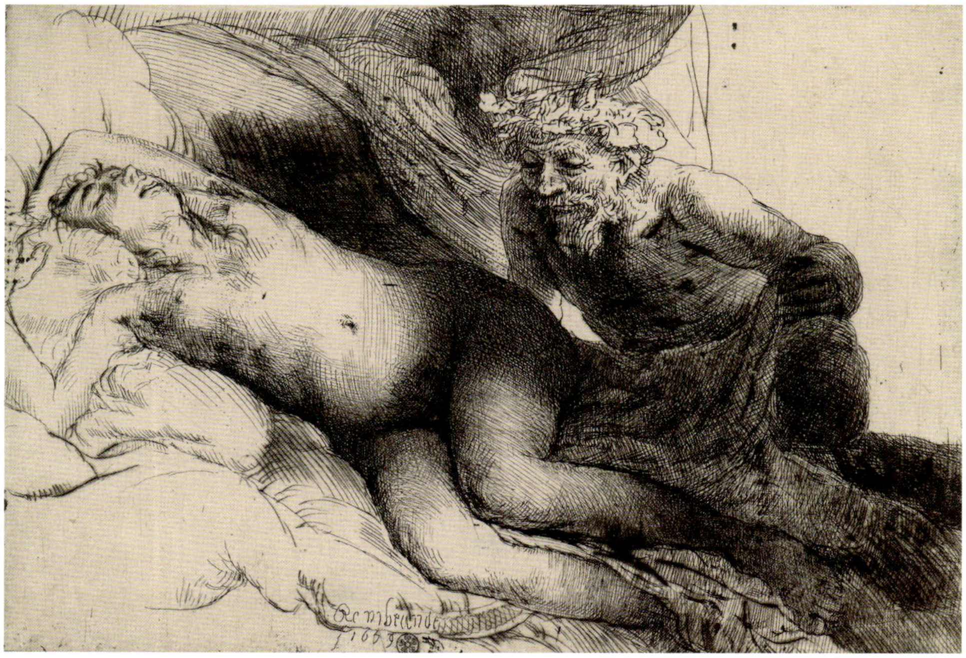

Rembrandt van Rijn, ***Jupiter and Antiope: The Larger Plate***, 1659; etching, burin and drypoint, printed on Japanese paper, 5⅜ × 8⅛ in. (13.8 × 20.5 cm); The Pierpont Morgan Library, New York

Picasso identifies himself with both the mythic and the tragic Rembrandt. In *Standing Nude with Flowing Headdress* and *Portrait of Rembrandt with Palette* (both 1934) he portrays Rembrandt as the successful painter with his model by his side. In compositions such as *Minotaur Holding Goblet and a Young Woman* (p. 47) and *Minotaur, Drinker, and Women* (p. 211), Picasso recalls Rembrandt's gay *Self-Portrait with Saskia* (1635). But Rembrandt also suffered great financial and personal misfortune. Three of his four children by his wife, Saskia van Uylenburgh, died in childbirth, and she herself died in 1642. Unable to remarry because of the financial provisions in her will, Rembrandt lived, amid public disapproval, with his model Hendrickje Stoffels, a twenty-three-year-old servant girl he met in 1649. His early financial and popular success in painting dwindled. By 1653 he faced financial ruin. His later self-portraits are immensely introspective.

Olga, who continued to torment Picasso with letters long after their separation in 1935, must have been particularly sensitive to Picasso's respect for Rembrandt. Writes Gilot: "Olga wrote him almost every day long tirades in Spanish, so that I wouldn't understand, mixed with Russian, which no one understood, and French, which she wrote so badly that it wasn't very understandable either.... Sometimes she would send a picture of Rembrandt on which she had written, 'If you were like him, you would be a great artist.'"[7]

Along with references to Rembrandt, Picasso also embedded in the Vollard Suite allusions to the bullfight, a theme he would develop more fully in *Minotauromachy*. A discussion of the figures of the horse and the dead bullfighter in *Minotauromachy* necessarily begins with Picasso's attitudes toward the bullfight. Gilot writes that "Picasso's definition of a perfect Sunday, according to Spanish standards, was 'mass in the morning, bullfight in the afternoon, whorehouse in the evening.' He had no trouble getting along without the first and last of these, but one of the major joys of his life was the bullfight, and we went often."[8] The bullfight was more than entertainment to Picasso; it was a ritual central to his life and art.

The bullfight is a complex drama in which each character plays a certain role. The matador and the bull are pitted in a heroic struggle. The picador's horse is often the tragic victim. Certainly within his Spanish tradition, the bullfight was one of Picasso's first subjects and appears consistently throughout his body of work. Of special note in relation to Picasso's work is Francisco Goya's 1816 print series *La Tauromaquia* (Bullfighting), from which derives the title for *Minotauromachy*. In Goya's prints, there are disemboweled horses, dead bullfighters, and dead bulls; Picasso's subject is not a new one. Picasso focused on the theme of the bullfight in 1919 in his set and costume design for *The Three-Cornered Hat*, a Ballets Russes production based on the novel by Pedro Antonio de Alarcón, set to music by Manuel de Falla, and first performed in London. The curtain opens to reveal a bullfight scene (painted by Picasso on the secondary drapery); spectators impassively observe as a slain animal is dragged away and a new bull enters the arena. Picasso's drawings for the set deal explicitly with the relationship between spectator and drama, the drama being one of death.

In 1922 Picasso painted a small Goyaesque bullfight scene with bull, horse, and toreador. The three figures are grouped closely together in the center of the picture on the stage of a stark, expansive arena. The bull seems triumphant, plunging into the horse, who cries in agony. The toreador lies slung over the bull's back. Far in the distance, spectators—dots on the picture—observe from behind the arena's walls. The toreador's pique lies on the ground beneath the group. The bull tramples the cape that the toreador, his arm slung over the bull's side, still clutches in his hand. The horse and female matador of *Minotauromachy* recall this original scene. In 1933 Picasso painted another small bullfight scene on wood, very similar to the 1922 picture.

7 Ibid., 154.

8 Ibid., 243.

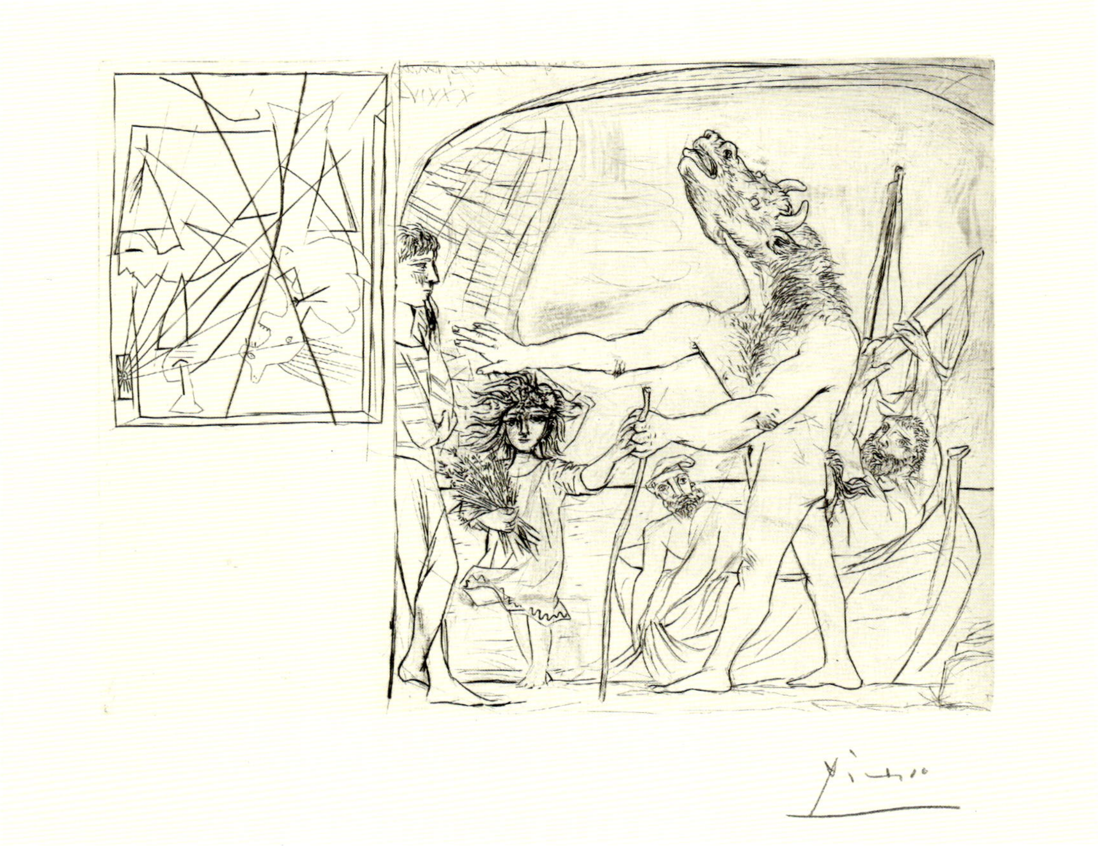

Pablo Picasso, ***Blind Minotaur Led by a Young Girl***, September 22, 1934

In this picture, however, the half-clothed female bullfighter of *Minotauromachy* is introduced. The bull is given much greater importance; both the smaller horse and the bullfighter are on the bull's back. In this picture, the matador's sword is deep in the bull's neck. Although the bull still charges forward, he must be near his own end.

The setting of *Minotauromachy* is not a Spanish arena, but rather a Mediterranean setting—the isle of Crete, perhaps, where one source for Picasso's female bullfighter can be found. Bullfights held in the Palace of Minos in ancient Crete have been said to be the true origin of the contemporary Spanish bullfight. These bullfights were centered on the acrobat toreador, who is, in most ancient illustrations, female. Although Picasso adopts a classical architecture in which to stage his bullfights, the acrobatic bullfights of ancient Crete are never literally illustrated in his work. Picasso absorbs what he needs from history or myth and changes it to suit his particular purposes. This is especially evident in the way Picasso deals with the myth of the Minotaur.

Although the title *Minotauromachy* derives from the term *tauromachy*, the print certainly does not illustrate a bullfight. There is no bull; instead, we recognize the mythological Minotaur, who is of great significance in Picasso's life and work. "If all the ways I have been along were marked on a map and joined up with a line," said Picasso, "it might represent a Minotaur."[9] Yet Picasso's Minotaur is mainly his own creation, only loosely based on traditional legend. The beast, usually represented with the body of a man and the head of a bull, lived, according to myth, in the fabled labyrinth in Crete. Young men and women from Athens were sacrificed to the beast regularly, until finally one day Theseus killed the Minotaur. Theseus found his way out of the maze with the help of Ariadne, following a long strand of thread he had strung from the entrance. Surrealist artists and writers adopted the myth of the Minotaur as their own, and the Minotaur came to symbolize man's bodily desires (the body of a man) and his irrationality (the head of a bull). The Surrealists' Minotaur, although blinded by natural light, sees in the darkness of the labyrinth of his own subconscious as others cannot. His labyrinth is within himself. The Minotaur first appeared in Picasso's work in 1928, and in 1933 Picasso illustrated the cover for the first issue of the new Surrealist magazine *Minotaure* (p. 15).

The Minotaur is the subject of several plates of the Vollard Suite. Two compositions, *Vanquished Minotaur* and *Dying Minotaur* (p. 39), depict a Minotaur down on his knees, stabbed. In both prints a crowd of spectators in classical garb looks on. In *Dying Minotaur*, a woman in the crowd reaches her hand out over the wall to touch the dying Minotaur; the others are dispassionate. Gilot quotes Picasso: "We're taught that Theseus came and killed a

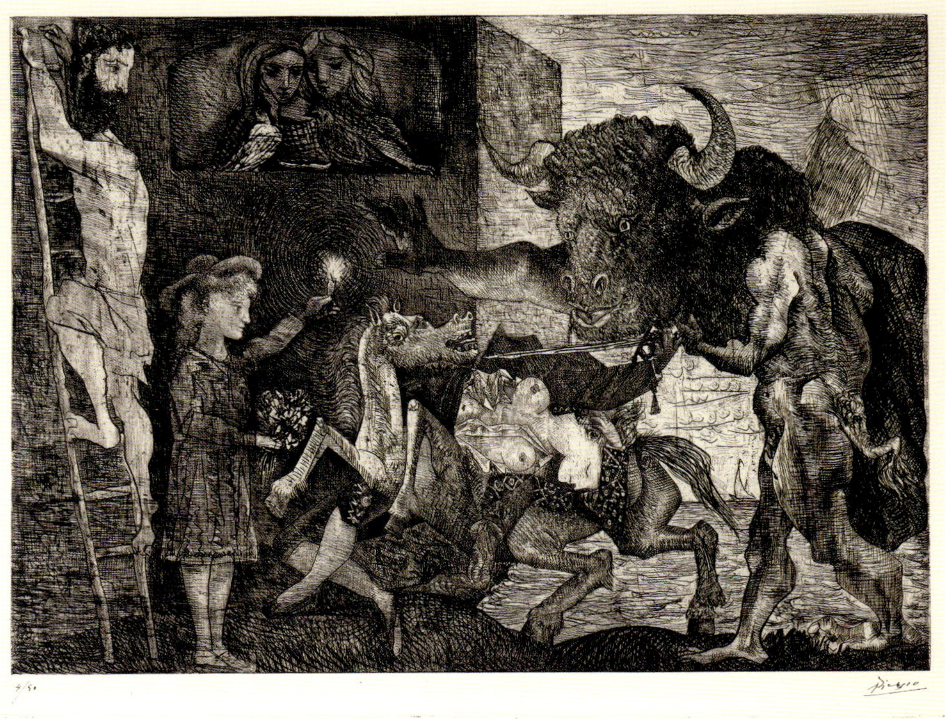

Pablo Picasso, ***Minotauromachy***, 1935; etching and engraving, PLATE 19½ × 27⅜ in. (49.6 × 69.6 cm); SHEET (IRREG.) 22⅝ × 29³⁄₁₆ in. (57.4 × 74.2 cm); The Museum of Modern Art, New York, Abby Aldrich Rockefeller Fund

9 Picasso quoted in *A Picasso Portfolio: Prints from the Museum of Modern Art*, ed. Deborah Wye (New York: Museum of Modern Art, 2010), 46.

Minotaur, but he was one of many. It happened every Sunday: a young Attic Greek came over from the mainland and when he killed a Minotaur he made all the women happy, especially the old ones. A Minotaur keeps his women lavishly but he reigns by terror and they're glad to see him killed."[10]

Picasso's story follows no accepted version of the myth and yet is not entirely inconsistent, combining elements of both the Minotaur myth and the history of the Cretan bullfight. Indeed, the Minotaur myth itself may have its origins in the ancient Cretan bullfights; the so-called labyrinth where the Minotaur lived could have been the labyrinthine palace complex of Knossos on the isle of Crete where the bullfights took place. Combining myth and history, Picasso draws a relationship between bull and Minotaur; both become victims in this case. But Picasso's Minotaur is at the same time lover, aggressor, and victim. Roaming the Mediterranean landscape, he is a character of complex emotions who, like Picasso, changes his mood frequently. Gilot quotes Picasso:

> All this takes place on a hilly island in the Mediterranean...like Crete. That's where the Minotaurs live, along the coast. They're the rich seigneurs of the island. They know they're monsters and they live, like dandies and dilettantes everywhere, the kind of existence that reeks of decadence in houses filled with works of art by the most fashionable painters and sculptors. They love being surrounded by pretty women. They get the local fishermen to go out and round up girls from the neighboring islands. After the heat of the day has passed, they bring the sculptors and their models for parties, with music and dancing, and everybody gorges himself on mussels and champagne until melancholy fades away and euphoria takes over. From there on it's an orgy.[11]

After viewing some of Picasso's drawings of Minotaurs, artist and writer Jaime Sabartés observed, "In all these designs, in the simplicity and firmness of line so characteristic of his emotional power, I sought Picasso and found him everywhere."[12] The Minotaur is Picasso; he feels what Picasso feels. Picasso begs sympathy for his Minotaur. Writes Gilot:

> Picasso was speaking very quietly now. "A Minotaur can't be loved for himself," he said. "At least he doesn't think he can. It just doesn't seem reasonable to him, somehow. Perhaps that's why he goes in for orgies." He turned to another print, a Minotaur watching over a sleeping woman. "He's studying her, trying to read her thoughts," he said, "trying to decide whether she loves him because he's a monster." He looked up at me. "Women are odd enough for that, you know." He looked down at the etching again. "It's hard to say whether he wants to wake her or kill her," he said.[13]

The character of the Minotaur is closely related to that of the sculptor in the Vollard Suite. It is the images of artist and model that dominate the suite, setting the tone for the Greek drama. The sculptor shares with the Minotaur an intuitive sense and many of the same emotions. As the Minotaur is to the intellectual rational man, so the sculptor is to the painter. Of painter and sculptor, Gilot quotes Picasso as saying: "The painters are a little out of contact with reality.... But at least the painters live a more orderly life than the sculptors. You'll notice that wherever there are orgies, there are beards. That's the sculptors: warm flesh in one hand, cool champagne in the other. No doubt about it, the sculptors are very much in contact with reality."[14]

10 Picasso quoted in Gilot, *Life with Picasso*, 50.

11 Picasso quoted in ibid., 49.

12 Jaime Sabartés, *Picasso: An Intimate Portrait* (Upper Saddle River, NJ: Prentice Hall, 1948), 130.

13 Gilot, *Life with Picasso*, 50.

14 Picasso quoted in ibid., 50.

Both the sculptor and the Minotaur possess the important sense of touch. The sculptor's sense of touch challenges the painter's sense of line. Somehow touch is more real. The gesture of touch is important in *Minotauromachy*, as it is in many of the prints of the Vollard Suite. The spectator in the prints of the dying Minotaur, for example, shows compassion toward the Minotaur in her gesture. The Minotaur's sense of touch is most explicit in *Blind Minotaur Led by Young Girl* and *Blind Minotaur Led by a Young Girl at Night* (pp. 214 and 215). Staff in one hand, the blind Minotaur reaches out to find his way; a little girl leads him. The profile of the girl, like the girl who holds the candle in *Minotauromachy*, is that of Marie-Thérèse, whose haunting face appears throughout Picasso's work of the 1930s. The blind Minotaur led by a girl brings to mind the story of Oedipus, who, stricken by tragedy, blinded himself and banished himself to Colonus, taking along his daughter Antigone. The blind Minotaur in relation to the sculptor is also a Tiresias figure, a sort of artistic prophet, stripped of sight but granted the gift of vision. "They ought to put out the eyes of painters as they do goldfinches in order that they can sing better," said Picasso in 1932.[15]

Picasso's Minotaur is many things at once; the sculptor/Minotaur also becomes Theseus, who followed Ariadne's thread out of the darkness of the labyrinth, just as Marie-Thérèse led Picasso away from his painful relationship with Olga. Theseus, of course, was later abandoned by Ariadne at Naxos. The anguish of Picasso's emotional situation is alluded to in the top of the image on the same plate as the first of the blind Minotaur prints (p. 42), which shows Picasso's version of *The Death of Marat* (1934) turned upside-down. Picasso depicts the moment of stabbing: Marat's monstrous-looking female assailant holds high a terrible dagger. Sun streaks in through the window onto the death scene, as it does in many of the bullfight scenes of the same period.

In Crete the sun may have been conceived of as a bull, and the bull as the sun. An anthropomorphic conception of the sun also existed as the Cretan Talos, described as a giant bronze man with a single vein extending from neck to ankle, where it was closed by a bronze nail. Poet Robert Graves has suggested that Talos's vein may be linked "to the mystery of early bronze casting by the *cire-perdu* method."[16] According to some sources, Talos was identified with the bull in Sardinia, and in both Crete and Sardinia came to be identified with the Minotaur. Talos was a guardian slain by the guile of Medea, who drove him mad, and several versions of his death are found in legend. One ancient depiction of his demise shows the Argonauts landing on the Cretan coast to catch him. Medea stands near, presumably keeping him under her magic spell. Two of the Argonauts have captured the helpless Talos. Portions of this myth can easily be related to the blind Minotaur prints.

In the large *Minotauromachy* print, the Minotaur is not blind, and the little girl no longer guides him with her body. She stands still, facing him, holding up a candle. The Minotaur extends his arm toward the light, right foot in front of left foot as he moves forward. Behind him, over his right shoulder, is a sack or possibly a matador's cape (in color proofs, it is blood red). Between the girl and the beast is a disemboweled horse. Draped over the horse's back is the half-clothed figure of a dead female matador, whose right hand, which almost touches the Minotaur's left hand, holds up a matador's sword. The figures stand near the sea,

15 Picasso quoted in *Picasso on Art: A Selection of Views*, ed. Dore Ashton (Boston: Da Capo Press, 1988), 78.

16 Robert Graves, *The Greek Myths: Complete Edition* (London: Penguin, 1992), 317.

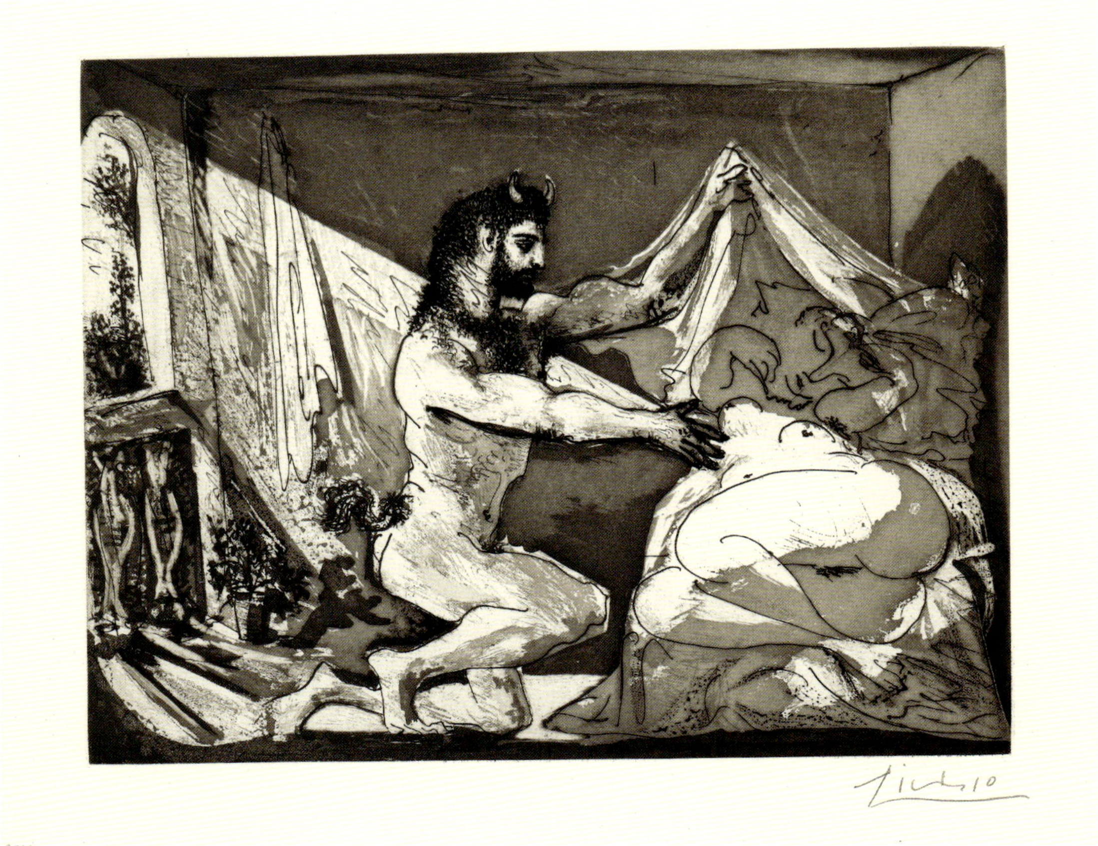

Pablo Picasso, ***Faun Uncovering a Woman***, June 12, 1936

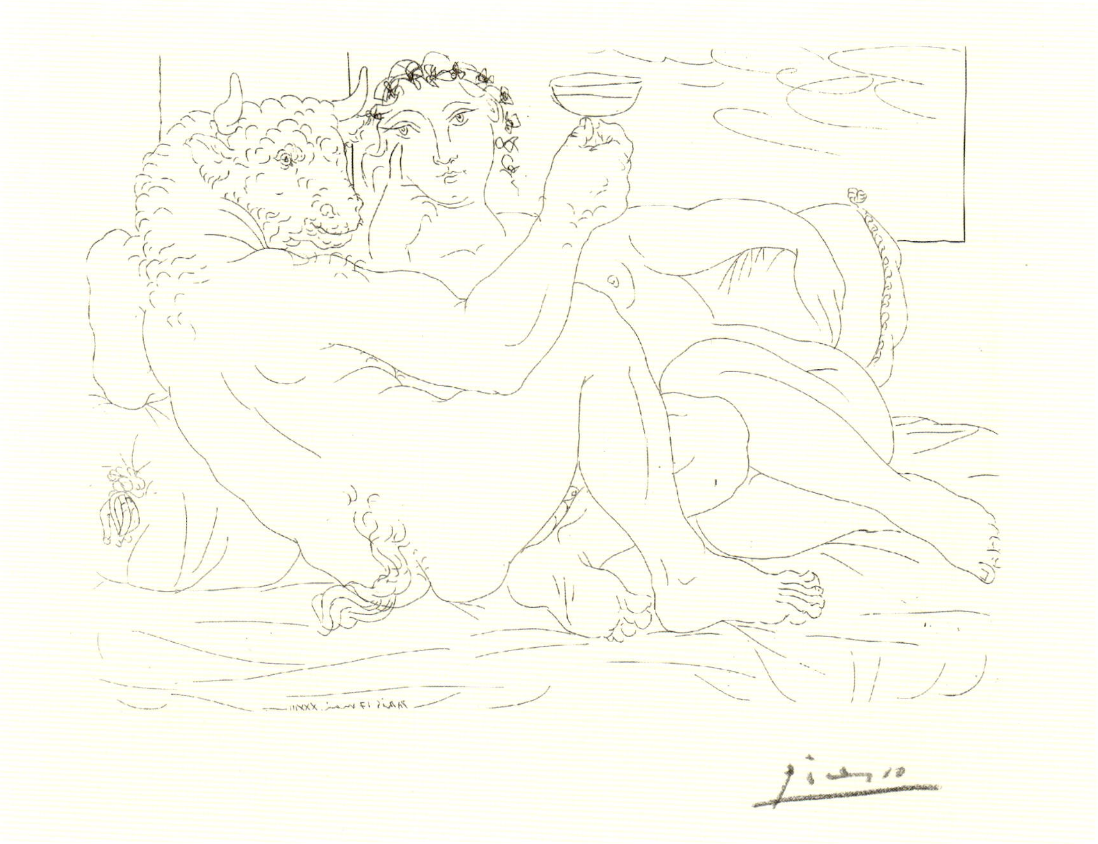

Pablo Picasso, ***Minotaur Holding Goblet and a Young Woman,***
May 17, 1933

17 Picasso quoted in André Malraux, *Picasso's Mask* (Boston: Da Capo Press, 1995), 41.

where a sailboat can be seen on the distant horizon. The sky is dark. In the left half of the etching, behind the main figures, is a simple building. A ladder leans against the wall on the far left; a bearded male figure wearing a simple loincloth looks down from it onto the scene. Above, in an arched window, two female figures also observe the scene.

The figures and composition are almost unchanged throughout the states of the print. The figure of the small girl is given a hat in the third state; also in the third state, the Minotaur's pack or cape is extended around his right shoulder. A wall of the building is added in the fourth state. None of these changes appear to have any significant bearing on the meaning of the print. The four earliest states reveal that what Picasso struggled with was not the composition, but rather the chiaroscuro. The drama is played out around light.

The composition centers around the extended arm of the Minotaur, his hand engaged with the light of the candle. The hand attempts to shield the light, yet the Minotaur's face is lit. The gesture is ambiguous. While the Minotaur seems to take an aggressive stance, the gesture of the hand is hesitant, approaching and shielding, but cautious. The gesture is related to the touch of the sculptor, the spectator, and the blind Minotaur we have observed in the Vollard Suite. The girl who holds the candle is obviously related to the girl guiding the blind Minotaur. She appears elsewhere in Picasso's work, most notably in *Guernica*, where her elongated figure stretches out of the window from above to light the scene of destruction. In an earlier 1934 drawing, the girl holds her candle over the edge of a wall in the *plaza de toros*, illuminating the scene of a bull disemboweling a horse; the bull himself is dying, stabbed by the matador's sword. Her candle illuminates death and destruction. As Picasso observed, Goya used light in the same manner. In reference to Goya's *The Third of May* (1814), which depicts the 1808 execution of Spanish rebels by French soldiers,

> [t]he black sky isn't a sky, it's blackness. As for the lighting, there are two types. One that we don't understand. It illumines everything like moonlight.... But it sheds far more light than the moon. It hasn't the same color. Then there's the huge lantern on the ground, right in the middle. And what does that illumine? The guy raising his arms, the martyr. If you look at it carefully, you'll see that it sheds light only on him. The lantern is Death. Why? No one knows. Not even Goya. But what Goya knew was that it had to be just like that.[17]

Picasso's lantern is also Death. In *Minotauromachy* the candle lights the dead female matador slung over the back of the disemboweled horse—the scene of destruction. The candle also sheds light on the Minotaur. His extended arm is lit from beneath by the candle's light, reflected off the bare breast of the female matador. The significance of the light in the Minotaur print is not simply one of death, however. Picasso's sources for this light and his various uses of it have mythological, classical, biblical, and other cultural origins. The worship of light and sun has many ancient sources—too many to rightfully bring into the context of Picasso's work. One, however, is particularly relevant within the Mediterranean/classical context and Picasso's own personal mythology—namely, Mithraism. Mithras, a god of light, in ancient sculpture is usually depicted slaying a bull, with one leg straight, foot on the ground, and the other leg bent on the bull's back as he plunges a petaloid knife into the bull's neck (p. 38). On either side of him stand two youths, one with an upright torch and the other with an inverted one. Around the figures are usually represented the sun and moon (sometimes Helios and Selene). Mithraism, with its roots in Zoroastrianism and other Persian mythology, was quite popular as a cult religion in Roman culture, especially among Roman troops around the third century CE.

Franz Cumont's *Mysteries of Mithras* (1903) popularized interest in the religious cult among French intellectuals and artists of the early twentieth century. In 1930 Georges Bataille wrote an essay, "Rotten Sun," connecting Picasso's interest in the bullfight with primitive sun worship, Mithraism, and the bull. According to Bataille, the bull itself in a slain state can be identified with the sun. One who stares at the sun is identified with the slain bull (along with Mithras and Prometheus) and the sun then becomes *destruction* as much as construction. He describes the Mithraic rite, including the priest's actual slaying of the bull, which produces a sudden spray of "hot blood, to the accompaniment of the bull's boisterous struggle and bellowing."[18] The rite becomes a "simple way of reaping the moral benefits of the blinding sun."[19] The sun mythologically can be connected to man slaying himself. The apex of elevation becomes confused with a sudden fall and violence.

Both *Vanquished Minotaur* and *Dying Minotaur* seem to derive directly from the image of Mithras, and to connect Mithras with a representation of the bullfight. Mithras, in his slaying of the bull, offered man a salvation. While modern scholarship is much more skeptical about the connection between Mithraism and Christianity, Cumont tried to prove that "if it has not inspired, it has at least contributed to give precise form to, certain doctrines of the Church, as the ideas relative to the powers of hell and to the end of the world."[20] In any case, the possibility of melding this ancient cult religion with his own Roman Catholic background, as well as with the bullfight, must have been an attractive one for Picasso.

The bearded sculptor figure on the ladder in *Minotauromachy* may offer insight into Picasso's engagement with Mithraism and its narrative of salvation. In the five states of the print, Picasso does not noticeably change him; he is completely in light from first to last. The image of the man in his simple loincloth may bring to mind the traditional composition of Christ's descent from the cross, although here our character is quite animated. Rembrandt's etchings *The Descent from the Cross by Torchlight* (1654) and *The Descent from the Cross: Second Plate* (1633) both provide strong visual evidence for such an interpretation.

The ladder is a motif that appears throughout Picasso's work. It is often part of the gear of traveling actors in Picasso's early output,

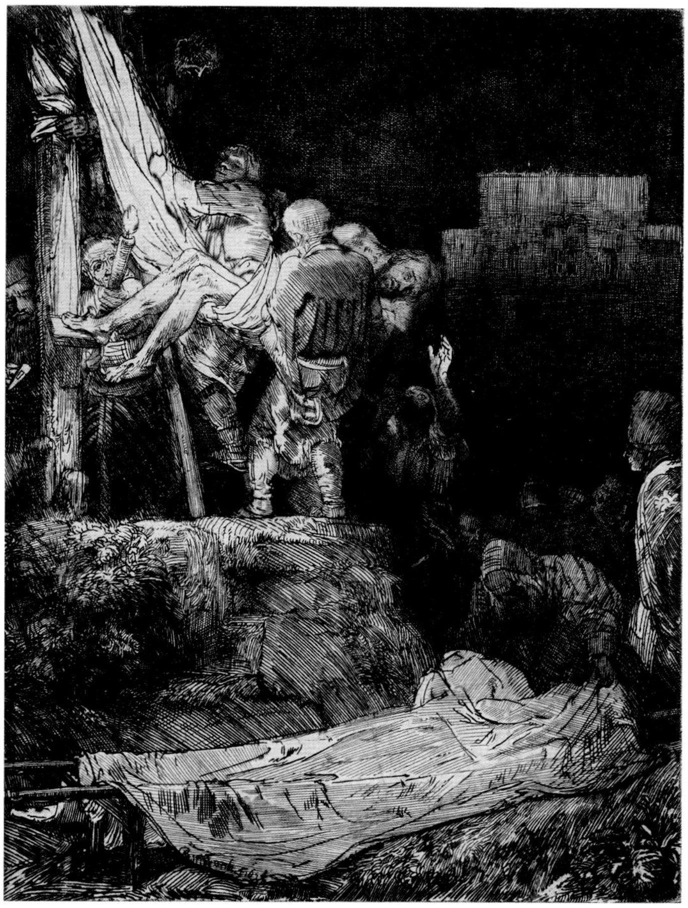

Rembrandt van Rijn, ***The Descent from the Cross by Torchlight***, 1654; etching and drypoint, SHEET 8⅜ × 6⅜ in. (21.3 × 16.2 cm); Los Angeles County Museum of Art, Art Museum Council Fund (M.62.3.3)

18 Georges Bataille, "Rotten Sun," in *Visions of Excess: Selected Writings, 1927–1939* (Minneapolis: University of Minnesota Press, 1985), 57.

19 Ibid.

20 Franz Cumont, *The Mysteries of Mithra* (Chicago: Open Court, 1903), vi.

21 Ibid., 128.

22 Gilot, *Life with Picasso*, 235–36.

and it is included in early sketches for the scenery of *The Three-Cornered Hat*, as well as in a 1930 painting of the Crucifixion. In both Christian and pagan imagery, the ladder is a common symbol of the path to heaven. The image of the ladder was also common in Mithraism: the seven steps symbolizing the ascent of the soul through the heavens became the seven steps of initiation into the cult of Mithraism, and by extension to salvation. Cumont connects this Mithraic salvation to the development of the Christian concept of salvation. Rembrandt's compositions of the descent from the cross, illuminated by streaks of light from the sky or by candlelight, illustrate the Christian significance of the ladder and Christ's death. By his death, Christ reopens the gates for humanity's ascent into Heaven. The ladder and the image of Christ's death, connected by light (the light of man, Christ), become symbols of an ultimate salvation.

Picasso's light, then, is both death and salvation. The girl with the candle stands between the scene of death and the image of salvation, echoing Cumont's statement that "Mithra was the 'mediator' between the unapproachable and unknowable god that reigned in the ethereal spheres, and the human race that struggled and suffered here below."[21] Her candle is a light for the Minotaur, guiding him like the girl guides the blind Minotaur. Yet the Minotaur is hesitant in his approach, touching the light of the candle, where death and salvation meet.

Picasso at this time was in anguish over his personal life. It was this anguish that inspired in the early and mid-1930s the images of death and suffering: the crucifixions, the death of Marat, the bullfights. The image of death is a continual one, which must be repeated over and over again as in the ritual of the bullfight. Intertwined with the image of death, however, is the image of escape. The female bullfighter of the bullfight scenes (p. 216), who resembles Marie-Thérèse, is connected to the horse as tragic victim, yet her image is also exactly that of the sleeping and dreaming Marie-Thérèse, Picasso's contemplative refugee. In the coexistence of these two senses lies the visual power of these images. Writes Gilot:

> Marie-Thérèse, then, was very important to [Picasso] as long as he was living with Olga because she was the dream when the reality was someone else. He continued to love her because he hadn't really taken possession of her: she lived somewhere else and was the escape hatch from a reality he found unpleasant. But once he had, in order to take fuller possession of that form of hers for which he had such an insistent desire, sent Olga away, then reality suddenly changed sides. What had been fantasy and dream became reality, and absence became presence—a double presence, since Marie-Thérèse was expecting a child. Then Marie-Thérèse replaced Olga as the one to escape from, in accordance with Pablo's form of logic.[22]

The theme of the conflict of dream and reality, and the artist's existence between the two, is prevalent throughout the Vollard Suite, in the images of artist and models, sleepers and their watchers, and, in a more complex sense, the bullfights. *Minotauromachy* is the culmination of the development of this theme, manifest in a confrontation of darkness and light, suffering and salvation. The artist's interior state of conflict is placed on a mythic scale. This shift of scale and complexity of meaning is achieved both through the pathos of figurative representation as well as through particular networks of meaning constructed by the artist's reference to various traditional iconographic sources, which he has developed in other images that surround the print. The characters that play out the drama in the print are not new in Picasso's work; each brings important associations with it. Picasso creates a recombination and new juxtaposition of the characters, forged by the synthesis of sources and references of personal relevance to the artist.

The light Picasso uses to define the symbolic forms of his composition is itself made up of many layers of reference. It points to powerful examples of the struggle between death and salvation, as represented in numerous Christian, pagan, and Spanish traditions. It is also an essential concept for the character of the artist, for it defines actually the physical word seen and represented by the artist. Yet a different sort of light offers the blind Minotaur a larger vision. Picasso was drawn to Rembrandt's infatuation with the light of illumination, the light of salvation, and the tragedy of the artist's blindness in both physical and symbolic terms. Rembrandt's introspective use of light served as a starting point for Picasso.

The importance of light to the Spanish bullfight is well known. "The theory, practice and spectacle of bullfighting have all been built on the assumption of the presence of the sun," writes Ernest Hemingway in *Death in the Afternoon*. "The sun is the best bullfighter, and without the sun the best bullfighter is not there. He is like a man without a shadow."[23] We have already observed the possible origins of the Spanish bullfight in the mythology of Crete. Many of Picasso's female bullfighter compositions of 1933–34 (known as *Death in the Sun*), as well as related compositions, prominently include the streaks of the sun's light.

The light also becomes a physical entity in itself, which can be "touched" by the sculptor/Minotaur, beyond being merely "seen" by the painter. Picasso synthesizes the earthly light that illuminates the painter's subject with the symbolic light of artistic vision, prophecy, and salvation. The light illuminates the scenes of ritual death like the bullfight. In *Minotauromachy* the light is placed in relation to the Minotaur so as to focus all of the associations that define Picasso's personal mythology. The print places the artist's personal battle on a dramatic scale in a public arena, like the heroic confrontation of life and death between matador and bull in the tauromachy. The two women in the window, Picasso's spectators, are there to witness the battle below. The conflict is represented again on the windowsill: the dove on the right is dark; the one on the left is light. Both turn their heads toward the man on the ladder.

23 Ernest Hemingway, *Death in the Afternoon* (New York: Simon & Schuster, 2002), 21.

Ultimately, the light is an object of attention, to be stared at intensely, like the sleeper/female matador and like the art object itself. Witnessing the battle of *Minotauromachy*, like witnessing Bataille's Mithraic rite, becomes a "simple way to reap morally the benefits of the blinding sun." The blinding sun is at once the apex of spiritual elevation and the fall of violent destruction; only in its contemplation is there any hope of escape or salvation.

Picasso's monumental *Guernica* takes on real historical events and, rare for the artist, suggests a collective rather than personal mythology. The composition of *Guernica*, like that of *Minotauromachy*, is organized largely horizontally, like a frieze, as if compressed into the shallow depth of a theatrical drama on a proscenium stage. Also like *Minotauromachy*, the imagery in *Guernica* is organized around light. In both, light illuminates death and suffering, as well as perhaps a path to salvation, inherent in Picasso's Cubist-like assembly of an iconography of light from ancient Mithraic rites to Christianity to the ritual bullfight.

Guernica is the quintessential example of Picasso drawing together a multiplicity of time and space. Analyzed in countless articles and books, Picasso's mural-scale protest against the destructive violence of the Spanish Civil War is a compendium of images of the evil inherent in unjustified violence, drawing on sources as diverse as the bullfight and the Roman narrative of the Rape of the Sabine Women, made visible through the light of truth, represented mythically in an Eye of Providence drawn to include the electric illumination of the modern age. Linear patterns of black dashes cover the disemboweled horse (from the bullfight) in the black and white paint of the entire painting, mimicking the text of the contemporary newspaper that speeds and imprints the awareness of evil instantaneously.

Picasso's composition is not simply a compendium of historical references embodied in different characters; rather, it is literally the embodiment of the victim through its historical and typological symbolism in the iconic drama of the bullfight and simultaneously the cry of the news of the moment. In a parallel fashion, Rivera developed an approach to painting and epic muralism, one that conjoins the origin stories of ancient Mexico with the narrative of its revolutionary present and future. It could be that while Rivera abandoned Cubism as a style, it remained a vital tool in opening possibilities of a new paradigm of the enlargement of the temporal dimension in painting. Rivera collapses time into his paintings in order to craft the image of a new politics and national identity, and Picasso, in *Guernica*, puts current events into a larger perspective of human nature and history.

This essay is based on work previously published in *The Minotaur & the Light: Sources for Picasso c. 1935* (Williamstown, MA: Williams College Museum of Art, 1985).

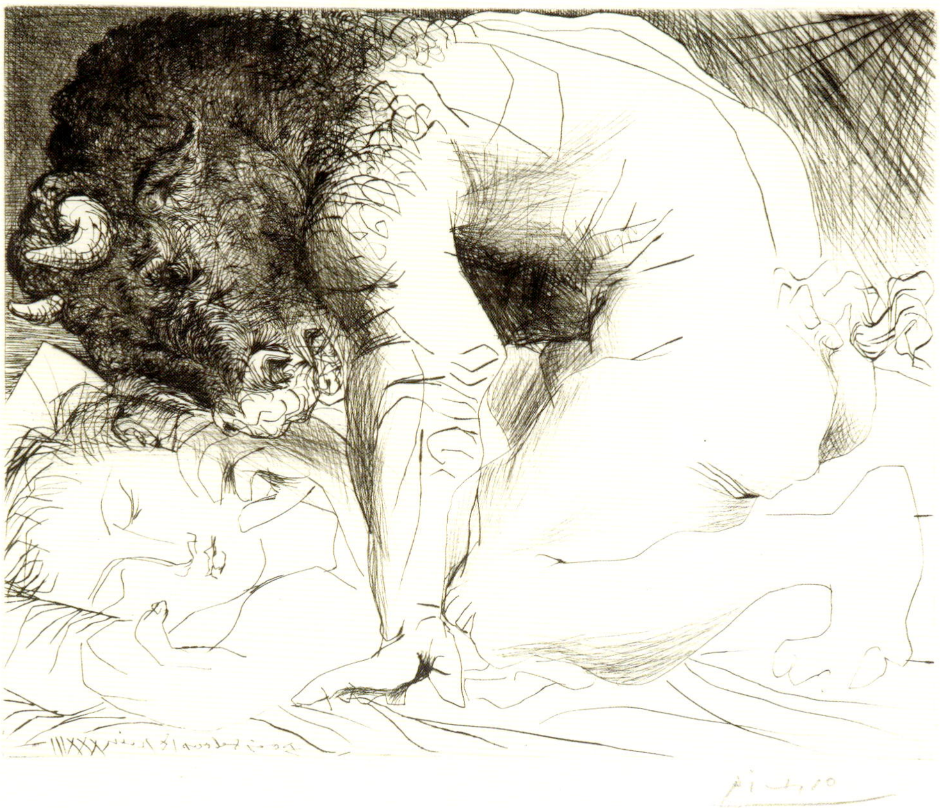

Pablo Picasso, ***Minotaur Caressing the Hand of a Sleeping Woman with His Muzzle,*** June 18, 1933

DIEGO RIVERA AND COATLICUE

TOWARD A MESTIZO HISTORY OF AMERICAN MODERNITY

DIANA MAGALONI

The great appeal of modernism in art, as Elizabeth Prettejohn points out, "has seemed to lie in a radical break with the past, a clean cut in which the rejection of the classical tradition opens the possibility to 'make it new,' in Ezra Pound's phrase."[1] Nonetheless, as Prettejohn indicates, this basis in rejection means that modernity in the arts cannot be defined without considering antiquity as its counterpart. That is, without a series of principles about what defines ancient art and the classic, we cannot trace the boundaries of modernism or assess its originality. Moreover, the ancient object is at once a contemporary construct and a historical reality. This essay explores the close relation between the art of the past and its transformation in the present in terms of two artists, Diego Rivera and Pablo Picasso. In particular it explores the ideas about ancient art that defined the modern in Rivera, and examines which of those critical concepts broke with the European modernist tradition so vigorously represented by Picasso.

1
Elizabeth Prettejohn, *The Modernity of Ancient Sculpture: Greek Sculpture and Modern Art from Winckelmann to Picasso* (London; New York: I. B. Tauris, 2012), 1.

2
Lisa Florman, *Myth and Metamorphosis: Picasso's Classical Prints of the 1930s* (Cambridge, MA: MIT Press, 2000), 7.

3
Ibid., 4–5.

4
Elizabeth Cowling and Jennifer Mundy, eds., *On Classic Ground: Picasso, Léger, De Chirico and the New Classicism, 1910–1930* (London: Tate Gallery, 1990), 11–19.

5
Prettejohn, *Modernity of Ancient Sculpture*, 171–200.

RIVERA AND PICASSO: THE CLASSICAL AS CATALYST

The concepts of "the ancient" and "the classic" play an important role in the works of both Picasso and Rivera. As contemporaries, they had similar educations, not only in their respective national academies in Spain and Mexico at the end of the nineteenth century but also, subsequently, as active members of the avant-garde in early twentieth-century Paris. Among the characteristics of classical art that critics in the 1920s considered most important to emulate were, as Lisa Florman asserts, purity, structure, harmony, order, constancy, and serenity.[2] Both Picasso and Rivera, however, took a stand by making these qualities not only part of their classicist works but also part of their Cubist works. These artists thereby reflect a position that embraces a diversity of artistic expressions rather than supporting the notion of a "stylistic evolution" toward the supposed perfection in art reached during the Greek Classical period, whose values are timeless and essential.[3] For example, Rivera based the neoclassical style and composition of his portrait *The Mathematician* on an openly Cubist scheme, as seen in the ink study for the painting, rendering both styles equivalent in their value as artistic forms (pp. 56 and 57). Picasso expressed this same inclusive principle in *Études*, in which neoclassical figures coexist at the same level as Cubist compositions (p. 59).

Furthermore, as Elizabeth Cowling and Jennifer Mundy indicate, Picasso and Rivera took part in an avant-garde movement that considered the past and the classical canon as catalysts for experimentation, whereas conservative neoclassicism advocated a return to the past through precise imitation of its forms.[4] Avant-garde artists wrought a profound transformation of classical art by deliberately disrupting the three-dimensionality of ancient sculpture—canonically considered the highest artistic expression—and making it two-dimensional in the picture plane.[5] Both Picasso and Rivera produced magnificent works in which ancient sculptures are brought to life in the picture plane and, in their perplexed modernity, reflect the past with a certain critical

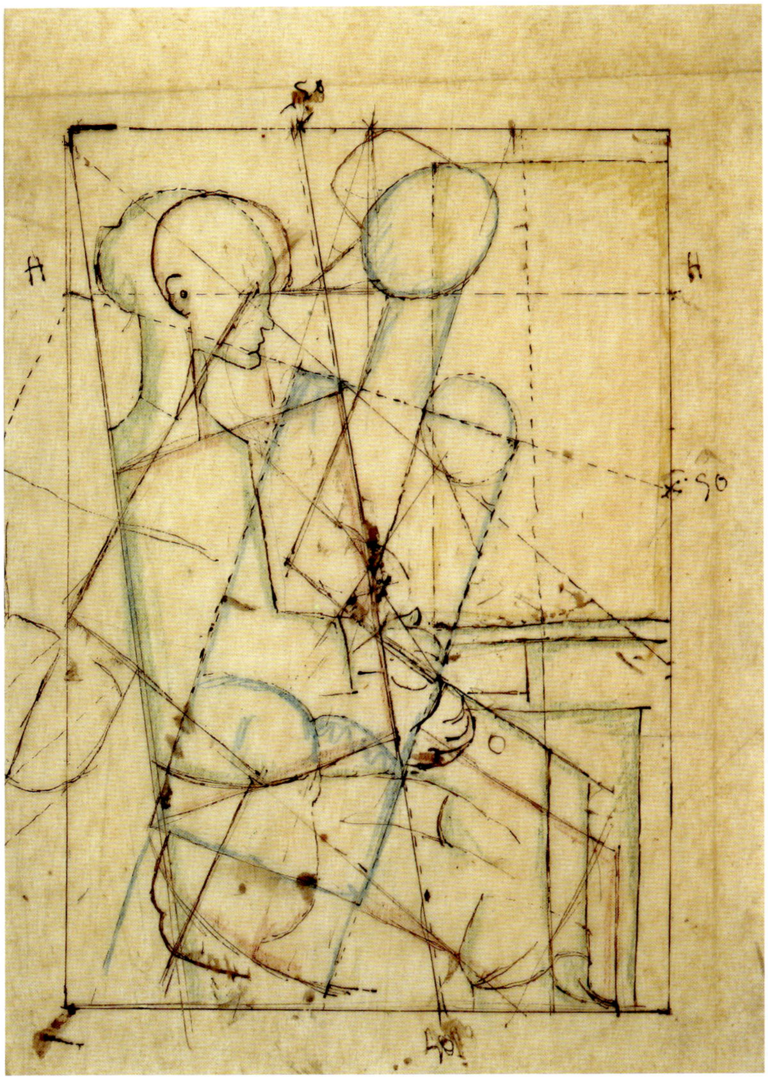

Diego Rivera, Sketch for *The Mathematician*, 1918

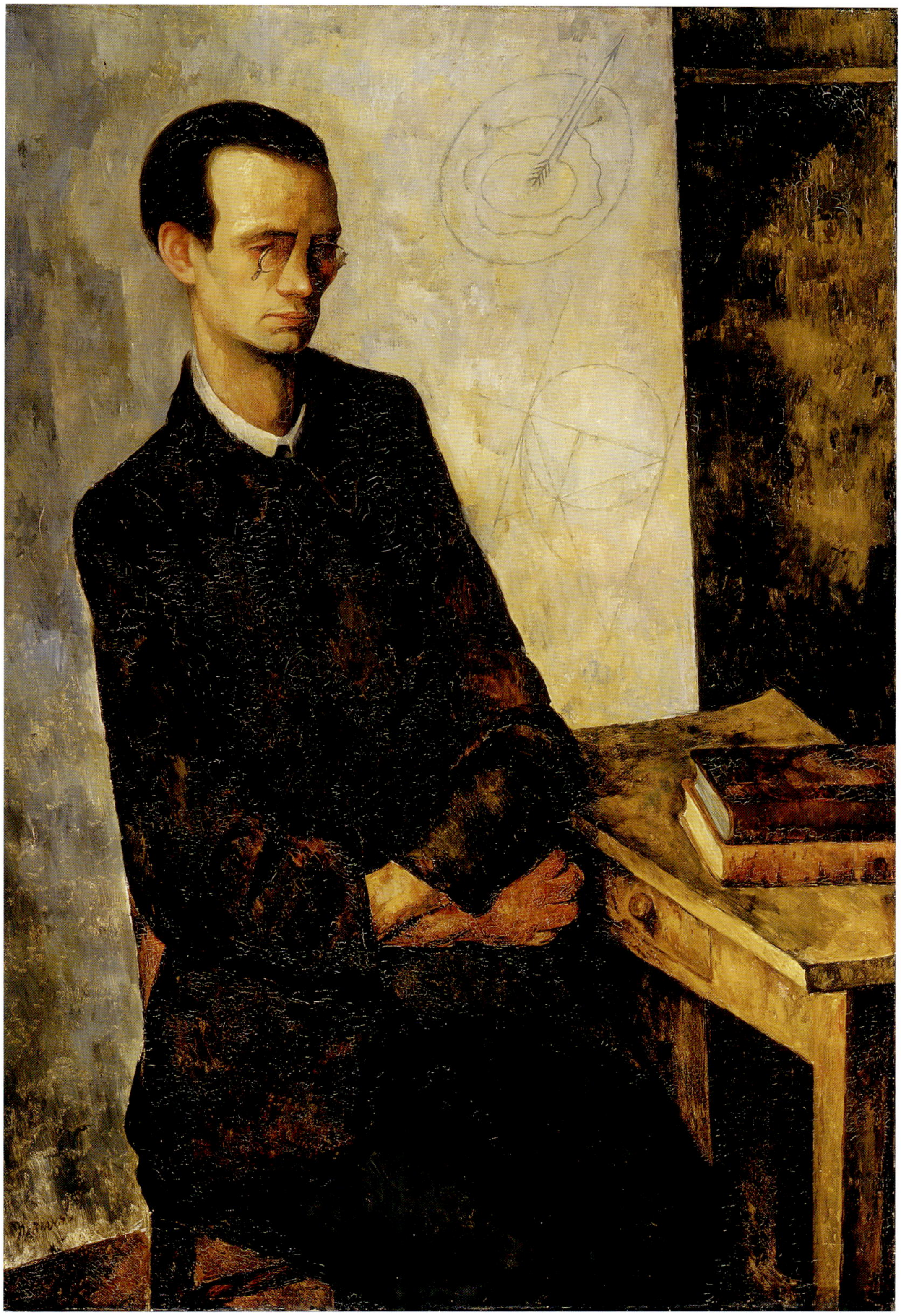

Diego Rivera, *The Mathematician*, 1918

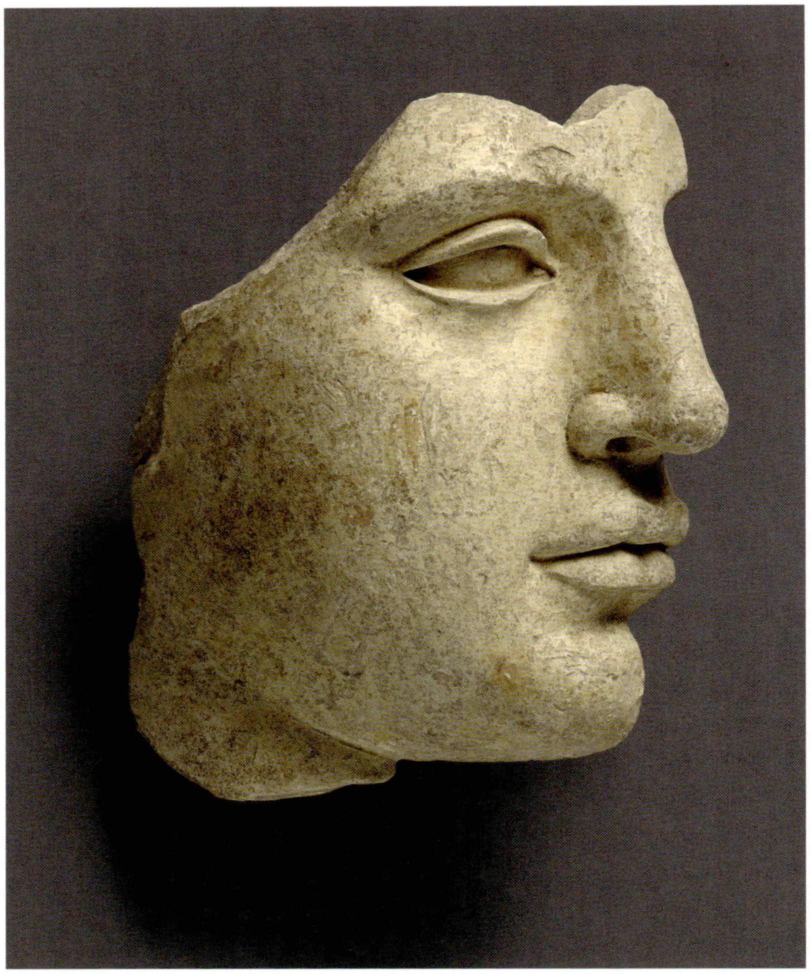

Fragment of a Head, Greek, Tarentum (Taras), 440–430 BCE

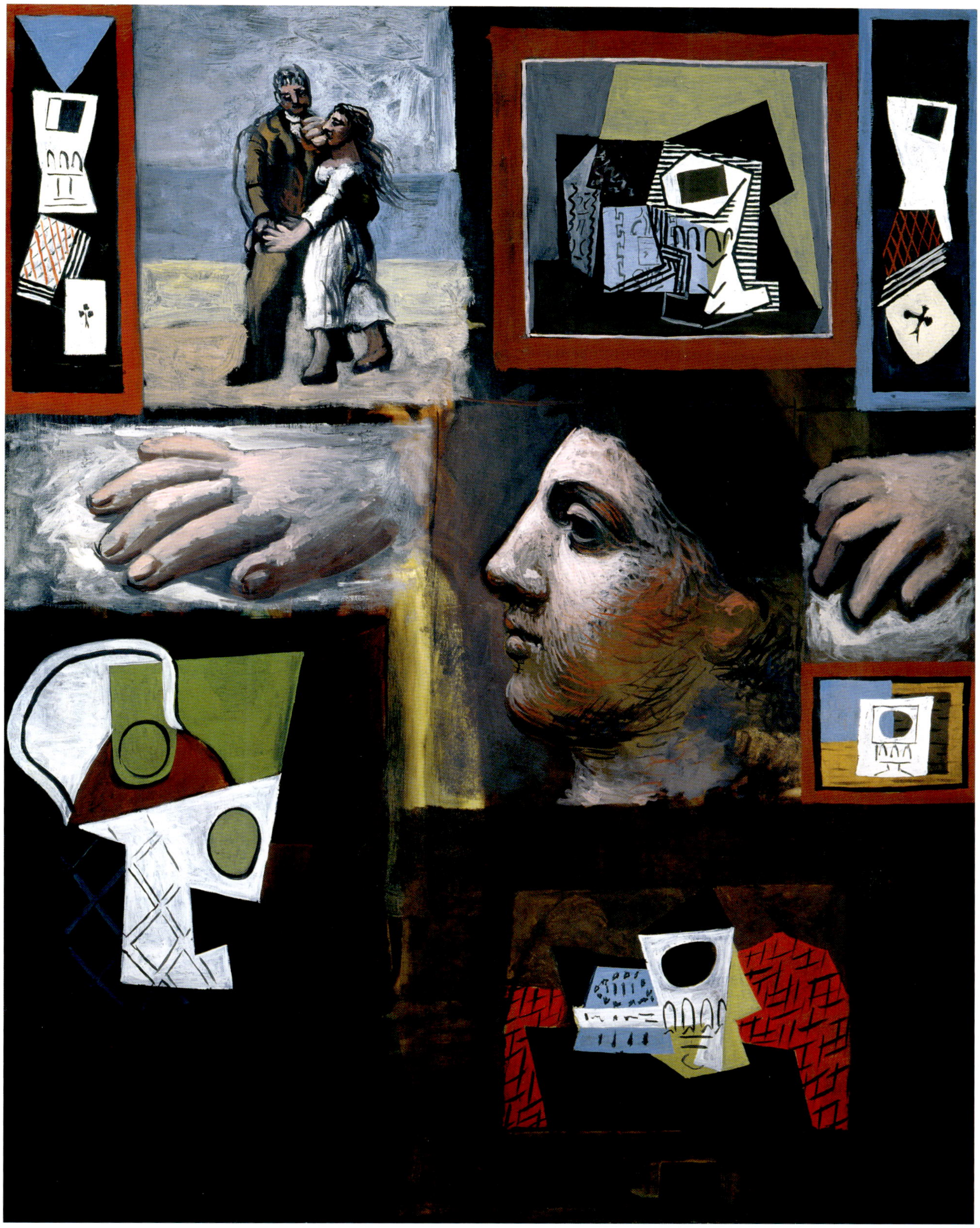

Pablo Picasso, ***Études***, 1920

distance. This is clearly seen in *Three Women at the Spring* (p. 115), in which Picasso uses the forms of classical Greek sculpture to represent three women who, in their simplicity, embody the dignity of the Mediterranean people. The same artistic operation takes place in Rivera's *Flowered Canoe* (p. 184), in which the oarsman of a *trajinera* (a traditional Pre-Columbian boat) resembles an ancient Aztec *macehual* (commoner), as can be seen by comparing this painting with the sculpture of an ancient *macehual* (p. 185). What distinguishes Rivera's painting, however, is that in merging the past and the present, the classical and the vernacular, the artist drew on a culture and history that did not then have a predominant place in either art history or modern art. At the time, the status of Aztec art was not remotely comparable to that of Greek art.[6] In the sixteenth and seventeenth centuries, Spanish conquistadors had condemned works of art from Pre-Columbian Mexico as abominable products of the devil,[7] while in the eighteenth and nineteenth centuries, these works were seen as admirable but incomprehensible products of a "savage" ancient civilization, as Leonardo López Luján demonstrates in his history of the reception of the marvelous sculpture of Coatlicue.[8]

THE TWO STONES, NEW SPAIN, 1790

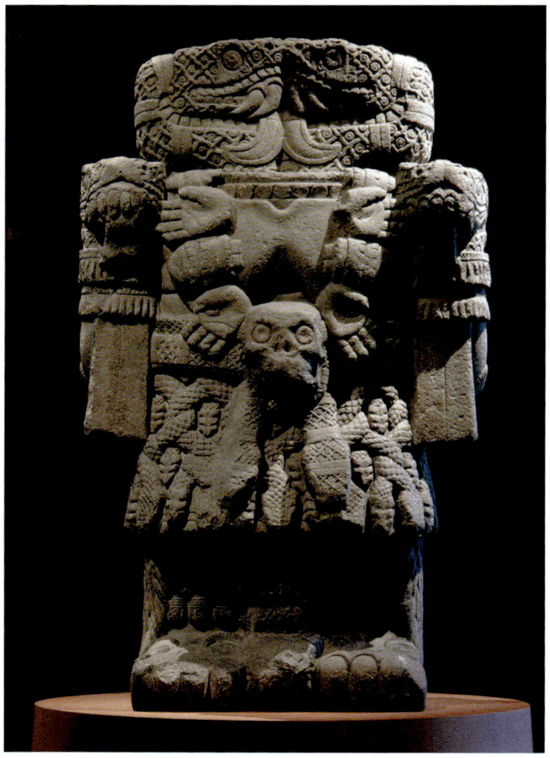

The history of Mexico's indigenous past is marked by a foundational event: the discovery of "the Two Stones," as renowned New Spanish astronomer Antonio León y Gama (1735–1802) called them, in Mexico City's Plaza Mayor. One, a statue of Coatlicue, was discovered on August 13, 1790, and the other, the Piedra del Sol, or Sun Stone (known during this period as the Calendario Azteca, or Aztec Calendar Stone), was found on December 17 of the same year.[9] In the 1790s, after centuries of colonial rule in which similar objects had been reviled and destroyed, such findings were, for the first time, considered historical artifacts of importance.[10] In fact, the *criollo* elites of New Spain's viceroyalty, with their Enlightenment values, were searching for their own classical American past in order to distance themselves from Spain.

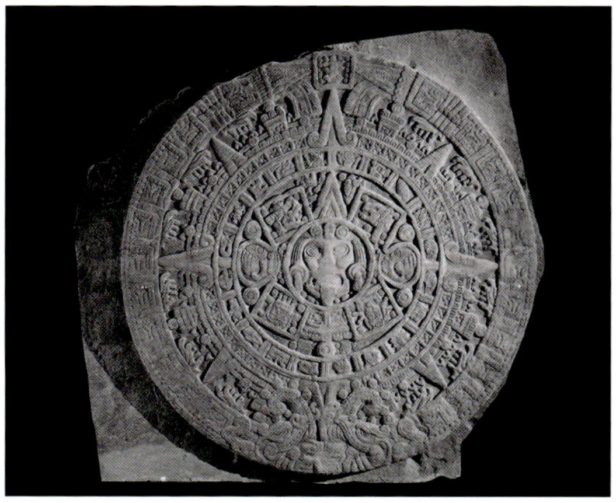

In his famous *Descripción histórica y cronológica de las dos piedras* (1792), Antonio León y Gama published the first news of these findings of great Aztec sculptures.[11] Eduardo Matos Moctezuma describes this event two ways: on the one hand, he rightly points out that the finding represents the beginning of Mexican archaeology;

Coatlicue (The Earth Mother), Aztec, late 15th century; stone, 137¾ × 51⅛ × 51⅛ in. (350 x 130 x 130 cm); Museo Nacional de Antropología, Conaculta-INAH

Sun Stone (Aztec Calendar Stone), Aztec, 1250–1521; basalt, DIAMETER 141 in. (358 cm); Museo Nacional de Antropología, Conaculta-INAH

6
For a discussion of the recognition of Amerindian art, see George Kubler, *Esthetic Recognition of Ancient Amerindian Art* (New Haven, CT: Yale University Press, 1991), 162–94, and "Aesthetics since Amerindian Art before Columbus," in *Collecting the Pre-Columbian Past: A Symposium at Dumbarton Oaks, 6th and 7th October 1990*, ed. Elizabeth Hill Boone (Washington, DC: Dumbarton Oaks Research Library and Collection, 1993), 35–48.

7
Serge Gruzinski, *La guerre des images de Christophe Colomb à "Blade Runner" (1492–2019)* (Paris: Fayard, 1990), 73–77. Published in English as *Images at War: Mexico from Columbus to "Blade Runner,"* trans. Heather MacLean (Durham, NC: Duke University Press, 2001), 42–45.

8
Leonardo López Luján, "La Coatlicue," in *Escultura monumental mexica*, ed. Eduardo Matos Moctezuma and Leonardo López Luján (Mexico City: GM Editores/Espejo de Obsidiana, 2009), 115–41.

9
An important analysis of these discoveries can be found in Eduardo Matos Moctezuma, *Las piedras negadas: De la Coatlicue al Templo Mayor* (Mexico City: Consejo Nacional para la Cultura y las Artes, 1998).

10
López Luján, "La Coatlicue," 133.

11
Antonio León y Gama, *Descripción histórica y cronológica de las dos piedras, que con ocasión del nuevo empedrado que se esta formando en la plaza principal de México, se hallaron en ella el año 1790* [1792] (Mexico City, 1832; facsimile edition, Mexico City: Instituto Nacional de Antropología e Historia, 1990).

on the other, he calls it "the return of the gods."[12] Matos Moctezuma's dual approach, combining the scientific and spiritual, accurately captures the response to these extraordinary and powerful works. The attitudes with which the statues were received, understood, and appreciated differ radically. These differences merit exploration because they convey the tension underlying modernity's relation to ancient indigenous art. At the same time, the story of these discoveries enables us to situate Rivera within the historical trajectory of understanding the indigenous past and to assess, from that perspective, his original and visionary artistic contribution.[13]

The first monolith to be uncovered was the statue of Coatlicue, goddess of the Earth. According to León y Gama, it was found during the construction of a canal near the Plaza Mayor "on August 13, 1790, a date that is memorable because it was the same day on which the king of Spain took possession of the city in the year 1521."[14] This coincidence was viewed as a premonitory sign of Coatlicue's power. The process of unearthing the stone monument was both arduous and portentous. A giant andesite figure was pulled from the earth, measuring nearly nine feet tall (2.7 meters) and weighing about three tons. The sculpture includes both human and animal features, with intertwined rattlesnakes forming a skirt, the claws and legs of an eagle, and a necklace (which covers the chest) made from human hands and hearts. Two large skulls with open eyes are placed on the sash that holds its skirt at the waist: one in front, on the sculpture's stomach, and the other on the back. The sculpture's forearms are truncated, replaced by fierce serpents that jut forward. Its supernatural face, arising from a decapitated neck, is also formed by two broad snakes that meet at the center and look at each other, forming a single frontal head. The sculpture's expression is made fierce by her sharp fangs. Today we understand that Coatlicue, as goddess of the Earth, is the first victim of sacrifice in Aztec mythology, and that the serpents that replace her arms and head symbolize the fertile blood of her immolation. The enormous sculpture represents the ritual moment par excellence, in which blood, transfigured as powerful serpents, nourishes life and fecundates death.[15] Obviously this great monument was not easy for the New Spanish to understand; indeed, we are still deciphering its messages, based in a myth that explains death by sacrifice as retribution on the universe, and trying to appreciate the brutal honesty of its artistic expression, which makes no attempt to sublimate the powerful exuberance and brutality of the sacrificial act.[16]

Nonetheless, the discovery of the statue in 1790 aroused two important social reactions. The first response was a combination of fearful curiosity, on account of its extraordinary size and frightful appearance, and appreciation, insofar as it represented "the ancient." The second is more complex, conveying the profound spiritual, cultural, and artistic distance between the indigenous and Western worlds, as well as the fear that this abyss provoked. The documents on the discovery clearly note that both the Spanish colonial governor,

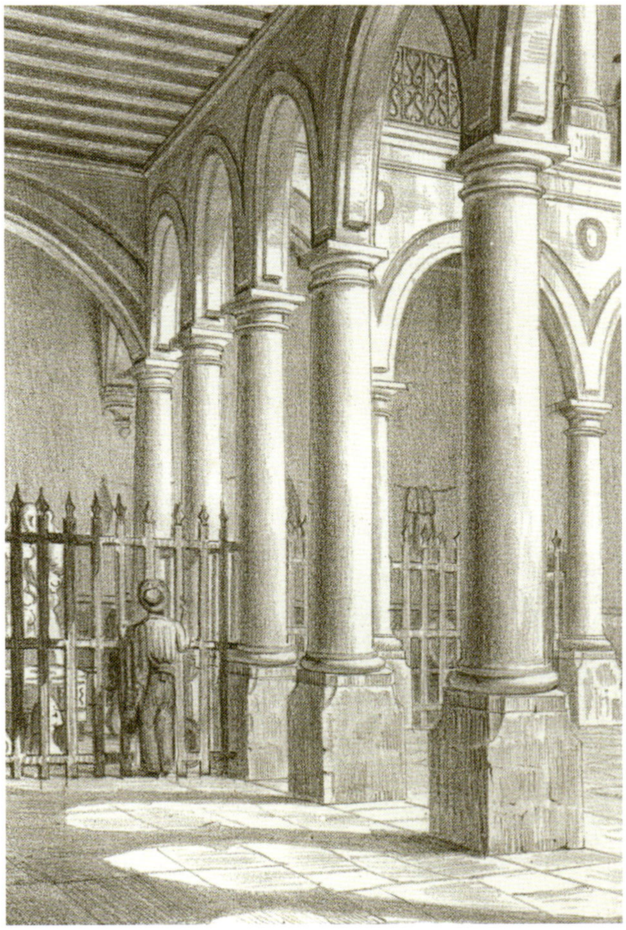

Pedro Gualdi, ***Interior of the University of Mexico***, 1841; lithograph from ***Monumentos de Mejico*** (1841)

12 Matos Moctezuma, *Las piedras negadas*, 17–18.

13 Indeed, during his years at the Academy of San Carlos, Rivera often visited the Museo Nacional, where these two important ancient monuments had been held since the museum's founding in 1825.

14 León y Gama, *Descripción histórica*, 9.

15 A complete analysis of the different interpretations can be found in López Luján, "La Coatlicue," 115–22. The interpretation presented here is based on Michel Graulich, "Les grandes statues azteques dites de Coatlicue et Yollotlicue," in *Cultures et sociétés, Andes et Méso-Amérique: mélanges en hommage à Pierre Duviols*, ed. Raquel Thiercelin (Aix-en-Provence: Université de Provence, 1991), 1: 387–400.

16 This idea of the monstrous as a reflection of the inclusive capacity of myth and portent is from Edmundo O'Gorman, "El arte o de la monstruosidad," in *Estudios sobre arte: sesenta años del Instituto de Investigaciones Estéticas*, ed. Martha Fernández and Louise Noelle (Mexico City: Universidad Nacional Autónoma de Mexico, 1998), 471–76.

17 López Luján, "La Coatlicue," 145.

18 Benito María de Moxó y de Francoli, *Cartas mejicanas* [1828], cited in López Luján, "La Coatlicue," 148–49.

19 Ibid.

Bernardo Bonavia, and the viceroy, Juan Vicente de Güemes, were interested in preserving the statue as evidence of the antiquity of the Americas.[17] To that end, the sculpture was moved to the Pontificia Universidad, where it was deposited in a remote corner with little visibility, as shown in Pedro Gualdi's 1841 lithograph (p. 61). The documents of the period also relate an important event that would result in the statue's fate being diametrically opposed to that of the Sun Stone, underlining the distance between myth as the source of explanation of the world for indigenous cultures and scientific rationality as the legitimizing thought system for Western cultures.

López Luján recounts that Benito Moxó, a Catalan Benedictine who lived in Mexico between 1804 and 1805, described the reasons that led to the removal of the statue of Coatlicue from the university courtyard and its reburial sometime between 1804 and 1805.[18] Even though, as Moxó acknowledges, the constant presence of indigenous people near the statue was initially interpreted as being motivated by "love for their nation, a trait no less typical of savages than of the civilized," the frequency of their visits and the growing number of visitors gave rise to the suspicion of some secret "religious motive"—leading to their eventual ban from entering the university courtyard. Nonetheless, Moxó reports, "at night Indians would be caught worshiping their goddess [Teoyaomiqui], some on their knees, others prostrate before the statue and holding lit candles in their hands, or some of the various offerings that their ancestors used to present to their Idols."[19]

As can be seen in the paintings of Coatlicue in the Florentine Codex (1575–77), the cult of the goddess entailed offering her products obtained from the Earth; Coatlicue, who is perhaps rendered in red to represent the sacrificial blood that covers her, is the giver of sustenance and the great devourer of death—like the Earth itself. Her cult was still present among the indigenous population of Mexico City in 1790, who related to her in a manner probably much in the way depicted two hundred years earlier in the Florentine Codex scene. The painting of Coatlicue and Moxó's description manifest the enormous gulf between the mentalities, practices, and needs of Mexico City's indigenous people versus those of the *criollos* and Europeans. For New Spanish Catholics, it was a mystery how the indigenous people could relate on a spiritual level to a formidable marvel such as the statue of Coatlicue; they wondered what hidden powers the monstrous goddess could awaken in the Indians, and worried about the significance of the Indians' ability to interact with this extraordinary idol. The statue's powerful aura not only inspired a cult among the city's indigenous population but also brought out, in palpable form, a deep fear of "otherness" on the part of those in power. Although the independence movement needed to invoke a glorious American

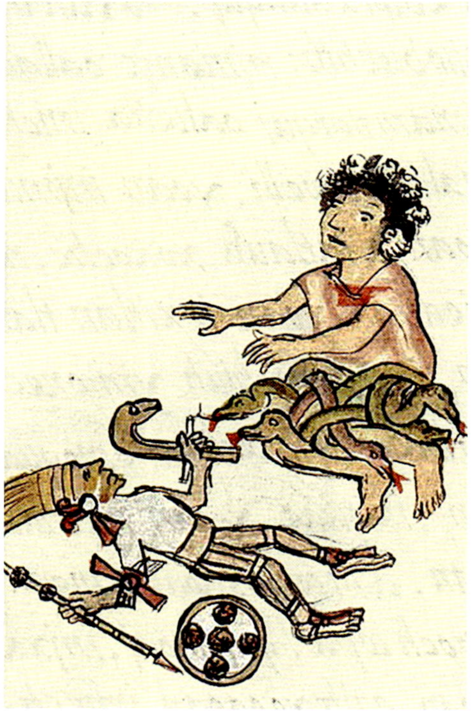

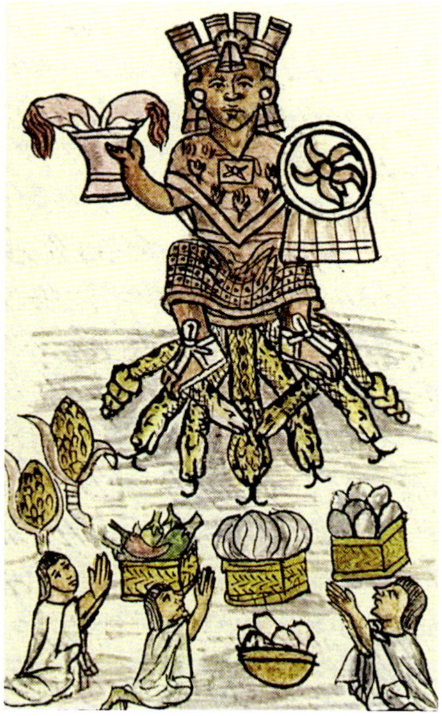

LEFT TO RIGHT Book 2 (p. 178) and Book 3 (p. 240) from the **Florentine Codex**, 1575–77; Biblioteca Medicea Laurenziana, Florence, Italy

antiquity in order to create a sense of pride in their heritage, the phenomenal Coatlicue, this monstrous goddess made of serpents and skulls, was seen as indomitable—and that is why she had to be reburied.

The Sun Stone was found only four months after the statue of Coatlicue, in the southeast corner of the Plaza Mayor, about three feet below the ground, with its carved side facedown. Its discovery and reception differ from the reception of Coatlicue, and in fact marks a distinct way of conceiving the past. León y Gama comments that of the two sculptures found that year, "this is the more peculiar and instructive one."[20] Indeed, since its discovery, the Sun Stone has drawn favorable attention from all who observe it. A perfect disk, it contains a series of concentric circles that radiate out from the center, where a face appears in frontal view. This face is framed within the sign Nahui Ollin (Four Movement), which is the name of the fifth cosmic era, or Fifth Sun, in which the Aztecs believed they were living. The face has been interpreted as that of the Sun god Tonatiuh, that of the Earth goddess Tlaltecuhtli, or a combination of the two. It is flanked by two fierce-looking sets of claws. This first circle surrounding the face is complemented by four quadrangular cartouches that contain the calendric symbols of the four eras, or Suns, that preceded the Fifth Sun of the Aztecs. The next circle contains the signs of the twenty days of the ritual calendar, beginning with Cipactli (Crocodile) and ending with Xochitl (Flower). Positioned along the perimeter of these two circles are eight solar rays in the form of inverted V-shapes. The outer circle that unites this set of rings is formed by two large serpents that meet face to face at the bottom. They have been identified as *xiuhcocoah* (fire serpents), who carry the Sun on its daily and nightly journey.[21]

Even though it was not fully understood at the time (beyond the day glyphs), the Sun Stone, from the moment of its discovery, served as proof of the rational, scientific, and mathematical abilities of indigenous people, offering an antidote to the fear that the Coatlicue statue provoked. In an influential study, León y Gama asserted that the carvings conveyed a system to measure time and calculate the movement of the stars, comparing the cosmic eras of Pre-Columbian mythology that are carved in the Sun Stone to Ovid's Ages of Man.[22] Here comparison with the classical world was used as proof of the artistic and intellectual capacity of ancient indigenous peoples, not taking into account the fact that Ovid's stories are filled with extreme suffering, murder, uncontrollable sexual desire, vengeance, and drama, as Jennifer Stager keenly points out in her contribution to this catalogue.[23] Nevertheless, the canons of the Metropolitan

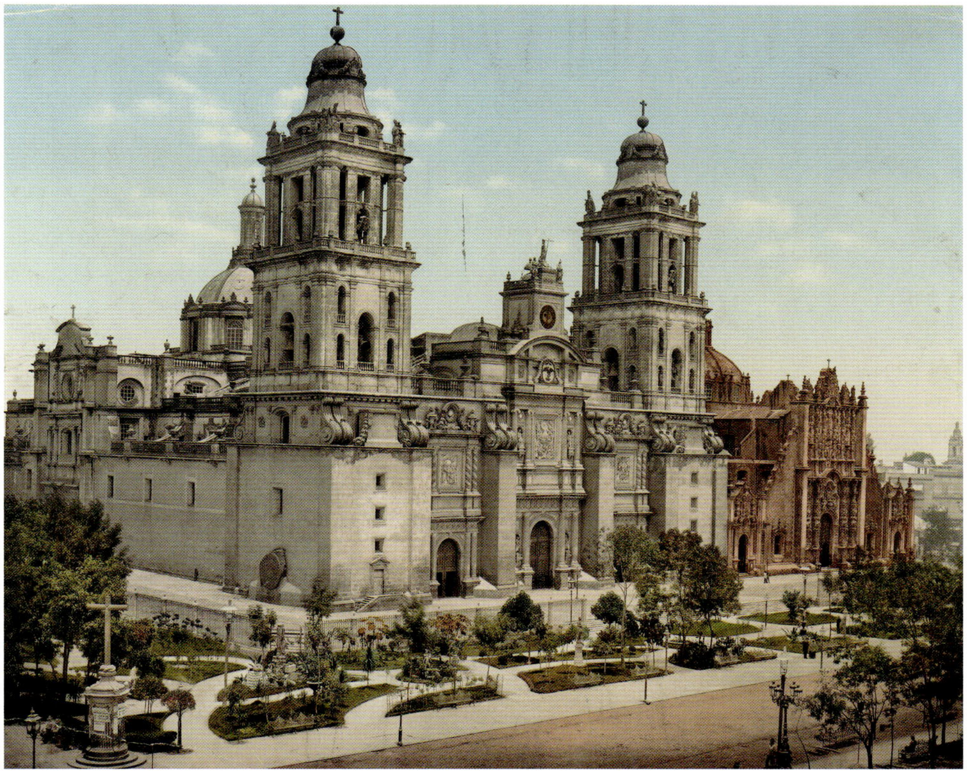

William H. Jackson, ***Mexico, the Cathedral, City of Mexico***, c. 1899; photomechanical print; Library of Congress, Washington, DC

20 León y Gama, *Descripción histórica y cronológica de las dos piedras*, 10.

21 Khristaan Villela and Mary Miller, *The Aztec Calendar Stone* (Los Angeles: Getty Research Institute, 2010), presents a historiographical review of interpretations of the Sun Stone.

22 Stacie Graham Widdifield, "The *Aztec Calendar Stone: A Critical History*," in Villela and Miller, eds., *The Aztec Calendar Stone*, 226.

23 The Hegelian idea that classical Greek art represents the pinnacle of humanity's artistic achievement has an unquestionable influence on the way that art history constructs hierarchies and values that exclude Mesoamerican art from the canon. See Prettejohn, *Modernity of Ancient Sculpture*, 42–60.

Cathedral were impressed by León y Gama's findings, and asked the civic authorities to have the Sun Stone moved to the cathedral.[24] Thus, the monument, which was possibly used as a receptacle for blood in sacrifices made to the Sun and the Earth, was placed vertically on the west side of the Metropolitan Cathedral, where it remained for more than a century, as can be seen in a hand-colored photograph by William H. Jackson from around 1899 (p. 63). The Sun Stone was now in the process of becoming the national icon par excellence, incorporated even into the image of the Mexican Catholic Church.

As Matos Moctezuma indicates, the first publications on the Sun Stone had a nationalistic function; since erudite thinkers, inspired by the ideas of Georges-Louis Leclerc, pointed out that Spain's conquest of the American lands did not—despite what the Spanish proclaimed—have the merit of subjugating "a barbarous people with no refinement or civilization."[25] Scholars criticized not only the moral weakness of the indigenous peoples but also the terrible imposition of the Catholic religion, the brutality suffered by the recently conquered, and the conquistadors' thirst for gold.[26] The discovery of the Sun Stone, its subsequent transfer to the cathedral, and the writings of León y Gama all furnished arguments against the negative opinions of these writers, and Mexico's image gradually improved among Europeans. León y Gama's *Descripción histórica cronológica de las dos piedras* was translated into Italian and published in Rome. Prussian explorer and naturalist Alexander von Humboldt, furthering León y Gama's ideas, wrote his own study of the statue of Coatlicue and the Sun Stone in *Vues des cordillères et monuments des peuples indigènes de l'Amérique* (1810–13), which was widely disseminated and translated.[27] Humboldt's praise for the Sun Stone brought it worldwide fame, and it became the most important tourist attraction among the Pre-Columbian monuments of Mexico.[28] The image of coherence and cultural greatness represented by the Sun Stone was adopted and reinforced by the nationalistic cultural politics of Porfirio Díaz, who governed the country from 1877 to 1910, when he was deposed by the Mexican Revolution. The Sun Stone, that perfect circle with its calendric signs, was promoted as the emblematic monument of the country; Mexican historian Enrique Krauze has rightly called it a "petrified symbol of the past."[29]

Matos Moctezuma observes that during the years in which the Sun Stone was embedded in the west wall of the Metropolitan Cathedral, no one came to worship it, as the Indians had done with the Coatlicue statue; rather, it was in the latter monument "that the indigenous people reencountered their past."[30] According to Edmundo O'Gorman, the problem with the Coatlicue statue is one of "contemplation"—that is, it lies in our capacity to take in the work of art from the past when we are historically conditioned by our present in very powerful ways.[31] The foundational tension expressed in the reactions to these two stones upon their discovery continues to be of significance in Mexico, which is still grappling with questions of indigenous otherness in the face of the indomitable power of Coatlicue.

24
León y Gama, *Descripción histórica y cronológica*, 10–11.

25
Eduardo Matos Moctezuma, "La Piedra del Sol o Calendario Azteca," in Matos Moctezuma and López Luján, *Escultura monumental mexica*, 249.

26
Ibid.

27
First published in Spanish as *Sitios de las cordilleras y monumentos de los pueblos indígenas de América*, trans. Bernardo Giner (Madrid, 1878); cited in Matos Moctezuma, "La Piedra del Sol," 256. Translated as *Views of the Cordilleras and Monuments of the Indigenous Peoples of the Americas: A Critical Edition*, ed. Vera M. Kutzinski and Ottmar Ette, trans. J. Ryan Poynter (Chicago: University of Chicago Press, 2012).

28
Eloise Quiñones Keber, "Humboldt and Aztec Art," *Colonial Latin American Review* 5, no. 2 (1996): 277–97.

29
Villela and Miller, *The Aztec Calendar Stone*, 37.

30
Matos Moctezuma, *Las piedras negadas*, 39.

31
O'Gorman, "El arte o de la monstruosidad," 472.

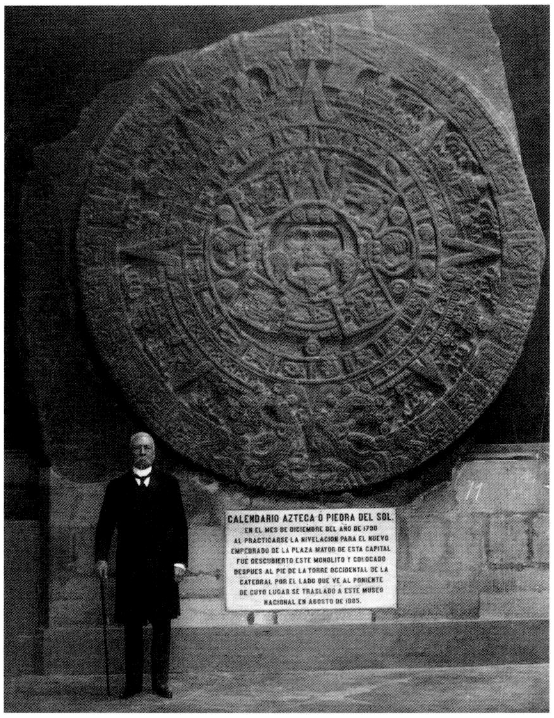

Porfirio Díaz in front of the Aztec Calendar Stone in the National Anthropology Museum, c. 1910 (photo by A. Carillo); Archivo General de la Nación

MODERN MEXICO, THE REEVALUATION OF PRE-COLUMBIAN ART, AND COATLICUE

Rita Eder has described three important conceptual moments in the reevaluation of Pre-Columbian art in the twentieth century that surely had an influence on Rivera because they changed the perception of the American indigenous past. First, German art historian and critic Carl Einstein offered a critique of ethnocentrism in his text *Negerplastik* (1915).[32] According to Eder, Einstein broke with the concept of stylistic evolution asserted by classicism, proposing instead that each artistic tradition should be considered in its own context, very much as Franz Boas had done for anthropological artifacts—which is what Picasso and Rivera had done with their own traditions, Cubist as well as classicist.[33] Einstein's rupture with classical aesthetics, Eder suggests, is based on a reinterpretation of Wilhelm Worringer's *Abstraktion und Einfühlung* (1908), one of the fundamental art history texts of the twentieth century.[34] Eder points out that Einstein and Worringer helped to introduce a reevaluation of Pre-Columbian art, whereby it was no longer seen as a product of classicist "naturalism" but rather as a formal and emotional art distinct from Western art that brought into question the latter's fixed principles.[35] The second new approach to the art of ancient Mexico, Eder continues, is represented by a 1928 essay by Georges Bataille, "L'Amérique disparue,"[36] and the subsequent debate over ethnography between Bataille and Einstein, which covered such topics as the nature of human sacrifice, the polyvalence of art that arose from these practices, and the aesthetic potential of violence. Finally, the third viewpoint that revised the understanding of Pre-Columbian art was that of André Breton, who in the 1940s valued Mexican culture as "originally" Surrealist and thus immensely creative. Breton's ideas influenced the Mexican Surrealist movement, in which Rivera participated.[37]

By the 1950s, these three positions had made it possible for Paul Westheim, a German historian living in Mexico, to offer an interpretation of the statue of Coatlicue that radically changed the way the monument was viewed.[38] Westheim speaks of the statue of Coatlicue as a dramatization of the goddess's power, which perpetuates the cycles of life and death in a world in which the supernatural is conceived as monstrous. He presents the paradox of Pre-Columbian art, in Eder's words, as "the more power and terror, the more aesthetic force."[39] Finally, in 1954 Justino Fernández, one of the founders of Mexican art history as an academic discipline, published his important book devoted to studying the goddess from the perspective of art history, primary sources, and the Nahuatl language. Fernández was the first to weave together the complexity of Aztec art, its mythical nature, its expressive power, and the relation of its forms to the Nahuatl language.[40]

The first decades of the revolutionary government were influenced by the ideas of anthropologist Manuel Gamio, whose policies and ideas on the close study of present-day indigenous communities in Mexico as a way to understand and recover ancient Pre-Columbian cultures created a new class of urban elites interested in their identity and heritage.[41] In this intellectual context, it is not surprising that Coatlicue was rediscovered after the revolution by Mexican artists who sought to represent national identity as mestizo and to describe the newfound emotions that being mestizo implies. The first powerful evocation of the goddess was

32 Carl Einstein, *Negerplastik* (Leipzig: Verlag der weissen Bücher, 1915); translated by Charles Haxthausen and Sebastian Zeidler as "Negro Sculpture," *October* 107 (2004): 122–38.

33 Rita Eder, "Benjamin Péret and Paul Westheim: Surrealism and Other Genealogies in the Land of the Aztecs," in *Surrealism in Latin America, Vivísimo Muerto*, ed. Dawn Ades, Rita Eder, and Graciela Speranza (Los Angeles: Getty Research Institute, 2012), 77. Barbara Braun, *Pre-Columbian Art and the Post-Columbian World: Ancient American Sources of Modern Art* (New York: Harry N. Abrams, 1993), 35.

34 Wilhelm Worringer, *Abstraktion und Einfühlung: Ein Beitrag zur Stilpsychologie* (Munich: Piper, 1908). Published in English as *Abstraction and Empathy: A Contribution to the Psychology of Style* (London: Routledge and Kegan Paul, 1948) and in Spanish as *Abstracción y naturaleza* (Mexico City: Fondo de Cultura Económica, 1953).

35 Eder, "Benjamin Péret and Paul Westheim," 78.

36 Georges Bataille, "L'Amérique disparue," in *L'art précolombien: L'Amérique avant Christophe Colombe*, ed. Jean Babelon (Paris: Beaux-Arts, 1928), 5–14.

37 Eder, "Benjamin Péret and Paul Westheim," 79.

38 Paul Westheim, *Arte antiguo de México* (Mexico City: FCE, 1950). Published in English as *The Art of Ancient Mexico* (Garden City, NY: Doubleday, 1965).

39 Eder, "Benjamin Péret and Paul Westheim," 91.

40 Justino Fernández, *Coatlicue: Estética del arte indigena antiguo* (Mexico City: Centro de Estudios Filosóficos, 1954), 33–161.

41 See Itzel A. Rodríguez Mortellaro's contribution to this volume.

42 James Oles, *Art and Architecture in Mexico* (London: Thames and Hudson, 2013), 222.

43 Enrique Krauze, *Mexico, Biography of Power: A History of Modern Mexico, 1810–1996*, trans. Hank Heifetz (New York: HarperCollins, 1997), 392–93.

by Saturnino Herrán, who in 1915 designed a radically innovative image of Coatlicue in his great work *Coatlicue Transformed*; it was intended to be the central panel of a mural called *Our Gods* (*Nuestros dioses*), but was left unfinished upon the artist's premature death. In this work, Herrán fuses the sacrifice of Christ on the cross, based (as James Oles has pointed out) on a painting by Spanish artist Ignacio Zuloaga, and that of Coatlicue into a single powerful figure, brilliantly equating the two.[42] *Coatlicue Transformed* seems to be a posthumous homage to the indigenous people who lay prostrate before the statue in the corridors of the university around 1790, when the cult of Coatlicue spread terror among the New Spanish authorities. In Herrán's painting, Coatlicue is transformed into Christ, thus becoming a mestiza goddess who does not forsake her indigenous roots. José Clemente Orozco painted her as well in the Hospicio Cabañas in Guadalajara and at Dartmouth College in New Hampshire, emphasizing terror and human sacrifice, but it was Rivera who truly explored Coatlicue's mythological meanings and turned her into a heroic figure of modernity. Significantly, he did so in two of his murals in the United States: one at the Detroit Institute of Arts and the other at the City College of San Francisco.

RIVERA AND COATLICUE

When Rivera returned to Mexico from Europe in 1921, he found a nation in search of itself, with a sense of urgency about the future. After the revolution (1910–20), peace was gradually restored and important intellectuals returned from exile. One of these was José Vasconcelos, who enabled the development of the vigorous artistic and cultural movement in which Rivera would actively participate. Vasconcelos would become the first minister of public education, and his vision was to unify a fragmented nation and to incorporate the indigenous population through a shared sense of identity. Under his brief but powerful leadership (1920–23), an education program was disseminated as rural teachers traveled throughout the country, and artists such as Rivera, Orozco, David Alfaro Siqueiros, and Fermín Revueltas threw themselves into the task of painting a revolutionary view of Mexican history on the walls of former colonial palaces, now converted into schools and public buildings.[43] This boundless energy—that of a country imagining itself in order to build itself—inspired Rivera in his artistic quest. Rivera, moreover, had a particular strength. He had been molded as an artist in the most creative, competitive, and demanding milieu of

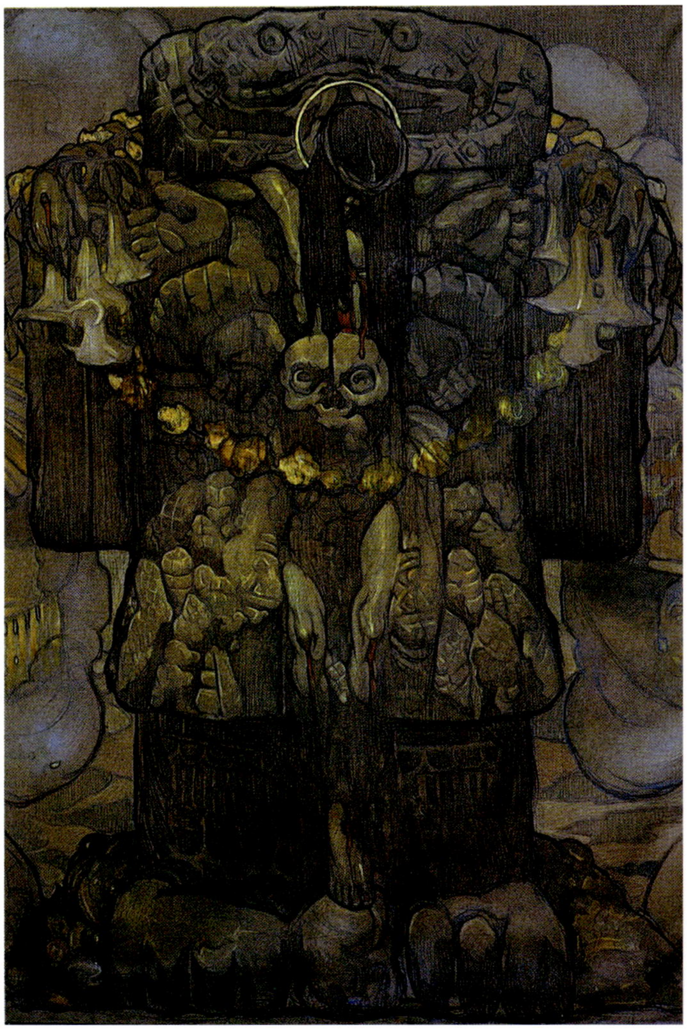

Saturnino Herrán, ***Coatlicue Transformed***, 1918, study for unfinished *Our Gods* mural; crayon and watercolor on paper; Museo de Aguascalientes, Conaculta-INAH

the period: namely, the Parisian avant-garde, in which Cubism and Surrealism were conceived and the principles of modern art were forged. In his biographies, we sense the young artist's internal struggle in Paris, where, as the poet Rubén Darío has said, Rivera had to play the role of "*sauvage*, much against his will."[44]

Having to find his artistic identity within the context of a colonialist sentiment that cast him as an exotic foreigner, while at the same time being nourished by his experience of the beginnings of modern art among such talented artists as Picasso, enabled Rivera to take a progressive stance with regard to the artistic and historical assessment of the Mexican indigenous past. When he speaks of what the Cubist adventure meant, for example, Rivera communicated an essential part of his capacity as an artist—what O'Gorman calls the capacity for "contemplation"—that was probably instrumental in how he chose to approach and represent the Pre-Columbian past in his art, and in particular how he dealt with Coatlicue. As Rivera explained, "Cubism constituted an extraordinary adventure.... As painters we discovered that vision is not produced by the ocular apparatus alone; rather, all the nervous organs take part in giving the sensation of colors and shapes and the perception of distance." He also referred to Cubism's ability to communicate "differences between smooth and rough, hard and soft, heavy and light" through the quality and nature of the brushstrokes, in works in which "density was just as important as color, and quality [as important] as form."[45]

Rivera's reflections on Cubism make clear that he considered art in its full sensory dimension: textures, densities, weights, and reliefs create an artistic whole, which in turn produces emotional responses. Imagine for a moment how Rivera would have approached the powerful statue of Coatlicue—a monument built like a great block of stone that imposes its presence on the viewer, and at the same time like an infinitude of meticulous textures that convey the scaly skin of the serpents interwoven in Coatlicue's skirt, the fleshy texture of the hearts and hands in her necklace, the lightness of the feathers of her eagle legs, the metallic smoothness of the rattlesnakes that hang from her skirt, and the sharp ferocity of fangs and claws. Remember, too, that Rivera was at once an extraordinary artist, an avid scholar of Pre-Columbian cultures, a believer in the powers held by ritual and myth, and an insatiable collector. As Juan Coronel Rivera points out, it was the artist's mythological vision, through which he seemed to perceive the ancestral and animistic forces that emanated from historical pieces, that led him to assemble his enormous collection.[46] Many of these objects—which he studied in detail with the help of archaeologist Ana Teresa Ordiales, who researched and catalogued his collection—figure in Rivera's murals and oil paintings. The depth of his dedication to the objects in his collection is evident in their research cards, which include drawings, glosses, and other information gathered by Rivera and Ordiales.

In reviewing his creations closely, we find specific works that Rivera studied and assimilated in order to paint his vision of the ancient civilizations that once populated Mexico. Roberto Velasco, studying the murals of the Palacio Nacional, identifies important groups of sources used by Rivera, such as the codices produced by indigenous artists in the sixteenth century, in particular *Primeros Memoriales*, the Florentine Codex, the Codex Mendoza, and the Codex Ixtlilxochitl. Velasco also identifies specific pieces, generally from Rivera's own collection or from the Aztec collections of the Sala de Monolitos at the Museo Nacional, depicted in the murals: pots representing the rain god Tlaloc, ceramic toys, Teotihuacán vessels, statues of porters (*tamemes*) and commoners (*macehuales*), figures of seated women, smiling faces from Veracruz, gourds sculpted in

44 Loló de la Torriente, *Memoria y razón de Diego Rivera* (Mexico City: Editorial Renacimiento, 1959), 2:53.

45 Ibid., 2:35.

46 Juan Coronel Rivera, "Diego Rivera: Idólatra," in *Diego Rivera: Coleccionista*, ed. Marte Rodolfo Gómez Segura (Mexico City: Museo Nacional de Arte, Instituto Nacional de Bellas Artes, 2007), 20–21.

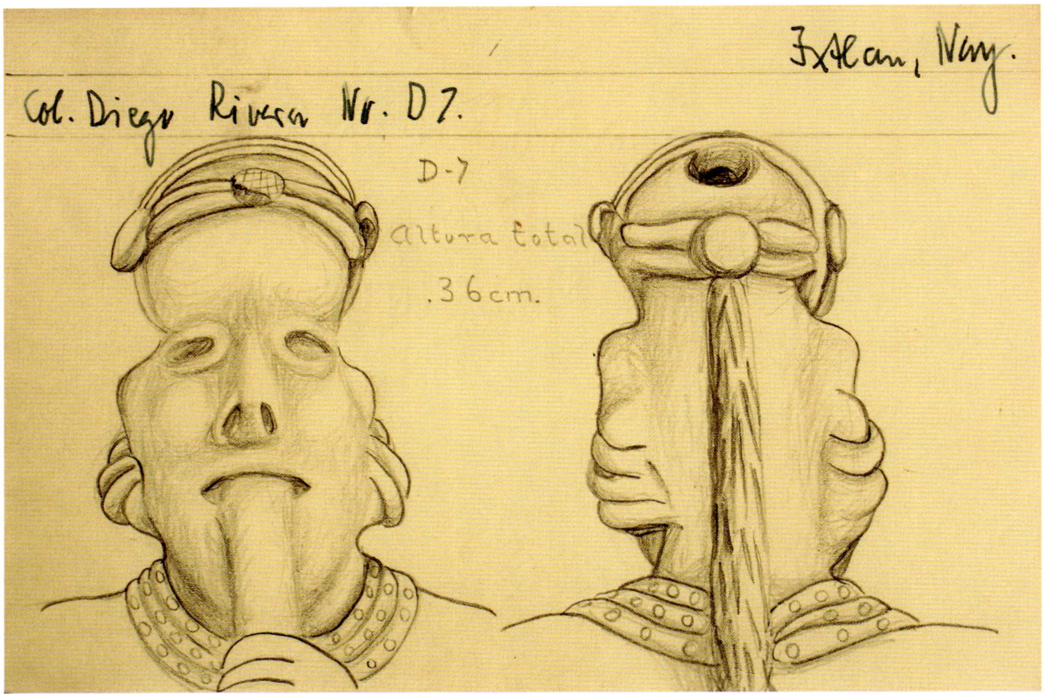

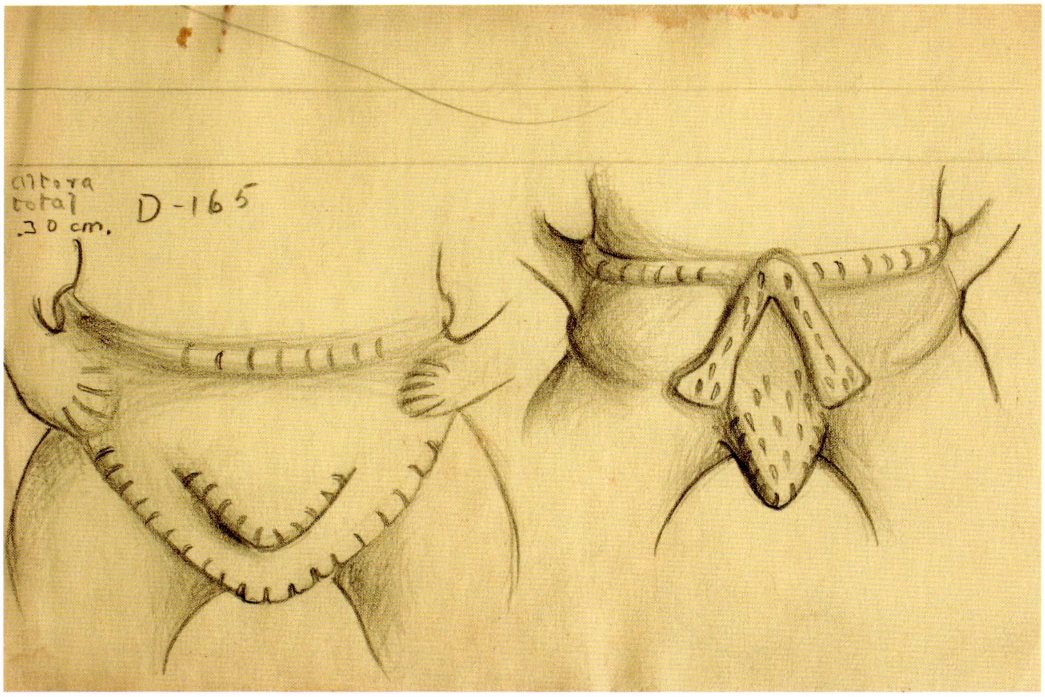

Diego Rivera, **Studies of Pre-Columbian Figurines**, c. 1955–56

stone, and Western rulers with their wives. Velasco's work systematically shows that Rivera eventually gained a deep knowledge of ancient objects and the skill to bring them to life in the present.[47]

The vision Rivera constructed with these objects collapses time and fuses disparate periods, as if the energy emanating from the past could transform the present and create a future. This impression is notable in comparing his magnificent painting *Flower Day* (p. 89) with a carving of the goddess Chalchiuhtlicue from his collection (p. 88). A characteristic example of representations of Chalchiuhtlicue, the painting shows the goddess as a noblewoman, seated on her heels with her feet tucked behind her, an impossible pose that Rivera copies exactly. In *Flower Day*, Rivera subsumes both contemporary and ancient Mexico within the body of the modern indigenous woman. In his murals portraying the history of Mexico, Rivera presents instead a vision of the ancient indigenous world as a timeless place, where, as Desmond Rochfort asserts, "conflict and culture, agriculture or slavery are treated with equal importance and assume no rank or hierarchy." Rivera suspends judgment when looking at the indigenous past, Rochfort continues, while harshly judging the violent European world that usurped this culture and its power.[48]

This vision attempts to re-create a lost world and give it reality in the present, erasing three hundred years of colonial history in one stroke. Considering this alongside Rivera's modernist stance from within the avant-garde—which, like Picasso's, led him to explore the art of the past without repeating tired formulas of cultural legitimation—we may begin to understand why Rivera never incorporated the Sun Stone into his murals or easel paintings; not a single reproduction or even reference to the Sun Stone exists in his oeuvre. For Rivera, the invocation of the "petrified symbol of the past" that the Sun Stone represents, to use Krauze's term, seemed a conservative formula, a way to repeat past forms and establish an idealized ancient world that is profoundly static and solitary. At the same time, and perhaps because of this formulaic political use, the image of the Sun Stone had become decorative, used and abused for commercial purposes. Rivera might have seen the Sun Stone as a tombstone recording the death of history, and its transformation into a cheap symbol of Mexican identity would have insulted his artistic conviction.

By contrast, Rivera invokes Coatlicue in an astonishing manner in his murals in the United States, at both the Detroit Institute of Arts and the City College of San Francisco.[49] In the Detroit imagery, Coatlicue is the machine that shapes steel to produce automobile exteriors (p. 70). Her heart is formed by chains, her face is that of a being from the future, a powerful and creative robot, her severed arms functioning as mighty flywheels that move the gears of the stamping press.[50] The goddess of the Earth—the mother of the gods and the first victim of sacrifice, with all her creative and destructive power, with her strangeness and monstrosity—resembles the machines of modernity, equally capable of creating and destroying, begetting and killing.

In the *Pan American Unity* mural at the City College of San Francisco, Coatlicue becomes a symbol of *mestizaje*, as in Herrán's *Coatlicue Transformed*. Here she is transformed into a hybrid creature: half past, half future; a half-mythical, half-mechanical being (p. 71). Her right arm, shown in human form and not yet severed, displays a palm with four blue circles, like inlaid turquoise, the symbol of the gods. Her right breast protrudes from the garment that covers her shoulders, showing her nipple—a conventional formula for representing goddesses in ancient Mixtec codices. Her fangs and face appear to be made of carved bone or sculpted

47 Roberto Velasco, "A raíz expuesta: fuentes historiográficas, arqueológicas y artísticas del códice Rivera," in *Epopeya del pueblo mexicano: los murales de Palacio Nacional*, ed. Arturo Chapa (Mexico City: Chapa Ediciones/Banco de México, 2010), 112–335.

48 Desmond Rochfort, *The Murals of Diego Rivera* (London: South Bank Board in collaboration with Journeyman, 1987), 59.

49 During the 1930s and 1940s, the American government instituted the Good Neighbor Policy, which promoted pan-Americanism through the collection and dissemination of Pre-Columbian art as part of American heritage. See Braun, *Pre-Columbian Art*, 42.

50 Linda Bank Downs, *Diego Rivera: The Detroit Industry Murals* (New York: W. W. Norton, 1999), 140–44.

and polished stucco—both precious materials used by Mesoamerican artists. Her skirt of serpents seems to be made of carved stone. The fangs faithfully reproduce those of the original sculpture and materially serve to transform the incarnated Mesoamerican Coatlicue into the metallic North American Coatlicue. The right side of the sculpture is a modern machine, similar to that of the Detroit mural but constructed of stainless steel, polished and gleaming. Coatlicue, at the center of the work, dominates the view captured by Rivera of the San Francisco Bay. It is as if the whole scene were produced by visions of the goddess. Indigenous creativity combines with industrial North American productivity. Coatlicue thus becomes the ancestral force behind North American prosperity, a deification of the modern mestizo being who is capable of uniting the southern and northern parts of the American continents.

Firmly associating ancient Mexico with modernity, Rivera breaks free of the Hegelian notion of the superiority of European classical culture and establishes the great works of the ancient Mexicans as the "ancestral canon" of the American continents. He does so, moreover, in a way that amounts to one of his greatest contributions to world art, because he manages to translate, in startling fashion, the fierce formal and spiritual power of the art of ancient Mexico, so far removed from the "classical" canon in its forms and basic precepts. Indeed, his large murals in the United States not only portray Coatlicue, the mother of all creation, as their protagonist, but also turn her into an archetype of the mestizo being of modernity, thus rewriting the past of the American continents, endowing it with a new mythic, historic, and artistic identity. His pictorial choice, that of fusing the indigenous past with the possibility of a pan-American future, is the most luminous aspect of Mexico's contradictory and painful relationship with its indigenous peoples and their astonishing capacity to honor diversity and embrace the future while conserving tradition.

Translated by ROSE VEKONY

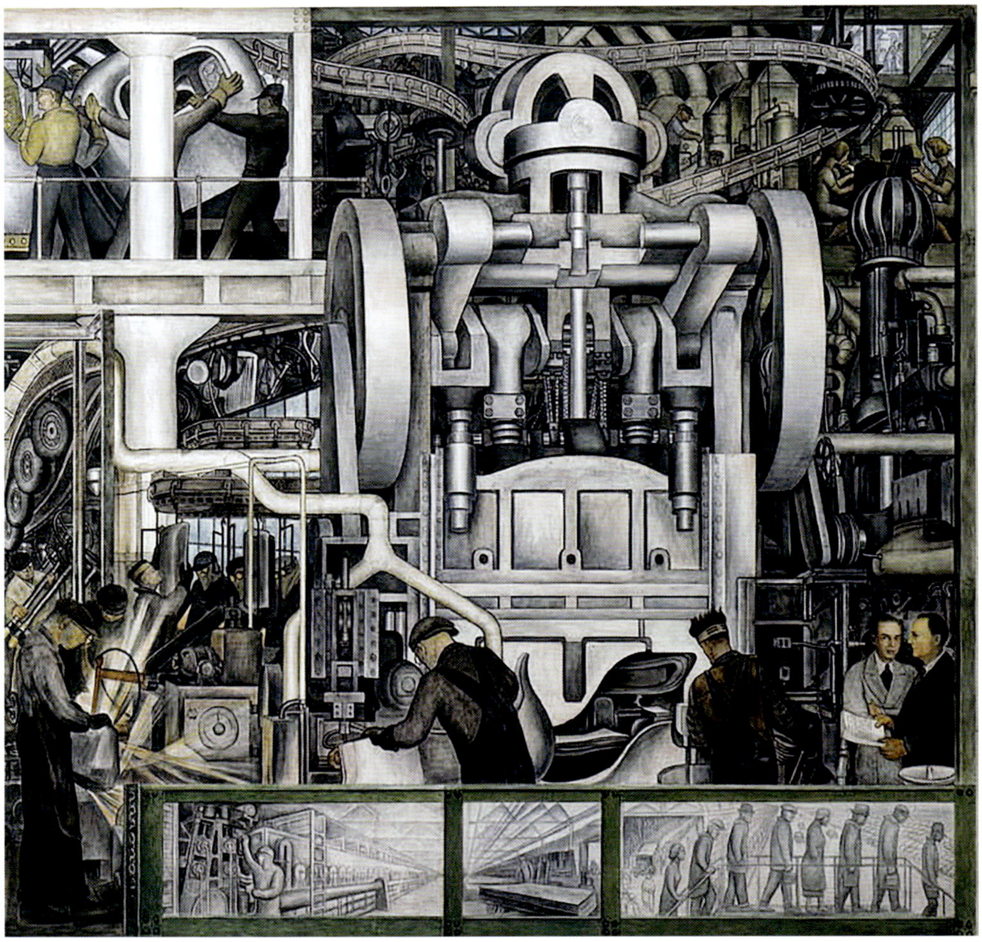

Diego Rivera, ***Coatlicue Mechanic*** (detail), 1932–33; South Wall, ***Detroit Industry***, Detroit Institute of Arts, gift of Edsel B. Ford

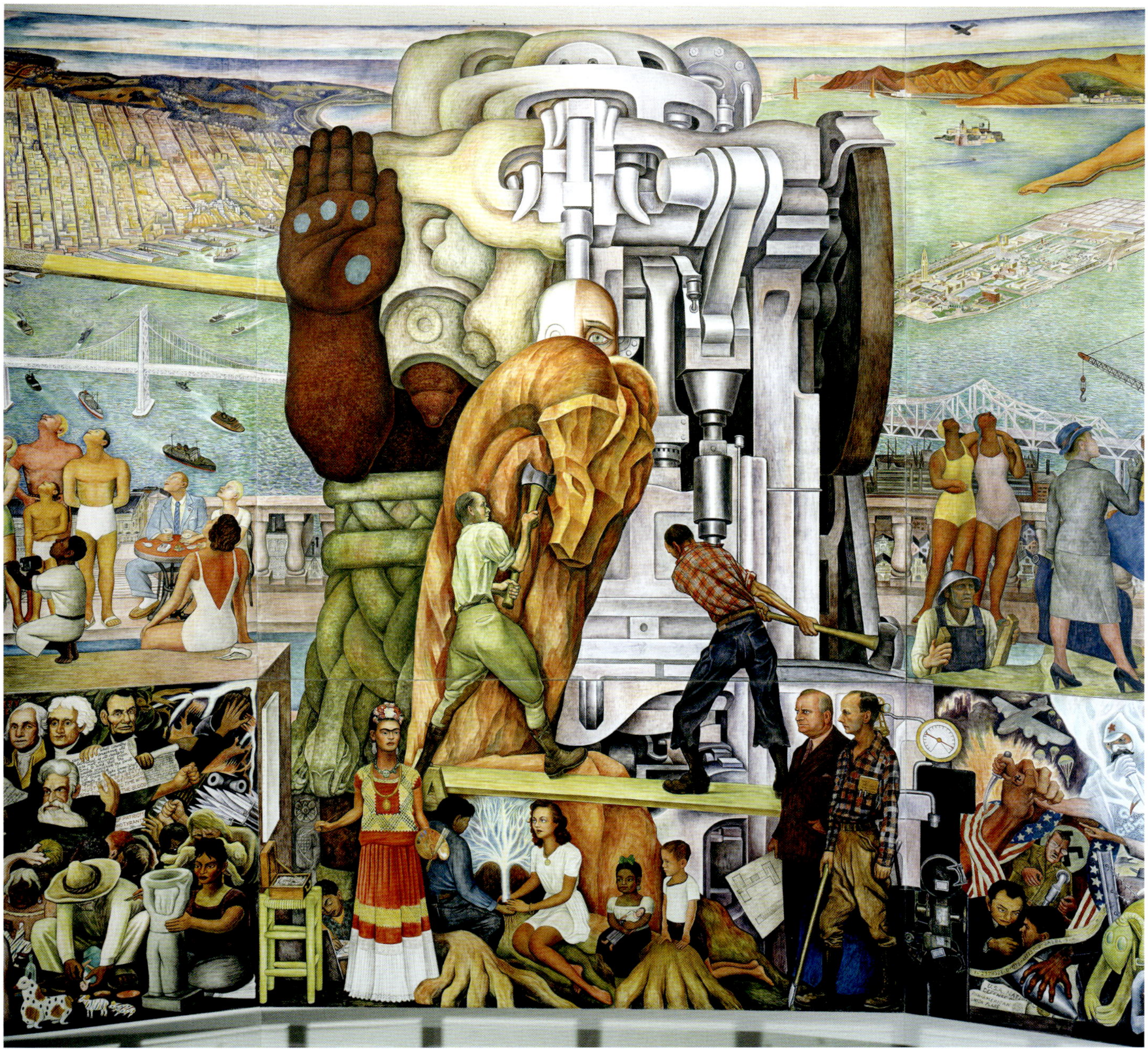

Diego Rivera, ***Pan American Unity: The Marriage of the Artistic Expression of the North and South of this Continent***, 1939–40; Panel 3, ***Pan American Unity***, City College of San Francisco, California

ORIGIN POINTS

ARCHAEOLOGY

AND THE SEARCH FOR AUTHENTICITY

CAMILLE MATHIEU

Lying on her back, with the top of her left shoulder facing the viewer, the subject of Diego Rivera's *Venus de Milo* of 1903 (p. 77) seems to be taking a well-deserved break from centuries of standing in her sensuous *contrapposto*. It requires a second look to recognize the Venus of Rivera's copy, as her iconic facial features—her aquiline nose, almond-shaped eyes, and seductive smile—are obscured by the angle at which she is rendered. Rivera also obscures the statue's curving hips that barely hold up the drapery falling precipitously down her legs, itself hinting at a moment of revelation that never comes. Rivera's drawn Venus, whose body is compressed by dramatic foreshortening, looks strangely as if she might not even possess a right leg. The artist has drawn in the features farthest away from the viewer with a lighter penciled touch, dutifully aiding in creating the impression of the figure's recession toward the back of the picture plane. Venus's hair, the element closest to us, is more meticulously defined in wavy, grouped strands; this emphasis highlights Rivera's interest in rendering traditionally unheralded aspects of the statue visible. The curve and muscular strength of her graceful back, the clover-like nature of the deformation marking the severance at her left shoulder, the brilliance and depth of the drill work defining her falling drapery, and the different impression of tactility (as opposed to the smooth flesh) that the fabric represents for the viewer are all prominently featured in the drawing.

Pablo Picasso's youthful rendering of the Venus de Milo (p. 76), one of a series of several undertaken from 1895 to 1896, represents the subject from a more traditional viewpoint: she is standing, and drawn from a three-quarter perspective.[1] Yet this rendering is not necessarily less innovative than Rivera's. Picasso emphasizes the top half of the body, only notationally marking the drapery folds. As in Rivera's image, the statue is lent a strength and power atypical to the constructs of sensuality and sexuality that usually characterize the figure.[2] This is due in part to the rigor of Picasso's shading technique. The drawn Venus's lips are almost obscured by the ferocity of their shading and by the prominent outlining of her chin, jaw, and neck. The flesh of Venus's stomach presents itself not as softly feminine, but as muscularly developed, shaded as if it were a series of so many sculpted and intersected planes, in a manner similar to Picasso's earlier treatment of the abdominal muscles of the Belvedere Torso (p. 75). The pronounced shading techniques and insistent definition of the statue's usually muted musculature reveal an eagerness on the part of each artist to show his mastery in both perceiving and rendering sculptural depth on paper, a two-dimensional format. Picasso and Rivera's keen understanding of sculptural depth and its translation to the canvas, as well as their attention to the materiality of the subject translated—both traditionally emphasized practices in art academies—would paradoxically aid both artists in developing their own avant-garde styles.

The Venus de Milos from which Rivera and Picasso copied were doubtless plaster casts, most likely reductions, as was common in contemporary art academies. The reduction can be read pictorially in both drawings through the large amounts of space in the picture plane surrounding the Venuses, making them look smaller. The Rivera drawing, in which the sculpture lies on its back in a manner unnatural to it and is positioned at the artist's eye level, implies an easy manipulation of the object being depicted. Both of these early drawings, in other words, define sculpture against its traditional attributes: the Venus is now an object to be manipulated and denaturalized, emphasized only in part as best served the artist. This defiance of sculpture's emblematic characteristics of obdurate materiality and immovability was an academic heresy only

1
Picasso's drawings from this 1895–96 series all represent the Venus de Milo from nearly the same viewpoint, with varying degrees of finish. For all of the reproductions in the series, see Natasha Elena Staller, *A Sum of Destructions: Picasso's Cultures and the Creation of Cubism* (New Haven: Yale University Press, 2001), 105.

2
See Francis Haskell and Nicholas Penny, *Taste and the Antique: The Lure of Classical Sculpture, 1500–1900* (New Haven: Yale University Press, 1981), 328–30.

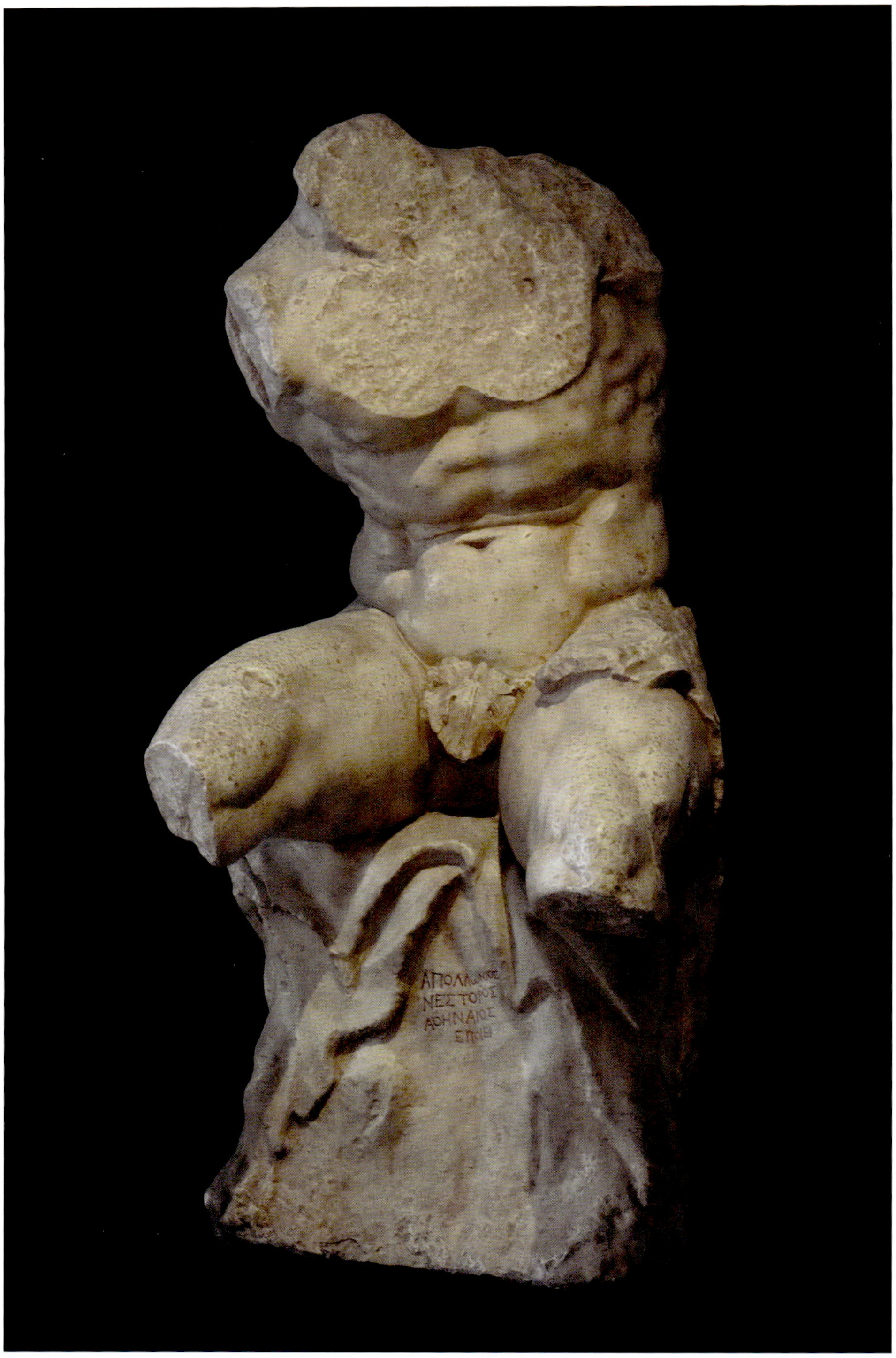

Belvedere Torso (Roman, 1st century BCE or CE), reduced copy, 2016

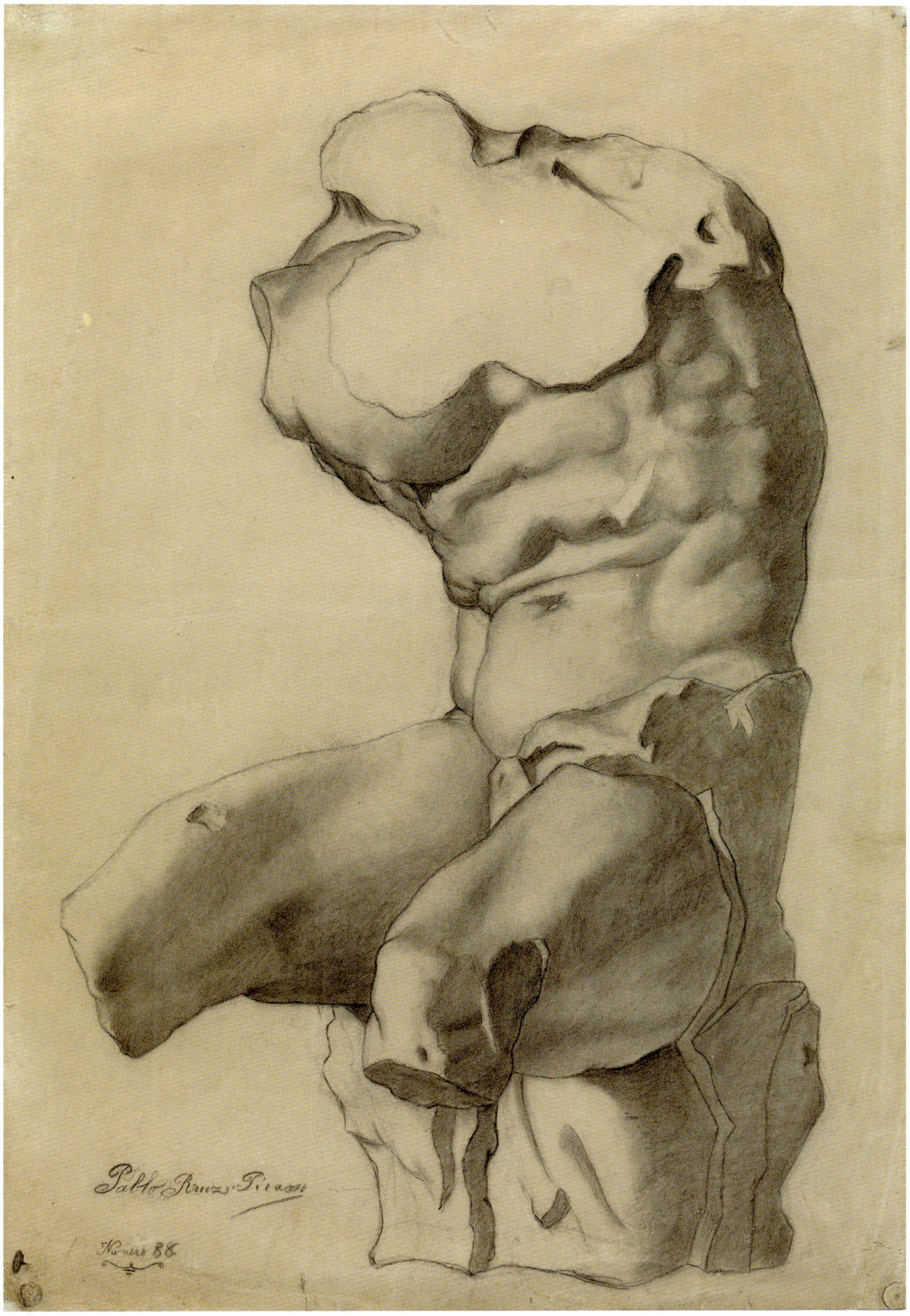

Pablo Picasso, ***Academic Study: Torso***, 1892–93

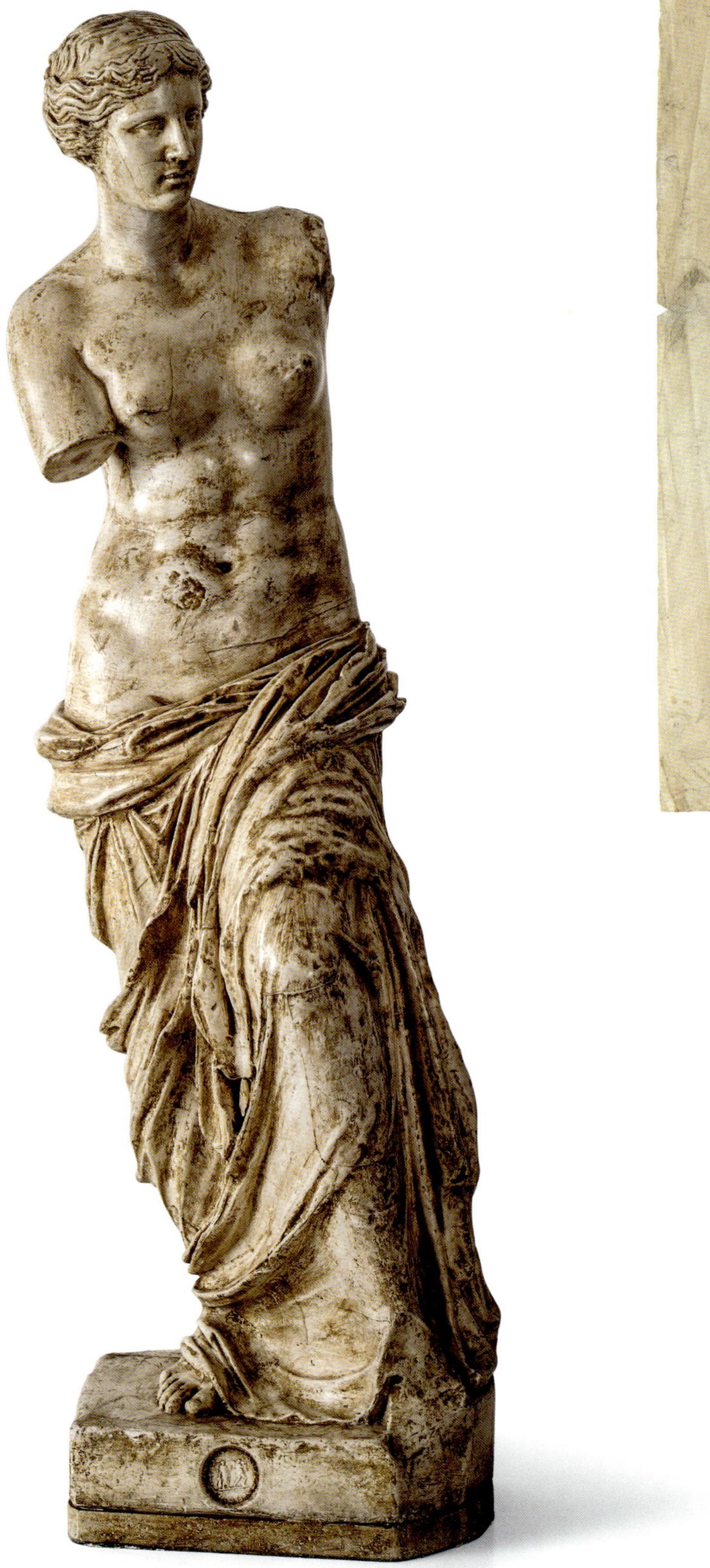

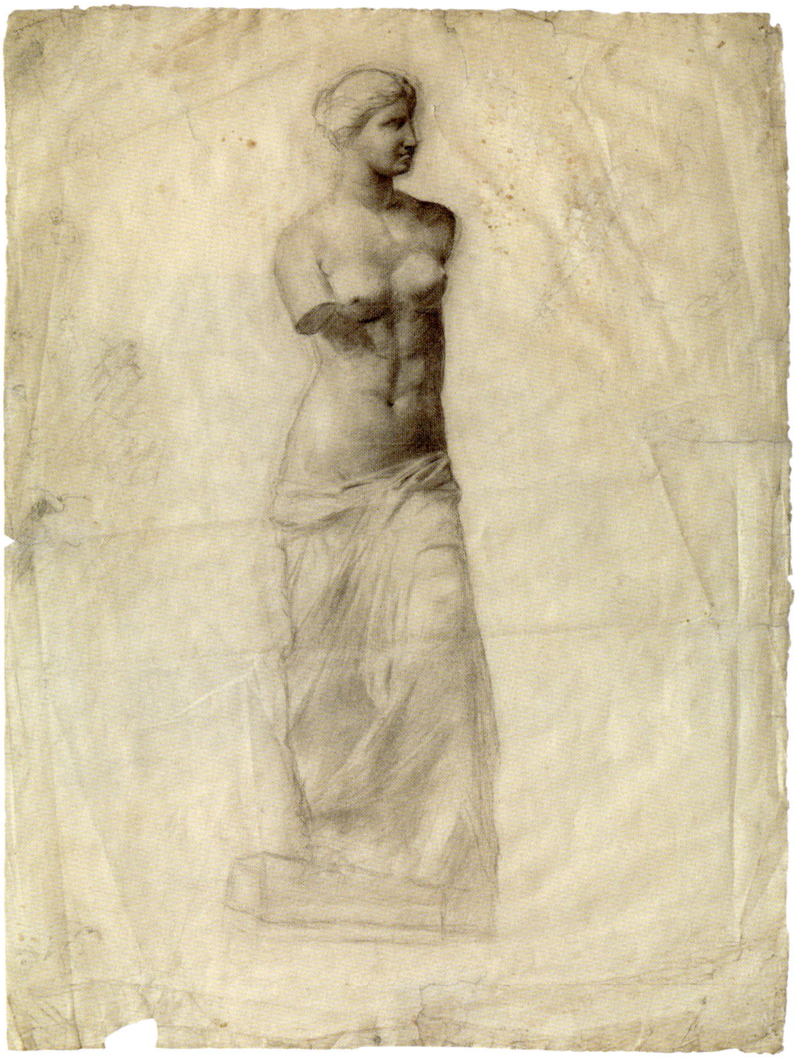

Venus de Milo (Greek, c. 130–100 BCE), reduced copy, 2016

Pablo Picasso, ***Venus de Milo***, 1895–96

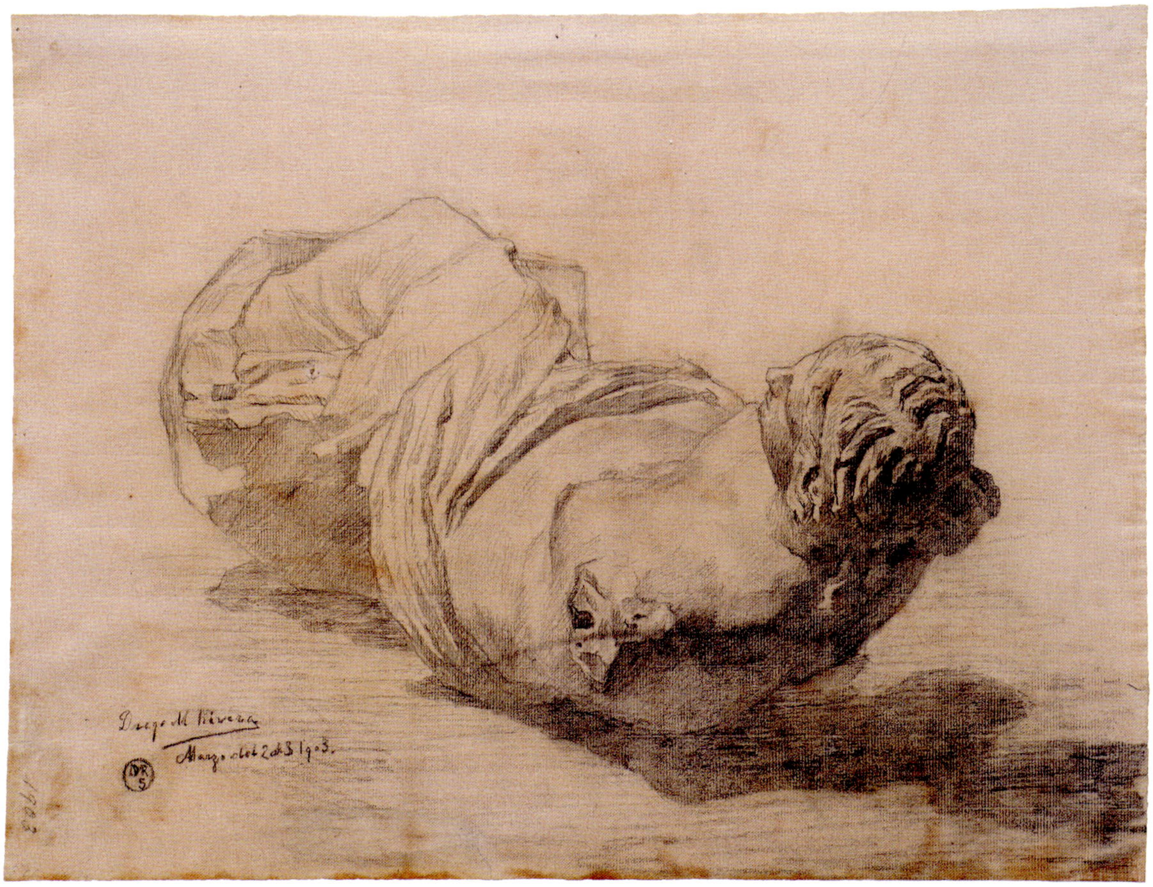

Diego Rivera, *Venus de Milo*, 1903

compounded, indeed worsened, by the origins of these statues in the mythologized and universalized Greco-Roman artistic canon. Works such as the Venus de Milo and the Belvedere Torso were deferred to in academies as canonical examples of the imitation of nature in art; to emulate them was therefore to drink at the source of art, and became a de rigueur student exercise.[3] Rivera's and Picasso's student drawings, however, suggest a malleability to classical art—both its artifacts and its canon—that the original objects were never meant to embody. The drawings reveal a willingness on the part of the artists not only to gain information from but also to play with and render anew forms handed down through tradition.

Both Picasso and Rivera began their precocious careers in art academies, institutions where rigorous copying of the antique and a ruthless adhesion to the principles it had come to represent were the chief means to a successful career. One such principle was that of its universality—namely, the ability of Greek sculpture to meld with Roman originals and copies into a collective classical entity that stood as the origin (and high point) of all culture in the civilized world.[4] In academic terms, these sculptures formed the building blocks of an artist's repertoire. They were the subjects from which an artist ought to draw inspiration, citing them either in part or in whole in the creation of new works. Artists developed this citational ability through extensive training in art academies, centered around learning to copy antique sculpture—first from engravings, then from plaster casts.[5] A typical example of such citation and recombination can be found in the youthful work of Jean-Auguste-Dominique Ingres, an artist greatly admired by both Rivera and Picasso.[6] His painting *Achilles Receiving the Ambassadors of Agamemnon* (1801) cites two antique sculptures in full (done from memory, as this work was produced for the prestigious Prix de Rome competition, where the participants were not allowed to consult outside images): *Phocion*, which Ingres translated into the character of Ulysses, and an *Apollo Sauroctonos*, whose form inspired that of Achilles's friend Patroclus.[7]

A reliance upon a lauded canon that revered sculptures from the past that had been appropriated by "civilized" men as the origin point of their culture was therefore drummed into Rivera and Picasso at a young age. Yet already by the end of their youthful academic careers, they had each begun exhibiting tendencies to undermine such a canon, if not the academic apparatus that brought them to it; their Venus de Milo drawings make this clear. For both men, it had become a question of relocating the origins of their own art in that of cultures that held greater meaning to them than classical Greece: ancient Iberian art for Picasso and ancient Mexican art for Rivera.

The abandonment of an adherence to a universalized Greco-Roman past for a more nationally relevant—if ultimately generalized—one occurred for each artist at a different time in his career. Though the artist's memoirs would have the reader believe that his interest in painting within a Mexican nationalist framework began with his early landscapes of 1904–7, Rivera's ambitions to make the artistic traditions and history of Mexico integral to avant-garde painting can be reliably dated to 1915, with *Zapatista Landscape* (p. 153).[8]

3
For more on the canonical nature of these Greco-Roman statues, see Haskell and Penny, *Taste and the Antique*, 93–107. For a standard description of the academic process as it had crystalized by the mid-nineteenth century in France, see Albert Boime, *The Academy and French Painting in the Nineteenth Century* (New Haven: Yale University Press, 1986).

4
Johann Joachim Winckelmann is considered the first art historian to have codified this academic trend. In the 1760s, he finished what many would call the first history of art, in which he suggested that Greek art was supreme over all other arts due in large part to climatic determinism. Once the supremacy of Greek art had been secured by Winckelmann, it was further bolstered by the work of Georg Wilhelm Friedrich Hegel and other philosophers to the point that for much of the eighteenth, nineteenth, and early twentieth centuries, a society's level of civilization was seen to be based on the ways in which its cultural productions measured up to this Greco-Roman ideal. See Johann Joachim Winckelmann, *History of the Art of Antiquity, 1717–1768* (Los Angeles: Getty Research Institute, 2006), and Rasheed Araeen, "From Primitivism to the Ethnic Arts," in *The Myth of Primitivism: Perspectives on Art*, ed. Susan Hiller (London: Routledge, 1991), 132–52. See also Whitney Davis, "Winckelmann Divided," ch. 9 in *Replications: Archaeology, Art History, Psychoanalysis* (University Park: Pennsylvania State University Press, 1996).

5
For more on the academic process as Picasso and Rivera experienced it, see David Craven, *Diego Rivera: As Epic Modernist* (New York: G.K. Hall, 1997), 10–15, and Susan Grace Galassi and Marilyn McCully, *Picasso's Drawings, 1890–1921: Reinventing Tradition* (New Haven: Yale University Press, 2011), 2–7.

6
One of Rivera's teachers at the Academy of San Carlos, Santiago Rebull, had been a student of Ingres. From Rebull, Rivera learned "not only the rudiments of draughtsmanship but also about the 'golden section' as a compositional device" (Craven, *Diego Rivera*, 12). In the years shortly following their Cubist periods (c. 1916–19), both Rivera and Picasso would produce several drawings in the style of Ingres; see Luis-Martin Lozano, "Diego Rivera, Classicus Sum," in *Diego Rivera: Art and Revolution*, ed. Luis-Martín Lozano, Agustín Arteaga, and William Robinson (Mexico City: Instituto Nacional de Bellas Artes: Landucci Editores, 1999), 132–37. For more on Picasso's lifelong relationship with Ingres's work, see Susan Grace Galassi, "Picasso and the French Tradition: Variations from 1903–1919," ch. 2 in *Picasso's Variations on the Masters: Confrontations with the Past* (New York: Harry N. Abrams, 1996).

7
See Pascale Picard-Cajan, ed., *Ingres et l'antique: L'illusion grecque* (Montauban: Musée Ingres; Arles: Actes sud, 2006), 296–97.

8
See Craven, *Diego Rivera*, 14–19, and Diego Rivera (with Gladys March), *My Art, My Life: An Autobiography* (New York: Dover Publications, 1991), 24. Craven explicitly argues that Rivera's depictions in these early landscapes of a Pre-Columbian archaeological site, the location of the execution of the emperor Maximillian, and the characteristic flora and fauna of Mexico—as well as the legendary volcano Popocatepetl—all reveal a willingness to adapt an avant-garde style (in this case, Impressionism) to local subject matter (Craven, 15–16).

This painting, realized in Paris after Rivera's initial trip to Spain during his Cubist phase, describes a mountainous region (perhaps the Valley of Mexico) as well as desert shrubbery, presided over by a sombrero, a rifle, and a woven serape. Rivera's use of traditionally Mexican objects, newly mobilized as symbols for the political left in the Mexican Revolution (which had begun in 1910), departs from the typical Cubist vocabulary of wineglasses, bottles, and pipes that characterized the daily lives of this avant-garde group of artists in Paris.[9] According to Rivera, his choice to mobilize this nationalist visual rhetoric in this painting led the Parisian Cubists to decry his work as too "exotic."[10] Such works as *Still Life with Gray Bowl*, however, seem to respond to this charge of exoticism by reinserting the Cubist vocabulary of bowls and fruit set upon tables, but offer the provocation of placing this fruit amid vibrant green shrubbery akin to that featured below the mountains of *Zapatista Landscape*. Furthermore, the still life includes what looks to be a fragment of a *petate* (straw mat).

But we should avoid conflating the placement of symbols of modern Mexican nationalist sentiment present in several of Rivera's Cubist works—even extending to portraits such as that of Martín Luis Guzmán (p. 142)—with Rivera's insertion of Pre-Columbian art–inspired imagery into his later works. The two projects are pursued at different moments in Rivera's career and take vastly different visual forms, though they stem undoubtedly from similar personal impulses. For it was only upon Rivera's return to Mexico in 1921 did he begin to systematically incorporate Pre-Columbian themes and sculptures into his painted works. That Picasso's discovery of his own "native" antiquity occurred before his Cubist phase while Rivera's occurred afterward should not preclude us from comparing the two. Both discoveries happened after each artist had moved away from the traditional pressures of the academies where they were trained and had become immersed in avant-garde circles in Paris. The mobilization of these new, "native" themes occurred in their work after encounters with archaeological artifacts from their respective homelands, as well as return visits to those homelands; for Picasso, it was Iberian objects in the Louvre and a 1906 visit to Gósol in Spain; for Rivera, it was the ruins of Chichén Itzá and Uxmal in the Yucatán peninsula—visited just after he returned to Mexico in 1921—as well as the city of Tehuantepec, visited a year later.[11]

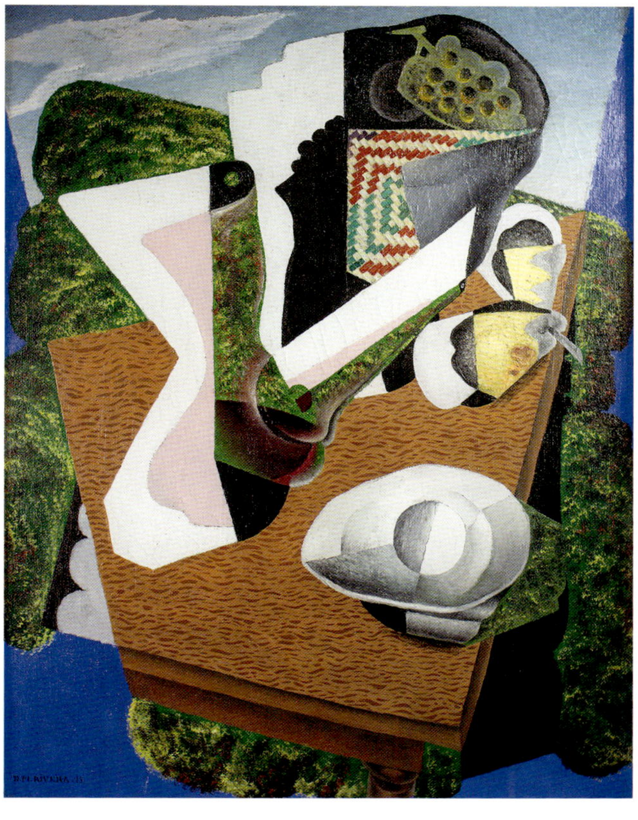

Thanks to the interests of a curator at the Louvre and two dedicated archaeologists, Pierre Paris and Arthur Engel, works from excavations undertaken in the late nineteenth century at ancient sites throughout southern and western Spain had been incorporated into the Louvre's collection of ancient Cypriot and Rhodesian art by 1901.[12] The Iberian works garnered

Diego Rivera, ***Still Life with Gray Bowl***, 1915

9
For more on *Zapatista Landscape*, see William H. Robinson "Cubist Heresies: Diego Rivera and the Parisian Avant-Garde, 1913–1917," in *Diego Rivera: Art and Revolution*, 118. For a traveler's account of trips to Tehuantepec, see Miguel Covarrubias, *Mexico South, the Isthmus of Tehuantepec* (New York: Knopf, 1947). See also Marta Turok, "Frida's Attire: Eclectic and Ethnic," in *Self Portrait in a Velvet Dress: The Fashion of Frida Kahlo*, ed. Denise Rosenzweig and Magdalena Rosenzweig (San Francisco: Chronicle Books, 2008), 51–174, especially 51–59.

10
See Craven, *Diego Rivera*, 34–35; Rivera, *My Art, My Life*, 65.

11
For more details on the Yucatán and Tehuantepec visits, see Laurance P. Hurlburt, "Diego Rivera (1886–1957): A Chronology of His Art, Life, and Times," in *Diego Rivera: A Retrospective* (New York: Founders Society; Detroit: Detroit Institute of Arts, in association with W.W. Norton, 1986), 53. For details about Tehuantepec as a mythological point of origin for avant-garde Mexicans in the early twentieth century, see Howard Campbell, ed., *Zapotec Struggles: Histories, Politics, and Representations from Juchitán, Oaxaca* (Washington, DC: Smithsonian Institution Press, 1993).

12
The *terminus ante quem* for the incorporation of the finds from Cerro de los Santos, the first group of Iberian reliefs to be systematically acquired by the Louvre, is 1897; see Pierre Rouillard, *Antiquités de l'Espagne* (Paris: Réunion des Musées Nationaux, 1997), 11. By 1901, finds from Elche and Redovan had been catalogued as well. For more on the history and exhibitions of the Louvre's antique Iberian collections, see Rouillard, *Antiquités de l'Espagne*, 5–16.

PICASSO'S IBERIAN HERITAGE

and *Les Demoiselles d'Avignon*

LILLY CASILLAS AND DIANA MAGALONI

In 1906, the twenty-five-year-old Picasso felt "he had the confidence, imagination, and power" to execute a painting that would "free art from its shackles" and "extend its frontiers."[1] This would be the revolutionary work known today as *Les Demoiselles d'Avignon* (p. 131), based on the synthetic yet authentic forms of ancient Iberian art.[2] Picasso told art historian Christian Zervos that "*Les Demoiselles d'Avignon* owed nothing to African art and everything to the reliefs from Osuna."[3] In fact, that same year, the Louvre acquired a collection of Iberian antiquities found in Osuna, from the artist's native region of Andalusia. Picasso keenly reflected upon the power that these primitive forms exerted upon him. By this time, he had become "dissatisfied with the conventional mode of expression," and—like other artists such as Matisse—was searching for a mode of expression that would disregard "conventional decorum" and the "emptiness of the accepted aesthetic canon."[4] Unlike the Fauves at the Salon d'Automne in 1905, he was concerned less with the effects of color and light than with the purposeful reduction of his style to the essentials, striving to produce an art without decoration that would offer new technical approaches to the quest to present reality in a new way.

Picasso began to locate this new manner of expression in Spain's ancient Iberian heritage, bringing into his practice an obsessive search of his origins as an artist. The numerous self-portraits that he produced in 1906 before painting *Les Demoiselles d'Avignon* reveal the extent to which Picasso studied the Osuna sculptures, particularly *Man Attacked by a Lion* (p. 82), which seems to have served as an alterego for the artist. In the *Self-Portrait* from 1906 (p. 83), Picasso depicts himself as if he were a man from ancient Osuna. Both have the same stoic gaze as well as the same head shape and marked hairline framing a masklike face with pronounced cheekbones, long narrow nose, close-lipped mouth, almond-shaped eyes, and elongated eyebrows. In *Self-Portrait with a Palette* from the same year (p. 29), Picasso is simultaneously an ancient Iberian and an avant-garde artist in Paris, "half-bohemian, half-workman."[5]

There are many studies for these two paintings, but the one at the Musée Picasso in Paris (p. 294) illustrates how much importance Picasso gave to these features—which are similar to those of three of the women in *Les Demoiselles d'Avignon*. This choice by Picasso was based on the supposedly "primitive" origins of ancient Iberian cultures; at the time, there was little known about them other than the fact that they had arrived from Africa to the Iberian peninsula around 3000 BCE, settling in Andalusia and migrating to Catalonia.[6] Picasso would have understood the art of Osuna as free from the restraints of the categorization of the classical canon; this mirrored his own search for an entirely new mode of expression outside the European tradition—one that would retain the power and simplified forms of the Osuna reliefs while propelling forward the future of art.[7] As Peter Stepan has argued, this primitivizing interest in Iberian art doubtless encouraged Picasso's interest in African art.[8]

By painting himself in a way intended to recall the ancient figure from his native Andalusia, Picasso linked himself to an ancient lineage while transforming his modernism into an approach anchored in expressive forms of the past. Indeed, he conceived of art as ever present: "To me there is no past or future in art. If a work of art cannot live always in the present it must not be considered at all."[9] This radical statement represents the origins of Picasso's personal artistic idiom, allowing for time to collapse and exist in a single, crystallized moment. Picasso was at once the man from Osuna facing the lion as well as the avant-garde artist facing with conviction the newly opened possibilities for modern art.

1 John Richardson, *A Life of Picasso*, vol. 1 (New York: Random House, 1991), 474.
2 James Johnson Sweeney, "Picasso and Iberian Sculpture," in *The Art Bulletin* 23, no. 3 (September 1941): 191–98. For a summary of the historical and current debates about the origins of the women's faces in *Les Demoiselles d'Avignon*, see Peter Stepan, *Picasso's Collection of African & Oceanic Art* (New York: Prestel, 2006)
3 Richardson, *A Life of Picasso*, 519.
4 Sweeney, "Picasso and Iberian Sculpture," 191–93.
5 Fernande Olivier, *Picasso and His Friends*, trans. Jane Miller (New York: Appleton-Century, 1965), 26.
6 Patricia Leighten, *Re-Ordering the Universe: Picasso and Anarchism, 1897–1914* (Princeton, NJ: Princeton University Press, 1989), 80.
7 Ibid., 81.
8 Stepan, *Picasso's Collection*, 29–34.
9 *Picasso on Art: A Selection of Views*, ed. Dore Ashton (New York: Da Capo, 1972), 4.

attention from their association with sources of indisputable pedigree (Greek art), which placed them in the line of antiquity that academic artists were encouraged to copy.[13] At the same time, these ancient Iberian works provided an alternate authority upon which to base an origin myth, one that was more specific, if still broadly universalized, to Picasso's own background. We know from the writings of Ardengo Soffici (an Italian writer, artist, and critic who was living in Paris at the time) that Picasso frequently visited the antiquities galleries of the Louvre.[14] While we do not know which artworks Picasso was specifically drawn to, we have a good idea of what he might have seen and we know what he later acquired.

By 1904 the Louvre had acquired enough of a collection from diverse find sites in Spain to devote an entire room of the "Antiquités orientales" galleries to these works.[15] The Iberian stone heads belonging to the Louvre that Picasso famously acquired from French poet Guillaume Apollinaire's former secretary Honoré Joseph Géry Pieret in the spring of 1907—*Head of a Man* and *Head of a Woman* (third century BCE)—came from the find at the site of Cerro de los Santos in the Spanish province of Albacete, itself one of the earliest sites to interest French archaeologists.[16] *Man Attacked by a Lion* (p. 82), which has been linked by scholar James Johnson Sweeney to Picasso's 1906 *Self-Portrait* (p. 83) due to its particular aesthetics and timely display in the Louvre in 1906, was found at Osuna in Andalusia, not far from Picasso's birthplace of Málaga.[17]

Géry Pieret's theft of Iberian artifacts from the Louvre is often connected with Picasso's work at Gósol, Spain, in 1906—though it should be noted that Picasso had not yet acquired the statuettes and therefore could have carried with him only his memory of seeing them amid a great group of Iberian antiquities.[18] What must have struck the artist was the overall depth, strong recession, and careful precision of the carved lines making up the statuettes' facial features. If we look at the *Head of a Man* or *Head of a Woman* that Picasso would eventually acquire, we note the prominent long nose, the deep recession of the eye area from the brow, the sharpness of the lines defining the eye's almond shape, and the depth of the cutting or drill work of the line separating the full-bodied lips. The emphasis on line in these statuettes readily translates to a two-dimensional rendering, provided that the thickness of the painted line can be made to signify the depth of the sculptural cut. As he did in his Venus de Milo sketch, Picasso would manipulate these Iberian heads to serve his aesthetic purposes. It is not surprising that scholar

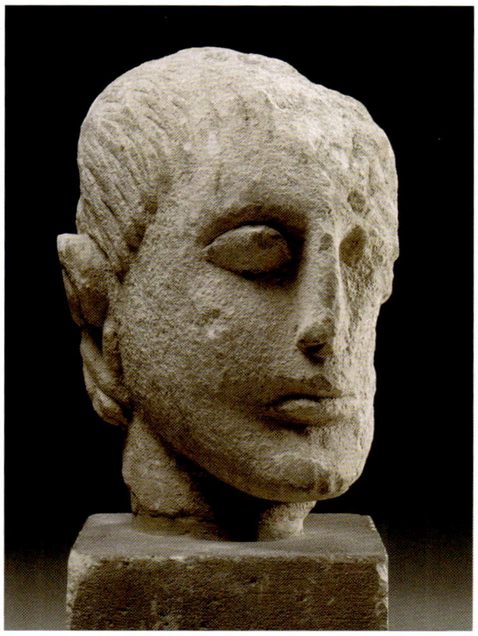

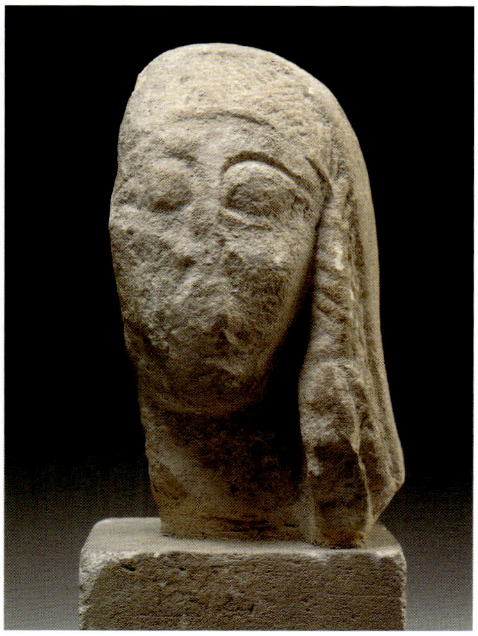

LEFT ***Head of a Man***, Iberian (Cerro de los Santos, Spain), 5th–3rd century BCE; limestone, 20 × 17.5 × 13 cm; Musée du Louvre, Paris (on loan to Musée d'Archéologie nationale, Saint-Germain-en-Laye) (AM 943)

RIGHT ***Head of a Woman***, Iberian (Cerro de los Santos, Spain), 5th–3rd century BCE; limestone, 18 × 11 × 13 cm; Musée du Louvre, Paris (on loan to Musée d'Archéologie nationale, Saint-Germain-en-Laye) (AM 1141)

13
For a description of the location of the Iberian works in the early twentieth century, see Ardengo Soffici, *Ricordi di vita artistica e letteraria* (Florence: Vallecchi, 1942), 365–66. See also Marilyn McCully, ed., *Picasso: The Early Years, 1892–1906* (Washington, DC: National Gallery of Art, 1997), 49 and John Richardson, *A Life of Picasso*, vol. 2, *1907–1917* (London: Jonathan Cape, 1994), 21–23. Richardson describes the layout of the Phoenician galleries at the Louvre using Géry Pieret's account from *Paris-Journal* (August 29, 1911) in his description.

14
See Soffici, *Ricordi di vita artistica*, 365–66.

15
See Rouillard, *Antiquités de l'Espagne*, 15.

16
For more on the theft, see Rouillard, *Antiquités de l'Espagne*, 15–16, and Richardson, *A Life of Picasso*, 21–24.

17
See Rouillard, *Antiquités de l'Espagne*, 7. Marilyn McCully discusses this link in "Eating Fire," in *Picasso in Paris, 1900–1907* (New York: Vendome Press, 2011), 195. For Sweeney's link between the works, see James Johnson Sweeney, "Picasso and Iberian Sculpture," *The Art Bulletin* 23, no. 3 (September 1941): 192–93. Thanks to Lilly Casillas for her research on this link and on the repatriation of Osuna statuary to Spain in 1941. The work's current location at the Museo Arqueológico Nacional in Madrid is deceptive; it was repatriated from Paris in the early years of World War II. For the repatriation process, see Antonio Garcia y Bellido, *La Dama de Elche y el conjunto de piezas arqueologicas reingresadadas en España en 1941* (Madrid: Consejo Superior de Investigaciones Cientificas, Instituto Diego Velazquez, 1943), 11–12.

18
For more on the chronology of Picasso's involvement with Iberian and African art in this period, see the chronology in Peter Stepan, *Picasso's Collection of African and Oceanic Art: Masters of Metamorphosis* (London: Prestel, 2006), 92–93.

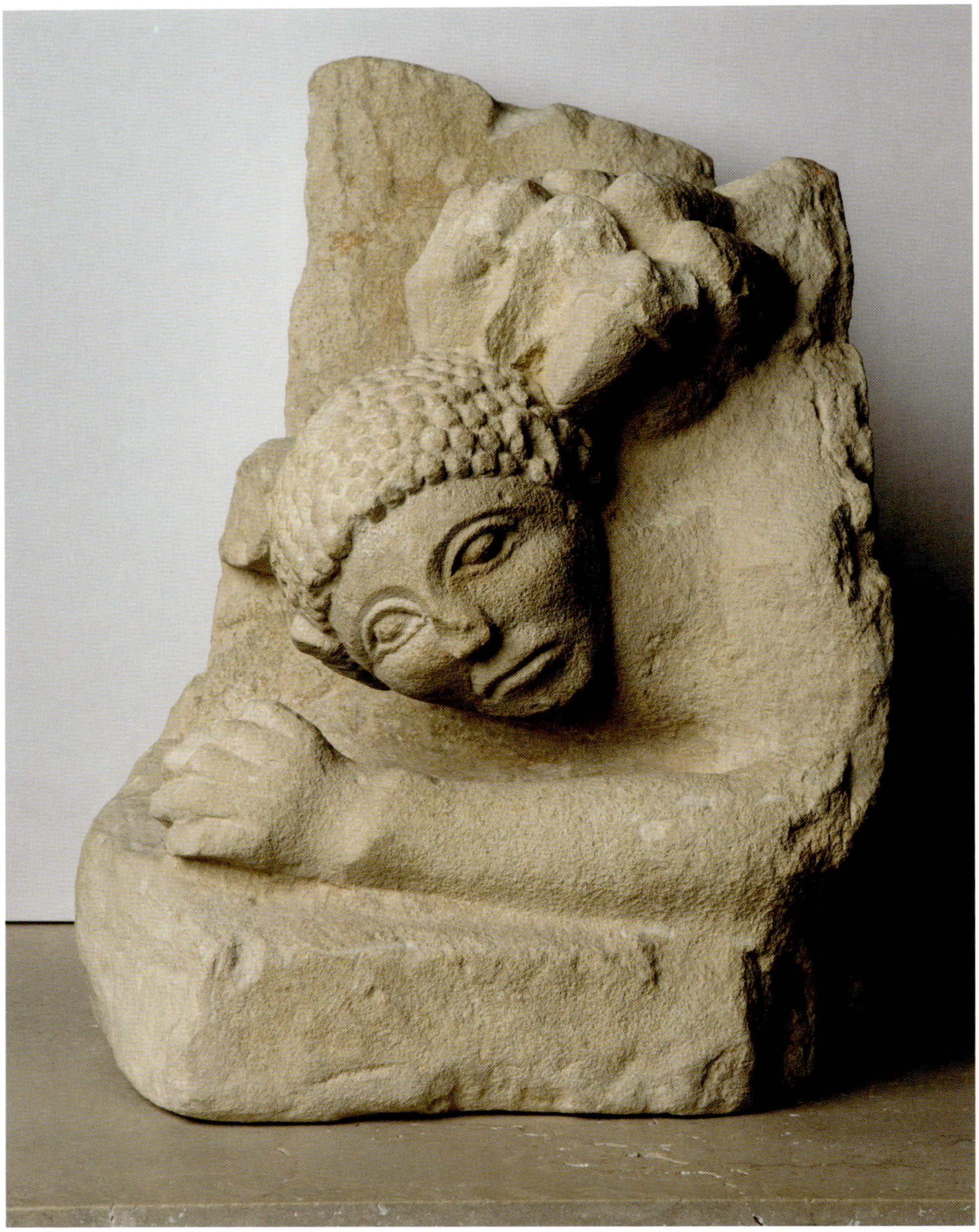

Man Attacked by a Lion, Iberian, Osuna, 6th–5th century BCE

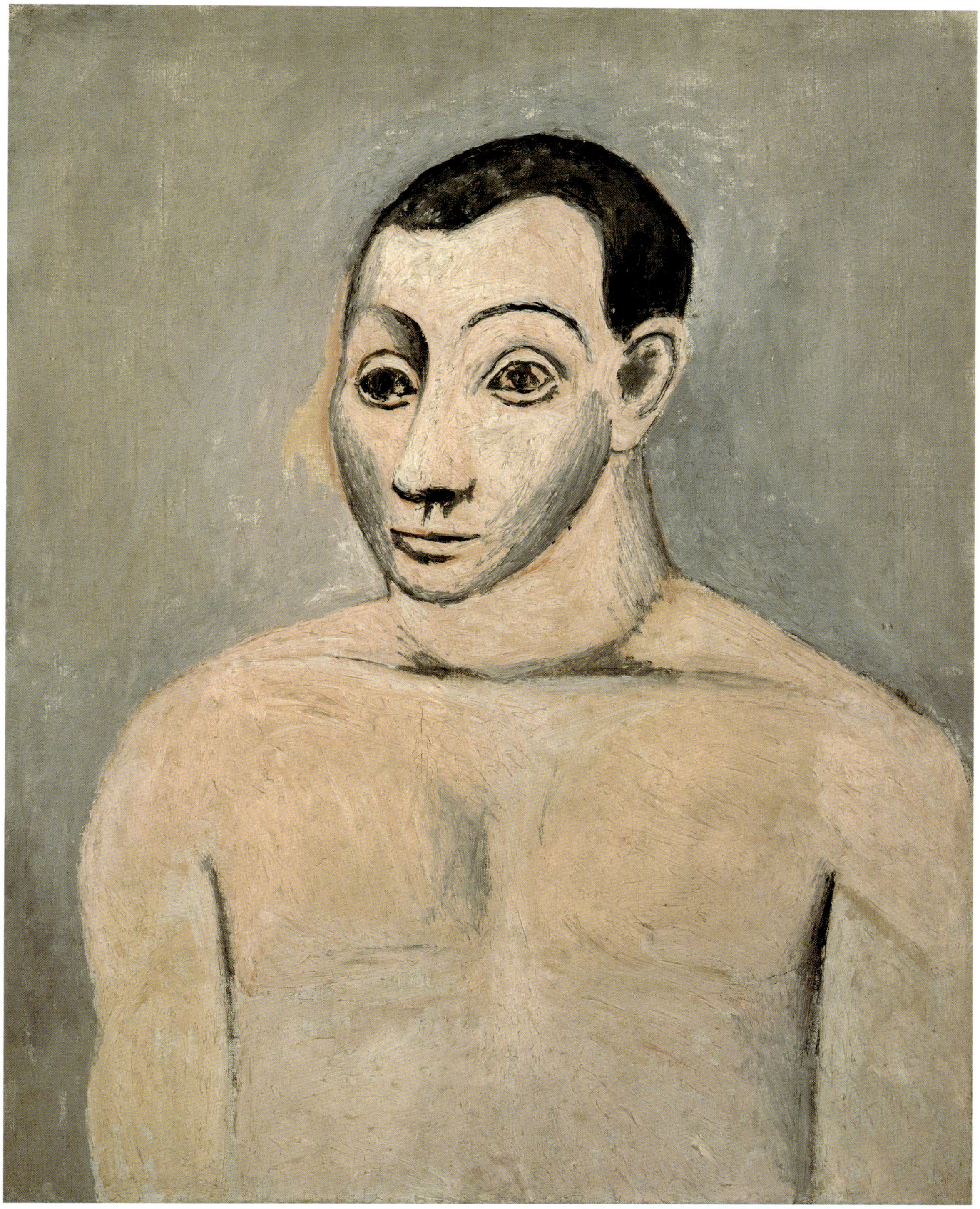

Pablo Picasso, ***Self-Portrait***, 1906

Werner Spies describes Picasso's aesthetic experiments in Gósol as "virtual sculpture"; the artist's Gósol works retained all suggestions of the Iberian objects' sculptural depth in painted form.[19] Robert Rosenblum has noted that "for Picasso, the Gósol summer… prompted many kinds of regression to ethnic and primitive roots, the Spanish equivalent, we might say, of Gauguin's and Bernard's sojourns in Pont-Aven."[20] Looking to one's origins to find an "authentic" version of the past, as Picasso did with pre-Roman Spain and Paul Gauguin did with Brittany (as opposed to appropriating from a culture far from their national origins, as Picasso would later do with pre-colonial Africa and Gauguin would do with Tahiti), seems for these artists to have been a vital step in the transition from accepting and repeating classical academic references to adopting a new aesthetic vocabulary.

The earliest works marking Picasso's engagement with Iberian sculpture exhibit a cut-and-paste aesthetic, as seen in the Iberian-inflected heads that appear atop more academically styled bodies in *Woman with Loaves*, *Reclining Nude* (*Fernande*), *Head of a Woman* (*Fernande*), and *Portrait of Gertrude Stein*. In both *Woman with Loaves* and *Reclining Nude*, the subjects' long noses define the features of their faces symmetrically, shaping the sculptural dynamic of their eyes and lips. This approach reflects stylistic attributes of the Iberian heads Picasso had seen in the Louvre (and would eventually acquire upon his return to Paris), in which the nose seems to exist chiefly to delineate and separate the eyes from each other, which are in turn dug deeply away from its bridge. The statuettes' wide, deeply carved, curved eyebrows highlight the eyes even more, while the depth of the carving stroke delineating the lips from each other accentuates their fullness. These features appear similarly sculptural in Picasso's paintings and drawings of the Gósol women. Each of these painted heads, it is often noted, seems disjointed from its body.[21] The face of the figure in *Woman with Loaves* is aggressively outlined and seems deeply recessed into the white scarf-like head covering that surrounds it, mimicking the qualities of an ancient Iberian sculpted head.

In both *Woman with Loaves* and *Reclining Nude*, however, Picasso also provides us with elements that mitigate the cut-and-paste aesthetic, such as a universal intensity of hue. This is particularly evident in the golden-brown, carefully shaded splendor of the subject's skin in *Woman with Loaves*. Her historically specific (ancient Iberian), "primitive" face—a facial type predating the modern canonization of the Greco-Roman type—is attached to her female body, also a symbol of the eternal primitive.[22] The subject's primitive female body is now assigned a more modern

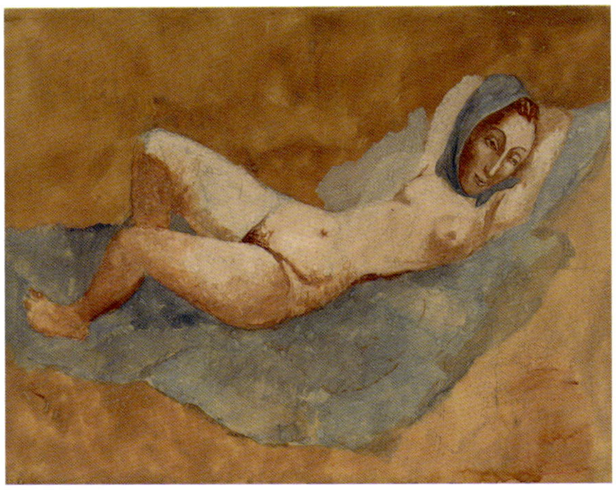

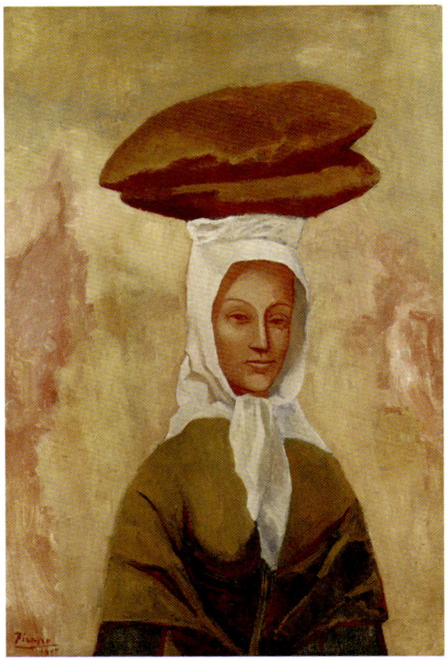

LEFT Pablo Picasso, ***Reclining Nude*** (***Fernande***), 1906; watercolor and gouache with pencil on paper, SHEET 18 9/16 × 24 1/8 in. (47.3 × 61.3 cm); Cleveland Museum of Art, gift of Mr. and Mrs. Michael Straight (1954.865)

RIGHT Pablo Picasso, ***Woman with Loaves***, 1906; oil on canvas, 39 3/16 × 27 1/2 in. (99.5 × 69.8 cm); Philadelphia Museum of Art, gift of Charles E. Ingersoll, 1931 (1931-7-1)

19
Werner Spies, *Picasso, das plastische Werk: Werkverzeichnis der Skulpturen* (Stuttgart: Hatje, 1983), 321n41. See also Stepan, *Picasso's Collection*, 28.

20
Robert Rosenblum, "Picasso in Gósol: The Calm before the Storm," in McCully, *Picasso: The Early Years*, 268.

21
Sweeney, in "Picasso and Iberian Sculpture," is one of the earliest sources to note this disjuncture.

22
For an artful exploration of the ways in which the feminine body was perceived to be closer to nature than the masculine one—and therefore, further from culture and civil society—in the late nineteenth and early twentieth centuries, see Mark Antliff and Patricia Leighten, "Primitive," in *Critical Terms for Art History*, ed. Robert S. Nelson and Richard Shiff (Chicago: University of Chicago Press, 1996), 220–25.

cultural specificity: namely, a Catalonian one as she is shown partaking in what we are meant to believe is a local Gósol activity. Fernande Olivier shares the head covering with the character from *Woman with Loaves* in *Reclining Nude*, where, even as her relaxed pose emulates Francisco de Goya's 1805 *Naked Maja*, she also lays claim to a certain Catalonian authenticity from having been the subject of Picasso's *Fernande on a Mule*. In this work, Olivier—dressed in a Spanish mantilla and the voluminous skirts common to the region—sits on the back of a mule, a typical local packhorse, and is silhouetted by Pedraforca Mountain, near Gósol, in the background.[23]

Such depth of immersion in a traditional culture, exhibited by an artist who was typically at the cutting edge of the avant-garde, could be likened to the sentimental nationalism Rivera painted into his Cubist *Zapatista Landscape*. Picasso, however, takes his lover, not political patriotism, as his subject matter. Paradoxically, he primitivizes and falsely nationalizes Olivier—who was French—in his search for authenticity. Rivera, too, frequently chose to portray his third wife, the painter Frida Kahlo, in various traditional Mexican clothing styles, but this is complicated by the fact that Kahlo herself often chose to wear these garments in order to denote her own nationalist pride. In his first painting of Kahlo, however—*Distributing Arms*, part of his 1928 *Apotheosis of the Mexican Revolution* cycle—Rivera depicts her in contemporary, Western-styled clothing, including a bright red shirt.[24] She represents not a quaint link to the past, as Olivier in a mantilla might, but a lethal and powerful instrument of modernity and progress. Unlike Fernande's face in *Reclining Nude*, her face is her own, not a primitivized one; she is active and ready to participate in the fight for her country, whereas Fernande simply reclines, the very picture of passivity.

Women were not the only subjects that Picasso painted in this primitivizing Iberian style in Gósol; the artist eventually submitted himself to a similar treatment, ultimately adopting an identity with the older, culturally specific (Iberian) antique he had used to render Olivier. In his 1906 *Self-Portrait*—probably started during the summer in Gósol and finished later that fall—Picasso adopts the same long nose, carefully delineated lips, and deeply set eyes from Iberian sculptures.[25] The eyebrows, each completed in what seems like a single, arching stroke, and the primitivized facial features support this interpretation.[26] To counter the flatness created by the universality of the skin tone, Picasso adds obvious strokes of grayed shading to the sides of the face and the collarbone area, almost in a parody of his technical academic training in which shading techniques are used to denote volume. This crude shading also appears on the area of his neck farthest away from his boldly outlined chin and in the area distinguishing

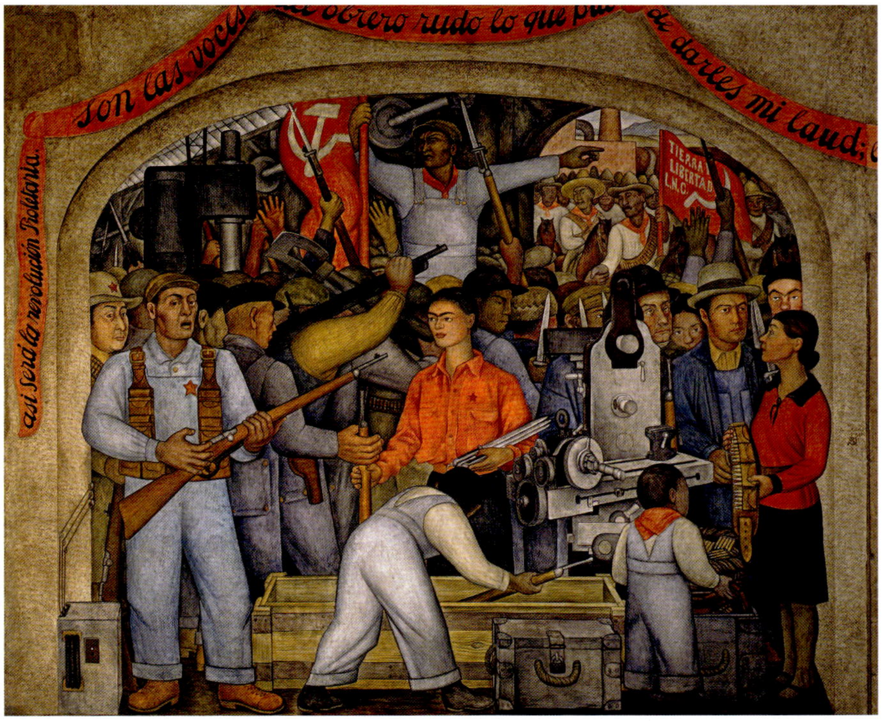

Diego Rivera, ***Distributing Arms***, 1928; Court of Fiestas, Level 3, South Wall, Secretaría de Educación Pública, Mexico City, Mexico

23
See Rosenblum, "Picasso in Gósol," 267. See also Galassi and McCully, *Picasso's Drawings*, 128.

24
For more on Frida Kahlo's dress styling, see Turok, "Frida's Attire," 52. For more on the nationalistic dress of women in Mexico in the early twentieth century, see Adriana Zavala, "Epilogue," in *Becoming Modern, Becoming Tradition: Women, Gender, and Representation in Mexican Art* (University Park: Pennsylvania State University Press, 2010), 271–74.

25
For more on this self-portrait's "masklike" aesthetic, see Stepan, *Picasso's Collection*, 28–29 (Stepan, mistakenly in my view, refers to the image as borrowing its expression from a Greek *kouros*).

26
An unpublished conversation between Christian Zervos and Picasso (documented and excerpted in Sweeney, "Picasso and Iberian Sculpture," 191n1) has allowed Sweeney to link the aesthetics of this self-representation specifically with the ancient Iberian sculpture *Man Attacked by Lion*. I agree with William Rubin's more general linkage of the work with the Iberian-influenced sculptural aesthetic that Picasso was developing at this time; see *Pablo Picasso: A Retrospective*, ed. William Rubin (New York: Museum of Modern Art, 1980), 59. Thanks to Lilly Casillas for her hard work in tracking down the origins of this conversation.

his right eye from his nose. Despite the rather unfinished quality of the bottom half of the torso, the painting nevertheless presents a more uniformly rendered body than Fernande's in *Reclining Nude*, in that the head seems to correspond better stylistically with the body upon which it has been set. Wide swaths of pink skin contrast with sharp black outlines, from which the artist builds up gray paint to signify volume in the planes of pectoral muscles; similar volume-creating tactics delineate his cheeks and chin. Picasso's experiments with placing Iberian-styled heads upon bodies not stylistically consistent with them come to their first resolution here, in his own self-image. Academically informed, sculpturally realized, and self-aggrandizing in the choice of both a Hispanicizing and an antique reference point, Picasso's 1906 self-portrait opens up embodied possibilities for a holistically conceived primitivizing style. Following visits to the Musée d'Ethnographie du Trocadéro, Picasso would further develop this style by switching reference points yet again: this time to Africa and Polynesia.[27]

In contrast, no existing self-portraits of Rivera bear any resemblance to the many Pre-Columbian art objects in his personal collection. Yet his extensive and deliberate citations of these objects in works made throughout his career shows such art to be at least as deeply embedded, if not far more so, in his identity of selfhood as ancient Iberian art was for Picasso.[28] Following a brief flirtation with an Ingresian classicism and a trip to Italy sponsored by the Mexican government to study the art of the fresco, Rivera left Paris permanently and returned in 1921 to an altered political landscape in Mexico. The country was now governed by Álvaro Obregón, one of the leading generals of the Mexican Revolution. Mexico's cultural sphere was presided over by José Vasconcelos, the young, dynamic minister of education.[29] Vasconcelos had developed a vast program to inspire social and cultural change that included integrating Mexico's diverse regions and ethnic populations into one collective and resolutely modern society. This included initiatives aimed at increasing literacy rates across the nation, promoting the history of pre-conquest Mexico and revitalizing the visual and performing arts.

As part of this national program, Vasconcelos initiated a plan to decorate prominent public buildings with murals.[30] In November 1921, before giving Rivera his first mural commission, Vasconcelos invited Rivera and other artists to accompany him on a government-sponsored trip to the Yucatán Peninsula. This trip and another journey a year later to Tehuantepec proved to be Gósol-like experiences for Rivera. Like Picasso, Rivera was inspired by the landscape, people, and artistic traditions of these new places. The jungles of the Tehuantepec isthmus appear in his first mural commission,

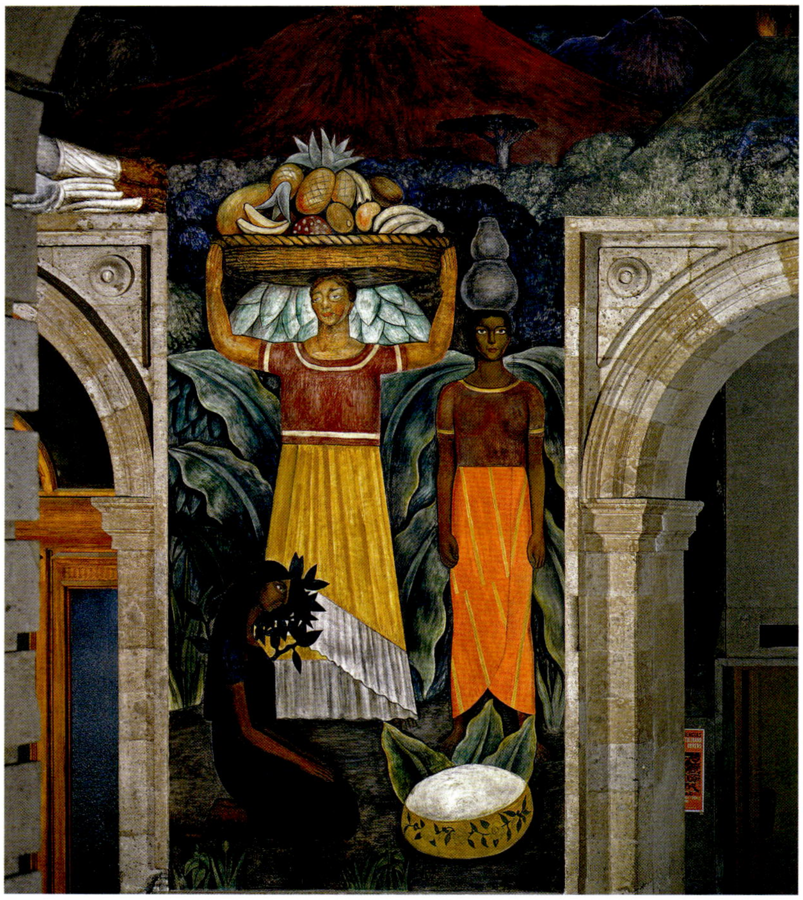

Diego Rivera, ***Tehuanas***, 1923–28; Court of Labor, Level 1, North Wall, Secretaría de Educación Pública, Mexico City, Mexico

27
See Hal Foster, *Prosthetic Gods* (Cambridge, MA: MIT Press, 2004), 29. See also Sieglinde Lemke, *Primitivist Modernism: Black Culture and the Origins of Transatlantic Modernism* (Oxford: Oxford University Press, 1998), 33–36, for an excellent discussion of the exact role of Iberian and African "primitive" sculpture in Picasso's art and Picasso's problematic relationship to admitting the importance of the African influence in his work. For the now famous description of Picasso's Musée d'Ethnographie du Trocadéro visit, see Richardson, *A Life of Picasso*, 24–27.

28
Certainly Picasso's interest in Iberian art was sustained for a far shorter period of his life than Rivera's for ancient Mexican art.

29
See Pete Hamill, *Diego Rivera* (New York: Harry N. Abrams, 1999), 73, 81. For a chronology of Rivera's activity from his Cubist period in Paris to his return to Mexico in July of 1921, see Laurence P. Hurlburt, "Diego Rivera: A Chronology," 37–53.

30
See Hamill, *Diego Rivera*, 81–84, and Stanton L. Catlin, "Mural Census," in *Diego Rivera: A Retrospective*, 242.

the fresco in the Simón Bolívar Amphitheater (1922–23). Women wearing clothing characteristic of the region are not only featured in this fresco, but also in his earliest frescoes at the Ministry of Public Education in Mexico City (1923–24).

On the Yucatán trip, Rivera visited the ruins of Chichén Itzá and Uxmal, recording not only the sites themselves but also the local people in his sketchbooks.[31] Though we cannot be certain that Rivera started collecting pre-conquest art as a result of his experience of these ruins, his first explicit integration of ancient Mexican sculpture into his murals follows closely on the heels of this trip. The kneeling women in the foreground of his *Day of the Dead* murals, including *First Friday of Sorrow on the Canal of Santa Anita* in the Court of the Fiestas at the Ministry of Public Education (1923–24), draw on the iconography of kneeling sculptural figures in basalt from the Aztec civilization, including statues of Chalchiuhtlicue and other fertility goddesses.[32] Also making an appearance in the foreground of canvas paintings from the 1920s such as *Flower Day* (p. 89), these kneeling women—their backs to the viewer and their attention focused on the scene before them—function as stand-ins for the experience of the viewer even as they enact the practice of viewing within the painting itself. These painted women further reflect the approach to sculpture Rivera first exhibited with his early version of the Venus de Milo. The female subject matter links the works in the first instance, as does the suggestion of the smaller size of the statue indicated by its easy visual manipulation—Rivera drew the Venus lying on her back, whereas he drew the Chalchiuhtlicue figures from the back (the Chalchiuhtlicue statues in the Rivera Collection at the Museo Anahuacalli are each around a foot high).[33] Finally, both address the question of artistic origin point. When Rivera began his studies, the classical past signified by the Venus was the subject of his emulation; by 1923, the ancient Mexican past had usurped its place.

Nearly all the photographs of Aztec Chalchiuhtlicue figures that appear in scholarly works highlighting their archaeological significance show the statues from the front. In contrast, books focusing on Rivera's use of them show both the fronts and backs, as the latter view was of greater interest to the artist. He carefully noted the details of their hair arrangements (most often braids) and their bare feet, folded beneath them, which make them easy to spot as a leitmotif in his work. In Rivera's 1920s images, the statues' painted facial expressions are often hidden from viewers. The material quality of basalt, a hardened volcanic stone that is as difficult as granite to carve, is reflected in the compact nature and relatively linear carving and angular modeling of the statues. Like Picasso with his Iberian heads, Rivera exploited the salient qualities of his source material. In *Flower Day*, he uses bold, black outlines for the toes and arms of the figures and color-blocked white shirts and dark skirts. The woman on the right's shirt line echoes the downward-pointed shawl line of a Chalchiuhtlicue figures from his own collection (p. 88). Rivera's kneeling women appear rectangular and solid, like the blocks of stone from which Chalchiuhtlicue figures were hewn. The painted women anchor Rivera's image but simultaneously seem demure and submissive in their poses and attitudes, which encourages viewers to primitivize them, even as we identify with them.

Scholars Patricia Leighten and Mark Antliff note that the concept of the "primitive" as it took root in late nineteenth- and early twentieth-century art comprised four elements: a regression in time or space from the modern, "civilized" world; the use of "native," non-white racial types to signify pre-"civilized" states; the projection of simplistic thought and activity onto the lower, often rural, classes; and the use of the female body to stand in for the most primal, or natural, of beings due in part to its

31
Hamill, *Diego Rivera*, 84. Many of the sketchbooks in question are in private hands.

32
For more on the history of these Chalchiuhtlicue figures in the collection, see *Diego Rivera Museum: Anahuacalli* (Mexico City: Organizing Committee of the Games of the XIX Olympiad, 1970), 105. See also the entry for *Head of a Water Deity* in "Heilbrunn Timeline of Art History," Metropolitan Museum of Art, http://www.metmuseum.org/toah/works-of-art/00.5.44.

33
Most of the statuary of the Anahuacalli collection is nonmonumental. See *Diego Rivera Museum*, 105.

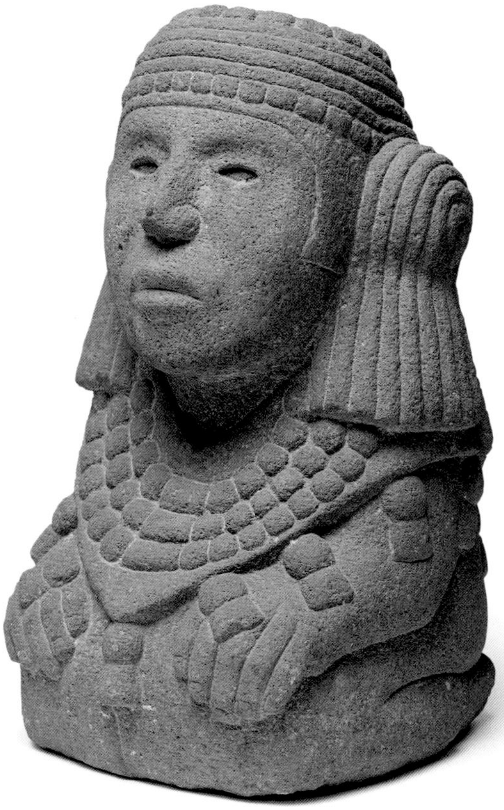

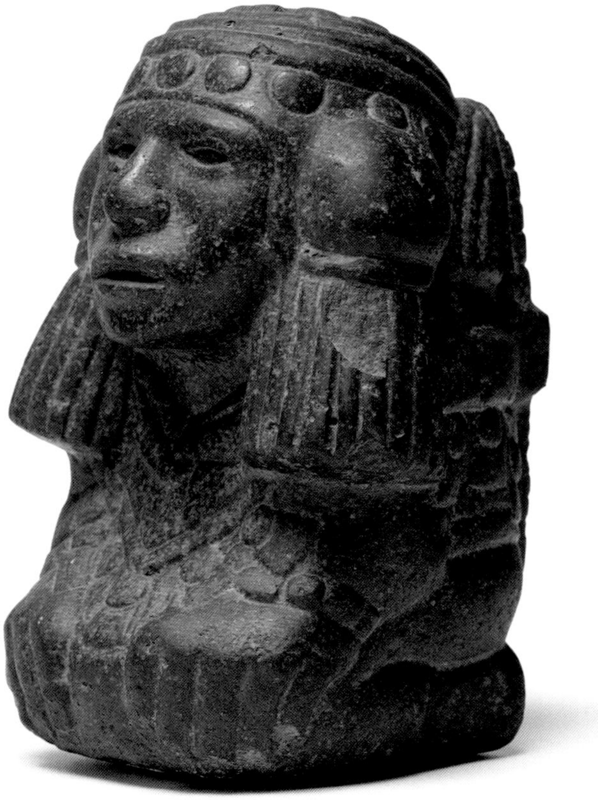

Chalchiuhtlicue (*Water Deity*), Mexico, Aztec, 1200–1521

Chalchiuhtlicue (*Water Deity*), Mexico, Aztec, 1200–1521

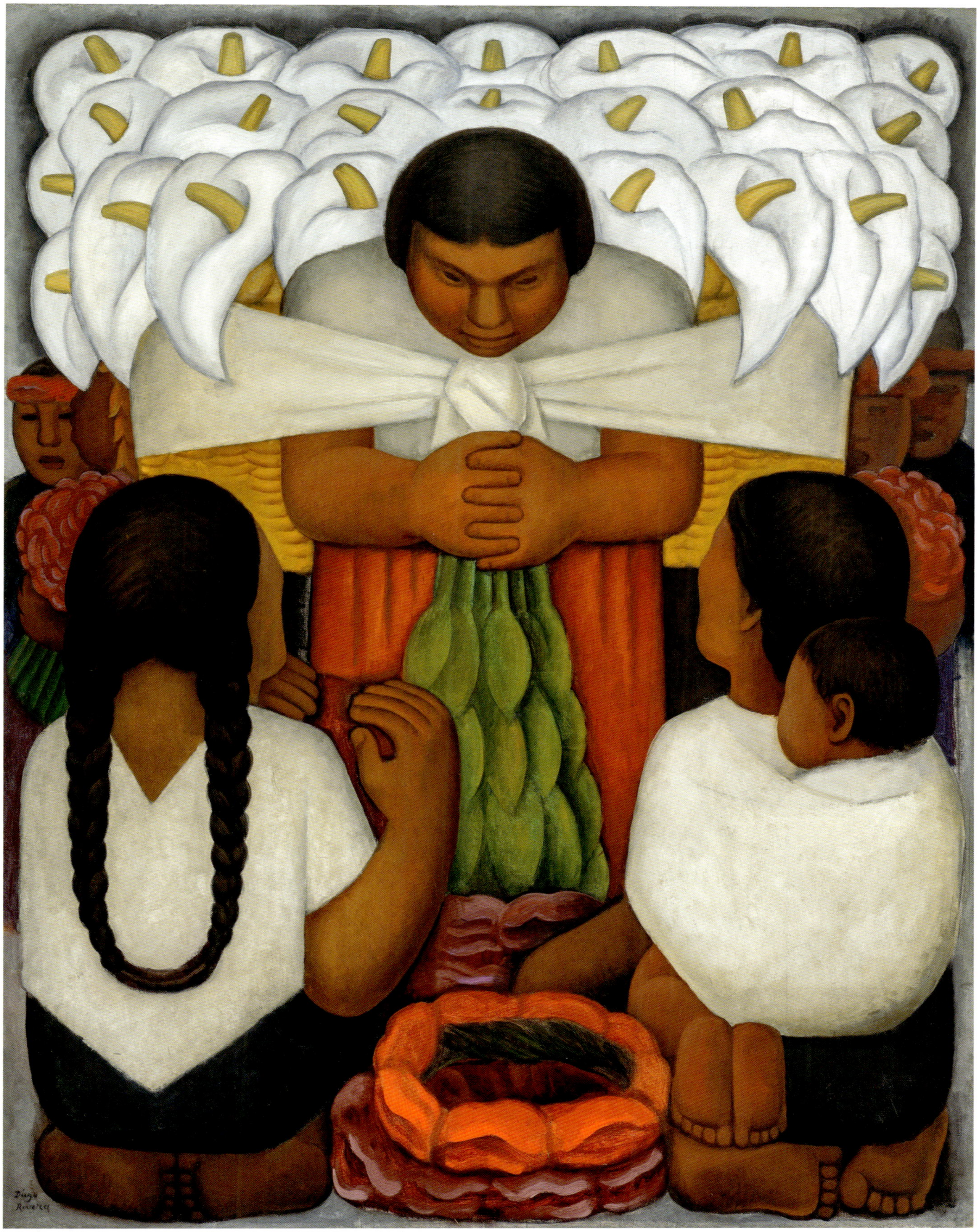

Diego Rivera, *Flower Day*, 1925

reproductive capacities.[34] Rivera's kneeling women are nearly always rendered as mestizos or "natives" in terms of their skin color. In this way, and in the heft with which they ground the images they occupy, Rivera projects primitiveness onto these women as a mythical origin point for a uniquely Mexican art that he nevertheless controls through his appropriation of their forms. While Rivera would continue to depict these kneeling women in his painting for the rest of his life, he did use this imagery—of the ancient Mexican witness—for himself in one instance. In his mural *The Making of a Fresco* at the San Francisco Art Institute (1931), Rivera himself sits at the center of a scaffold, back to the viewer, watching others labor over a mural depicting labor. He appropriates their actions: he stands in for the viewer's experience while he himself views the mural. But he is also creator here and, as such, is placed in a position much higher off the ground than his Chalchiuhtlicue-like women would usually occupy.

Like Picasso before him, Rivera adapted the primitivizing motif he had projected onto contemporary women for himself only once he had mastered it. But whereas Picasso built a career on shifting identities—from Spanish to French nationalities, from Cubist to neoclassical styles, from Iberian to African and Polynesian antique reference points—Rivera built his career on his identity as a proud Mexican nationalist. This work began with generalized expressions of nationalism, like that exhibited in the women of Tehuantepec (Tehuanas) in their regional dress in the early panels of the fresco cycle at the Ministry of Public Education and *Dance in Tehuantepec* (1928). It then progressed to include specific imagery grounded in Mexico's antique past—citations of gods and goddesses from ancient Mexican art appear in mural paintings throughout his career—a past he both collected and promoted through his public mural-making.

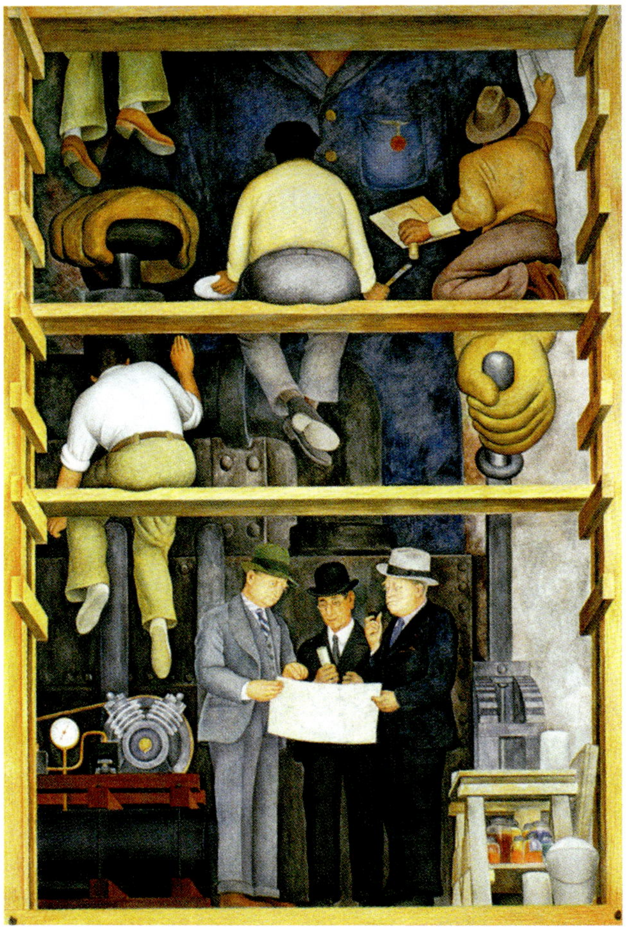

Diego Rivera, ***The Making of a Fresco*** (detail), 1931; Central Wall, Diego Rivera Gallery, San Francisco Art Institute

At the same time that Rivera was turning Chalchiuhtlicues into kneeling Tehuanas, he was also sketching indigenous "Indians"—possibly in the Yucatán or in Tehuantepec; these faces would in turn be informed by death masks excavated from the ancient city of Teotihuacán (p. 92). Though the site had caught the attention of foreign explorers as early as 1675, it was not until 1905 that Teotihuacán began to be fully exploited by local archaeologists.[35] Work undertaken after the 1910 Revolution was further encouraged as a nationalistic celebration of the glorious past of Mexico and its indigenous people.[36] By the time Rivera returned to Mexico and had begun painting images of its "native" people, the excavations at Teotihuacán had only become more sophisticated and widespread.[37] Results of newer excavations were published beginning in 1922; it is possible that Rivera not only read these publications but also went to the archaeological site himself, given its proximity to Mexico City and his interest in Pre-Columbian art.

The archaeological objects most associated with Teotihuacán are death masks, as so many have been uncovered there during excavations. Rivera procured many such masks for his collection. Drawings from his sketchbooks

34
See Antliff and Leighten, "Primitive," 220–25.

35
For a history of exploration of the site, both local and foreign, see Mari Carmen-Serra Puche, "The Role of Teotihuacan in Meso-American Archaeology," in *Teotihuacan: Art from the City of the Gods*, ed. Kathleen Berrin and Esther Pasztory (New York: Thames and Hudson; San Francisco: Fine Arts Museums of San Francisco, 1993), 65–66. The site's first chief excavator from Mexico, Leopoldo Borras, was charged with the excavation of the Pyramid of the Sun by then president Porfirio Díaz—the sponsor of Rivera's trip to Italy—who wanted to have it ready for foreign luminaries to visit on the centennial of Mexican Independence in 1910.

36
Ibid., 67.

37
Ibid., 67–68; this included interdisciplinary studies of the geography of the region, as well as an investigation into the Temple of the Serpent.

show that he must have come into contact with them at an early stage in his career. Like the basalt Aztec Chalchiuhtlicue figures, the death masks from Teotihuacán exhibit a linear carving aesthetic which Rivera emphasized in order to capture their essence in carefully sketched two-dimensional line drawings. In one sketch (p. 93), Rivera faithfully copied the mask, noting the indented features (dimples) of the cheeks, the pronounced nose, the heavyset jaw, the deep relief of the eyes and parted lips, and the ears sticking out prominently from the face. In another contemporary drawing, he adapts those features—the prominent nose, the almond eyes, and the full lips—to the head of a "native" woman (p. 93). In a 1938 series of pastels, Rivera again drew on these death masks to help shape the faces of "native" women selling flowers. Their bodies obscured by the flowers they sell, the women stand against massive, dark stone walls of the kind that would later define the Museo Anahuacalli, itself a blend of Toltec and Mayan architectural styles.[38]

This primitivizing association of contemporary indigenous Mexican women with Mexico's ancient past through the citation of a distinctive facial type endemic to Teotihuacán death masks is superficially similar to Picasso's appropriation of ancient Iberian heads. Picasso's interest in Iberian art was academically and personally informed but ultimately more useful to him as a style to be tried on and tried out, then cast aside when no longer useful. Rivera's use of ancient Mexican art infiltrated his style to the point that the two cannot always be torn asunder. Rivera so strongly identified the particular facial style embodied in the death masks of Teotihuacán with the indigenous peoples of the Americas that he replicated it in his murals in the Detroit Institute of Arts in 1932. No doubt in the absence of any part of his Pre-Columbian collection, Rivera used the facial type of the Teotihuacán death mask to inform (and to differentiate from the other races) the "Red Race," or Native American, figure (p. 94).

Rivera would replicate the Teotihuacán-inspired faces over and over again; like the kneeling women, they are present throughout his corpus, in such diverse works as the Palacio Nacional murals (1929–30), the Palace of Cortez murals (1930), *Pan American Unity* at City College of San Francisco (1940), and *Dream of a Sunday Afternoon in the Central Alameda* in Mexico City (1947–48). Like the works of classical art he copied at the beginning of his career, these faces became building blocks for his art. On them, Rivera constructed a pedagogically and politically oriented mural painting that was, in spite of its primitive undertones, profoundly steeped in the history of Mexico—not just in content but also in form.

That form, however, was ultimately somewhat generalized and universalized, as the diversity and arrangement of his collection at the Museo Anahuacalli makes clear. Over the course of his lifetime, Rivera

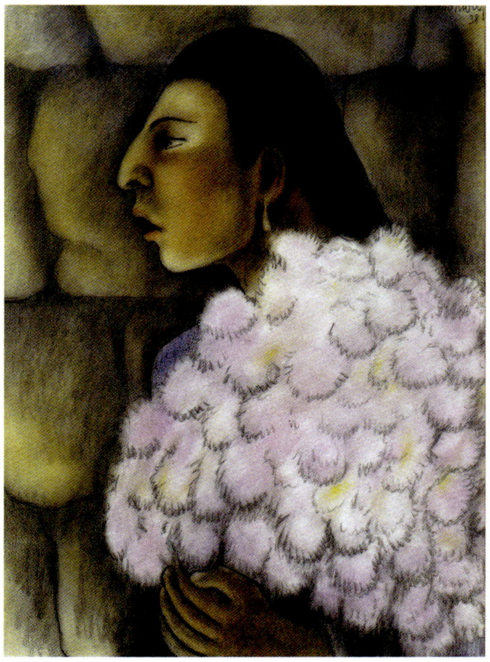

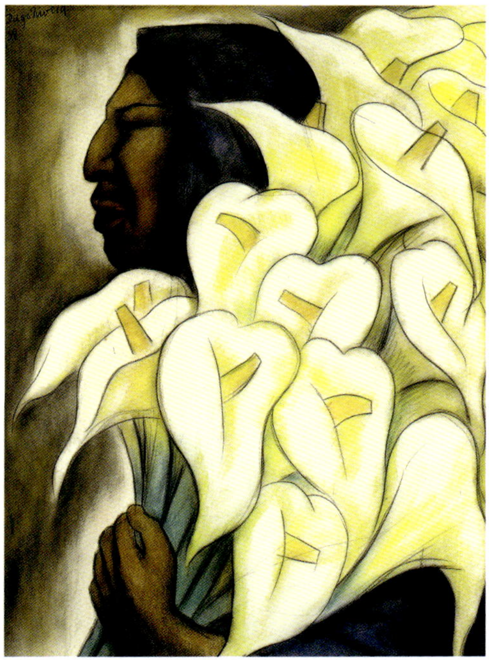

LEFT Diego Rivera, ***Profile of an Indian Woman with Lilacs***, 1938; charcoal and pastel on paper, 24⅞ × 18¾ in. (63.2 × 47.6 cm); Milwaukee Art Museum, gift of Mr. and Mrs. Richard E. Vogt (M1980.139)

RIGHT Diego Rivera, ***Profile of a Native with Calla Lilies***, 1938; charcoal and pastel, 23¾ × 18¾ in. (62.9 × 47.5 cm); Mr. and Mrs. Kenneth E. Hill Collection

[38] Ibid., 27.

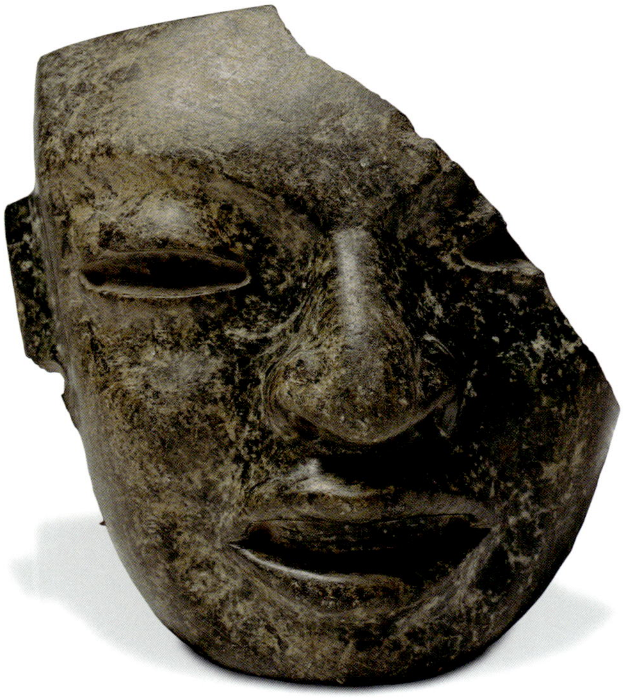

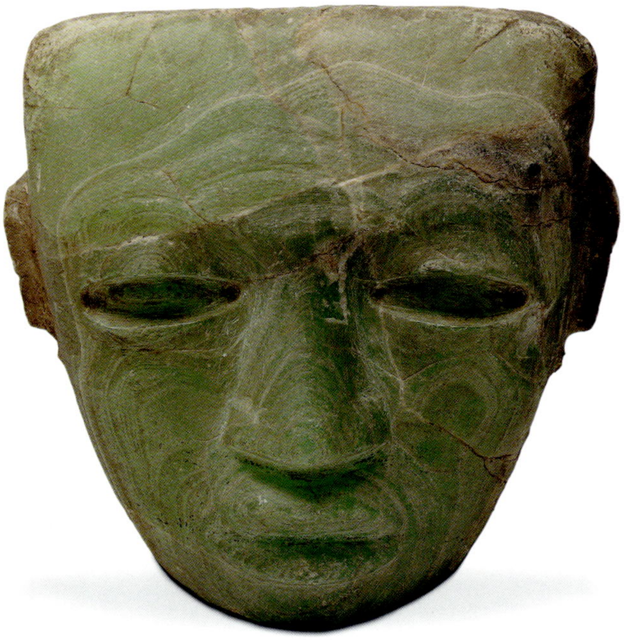

Mask, Mexico, Teotihuacán, 200–650

Mask, Mexico, Teotihuacán, 200–650

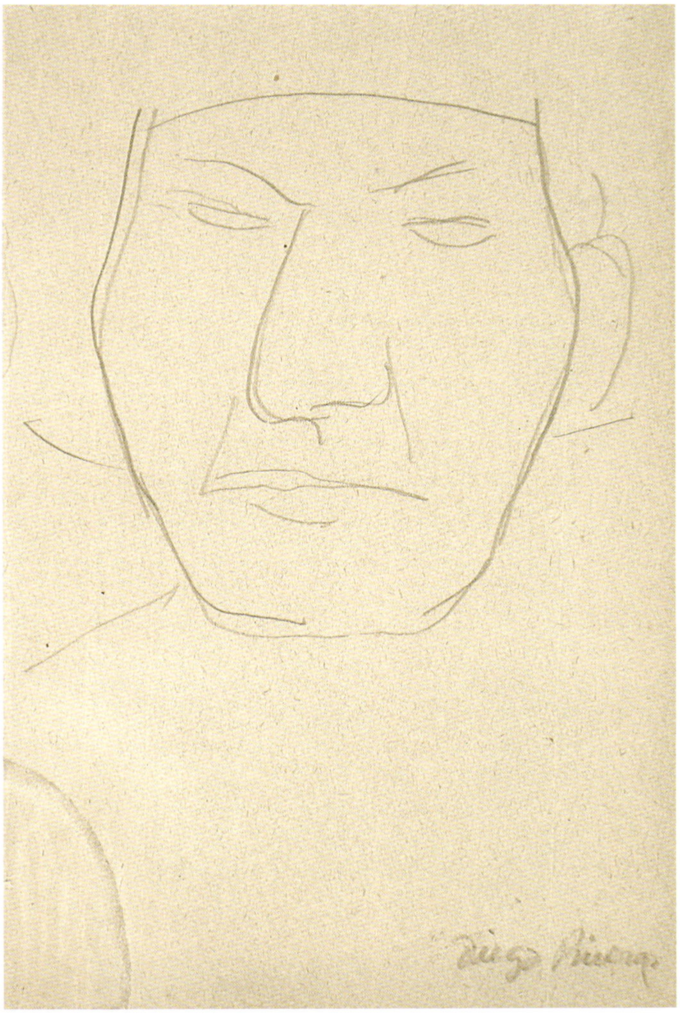

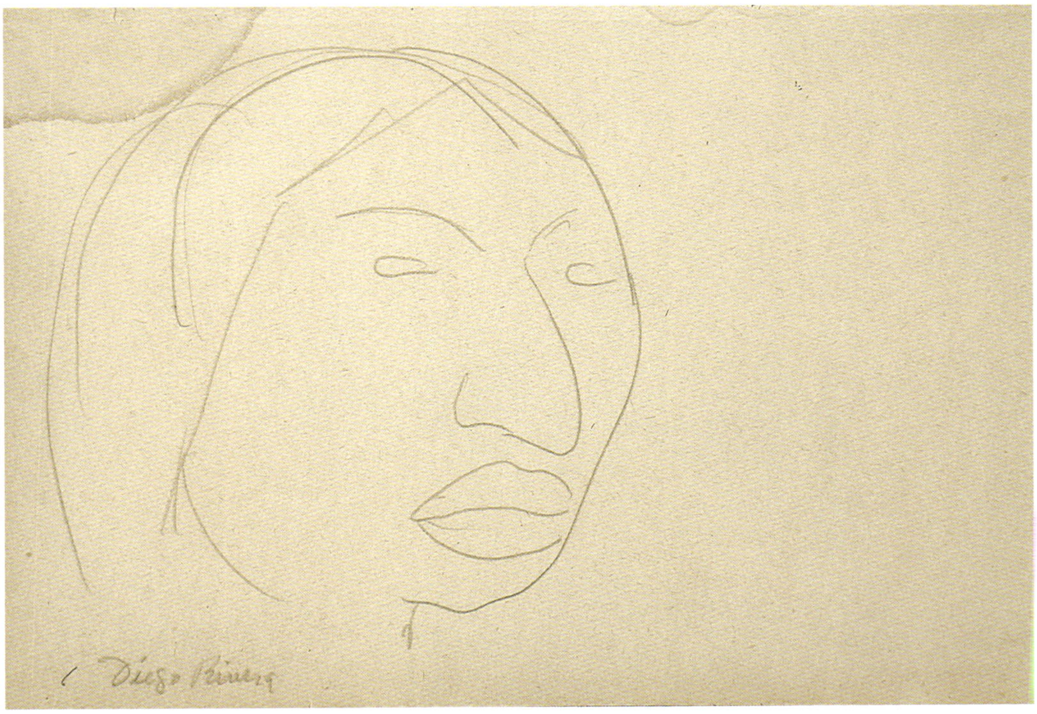

Diego Rivera, *Untitled* (*Face*), 1923–25

Diego Rivera, *Untitled* (*Head of an Indian Woman*), 1923–25

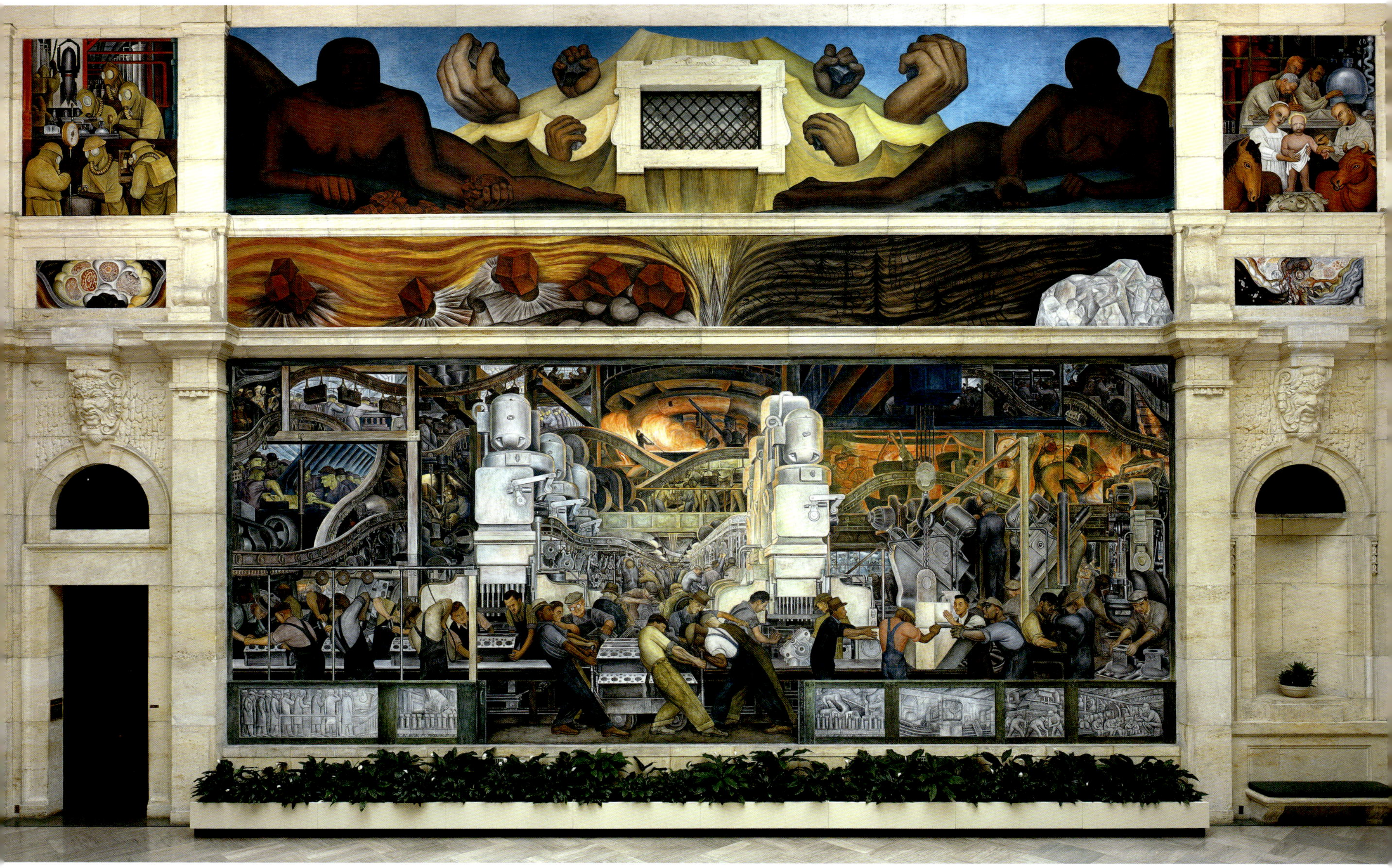

Diego Rivera, ***Detroit Industry***, 1932–33; North Wall, Detroit Institute of Arts, gift of Edsel B. Ford

amassed an important number of stone sculptures, bas-relief fragments, baked-clay figurines, temple models, and ceramic pottery from many different indigenous Mexican civilizations. The Aztec culture is well represented, as is earlier art from Colima and Tlatilco in the Valley of Mexico.[39] This geographically, historically, and materially diverse collection also includes Oaxacan objects from the Zapotec and Mixtec cultures (for pieces from Rivera's collection now in the Museo Anahuacalli, see pp. 22, 88, 92, 193, 218, 220, 224).[40] However, in an altar-like space he built in the museum to showcase different works in his collection, objects from the Teotihuacán, Aztec, and Toltec cultures are interspersed with one another as opposed to distinguished by origin, encouraging the viewer to imagine the Mexican past as a collective, generalizable whole.[41]

As Picasso's 1907 painting *Les Demoiselles d'Avignon* elides Iberian cultures with African and Polynesian ones to create a sort of universalized primitivism, so too do Rivera's Mexican-themed works of the 1920s and 1930s invoke specific cultural references in the service of the general. Indigenous women kneel in his canvases as Aztec Chalchiuhtlicues, but when they face the viewer in other images, their facial features are borrowed from pre-conquest Teotihuacán.[42] Ultimately, this generalization between ancient Mexican cultures serves Rivera's lifelong political goal of celebrating both Mexican people and their art, as well as exposing Mexicans and foreigners alike to ancient Mexican motifs in his pedagogically oriented murals in public spaces. Because Picasso's self-synthesis with Iberian art (in his 1906 *Self-Portrait*) is imperfect, its clear stylization sends scholars hunting for the sources that make up its parts. Rivera's choice to merge his identity with that of ancient Mexican art results in works that are endlessly circular—by the time he painted himself in the position of a Chalchiuhtlicue kneeler on the scaffolding at the San Francisco Art Institute, he was citing his own earlier transformations of these ancient forms. Picasso's multiple and varied citations represent, in his pre-Cubist years, a struggle to distance himself from an anchored past. Rivera's citations of ancient art in his post-Cubist phase perform the same struggle to separate from the Greco-Roman canon while seeking out a different canon to replace it: one based on pre-conquest Mexican art. Ultimately, then, the majority of Rivera's work is always already performing Mexico's past—and his own history with it.

39
There is very little information available in the English-language scholarship as to the exact time periods in which Rivera amassed the specific objects in his collection. He must have begun his collecting, as Picasso did, relatively early on in his career. By 1942 he had a collection of sixty thousand pieces of art. See Patrick Marnham, *Dreaming with His Eyes Open* (New York: Knopf, 1998), 321–22. His citation of a wide variety of Pre-Columbian works throughout his post-1921 oeuvre suggests that the process of acquisition was a lifelong project. For a good description of the kind of work and the variety of cultures represented in the Museo Anahuacalli's collection, see *Diego Rivera Museum*, 27–28.

40
Ibid.

41
Ibid., 26.

42
Certainly, Rivera's later works, including murals for the Palacio Nacional (1929–30) depicting the history of Mexico from the Fall of Teotihuacán in 900 CE to the beginning of 1935, do distinguish between Mayan, Toltec, and Aztec civilizations; see Catlin, "Mural Census," 261.

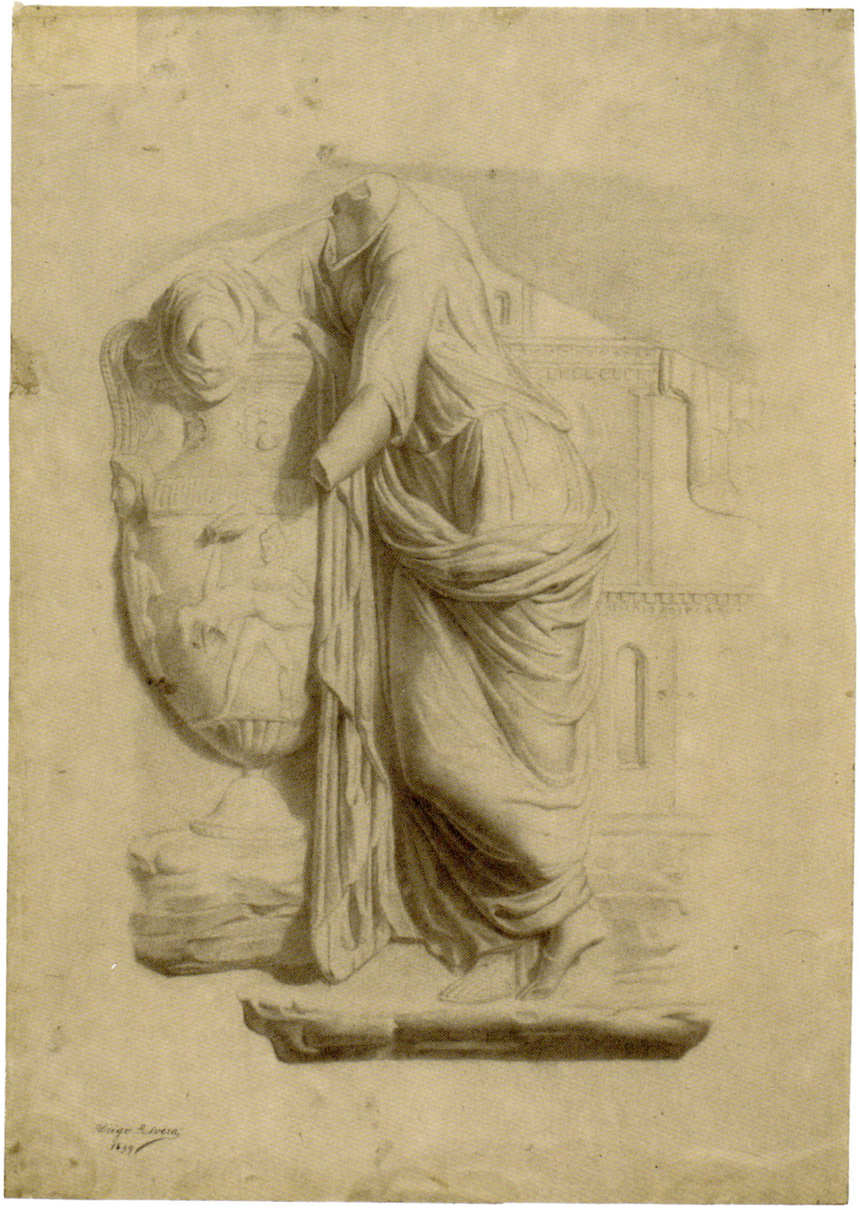

Diego Rivera, *Classical Standing Figure*, 1899

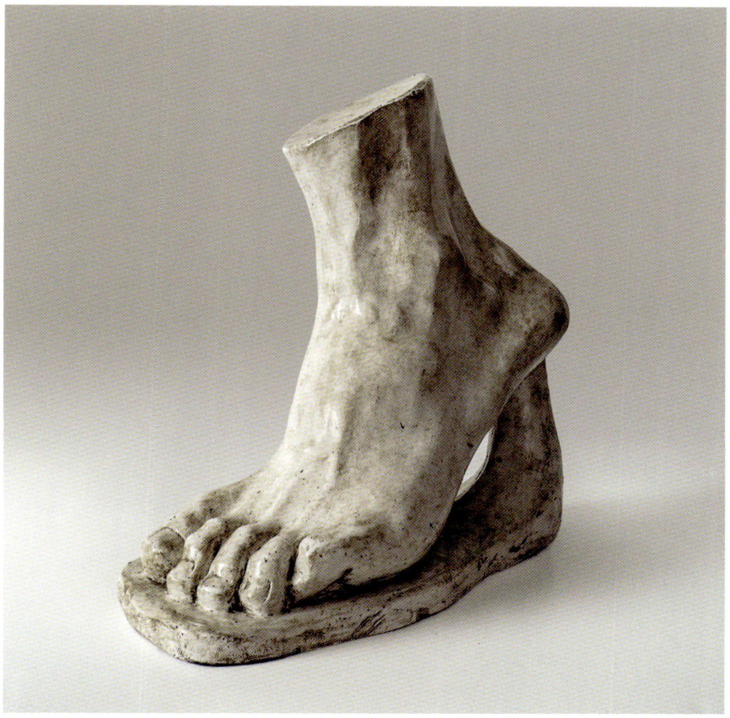

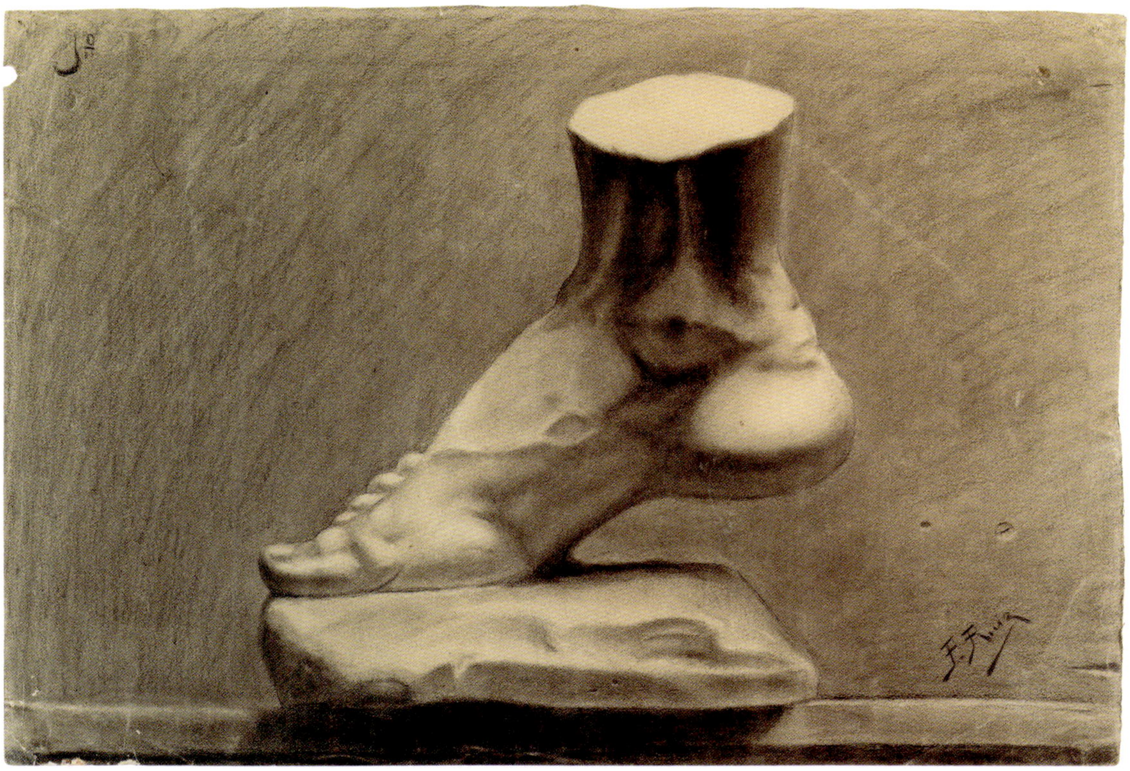

Foot (possibly Greek, c. 400–100 BCE), reduced copy, 2016

Pablo Picasso, ***Academic Study: Foot***, 1894

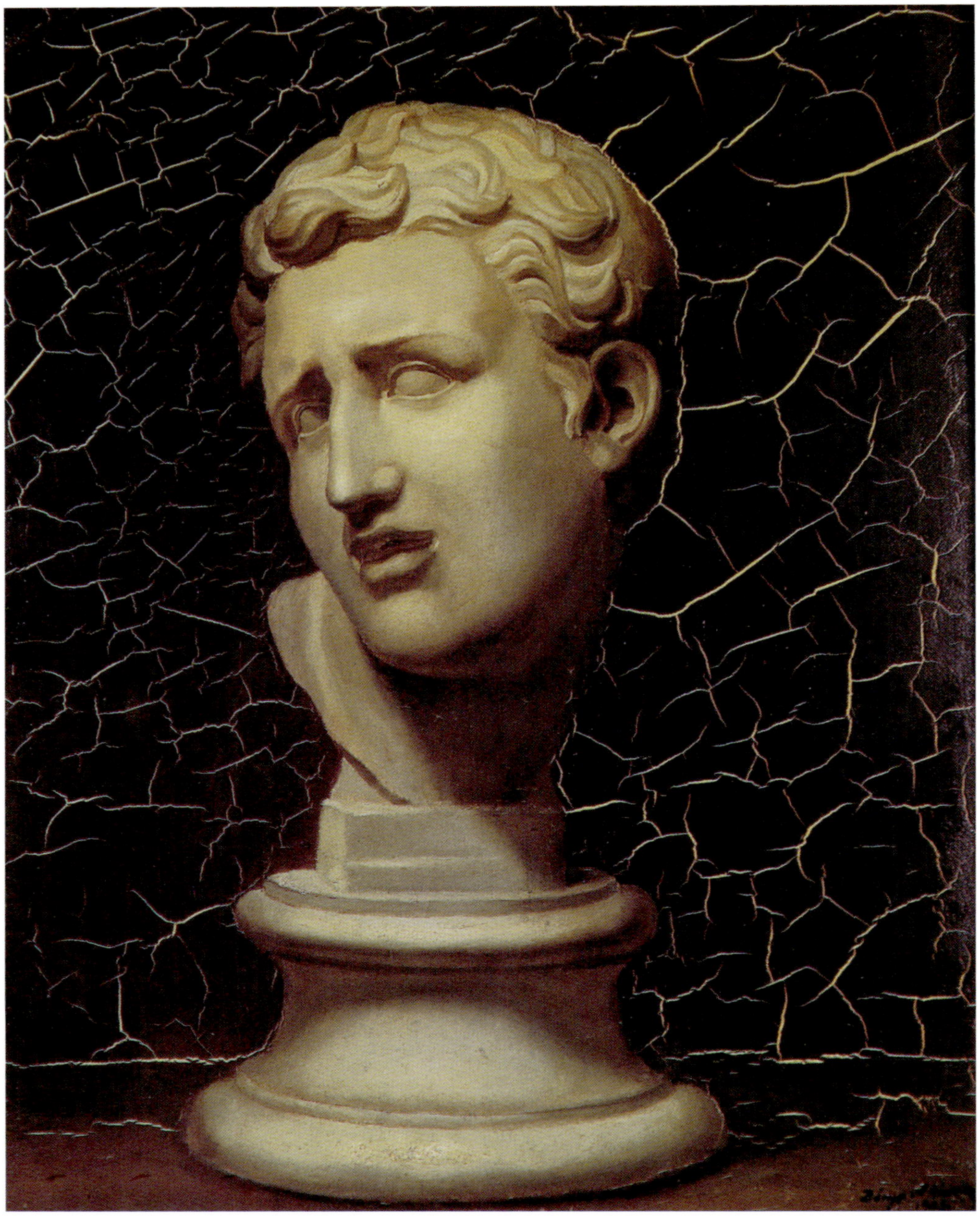

Diego Rivera, *Classical Head*, 1898

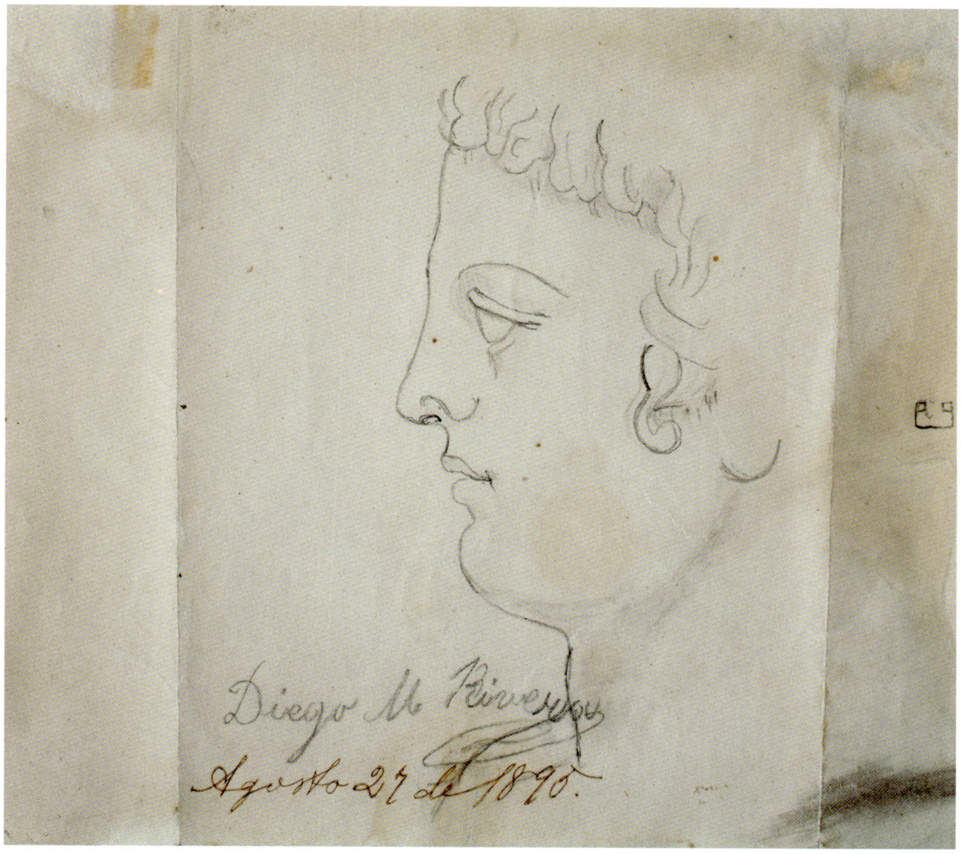

Diego Rivera, ***Classical Head,*** 1898

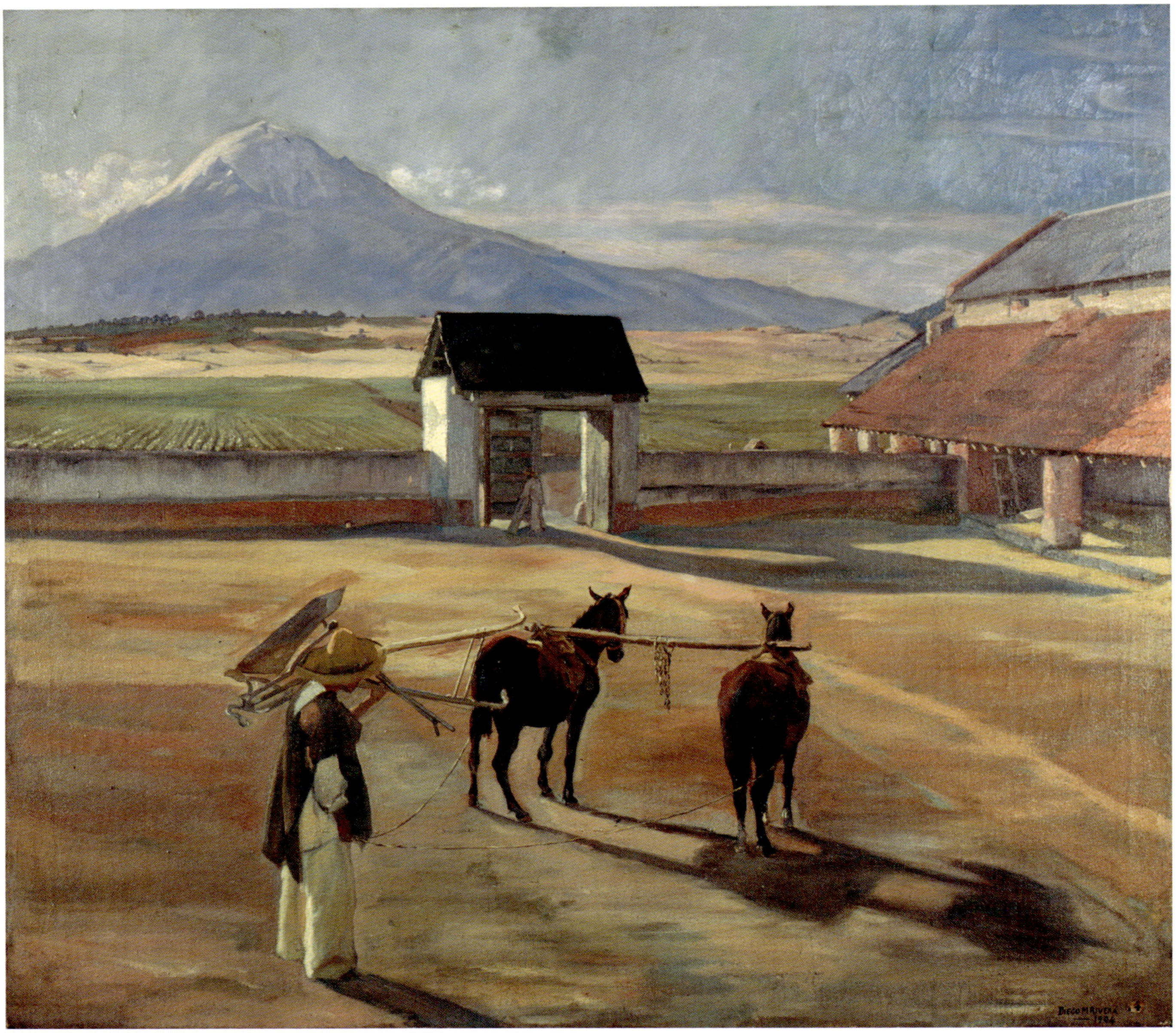

Diego Rivera, *The Era*, 1904

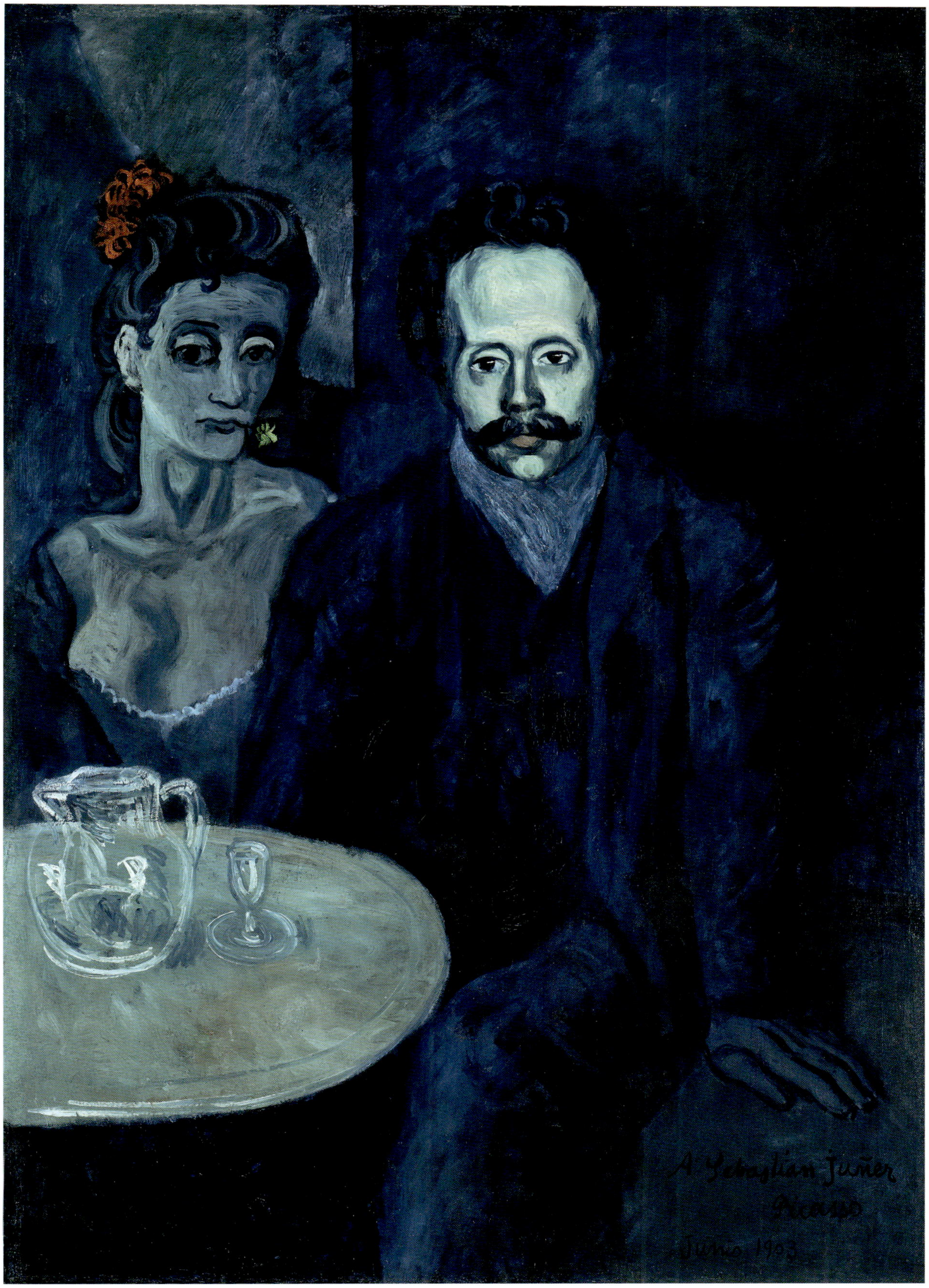

Pablo Picasso, ***Portrait of Sebastià Junyer Vidal***, June 1903

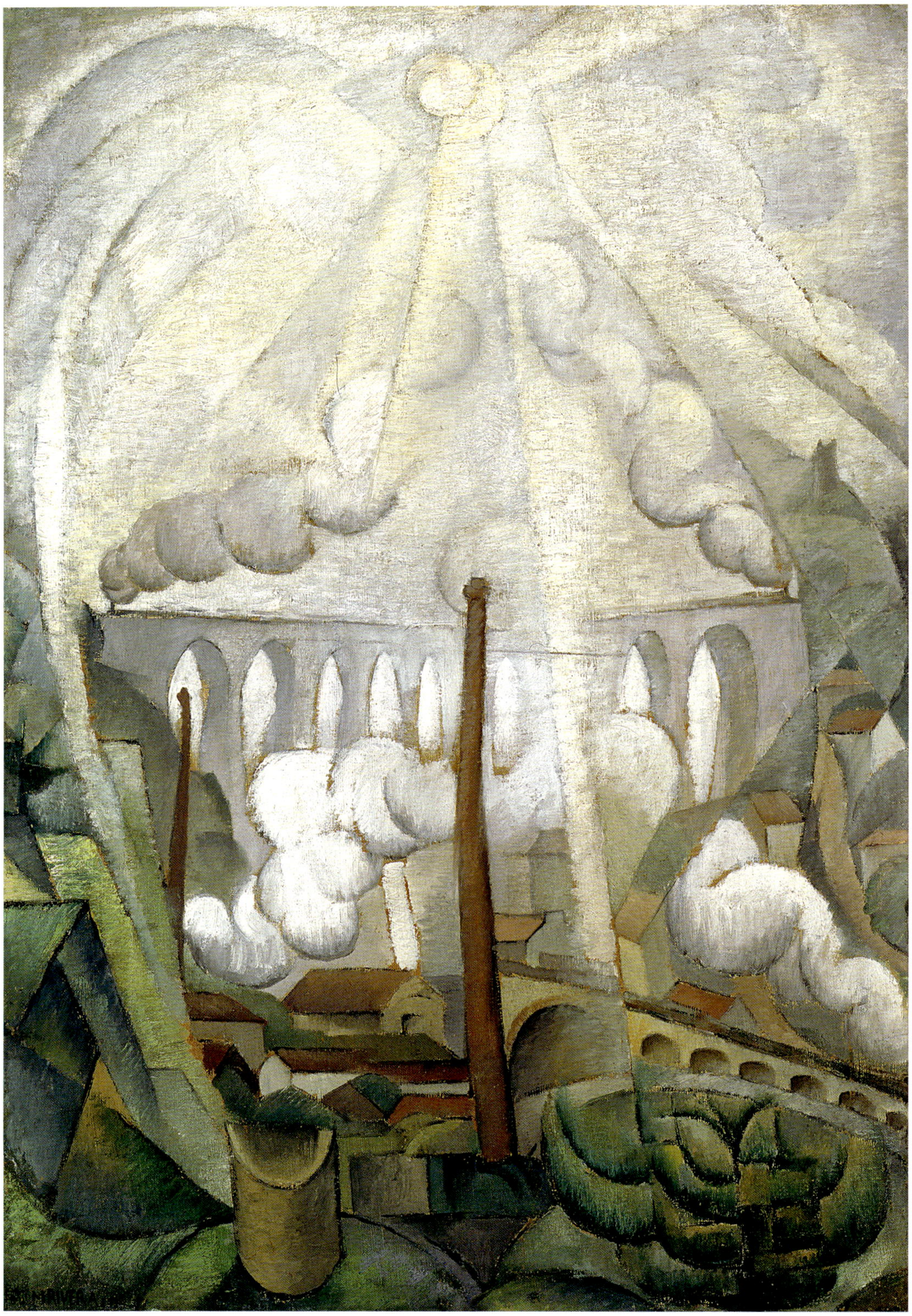

Diego Rivera, ***Sun Breaking through the Fog***, 1913

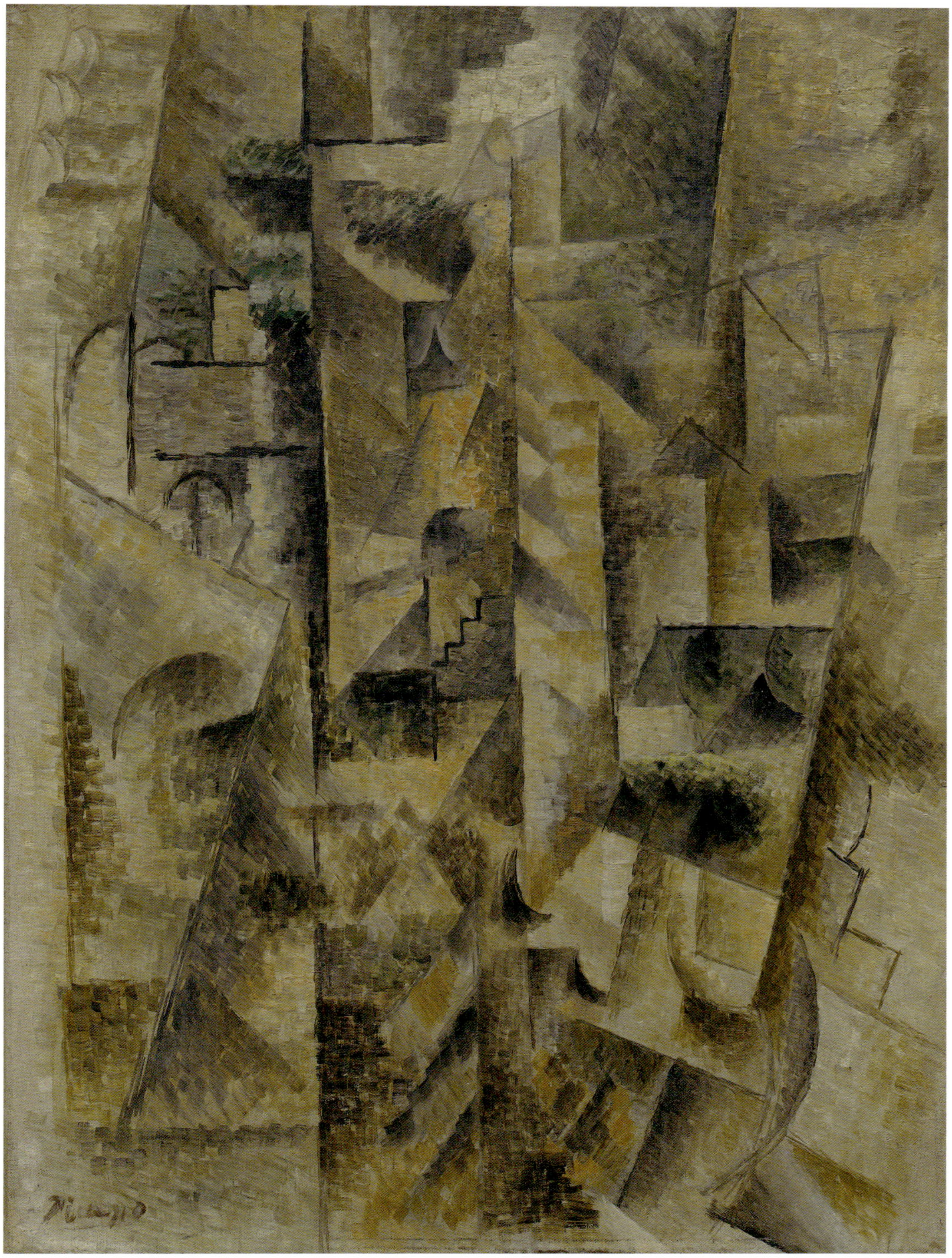

Pablo Picasso, ***Landscape at Céret***, 1911

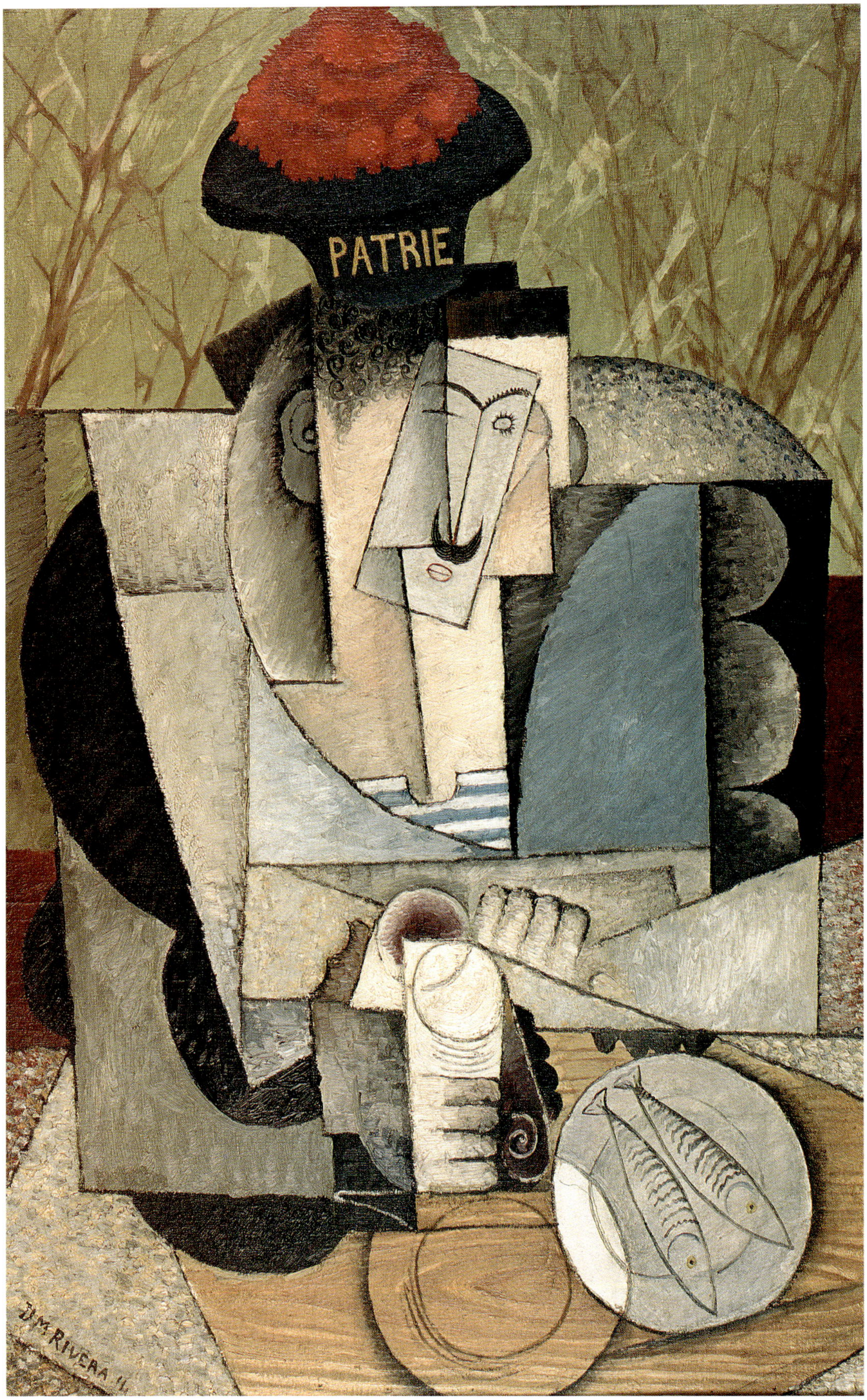

Diego Rivera, *Sailor at Lunch*, 1914

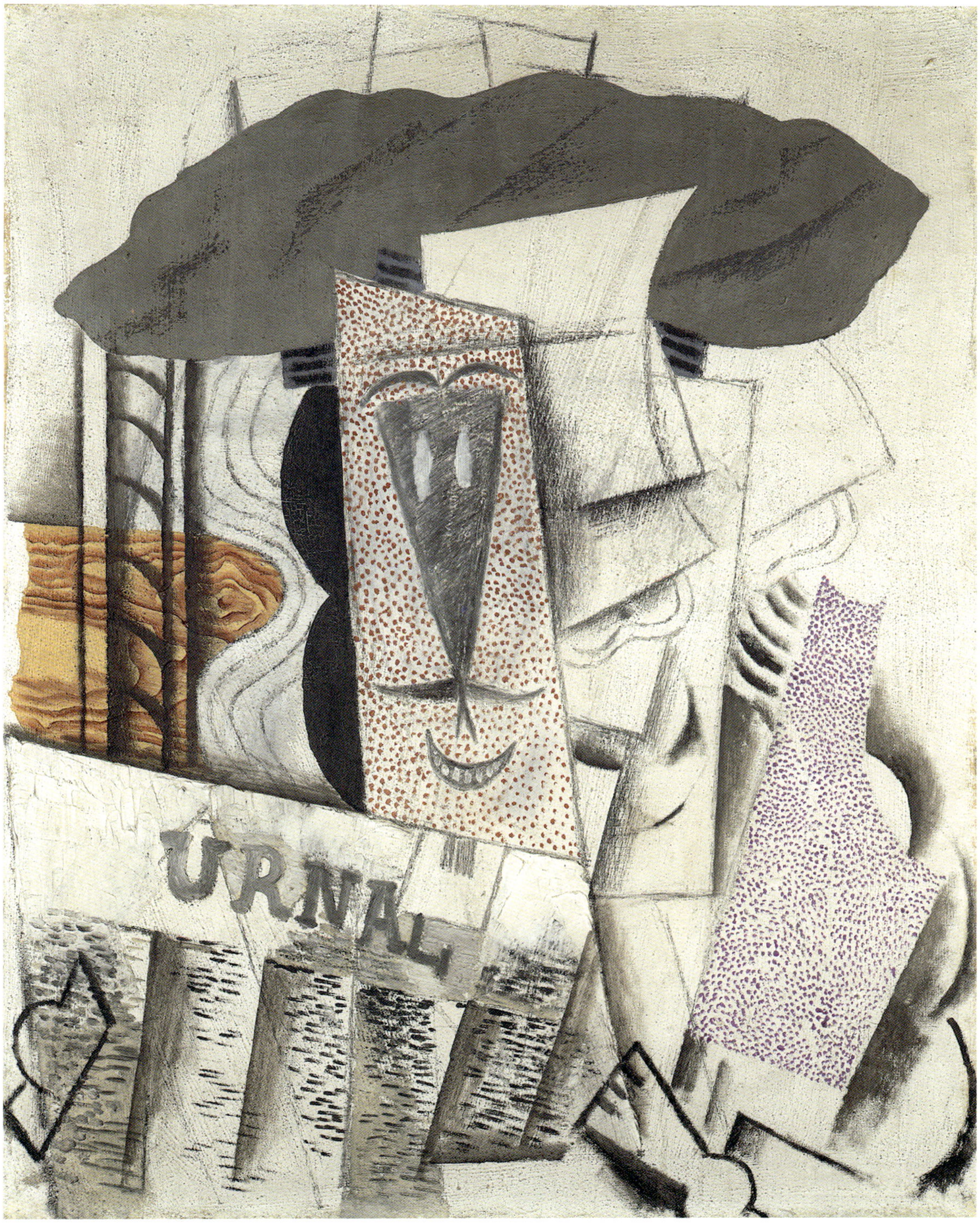

Pablo Picasso, ***Student with Newspaper***, 1913–14

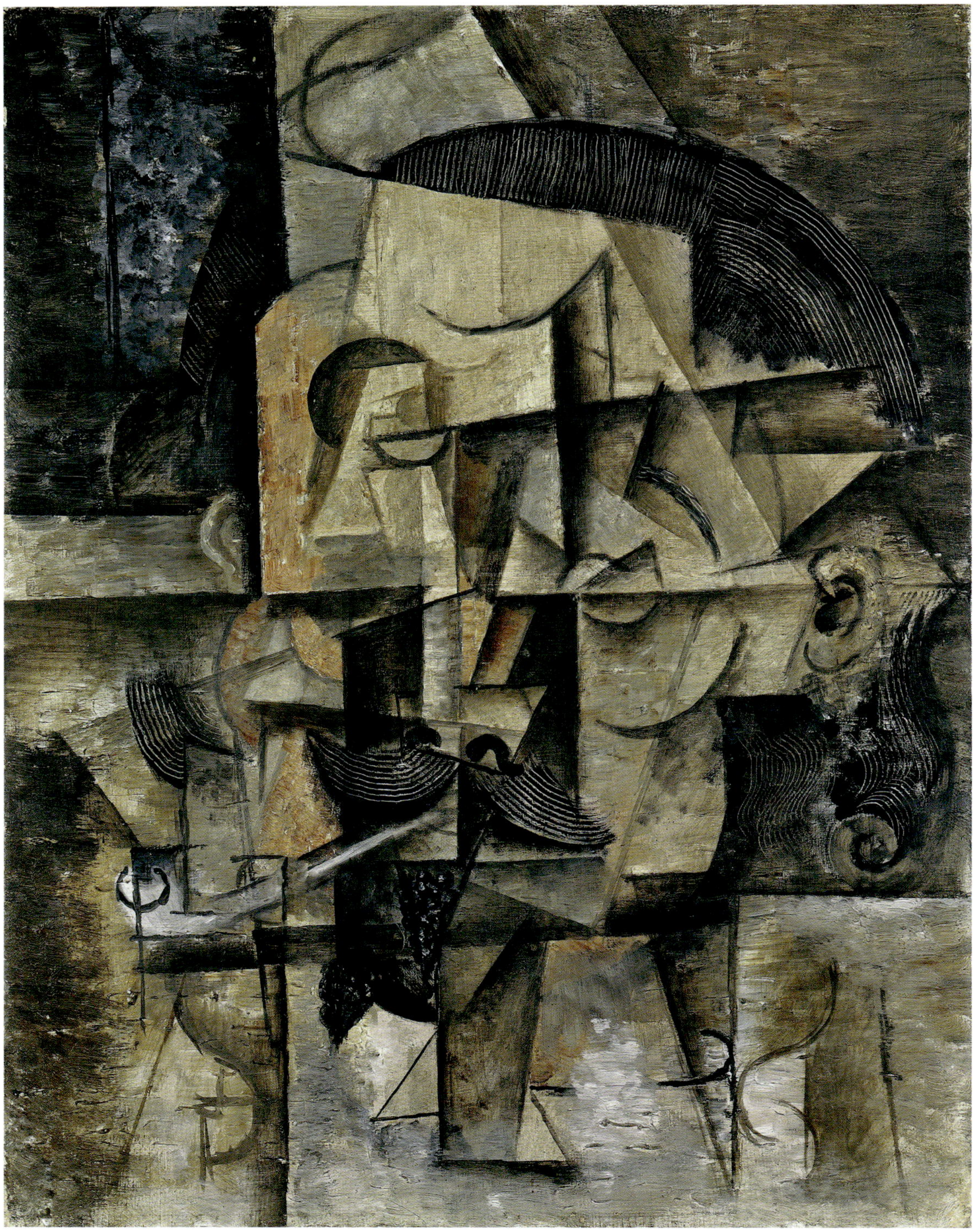

Pablo Picasso, *The Poet*, 1912

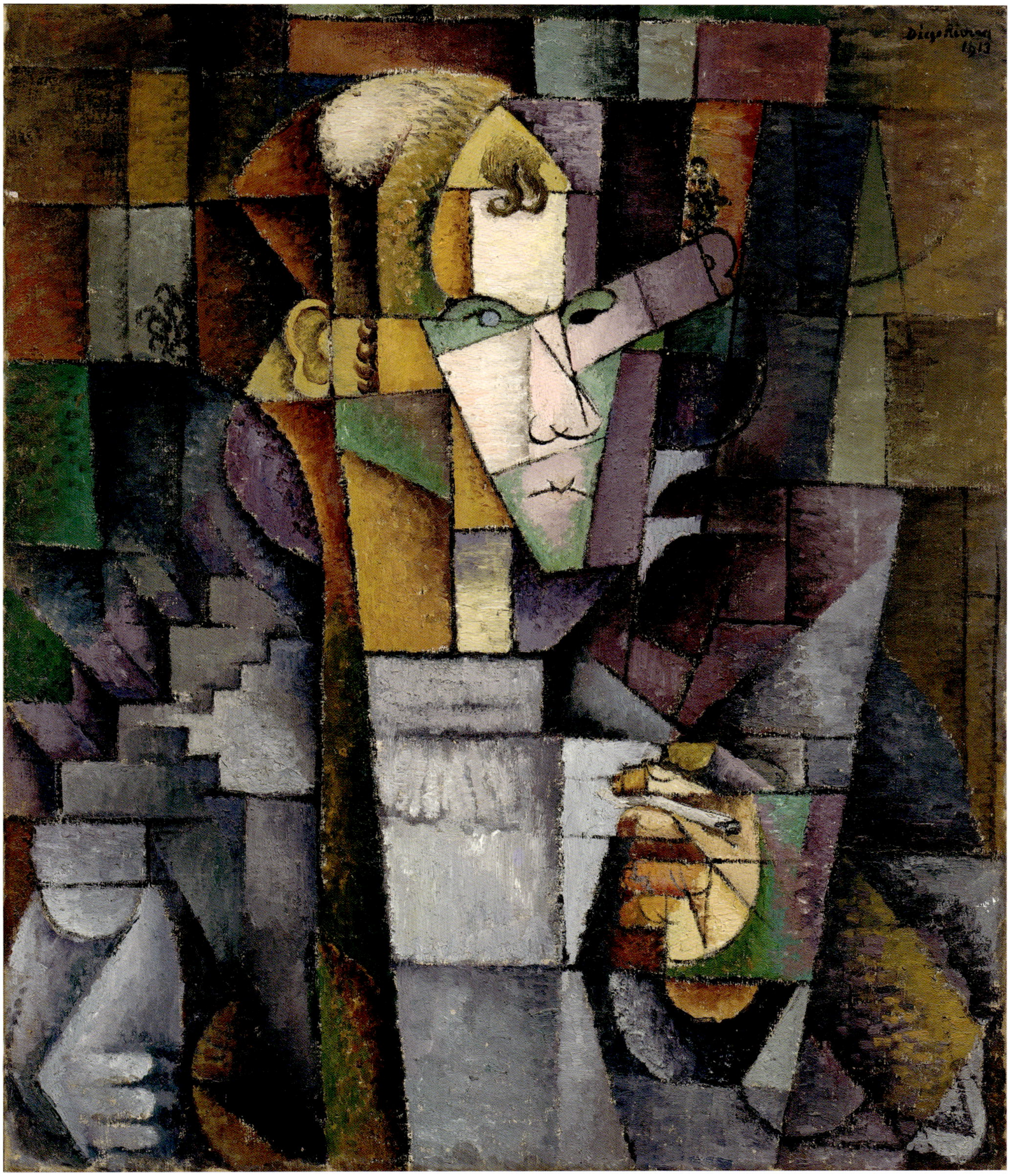

Diego Rivera, ***Portrait of Sculptor Elie Indenbaum***, 1913

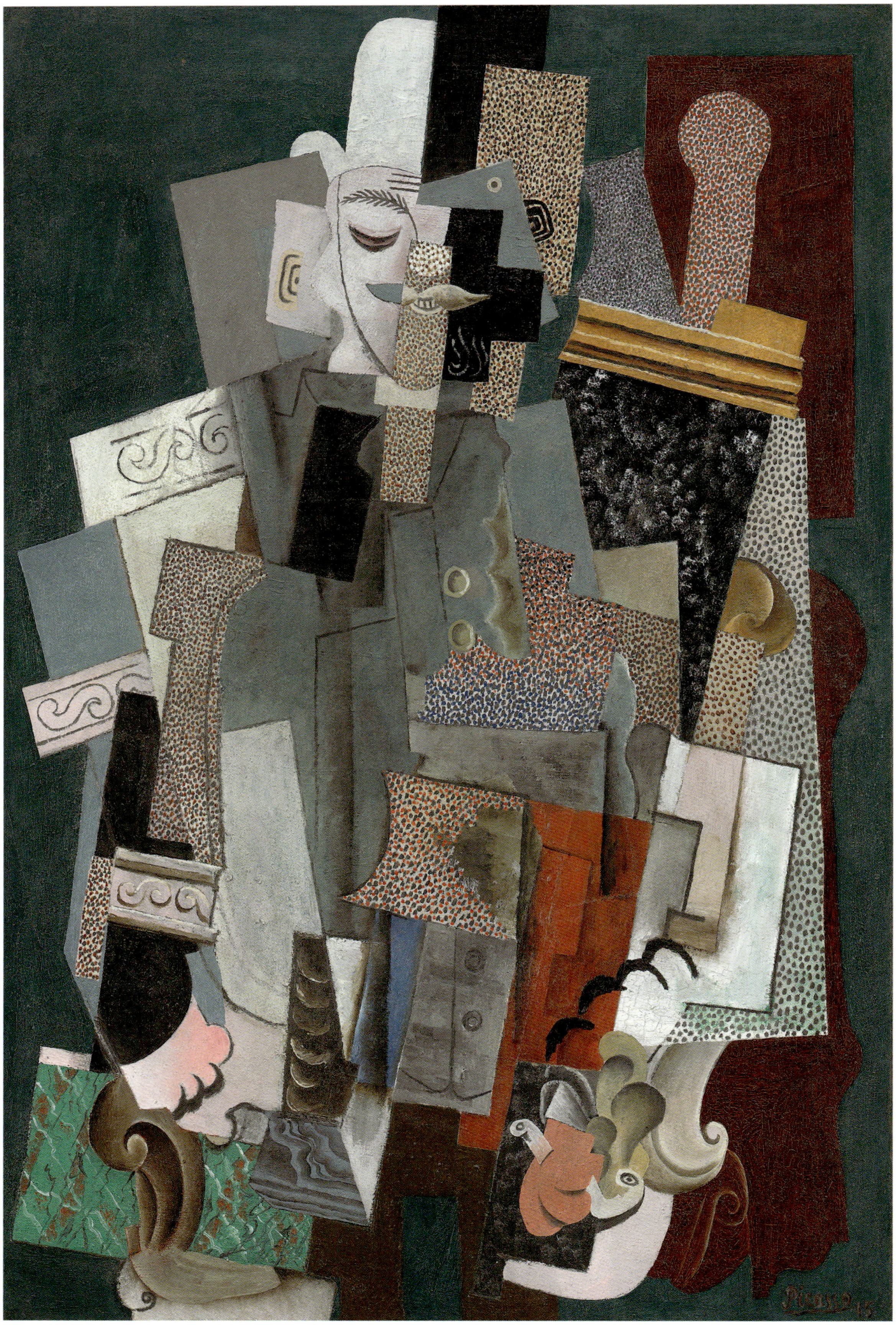

Pablo Picasso, *Man with a Pipe*, 1915

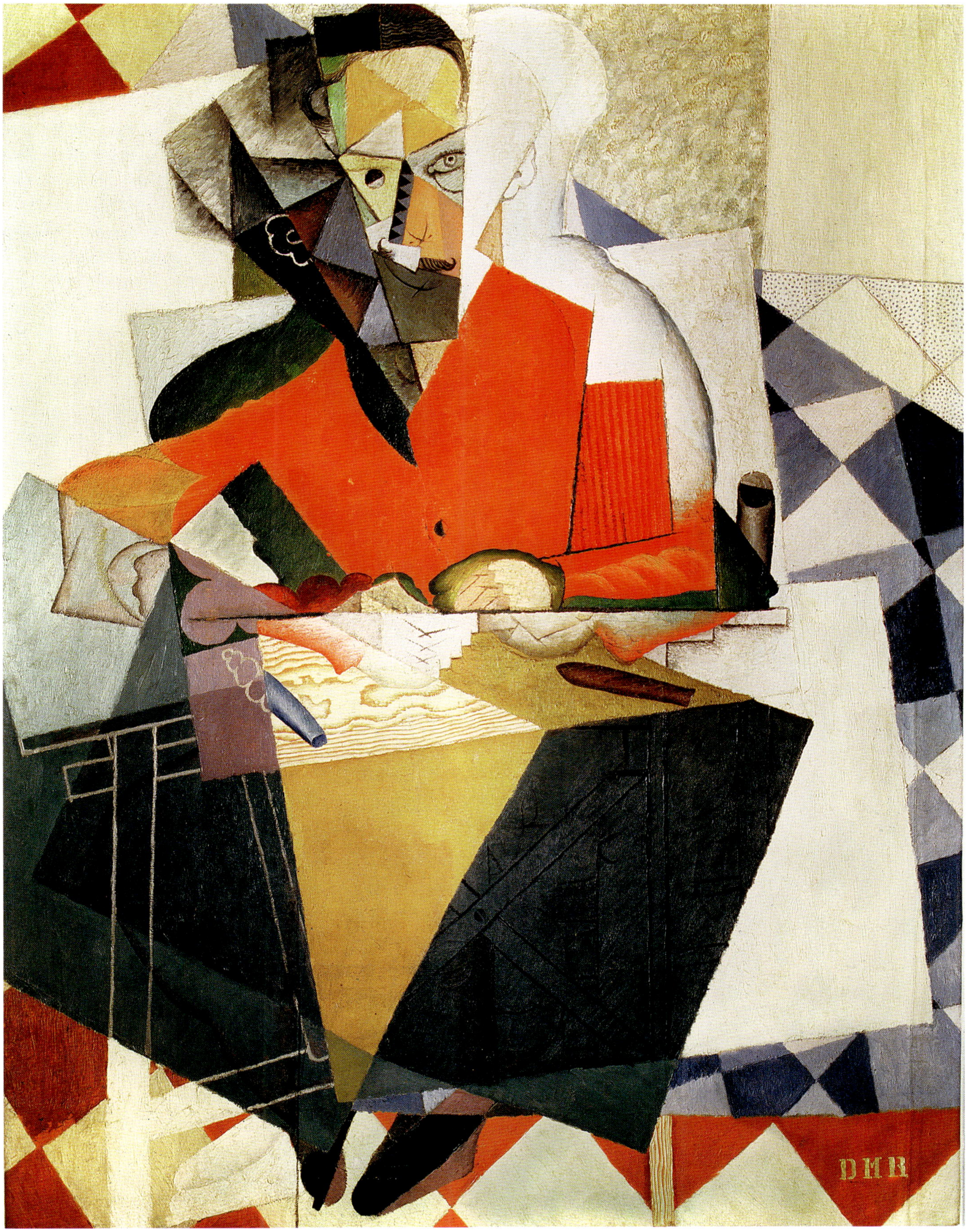

Diego Rivera, *The Architect* (*Portrait of Jesús T. Acevedo*), 1915

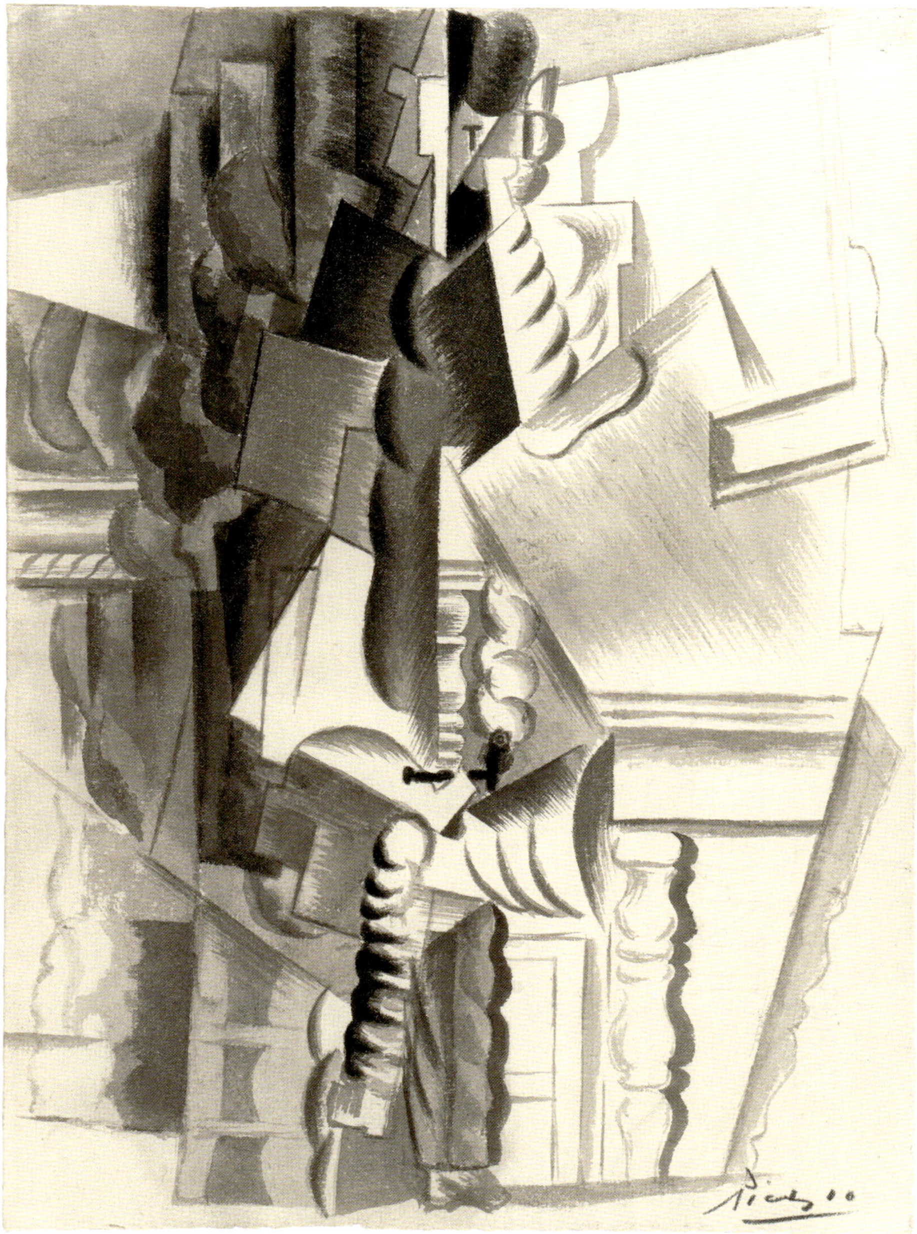

Pablo Picasso, ***Man Leaning on a Table***, 1914

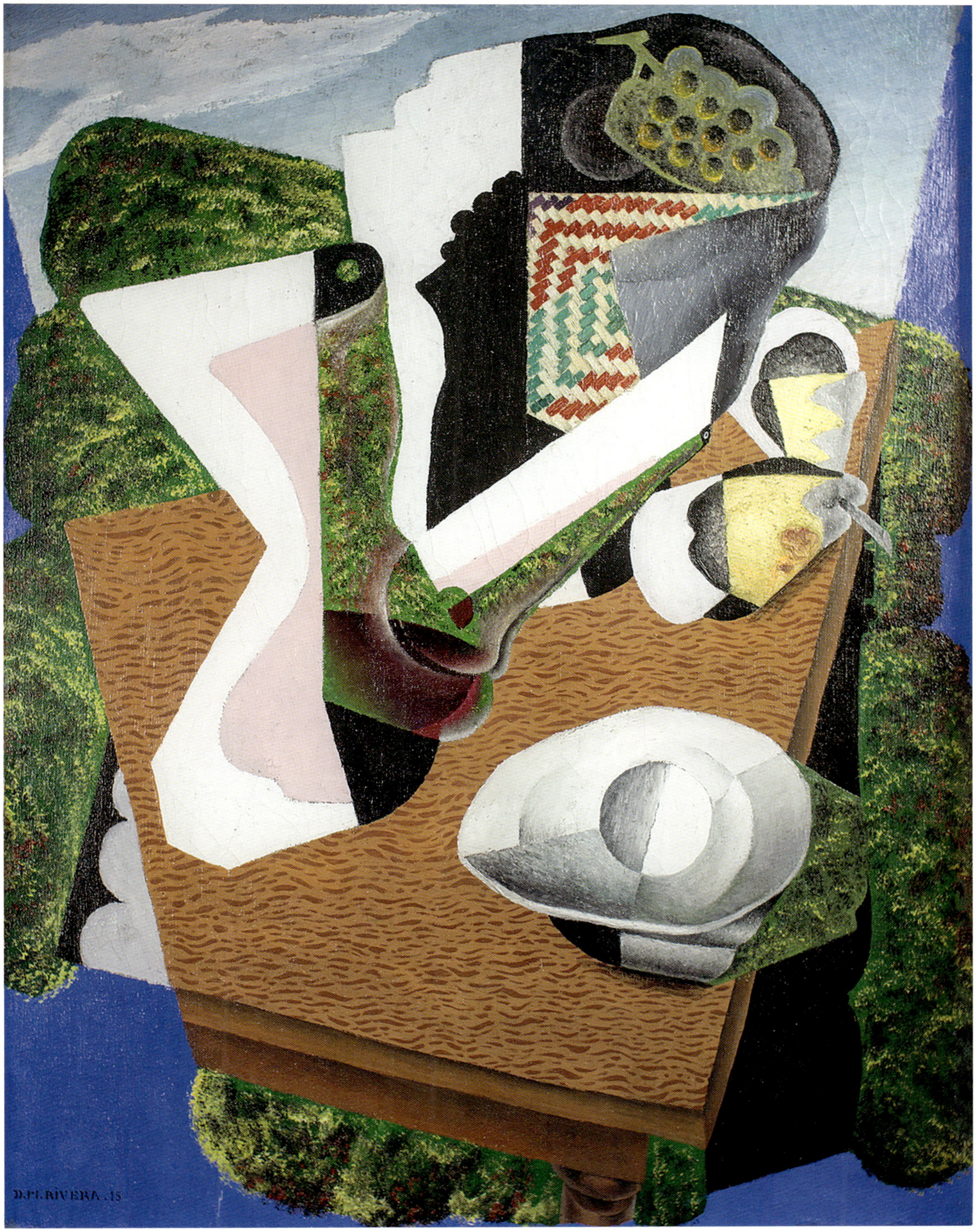

Diego Rivera, ***Still Life with Gray Bowl***, 1915

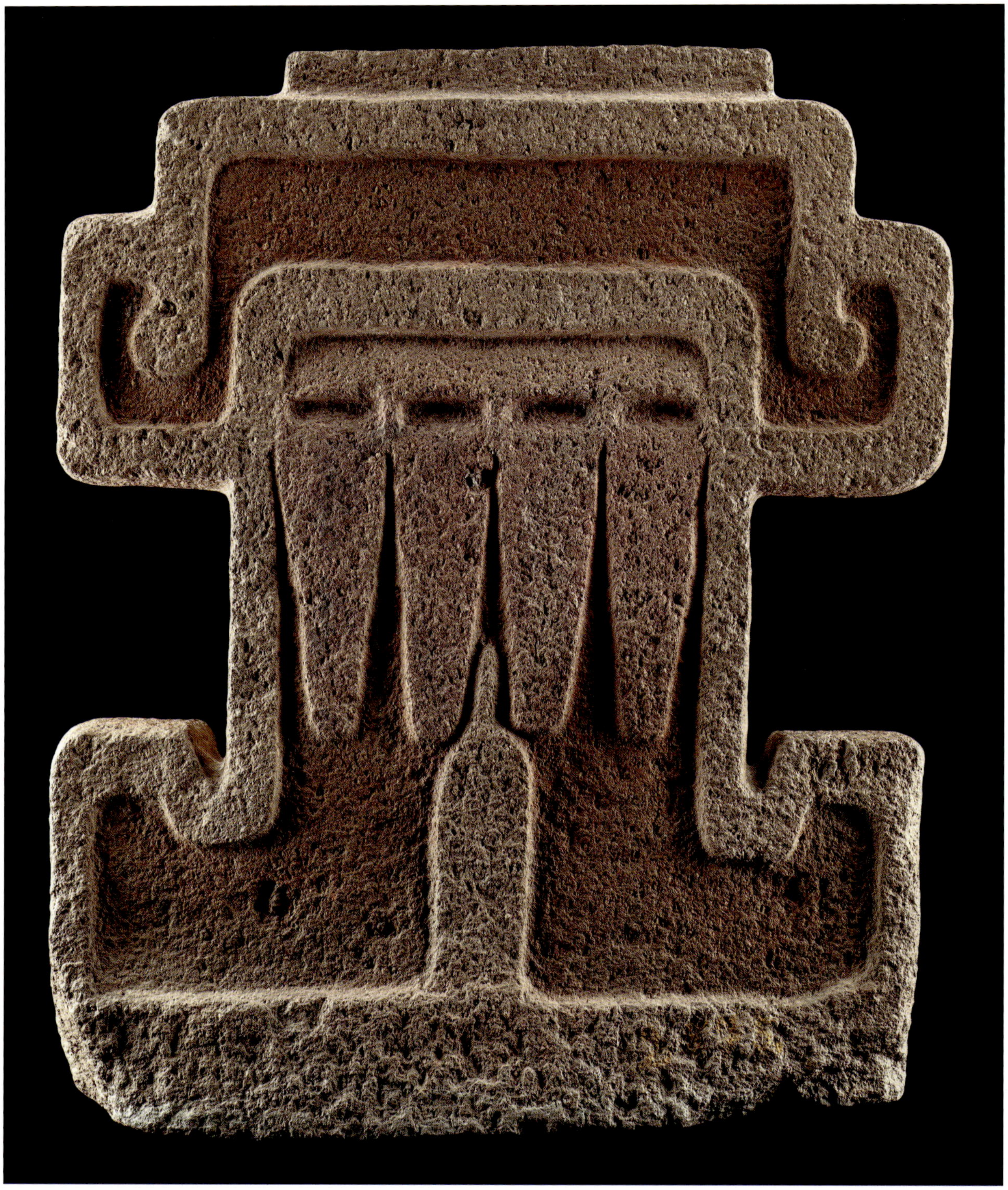

Roof Ornament with Tlaloc Emblem, Mexico, Teotihuacán, 250–650 CE

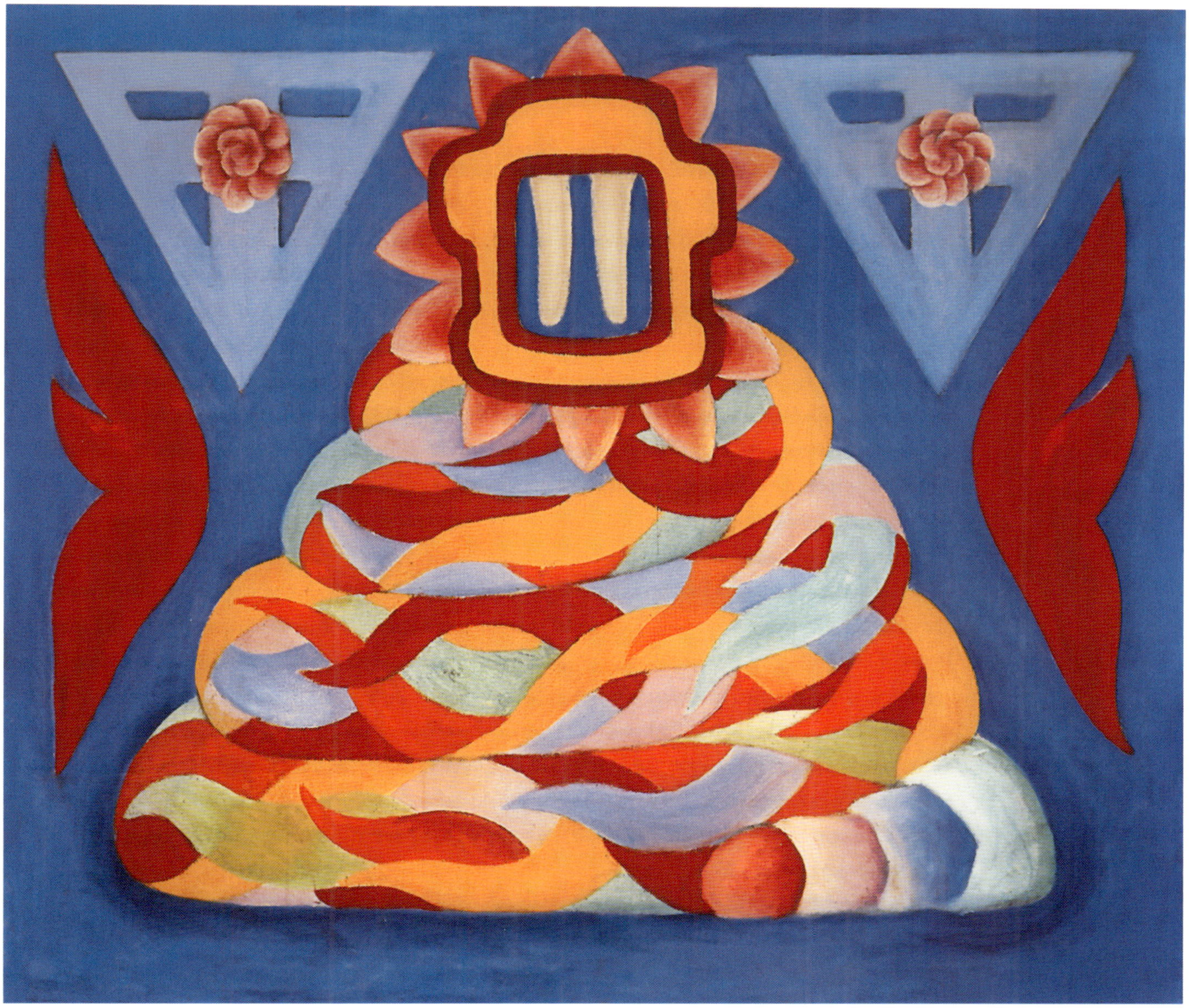

Diego Rivera, ***Feathered Serpent***, 1926

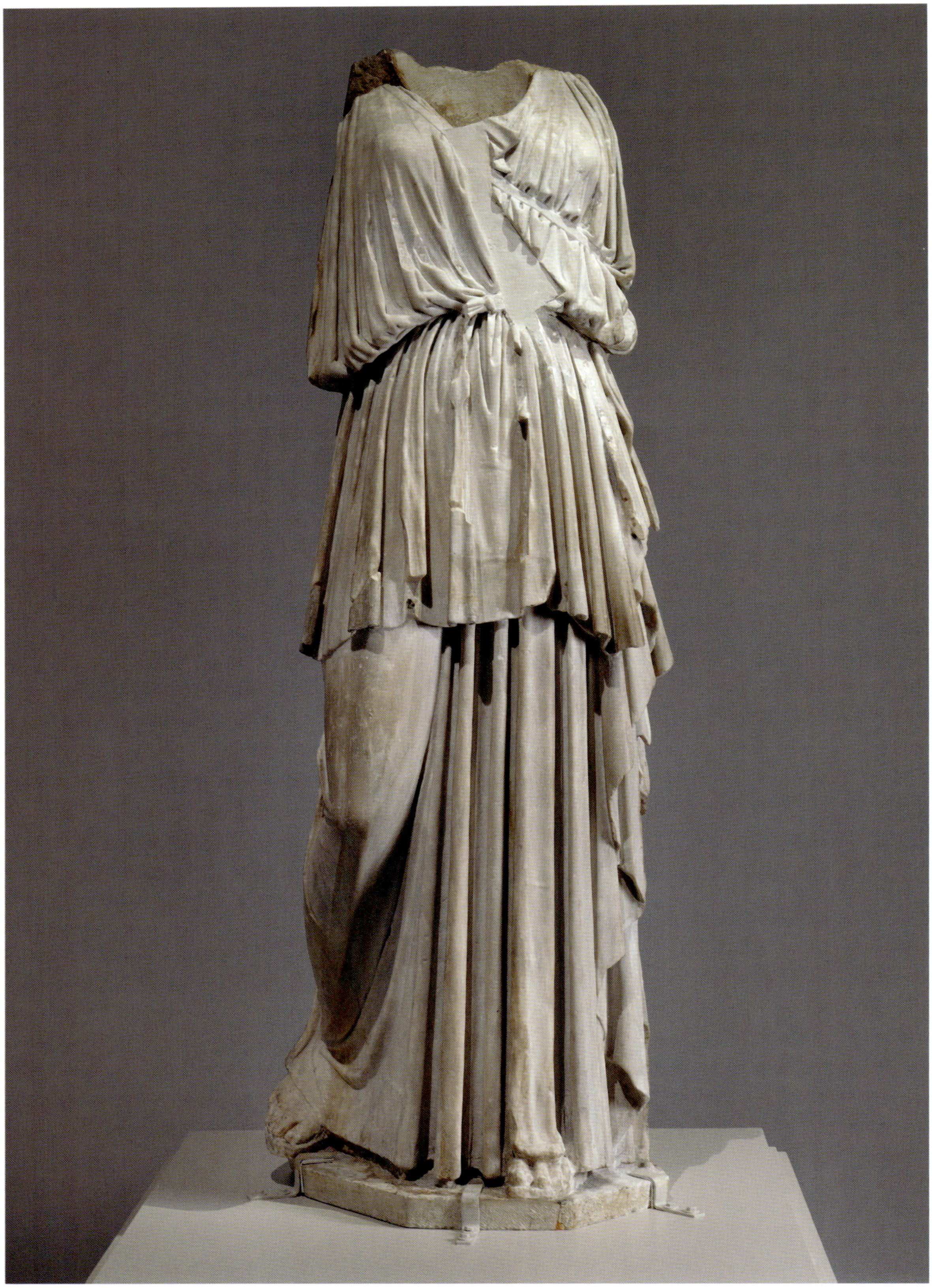

Lansdowne Artemis, Roman, 1st century BCE or 1st century CE

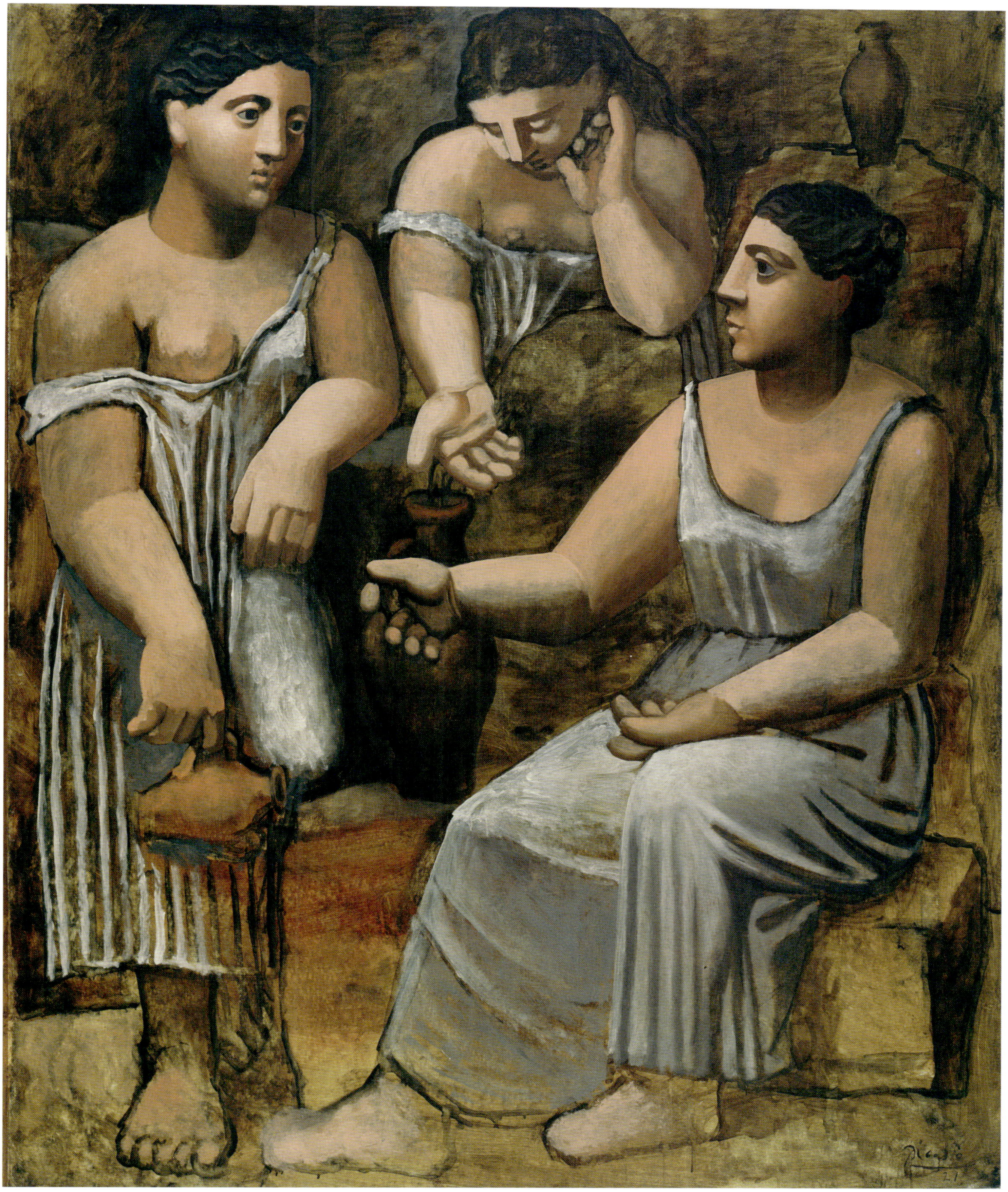

Pablo Picasso, ***Three Women at the Spring***, Summer 1921

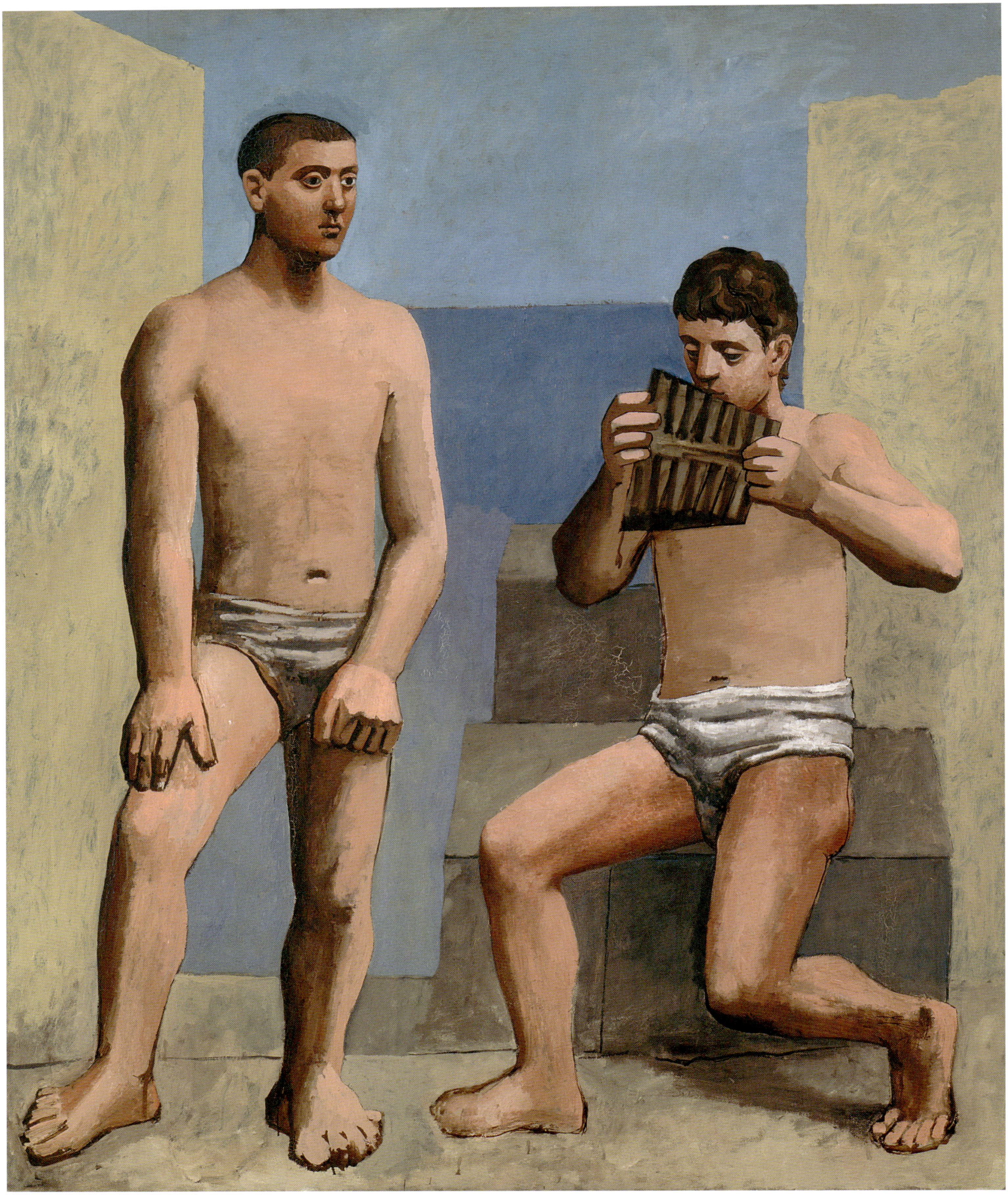

Pablo Picasso, ***The Pipes of Pan***, Summer 1923

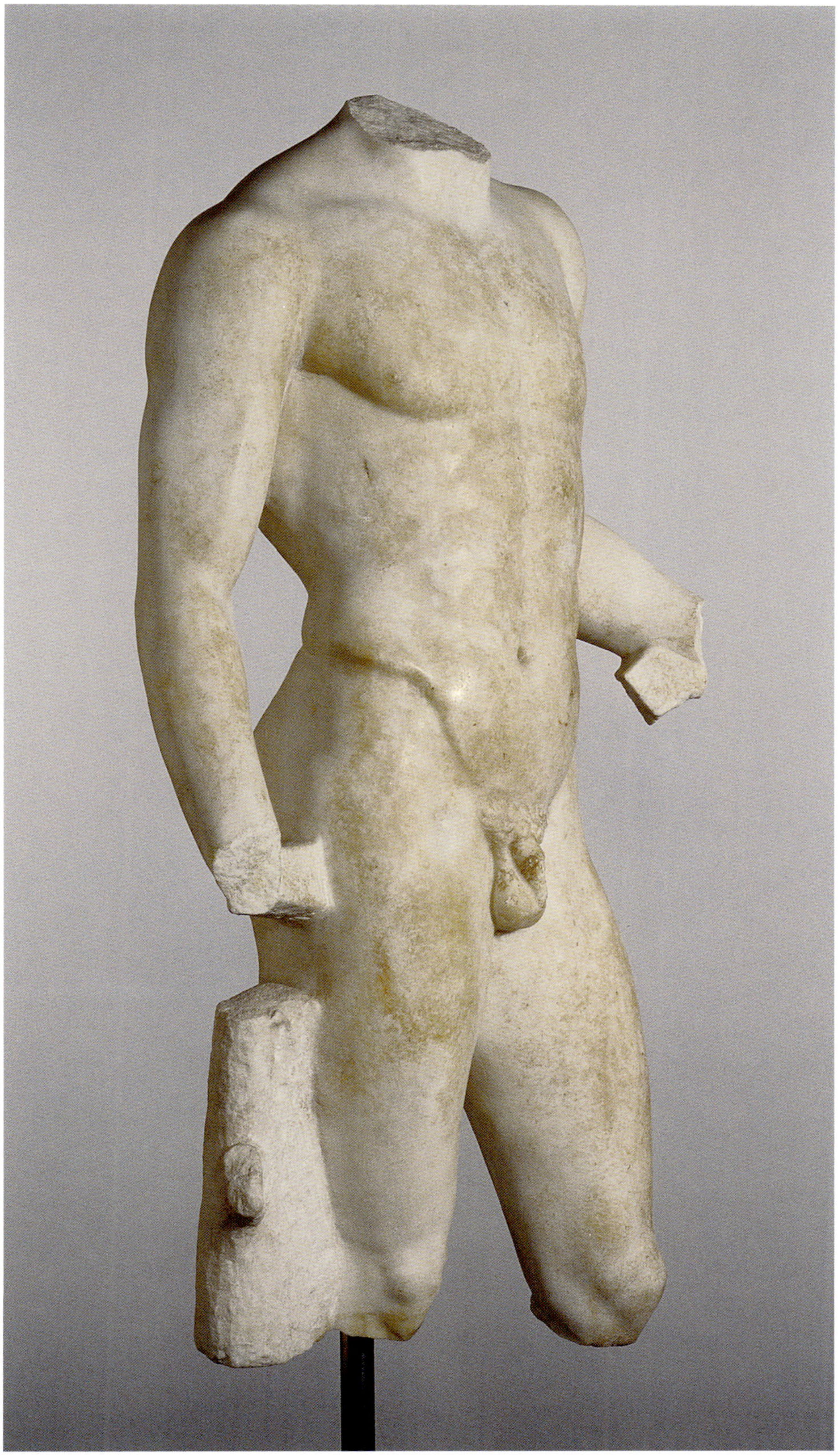

Male Torso, Roman, 100 CE

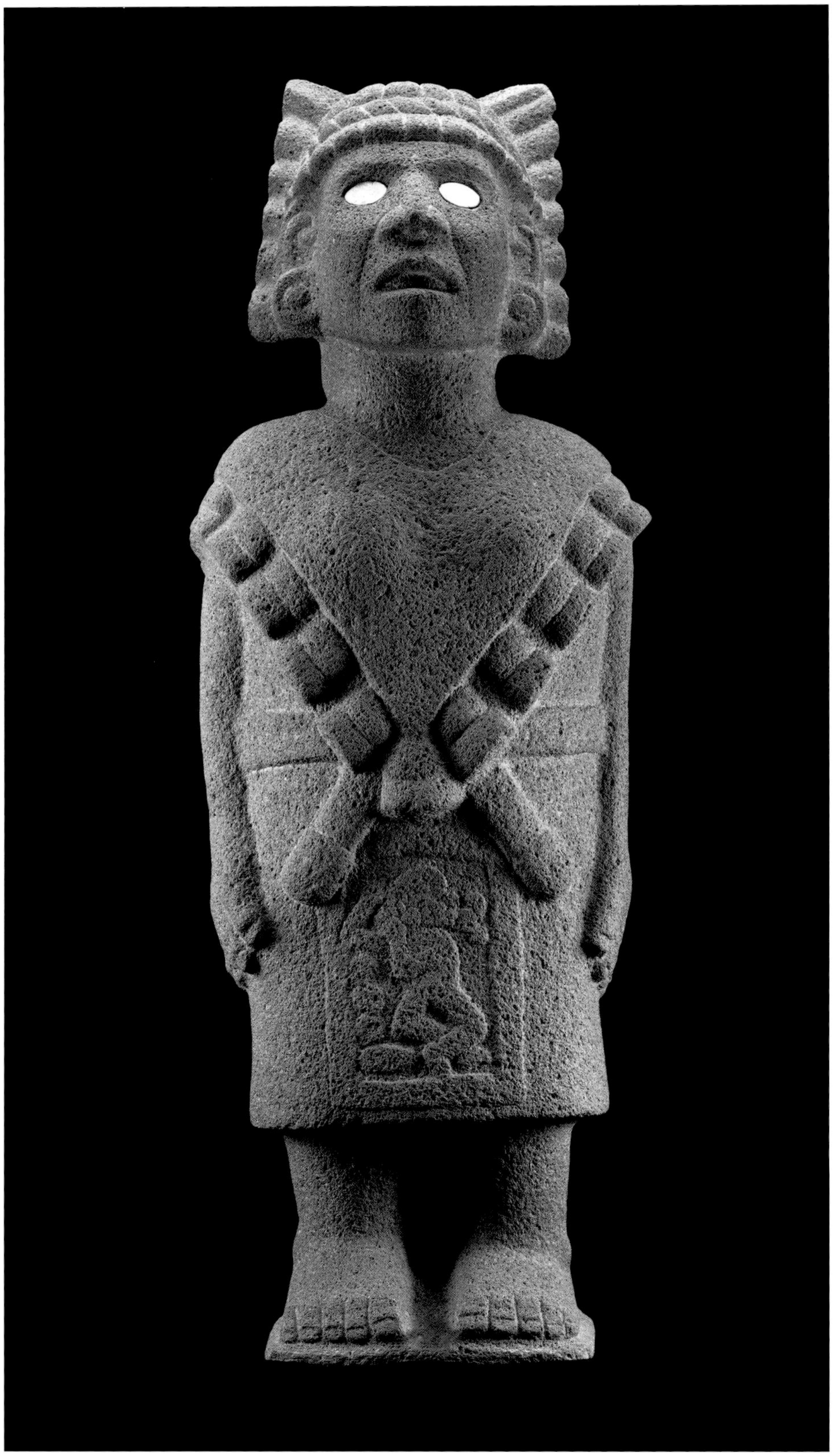

Goddess from Tlalmanalco, Mexico, Aztec, Tlalmanalco, 1250–1521

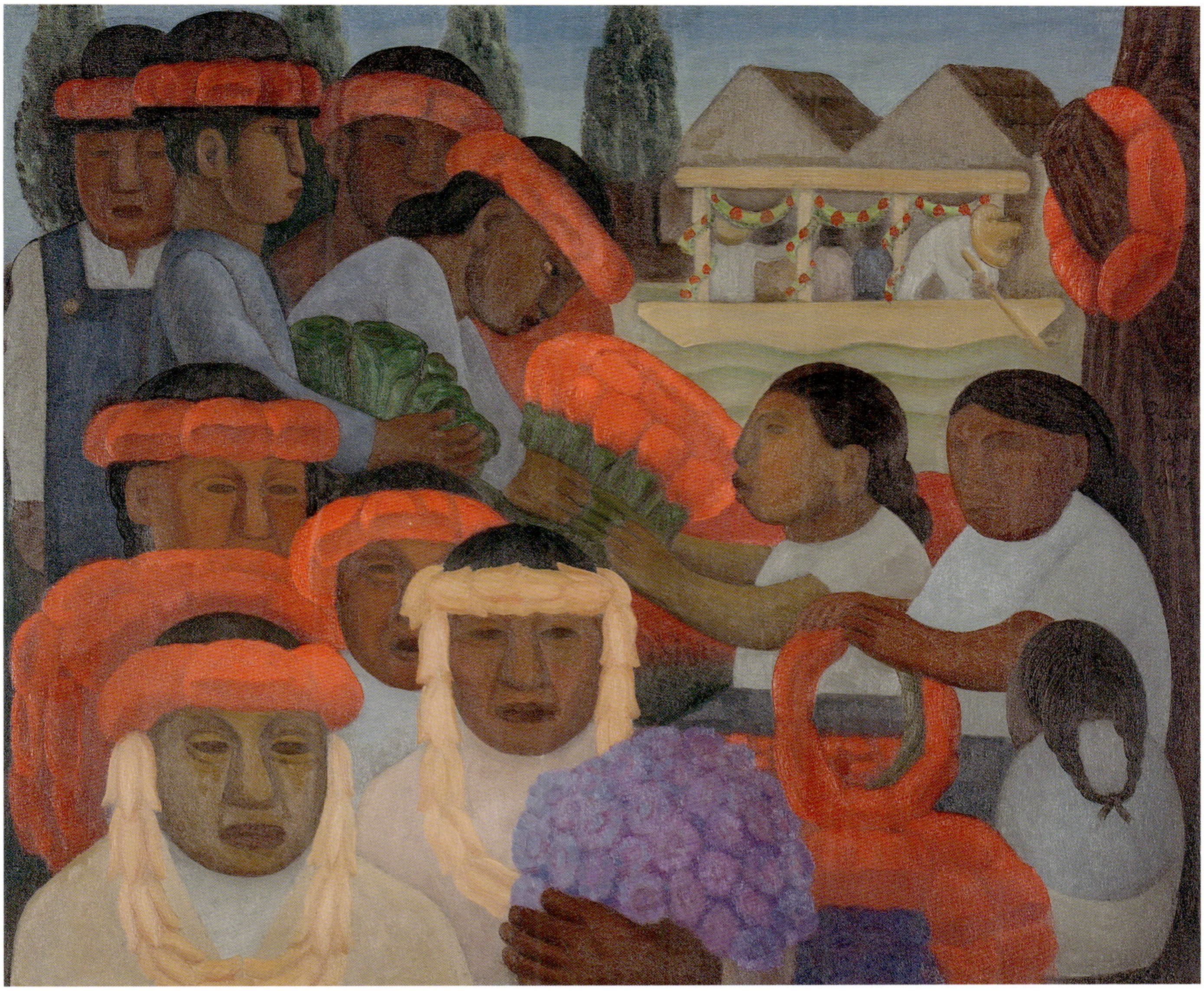

Diego Rivera, *Flower Day, Xochimilco*, 1926

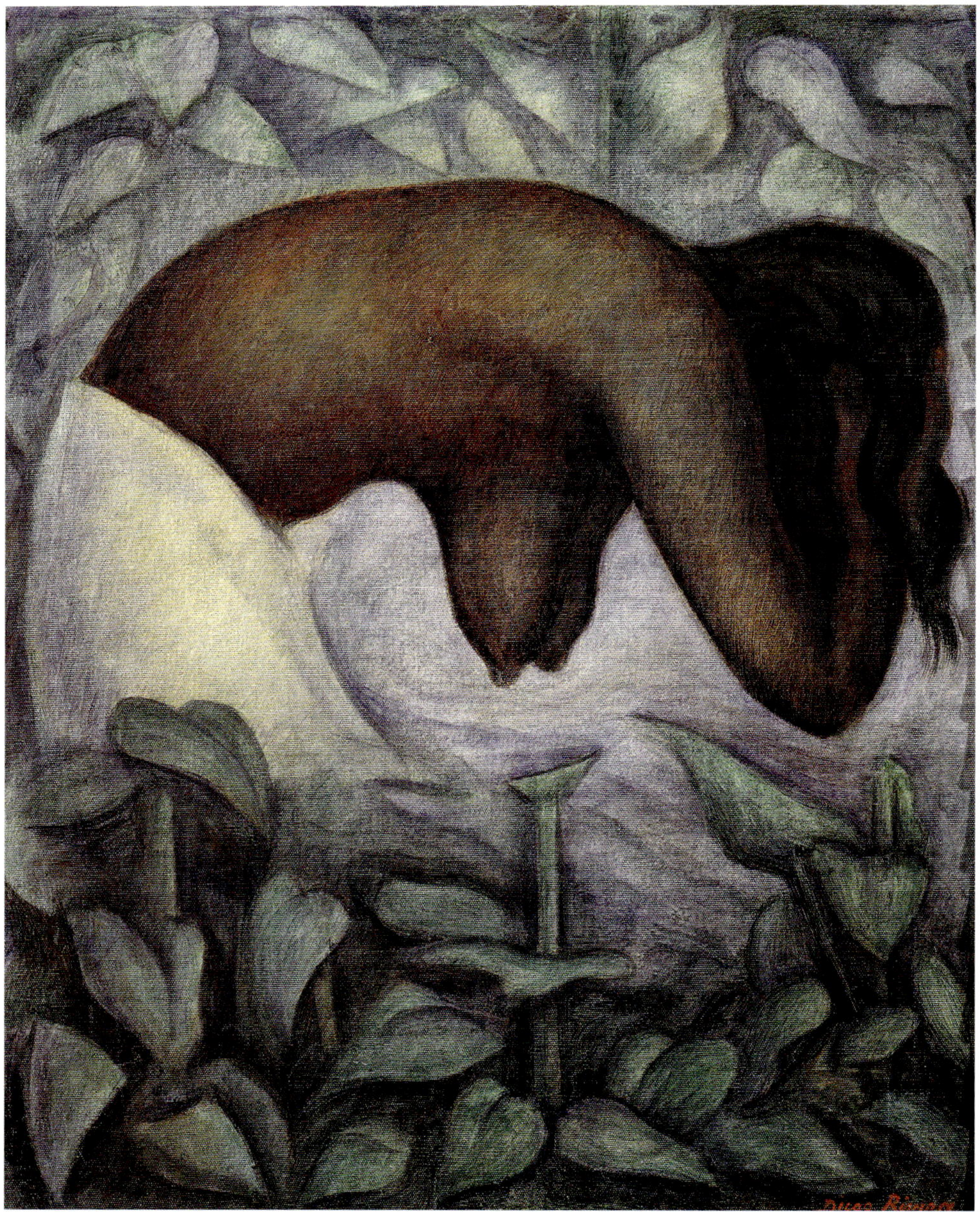

Diego Rivera, ***Bather in Tehuantepec***, 1923

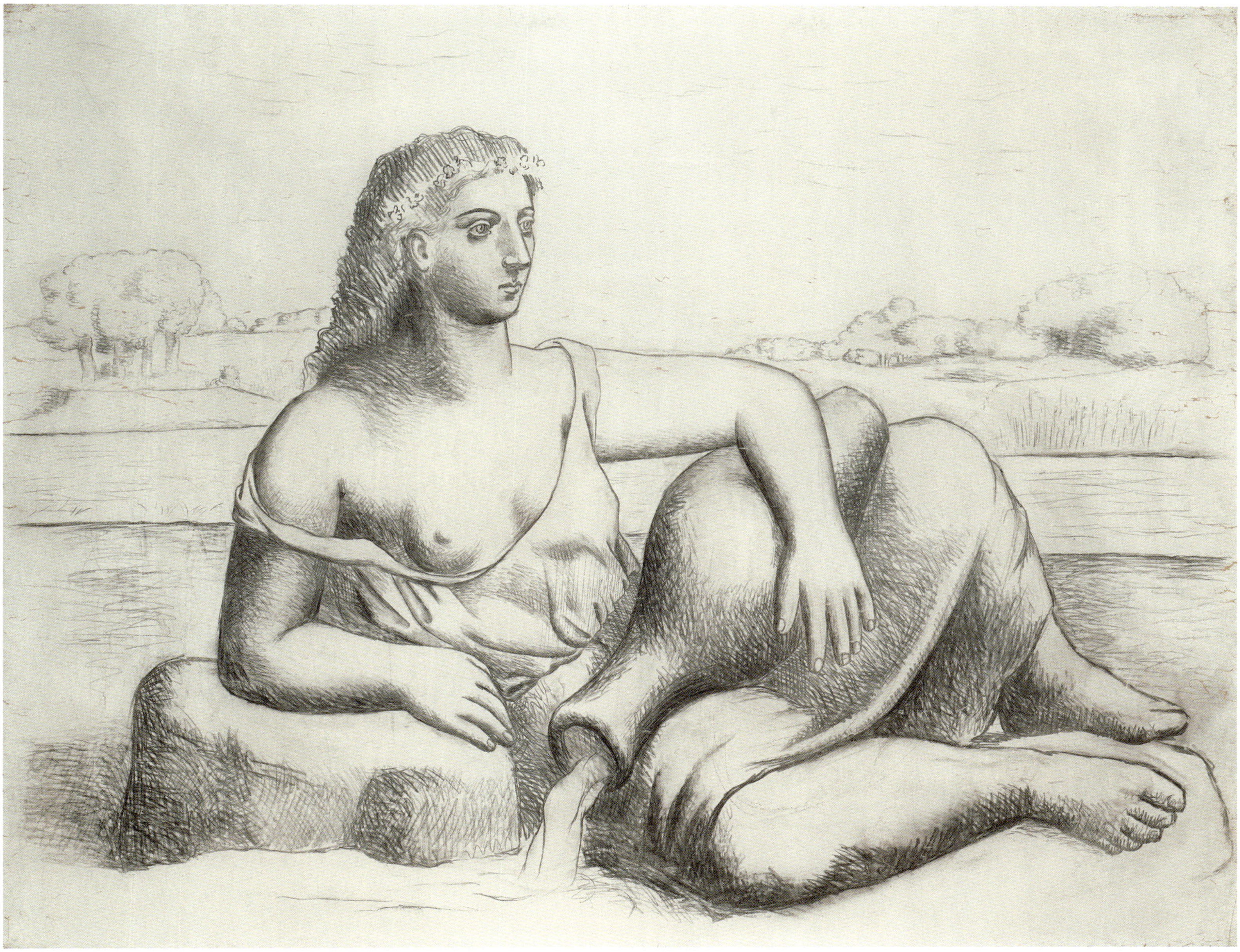

Pablo Picasso, ***The Source***, Summer 1921

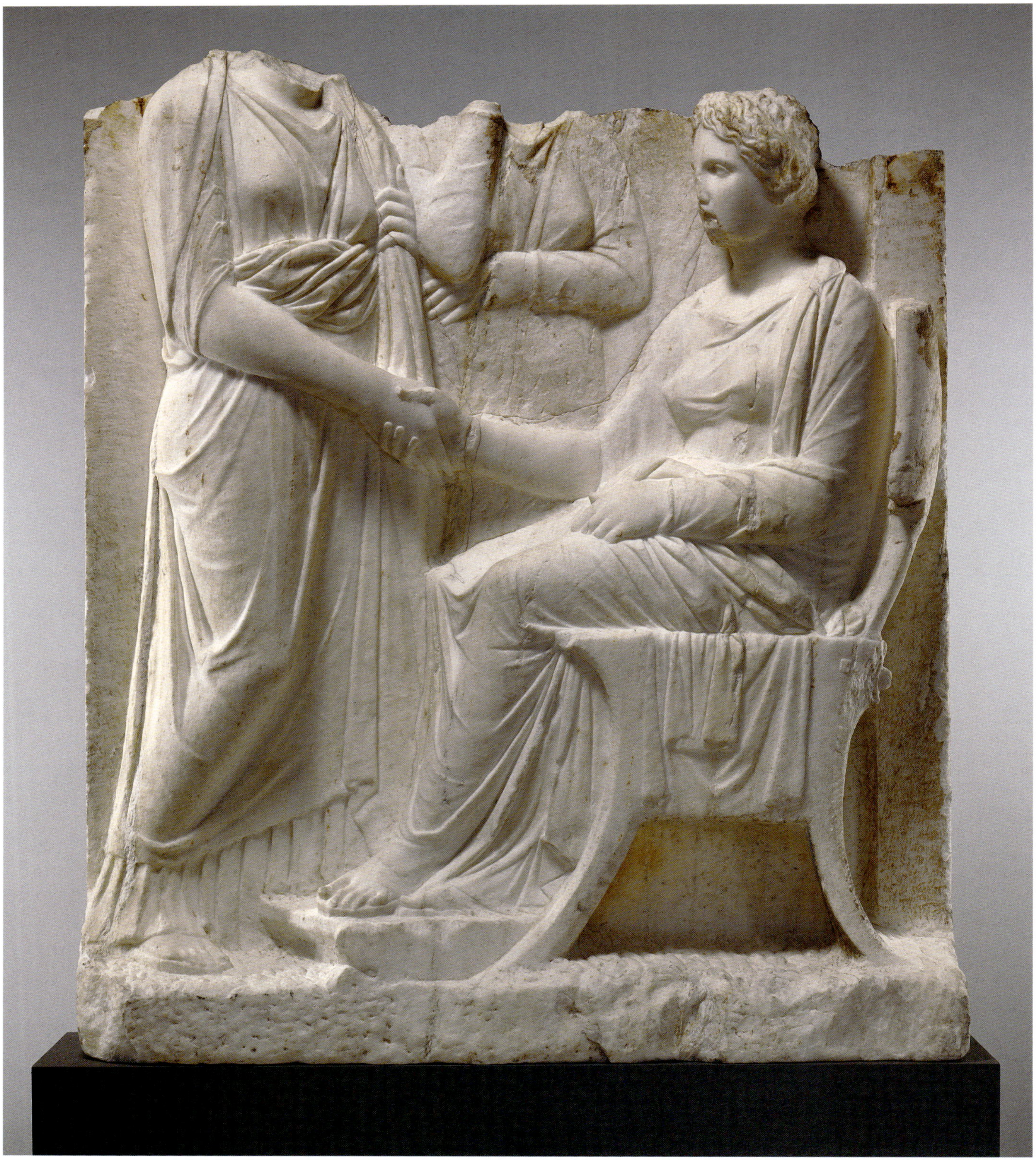

Grave Naiskos of a Seated Woman with Two Standing Women,
Greek, Athens, c. 340 BCE

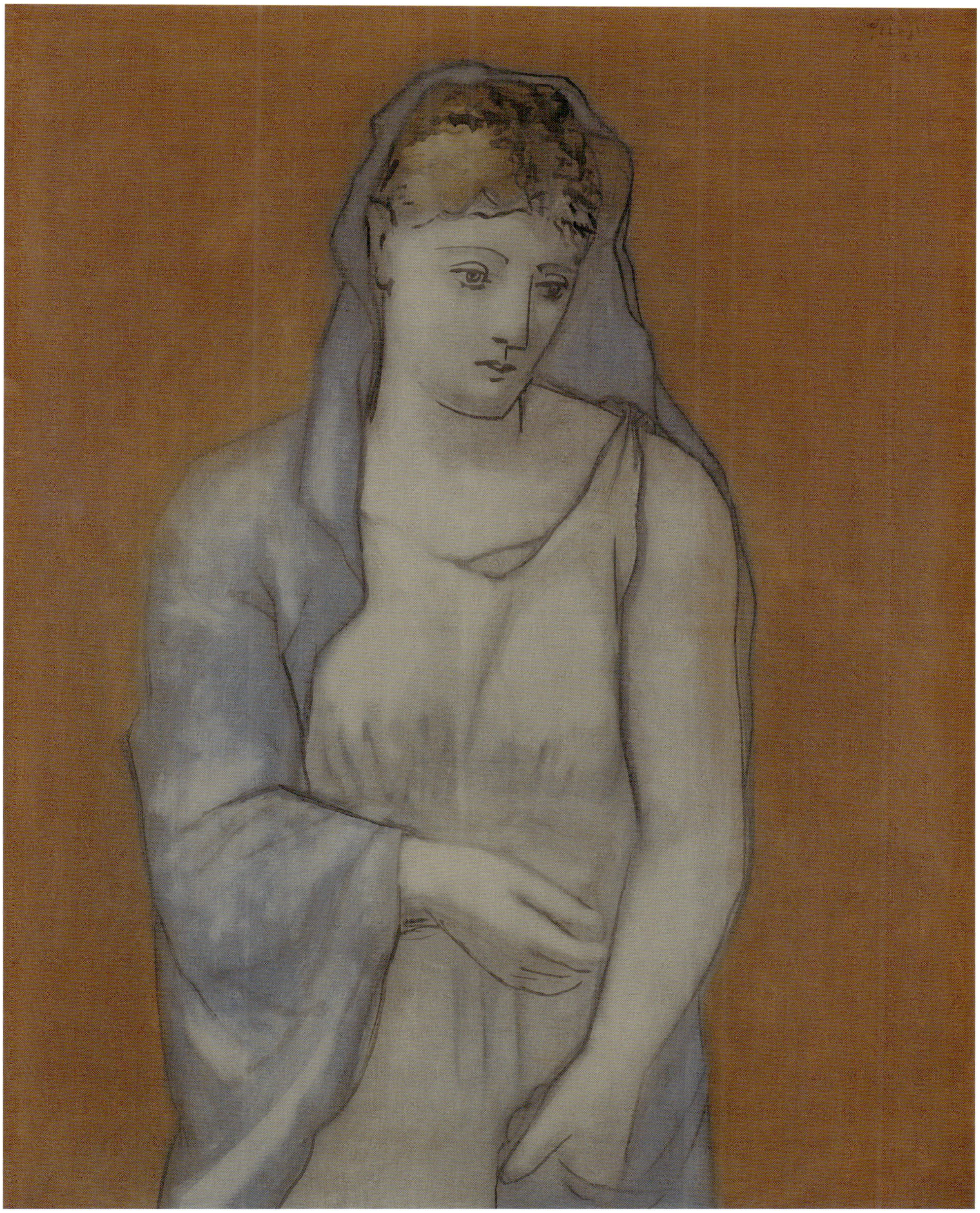

Pablo Picasso, ***Woman in Blue Veil***, Fall 1923

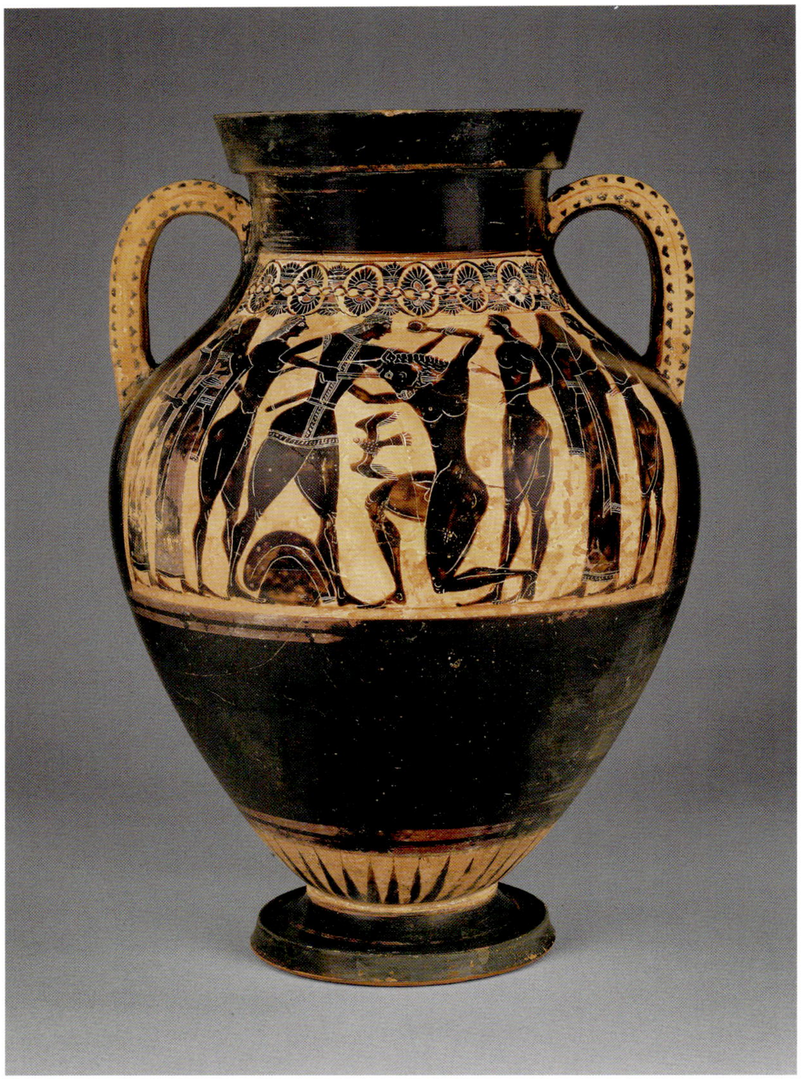

Attic Black-Figure Amphora, Greek, Athens, 550–540 BCE

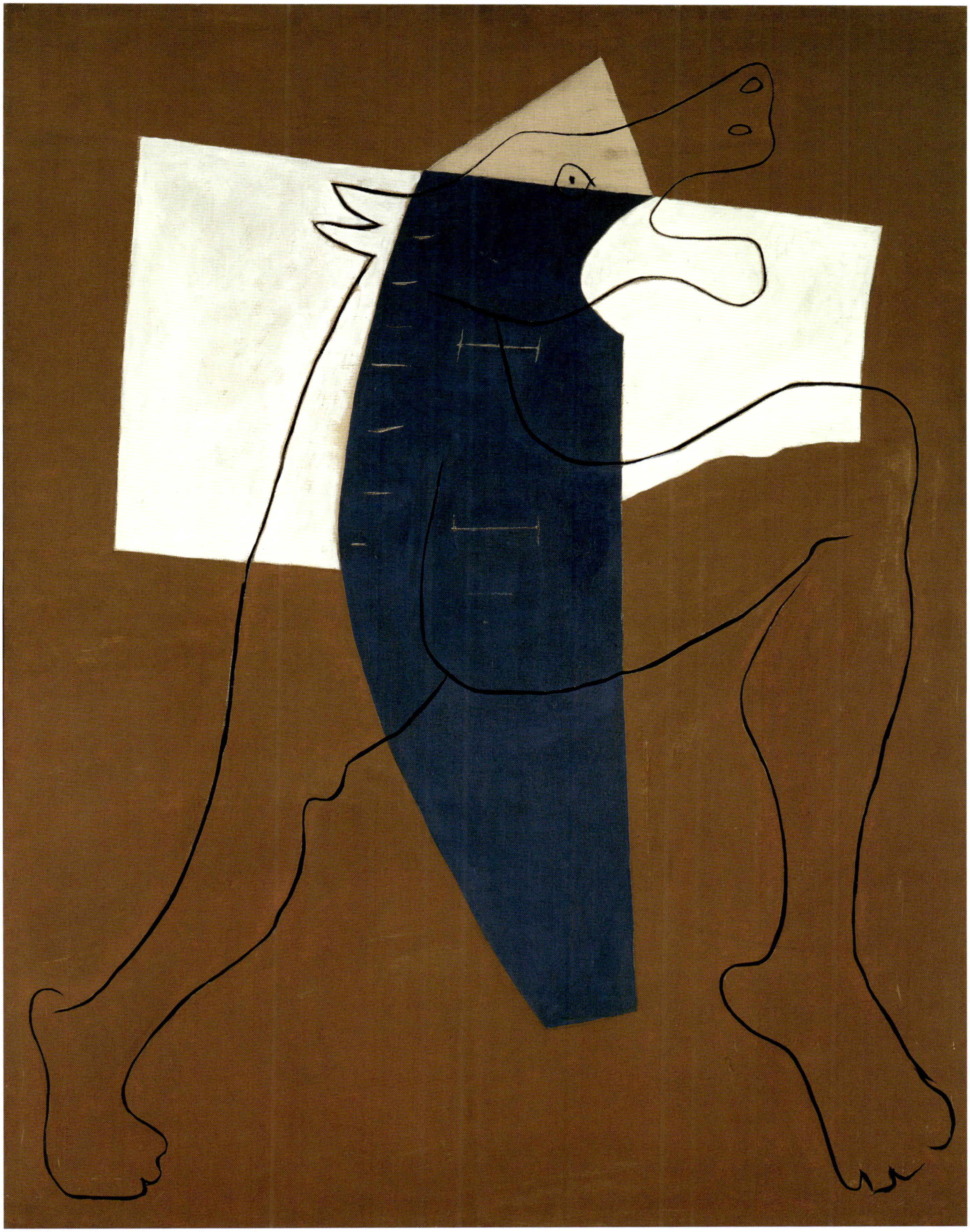

Pablo Picasso, ***Running Minotaur***, 1928

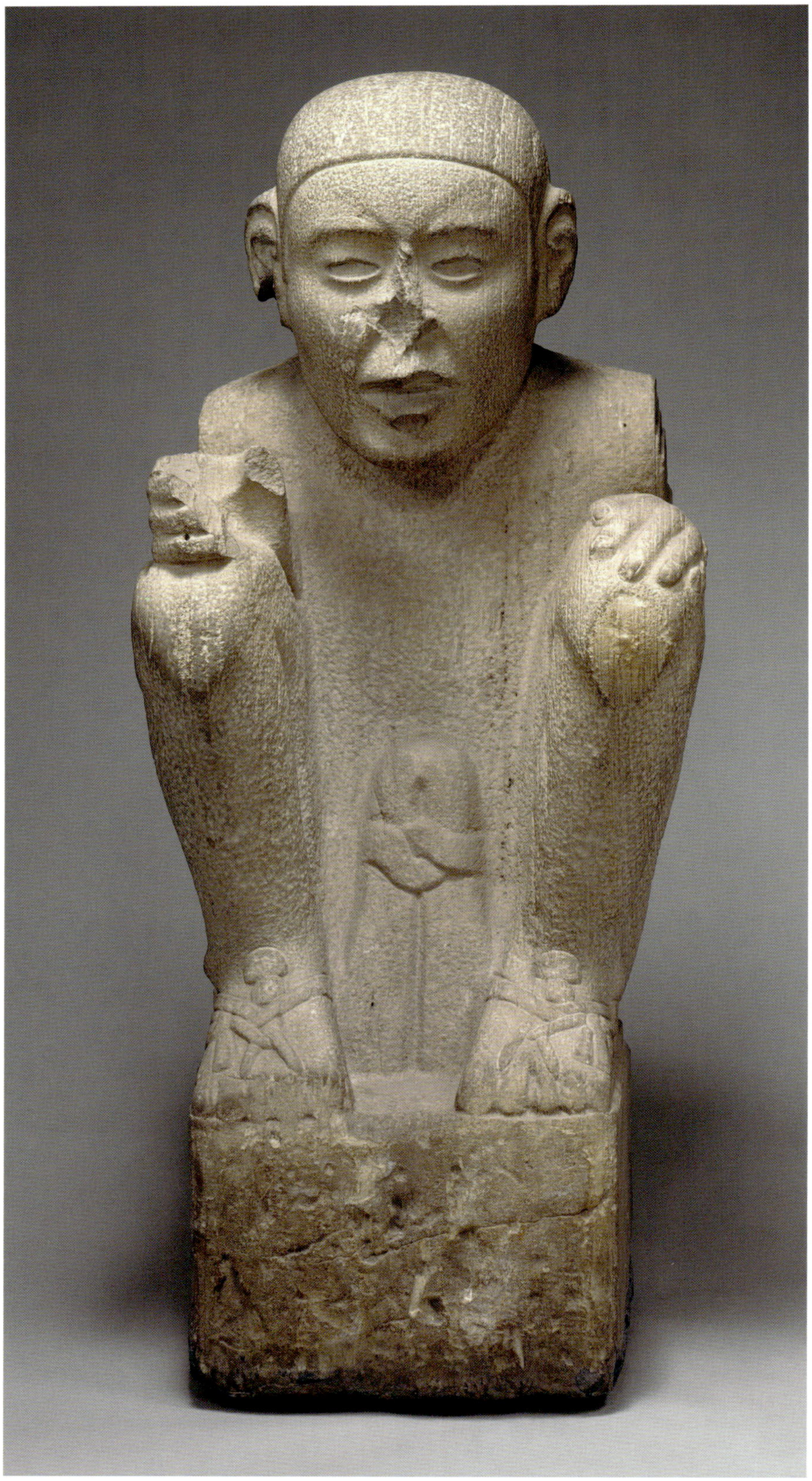

Seated Standard Bearer, Mexico, Aztec, Veracruz, 1250–1521

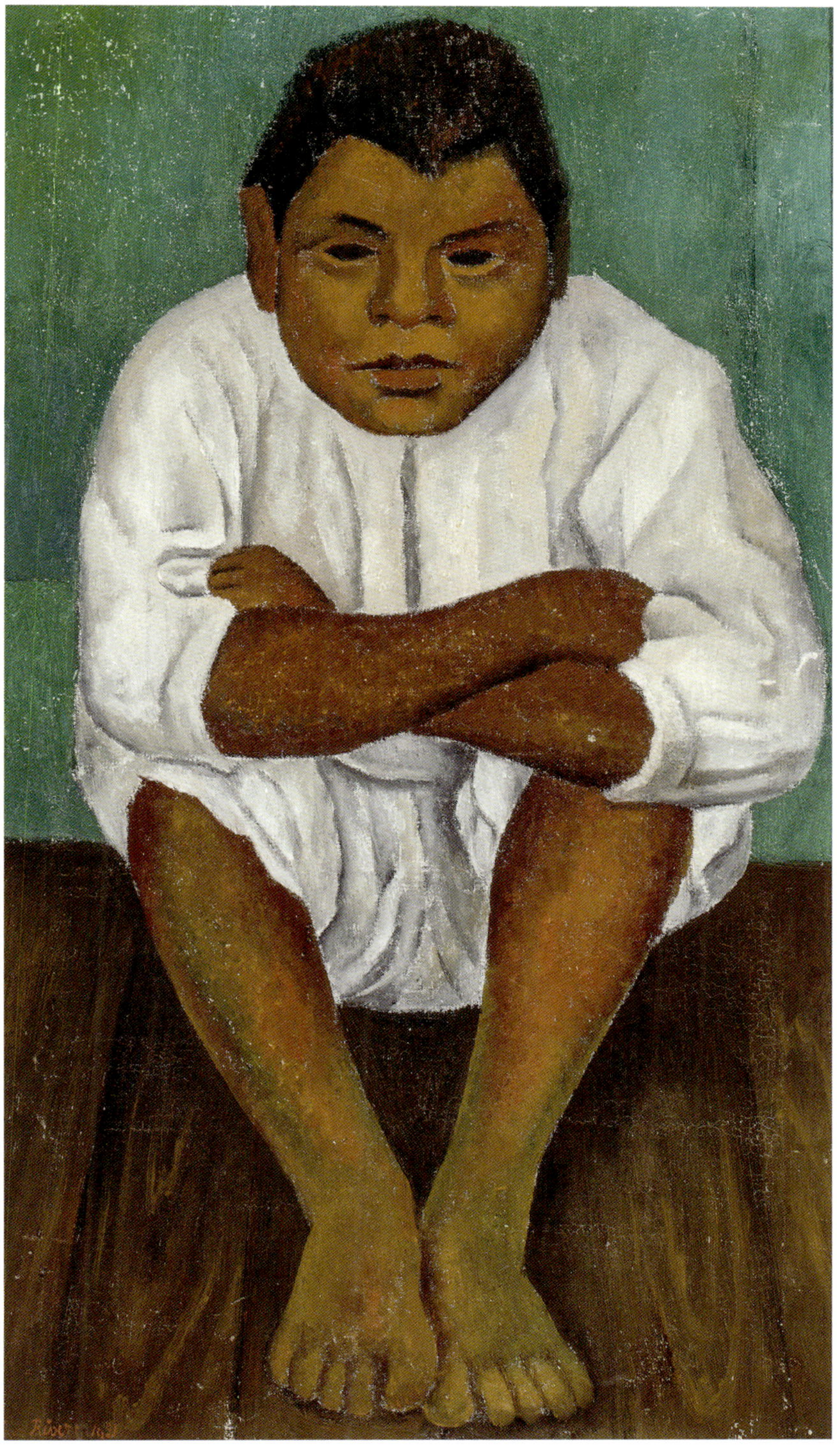

Diego Rivera, ***Frida's Friend***, 1931

PICASSO EMBATTLED RIVERA CUBISM AND WORLD WAR I

PATRICIA LEIGHTEN

1 Gustave Kahn, *Première poèmes; avec une préface sur le vers libre*, 2nd ed. (Paris: Société du Mercure de France, 1897), 24, trans. in Eugenia Herbert, *The Artist and Social Reform: France and Belgium, 1885–1898* (New Haven: Yale University Press, 1961), 54.

As this exhibition demonstrates, both Pablo Picasso and Diego Rivera were trained from an early age in academic styles of painting deeply rooted in the classical tradition, which was devoted to ancient Greek and Roman art as foundation stones of artistic practice. Equally clearly, both artists rebelled against this training as a hallmark of their varied careers. Having undergone a rapid series of stylistic transformations, each artist arrived at an exaggerated form of abstraction during World War I. Yet both remained committed throughout their lives to the notion that avant-garde art draws on various forms of ancient art. In Picasso's case, in works like *Self-Portrait* from 1906 (p. 83), he first embraced Iberian art, a western Mediterranean style echoing archaic Greek sculpture, as in *Man Attacked by a Lion* (p. 82). By incorporating aspects of its style, he transformed his painting via an alternative model at once "primitive" and inherently Spanish; this formed a pattern that he later substituted in his early Cubist period with Oceanic and African art, imagined as "timeless." Rivera likewise transformed his early academic art by embracing El Greco's exaggerated Mannerist style as an alternative model, later substituting the forms of Mexican popular culture and ancient Mesoamerican art, an equally primitivist and nationalistic act of self-discovery. During their early careers, furthermore, both artists were influenced by the anarchist movement—with its revolutionary appeal and vision of a just world—in ways that transformed their thinking and informed their art.

Yet, despite these strong parallels, as well as several others explored below, there was only one period during which these two major figures in modern art participated in the same artistic movement at the same time and came to know each other intimately. Both were Cubists and noncombatant foreigners living in Paris during World War I, and their art from this time shares significant aesthetic aims and appears strikingly close. In this period, art criticism representing the entire range of political opinion from right to left reveals how deeply French culture was saturated in a politicized rhetoric that saw ideological implications everywhere, especially in art, and especially in the rebellious art that Picasso and Rivera practiced. From 1908 until after the war, Cubism was consistently both attacked and celebrated on the assumption that traditional artistic canons reflected stable social conventions. As the anarchist and Symbolist poet Gustave Kahn wrote in 1897 in his defense of free verse, "any serious critic realizes that in shattering a fragment of the artistic façade one touches the social façade; it is this that explains why artistic demands once made encounter such aggressive resistance."[1] Though an ambivalent marker, style could thus encode a rejection of status quo social values, which explains how politics could operate in even the most abstract reaches of Picasso's and Rivera's art. This politicized environment heated to a xenophobic pitch as the war approached.

Cubism was also viewed, by both its defenders and detractors, as a "primitive" expression rooted in the same atavistic impulses that had created cave art and continued in the art of non-Western peoples and folk art. Concepts of primitivism encompassing the exotic, the ancient, and the infantile—in the name of authenticity or of degeneracy—shaped the whole of the Cubist movement throughout the period and are rife in the primary literature on Cubism right up to the war, in both texts sympathetic to the artists and those opposing them.[2] Critics who defended Cubism repeatedly evoked primitivist tropes, arguing that Cubism drew on cave art, children's art, and historically or geographically distant non-European cultures in the name of authenticity, spontaneity, and direct expression, all of which were at the heart of the new painting.[3] Further, the notion of the universal expressed in this modernist primitivism was sparked by the global phenomenon of colonialism. For example, Picasso responded to forms of African and Oceanic art brought to France by missionaries and colonial administrators, on view in the Musée d'Ethnographie du Trocadéro, while Rivera was sensitive to the fact that he was from a country that was still struggling with its legacies, especially its relations with its indigenous population. Given both artists' anticolonial political positions, this background gives us perspective on their attempts to act as historical and critical agents in their social environments, rather than as passive celebrants.[4] Their Cubist abstraction expressed deep roots in "primitive" creativity, contrasting with their later, more overt ways of engaging the myths and imagery of ancient Greece and Mesoamerica, respectively, in the 1920s and 1930s.

ARTISTIC AND POLITICAL BACKGROUNDS

When Picasso joined the French Communist Party in 1944, he stated, "I am conscious of having always struggled by means of my painting, as a true revolutionary."[5] Despite the many formalist interpretations that see Picasso's art as solely reflective of his inner emotional life, this statement regarding his political engagement was wholly true. Trained at a young age by his father, a Spanish academician, Picasso was drawn into the *moderniste* movement in Barcelona in his teens. This movement was steeped in anarchism as well as regional Catalan separatism, so the period from 1897 to 1904 constituted for him both an introduction to modernist art and an education in radical antiauthoritarian politics. *Anarchism* literally means "without rulers," and anarchist ideology calls for an end to a centralized government, army, and judicial system in favor of decentralization, direct democracy, and voluntary communities in loose federations. In the artistic café Els Quatre Gats, Picasso learned how these rebellious artists expressed new ideas in novel aesthetic forms, based on a rejection of academic precepts and an embrace of modern life, while expressing criticism of the government. The radicalism of the themes and styles of such artists as Ramón Casas and Isidre Nonell was of central importance in Spanish and Catalan modernism and would have a profound effect on the young Picasso.[6] His immersion in

2
For an extensive discussion of this aspect of Cubism, see Patricia Leighten, *The Liberation of Painting: Modernism and Anarchism in Avant-Guerre Paris* (Chicago: Chicago University Press, 2013), 85–110.

3
See Mark Antliff and Patricia Leighten, "Primitive," in *Critical Terms for Art History*, ed. Robert S. Nelson and Richard Shiff (Chicago: Chicago University Press, 2003), 217–33.

4
On Picasso, see Leighten, *The Liberation of Painting*, 57–84. On Rivera, see David Craven, *Diego Rivera: As Epic Modernist* (New York: G. K. Hall, 1997), 35–41 and 49.

5
Pablo Picasso interviewed by Pol Gaillard, "Pourquoi j'ai adhéré au Parti Communiste," *L'Humanité*, October 29–30, 1944. The full statement in the original French is in Alfred Barr, *Picasso: Fifty Years of His Art* (New York: Museum of Modern Art, 1946), 267–68.

6
The group included Ricard Canals, Ricard Opisso, Ramon Pitxot [Pichot], and Joaquim Mir. See Joseph Cervera, *Modernismo: The Catalan Renaissance of the Arts* (New York: Garland, 1976), 62–64; Patricia Leighten, *Re-Ordering the Universe: Picasso and Anarchism, 1897–1914* (Princeton: Princeton University Press, 1989), 6–7, 18–19, 25–32; and Temma Kaplan, *Red City, Blue Period: Social Movements in Picasso's Barcelona* (Berkeley: University of California Press, 1992), 74–77.

7
See Alain Corbin, *Les filles de noce: Misère sexuelle et prostitution aux dix-neuvième et vingtième siècles* (Paris: Aubier Montaigne, 1978); and Hollis Clayson, *Painted Love: Prostitution in French Art of the Impressionist Era* (New Haven: Yale University Press, 1991). On Picasso and prostitution, see Michael Leja, "'Le vieux marcheur' and 'Les deux risques': Picasso, Prostitution, Venereal Disease, and Maternity, 1899–1907," *Art History* 8 (March 1985): 66–81; Leighten, *Re-Ordering the Universe*, 13–47; and Josep Palau i Fabre, *Picasso: The Early Years, 1881–1907* (New York: Rizzoli, 1981).

8
Palau i Fabre, *Picasso*, 200–203; Maria Teresa Ocaña, "Chronicle from Paris," *Picasso and Els 4 Gats: The Early Years in Turn-of-the-Century Barcelona* (Barcelona: Museu Picasso, 1995), 52–56; and Leighten, *Re-Ordering the Universe*, 51.

9
Herbert, *The Artist and Social Reform*, 14–25 and 99–143, and Richard D. Sonn, *Anarchism and Cultural Politics in Fin de Siècle France* (Lincoln: University of Nebraska, 1989), 141–80. Both detail the widespread influence of the anarchist movement among many Symbolist artists in France.

10
On Apollinaire's aesthetic, see Marcel Adéma, *Apollinaire*, trans. D. Folliot (New York: Grove Press, 1955); Roger Shattuck, *The Banquet Years: The Origins of the Avant-Garde in France, 1885 to World War I*, rev. ed. (New York: Random House, 1968); LeRoy C. Breunig, *Guillaume Apollinaire* (New York: Columbia University Press, 1969); Peter Read, *Picasso et Apollinaire: Les métamorphoses de la mémoire, 1905/1973* (Paris: Éditions Jean-Michel Place, 1995); and Adrian Hicken, *Apollinaire, Cubism and Orphism* (Aldershot: Ashgate, 2003). On Apollinaire and anarchism, see Leighten, *Re-Ordering the Universe*, 53–63.

11
See the range of essays treating this subject in *Picasso's "Les Demoiselles d'Avignon,"* ed. Christopher Green (Cambridge: Cambridge University Press, 2001). For the colonial context of Picasso's embrace of African art in 1907, see Leighten, *The Liberation of Painting*, 57–84; and Patricia Leighten, "Colonialism, *l'art nègre*, and *Les Demoiselles d'Avignon*" in *Picasso's "Les Demoiselles d'Avignon,"* 77–103.

Barcelona's anarchist aesthetic movement encouraged images of social outcasts and street life in his early work and led directly to his Blue Period paintings of prostitution, starving artists, and the poor, as in *Portrait of Sebastià Junyer Vidal* (p. 101).[7]

When he arrived in Paris in 1900, Picasso sought out a radical culture parallel to the one he had inhabited in Barcelona—partly through his many contacts among Catalans living in Paris[8]—and painted similar subjects: working-class cafés, dance halls, and nightclubs, as well as the poor outskirts of the city. After settling in Paris permanently in 1904, Picasso became a member of the city's "Spanish colony" while also entering the most experimental reaches of cosmopolitan Parisian culture. Among his new friends in the French avant-garde were André Salmon and Guillaume Apollinaire, two neo-Symbolist poets with a history of anarchist thought.[9] Picasso met Apollinaire in 1904 and over the next decade came to share an aesthetic position dedicated to revolution in the arts.[10] In his Rose Period, Picasso continued his earlier explorations of socially conscious subjects, depicting hungry and marginalized acrobats and street entertainers. In his African Period, he produced *Les Demoiselles d'Avignon*, a major work on the theme of prostitution that was fully in tune with the contemporaneous anarchist critique of economic conditions that fostered the practice.[11] In his Cubist period, Picasso took his antiacademic art to the point of near-total abstraction.

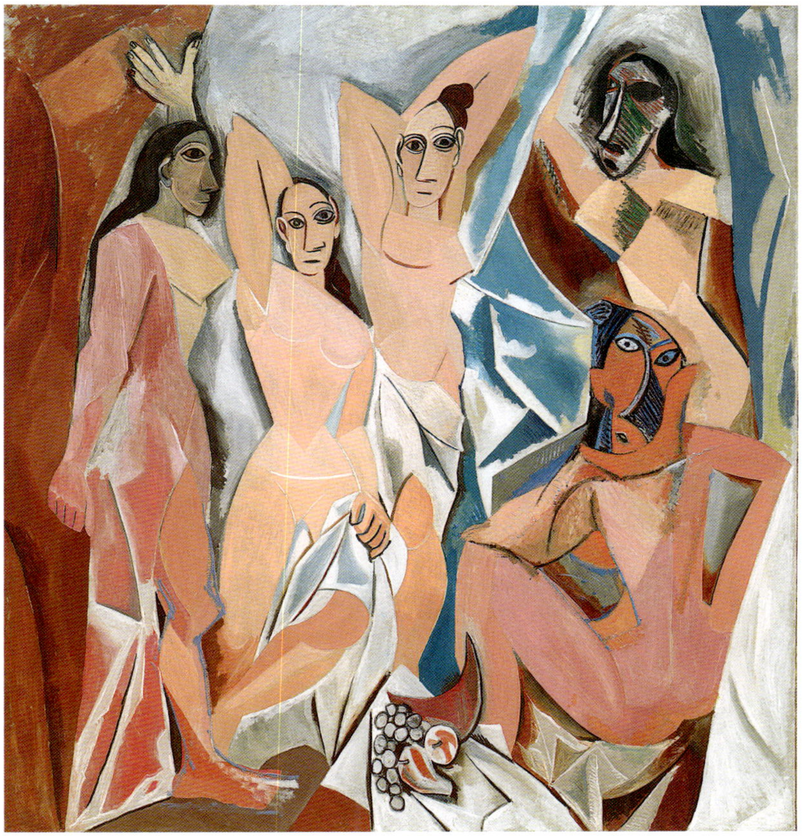

The Cubist movement was a complex development of the prewar period, involving numerous artists from around the world. While sharing a number of key theories—from simultaneity and Bergsonian intuition to the "fourth dimension" and n-dimensional mathematics—each artist worked in a style uniquely his or her own. Picasso and Georges Braque developed a geometrized style as early as 1907, while others, such as Robert Delaunay and Jean Metzinger, approached abstraction via late neo-Impressionist color. Their politics varied as much as their styles, ranging from French nationalism to anarchism.

Picasso's anarchist approach to Cubism shows in two important ways: first, in his nearly systematic subversion of tradition and the academic rules of art, and second, in his introduction of themes relevant to anarchist critique in his pasted-paper collages. Apollinaire and Picasso identified artistic novelty with new ways of thinking and a concomitant break from a bourgeois order allied with imitative academicism. *Les Demoiselles d'Avignon*, Picasso's meditation on sexuality and its commodification as a parallel to colonialism, already reveals his strategy of subverting and violating, point for point, academic rules of painting; this technique may be observed

Pablo Picasso, ***Les Demoiselles d'Avignon***, 1907; oil on canvas, 96 × 92 in. (243.9 × 233.7 cm); The Museum of Modern Art, acquired through the Lillie P. Bliss Bequest

throughout his increasingly abstract Cubist period. *The Poet* from 1912 (p. 106)—with its lack of tactile form, arbitrary distribution of light and shadow, suppression of color, abstract linear rhythms, and bewildering lack of recognizable detail—not only successfully refuses the world of bourgeois taste but openly satirizes it. And in his Cubist collages, by incorporating newsprint relating to the First and Second Balkan Wars, Picasso meditated on war and militarism in the period leading directly to World War I.[12] When he and Braque began to develop their pasted-paper technique in 1912, as in *Bottle of Suze*, Picasso chose to include newspaper articles relating to the coming pan-European war among his materials. In radically simplified compositions countering traditional depictions of space and form, he was able to create an updated version of the "painting of modern life" by suggesting the content of conversations among his friends in the cafés where they gathered. Pierre Daix, who met Picasso through the French Communist Party, later asked him whether he had purposely incorporated newspaper articles reporting on mass antiwar demonstrations. Picasso replied: "Of course I did it on purpose, because it was an important event involving a hundred thousand people.... Oh yes, I found that in the newspaper, and it was my way of showing I was against the war."[13]

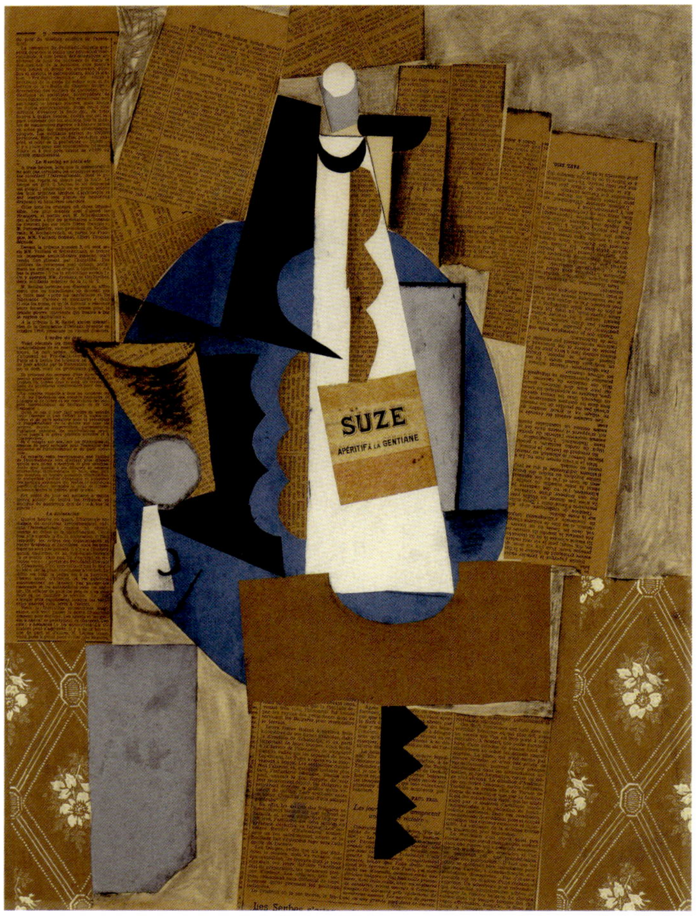

Rivera, five years younger than Picasso, was likewise academically trained in his youth, entering the Academy of San Carlos in Mexico City at the age of twelve. Mastering drawing, perspective, and painting techniques rooted in eighteenth-century Spanish traditions, he was a model student and was given government support to study in Europe.[14] In 1907, at age twenty, Rivera went to Madrid, where he spent two years learning from academic realist Eduardo Chicharro.[15] He then spent a period in Paris, where he was first exposed to Parisian modernism, returning to Mexico for a successful exhibition of his still-academic works in 1910. Rivera's own developing modernism slowly emerged during the subsequent few years, which he spent mostly in Madrid and Paris. Initially, having studied El Greco closely in the Prado Museum, Rivera adapted that artist's formal and spatial distortions to his own images of landscapes and figures. It may seem strange to consider El Greco "primitive," but for modernists like Rivera and Picasso (who had his own El Greco phase in 1906),[16] employing any model that helped divert their work from academic illusionism constituted an act of primitivism, allowing them to transform their expressive visions.

Pablo Picasso, ***Bottle of Suze***, 1912; pasted papers, gouache, and charcoal, 25¾ × 19¾ in. (65.4 × 50.1 cm); Mildred Lane Kemper Art Museum, Washington University in St. Louis, University purchase, Kende Sale Fund, 1946

12
Patricia Leighten, "Picasso's Collages and the Threat of War, 1912–13," *The Art Bulletin* 67 (December 1985): 653–72.

13
Picasso quoted in *Picasso and Braque: A Symposium*, ed. Lynn Zelevansky (New York: Museum of Modern Art, 1989), 75–76. A number of Picasso's friends were also against the war, for instance Juan Gris and André Salmon; the latter nonetheless fought in the war and later wrote *Le Drapeau noir* [The black flag] (Paris: La Cité des Livres, 1927), detailing his and his generation's intense conflict over reconciling their anarchist antimilitarism with the call of key anarchist leaders in 1914 to "defend civilization." On Gris's pacifism, see Leighten, *The Liberation of Painting*, 111–22, 138–44; on a wide range of artists' responses to the war, see Kenneth E. Silver, *Esprit de Corps: The Art of the Parisian Avant-Garde and the First World War, 1914–1925* (Princeton, NJ: Princeton University Press, 1989).

14
Ramón Favela, *Diego Rivera: The Cubist Years* (Phoenix: Phoenix Art Museum, 1984), 9, 12. San Carlos was closely modeled on the San Fernando Royal Academy in Madrid.

15
Ibid., 21.

16
See *Picasso and the Spanish Tradition*, ed. J. Brown (New Haven: Yale University Press, 1996).

Gradually abandoning the influence of Ignacio Zuloaga and Ángel Zárraga—who both worked in an El Greco style themselves—Rivera turned his ambitions to more full-blown modernist abstraction, looking to the new Cubist movement. Charting the development of Rivera's Cubism, Ramón Favela rightly argues that the artist's initial phase in 1912 was influenced by Dutch painters Lodewijk Schelfhout and Piet Mondrian, and then by the so-called Salon Cubists, especially Fernand Léger, Albert Gleizes, and Robert Delaunay.[17] *The Viaduct* (*Sun Breaking through the Fog*) (p. 102), from 1913, is a clear example of Rivera's absorption of Salon Cubist styles. Like many of these artists, Rivera adhered to a deeply theoretical and systematic approach; he was driven by a spiritualized interpretation of the "fourth dimension," yet his aims shared the extreme individualism of the movement as a whole.[18] By 1914, when the war broke out, Rivera had fully grasped the whole range of Cubist styles and developed a unique form of Cubism, but one more indebted to Picasso and Juan Gris than to the Salon Cubists.

Rivera, like Picasso, was immersed in anarchist thought as a young man. David Craven has established that Rivera's testimony to this effect is important and reliable, preceding his later transition to Leninist Marxism and his joining of the Mexican Communist Party in 1922.[19] Rivera maintained he was galvanized by Emiliano Zapata in the early days of the Mexican Revolution, and even claimed to have fought in the uprising for six months in 1910.[20] While few are convinced of the latter assertion, Craven takes very seriously Rivera's support of the anarchist character of Zapata's call for agrarian reform in his 1911 Plan of Ayala, with its proposal for the mass redistribution of land and fundamental opposition to a professional army and national government.[21] He points out that "Zapata's project was also distinctly anarchist in character and it was, in many ways, the heir to the earlier anarchist insurgency led by Enrique and Ricardo Flores Magón of the PLM [Partido Liberal Mexicano]."[22] He concludes that "[t]he fact that Rivera would paint Zapata's portrait almost forty times, with several of these depictions being located in large federally financed public murals that are an ironic testimony to the centralized state consolidated after 1920, alerts us to an important strain of ideological continuity in Rivera's long career."[23]

Rivera's long and intimate association with Mexican artist Gerardo Murillo, better known as Dr. Atl (the Nahuatl word for *water*), would have powerfully affirmed his engagement with anarchism as an ideology. Atl had befriended Rivera as a student, and they were reunited in Paris in 1912 among a group of expatriate Latin American artists and writers.[24] As Rivera attested, "Like me, Atl was politically an anarchist, a product of the discontented middle class. Our common political and artistic interests brought us very close."[25] Atl is a major figure in the history of Mexican modernism, both as an artist and as a supporter of the Mexican muralist movement. He studied art at San Carlos and in Rome, where he moved in anarchist circles, passionately embracing the work of Georges Sorel, the theorist of anarchist syndicalism.[26] An active participant in the Mexican Revolution in 1910, Atl returned to Paris in 1911, and

17
Favela, *Rivera: The Cubist Years*, 36 and 43–53; in 1912 Rivera moved into the same building with Schelfhout, Conrad Kikkert, and Mondrian.

18
Gino Severini, during his wartime Cubist phase, was an excellent witness to this: "As the painter Rivera, following Poincaré, justly observed, 'A being living in a world with varied refractions, instead of homogenous ones, would be bound to conceive a fourth dimension.' This milieu with different refractions is realized in a picture if a multiplicity of pyramids replaces the single cone of Italian perspective. Such is the case with certain personal experiments made by Rivera, who sees in Poincaré's hypothesis a confirmation of some intuitions of Rembrandt, Greco and Cézanne." Gino Severini, "La peinture d'avant-garde," *Mercure de France* (June 1, 1917): 451–68, trans. in Jean Charlot, *The Mexican Mural Renaissance, 1920–1925* (New Haven: Yale University Press, 1963), 124. My thanks to Laura Moure Cecchini for this quotation.

19
Craven, *Rivera: As Epic Modernist*, 17–19 and 35–41. Rivera was later expelled from the party in 1929 for Trotskyite sympathies.

20
See ibid., 40–41; and Favela, *Rivera: The Cubist Years*, 24–29.

21
Craven, *Rivera: As Epic Modernist*, 40.

22
Ibid. The PLM, or Mexican Liberal Party, was founded by the Regeneration group and led in exile by Ricardo Flores Magón and his brothers. "In 1906 the Regeneration group published a comprehensive program in the form of a manifesto that had wide, if clandestine, circulation in Mexico. It advocated a one-term presidency, guarantees of civil liberties, breaking the hold of the Roman Catholic Church, vast expansion of free public education, and land reform. It asked that Mexican citizenship be a prerequisite to property ownership and that unused land be distributed to the landless. The manifesto proposed confiscation of the wealth that [dictator Porfirio] Díaz and the *científicos* had illegally acquired, the abolition of child labour, guaranteed minimum wages, and improved conditions for workers." *Encyclopaedia Britannica Online*, s.v. "Mexico, La Reforma," http://www.britannica.com/place/Mexico/La-Reforma.

23
Craven, *Rivera: As Epic Modernist*, 41.

24
When Rivera first went to Europe, he took a letter from Atl introducing him to one of Madrid's most important painters, Eduardo Chicharro, and he traveled on funds raised by an exhibition Atl had organized in San Carlos of fifteen Rivera landscapes; see ibid., 16, 19.

25
Diego Rivera (with Gladys March), *My Art, My Life: An Autobiography* (New York: Citadel Press, 1960), 47.

26
Olfa Sáenz, "Pintor de Mitos y Realidades," in *Dr. Atl: Obras Maestras* (Mexico City: Museo Colección Blaisten, UNAM, 2012), 34. For biographical information on Dr. Atl, see also Miguel A. Rosas, "Dr. Atl: Breve Cronología de su Actividad Plástica," in ibid., 363–67; Xavier Moyssén, "Atl, Dr.," *Grove Art Online*, *Oxford Art Online*, Oxford University Press, http://www.oxfordartonline.com/subscriber/article/grove/art/T004871; and "Atl, Dr.," *Benezit Dictionary of Artists*, *Oxford Art Online*, Oxford University Press, http://www.oxfordartonline.com/subscriber/article/benezit/B00008264.

by 1913 was a full member of the Bergsonian anarchist-individualist group known as the Artistocrats, publishing in their journal *L'Action d'art*.[27] Here Atl railed against both the salon system and galleries as exploitative commercial enterprises and condemned oil paint on canvas as catering to the market. Instead, he advocated his own mixture of pigmented encaustics—which he called "Atl colors"—claiming that these were appropriate for public, rather than collectable, privatistic art.[28] Having already promoted mural painting before the Mexican Revolution,[29] Atl remained consistent with his earlier, politicized notions of art. As Mark Antliff explains, according to Atl,

> "Artistocratic art was beautiful by virtue of its utter individuality.... It is 'the integral action of the self' that engenders true art, and art of this type will 'harmonize lines, colours, and volumes of a decoration with the structure of an edifice or with the dimensions of a great idea.'"[30]

Atl believed that the epic idea of the Artistocrats produced a "decorative rhythm" that could even give easel painting the volumetric force of a wall fresco.[31] In his review of the 1913 Salon des Indépendants, Atl found this rhythm in the work of the Cubist Albert Gleizes. He transformed his own landscapes along similar, if less radically abstract, lines, embracing the Cubists' non-Euclidean perspectives and the curvilinear Riemannian space that he saw in the work of Jean Metzinger. Atl's admiration for these artists could have served to reinforce Rivera's interest in this style of avant-garde painting once Rivera was reunited with his forceful friend, whose "violent individualism" he vividly remembered.[32] Rivera eagerly embraced the Salon Cubists' excitement about non-Euclidean geometry and the fourth dimension. As Antliff concludes, "the political aspirations that led Atl to condemn oil on canvas were not unlike those that inspired Picasso to invent collage, for both artists abandoned easel painting's traditional medium as a form of protest against state-sanctioned academicism."[33]

In his memoirs, Rivera is explicit about his anarchist sympathies leading into the war, stating that he participated with other leftist writers and artists who "risked their necks in workers' demonstrations against war" in 1913 and 1914; he later claimed that attending these mass rallies—for instance, to hear the powerful antiwar

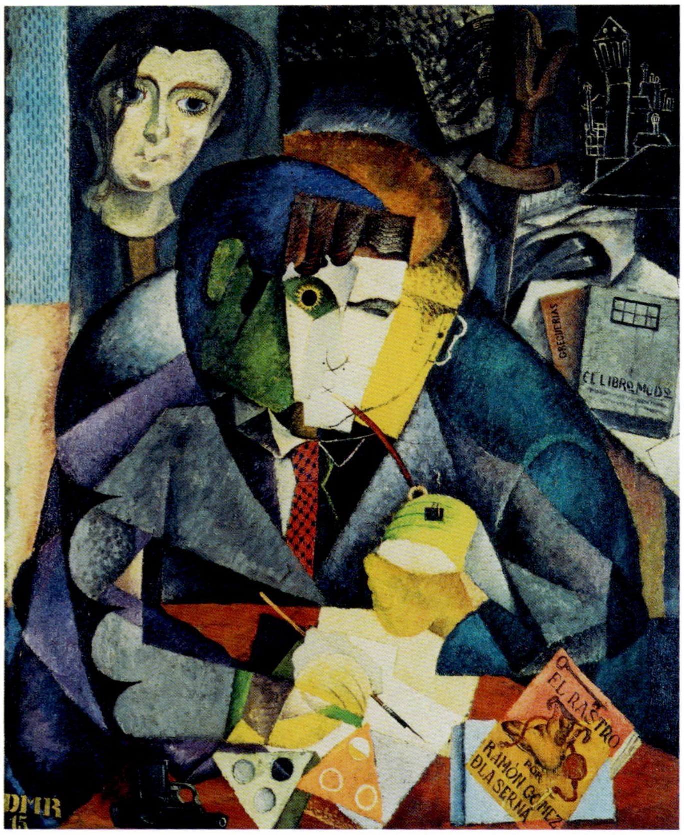

Diego Rivera, ***Portrait of Ramón Gómez de la Serna***, 1915; oil on canvas, 42 7/8 × 35 3/8 in. (109 × 90 cm); private collection

27 Mark Antliff, "Cubism, Futurism, Anarchism: The 'Aestheticism' of the *Action d'art* Group, 1906–1920," *Oxford Art Journal* 21, no. 2 (1998): 99–120. For the importance of Henri Bergson's philosophy to modernism and Cubism, see Mark Antliff, *Inventing Bergson: Cultural Politics and the Parisian Avant-Garde* (Princeton: Princeton University Press, 1993); and Mark Antliff and Patricia Leighten, *Cubism and Culture* (New York: Thames & Hudson, 2001), 64–110.

28 Antliff, "Cubism, Futurism, Anarchism," 109.

29 "Atl, Dr.," *Benezit Dictionary of Artists*.

30 Antliff, "Cubism, Futurism, Anarchism," 109.

31 Ibid., 110; quotations from Dr. Atl from "Une Orientation s'impose," *L'Action d'art* (February 15, 1913): 1–2; and "Le Salon des Indépendants," *L'Action d'art* (March 15, 1913): 2.

32 Rivera, *My Art, My Life*, 48.

33 Antliff, "Cubism, Futurism, Anarchism," 110.

34 Rivera, *My Art, My Life*, 121.

35 Ibid., 111–13. See also the discussion in Craven, *Rivera: As Epic Modernist*, 36; and in Favela, *Rivera: The Cubist Years*, 96–97.

36 Henri Bergson, "La force qui s'use et celle qui ne s'use pas," *Bulletin des armées de la République*, November 4, 1914, 1.

37 Peter Marshall, *Demanding the Impossible: A History of Anarchism* (London: Fontana, 1993), 332.

speeches by Jean Jaurès—influenced his murals.[34] In 1915, while living in Madrid, Rivera delighted in the public outrage over the exhibition in a local gallery window of his *Portrait of Ramón Gómez de la Serna*, whose depiction, Rivera asserted, "had the appearance of an anarchist demon, inciting crime and the general overthrow of order. In this Satanic figure everyone recognized the features of Serna, notorious for his opposition to every conventional, religious, moral, and political principle."[35]

WARTIME CUBISM

The period from the outbreak of World War I in August 1914 to its conclusion in November 1918 radically transformed every aspect of French society. The French—like the British and Germans—entered the war enthusiastically, assuming it would be over by Christmas. But after three months, it was already clear that any chance of a decisive military victory had been lost; the war was a stalemate. Parallel fortified trenches on either side of a 230-meter no-man's-land—the machine gun's range roughly determined its width—stretched hundreds of kilometers across northeastern France, from the Swiss border into Belgium. This stalemate guaranteed a war of attrition, regularly punctuated by massive and fruitless assaults by both sides, resulting in human slaughter on a historically unprecedented scale. By the war's end, more than 1,350,000 French soldiers alone had been killed and another 4,250,000 were wounded, a cost of lives that would have been unimaginable at the start of hostilities. The best word for the state of culture was "traumatized," a condition that slowly unfolded during the four long years of the war and through the period that followed.

France's cultural and political elite responded forcefully to the outbreak of war. Philosopher Henri Bergson turned the conflict into a spiritual battle between the forces of despotism (Germany) and those of freedom (France), disseminating his views in the November 4, 1914, issue of the *Bulletin des armées de la République*.[36] His ethical interpretation of the conflict was echoed by the leading anarchist theorist Peter Kropotkin, who supported the French war effort as a defense of the revolutionary tradition against the forces of political reaction, rejecting international class solidarity in the name of France's "civilization and her ideas of liberty, communism, and fraternity."[37] In 1912 the anarchist-syndicalist trade union Confédération Génerale du Travail (CGT) had fomented a general strike against the jingoistic buildup of armaments in France, but in August 1914, under the leadership of Léon Jouhaux, the CGT declared the war a battle for justice and republican liberty against German militarism, agreeing not to oppose the government or call for strikes. The vast majority of able-bodied men in Paris were now in uniform.

PICASSO AND RIVERA

Exchanges between Artists

LILLY CASILLAS AND DIANA MAGALONI

After meeting in early 1914, Picasso and Rivera developed a friendship that included both personal closeness and conflict. As James Oles discusses (p. 160), they fell out in August 1915 at least in part over a specific stippling technique used to create the illusion of foliage, which Rivera laid claim to having invented and which Picasso, in turn, used without consultation. This incident has led many scholars to believe that Picasso and Rivera's friendship was only brief and of little consequence, particularly for Picasso. But new evidence provides a counterargument to this assumption.

Rivera's memoir vividly reconstructs the early days of their friendship, recalling the four recent works that Picasso saw when he first visited Rivera's studio: two portraits, *Sailor at Lunch* (p. 104) and *Young Man with a Stylograph* (1914, Museo Dolores Olmedo), and two still lifes, *Still Life with Balalaika* (1913, Bergen Kunstmuseum) and a painting he calls *Bottle of Spanish Anis*, which we believe is the work known today as *Cubist Composition* (*Still Life with Bottle of Anis and Inkwell*). This painting provides a key to our understanding of their friendship. There are six known Cubist works by Rivera portraying a bottle of anis, with only two dating to the time of Picasso's visit: the study for *Cubist Composition*, known now as *Spanish Still Life* (1914, Museo Casa Diego Rivera), and *Cubist Composition* (*Still Life with Bottle of Anis and Inkwell*).

Picasso acquired the latter in 1915. It is now part of the Almine and Bernard Ruiz Picasso Foundation, and its inclusion in *Picasso and Rivera: Conversations Across Time* marks the first time it is known to have been published and exhibited. Though Picasso acquired one of Rivera's paintings (whether as a gift or as a purchase is unknown), Rivera is not known to have acquired any of Picasso's works. Instead, he had a photograph of one of Picasso's earlier Cubist collages, *Gas-Jet and Guitar* (1913, National Gallery, Prague), which Picasso gave to Rivera after their first meeting.[1] Picasso inscribed the photo (evidently at a later date) in both Spanish and French: "A mi querido amigo Diego Rivera, en tout d'accord" (To my dear friend Diego Rivera, we agree on everything).[2] This document from Picasso to Rivera is also published here for the first time.

Rivera's *Cubist Composition* is one of the few works in which he experimented with sand and other nontraditional materials, and this may have been due in part to the conversations Rivera and Picasso shared in these years. Rivera seems to have been particularly inspired by Picasso's collages, as suggested by the strong similarities between Rivera's *Sailor at Lunch* and a number of Picasso's works at the time, such as *Student with Newspaper* (p. 105) and *Student with a Pipe* (1913–14, Museum of Modern Art).

Picasso's personal art collection contained works by many of his contemporaries, including Matisse, Braque, Modigliani, and others. He referred to the works in his collection as his "friends," remarking to his art dealer, Daniel-Henry Kahnweiler, in February 1934: "Why shouldn't one inherit from their friends? In essence, what is a painter? A collector who consolidates a collection for himself by making other people's paintings that he likes."[3] The fact that Picasso kept Rivera's painting as part of his collection of "friends" suggests the importance he attributed to his time with Rivera in Paris.

Other documents attest to their continuing friendship, or at least to Rivera's desire to remain in contact. Rivera is known to have written to Picasso on two occasions, in 1949 and 1957.[4] These letters evince the respect Rivera had for his "muy admirado y querido maestro y amigo" (much admired and loved teacher and friend), as he refers to Picasso in his letter from 1949. In the same letter, Rivera includes an update regarding Frida Kahlo's health: "Frida ha estado muy enferma. Ahora parece fuera de peligro. Lo saluda con mucho cariño" (Frida has been very sick. Now she seems safe from danger. She sends you her fondest regards). These gestures suggest a familiarity and camaraderie (both professionally and personally) that allow us to understand their relationship in a new light.

1 Rivera recalled leaving Picasso's studio "pressing the photograph to his chest as if it were his passport to glory." *Diego Rivera: Illustrious Words*, vol. 1, 1886–1921, ed. Juan Rafael Cornel Rivera (Mexico City: Instituto Nacional de Bellas Artes, 2007), 303–4. See also Loló de la Torriente, *Memoria y Razón de Diego Rivera*, vol. 2 (Mexico City: Editorial Renacimiento, 1959), 14–15.

2 Picasso's inscription is dated May 12, 1915. We are grateful to Hilda Trujillo and Verónica Rincón for providing access to the Diego Rivera and Frida Kahlo Archive.

3 Anne Baldassari and Philippe Saunier, *Picasso & His Collection* (Sydney: Art Exhibitions Australia, 2008), 44.

4 We are grateful to Sophie Annoepel-Cabrignac at the Musée Picasso Paris for providing access to these documents.

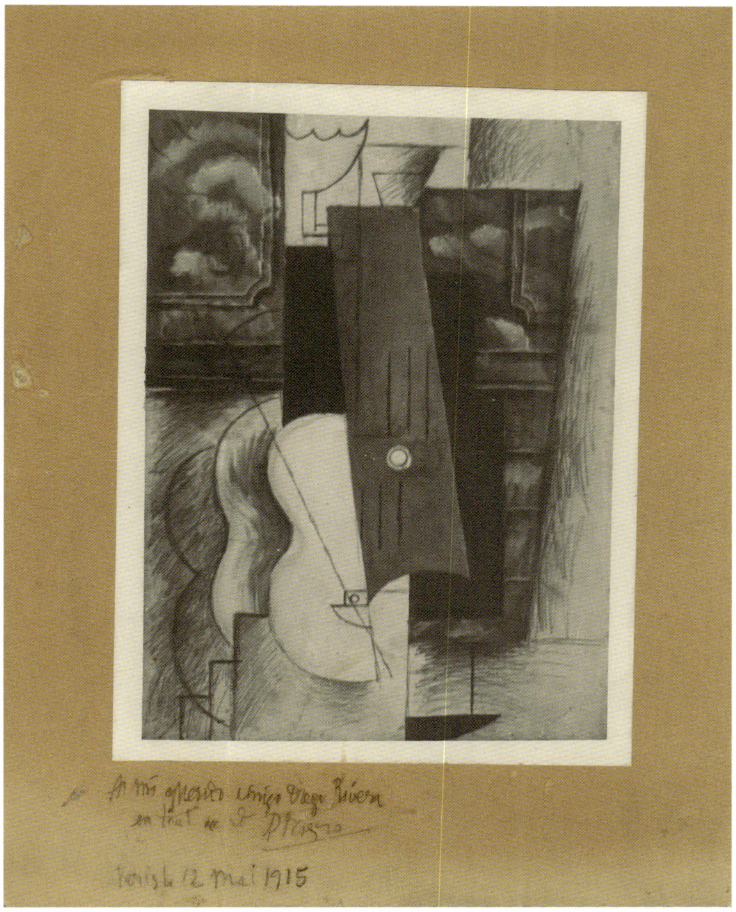

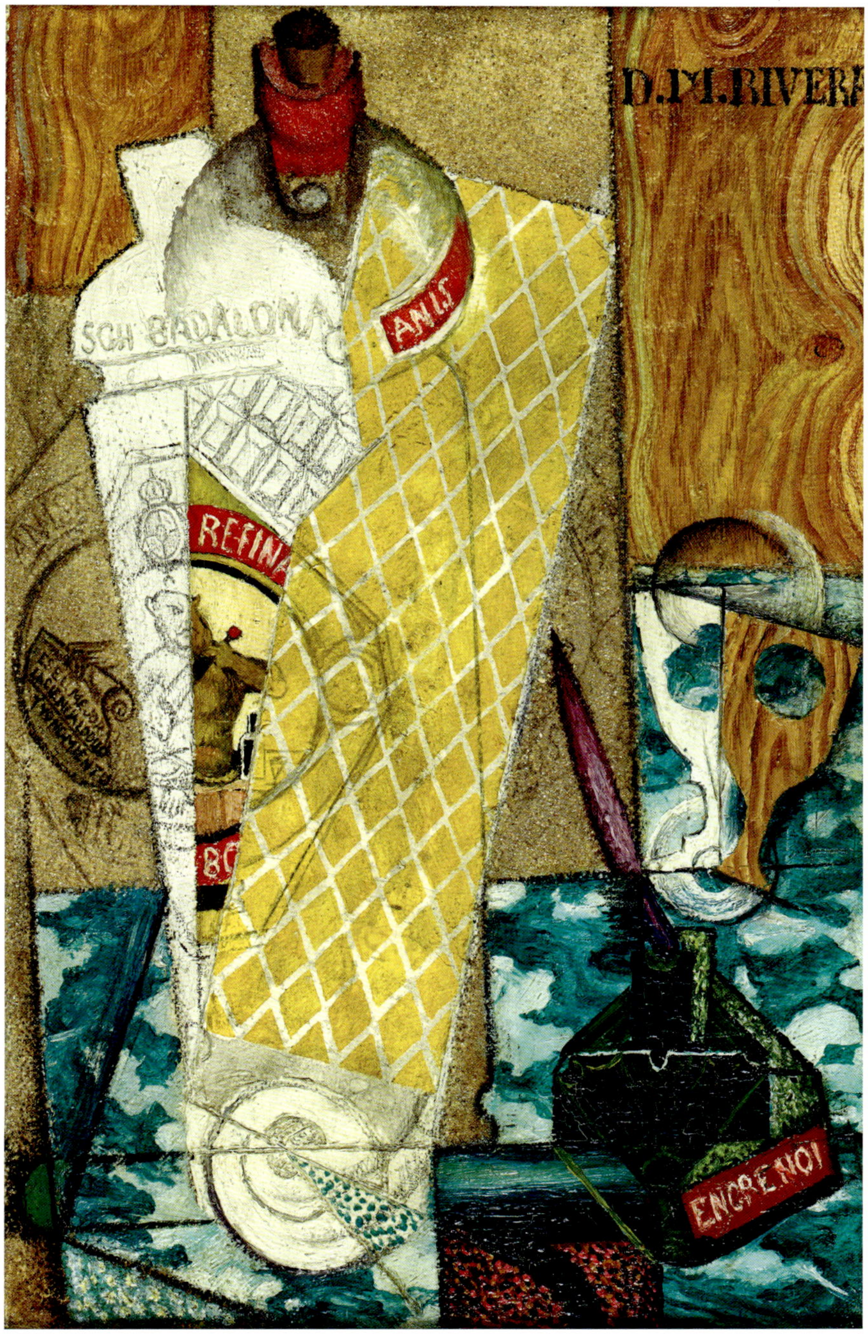

LEFT Photograph of Pablo Picasso's *Gas-Jet and Guitar* (1913), with inscription from Picasso to Rivera: "A mi querido amigo Diego Rivera, en tout d'accord. 12 mai 1915, Paris." Diego Rivera and Frida Kahlo Archive, Mexico City

RIGHT Diego Rivera, ***Cubist Composition*** (***Still Life with Bottle of Anis and Inkwell***), 1914–15

38 Leighten, *Re-Ordering the Universe*, 143–46.

39 Apollinaire became a French citizen; the others joined the Foreign Legion. See Antliff and Leighten, *Cubism and Culture*, 197–214, and Leighten, *Re-Ordering the Universe*, 143–45.

The Cubists and their literary supporters were swept up in these events, which transformed the Parisian cultural landscape in which Cubism had flourished. Kenneth Silver, in his book on the Parisian avant-garde and the war years, has charted the impact: whereas Picasso, Gris, and Rivera remained noncombatants throughout the conflict (Picasso and Gris were in fact in default of their Spanish military service obligations), most Cubists either volunteered or were conscripted.[38] Braque, Gleizes, Léger, Metzinger, André Derain, Raymond Duchamp-Villon, Roger de La Fresnaye, and Jacques Villon were all at the front by the first winter of the war. Foreigners

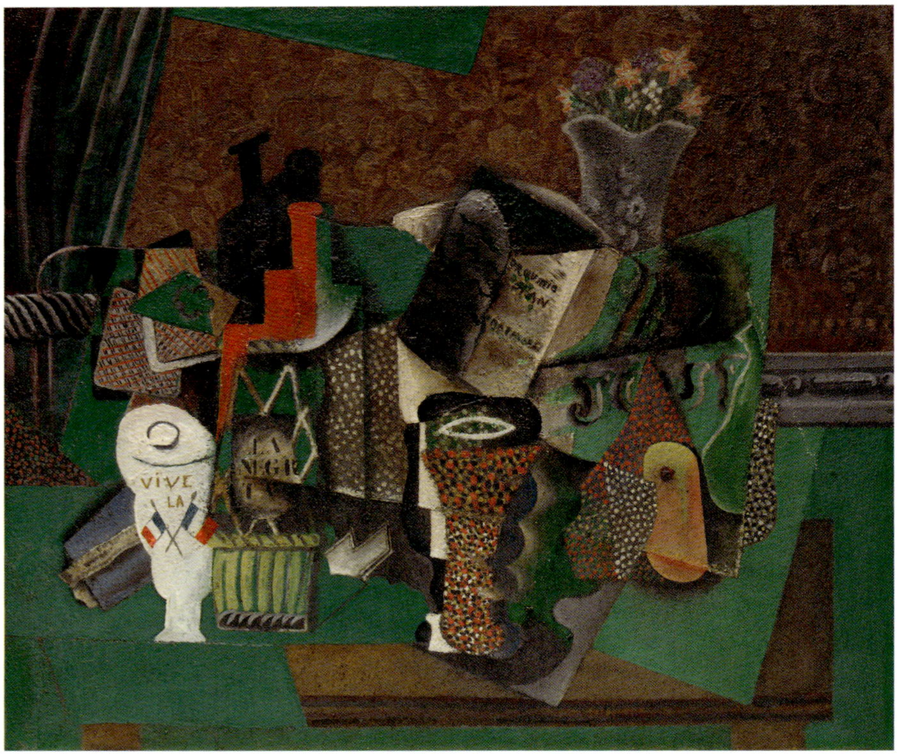

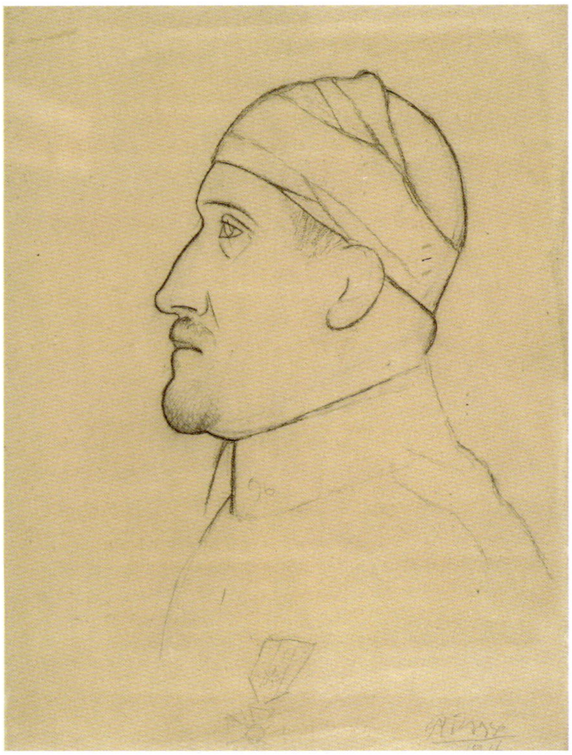

such as Apollinaire, Moïse Kisling, and Louis Marcoussis found ways to join the French troops.[39] Those of German citizenship were either arrested or forced to flee: art dealer Daniel-Henry Kahnweiler was in Italy when the war broke out and sought refuge in Switzerland, while painter Marie Laurencin, who had married her German husband in June 1914, fled to neutral Spain for the war's duration. Still others signaled their opposition by leaving France: Robert and Sonia Delaunay lived in Portugal and Spain throughout the war, Henri Le Fauconnier settled in neutral Holland, and Marcel Duchamp left France for the still-neutral United States in 1915, followed by Gleizes, when he was demobilized the same year.

In Paris, Cubism was now journalistically viewed as part and parcel of a prewar cultural invasion of Paris that had undermined the French spirit and prepared the way for the military invasion that followed, and was frequently dismissed as *bôche*,

LEFT Pablo Picasso, ***Playing Cards, Glasses, Bottle of Rum: "Vive la France,"*** 1914/1915; oil and sand on canvas, 20½ × 25 in. (52.1 × 63.5 cm); The Metropolitan Museum of Art, promised gift from the Leonard A. Lauder Cubist Collection

RIGHT Pablo Picasso, ***Portrait of Guillaume Apollinaire with Bandaged Head***, 1916; black chalk, 11¾ × 8⅞ in. (29.7 × 22.5 cm); Musée Picasso, Paris (MP1993-5)

[40] Pierre Daix, *Picasso: Life and Art*, trans. Olivia Emmet (New York: HarperCollins, 1993), 142.

[41] Guillaume Apollinaire, "Living Art and the War," *Le Petit Messager des Arts et des Industries d'Art*, March 1, 1915, in *Apollinaire on Art: Essays and Reviews, 1902–1918*, ed. LeRoy C. Breunig, trans. Susan Rubin Suleiman (New York: Viking, 1972), 439–40.

a French slur for "German." Throughout the war, Picasso, Gris, and Rivera drew and painted, staying mostly in a Paris that was by now thoroughly militarized. As healthy men in their prime (Picasso was thirty-three, Rivera was twenty-eight, and Gris was twenty-seven), they were at a certain risk from angry soldiers on leave during the war; Picasso was more than once challenged in the street.[40] Traveling in Spain when the war began, Rivera stayed in Madrid until the spring of 1915, when he returned to Paris, participating in a diminished, fragmented, and rather demoralized circle of largely foreign vanguard artists.

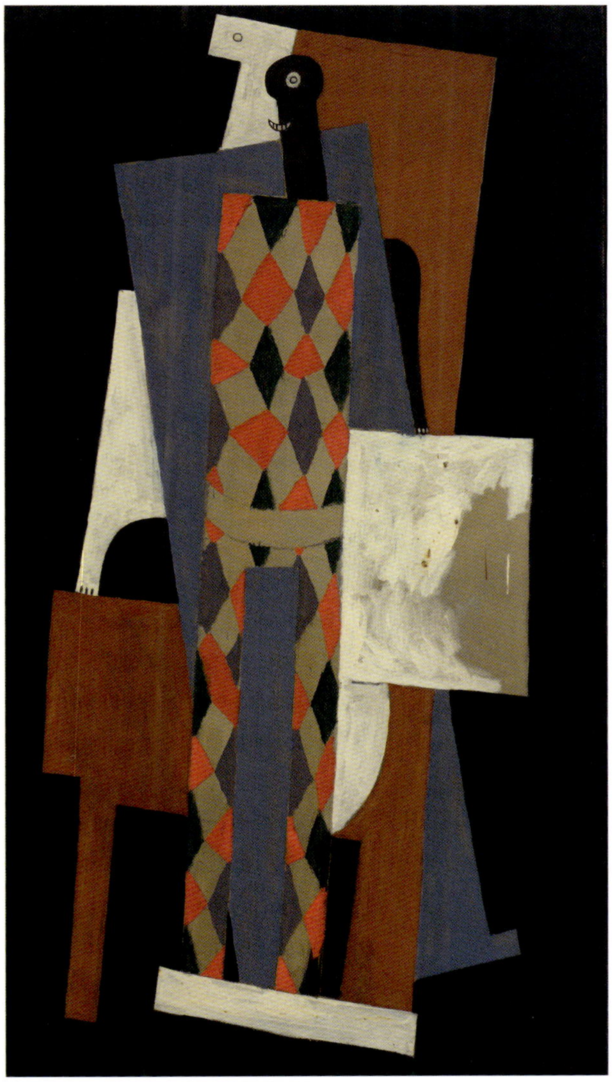

At the beginning of the war, Picasso painted relatively lighthearted works, in some cases humorously evoking his friends' patriotic fervor. *Playing Cards, Glasses, Bottle of Rum: "Vive la France"* incorporates into a still life the words "Long Live…" followed by a pair of crossed French tricolor flags. The pointillist dots of color seem equally celebratory, evoking the mood of a goodbye party. But Picasso's playful dialogue with French culture gave way to a more somber politics of appeasement, indicative of his suppression or reevaluation of his prewar anarchist sympathies. Starting in 1914, Picasso eschewed the language of Cubism in favor of a traditional naturalism, in works such as his *Portrait of Guillaume Apollinaire with Bandaged Head*. Apollinaire, in an article written from the front before he received a serious head wound, underscored the point by announcing that Picasso, "whose health is too weak to allow him" to fight, had "outdone Ingres" in his recent drawings.[41] By lamenting Picasso's "illness," Apollinaire created a fiction that accounted for his fellow artist's status as noncombatant during a period when those who refused to fight were labeled "defeatist." It is telling, therefore, that Apollinaire praises Picasso's emulation of Ingres, the nineteenth-century French artist most celebrated by the reactionary right, as a sign of his wartime contribution. In the absence of Picasso's military service, his "defense" of French culture in the guise of Ingresque portraits could stand in as evidence of his loyalty.

Yet simultaneously Picasso continued his exploration of Cubism, which was becoming increasingly abstract and bold. At a time when his partner, Eva Gouel, was tragically dying of cancer, Picasso painted a series of highly abstract works, culminating in *Harlequin* in the fall of 1915. These paintings echo his earlier images of *saltimbanques* (clowns or itinerant entertainers), which he had characteristically treated as allegorical self-portraits; he returned to this

Pablo Picasso, ***Harlequin***, 1915; oil on canvas, 72¼ × 41⅜ in. (183.5 × 105.1 cm); The Museum of Modern Art, New York, acquired through the Lillie P. Bliss Bequest

42
See Pierre Daix and Joan Rosselet, *Le Cubisme de Picasso: catalogue raisonné de l'oeuvre paint, des papiers collés et des assemblages, 1907–1916* (Neuchâtel, Switzerland: Ides et Calendes, 1979), nos. 762, 844, 845, 846, 849, 850, 856.

43
Daix and Rosselet, *Le Cubisme de Picasso*, nos. 873, 874.

44
Leighten, *The Liberation of Painting*, 111–22.

45
Leighten, *Re-Ordering the Universe*, 122–34.

46
See Lewis Kachur, "Gris, Cubismo y Collage," in *Juan Gris (1887–1927)*, ed. G. Tinterow (Madrid: Salas Pablo Ruiz Picasso, 1985), 33–44.

47
Juan Gris to Maurice Raynal, December 20, 1914, in *Letters of Juan Gris (1913–1927)*, ed. Daniel-Henry Kahnweiler, trans. Douglas Cooper (London: Humphries and Co., 1956), 20. For the impact of the war on these artists, see Leighten, *Re-Ordering the Universe*, 143–45; and Silver, *Esprit de Corps*, passim.

48
Gris to Raynal, October 17, 1916, in *Letters of Juan Gris*, 42.

theme later in naturalist form.[42] Depicted alone, the figure in the 1915 *Harlequin* stands or sits in a dark, geometric interior space, tilted awkwardly. Similarly, at the beginning of 1916, Picasso painted two works centered on a highly geometrized figure seated in a chair reading *Le Journal*,[43] a newspaper filled with little more than war news at the time. This lonely figure culminated in *Seated Man* (*Man Leaning on a Table*), where he is reduced to a pair of blank eyes looking out from the upper right. All these works are increasingly and rigorously rectilinear, this last one an unrelenting series of overlapping vertical rectangles.

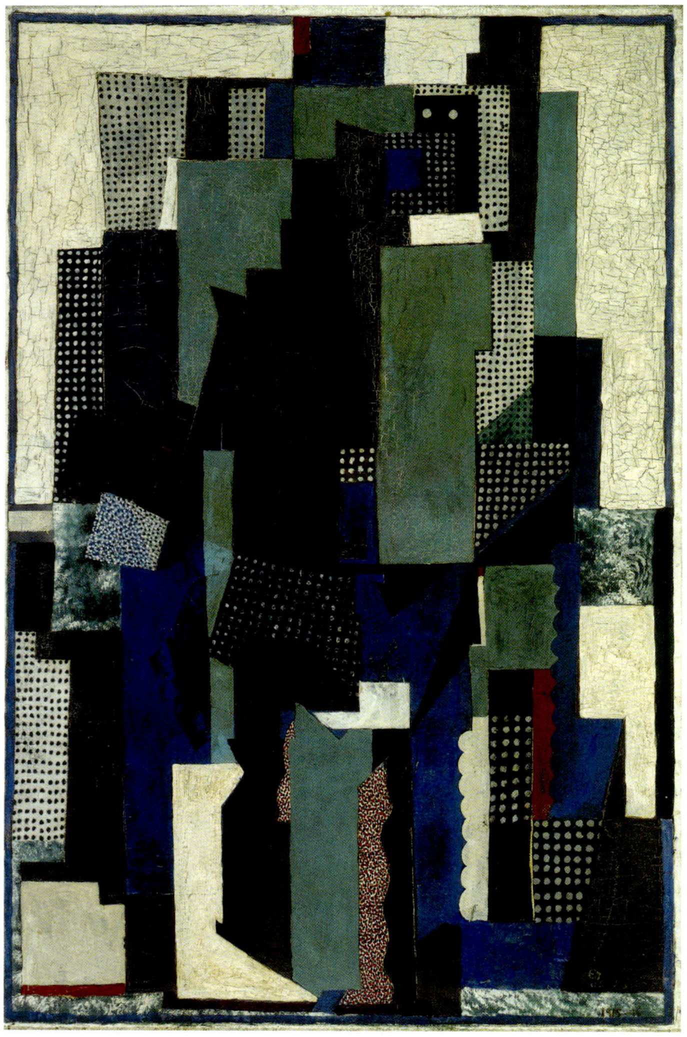

Gris, the other most important influence on Picasso in this period, likewise expressed anxiety and isolation during the war. He had had his own period of radical leftism—he was an accomplished satirist, contributing cartoons to the anarchist journal *L'Assiette au beurre*[44]—but he, like Picasso, suppressed overt politics in his Cubist work of this period. In 1912, through his use of pasted newsprint, Picasso had purposefully incorporated anarchist themes—war, pacifism, armaments profiteering, strike-breaking—at a moment of international crisis.[45] By manipulating public events like anti-war demonstrations in his first collages, Picasso negotiated his relation to the ideological views of pacifists, socialists, and anarchists opposed to the impending war. By contrast, Gris made most of his collages later, during the height of nationalist sentiment in France. When he occasionally included newspaper references to political controversies (such as the debate over expanding the draft from two years to three) in several collages of 1914,[46] the allusion is barely legible, muffled rather than amplified.

That Gris knew perfectly well the potential of such newsprint allusions is subtly visible in numerous works made during the war, as, for example, when he carefully painted the headline "Official Communiqués" on a newspaper in *Still Life with Checked Tablecloth*. He did this at a time when, as he wrote to a close friend, art critic Maurice Raynal, "I don't even like reading the newspapers because I am so impressed and terrified by what is happening."[47] Gris wrote later to Raynal, who was at the front in 1916, "I can't understand as you do this urge to massacre, to exterminate.... Ever since war broke out, all the civilians I come in contact with have their minds warped by events. There's not one of them intact; all have broken down under the pressure of war."[48] His works of this period reveal dark, shuttered interiors, at a time when public spaces were taken over by combatants openly hostile to

Pablo Picasso, ***Seated Man*** (***Man Leaning on a Table***), 1916; oil on canvas, 78¾ × 52 in. (200 × 132 cm); Pinacoteca Giovanni e Marella Agnelli

able-bodied civilian men, as in Louis Rémy Sabattier's *Café de la Paix in Wartime* (1917).[49] In *Still Life with Newspaper*, Gris seems to comment on his own immovable pacifism: the gloomy painting contains one bright and bitter spot of citron intersecting with the lighted masthead of the newspaper *The Intransigent*. Such works are perfectly in tune with his private, inward-turned world of wartime Cubism.

Perhaps partly because he missed the onset of the war by staying in Madrid, and partly because he was still relatively new to the Parisian scene, Rivera did not

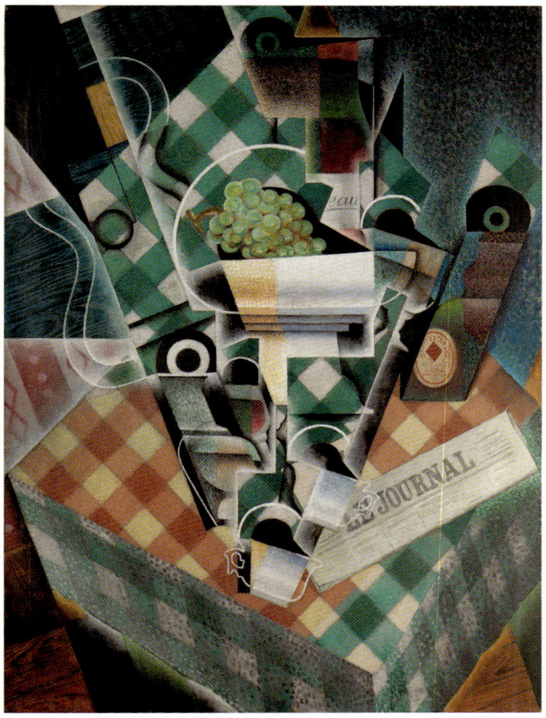

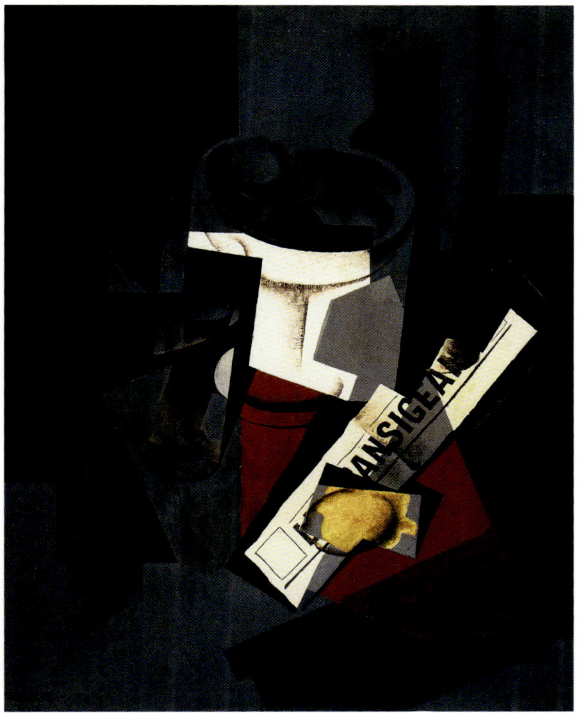

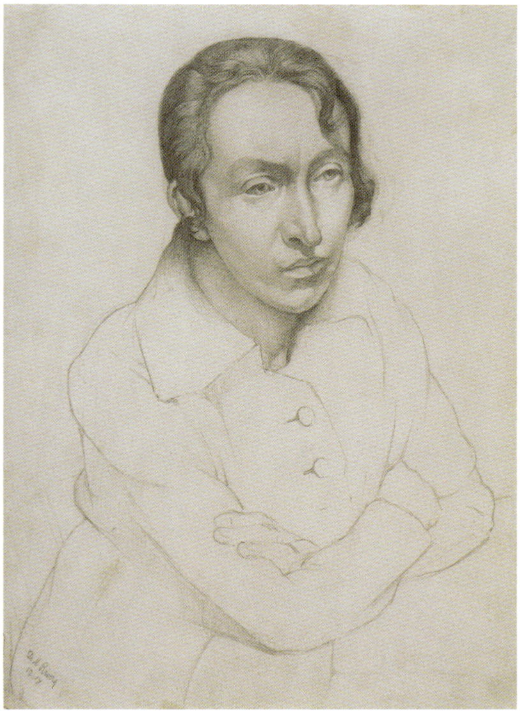

respond to the European war in the same way as Picasso and Gris. Mexican writer Alfonso Reyes had reported from Madrid that "Rivera was all fired up for getting back to France and going to war,"[50] but the artist did not act on this impulse. By the time he returned to Paris in 1915, the war had already descended into attrition and mass slaughter. Likewise, his developing friendship with Picasso and Gris may have tempered his enthusiasm for the European war. Having also spent time in Madrid with an old friend, novelist Martín Luis Guzmán, who had joined the Mexican Revolution in 1910, Rivera was newly aware that his own homeland was in turmoil, and he took advantage of the war period as a fertile time for the development of his art. He rivaled Picasso in a series of Ingresque pencil studies, drawing on his equally long and excellent academic training in such beautiful works as *Portrait of Angelina Beloff*.

LEFT Juan Gris, ***Still Life with Checked Tablecloth***, 1915; oil and graphite on canvas, 45 7/8 × 35 1/8 inches (116.5 × 89.2 cm); The Metropolitan Museum of Art, Leonard A. Lauder Cubist Collection, Purchase, Leonard A. Lauder Gift, 2014 (2014.463)

CENTER Juan Gris, ***Still Life with Newspaper***, 1916; oil on canvas, 29 × 23 3/4 in. (73.7 × 60.3 cm); The Phillips Collection, Washington, DC, acquired 1950

RIGHT Diego Rivera, ***Portrait of Angelina Beloff***, 1917; pencil on paper, 13 1/4 × 10 in. (33.7 × 25.4 cm); The Museum of Modern Art, gift of Mrs. Wolfgang Schoenborn in honor of René d'Harnoncourt

49
Published in *L'Illustration*, January 26, 1918. On the war and the wartime xenophobic atmosphere, see Leighten, *Re-Ordering the Universe*, 143–45; and Fae Brauer, "Commercial Spies and Cultural Invaders: The French Press, *Pénétration Pacifique* and Xenophobic Nationalism in the Shadow of War," in *Printed Matters: Printing, Publishing and Urban Culture in Europe in the Modern Period*, ed. Malcolm Gee and Tim Kirk (Aldershot, UK: Ashgate, 2002), 105–31.

50
Favela, *Rivera: The Cubist Years*, 91.

51 Ibid., 18.

52 Ibid., 70; Favela also discusses its relation to Rivera's circle of Russian friends, especially Ilya Ehrenburg, who celebrated folk art. Craven points out that this circle included revolutionary writer Anatoly Lunacharsky and modernist artists Natalia Goncharova, Ossip Zadkine, and Lipchitz, and asserts that "it was these latter associations, which caused 'Diego Diegovich' to learn Russian in order to participate more directly in their animated political discussions. Ultimately, these friendships served as a more enduring marker of the maturation of Rivera's radicalism during his years in Paris." Craven, *Rivera: As Epic Modernist*, 32.

Most importantly, in 1914 he arrived at his own mature Cubist style, while his work came far closer to the contemporaneous paintings of Picasso and Gris. Rivera's *Sailor at Lunch* (p. 104) is a brilliant synthesis of lessons learned from both artists, inscribed with Rivera's own flair. The painted faux-marble and wood grain are hallmarks of Picasso's and Gris's collage phases and subsequent paintings, while the cartoon-like face and ear are echoes of works such as Picasso's *Student with Newspaper* (p. 105). The perfect legibility of the plates and fish takes a page from Gris's play between abstraction and illustrational realism; this differs from Picasso's more obscured if equally humorous play on abstraction and realism in works such as *The Poet* (p. 106) and *Man with a Pipe* (p. 108), each with his mustache and a cheap clay pipe. Also like Gris, Rivera carefully planned the overall geometry and compositional structure in accordance with the golden section, a harmonic proportional ratio first studied in ancient Greece that Rivera had learned about in Mexico.[51] The dynamic curves that unite the layering of planes, however, and the rhythmic textural surface and overall boldness reflect Rivera's personal style, and his unusual choice to depict a military figure—including the sailor's red-and-blue hat, printed prominently with the word "PATRIE" (fatherland) in gold—may express the French patriotism he felt on the eve of the war but did not share with Picasso and Gris.

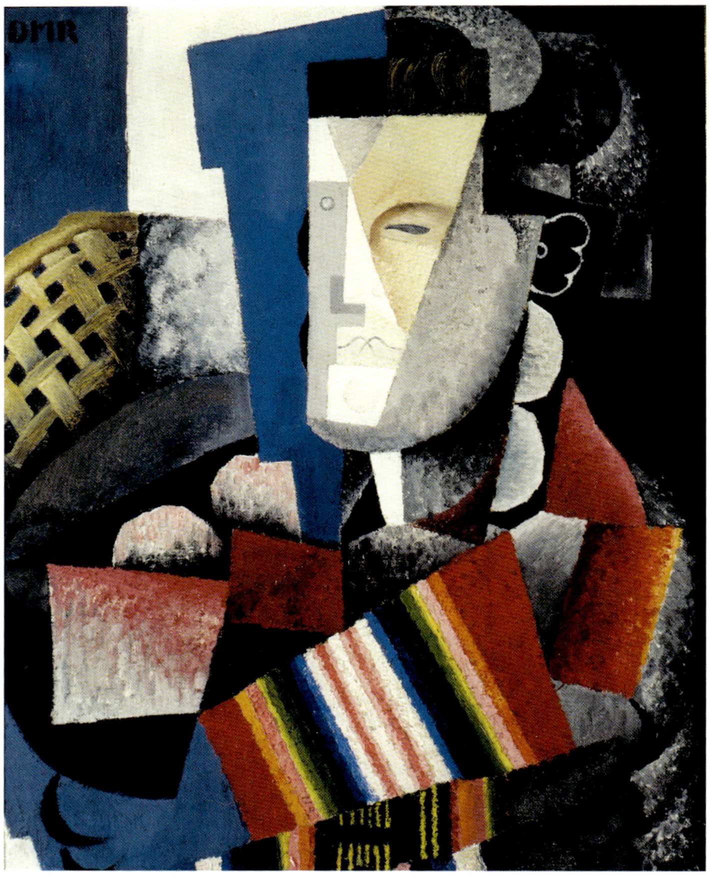

The most significant work of Rivera's wartime Cubism was *Zapatista Landscape* (p. 153). He achieved a unique and powerful Cubist style in a painting that summed up his own history and intellectual engagements, of which he was especially proud, as revealed by a period photograph of Rivera in his Paris studio with the painting (p. 11). Early in his career, Rivera had suppressed his Mexican origins, being concerned initially with mastering Spanish academic style, then grasping various techniques of European modernism. But in 1914 he began to assert his Mexican identity in his art for the first time, inserting the decorative, brightly colored stripes of a serape in *Jacques Lipchitz: Portrait of a Young Man* (1914; Museum of Modern Art, New York). He would repeat this motif in several other works,[52] appearing most prominently in his portrait of Martín Luis Guzmán,

Diego Rivera, ***Portrait of Martín Luis Guzmán***, 1915; oil on canvas, 28½ × 23⅜ in. (72.3 × 59.3 cm); Fundación Televisa, A.C. Mexico City

53
Favela, *Rivera: The Cubist Years*, 21, 90.
54
Guzmán remained in exile from 1914 to 1934.
55
Rivera again shared an interest in this subject with Dr. Atl, who published *Las artes populares en México* (México Libreria "Cultura") in 1921.
56
See Favela, *Rivera: The Cubist Years*, 107.
57
Rivera, *My Art, My Life*, 114, cited in Favela, *Rivera: The Cubist Years*, 108.
58
Atl had an exhibition of his "Landscapes of Mexico" in Paris in 1914: *Les Montagnes du Mexique du 1er Mai au 15 Mai 1914* at the Galerie Joubert et Richebourg. The exhibition catalogue cover is reproduced in Jean Charlot, *The Mexican Mural Renaissance, 1920–1925* (New Haven: Yale University Press, 1963), 48; see also Craven, *Rivera: As Epic Modernist*, 16. Favela notes that Rivera's Mexican landscapes are now lost. Favela, *Rivera: The Cubist Years*, 31.

who had served as a colonel under Pancho Villa until 1914.[53] Sitting in an *equipal* (a type of Mexican woven chair) and wrapped in a serape, Guzmán appears as an exiled man of action, forced into a dark interior.[54] The tension between the realist and abstract depictions of his face, chair, and serape are reinforced by the ambivalence of forms and spatial planes throughout the painting. No mere nationalistic reference, the serape evokes Mexican folk culture, both a symbol of the peasant uprising and a primitivist maneuver on Rivera's part, laying claim to his own creative authenticity and *mexicanidad*.[55]

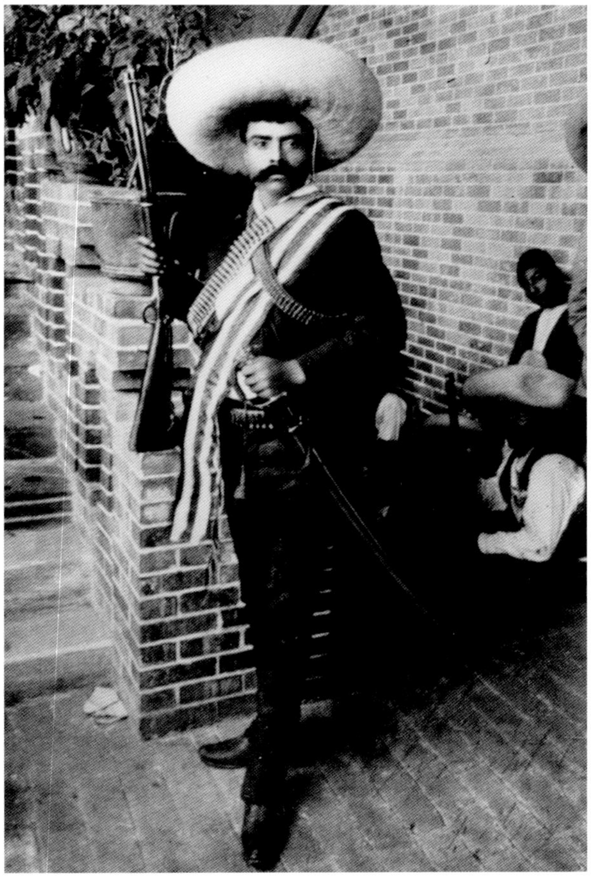

In *Zapatista Landscape*, Rivera confronts the revolution head-on. Based loosely on a photograph of Emiliano Zapata wearing a wide hat, serape, and cartridge belts while holding his rifle,[56] the painting was later described by Rivera this way:

> I recall that, at this time I was working in order to bring into focus the inmost truth about myself. The clearest revelation came from a Cubist canvas, *The Zapatistas* [*sic*] which I painted in 1916 [*sic*]. It showed a Mexican peasant hat hanging over a wooden box behind a rifle. Executed without any preliminary sketch in my Paris workshop, it is probably the most faithful expression of the Mexican mood that I have ever achieved.[57]

The "Mexican mood" in 1915, if Zapata is our reference point, was in revolt against attempts to stabilize a new government without the egalitarian changes demanded by revolutionaries like Zapata. Through its location and his focus on the accoutrements of this revolutionary leader, Rivera positions himself in Mexico and with the Zapatistas. The brilliant Cubist layering of planes, forms, and a variety of decorative surfaces—including the serape, wood grain, striped wallpaper, and pointillist dots—cluster in front of a grisaille landscape of volcanic mountains in the Valley of Mexico, familiar from earlier work by Dr. Atl and Rivera himself.[58] The simplified planarity and overlapping recession of the mountains contrast with the complex cluster of Cubist forms in the center. Rivera even seems to remind the viewer of his roots in Spanish academic realism with the trompe l'oeil image of a note pinned to the bottom right of the canvas. By drawing on a variety of approaches—from realism

Emiliano Zapata in Cuernavaca, Morelos, during the Mexican Revolution, c. 1911 to abstraction—Rivera's painting takes us on the long journey of his career from art student to modernist, simultaneously Mexican and international. As Craven notes, "one of the visual facts that stands out prominently is the conjunction of an internationalist and cosmopolitan language with the *campesino*-inspired regionalism of the scene being evoked."[59] The work celebrates the promise that Mexico was at last throwing off the yoke of Spanish colonialism—an absolute principle among anarchists—and of its heirs, the Mexican upper classes who aspired to imitate European and American models and despised the indigenous population.

Zapatista Landscape became a point of contention between Rivera and Picasso, who was working on an early version of *Seated Man* (*Man Leaning on a Table*) at the same time. It is evident from the photograph of Picasso in his studio in 1915 (p. 11) that *Seated Man*—at the time titled *Man Seated in Shrubbery*—was also pyramidal in structure and borrowed a green-over-black stippled foliage technique from Rivera's painting (seen on the left and right sides in *Zapatista Landscape* and even more in *Still Life with Gray Bowl*, p. 111). Picasso used this effect extensively in *Man Seated in Shrubbery* but subsequently converted *Seated Man* into an interior, possibly in response to Rivera's accusation that Picasso had stolen his technique. Ironically, exploring the subjects and styles of other painters was a hallmark and strength of both artists' development. Each had worked through numerous academic and modernist styles in arriving at his own, and each was a magpie in noticing effective aspects of the works of fellow artists. Sadly, this episode resulted in coolness in Rivera and Picasso's friendship, and they went their separate ways.[60]

Yet historically these two great Hispanic artists will always remain parallel. Certainly aspects of Cubism underlie all their future work.[61] Craven concludes:

> It is precisely because modernist art was a dehierarchizing and demotic critique of the overarching conventions of official Western art that the "collage" aesthetic could become so effective at accommodating a multicultural interplay of Western and non-Western elements on equal terms.… The Cubist contestation of Western cultural hegemony is precisely what allowed Diego Rivera to recruit Cubist collage and modernist space on behalf of the Mexican Revolution of 1910–20, with its unequivocal commitment to constructing a non-Eurocentric and postcolonial national identity.[62]

59
Craven, *Rivera: As Epic Modernist*, 39.

60
For differing interpretations of this story, see Favela, *Rivera: The Cubist Years*, 109–10; and John Richardson, *A Life of Picasso: The Cubist Rebel, 1907–1916* (New York: Knopf, 2007), 412–14. However, the fact that Picasso kept Rivera's *Cubist Composition* (*Still Life with a Bottle of Anis and Inkwell*) (1914–15) throughout his life, as well as two letters from Rivera to Picasso dated 1949 and 1957 (Fundación Almine y Bernard Ruiz-Picasso para el Arte), prove the two artists' continued connection; thanks to Diana Magaloni and Lilly Casillas for providing this information.

61
See also Anna Indych-López, "'An Abstract Courbet': The Cubist Spaces of Rivera's Murals," in *Diego Rivera: The Cubist Portraits, 1913–1917* (London: Philip Wilson, 2009), 137–55.

62
Craven, *Rivera: As Epic Modernist*, 50–51.

63
Herschel Chipp, *Picasso's Guernica: History, Transformations, Meanings* (Berkeley: University of California Press, 1988).

Craven acknowledges here the innovative ways in which Rivera dealt with space in his later murals and continued to structure his work in accordance with the golden section. Nonetheless, he did this in the form of readably modernist and primitivizing public paintings that were aimed at the general public as well as ruling elites, and that celebrated Mexico's multiclass and multicultural society, which was rooted in indigeneity. For his part, Picasso took a more abstract path, drawing more recognizably on Cubist techniques in his subsequent work. Yet his famous 1937 mural, *Guernica* (its composition visible in a study, p. 235), which overtly invokes ancient art and represents the culmination of all of his postwar work, was also aimed at the public. This work, an outcry against the deliberate aerial bombing of civilians at the start of the Spanish Civil War, was designed to be seen by visitors to the Spanish Pavilion at the 1937 Paris International Exposition.[63] Picasso and Rivera shared social and political views that first found expression in their early work and that remained relevant in their subsequent careers, and both continued to employ Cubist forms and techniques in their later art. Wartime Paris, despite its horrors and deprivations, fostered for both artists an exploration of ongoing Cubist forms of primitivism and remains central to understanding their work.

RIVERA'S TROPHY

JAMES OLES

1 Diego Rivera (with Gladys March), *My Art, My Life: An Autobiography* (New York: Citadel Press, 1960), 105–6. The interviews were conducted mainly in 1944 and 1945. John Richardson (who relied on Ramón Favela, see note 5) provides no further details in his masterful biography, *A Life of Picasso: Volume II, 1907–1917* (New York: Random House, 1996), 369–70. The two artists lived on either side of the Montparnasse Cemetery: Picasso at 5 bis, rue Victor Schoelcher, and Rivera at 26, rue du Départ. I like to think of them playing around, much like Picasso, Ortiz de Zárate, and others did on that afternoon in 1916 as delightfully recounted in Billy Klüver's *A Day with Picasso* (Cambridge, MA: MIT Press, 1999).

Although the paper trail is scant, Pablo Picasso and Diego Rivera first met sometime in the spring of 1914. What we know about this meeting depends entirely on what Rivera told American journalist Gladys March many years later (for the full account, see p. 154). According to Rivera, he was introduced to Picasso by his friend, Chilean painter Manuel Ortiz de Zárate:

> I went to Picasso's studio intensely keyed up.... My friends and I were absorbed for hours, looking at his paintings. Our interest so pleased him that he let us see his most intimate sketchbooks. Finally,... when I made a motion to go, Picasso asked me to stay and have lunch with him, after which he went back with me to my studio. There he asked to see everything I had done from beginning to end.... After I had showed Picasso these paintings, we had dinner together and stayed up practically the whole night talking. Our theme was Cubism—what it was trying to accomplish, what it had already done, and what future it had as a "new" art form.... In Paris, Picasso and I used to have the best times, especially when we were by ourselves. Then we would say things about other painters which we would never tell anybody else.[1]

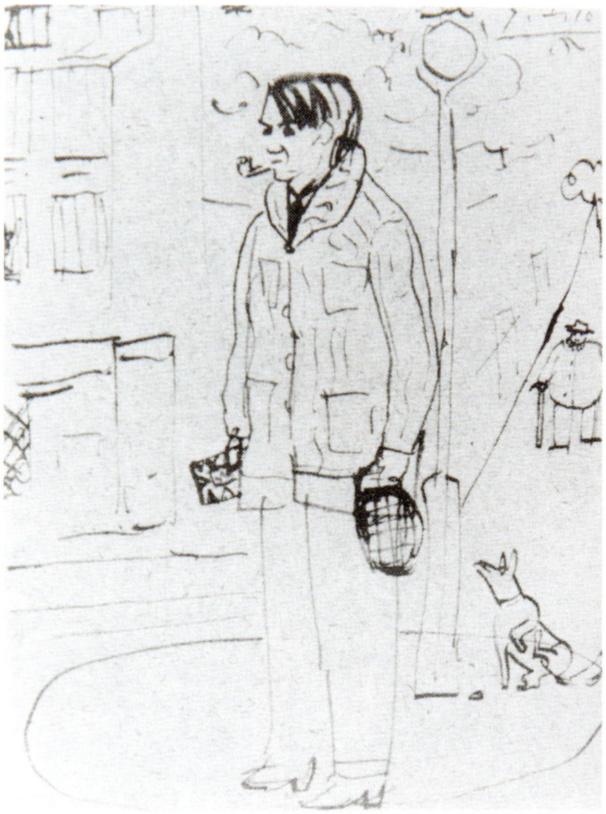

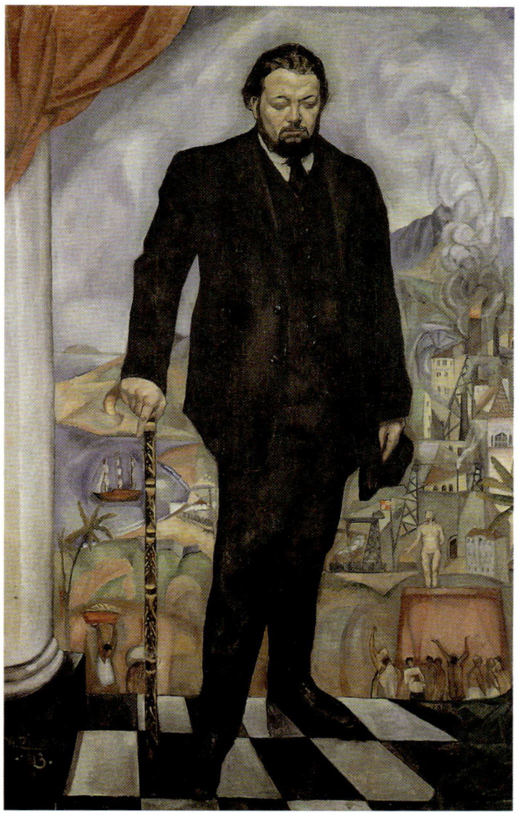

LEFT Pablo Picasso, ***Self-Portrait as Suitor***, 1915; pen and ink on paper, 5⅞ × 4½ in. (15 × 11.5 cm); Sala Gaspar, Barcelona

RIGHT Alexandre Zinoviev, ***Portrait of Diego Rivera***, 1913; oil on canvas, 76½ × 50 in. (194.3 × 127.3 cm)

This passage reveals a nervousness followed by a quick intimacy, partly based on their shared language, and the details seem wholly reliable despite Rivera's propensity for retrospective exaggeration about other aspects of his life.[2] In earlier accounts, however, Rivera was far less wordy about the encounter,[3] and his most important biographers, Bertram Wolfe and Loló de la Torriente, do not even mention the meeting. We have almost no evidence of this friendship from Picasso's side, for he appears not to have thought too much about Rivera in later years, just as a movie star forgets the fan for whom meeting the star is a life-changing event. Picasso's best-known record of Rivera is a self-portrait sketch he made in 1915, in which the Mexican artist—identified unmistakably by his girth and carved walking stick—appears in the distance (p. 147). According to John Richardson, this drawing hints at sexual rivalries, but it is painterly rivalries that are the subject of this essay, and on that topic, Picasso had even less to say.[4]

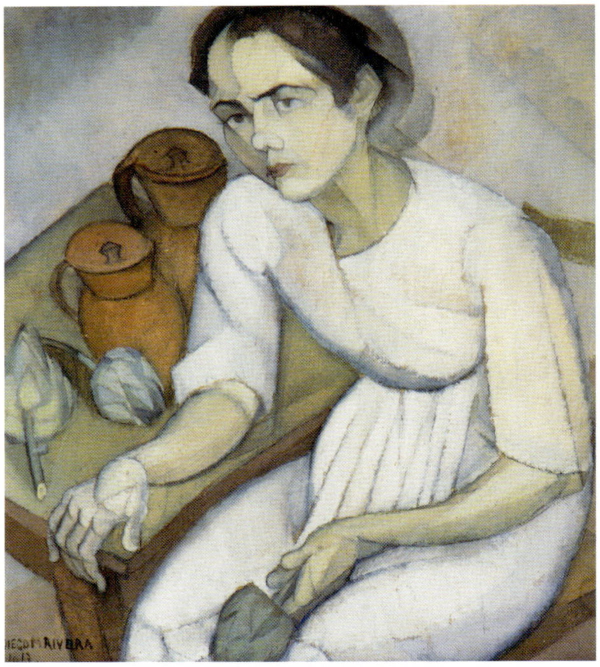

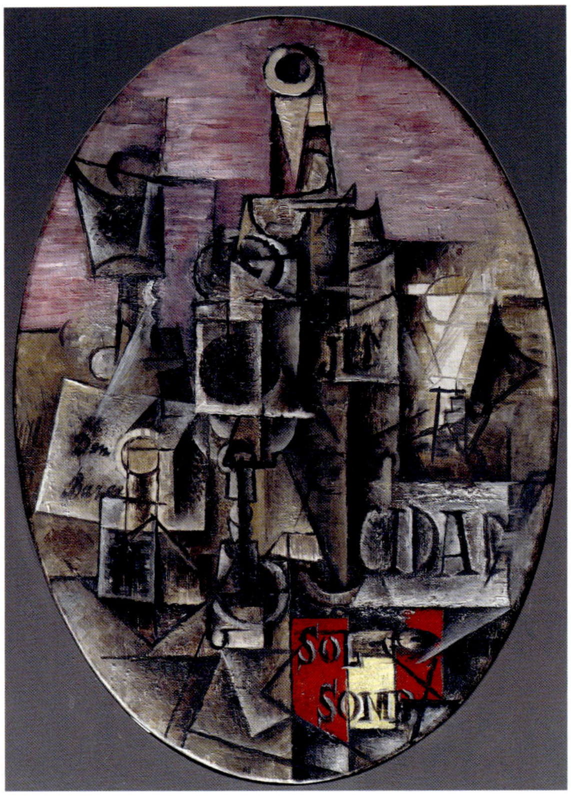

By the time he met Picasso, Rivera had advanced quickly in the competitive Parisian art world. He came to Cubism rather late, via a circuitous route that had taken him from Mexico City (where he had been the star pupil at the conservative Academy of San Carlos) to Madrid and Toledo, before setting up a studio in Montparnasse in the fall of 1912. He enjoyed some critical success after showing three Cubist paintings completed in the spring of 1913, including *Girl with Artichokes*, at the Salon d'Automne that November. Rivera was then picked up by Picasso's former dealer, Berthe Weill, who gave him his first one-man show in Paris in April 1914, around the time he first visited Picasso's studio.

The complex story of Diego Rivera's "Cubist years" has been told in detail by other scholars.[5] My research focus has been on a small group of works from around 1915 that include explicit references to Mexico. Although their nationalist characteristics have been somewhat overdetermined or exaggerated by scholars, these visual souvenirs do reveal nostalgia for the nation he had left behind in 1907. They are hardly unique in this, since references to the local rippled through prior Cubist paintings, as in Picasso's own *Spanish Still Life* (1912), with its bright Spanish flag, Barcelona newspaper, and textual references to the bullfight. Indeed, some of Rivera's still lifes also include Spanish iconography (the *porrón*, the bottle of anis), not surprising given his extended residence there.

LEFT Diego Rivera, ***Girl with Artichokes***, 1913; oil on canvas, 31¾ × 29½ in. (80.5 × 75 cm); private collection

RIGHT Pablo Picasso, ***Spanish Still Life*** (***Sun and Shadow***), 1912; oil and enamel on canvas, 24¾ × 18⅛ in. (63 × 46 cm); Lille Métropole Museum of Modern, Contemporary and Outsider Art

The Mexican images raise several fascinating theoretical issues, some of which are beyond the scope of this essay. All juxtapose or combine urban/international and rural/Mexican messages, as David Craven emphasized in his discussion of Rivera's 1915 paintings, though perhaps in a way that overstated their revolutionary or critical purpose.[6] It might be more helpful to see Rivera's "Mexicanized" Cubism as a manifestation of that "marginal cosmopolitanism" described by Natalia Majluf, in which the French art system encouraged cosmopolitans from abroad (especially Latin Americans) to perform cultural difference once in Paris, as a means of preserving French artistic hegemony.[7] But it is also true that a least a few of Rivera's Cubist paintings were forms of resistance, not only to the "internationalism" of Cubism, but to the charged rhetoric of French nationalism, which increased with the outbreak of war in 1914, threatening numerous foreigners and marginalizing those not required to fight.[8]

In this essay, I want to concentrate on a singular picture that Rivera created in the summer of 1915, midway through his Cubist adventure, that is both his most acclaimed Cubist painting and one of the most famous and complex avant-garde works ever produced by a Latin American artist: the work known today as *Zapatista Landscape* (p. 153). The distorting lens of that title has colored all subsequent interpretations, which invariably conclude that the work provides evidence of Rivera's sympathies with the Mexican Revolution—a bitter civil war then under way across the Atlantic—and particularly with the peasant revolt led by General Emiliano Zapata. Such political readings, whether inaccurate or merely limited, have obscured the actual history of the painting and the *artistic* battles that more immediately shaped its forms and content (thus, to the extent possible, I will avoid using the traditional title). For beyond any period letters or reviews, or subsequent memoirs or interviews, this painting provides the most compelling and direct evidence of Rivera's specific relationship to Picasso, as both mentor and rival.

A PAINTING AND ITS TITLE

Rivera, who had been living in Spain since the summer of 1914, returned to Montparnasse in the spring of 1915, a difficult and "insular" time for artists living in France: the war caused economic hardship, though it also forged tight artistic and personal alliances.[9] As Bertram Wolfe noted, Rivera "painted all through the war, even when fuel was lacking and his fingers were numb, [working] swiftly with unceasing energy."[10] The painting known today as *Zapatista Landscape* was completed in June or July of 1915; it was one of Rivera's largest Cubist compositions, hard evidence of its importance to the artist.[11] Surprisingly, it seems it was never exhibited in the period; instead, it was the first of his paintings purchased by Rivera's then dealer, Léonce Rosenberg.[12] A receipt dated November 3, 1915, in the

2
I have explored Rivera's invented relationship with Cézanne in an unpublished essay, "Cézanne Effects in Latin America: From Diego Rivera to Jesús Rafael Soto."

3
"From my early days in Paris, I was first the disciple of Picasso, and later his friend." Diego Rivera, as told to Katherine Anne Porter, "From a Mexican Painter's Notebook," *The Arts* 7 (January 1925), 21. In another interview, he implied that he had met Picasso before his brief return to Mexico in 1910–11. Ernestine Evans, *The Frescoes of Diego Rivera* (New York: Harcourt Brace, 1929), 25.

4
Richardson, *Life of Picasso*, 367. Based on an interview with the original owner, Picasso's lover Gaby Depeyre, Richardson believes the sketch shows Picasso waiting for his rival to leave so he can visit Depeyre's apartment. Rivera, however, is walking *toward* Picasso, not away from him.

After this essay was completed, I learned that a mounted photograph of Picasso's *Gas-Jet and Guitar* (1913; National Gallery, Prague) had been discovered in the archive at the Museo Frida Kahlo in Mexico City. A pencil inscription signed by Picasso and dated May 12, 1915, seems to indicate close camaraderie though not excessive generosity, since it is only a reproduction. A 1915 painting by Rivera located in the Picasso estate during the organization of this exhibition, and previously unpublished, was possibly acquired by Picasso around the same time, but whether a gift or purchase, directly from the artist or not, are facts yet to be determined. For one interpretation of the significance of this new evidence, as well as of much later letters Rivera wrote to Picasso, see pp. 136–37.

5
Rivera's Cubist period was explored simultaneously by Olivier Debroise, *Diego de Montparnasse* (Mexico City: Fondo de Cultura Económica, 1979), and Ramón Favela, first in his doctoral dissertation ("'Rivera Cubista': A Critical Study of the Early Career of Diego Rivera, 1898–1921," University of Texas at Austin, 1984) and then in *Diego Rivera: The Cubist Years* (Phoenix: Phoenix Art Museum, 1986). Subsequent exhibitions and publications include *Memory, Politics, Place: The Cubist Paintings of Diego Rivera* (National Gallery of Art, Washington, DC, 2004), Luis-Martín Lozano, *Diego Rivera cubista: De la Academia a la Vanguardia (1907–1921)* (Malaga: Fundación Unicaja, Municipalidad de Malaga, 2011), and Silvia Navarrete et al, *Diego Rivera: The Cubist Portraits, 1913–1917* (Dallas: Meadows Museum, SMU, in association with Philip Wilson Publishers, 2009).

6
See David Craven, *Diego Rivera: As Epic Modernist* (New York: G. K. Hall, 1997), 38–41, 50–51; see also Craven, "Postcolonial Modernism in the Work of Diego Rivera and José Carlos Mariátegui, or New Light on a Neglected Relationship," *Third Text* 15:54 (Spring 2001), 3–16.

7
Natalia Majluf, "Ce n'est pas le Pérou, or, the Failure of Authenticity: Marginal Cosmopolitans at the Paris Universal Exhibition of 1855," *Critical Inquiry* 23:4 (Summer 1997), 868–93.

8
Picasso's wartime references to French nationalism—as in *Playing Cards, Glasses, Bottle of Rum: "Vive la France"* (1914/15, Metropolitan Museum of Art)—have been alternately interpreted as patriotic and ironic. See, for example, Richardson, *Life of Picasso*, 351.

9
Favela, *Rivera: The Cubist Years*, 99.

10
Bertram Wolfe, *Diego Rivera: His Life and Times* (New York: Knopf, 1939), 106.

11
Favela, "Rivera Cubista," 581.

12
Wolfe, *Life and Times*, 106; Favela, *Rivera: The Cubist Years*, 108.

Rosenberg archive in Paris registers the work as simply "Nature morte mexicaine" (Mexican still life), a descriptive title in all likelihood assigned by the dealer without much input from the artist.[13]

Although Rosenberg had aggressively built up his stock during the war, sales were few, and the painting probably remained in gallery storage after his break with Rivera in 1917 following the bitter quarrels known to insiders in Paris as *l'affaire Rivera*.[14] Writing in 1918, David Alfaro Siqueiros informed his Mexican readers that "a major part of the [Cubist] work of Rivera is in the hands of a Jewish *'marchand'* [merchant] who hides it maliciously, and from whose tyrannical control Rivera has freed himself."[15] Siqueiros's anti-Semitism obscures what was probably a wise business decision: Rosenberg (in alliance with poet Pierre Reverdy) may have had specific disagreements with Rivera's general approach to Cubism (attacking his embrace of local references and identifiable portrait subjects, for example), but Rivera's total rejection of Cubism by 1918—which challenged its general validity as an artistic language—had also depreciated the value of his Cubist paintings. There is some evidence that Rosenberg dumped them on the market in the early 1920s, after Rivera had left for Mexico.[16] The picture was later acquired by the Mexican politician and agronomist Marte R. Gómez, a close friend of the artist who had been the patron of his mural cycle at the National Agricultural School in Chapingo in the 1920s. Rivera had probably set him on the trail of specific paintings formerly owned by Rosenberg, but the precise circumstances of the acquisition remain unclear.[17]

The earliest published reference to the 1915 picture appears in an article by Martín Luis Guzmán, written just a couple of months after it was finished. Guzmán focused mainly on the experience of having his own portrait (p. 142) done by Rivera but, in an aside, described the artist's "latest painting" as "a material and spiritual landscape of the Mexican highlands."[18] In a letter to Guzmán dated February 1916, Rivera referred to the work as "mi trofeo mexicano" (my Mexican trophy), and this must have been how he referred to the painting in general, for that same month another friend, poet and critic Max Jacob, mentioned Rivera's "trophée mexicaine" in a humorous conservation, published in Alfred Stieglitz's magazine 291. Jacob's wordplay is difficult to capture in English, but at one point an art critic turns to Rivera and says: "I have seen a Mexican trophy of yours that I was tempted to mistake for a Picasso. If this mistake is not in my favor, it might prove very much to be in yours." The painter responds: "Let's prefer mistake [*méprise*] to surprise, which would hide some contempt [*mépris*]."[19] We will return to this confusion, which might not have been taken so lightly by either artist at the time.

Some variant of the current title (in Spanish, *Paisaje zapatista*) was probably given to the work around the time it was acquired by Gómez, though it does not appear in print until 1951, when the catalogue to Rivera's 1949 retrospective at the Palacio de Bellas Artes was published.[20] Rather than being eternally fixed, titles sometimes evolve over time or are transmitted in casual conversation rather than written down.

13
Michele Greet generously shared this information with me. Although the receipt includes neither photograph nor dimensions, I think it likely this French title applies to the present *Zapatista Landscape* rather than *Still Life with Gray Bowl* (p. 111), since the Mexican imagery in the latter is far less prominent. On titles, see Daniel-Henry Kahnweiler, *The Rise of Cubism* (New York: Wittenborn, Schultz, 1949), 89; Jean Sutherland Boggs et al., *Picasso & Things* (Cleveland: Cleveland Museum of Art, 1992), 97.

14
For details, see Favela, *Rivera: The Cubist Years*, 121–51; See also Christopher Green, *Cubism and Its Enemies: Modern Movements and Reaction in French Art* (New Haven: Yale University Press, 1987), 7–11.

15
David Alfaro Siqueiros, "Diego M. Rivera, Pintor de América," *El Universal Ilustrado* 5, no. 217 (July 1918), 20–21.

16
The Rosenberg archive includes a letter to Rivera informing him of an auction of works held on February 14, 1921; the envelope was marked "return to sender." See also William H. Robinson, "Cubist Heresies: Diego Rivera and the Parisian Avant-Garde, 1913–1917," in *Diego Rivera: Art & Revolution* (Mexico City: INBA/Landucci, 1999), 123, 125.

17
Favela, "Rivera Cubista," 598, n151. Gómez told Favela that it had been bought by "a member of his staff." He was Mexico's ambassador to the League of Nations, later Mexico's minister plenipotentiary in France in 1935–36, but according to a recent study of his collection, the work was acquired in 1946. María Elena Durán Payán and Ana María Rodríguez Pérez, *Marte R. Gómez y Diego Rivera: Historia de una colección* (Guanajuato, Mexico: Ediciones La Rana, 2012), 41. The Instituto Nacional de Bellas Artes acquired Gómez's important collection of works by Rivera in 1966.

18
Martín Luis Guzmán, "Diego Rivera y la filosofía del cubismo" (finished by September 1915), in *Obras completas de Martín Luis Guzmán*, vol. 1 (Mexico City: Compañía General de Ediciones, 1961), 86; cited in Favela, *Rivera: The Cubist Years*, 107.

19
Rivera to Guzmán (February 2, 1916); Max Jacob, "La Vie Artistique," 291, 12 (February 1916), back cover; both cited in Favela (107) but the latter is newly translated here (with generous assistance from Isidore Bethel). The original reads:

> Le Critique d'art: […] j'ai vu de vous un trophée mexicain que j'ai eu la tentation de prendre pour un Picasso. Si la méprise ne prouve pas en ma faveur elle prouve beaucoup en la vôtre.
> Mr. Rivera: Préferons méprise à surprise qui cacherait quelque mépris.

20
Diego Rivera: 50 años de su labor artística (Mexico City: Instituto Nacional de Bellas Artes, 1951), illustrated in color but not discussed.

In his own discussions of the picture in the 1940s and 1950s, Rivera provided several alternatives, none of which exactly match the current title. In the longest of these statements, made to Gladys March, he said: "I recall that, at this time I was working in order to bring into focus the inmost truth about myself. The clearest revelation, however, came from a Cubist canvas, 'The Zapatistas,' which I painted in 1916 [*sic*]. It showed a Mexican peasant hat hanging over a wooden box behind a rifle. Executed without any preliminary sketch in my Paris workshop, it is probably the most faithful expression of the Mexican mood that I have ever achieved."[21] Cuban journalist Loló de la Torriente provided two titles, *El guerrillero* or *Paisaje y naturaleza muerta zapatista* ("The Guerilla" or "Zapatista Landscape and Still Life"), but barely discussed the work, except to assert that it was a "direct projection of the Mexican Revolution within Cubism."[22]

I think it is likely that Rivera, presented with the picture after all those years, and probably not remembering that Rosenberg had called it "Mexican Still Life," invented—rather than recalled—that the painting had something to do with the rebellious forces unleashed during the Mexican Revolution. As a former minister of education and director of the National Agricultural School, Gómez surely would have embraced a title that referred to agrarian reform, and Rivera might have catered to his friend's concerns. But the artist, a great storyteller, also had a *personal* interest in giving the painting a revolutionary pedigree: it was a way of healing an unhealed wound.

In the 1910s, Rivera had basically missed the defining event of his generation, unlike those witnesses and participants who would become, once back in Mexico, his closest colleagues—foremost among them, José Clemente Orozco and David Alfaro Siqueiros. This is why, beginning in the 1920s, he told interviewers that during the brief hiatus in his European sojourn—from October 1910 to June 1911, when he returned to Mexico to exhibit his works at the Academy of San Carlos and witnessed the fall of Díaz—he had been deeply affected by the revolution. In the 1930s, when he was often under assault from some on the left for "reactionary" alliances, he embellished the story further, telling Wolfe that he had "watched the incredibly swift flow of events from close by in the State of Morelos. He was so stirred he forgot to paint, even to make pencil sketches."[23] Wolfe was healthily suspicious about such stories—including one March recorded about Rivera's "six months as an active rebel" when he had "joined Zapata's peasant partisans in the state of Morelos"—calling them such "fantasies" that he was unable to find within them any "solid kernel of prosaic fact."[24]

We know that Rivera was in close contact with Mexican exiles in Paris, particularly Guzmán, a follower of Pancho Villa who escaped to Europe in March 1915; he could also have read any number of newspaper or magazine articles about the war, many of them illustrated with photographs.[25] But there is no documentary evidence—not a single letter—that indicates what Rivera thought about the Mexican Revolution

21
Rivera, *My Art, My Life*, 114.

22
Loló de la Torriente, *Memoria y razón de Diego Rivera*, vol. 2 (Mexico City: Editorial Renacimiento, 1959), 68. In another interview, Rivera called it simply *El guerrillero*. Luis Suárez, *Confesiones de Diego Rivera* (Mexico City: Era, 1962), 122.

23
Wolfe, *Life and Times*, 62.

24
Rivera, *My Art, My Life*, 91; Wolfe, *Life and Times*, 63. See also de la Torriente, *Memoria y razón*, vol. 1, 347–48.

25
Guzmán's early account of the revolution, *La querella de México*, was published in Paris in 1915, after Rivera had completed *Zapatista Landscape*. He was actually a staunch anti-Zapatista.

26
Richardson (*Life of Picasso*, 343) notes that when Pierre Daix asked Picasso if an antiwar speech included in the newspaper clippings in *Bottle of Suze* (p. 132) related to his wartime pacifism, he responded: "Well, I knew people would find this later and understand."

27
Favela, *Rivera: The Cubist Years*, 108; Craven, *Rivera: As Epic Modernist*, 50.

during the Mexican Revolution itself. (Although one might say the same about Picasso and his ideological view of World War I, there is actually physical evidence he used his early collages to express his pacifist sympathies.)[26] Suddenly, when Gómez repatriated his lost "Mexican trophy" from 1915, Rivera had the "solid kernel of prosaic fact" he needed: a bellicose picture armed to the teeth, a portrait of a warrior. Here was incontrovertible visual proof that he had not been just a bourgeois practitioner of art-for-art's-sake far from home, but rather a Zapatista sympathizer, way back in the summer of 1915.

Rivera's sly maneuver was unbelievably successful, for every single analysis of the painting since that time—no matter how much attention was paid to the facts just discussed—has connected it directly to the Mexican Revolution. According to Ramón Favela, the "meaning of the painting in its Parisian context was obvious. It was about the accoutrements of a civil war and revolution existing in the sky-blue realm of the artist's detached consciousness." David Craven relied extensively on the work's supposed historical references in his extended discussion of Rivera's radical modernism, which theorizes Rivera's "postcolonial" recruitment of "Cubist collage and modernist space on behalf of the Mexican Revolution of 1910–20" (going so far as to highlight the work's "non-Western" elements).[27] A lot rests, then, on what the painting actually depicts.

BRAVURA AND BRAVADO

The composition basically consists of a still life dominated by a broad-brimmed felt sombrero and woven serape, placed upon a blond wooden box set atop a low table; a rifle is propped up in front, while a leather belt, some fruit, and ambiguous clusters of green and brown forms are set to the sides. The floor and walls of the artist's studio are signaled by the gray trapezoidal field, but the still life seems to have been transposed to another realm. An unmodulated field of blue fills the lower part of the canvas, separated by mottled shrubbery from the upper part, which is dominated by a snowcapped volcano (Popocatepetl) and the ash cones typical of the Valley of Mexico, a reference noticed from the very beginning by Guzmán. At lower right, a trompe l'oeil sheet of blank paper looks like it was unfolded before being nailed to the surface. The signature and date "D. M. RIVERA 15" are written in small, black, stencil-like lettering at the lower left.

Rivera's painting is a tour de force of Cubist practice. Objects are rendered in two- and three-dimensions, shown front and back, inside and out, near and far, colorful and colorless, as presence and as absence, solid and void, falsely real and really false. Some details, such as the ropes around the sombrero's crown or the wood of the rifle stock, are rendered with representational fidelity, while others have been abstracted almost beyond recognition. These qualities coexist not only within the entire pictorial space but within individual objects: most are progressively deconstructed from right to left, as if placed on a continuum from realism to abstraction. The sombrero, for example, is fractured into some twenty parts in order to emphasize differing colors, materials, textures, and volumes.[28] The contrast between representational systems is nowhere clearer than in the difference between the two blue backgrounds.

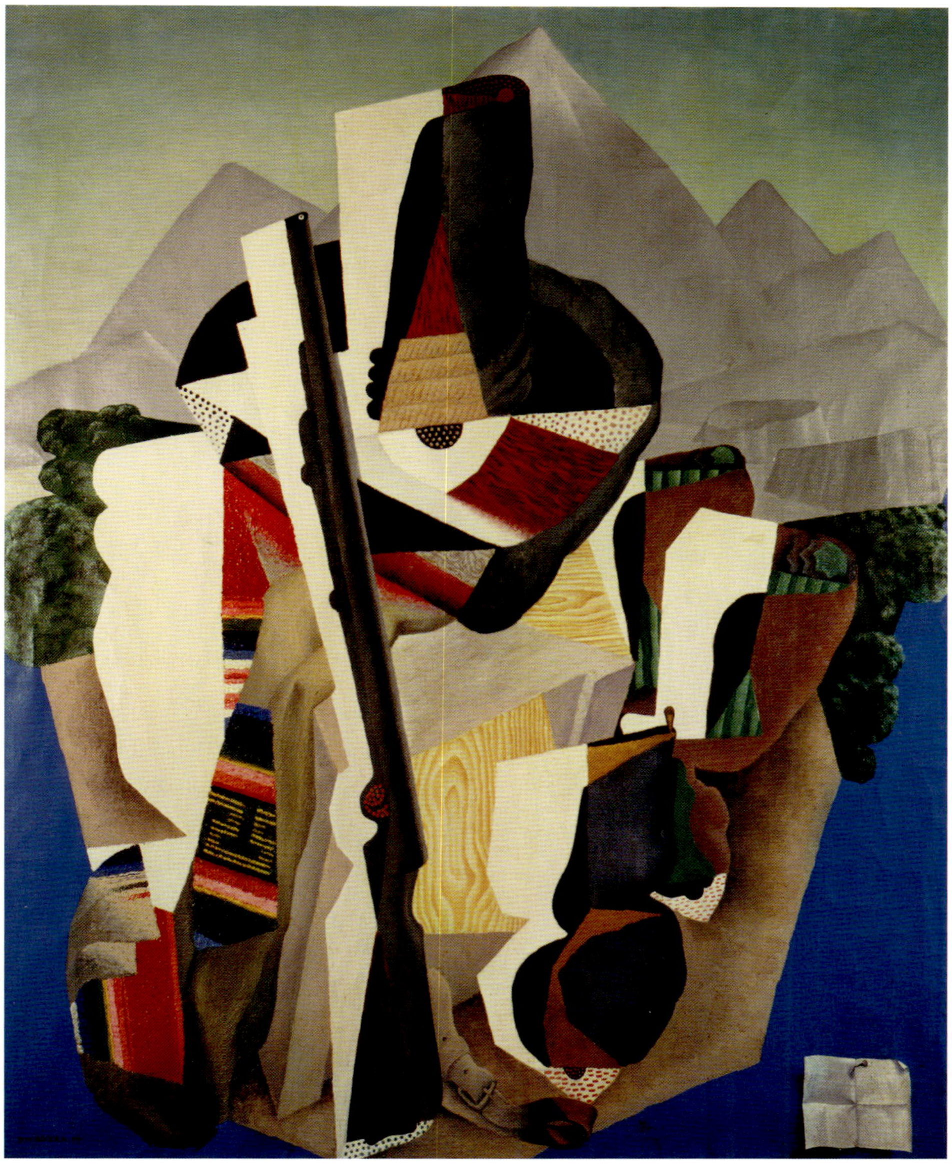

Diego Rivera, ***Zapatista Landscape***, 1915

The still life includes several formal devices typical of the synthetic Cubist style Rivera had developed by 1915—which was labeled "Classical" or "Crystal" Cubism at the time—and that are evident in other works of the same year, including *Still Life with Gray Bowl* (p. 111). Without denying the originality of Rivera's language, his innovative selection, appropriation, and assembly of these devices, or the multiplicity of histories and sources behind any particular detail, I would like to emphasize that most of these Cubist devices—but only a few of the objects—were clearly lifted from Picasso, who had often lifted them from Braque. The one prominent exception is Rivera's technique of creating an illusion of foliage by stippling paint with a brush or sponge. In no particular order, the stolen goods include crisply defined forms that overlap each other like sheets of colored paper in a collage (especially bright blue paper); "pointillist" undersides (spaces we know are there but cannot see); ghostly white areas that echo objects and indicate either the space they vacate as the painter shifts his viewing angle or geometric abstractions of the objects themselves; stencil lettering, though here used for the signature on the front of the canvas, personalizing a formal device that had been about *impersonality*; and trompe l'oeil jokes and wood graining.[29] This array of elements proved how much Rivera had learned since arriving in Paris; that he had, in fact, caught up.

Besides these iconographic details, the picture's composition also alludes to prior Cubist practice. The roughly oval arrangement of the central section, for example, finds its origins in paintings by Braque and Picasso from early in the decade. The witty conflation of still life and landscape, though following a long tradition in European painting, also seems a direct reference to the contemporaneous work of his rivals, especially Picasso and Gris.[30] In fact, in the spring or summer of 1915 Rivera created four paintings that Favela called "still lifes in landscapes and landscapes in still

28
A diagonal rectangle with incised motifs is probably the embroidered area beneath the brim. The ropes around the crown are in low relief, and might have been impressed with actual cordage to create a realistic texture.

29
It may be pure coincidence, but the first paintings—rather than collages—by Braque (*Homage to J.S. Bach*) and Picasso (*Souvenir du Havre*) to use wood graining were, like Rivera's painting, tied to specific persons or places.

30
Favela, "Rivera Cubista," 580. Favela is noncommittal about who was the first to engage in such genre-bending.

MEETING PICASSO

Rivera's Recollections

In 1913 I had reached the Cubist phase of my development. I worked hard at my Cubist paintings all through that year and the first half of 1914, because everything about the movement fascinated and intrigued me.

It was a revolutionary movement, questioning everything that had previously been said and done in art. It held nothing sacred. As the old world would soon blow itself apart, never to be the same again, so Cubism broke down forms as they had been seen for centuries, and was creating out of the fragments new forms, new objects, new patterns, and—ultimately—new worlds. When it dawned on me that all this innovation had little to do with real life, I would surrender all the glory and acclaim that Cubism had brought me for a way in art truer to my inmost feelings....

The greatest of the Cubists and my idol at the time was Pablo Picasso. I was eager to meet this already celebrated Spaniard, but my shyness prevented me from approaching him directly. Somehow, however, Picasso learned of my feelings towards him and one day he sent me a message through a mutual friend, [Chilean painter Ortiz de Zarate]....

I went to Picasso's studio intensely keyed up. My feelings were like those of a good Christian who expects to meet Our Lord, Jesus Christ.

The interview was marvelous. Picasso's studio was full of his exciting canvases; grouped together they had an impact more powerful than when shown by dealers as individual masterpieces. They were like living parts of an organic world Picasso had himself created.

As for the man, will and energy blazed from his round black eyes. His black, glossy hair was cut short like the hair of a circus strong man. A luminous atmosphere seemed to surround him. My friends and I were absorbed for hours, looking at his paintings. Our interest so pleased him that he let us see his most intimate sketchbooks. Finally, [the others] said good-bye and left; but when I made a motion to go, Picasso asked me to stay and have lunch with him, after which he went back with me to my studio.

There he asked to see everything I had done from beginning to end. I had completed my painting *Sailor Eating and Drinking* [now *Sailor at Lunch*, p. 104], and several others that I liked: a second portrait of Adolfo Best [Maugard] called *The Man in the Stilograph*... and the still lifes *Balalaika* and *Bottle of Spanish Anise* [believed to be *Cubist Composition* (*Still Life with Bottle of Anis and Inkwell*), p. 137].

After I had showed Picasso these paintings, we had dinner together and stayed up practically the whole night talking. Our theme was Cubism—what it was trying to accomplish, what it had already done, and what future it had as a "new" art form.

With this meeting, Picasso and I became great friends. He brought all his own friends to visit my studio: the writers Guillaume Apollinaire and Max Jacob; the painters Georges Seurat [*sic*], Juan Gris, and others. Picasso's enthusiasm for my work caused a sensation in Montparnasse. My contemporaries who felt kindly toward me were gratified and those who did not were surprised and outraged.

Being accepted by the master of Cubism himself was, of course, a source of tremendous personal satisfaction to me. Not only did I consider Picasso a great artist, but I respected his critical judgment, which was severe and keen.

My enthusiasm for Picasso has not lessened, though today I would qualify it by two reservations. It seems to me that, in every one of his periods, Picasso has shown more imagination than originality, that everything he has done is based upon the work of somebody else. Also, I have come to feel that Picasso appeals chiefly to the emotions of the upper classes. In contrast with an artist like Renoir, for instance, he lacks a genuine universality. Renoir's first paintings were bought by such ordinary people as his wood dealer and his butcher. It would be hard to imagine Picasso's canvases hanging in any kind of worker's home.

In Paris, Picasso and I used to have the best times, especially when we were by ourselves. Then we would say things about other painters which we would never tell anybody else.

We would walk through the art galleries and take off on other artists' styles on the backs of matchboxes. In a spirit of pure mischief, we would often play tricks on our women acquaintances, among whom I had acquired a terrible reputation.

When one of them would come to his studio, Picasso would hide me behind a door. In the course of the conversation, Picasso would happen to mention my name. This would inevitably provoke a stream of epithets from his unsuspecting guest. Picasso would laugh heartily, shrug his shoulders, and say, "Well, *I* said he was an angel."

Excerpted from Diego Rivera, *My Art, My Life: An Autobiography*, ed. Gladys March (New York: Citadel Press, 1960; republished by Dover, 1991), pp. 58–61.

[31] Richardson, *Life of Picasso*, 407.

lifes": *Still Life with Gray Bowl*; *Still Life* (*Mallorca*) and *Still Life with Bread Knife* (both Columbus Museum of Art); and *Still Life with Bottle* (Kröller-Müller Museum, Otterlo). As in Picasso's *Still Life in a Landscape*, these works all intercut or interweave the two genres—the stippled green vegetation runs across the surface, glimpsed behind glass vessels or through the sound hole of a guitar. And yet these are all comparatively small paintings; the far larger *Zapatista Landscape* also combines genres, but here the still life seems pasted onto the landscape, connected less by the vegetation than by witty visual rhymes: natural mountains and a mountain of objects; a conical volcano and a conical sombrero. And crucially, the landscape—as in none of the other works—is now localized rather than generic, illusionistic rather than abstract.

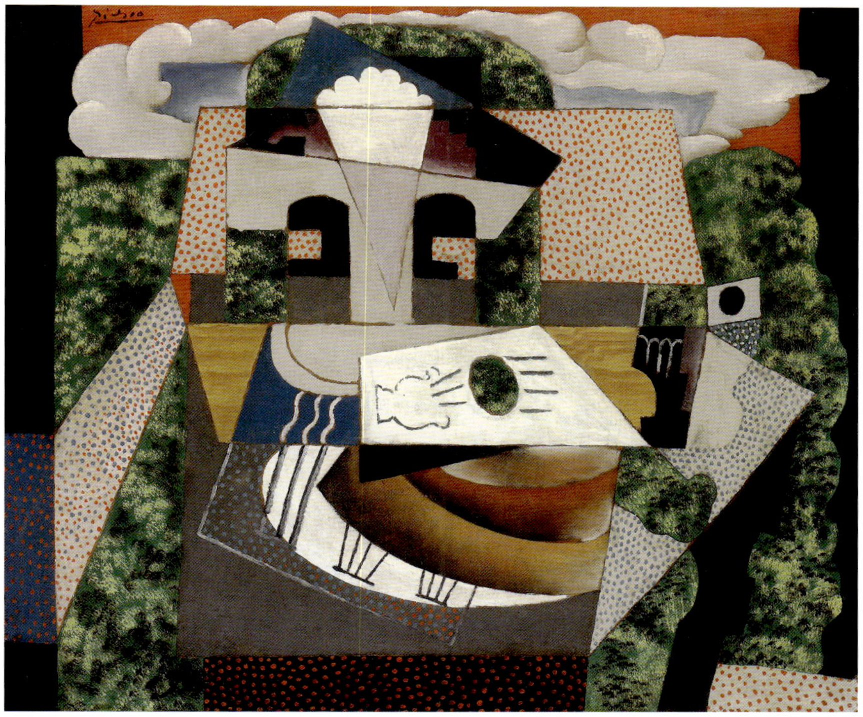

Compared to the brilliant objects in the still life, the landscape is pale: seen through a dusty haze or the haziness of memory (a fading that increases with distance, like atmospheric perspective) compared to what is crisp and close at hand in Rivera's Paris studio. Like the analysis of individual objects, the painting as a whole contrasts and conjoins exterior (landscape, being in the world, his history, his background) and interior (studio, a life of the mind). Time, geographic space, and artistic style are all in play here. The mountains are locked not only in a geological past, but in Rivera's own past: Mexico looms behind Paris just as the "realism" of José María Velasco—his former professor in the Academy of San Carlos back in Mexico City—precedes the formal experiments of Picasso.

Rivera's painting seems to inventory or index Cubist practice and then declare its difference. Even without subsequent titles like "The Guerilla" to guide us, the still life is overwhelmed by a powerful anthropomorphism—the roughly pyramidal arrangement of forms surmounted by a hat; the serape draped as if over a shoulder. Seated male figures were an essential part of Picasso's wartime repertory, though according to Richardson, they had "no symbolical or allegorical meaning."[31] In Rivera's work, however, the iconographic details (or attributes) assert a subjecthood beyond the generic icon, and inescapable symbolical and allegorical details give it a specifically Mexican identity. Although faceless and disembodied (unlike Rivera's seated male portraits from this period, which all depict known sitters), this is most certainly a portrait, though as we will see, certainly not of Emiliano Zapata.

If the "landscapes in still lifes" were themselves already commentaries on the slippage of traditional academic genres in modernist painting, Rivera's painting goes much further: landscape and still life are now joined by portraiture and, as I discuss below, self-portraiture, genre or *costumbrista* painting, and perhaps even

Diego Rivera, ***Still Life in a Landscape***, 1915; oil on canvas, 24½ × 29½ in. (62.2 × 75 cm); Meadows Museum, SMU, Dallas, Algur H. Meadows Collection

history painting. These genres provide multiple, coequal angles of simultaneously considering and understanding this single work—a neat parallel to Cubism's visual language, in which we understand *form* through a multiplicity of points of view recorded over time. Yet Rivera's most blatant declaration of originality lies not in the forms (not even that stippled shrubbery), nor in the composition, nor in the conflation of genres: rather, what makes us remember the painting known as *Zapatista Landscape*—indeed, what determined its fame as an icon of the Latin American avant-garde—is the extraordinary selection of objects, unlike those in any other Cubist picture of its time.

Regarding the subject matter, we might first dispatch some easy correspondences with earlier still-life paintings by Picasso and others: the serape-cum-tablecloth whose prominent folds also echo Cézanne; the two sensuous pieces of fruit that are probably pears, which are not ripe in the summer and thus must have been remembered or copied from other paintings;[32] the black silhouette just to the left of the pears, whose outline resembles the dried gourds (*guajes*) used as water containers in Mexico, but that also appeared in Picasso's *Vase, Gourd and Fruit on Table* (1908; Yale University Art Gallery).[33] But rather than emphasizing such ordinary objects—clichés of the genre, like the controlled variables in a science experiment—Rivera has pushed them to the side in favor of more interesting things.

Although fragments of the same serape appear in Rivera's portrait of Martín Luis Guzmán, the prominent sombrero and rifle are unique to this picture: all three elements are unquestionably Mexican and unquestionably his own. On one level, Rivera is showing his viewers that he not only can cite Cubist theory but also can apply it to original subjects in original ways.[34] But the sombrero, serape, and rifle are also loaded with cultural meanings, and from the start guided interpretations of the picture as related to the Mexican Revolution. Indeed, Zapata sometimes wore a fancy embroidered felt sombrero and carried a rifle, as seen in an oft-reproduced portrait of the general taken in 1911 that some scholars—especially Favela—imply was the source for *Zapatista Landscape* (p. 143).[35] I think this is unlikely, for it ignores that the painting features one costume element that is *never* associated with Zapata or his troops—the vibrant serape from northern Mexico—while at the same time it lacks another almost *always* associated with Zapata and his troops: the cartridge belt.[36] Nevertheless, scholars have been so certain that the painting shows the accoutrements of a revolutionary soldier that they have found "cartridge belts" (Favela) and an "ammunition box" (Lozano) where in fact there are only generic objects, and source photographs where there are only the most superficial of connections.

The costume elements and weapon in the painting are instead, and most directly, associated with the Mexican *charro* (horseman), whose costume, including the fancy sombrero, had been appropriated by Zapata as a sign of legitimacy and social status (distinguishing himself from the peasant status of his troops).[37] This costume includes

32
See Sutherland Boggs, *Picasso & Things*, 167.

33
Favela (*Rivera: The Cubist Years*, 104) calls these "Mexican *guajes* [gourd canteens] metamorphosing out of Parisian pears."

34
Rivera apparently brought some Mexican objects with him to Paris in 1911, but they do not appear in known photographs. Rivera surely had a serape (or serapes) in his studio; to paint the hat and rifle, he might have relied on photographs or drawn them from his memories of hacienda life.

35
Such images began to circulate internationally after Zapata's entry (with Francisco Villa) into Mexico City in December 1914. On this particular image, see Ariel Arnal, "Construyendo símbolos: fotografía política en México: 1865–1911," in *Estudios interdisciplinarios de América Latina y el Caribe* 9:1 (January–June 1998); Arturo Guevara Escobar, "En busca del fotógrafo de Zapata" (2010), available online at http://fotografosdelarevolucion.blogspot.mx/; see also Luis Adrián Vargas, "Emiliano Zapata: cuerpo, tierra, cautiverio," in *El éxodo mexicano: los héroes en la mira del arte* (Mexico City: Museo Nacional de Arte/UNAM, 2010), 440, 446.

36
Zapata's poorer soldiers might have carried blankets, but not brightly colored ones from Saltillo or Zacatecas. Serapes do appear in Fernando Leal's *Zapatistas at Rest* (1922; private collection), but this is an artificial and postwar construction, with no documentary value.

37
Rosa King said Zapata wore "the charro suit of the ranchman, always neat even when made up, as his was, in coarse materials." *Tempest over Mexico: A Personal Chronicle* (Boston: Little, Brown, 1935), 73.

38
Perhaps a hidden message for future critics, not unlike the headline inserted by Picasso (see note 26).

39
My reading of charros is indebted to conversations with Ricardo Pérez Montfort, as well as his "De Charros y Charrería: la construcción de un estereotipo mexicano," in *Charrería* (Mexico City: Federación Mexicana de Charrería, 2010).

40
The charro was also associated with the agricultural Bajío, where Rivera was born (though in the city of Guanajuato rather than on an hacienda). Because the charro occupied a "middle" social class, between elite and *campesino*, between Spaniard and Indian, he would be of great symbolic utility in the post-revolutionary attempt to unify the nation's social and ethnic diversity. Pérez Montfort, "De Charros y Charrería."

41
It is possible that just as Manet faced the challenge of depicting Maximilian's assassination from a distance (from the same distance, in fact), so Rivera didn't really know what Zapata or Zapatistas wore. On the other hand, if he knew enough about Zapata to honor him, he had probably seen reliable photographs (more common and more speedily available than in the 1860s) that would have allowed a more accurate reference to his military costume.

the mysterious elements above the pears, which Favela identified as "possible saddle bags," but that actually represent pants and chaps (or a shirt and jacket) made from brown leather or suede and the striped green wool fabric called *jercha*, perhaps decorated with metal clasps or epaulets. The outfit, apparently folded, is shown awkwardly, unintelligible to all but those already familiar with Mexican haciendas.[38]

Rather than a contemporaneous war, Rivera's painting looks to the past. In the nineteenth century, the charro (and his antecedent, the *chinaco*), heir to long-standing Spanish equestrian traditions, emerged as a patriotic figure, especially during the French invasion in the 1860s; this is why, in his first and inaccurate version of the *Execution of Maximilian* (1867; Museum of Fine Arts, Boston), Manet dressed the firing squad in charro gear. By the turn of the century, just before Rivera left for Europe, the charro embodied Mexican bravery and virility, and served, according to cultural historian Ricardo Pérez Montfort, "to vindicate national and local culture in the face of international styles."[39] But these charros were hardly revolutionaries: instead they were linked to the hacienda system and its great defenders, the repressive if brave federal forces known as the *rurales*.[40] It was not until *after* the revolution—and particularly with the popularity of Mexican films in the 1930s featuring charros—that charro imagery was detached from its more elitist and repressive connotations, and subsumed within a unified and useful national identity. It is the charro imagery, in fact, that connects the picture to genre (or *costumbrista*) painting, as in the popular hacienda scenes of painter Ernesto Icaza, and perhaps to history painting as well.

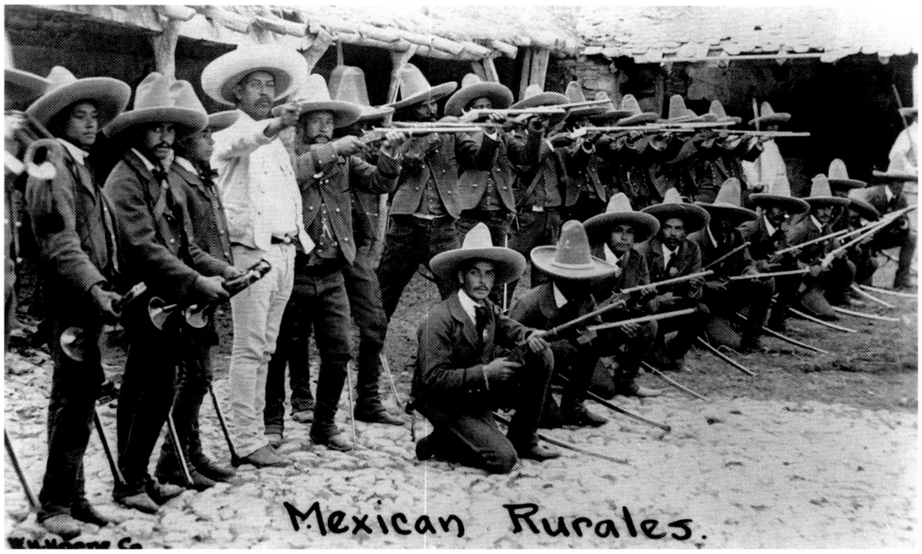

It is impossible to prove that Rivera's painting has absolutely nothing to do with Zapatistas or *Zapatismo*: he may have conflated generic *charrería* imagery with an *imagined* understanding of Zapata (or his followers) as the perfect charros. But as a visual document, the painting refers mainly to the charro, as both an embodiment of Mexican virility and a threat to foreign (French) imperialism: if some charros were already revolutionaries, then it only underscored his point.[41] Rivera, of course, was not a charro. But like vaudeville performers and tourists in Tijuana, he dresses as one in this covert self-portrait, wearing the costume of the most "Mexican" male stereotype he could imagine. His performance of Mexican identity here is theatrical—set before a backdrop as artificial as that in a photographer's studio—but is nonetheless a sign of rebellion and an assertion of difference. The painting is thus not only an assertion of formal skills but self-assured and even threatening (the phallic rifle might have been particularly annoying to a pacifist like Picasso), a throwing down of the gauntlet: bravura and bravado at the same time.

Mexican *rurcles* taking aim with their rifles, 1916 (photograph by Walter Hcrne)

42
On Rivera's reuse of canvases, see Joanne Klaar Walker, "Textual Techniques in Diego Rivera's Cubist Paintings," in Navarrete, *The Cubist Portraits*, 125–26; in the same publication, see also "Catalogue," 46.

43
In his 1915 essay (see note 18), Rivera's ally Guzmán favorably compared the Mexican's Cubism, which he called "unexpected, dominant, unalterable" (*súbito, dominante, inconmovible*) to Picasso's, which he labeled "flexible, vaporous, whispering" (*flexible, vaporoso y susurrante*). The comparison seems unfair, at least if he were comparing their work of 1915, but might reveal a shared Mexican attempt to highlight the tough masculinity of Rivera's work, its *elán vital*, to use a term much bandied about at the time.

44
Essential sources are *Picasso and Braque: Pioneering Cubism* (New York: Museum of Modern Art, 1989); *Picasso and Braque: The Cubist Experiment, 1910–1912* (Santa Barbara, CA: Santa Barbara Museum of Art, 2011); and Sebastian Smee's *Side by Side* (Sydney: Duffy & Snellgrove, 2002), a study of the relationship between Picasso and Matisse.

45
Smee, *Side by Side*, 3, 164.

Rivera's new still life showing charro gear was an aggressive act in another way. A decade after it was acquired by the Mexican government, conservators discovered that a layer of purple paint on the verso obscured a 1913 painting, now known as *Woman at the Well*, a Cubofuturist scene rendered in bright Mannerist colors, reminiscent of the work of Albert Gleizes and Jean Metzinger, the so-called Salon Cubists.[42] Rivera had reused this canvas and—adding insult to injury—had also inverted it in the process, thus leaving the older picture upside down. Such reuse is hardly surprising, given Rivera's ongoing penury and the shortage of art supplies during the war. But by doing so, he symbolically stamped out the past: the new painting emphasized primary rather than secondary colors, permanence rather than movement, hard rather than soft forms, local rather than generic imagery, male rather than female subject matter, and perhaps above all, an affiliation with Picasso rather than Gleizes and Metzinger, with a Spaniard rather than the French.[43] Whether Rivera considered his act one of erasure or just economy, is hard to say today.

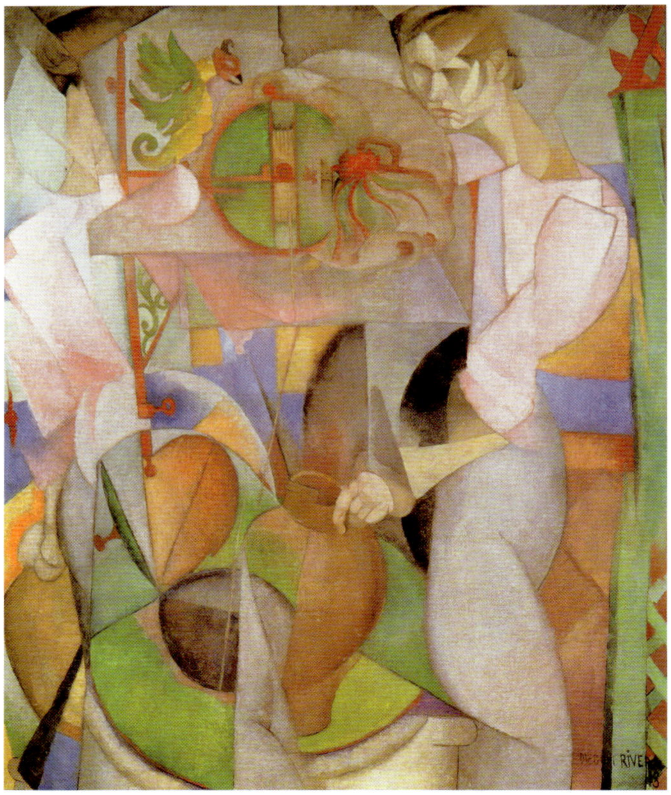

Diego Rivera, ***Woman at the Well***, 1913; oil on canvas (verso of *Zapatista Landscape*), 57 1/8 × 49 1/4 in. (145 × 125 cm); Museo Nacional de Arte, CONACULTA, INBA, Mexico City

A PYRRHIC VICTORY

In the summer of 1915, artistic battles were being fought on multiple fronts and were often exaggerated to justify their importance or intellectual significance, especially after 1914, since these particular warriors often felt guilty for escaping the muddy trenches of France. As is much discussed in the literature and surveyed elsewhere in this catalogue, throughout his life Picasso not only wrestled with historical sources (the archaic Mediterranean world, Spanish Baroque painting) but also with his close contemporaries, especially Braque and Matisse as well as Juan Gris and, for a short time in the summer of 1915, while Braque was away at war, with Diego Rivera.[44] To put it another way, Picasso stole as much from the present as from the past, relying on "creative foils" to constantly goad and inspire himself: Matisse once called him a "bandit waiting in ambush."[45] Picasso even incorporated references to these battles of primacy and genius directly into his art, as in his much-discussed inclusion of the newspaper headline "La Bataille s'est engagé[e]" in his collage *Guitar, Sheet Music, Glass* (1912; McNay Art Museum), a statement that referred more to his rivalry with Braque than to the tensions of the Balkan War.[46]

46
It is likely that Picasso was thinking of local artistic battles rather than the war referred to in the headline; exactly *who* was thus engaged is the subject of some debate. See William Rubin and Lynn Zelevansky, eds., *Picasso and Braque: A Symposium* (New York: Museum of Modern Art, 1992), 153, 161–63.

47
This story is based on facts and guesses in the accounts published by Favela and Richardson, but here I narrate what I believe to be a more logical possible sequence of events.

48
Richardson (*Life of Picasso*, 337–38) discusses Picasso's reliance on photographs of his work; the pose he takes in the image discussed here is distinct from those in other shots from the same year (see ibid., 378, 415).

49
This Flemish baroque subject was picked up by French artists, including Chardin and Monet (*Hunting Trophy*, 1862; Musée Fabre, Montpelier): over time the shotgun became a more prominent device.

50
Favela (*Rivera: The Cubist Years*, 107) hints at this meaning ("a classically traditional art form") but does not explore it further.

But Rivera was plenty pugnacious himself. As he staked his claim as a leading Cubist—not just a follower, but a theorizer—he was also embroiled in controversies that were as bellicose, if not as deadly, as actual military encounters. Sometimes Rivera suffered collateral damage through no (real) fault of his own, as when Berthe Weill took advantage of his one-man show in 1914 to publish a note critical of Picasso in the tiny catalogue. But he was also an instigator and a thief, at times simply engaged in the playful macho posturing typical of the boys of Montparnasse but—more than Picasso—also increasingly convinced that he had found "truths" that no one else could see: a dangerous proposition, in art as elsewhere.

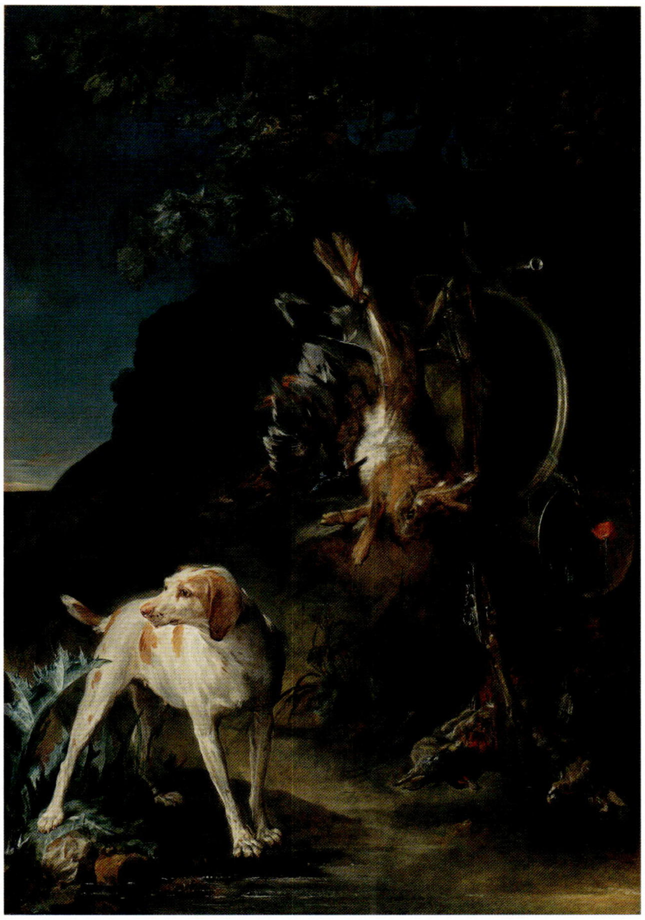

Picasso and Rivera's friendship-turned-rivalry reached a crescendo in the late summer or fall of 1915, when each posed in his studio next to a large painting of a male subject, partly surrounded by foliage (p. 11).[47] Picasso relied on such photographs to track his progress, and several images of him posing with paintings survive, whereas the portrait of Rivera, looking directly at the camera, is unlike any other in his archive. But why are the two artists in exactly the same position, on the same side of the easel, holding the brush and palette identically? Who was copying whom?[48]

We might now return to Rivera's original title: his "Mexican trophy." Rather than commemorating a military victory—and there were few, in France or Mexico, to celebrate that summer—the term returns us to art history, and Cubism's delight in the genres of the past. Rivera might have been referencing painted trophies of the hunt, in which pyramidal displays of game are placed in a landscape, accompanied by a prominent shotgun.[49] Though more genteel, this was a form of battle, albeit against nature. More likely, however, Rivera was thinking of the classical source behind those hunting scenes: representations of the *tropaion* (the word, from which our "trophy" comes, has its own origins in the term for "rout"), an assemblage of weapons, armor, shields, and other spoils of a defeated army set up on a wooden post, either on the battlefield or back home, as a memorial of victory to the winner and a reminder of defeat to the loser—a form that was endlessly repeated on monuments and prints (pp. 160–61).[50]

Of course, Rivera's trophy features elements—the sombrero and rifle, above all—that represent the artist's own nationalist costume; what parallels the captured game or soldier's armor in the historical sources are the tricks and tools of the leading Cubists, their visual weaponry, displayed on a wooden form and set before a landscape. Rivera may have even been referencing another weapon of Picasso, the classical past, embodied in the ancient trophy motif. In any event, the painting marked a momentary and very Mexican triumph on the battlefields of Montparnasse: a public assertion that he had beaten the Cubist leaders at their own

Jean-Baptiste-Siméon Chardin, ***Dog and Game***, 1730; oil on canvas, 67¾ × 54¾ in. (172 × 139 cm); Norton Simon Museum

game and on their own territory. And this—rather than a vague reference to Zapata, a different sort of leader, whom he had never met and whom few in Paris would have known or cared about—surely explains why Diego Rivera stood so proudly next to this one painting, his self-awarded trophy, and faced the camera (p. 11).[51]

If it was a trophy, however, it commemorated a battle won but a war ultimately lost. After completing his cocky display of all he had stolen, Rivera went with Guzmán to Picasso's studio in August 1915, only to discover that Picasso had turned around and stolen his technique of painting shrubbery (which Richardson unhelpfully called "virtually [Rivera's] only original contribution to Cubism") in a pair of still lifes (including *Still Life in a Landscape*) and quite prominently in a much larger painting, *Man Seated in Shrubbery*, then probably on the easel.[52] Wolfe later wrote that despite their earlier allegiance, "in the end Diego quarreled with Picasso—over what, I could no longer find out from either of them. I doubt whether either rightly remembers."[53] Richardson suggests it was Rivera's rage over the theft: "By accusing Picasso of plagiarism, the little-known Rivera made a name for himself; worse, he gave Cubist hacks a pretext for barricading studio doors against the artist to whom they owed so much."[54] But I think Rivera's anger may have been due to more than just being ripped off by the master.

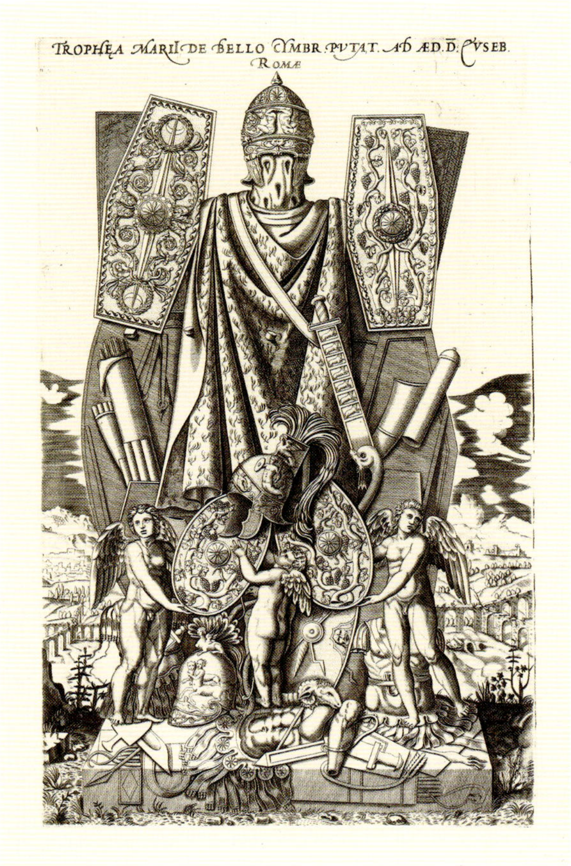

Not too long after that visit, Picasso reused his canvas, as Rivera had done in 1915, but rather than painting on the verso, he practically obliterated *Man Seated in Shrubbery*, replacing it with the more abstract *Seated Man* (p. 140). Richardson, who devotes a whole chapter to this painting, discusses the change in relation to formal decisions, camouflage units, New York skyscrapers, and even Balzac, but what is also true is that Picasso worked obsessively to destroy the one Picasso that was closest to a Diego Rivera. Rather than just a way to "exorcise Cubism," perhaps the repainting was a way to exorcise Rivera's type of Cubism, or any evidence he might be confused with Rivera.[55] Max Jacob's joke about mistaking a Rivera for a Picasso (which appeared eventually in the pages of 291 but must have circulated before) might have left Rivera smiling at the mistake and Picasso furious at the surprise.[56] Thus Rivera's rage: just at the moment Rivera declared victory, Picasso changed the rules.

A Roman Trophy, Italian, c. 1550; engraving on paper, 15 × 9⅝ in. (38 × 24.3 cm); Victoria and Albert Museum, London (24486:1)

51
I suspect Rivera was inspired by Picasso's photographs, but whether he was imitating the particular photograph of Picasso standing before *Man Seated in Shrubbery* is impossible to say.

52
Richardson, *Life of Picasso*, 412. On Picasso's theft of Rivera's technique, see Marevna Vorobëv, *Life with the Painters of La Ruche* (London: Constable & Robinson, 1972), cited in Favela, *Rivera: The Cubist Years*, 111. See also Jean Cocteau's account, cited in Richardson, *Life of Picasso*, 414.

53
Wolfe, *Life and Times*, 114.

54
Richardson, *Life of Picasso*, 414.

55
Picasso left two small "windows" that reveal Rivera's shrubbery, intact from the first version of the painting; this have might have been a further affront, as if to say, see, *Rivera, I've painted you over and want everyone to know*. I thank Diana Magaloni for pointing out this detail.

56
See note 19 for the original French, which plays on the similarity between the words *méprise* (mistake), *surprise* (surprise), and *mépris* (contempt).

Rivera continued fighting Cubist battles through 1916, but in March 1917, he pushed too far: his claim to have discovered a way to represent the "fourth dimension" culminated in a series of critical and xenophobic attacks, including a physical altercation with Pierre Reverdy, a break with Léonce Rosenberg, and an ensuing loss of friends that must have been particularly disheartening. André Salmon summed up the whole mess as *l'affaire Rivera*, and more than two decades later, Wolfe captured the essence of this stormy moment (which also seems to confirm that the great 1915 painting is indeed a self-portrait): "Like a Mexican *caudillo* [Rivera] seemed bent on organizing a band of his own, or fighting independently, a lone outlaw.... Picasso, arch-experimenter and restless investigator of myriad phenomena in turn, viewed the whole controversy with amused indifference. Lesser men were more annoyed at this latecomer who would not stay in line, who kept insisting, sometimes with and sometimes without reason, on his own originality."[57]

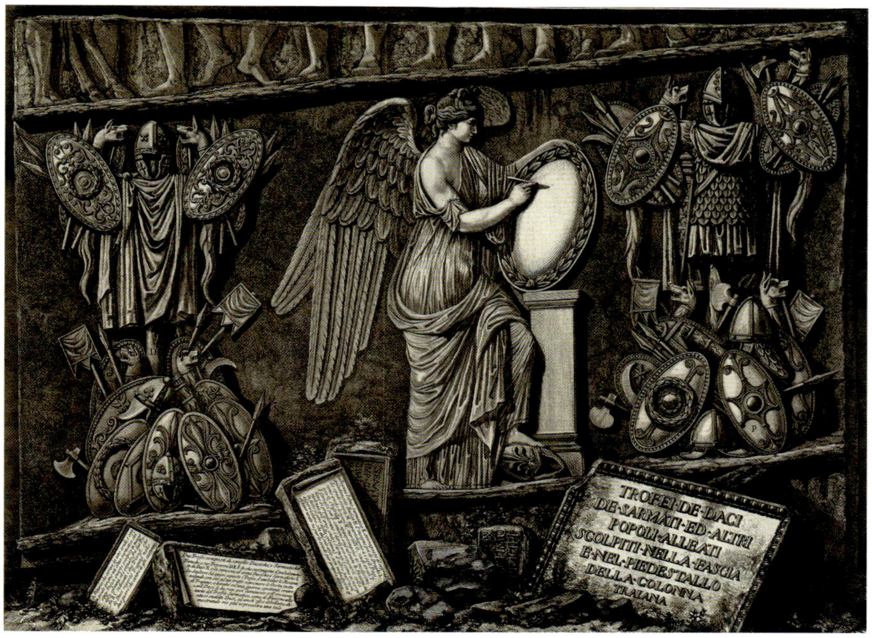

It would take Rivera a few short years to discover that originality, though he first had to also conquer Ingres, Renoir, Cézanne...and Giotto. In July 1921 he disembarked in Mexico armed with a new classicism, soon to rediscover the *tehuanas* and pyramids of his own country, taking the *retour à l'ordre* of postwar France and transferring it to walls on a scale no one had ever seen before. In the mid-1940s, now as a confident and seasoned warrior, Rivera would turn to Gladys March and say: "I have come to feel that Picasso appeals chiefly to the emotions of the upper classes.... It would be hard to imagine Picasso's canvases hanging in any kind of worker's home."[58] What Picasso might have said in retort, we will never know.

This essay builds on the crucial foundational research of Ramón Favela, a scholar who has unfortunately disappeared from the scene. It also benefited from the insights of colleagues in the Wellesley College Art Department, especially Patricia Berman, as well as George Flaherty, Luis Adrián Vargas Santiago, and others at the Center for Latin American Visual Studies (CLAVIS) at the University of Texas, Austin, where I gave an early reading of my findings. Alicia Reyes Mota, director of the Capilla Alfonsina, facilitated access to Alfonso Reyes's file on Diego Rivera, which includes the invitation and pamphlet for Rivera's 1914 exhibition at Berthe Weill's gallery. A shorter version was commissioned for the final volume of the catalogue of the permanent collection of Mexico's Museo Nacional de Arte.

Giovanni Battista Piranesi, ***Victory Inscribing a Shield Surrounded by Trophies of the Dacians, the Sarmatians, and Other Allies*** (detail), 1774–79; copperplate engraving, 29¾ × 37½ in. overall (75.6 × 95.3 cm), Metropolitan Museum of Art (2012.136.956[9])

57 Wolfe, *Life and Times*, 115.

58 Rivera, *My Art, My Life*, 106.

CLASSICISM AND MONSTROSITY TORN BODIES IN PICASSO'S ILLUSTRATIONS OF FOR PLEASURE OVID'S *METAMORPHOSES*

JENNIFER STAGER

Orpheus slumps over his lyre, his left hand clasping the instrument's upper curve. The lyre seems to be used to anchor the body that sprawls across his lap, its limbs falling limply to either side. The specifics of how many bodies are being shown and to whom they belong are not immediately evident here, for Pablo Picasso's lines do not allow us to parse the figure(s) easily. This drawing, executed on September 1, 1930, is known as *The Death of Orpheus*. The study was Picasso's initial experimentation with imagery for Albert Skira's 1931 French translation of Ovid's *Metamorphoses*, to which the artist contributed fifteen full-page etchings and fifteen half-plates to use as frontispieces for each of the books of Ovid's epic.[1]

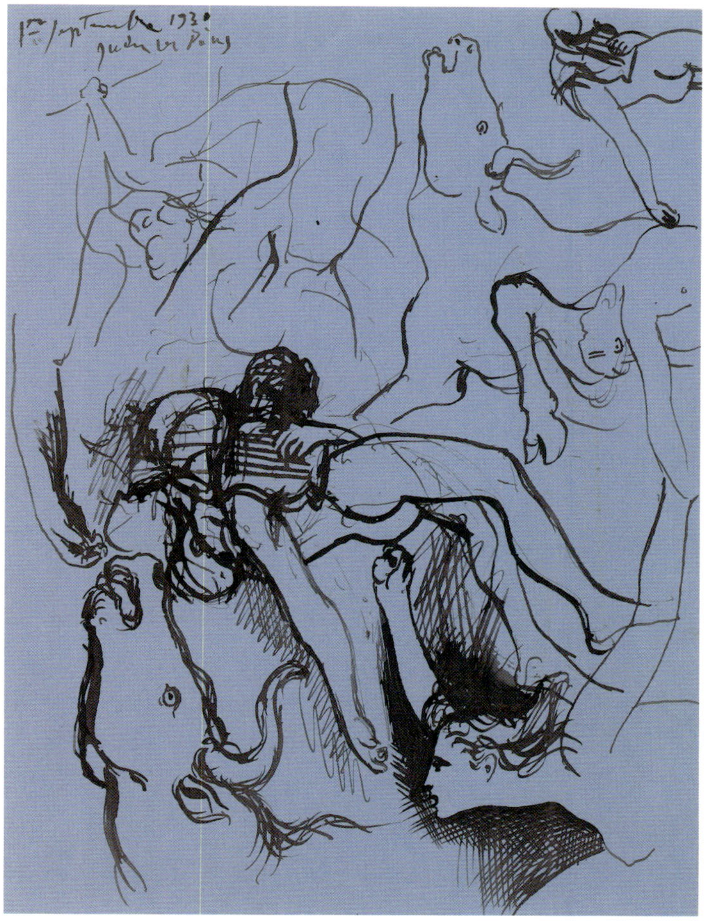

The Roman poet Ovid published the *Metamorphoses* in Latin in 8 CE; his text, which escapes traditional genre designations, retold more than two hundred and fifty Greco-Roman myths, stretching from the creation of the world through the deification of Julius Caesar in 42 BCE, a year after Ovid's birth. Through his focus on changing forms and bodies, on the process of becoming (often through violent means), Ovid thematizes the very acts of rewriting and reworking.[2] Surely Ovid's authorial control and revision of a vast array of familiar Greco-Roman stories appealed to Picasso, who practiced a similar selective canonical absorption and modification in his own work. Just as Ovid's text influenced and inspired later writers such as Dante Alighieri, William Shakespeare, Geoffrey Chaucer, and Giovanni Boccaccio, so too did many visual artists, including Sandro Botticelli, Nicolas Poussin, Peter Paul Rubens, and Odilon Redon, take up specific Ovidian tales in painting, sculpture, and graphic work.[3] Picasso's choice of Ovid's text for his venture with Skira thus participates in a long-standing literary and visual tradition. For both Ovid and Picasso the appeal of tradition lay in remaking it.[4]

With the exception of an unpublished illustration of Actaeon becoming a boar, Picasso avoided depicting an actual metamorphosis. Instead, he used linear style to show bodily interaction and exchange, the movements of bodies into one another. Many of Picasso's preliminary drawings for the *Metamorphoses* work through ideas that had long engaged him in his academic training, in his attention to the inherent fragmentation of the body through Cubism, and in the pressure he places on what a classical body can be in large paintings from the early 1920s. During this time, Picasso's large-scale work engaged directly with classicism, while in the later part of the decade his large-scale painting did not quote classical art explicitly. If

Pablo Picasso, ***The Death of Orpheus***, study for Ovid's ***Metamorphoses***, September 1, 1930; pen and ink, 10⅝ × 8¼ in. (27 × 21 cm); Musée Picasso, Paris, France (Inv. MP 1033 recto)

1 *Metamorphoses* was Skira's first publication, and these were Picasso's first book illustrations. See Marilyn McCully, "Boisgeloup, l'Olympe de Picasso," in Jean Clair, *Picasso érotique*, exh. cat. (New York: Prestel, 2001), 138–52. See also Lisa Florman, *Myth and Metamorphosis: Picasso's Classical Prints of the 1930s* (Cambridge, MA: MIT Press, 2000), 16.

2 Richard Tarrant, "Ovid and Ancient Literary History," in *The Cambridge Companion to Ovid*, ed. Philip Hardie (Cambridge: Cambridge University Press, 2002), 21. On Ovid's becoming as coterminous rather than fixed, see Charles Boer, "Introduction," *Ovid's Metamorphoses*, trans. Charles Boer (Dallas: Spring, 1989), xi.

3 On the *Metamorphoses* in Western art, see Paul Barolsky, *Ovid and the Metamorphosis of Modern Art from Botticelli to Picasso* (New Haven: Yale University Press, 2014).

4 On the complication of Ovid's classicism, see Florman, *Myth and Metamorphosis*, 24, and Barolsky, *Ovid and the Metamorphosis*, 43–61.

the classical tradition up to this time had emphasized wholeness, even as fragments, Picasso played with this ideal of wholeness in paint, often flattening or compressing parts of even his most sculptural bodies.[5] However, he remained engaged throughout the 1920s with inquiries toward which he directed the classical in the period of 1921–23. What he moved away from over the decade and returned to again at its close is the deployment of imagery that bears a formal relationship to a classical poetics of the body. Of the many interwar paintings executed in this large, lumbering sculptural style, I present two as typical: *Three Women at the Spring* and *The Pipes of Pan*.

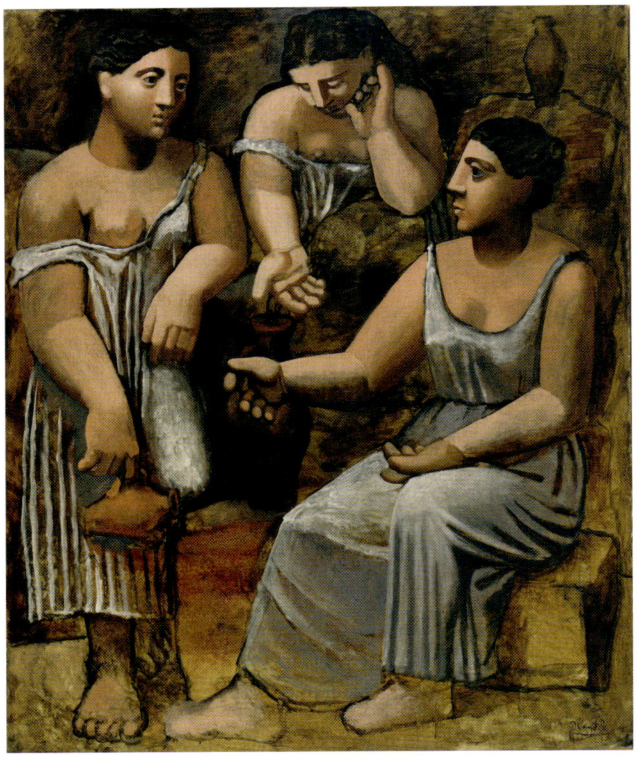

Pablo Picasso, ***Three Women at the Spring***, Summer 1921

Picasso executed at least twenty full studies for *Three Women at the Spring*, not counting the many related drawings and paintings preceding it and studies of individual body parts, in particular of hands.[6] The women's loosely modeled masses define the space taken up by their bodies. The rocks and the small water jugs place these women in an undefined, somewhat pastoral setting. Each woman is an iteration of her companions in the manner of ancient Greek *korai*, or maidens.[7] The thick, vertical drapery of their garments evokes the solid fluting of Doric columns as well as the folds of the ancient Greek *peplos* (outer garment). These women are not the sensuous female Aphrodites, the smooth bathing nudes that populate paintings by Jean-Auguste-Dominique Ingres, nor are they like the three nymphs traced out by delicate lines as shown, for example, in Picasso's *Sculptor with a Sculpted Group (Homage to Carpeaux)* (1934) from the Vollard Suite (1930–37).[8] The women at the fountain are decidedly not graces. Picasso depicts the restrained chignons of the figures in *Three Women at the Spring* as though they are carved. Dark, almost vacant eyes look out from sculptural faces, recalling Picasso's 1906 portrait of Gertrude Stein, as well as the empty gazes of innumerable Greco-Roman sculptures.[9] Picasso depicts the semblance of sculpture, of the completed presence of the figure in the round that characterizes the plastic body, yet in certain passages he collapses the three-dimensionality of his figures. In the lower right-hand corner, for example, he drips paint from the woman's feet, flaunting the medium from which she emerged. Shading at the women's necks suggests Picasso's choice, in the later 1920s, to sever bust or face from body, both the cleaving and its reconstitution. Their bodies, however, remain solidly bounded.

In *The Pipes of Pan* (p. 116), Picasso's youths have the same angular faces as his maidens. They share their heavy-footed weight, but Picasso flattens the youths' plastic presence. The passage of dripping paint at the foot of *Three Women* that marked their medium becomes the flattened volumes of the pipes, parts of the figures' chests, and the relationship of their legs to architecture. The painted body begins to lose its

5
On fragments and the body, see William Tronzo, *The Fragment: An Incomplete History* (Los Angeles: Getty Research Institute, 2009).

6
Elizabeth Cowling, *Picasso: Style and Meaning* (London: Phaidon, 2002), 429.

7
Although *kouroi* and *korai* were types, individuation was a significant aspect of their value. As the representative of the dedicator, *kouroi* and *korai* display their individuality in terms of hairstyles (both coiffure and pubic hair), scale, color, and attributes. See Katerina Karakasi, *Archaic Korai* (Los Angeles: J. Paul Getty Museum, 2003).

8
Cowling, *Picasso: Style and Meaning*, 548.

9
On inlaid eyes in ancient Greek art, see Jennifer Stager, "The Embodiment of Color in Ancient Mediterranean Art" (PhD diss., University of California, Berkeley, 2012). On the debate among modern artists about the sculptural gaze and whether to sculpt the eyes smoothly or drill a pupil, see Jacqueline Lichtenstein, *La Tache aveugle: essai sur les relations de la peinture et de la sculpture à l'âge modern* (Paris: Gallimard, 2003), 86–92.

10
John Richardson suggests that Skira was responsible for Picasso's selection of myths and shifts in style from the studies to the finished products; see John Richardson, *A Life of Picasso: The Triumphant Years, 1917–1932* (New York: Knopf, 2010), 384. Yet the young publisher-to-be had no authority on which to manage the famous artist, whose contribution to his nascent publishing venture was career-making; the choice of book to publish, possibly at the casual suggestion of Pierre Matisse, and the selection of myths from that book and the styles in which they are executed were all Picasso's own. On Pierre Matisse, see Florman, *Myth and Metamorphosis*, 14–15; McCully, "Boisgeloup, l'Olympe de Picasso," 140.

11
Older illustrated editions of Ovid's *Metamorphoses* often included multiple plates per myth, illustrating sequential scenes from an ongoing narrative. For example, the Latin-to-German version published in Cologne in 1607, now in the collection of the Getty Research Institute, contains over 130 engravings with elaborate borders.

sculpted integrity. Just as Picasso's women evoke ancient Greek *korai*, so do these young men recall ancient Greek *kouroi* (youths), archaic Greek dedications that play between individuation and type. Both *Three Women at the Spring* and *The Pipes of Pan* present the illusion of individual bodily integrity, of *presence* in a world constructed with and in relation to other bodies.

Not only did Picasso edit his own preliminary sketches for *Metamorphoses* to settle on a very clear, curvilinear style that joins all thirty drawings, but he also carefully selected which Ovidian tales to illustrate, reworking the style in which he responded to them.[10] His selection is as important for which stories he leaves out (such as Proteus, Pygmalion, Narcissus, and the Minotaur) but which, I would argue, he picks up in other contexts. Some of what Picasso excluded from his tightly edited 1931 edition of Ovid's *Metamorphoses* finds expression in both the Vollard Suite and *Guernica*.

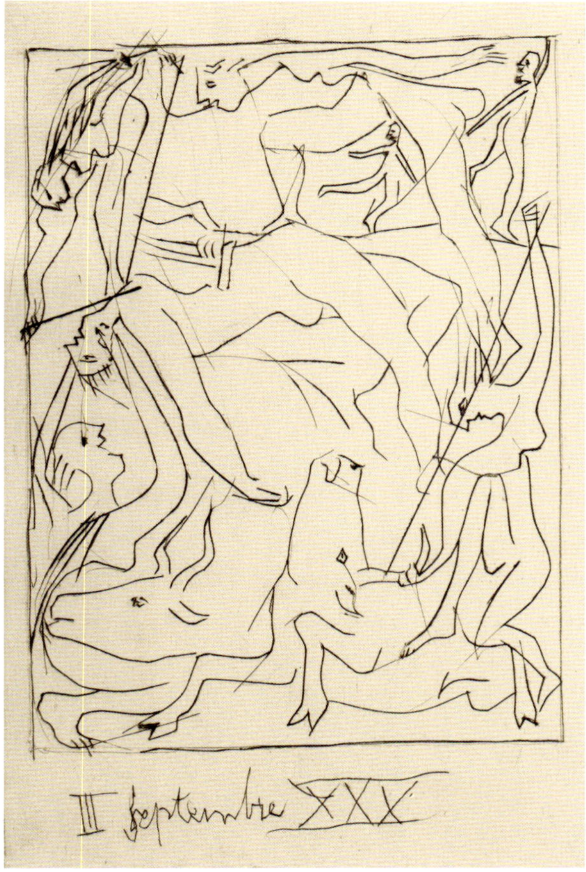

In earlier editions of the *Metamorphoses*, artists matched sequential, didactic illustrations to Ovid's narrative, which often includes several connected myths in each book. Picasso, in contrast, presents a synchronic image of an event from a single myth per book.[11] The collected images still present a continuous narrative, but Picasso's tight editing gives his selection much more visual power. In the only instance of repetition within the series, he devotes two of his fifteen full plates to different components of the story of Orpheus and Eurydice (*Eurydice Bitten by a Serpent* and *Death of Orpheus*). He also includes half-sized, non-narrative frontispiece images of faces and fragments of bodies; he executes these in the same clean lines as the larger illustrations, unifying his style across all thirty final images. These half-plates of faces and fragments of bodies offer up witnesses to Ovid's account within each book. Picasso depicts both selected moments in the narrative, and fragments of an audience. In this way, Picasso departs from the didacticism of his predecessors in favor of directing a collective theatricality.

ORPHEUS

Picasso began his experiments with Ovid and Orpheus with the study from September 1, 1930, and in the following three weeks he went on to produce at least two other studies, specifically of the *Death of Orpheus*, among his many preliminary drawings for the full series. Depictions of the myth of Orpheus appear as early

Pablo Picasso, ***Death of Orpheus***, illustration for Ovid's ***Metamorphsis*** (first plate). September 3, 1930. Drypoint on Arches paper, 22.5 x 17.1 cm; Musée Picasso, Paris, France

12
Apollo was, among other things, the god of music, and Calliope is the muse invoked at the beginning of epic poetry, such as Homer's *Iliad* and *Odyssey*, or Vergil's *Aeneid*. Ovid tells the story of Apollo's pursuit of the nymph Daphne, who turns into a tree to escape him, in Book 1 of the *Metamorphoses*.

13
In Vergil's account, Eurydice is running to escape rape by a satyr; in Ovid's account, she is dancing with the Naiads on the day of her wedding to Orpheus when the serpent bites her.

14
Ovid, *Metamorphoses* 11.71–74. The edition cited here and below (unless otherwise noted) is *Metamorphoses: A New Translation*, trans. Charles Martin (New York: W. W. Norton, 2005).

as the fifth century BCE, such as on an ancient Attic red-figure calyx krater now in the collection of the Getty Villa: the painter has depicted a scene of maenads attacking Orpheus on one side (p. 201), while the other side shows a more generalized Dionysiac scene. Orpheus, whose story is recounted in Books 10 and 11 of the *Metamorphoses*, was the child of Apollo and Calliope, the Greek muse of epic poetry.[12] Orpheus falls in love with Eurydice, who is bitten by a serpent on their wedding day and killed.[13] Orpheus follows Eurydice into the underworld to negotiate with Hades, who, swayed by Orpheus's musical lament, agrees to return Eurydice to the living world, on the condition that Orpheus not look back at Eurydice as she follows him out of the underworld. Of course, just before they would have emerged, Orpheus indeed looks back, and Eurydice is lost to the underworld forever. Orpheus mourns Eurydice and his music arrests the natural world surrounding him until a group of Thracian maenads in a Bacchic frenzy slaughter him with stones, branches, *thyrsoi* (Dionysiac staffs), and their bare hands. Orpheus's lyre and severed head float down the river Hebrus: "the plaintive lyre makes some kind of moan, the lifeless tongue moans along with it, the moaning riverbanks respond in turn."[14]

Picasso avoids depicting Ovid's triumphant *ekphrasis* (vivid description) of Orpheus's lyre and postmortem tongue continuing their low lament. In the sketch Picasso made on September 1 (p. 163), the passage at the center, identifiable only by Orpheus's lyre, seems to show Orpheus grasping at a falling body. His lyre and head are joined in such a manner that the lyre seems to cover part of his face and mouth. The falling body in the central passage could be his own, or possibly Eurydice's, whose fall precedes and precipitates Orpheus's own death in Ovid's narrative. In the published version (p. 201), the falling body has definitely become Orpheus's, but in the study (p. 163) Picasso appears to be exploring the relationship of one death to the other. Picasso's rendering is ambiguous regarding the boundaries between bodies and body parts, a practice that he repeats in other drawings and etchings, as well as in other media. In the upper right corner, Picasso reiterates this coterminous figure of head, lyre, and body, using less shading and even more weight to depict the falling limbs. The figures remain difficult to parse, but just below the pair, Picasso depicts again the twisting, falling body, as though describing the path of its fall. Orpheus has lost his grip. The figure's slack arm merges with the raised arm of the personified wind blowing in from the right. Hatched shading highlights her profile and attack. Her right hand wields a raised blade, moving straight toward the central figure of Orpheus. She is at once a maddened maenad and the wind that scatters Orpheus's limbs and carries his lyre and head, still lamenting, down the river. Limbs and torsos fill the upper left section of the study, conveying action but not its narrative particulars. One hand grips a bow that points upward. The lowing bulls, one in the lower left foreground and the other in the upper right background, set the pastoral, Orphic setting and hint at formal qualities that Picasso would later bring to *Guernica*.

15
On Etruscan mirror engravings and Picasso, see Florman, *Myth and Metamorphosis*, 18–21, especially 18, and *Cahiers d'art* 4 (1929), edited by Christian Zervos, which featured an article on the liminal "classical" status of Etruscan art. Etruscan mirrors are traditionally cited as the source material for Picasso's style, and they are certainly relevant; ancient Greek vases were as readily available and as stylistically important for Picasso in 1930.

16
Barolsky, *Ovid and the Metamorphosis*, 112.

17
Johann Joachim Winckelmann, *Reflections on the Painting and Sculpture of the Greeks: With Instructions for the Connoisseur, and an Essay on Grace in Works of Art*, trans. Henry Fuseli (London, 1765). Alex Potts notes *stille*'s connotations of the stillness and calm after death, which the typical translation "quiet" does not fully capture, but which seems relevant to Picasso's engagement with Ovid. Alex Potts, *Flesh and the Ideal: Winckelmann and the Origins of Art History* (New Haven: Yale University Press, 2000), 1.

18
On Winckelmann and the classical tradition, see Potts, *Flesh and the Ideal*.

A preliminary sketch for *Death of Orpheus*, dated September 16, 1930, deploys the heavy shading that Picasso works through some of his etchings in the Vollard Suite. Here, he takes on Orpheus's violent death directly; maenads stab Orpheus's falling body with their *thyrsoi*. His bearded head, still attached to his body, falls back as a maenad from the bottom right—a new version of the previous study's wind-like woman—claws at his jaw and mouth, about to rip his head from his neck. The lowing bulls of the earlier study are now actively put to use, with maenads grabbing their horns for use in rending Orpheus limb from limb. Like ancient depictions of the event, Picasso stays close to Ovid's text.

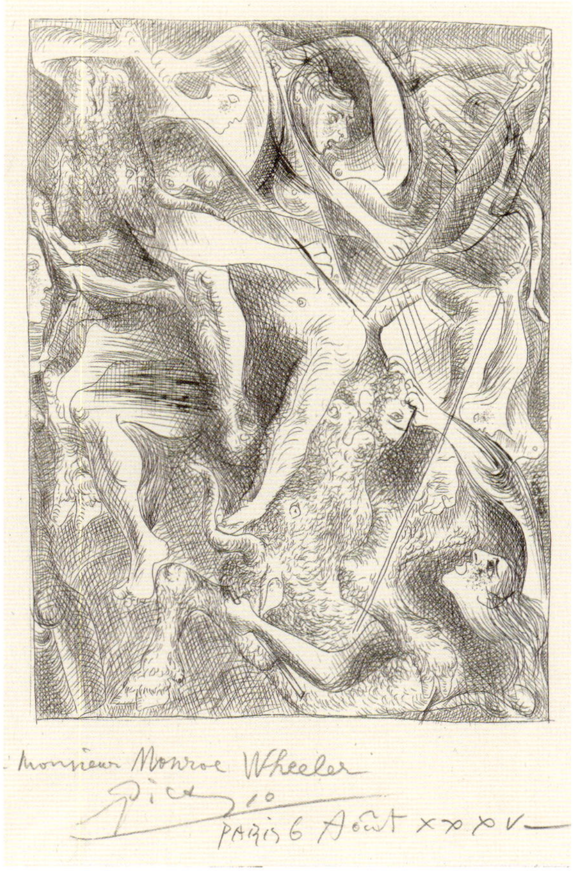

None of Picasso's preliminary drawings resemble the stripped-down published etching, a style that owes much to the sleek lines carved on Etruscan bronze mirrors and painted on Attic vases, examples of which were abundantly available at the Louvre, where Picasso would have viewed them.[15] In his initial studies of September 1930, Picasso tests his overall approach to the *Metamorphoses*, paying particular attention to the Orpheus myth. His passages of heavy shading, especially in the September 16 study, match the heaviness of Ovid's stories, which are primarily tales of change wrought by destruction, as well as of subjectivity dispersed across different and diffuse forms. Ovid, however, retells these tales of horrific abasement and transformation with masterfully deft, even light, verse.[16] Picasso, in turn, riffs on Ovid's opposition of form and content. He depicts the most gruesome myths in a classicizing style bearing the conservative weight of tradition, aligned with Winckelmann's famous mid-eighteenth-century pronouncement concerning classical Greek art's *edle Einfalt und stille Größe* (typically translated "noble simplicity and quiet grandeur"), a predicament from which classical antiquity has never fully escaped.[17] In their juxtaposition of form and content, both Ovid and Picasso contest this Winckelmannian ideal, as it has been conventionally received.[18]

In his published illustration of the *Death of Orpheus*, dated September 18, 1930, Picasso has stripped the image of its violent specifics: no blood, no torn limbs, no severed head, no murmuring, lifeless tongue. Orpheus is shown in profile as he falls downward, arms flailing over his head as his body arches in flight. A kneeling cow is shown below him and three women huddle together behind him, each clutching a branch or bow in her right hand. The three women track Orpheus's descent. The cow's hoof appears as the left leg of the crouching woman at far right. Her companion at the far left springs up and arches forward in an inversion of

Pablo Picasso, ***Death of Orpheus***, unpublished plate from Book 11 of Ovid's ***Metamorphoses***, September 16, 1930; etching, 12 5/16 × 8 11/16 in. (31.2 × 22.1 cm); The Museum of Modern Art, New York

19
Ovid, *Metamorphoses* 3.10–11.
20
Ovid, *Metamorphoses* 6.
21
Ovid, *Metamorphoses* 2.

Orpheus's backward-arching fall. Her left leg bends at the knee and her right leg rises straight up from where her foot touches Orpheus's bent right leg. She rises as he falls, directed by her gaze.

Eurydice's death is similarly serene. She has fallen, and the torqued lines of her body from right leg through hips and spine suggest motion, even as she appears to rest in the arms of one of her attendants. Her garment spreads out beneath her. Three women attend her as a fourth turns away at far left. One woman gazes at Eurydice as she lifts her by her armpit, while behind her another figure moves forward, simultaneously a former iteration of the kneeling woman and a separate figure. The central woman kisses and clasps Eurydice's right foot, where the snake bit. A fourth woman, wearing a *peplos*, faces away; she might be an iteration of Eurydice several moments earlier, running before the fatal snake bite. Eurydice, dead or dying, looks toward the snake on the ground. Picasso reduced the snake itself to comic proportions, a mere squiggle beneath Eurydice's forearm and dying gaze.

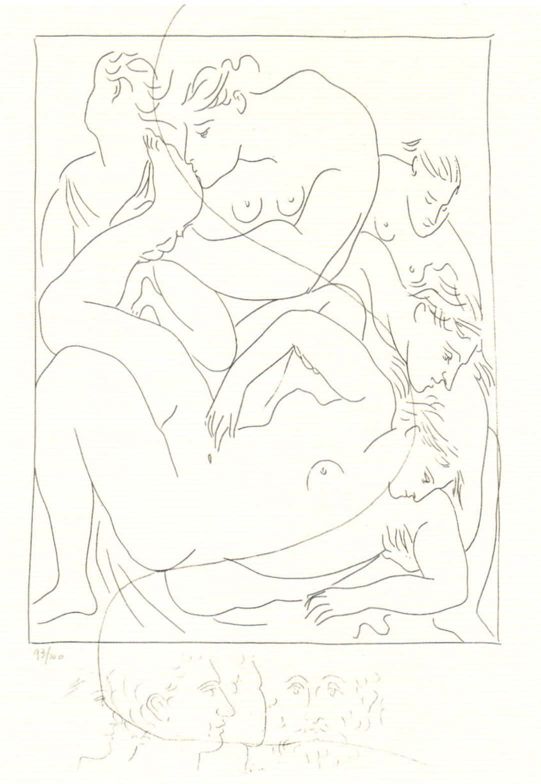

Picasso maintains a light, streamlined style in depicting Eurydice's violent death, just as he does with her lover's. He avoids showing the actual attacks, scenes of the underworld, or Orpheus's fatal look back. Picasso never competes with Ovid's *ekphrasis*, but his dissolution of bounded, individuated bodies, to which he gestured in his paintings of the early 1920s, responds to the death and dismemberment in Ovid's stories. In the *Metamorphoses*, Orpheus dies at the hands of Thracian women, Eurydice from a serpent bite, Semele from Zeus's thunderbolt.[19] Proteus changes rapidly—from lion to boar to serpent to bull to tree to water, and finally to flame.[20] Phaethon, intoxicated by the hubris of youth, tries to command his father's chariot, scorches the earth, and Zeus smites him dead.[21] Change is violent; love is violent; history is violent; humanity is violent. Picasso depicts it all with exquisite line. This duality of formal restraint and internal violence constitutes one of Picasso's commentaries on classicism itself. For Ovid the soul remains intact through each subsequent change in form; Picasso, in contrast, shows us the myth of a body's solidity, of its bounded individuation.

Pablo Picasso, ***Eurydice Bitten by a Snake***, illustration for Ovid's *Metamorphoses*, 1930; etching on Rives BFK paper, 12 5/16 x 8 3/4 in. (31.2 x 22.2 cm); California Palace of the Legion of Honor, Achenbach Foundation, Bruno and Sadie Adriani Collection, 1971.28.69

22
Ovid, *Metamorphoses* 6.412–674. On repetition and Picasso, see Jeremy Melius, "Inscription and Castration," in *October* (2015), 61.

PHILOMELA

Picasso executed four illustrations over a month (September 18–October 18, 1930) depicting the Thracian king Tereus's rape and disfigurement of his sister-in-law, Philomela.[22] In Ovid's narrative, Tereus travels to Athens to fetch Philomela from her father; he then brings her back to Thrace, where he takes her into the woods and repeatedly rapes her. After the first rape, Philomela says that she wishes she had died and that she will tell others what Tereus has done. Tereus cuts out her tongue

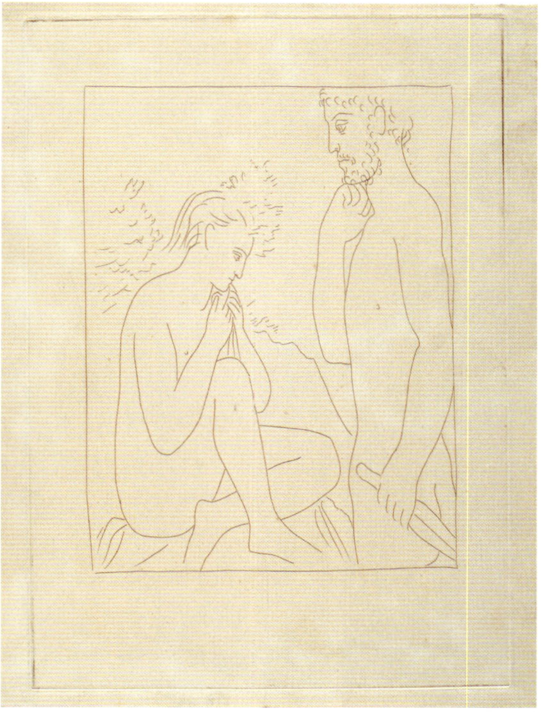

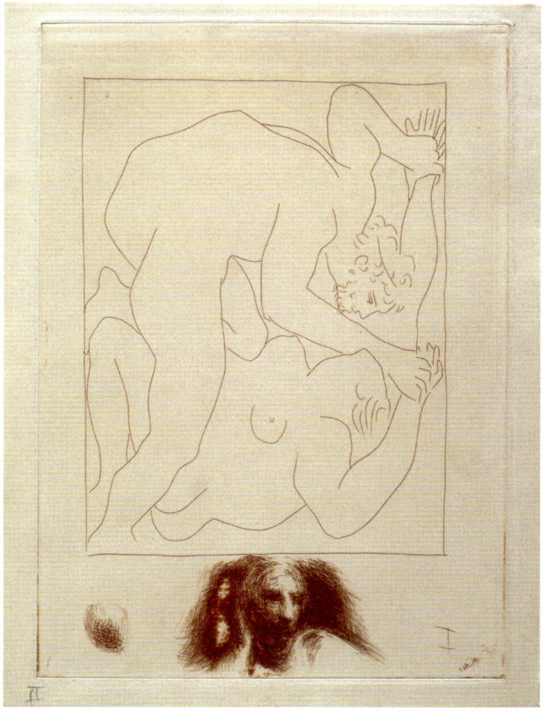

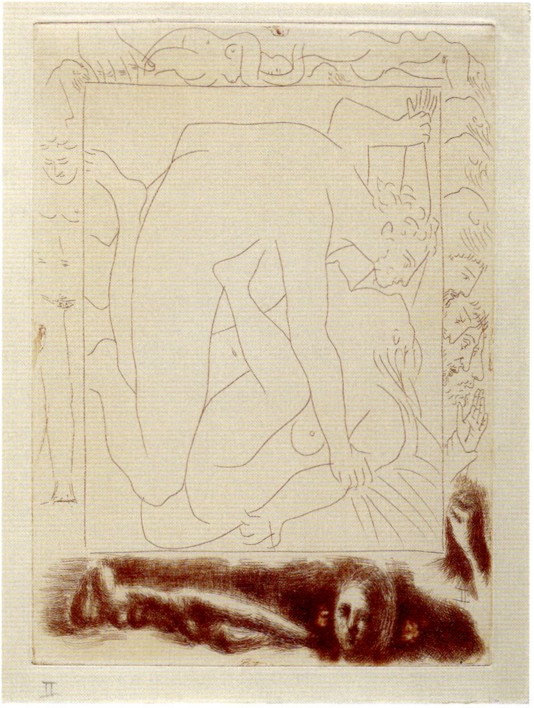

and rapes her again, then abandons her brutalized body to return to her sister, his wife, Procne. Here is Charles Boer's translation of the scene:

> King drags Pandion's daughter to high stable / hidden in ancient forest; locks her in, / pale & trembling, scared of everything; she asks with tears / where's sister? He admits evil & rapes solitary / girl; she calls in vain for father, sister, great / gods above…
>
> Soon herself again, she tears rumpled hair / like mourner, arms cut striking / …why not take my life too? / that crime's left: I wish you had, / before evil copulation! My ghost then innocent; / …you'll pay! Shame aside, I'll tell!…
>
> Tyrant's anger aroused, & fear: driven by both, / he frees sword from scabbard on belt, grabs her by hair, / ties hands behind back; seeing sword, / Philomela offers throat, hoping for death; he grips / indignant tongue (struggling to speak & calling / father's name) with

LEFT Pablo Picasso, ***Tereus and Philomela***, illustration for Ovid's ***Metamorphoses***, September 18, 1930; etching on vellum, 8⅞ × 6¾ in. (22.4 × 17.2 cm); Musée Picasso, Paris (Inv. MP 2151)

CENTER Pablo Picasso, ***Struggle between Tereus and Philomela***, illustration for Ovid's ***Metamorphoses***, October 18, 1930; etching on vellum, 8¾ × 6¾ in. (22.2 × 17.1 cm); Musée Picasso, Paris (Inv. MP 2155)

RIGHT Pablo Picasso, ***Struggle between Tereus and Pilomela***, illustration for Ovid's ***Metamorphoses***, Plate II, October 18, 1930; etching on vellum, 8¾ × 6¾ in. (22.3 × 17.2 cm); Musée Picasso, Paris (Inv. MP2156)

CLASSICISM AND REVOLUTION

JENNIFER STAGER

Picasso executed the series of one hundred prints known as the Vollard Suite over the decade of the 1930s, deploying a range of techniques and depicting a range of subjects (including circus performers, the Minotaur, faun and maiden scenes, and studio scenes), and yet a clear connection between prints continues to evade summary analysis.[1] Ambroise Vollard, Picasso's dealer from 1901 until Vollard's death in 1939, commissioned the series in 1931. Unlike much of Picasso's graphic work of the late 1920s and early 1930s, such as his illustrations for Aristophanes' *Lysistrata* and Ovid's *Metamorphoses*, the Vollard Suite was not structured around a specific text. While diverse in technique and subject matter, the series of images that comprise the suite share a consistent integration of forms and subjects from the antique past in modern contexts.

Sculptor Reclining before Nude (p. 207), from the loose subset of images of studio sessions within the Vollard Suite, is paradigmatic: the scene depicts a classicizing sculpture that recalls, but does not strictly imitate, the Aphrodite of Knidos, reportedly the first female nude sculpture in ancient Greek art, as well as the slightly later crouching Aphrodite, also naked (p. 206).[2] A base affirms that this naked figure is a statue, although she is in the act of drying her right arm with a towel and her face turns towards the viewer over her right shoulder. A bearded man reclines naked on a bed or couch in the arms of a woman whose head is visible in profile, suggesting a bust, but for her hands clasping the man. The scene, indeed all of the Vollard Suite, plays with Pygmalion-esque boundaries between art and life. Another etching, *Masked Characters and Bird-Woman* (p. 213) literalizes the fluidity of boundary in the suite by situating the scene within the world of the theater. Three naked figures approach the sculpted bird on a pedestal. Each wears a different mask—a bearded male, a Minotaur with his cane, and a woman holding up a male mask to her face. The Dionysiac world of the theater in ancient Greece was foremost a space of religious, political, and civic expression.[3] There is a politics to Picasso's classical theater here as well—and a contemporary (but independent) etching offers a key.

In 1937, Picasso produced a standalone graphic work, *The Dream and Lie of Franco I* and *II*, against the fascist regime of Francisco Franco in Spain. Nine graphic novel–style panels, arranged in three rows of three, comprise each of two plates. The first plate depicts Franco in each panel, moving through various acts of destruction while mounted on a horse. In the third scene, upper left of the plate, Franco attacks with a pickax a classical (or classicizing) bust that looks like one of Picasso's studio images from the Vollard Suite.

Given the tyrannical hold of the classical Greek and Roman past on the history of Western art and the association of classical antiquity with a kind of conservative, elite culture in the modern West, a classical bust might seem a strange object for a fascist to attack. Indeed, elsewhere in Europe, Hitler and Mussolini put the classical past to their own use; it is, for example, that very moment of art produced under the short-lived Athenian democracy that Leni Riefenstahl coopted for Hitler in her film *Olympia* (1938). In this way, classical culture became a tool of conservative governments and social groups. Picasso, in contrast, sought out the multifaceted and ambiguous aspects of antiquity and drew them into his own modernism. Franco's axe attack could be taken at face value, as an iconoclastic act of a dictator. Picasso's classicism, however, is rarely so straightforward. Under Franco's axe is classicism itself, which for Picasso is always already multifaceted and fragmented.

In the Vollard Suite Picasso repeatedly depicts the blind Minotaur. In the version from September 22, 1934 (p. 42), the scene of the blind Minotaur is contiguous with another canvas, a variation on his July 22 linear sketch for *The Death of Marat*. The sketch is a citation of Jacques-Louis David's painting of the murdered French revolutionary. Picasso's executes this image within an image in a distinctly sparse and linear style, abandoning the curving lines of his classicizing figures. Here within these repeated depictions of ancient players and forms, Picasso eulogizes a modern revolutionary. In this way, Picasso's Vollard Suite depicts the potential for revolution within even the most classical of forms.

1 On the history of the Vollard Suite and its status as a cohesive unit, see Lisa Florman, *Myth and Metamorphosis: Picasso's Classical Prints of the 1930s* (Cambridge, MA: MIT Press, 2000), 70–73.
2 See Christine Mitchell Havelock, *The Aphrodite of Knidos and Her Successors: A Historical Review of the Female Nude in Greek Art* (Ann Arbor: University of Michigan Press, 1995).
3 See Mary Louise Hart, *The Art of Ancient Greek Theater* (Los Angeles: J. Paul Getty Museum, 2010).

> forceps, extracts it with sword; / last of tongue root quivers: tongue lies / trembling, murmuring on dark ground: like snake's / tail, lopped off & wanting to leap, it throbs, / & dying, seeks mistress's feet; (& they say / after this horror—I can hardly believe it— / he took her torn body for pleasure again & again).[23]

Philomela survives and weaves the events into a tapestry that she sends to her sister. In revenge, the sisters kill Itys, Tereus and Procne's son, and serve his flesh to Tereus at a banquet. After the king has eaten his son's flesh, Philomela emerges with the head of Itys on a platter. The acute violence of Philomela's story is nominally mitigated by her final transformation into a nightingale. It was no doubt significant for Picasso that Philomela's story emerge as something of an *Ur-eine* (primal being) for modern poetry. The tale reappears most famously in Shakespeare's *Titus Andronicus* and T. S. Eliot's *The Waste Land*.[24]

While Ovid offers extreme details of the story's violence, like Philomela's severed tongue writhing on the ground and still struggling to call for her father, Picasso depicts in synchronic narrative the repeated rapes and the dissolution of the body that these rapes engender. In his four versions, Picasso works through the violent story to settle on a version in which the dissolution of the boundary between Philomela's and Tereus's bodies conveys its violence. In the September 18 study (p. 169 left), he depicts Tereus and Philomela as separate and defined bodies at rest. Only the disfiguring dagger at Tereus's hip registers any aspect of Ovid's narrative. In his three other versions, Picasso discards the direct reference of the dagger to specific tortures, focusing instead on the more generalized penetration of one body by another.[25]

Picasso's published etching (p. 200) depicts Tereus moving into a resistant Philomela, although the ambiguity or at least restraint of her resistance sets Picasso's drawing decidedly apart from Ovid's text. Tereus simultaneously stands over Philomela and lunges into her; his right leg appears both straight and bent-kneed, while his left is braced to the side. Philomela's right foot merges with Tereus's torso, pushing into him, in vain. The limb itself is not fully enclosed or defined but open to the invasion. Her left leg kicks against Tereus's standing right leg and opens against the movement of his bent right leg. Philomela fights and flails before our eyes and in the same figural moment. The lack of bodily enclosure, particularly of torsos and genitals, registers the merging of their bodies, of his movement into her. Tereus's hands clasp Philomela's back and neck, holding her to him. She averts her face. The strands of her hair recall Picasso's earlier, electric paintings from the late 1920s. Of his four studies of this story, Picasso chose the most domesticated for publication. Without Ovid's words, the image might register as sex-play, an ambiguity that pervades different episodes throughout the Vollard Suite.

23
Ovid, *Metamorphoses* 6.6.125–26.

24
In *Titus Andronicus* (act 2, scene 4), Lavinia is raped by two men, who cut off not just her tongue but also her hands, to prevent her from weaving or writing an account of their crime, as Philomela did. Eliot references the rape of Philomela in *The Waste Land* at lines 98–103.

25
The dagger returns later in the hands of the Minotaur in a group of five etchings dated April 11, 1933. The story appears in *Metamorphoses* 8.

26
The illustrated border does not appear in Florman's *Myth and Metamorphosis*, but does appear in the 2001 exhibition catalogue *Picasso érotique*, 104–5. The catalogue includes only two studies, perhaps because the first and final versions were not sufficiently "érotique."

Picasso's third study most fully articulates the breadth of his engagement with Philomela's rape. He composed the scene within a central rectangular frame but filled the border with sketches (p. 169 right).[26] While the border images are themselves studies in some respects, they contribute to the image's overall sense of repeated movement. This study also articulates a relationship between Picasso's graphic works of 1930–31 and what he put to the test of large-scale painting in 1931–32. In the study's central panel, Picasso depicts Tereus's bulky frame pressing down on the resistant Philomela, who shoves at her attacker with her left leg. Tereus restrains her arms, pushing her to the ground. Hash marks radiate from Tereus's grip on Philomela's left arm, a feature that is not retained in the other studies. The marks add a somewhat comic urgency that counters the gravity of the violation under way. Philomela's spreading body—her navel floating to the left, Picasso's trademark composite rear-frontal view, her impossibly rotated left leg—attests to her effortful struggle. She averts her face from both Tereus's and the viewer's gaze. Philomela's turned-away face obscures the chronology of events: are we seeing the rape before or after Tereus has cut out her tongue? This chronological ambiguity registers rape's repetition, its iterative impact.

Picasso *figures* the repeated rape in the multiple faces around the border. At the bottom of the frame, he deploys a shaded, volumetric style that is entirely different from the linearity of the central frame and the rest of the border. A lush nude figure reclines at left. She lies on her right side, right leg drawn up beneath her and head propped in her right hand. Her round breasts press forward, framed by her left arm, which drapes along the curves of her torso. Her hand falls strategically to cover her genitals in a coquettish gesture that invokes the classical Venus pudica ("modest Venus"), a figure with whom Picasso feels entirely at home. Two similarly shaded busts appear at the right. At the margins, Picasso returns to the weightier presence of figures in the round. The right border begins with one hand gripping another at the wrist, with great attention paid to the lines and contours of both hands. By contrast, the hands and feet in the central frame are much less complete, their digits unfinished or open-ended. Above the hands, Tereus's bearded profile, with eyes downcast toward the hands as well as toward the defeated Philomela, appears in quadruplicate. His expression here is far less predatory, more observant, than in the main scene. The short strands of Tereus's hair give way to Philomela's averted face in triplicate along the upper right border. A fourth face attaches to a twisting, prone torso that runs along the top border. Her limbs are absent. This body bears a strong formal resemblance to the body twisting from Orpheus's arms in the September 1 study. Another averted face, in profile, appears beneath Philomela's leg. How many times must she turn away?

27
The second study, executed on the same day, resembles the third but includes only a bust along the bottom border. In its central panel, Philomela battles her attacker more animatedly than in the final version, but her body is less dispersed than in the third study.

28
Two sculptures from 1928, *Metamorphose I* and *Metamorphose II*, bear mention at this junction, for their fused limbs present a being that perpetually merges with itself.

At top left, in an inversion of the twisting Philomela at right, a lush sleeper reclines. She evokes another study from early September that Picasso executed on the back of an envelope, in which a sleeper cushions her head on outstretched arms. The organic modeling of the body, with its apple-shaped breasts and belly and scythe-like legs, reappears two years later as aspects of *Figures by the Sea*, and more calmly in the series of *Sleeping Woman* paintings of 1932. In the Philomela sketch, the sleeper's pliant sensuality is contrasted by its pendant at right and the brittle linearity of the resistant Philomela's body in the central frame. If Picasso took from his study of Philomela a preference for her sleeping figure opposite, he seems to have worked through some of that logic here at the margin. A frontal nude takes up most of the left border, and just above her head is another averted profile.[27]

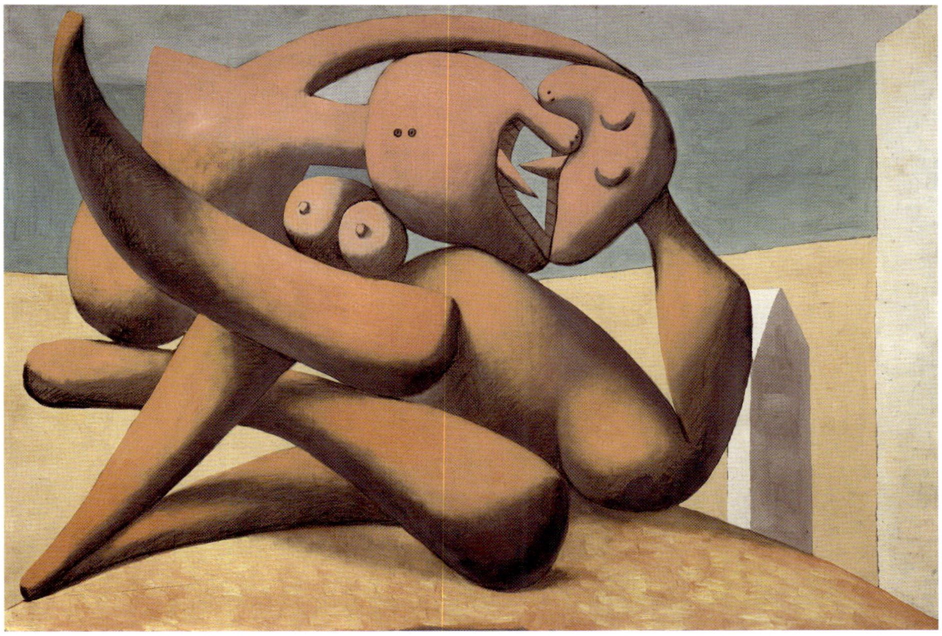

In his paintings of the early 1920s, Picasso explored light subjects—ladies by a spring, boys piping, couples on the beach—with a weighted, sculptural style, and only hinted at the illusion of a body's bounded integrity. In 1930, he brought the simplicity of line to bear on debasement. The lack of enclosure of Philomela's body articulates an idea that is similar to the one implied by the paint dripping from the foot of the woman at the right in *Three Women at the Spring*: the impossibility of individualism, of a body's bounded independence. The solid, substantial bodies of the early 1920s reappear a decade later as the merging of modular body parts at the beach, entwined and indistinguishable, as in *Figures by the Sea*. The figure(s) here work their semblance of boundedness and individuation, a semblance that is only partially performed. In *Figures by the Sea*, as in Picasso's *Metamorphoses* illustrations—especially those of Tereus and Philomela—it is impossible to isolate one body from another or to assemble the parts into a unified whole. The truth of the plastic body's nonindividuation appears before the viewer, made (barely) tolerable by paint. Picasso has captured these forms, sculpted out of the sand on which they rest, in their full, illusory presence, but at a moment whose imminent dissolution is figured in our inability to articulate individual bodies. If Picasso's paintings of the early 1920s hint at bodily replication, *Figures by the Sea* pictures that replication in terms of exchange or interchange between bodies, an interchange that occurs at the expense of individuation. Metamorphosis demands the breakdown of illusory bodily integrity.[28] While this painting bears no obvious formal relationship to classical imagery, it engages the same questions of the body's coherence and solidity. From *Three Women at the Spring* to *Figures by the Sea*, Picasso's engagement with the body and the ancient Mediterranean develops over the course of a decade.

Pablo Picasso, ***Figures by the Sea***, January 12, 1931; oil on canvas, 51⅛ × 76¾ in. (130 × 195 cm); Musée Picasso, Paris, France

The border of Picasso's third study for the *Rape of Philomela* allows us to understand the sleepers who make up the majority of his large-scale paintings between 1931 and 1932 within the context of his particular engagement with Ovid. The series of sleeping women makes this connection to his Ovidian figures rather obviously by depicting a sleeping body that seems to be both human and composed of ripe fruit. With this sleep sequence, Picasso approaches the process of bodily change that he distinctly avoided in his illustrations of the *Metamorphoses*, precisely because his version of metamorphosis differs from Ovid's. In an Ovidian version of the scene, the woman would become a cornucopia with womanly desires, her soul intact within her transformed body; in Picasso's depiction, she is both woman and fruit. In his *Girl with Guitar* (January 10, 1932) the paneling of the *Figure* sequence from the late 1920s is recognizable. The paneling gives way to the back of her chair, disjointed by the head in profile. The familiar white shape highlights the girl's head and its separation from her body. Picasso takes pains to suture this head to its body, to depict the imperfect process of melding a face and figure. He has smoothed the face's electric strands of hair and given it the elegant lines of his illustrations for Ovid. Her breast is both apple and fern, her belly the guitar that in an earlier incarnation stands in some relation to the face (compare with the September 1 study for *The Death of Orpheus*). Her limbs merge with the chair in which she sleeps.

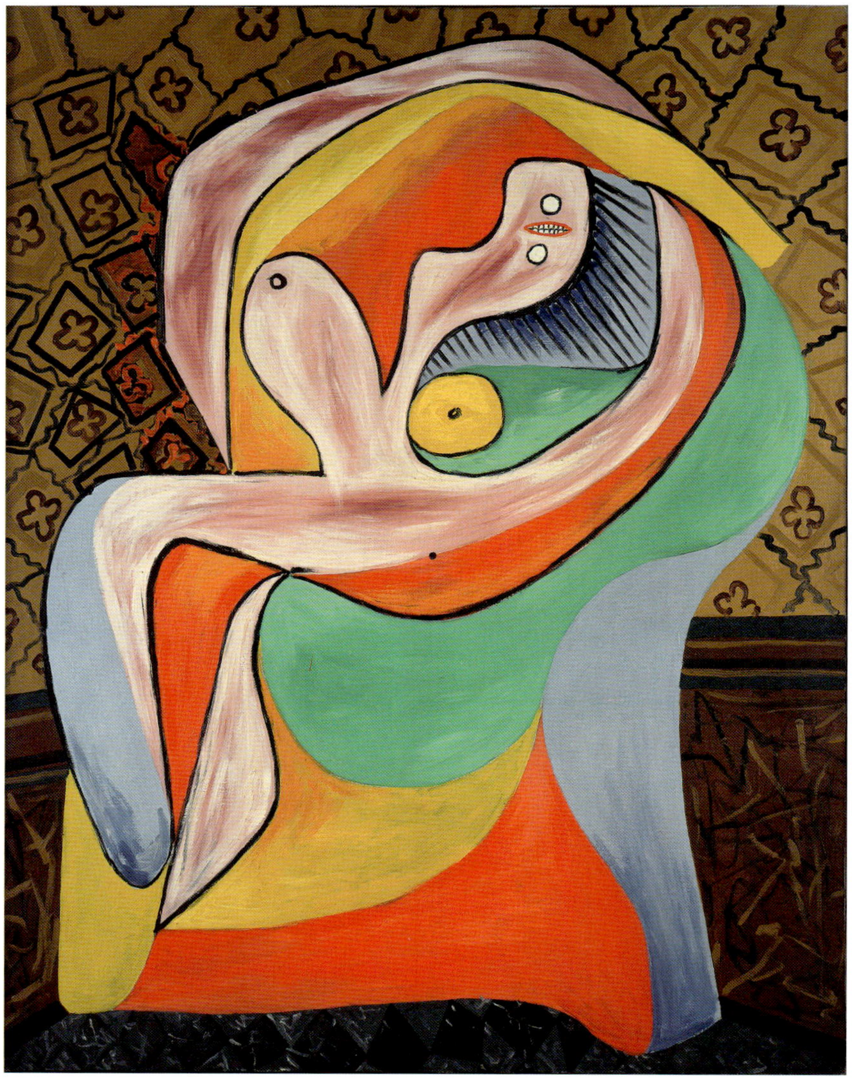

In *Reading*, painted the previous day (January 9, 1932), Picasso grafts the figure's head more securely to her body, its sutures smoothed. If the Ovidian prints concerned themselves with the interpenetration of multiple bodies, or with the openness of one body to another as the sign of its fiction, the sleep sequence, which Picasso worked out in the context of illustrating Ovid, explores the reconstitution of face and body from constituent organic parts, and the penetration of a body by its own constituent parts. Guitar, fern, and face create a woman.

Pablo Picasso, ***Rest***, January 22, 1932; oil on canvas, 63¾ × 51¼ in. (161.9 × 130.2 cm); private collection

Two images in the sleep sequence painted January 22 and 23, 1932, display the all-at-once-ness toward which Picasso had been working. On January 22, he painted *Rest*. But this is hardly the body at rest. We recognize the wild profile with its electric hair and its displaced carnivorous mouth between two vertical eyes, somehow replicated in a gaping scream emanating from the profile. This head meets its body seamlessly; body and face form a monstrous, unified whole.[29] Vivid color—bright reds, yellows, greens, and blues—advertises the figure's madness, juxtaposed against jaunty parlor wallpaper. Here is the creature that stoned Orpheus. The next day, with *Sleep*, Picasso returns to the comfort of apparent legibility: clear lines, soft color, a calm moon-face, rounded breasts and belly, the closed hairless lips of prepubescent genitals. We can almost hear a light snore. In his selections for the *Metamorphoses*, Picasso deliberately depicted the most shattering of narratives with exquisite line. By the same token, Picasso painted *Sleep* one day after *Rest* not to sublimate the terrible with the beautiful but to declare the two as one, existing in a state of unending and simultaneous metamorphosis in which beauty and monstrosity inhabit the same form.

Many thanks to Diana Magaloni and Michael Govan for inviting me to participte in this exhibition in such good company, to the the indefatigable Lilly Casillas for her incredible research skills, to Sara Cody for her deft editing, to Camille Mathieu for sharing her knowledge of early archaeology, art history, and modernism so generously, and to Jeremy Melius, Shahrzade Ehya, and Tim Clark for the opportunity to begin thinking through Picasso and Ovid in their company early in my time at Berkeley. All errors remain my own.

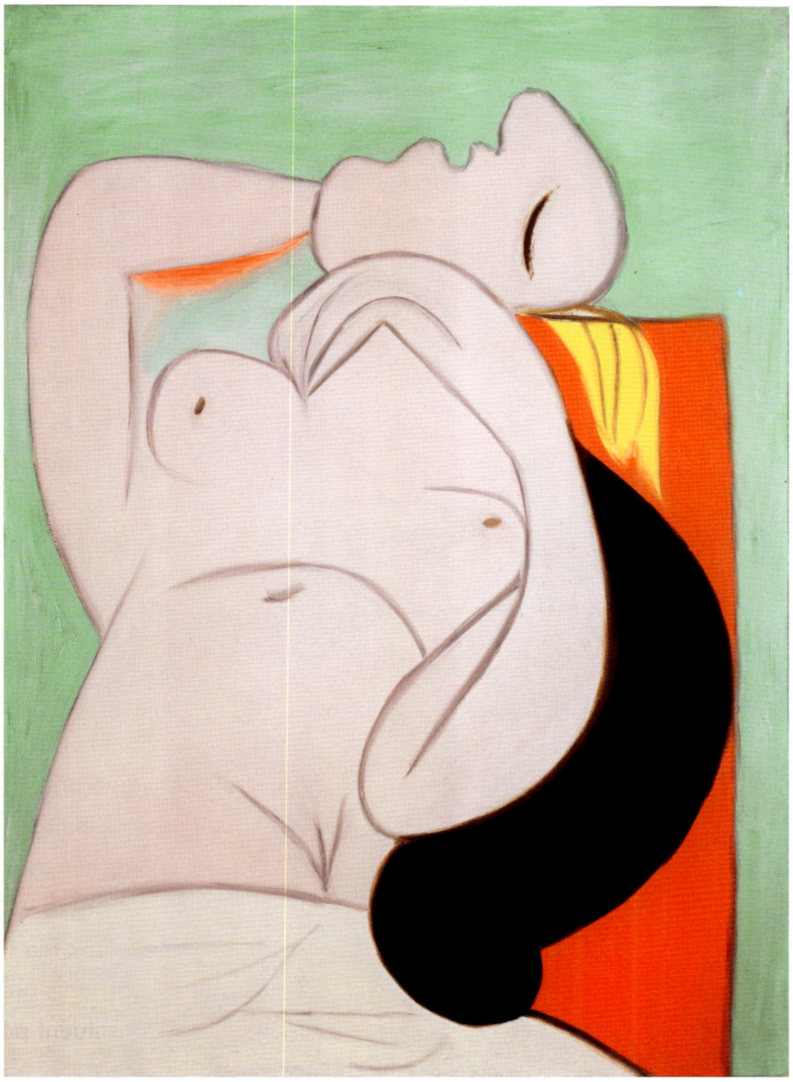

Pablo Picasso, ***Sleep***, 1932; oil on canvas, 51¼ × 38¼ in. (130.2 × 97 cm); private collection

29 On monstrosity and Picasso, see T. J. Clark, *Picasso and Truth: From Cubism to Guernica* (Princeton, NJ: Princeton University Press, 2013), 173–90.

GUERNICA AND THE TRADITION OF MURALISM AND CONTEMPORARY URBAN ART

ÉMILIE BOUVARD

1 Picasso did not respond to the invitation.

The rise of totalitarianism in the 1930s made explicit the crucial relationship between art, politics, and history, both within and outside such regimes. In January 1937, two events occurred in the lives of Diego Rivera and Pablo Picasso that typified this relationship. That month, Frida Kahlo and Diego Rivera welcomed Leon Trotsky and his wife, Natalia Sedova, to Casa Azul, their home in Mexico City. The Trotksys had fled the Moscow Trials in the Soviet Union that aimed to purge all opposition to Stalin within the Communist Party through silence, prison, or death. The reception of Trotsky and his wife by Diego and Frida had placed them in a dangerous position internationally and within the Mexican Communist Party. Meanwhile in Paris, Picasso was commissioned that same month by a delegation of Spain's Popular Front—a coalition of Spanish socialist and communist parties elected in 1936—to create a large-scale painting to cover one of the walls of the Spanish Pavilion at the International Exposition that would open in Paris that summer. From this commission, Picasso would produce *Guernica*, which would eventually become one of the most widely recognized paintings of the twentieth century.

European politics were increasingly tense in this period, and *Guernica*—created in the aftermath of the aerial bombardment of the small Basque village by German forces in support of Franco—was a powerful denunciation of the atrocities. No doubt the political situation in Spain was discussed at Casa Azul, as Frida Kahlo and Diego Rivera were themselves supporters of the Popular Front, which had been fighting a civil war to defend the Spanish Republic against the far-right nationalist forces of General Francisco Franco. Spain appeared as a miniature theater scene, or a macabre rehearsal for the global conflict to come: Hitler and Mussolini supported the Nationalists, while the Soviet Union supported the Republican forces.

Rivera's murals of this period would have been known by Picasso; Rivera and other Mexican muralists had risen to prominence through the 1920s, and in 1932 both Rivera and Picasso were invited to paint a mural at Rockefeller Center in New York.[1] They also shared friends in common, such as André Breton, for they had been part of the same avant-garde milieu from 1907 to 1920 in Paris. Nevertheless, the mural as an artistic form as it developed in Mexico is not likely to have been on Picasso's mind during the making of *Guernica*, or at least we have no evidence that it was. We could just suggest that *Guernica*—inspired as it is by the traditional genre of history painting in its scale and theme, and by the genre's shift in representation from scenes from antiquity to those of recent history (e.g., Francisco de Goya's *The Disasters of War*, 1810–15)—was one of the most striking examples of the contemporary reinvention of history painting in the 1930s. Rivera was also an active participant in this process (his historic murals at the Ministry of Public Education and the Palacio Nacional in Mexico City are key examples), as were other painters such as Otto Dix (*The War*, 1929–32).

Prior to the attack on Guernica, Picasso was working on the series of etchings later collected as the Vollard Suite, and focused on such themes as the minotaur and the painter and his model. However, the bombing of the village on April 26, 1937, followed by radio reports and the photographs of the destruction published in French newspapers, provoked the sudden shift toward the scene that we all know (p. 235). Dora Maar photographed the painting in process (p. 17): the monumental canvas (nearly 3.5 x 7.8 m, or 11.5 x 25.5 feet) leans on the far wall of his studio in the rue des Grands Augustins, with its wooden ceiling beams visible. Maar's photographs of Picasso's process in painting *Guernica* must have influenced the artist, for he changed the outdoor scene of destruction of Guernica as a town into an indoor scene of a house on fire, the fusion of the creative space—his studio—and the real space where the bombings occurred—transforming both the painting and the process of its making into a surrealist experience. As a result, his studio wall becomes the first wall to transform *Guernica* from a "painting" into a "mural."

The inherent confusion of terms referring to *Guernica* is illustrated in a number of semantic considerations. As a French speaker, I was surprised the first time I heard and read *Guernica* described as "a mural," in both Spanish and English; in French, it is always referred to as *la peinture* or *le tableau*. In 1937, in his discussion for the opening of the Spanish Pavilion, Max Aub described it in French as follows: "At the entrance, on the right, Picasso's great painting leaps into view."[2] That summer's issue of *Cahiers d'art*, devoted exclusively to *Guernica* and Picasso's creative process, also refers to it in the language of "painting" and "canvas."[3] A decade later, in his notes for a 1947 symposium about *Guernica*, Alfred H. Barr Jr., director of the Museum of Modern Art, refers to it never as "a mural," but only as "a painting."[4] In 1956, in the catalogues for the painting's European tour, Daniel-Henry Kahnweiler, Picasso's long-time friend and dealer, also refers to it as a "picture" or a "painting."[5]

Nevertheless, the way *Guernica* was received—and referred to—by the public and press varied in this regard. Articles in Picasso's private archives refer to a "painting," but very often they also refer to it as a "fresco," underlining the monumentality of the work.[6] Emily Genauer, one of the first American journalists to review the Paris Exposition, quoted Picasso as speaking of a "panel" in reference to the work.[7] In London, where it was exhibited in 1938 to raise funds for Spanish refugees, British poet Herbert Read referred to it as a "painting," a "canvas," and a "fresco" (in a slightly metaphoric sense).[8] A year later, when it was exhibited at the Valentine Galleries in New York, Elizabeth McCausland titled her review "*Guernica*, Picasso's Great Mural, Shown."[9] By contrast, Henry McBride evoked a "painting" in the *New York Sun*,[10] as did Doris Brian in *Art News*.[11] James Thrall Soby, who saw *Guernica* in Paris, praises it solely as a "mural" (three occurrences) in reviewing the retrospective *Picasso: Forty Years of His Art* a few months later.[12] Jerome Seckler, in his famous 1945 interview with Picasso for the communist magazine *New Masses*, asked Picasso about the "mural."[13] In 1947, Ad Reinhardt called *Guernica* "a mural that was to become the greatest anti-fascist work of art."[14]

2
Max Aub, *Hablo como Hombre* (Mexico City: Joaquín Motiz, 1967), 11–13; Ellen C. Oppler, ed., *Picasso's Guernica* (New York and London: Norton, 1988), 204.

3
Cahiers d'Art 12, no. 4/5.

4
Guernica: Symposium, incl. drafts, notes, and material by AHB, November 25, 1947, Alfred H. Barr Jr. Papers, 12.II.F.3, Museum of Modern Art Archives, New York.

5
Daniel-Henry Kahnweiler, *Picasso: Guernica* (Brussels: Palais des Beaux-Arts; Amsterdam: Stedelijk Museum; Stockholm: National Museum, 1956).

6
Fonds 515AP, Pablo Picasso's private archives, Musée National Picasso, Paris, boxes H21 to H40.

7
Picasso quoted in Emily Genauer, "Picasso's Mural Draws Throng: Painter Says Work Defends Loyalists," *New York World Telegram*, August 21, 1937; quoted in Oppler, *Picasso's Guernica*, 224.

8
"Picasso's great fresco is a monument to destruction, a cry of outrage and horror amplified by the spirit of a genius," Herbert Read, *London Bulletin* VI (October 1938): 6; see also Archives, Musée national Picasso-Paris, Paris.

9
Elizabeth McCausland, "*Guernica*, Picasso's Great Mural, Shown," *Springfield Republican*, May 21, 1939; quoted in Oppler, *Picasso's Guernica*, 226.

10
Henry McBride, "Picasso's Guernica Here," *New York Sun*, May 6, 1939; quoted in Oppler, *Picasso's Guernica*, 227.

11
Doris Brian, "Picasso Premiere: Guernica and Studies in Benefit Exhibition," *Art News*, May 20, 1939; quoted in Oppler, *Picasso's Guernica*, 229.

12
James Thrall Soby, "Picasso: A Critical Estimate," *Parnassus* 11 (December 1939); quoted in Oppler, *Picasso's Guernica*, 230.

13
Jerome Seckler, "Picasso Explains," *New Masses*, March 13, 1945; quoted in Oppler, *Picasso's Guernica*, 145; see also Picasso Archives, Musée National Picasso, Paris.

14
Ad Reinhardt, "How to Look at a Mural," *P.M.*, January 5, 1947.

15
Picasso quoted in Seckler, "Picasso Explains," *New Masses*, October 24, 1944, 11.

16
Simone Téry, "Picasso n'est pas officier dans l'armée française," *Les Lettres françaises* (March 24, 1945); see also Archives, Musée National Picasso, Paris.

17
Picasso quoted in Oppler, *Picasso's Guernica*, 153.

18
Picasso quoted in "Guernica ne reviendra en Espagne qu'avec la République," *Le Monde*, November 14, 1969.

And what did Picasso say about *Guernica*? In Seckler's 1945 interview, he spoke of it as a "mural": "My work is not symbolic. Only the *Guernica* mural is symbolic. But in the case of the mural, it is allegoric."[15] Just a few months later, he spoke of it to Simone Téry as "my canvas,"[16] followed by a written political artistic statement in which he stated: "No, painting is not done to decorate apartments. It is an instrument of war for attack and defense against the enemy."[17] More than two decades later, in 1969, in stating that *Guernica* should be returned to Spain once the republic is restored, he referred to it as the "work."[18] A year later, in a letter to the Museum

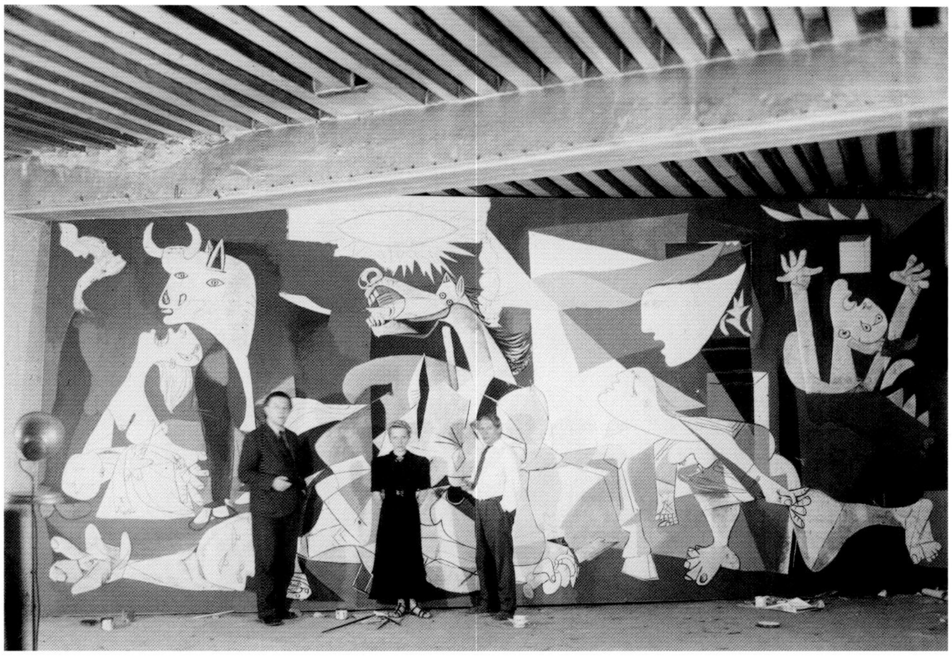

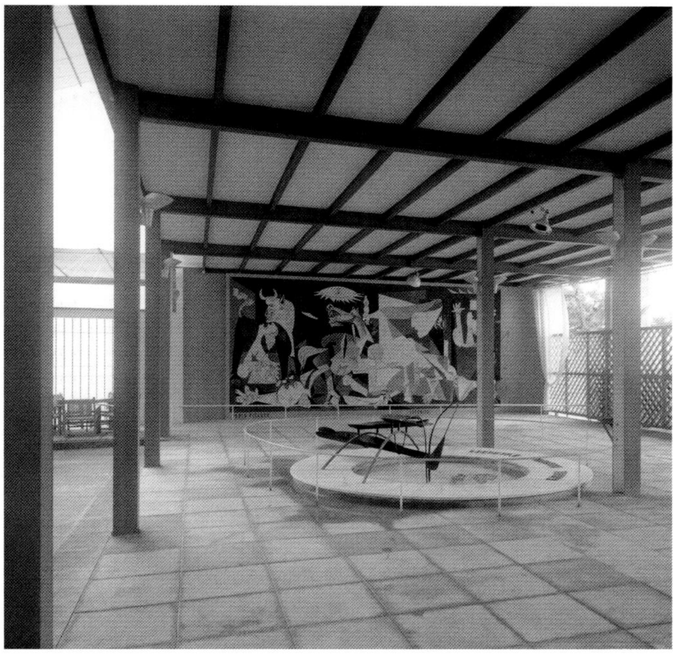

of Modern Art, he refers to it in French as *le tableau*. Finally, on November 8, 1974, more than a year after Picasso's death, MoMA curator William Rubin wrote to Spain's representative José Mario Arnero referring to *Guernica* as a "painting."

This brief history of the many ways *Guernica* has been referenced point to a striking conclusion: *Guernica* is described specifically as a mural when an author deals with its political reception. Even in the absence of documents supporting the idea that Picasso specifically had Rivera's murals in mind when he conceived of *Guernica* as a monumental work, the dimensions of the painting as well as Picasso's above-mentioned intention to create "an instrument of war" are those of a fresco. Frescoes functioned historically to address large numbers of people, like the Renaissance frescoes in religious and civic establishments and Rivera's modernist frescoes in Mexico and the United States. *Guernica* functioned as a different kind of mural: a "moveable fresco" that could be moved as needed.

LEFT Pablo Picasso (right), with Andre Breton and Jacqueline Lamba in front of *Guernica* at Picasso's rue des Grands-Augustins studio, May–June 1937 (photo by Dora Maar); Musée National d'Art Moderne, Centre Georges Pompidou, Paris

RIGHT Picasso's *Guernica* and Calder's *Mercury Fountain* at the Spanish Pavilion, International Exposition, Paris, 1937 (photo by Henri Baranger); Médiathèque de l'Architecture et du Patrimone, Paris

19 Max Aub to Luis Quintanilla, January 23, 1970, quoted in Herbert Routledge, *Guernica! Guernica! A Study of Journalism, Diplomacy, Propaganda, and History* (Berkeley: University of California Press, 2015), 479. Emphasis added.

In that context, it is interesting to read Max Aub's letter to the artist Luis Quintanilla, written in 1970, in which he recalls the painting's commission in 1937: "As cultural attaché to the Spanish Embassy in Paris and subcommissioner of the Spanish Pavilion in the 1937 Exposition, I ordered a painting—*or a fresco*—from Picasso for the entrance of the building conceived and built by the architects Lacasa and Sert."[19] In the 1937 Pavilion, Picasso's work was as large as the far end wall of the entrance hall; it could easily appear as an actual fresco, particularly in photographs. This impression was furthered by its installation in a large patio (where Alexander Calder's *Mercury Fountain* was also installed) that opened onto a garden where readings and performances were held. On the upper floors of the pavilion, visitors encountered politically engaged paintings and sculptures, as well as propaganda posters promoting the Republic and the Popular Front. With *Guernica*, Picasso might have preferred to create a "painting"—that is, a long-lasting work rather than an ephemeral one—but through its monumentality and subject matter, it was a painting that forever took on significant muralistic qualities.

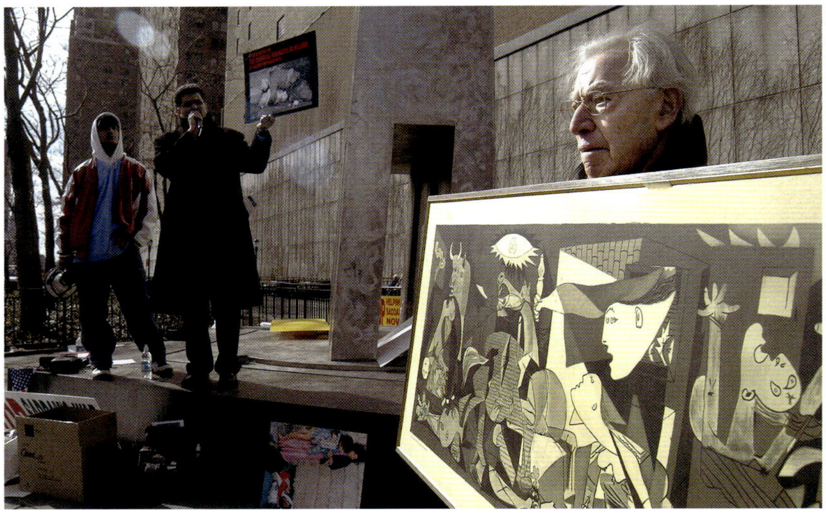

The qualities that contribute to *Guernica*'s reception as a mural also make it an inspiration for countless contemporary murals and graffiti around the world. Unsurprisingly, Spain is the country in which the highest number of *Guernicas* can be found. In the city of Guernica itself, a mural in ceramic representing the painting was installed in Pedro de Elejalde Street to commemorate the bombing as well as to advocate for bringing the painting to the city. *Guernica* generally appears in Spain in a pacifist context; additionally, it is sometimes presented as part of Spanish national heritage. It also has leftist political connotations, especially in demonstrations against the war in Iraq. Other representations utilize a newer interpretation of *Guernica*—namely, as an enactment against poverty, exclusion, and injustice. Picasso appears as a defender of the poor, and perhaps as an exile himself. His membership in the French Communist Party after World War II is likely influential in this regard, as might be his promotion of non-Western art—both factors that encourage the conception of Picasso as an artistic and political revolutionary in art. The *Guernicas* found throughout Latin America and South America (including Mexico, Argentina, and Brazil) also contain a similarly leftist content; reproduced mostly in poor areas, they denounce poverty and injustice, and are an appeal for equality.

Along similar lines, James De La Vega, a Puerto Rican street artist in New York, has painted two notable reinterpretations of *Guernica* in Harlem: *Homage to Picasso* (from 1996, at Lexington Avenue and 111th Street) and *Ode to Picasso* (from 1999, at Lexington Avenue and 124th Street). *Homage to Picasso*, against a red background,

A man holds a copy of Picasso's *Guernica* outside the United Nations in New York on February 5, 2003, to protest U.S. military action against Iraq

20 James De La Vega quoted in "Interview with James De La Vega," *Trip to El Barrio*, n.d., http://macaulay.cuny.edu/student-projects/2005/neighborhoods/2/EastHarlem/Shivani/Page/delavega.htm.

21 Gerry Adams, "Guernica Mural Unveiled," August 12, 2007, http://www.sinnfein.ie/contents/9723.

includes an aggressive-looking dog that competes with the bull in creating a disquieting mood and suggests the real-life dangers the neighborhood's residents may have felt at the time. The brightly colored *Ode to Picasso* (painted collectively with Nelson Caban, Michel Britto, PJ Pierre, and Victor Melendez) quotes *Guernica*'s structure but tells a different story. The mural gathers characters rendered in various shades of brown, black, white, and yellow (including a woman embracing a dog, an elderly man with a white beard, a drinker with a bottle in his hand, and a devil being pushed down by the dog's paw) around a green-hued Christ on the cross. In

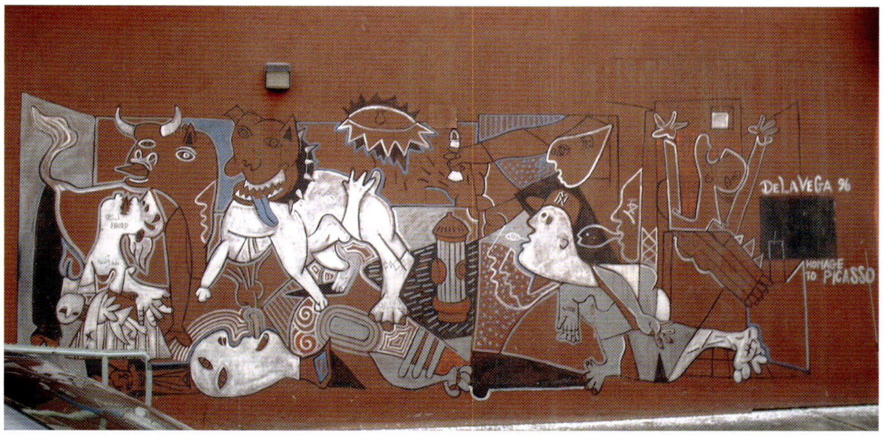

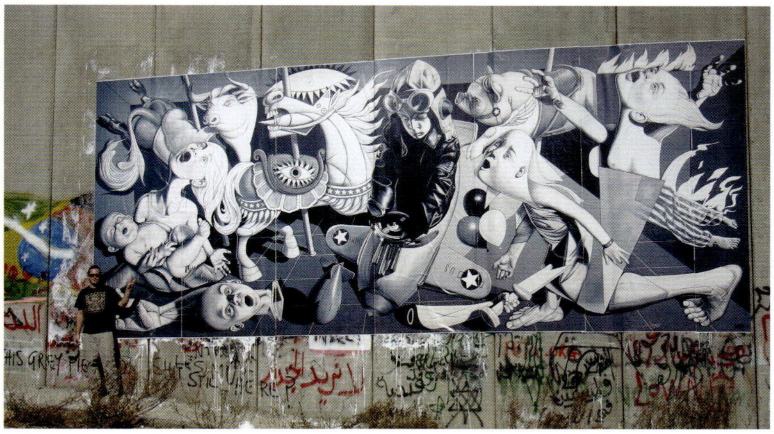

both works, De La Vega denounces the oppressive nature of poverty, as well as drugs and perhaps even the fascination with religion. In a 2005 interview, he noted that he "wanted to show that war also goes on in poor neighborhoods."[20]

The final group comprises walls within contested territories. At least one *Guernica* is documented to have been painted on the Berlin Wall. There have been at least three *Guernicas* in Belfast, including one on the so-called Solidarity Wall in Falls Road, which regularly features Irish republican murals (including one honoring the International Brigades that fought on the side of the Spanish Republic in 1936–39). Another one—a faithful reproduction of the painting—was inaugurated by Irish republican leader Gerry Adams in 2007. In his speech, he drew parallels between Belfast's Divis Street (the site of riots in 1964), the Palestinian border, the war in Iraq, and the bombing of Guernica.[21] Indeed, one of the most remarkable contemporary locations of *Guernica*'s presence is on the West Bank wall separating Israel and Palestine, which includes at least two *Guernicas*: one faithful to the original and another titled *Grade School Guernica* by street artist Ron English. English's mural retains Picasso's general composition and some distinctive details (electric bulb, horse, bull, fire), but strikingly he portrays only children in the scene, both as victims and, in the central figure, as a bomber. Beyond these two, at least one other *Guernica* has been created in Fallujah, Iraq, not to mention its presence as a "movable mural" appearing in antiwar demonstrations, particularly in 2003 against the Iraq War, and in Gaza. Eighty years after it was first created, *Guernica*'s effect is more powerful than ever.

LEFT James De La Vega, ***Homage to Picasso***, 1996; Harlem, New York City

RIGHT Ron English, ***Grade School Guernica***, 2007; West Bank, Palestine

PLATES II

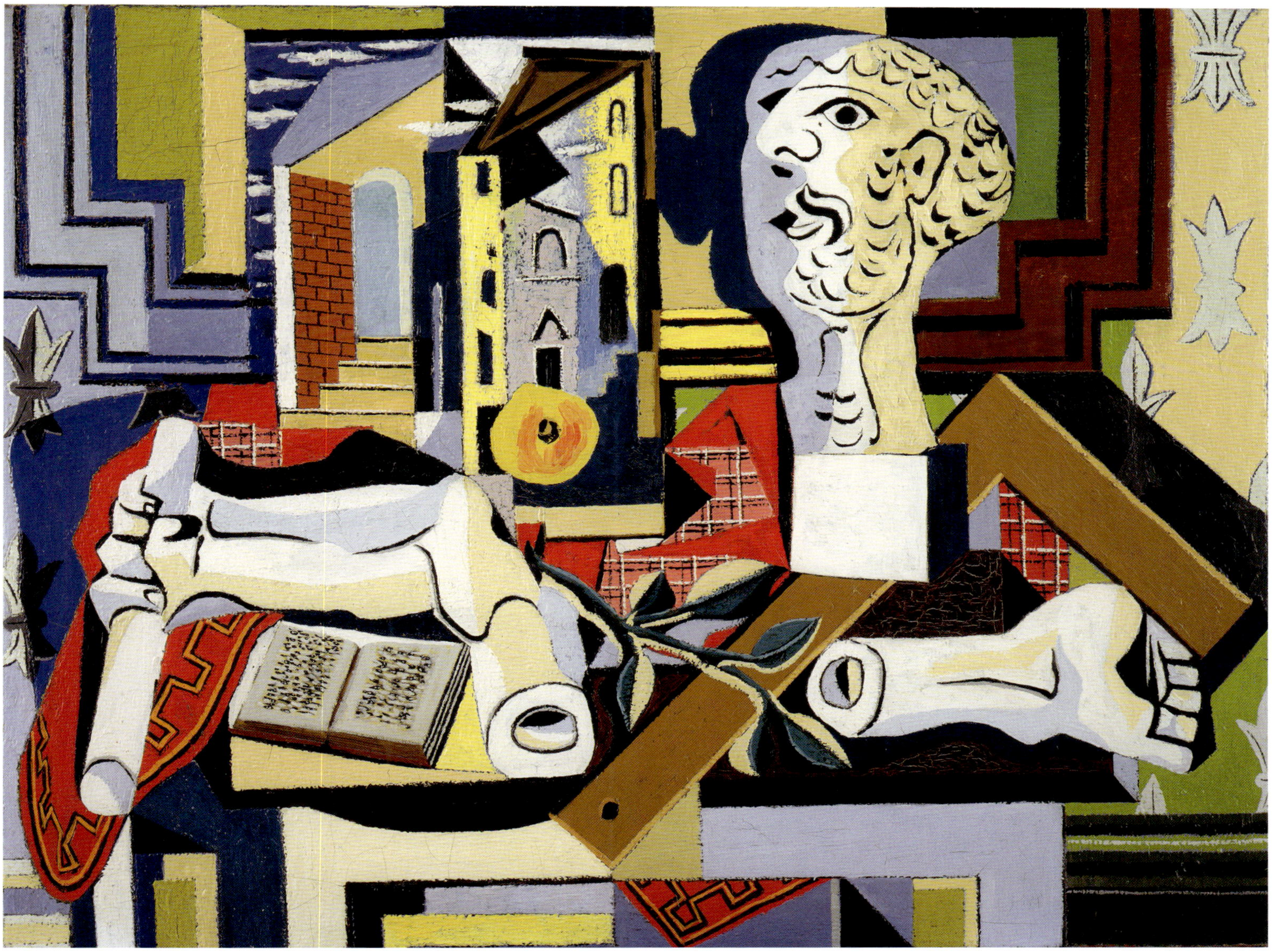

Pablo Picasso, ***Studio with Plaster Head***, June 1925

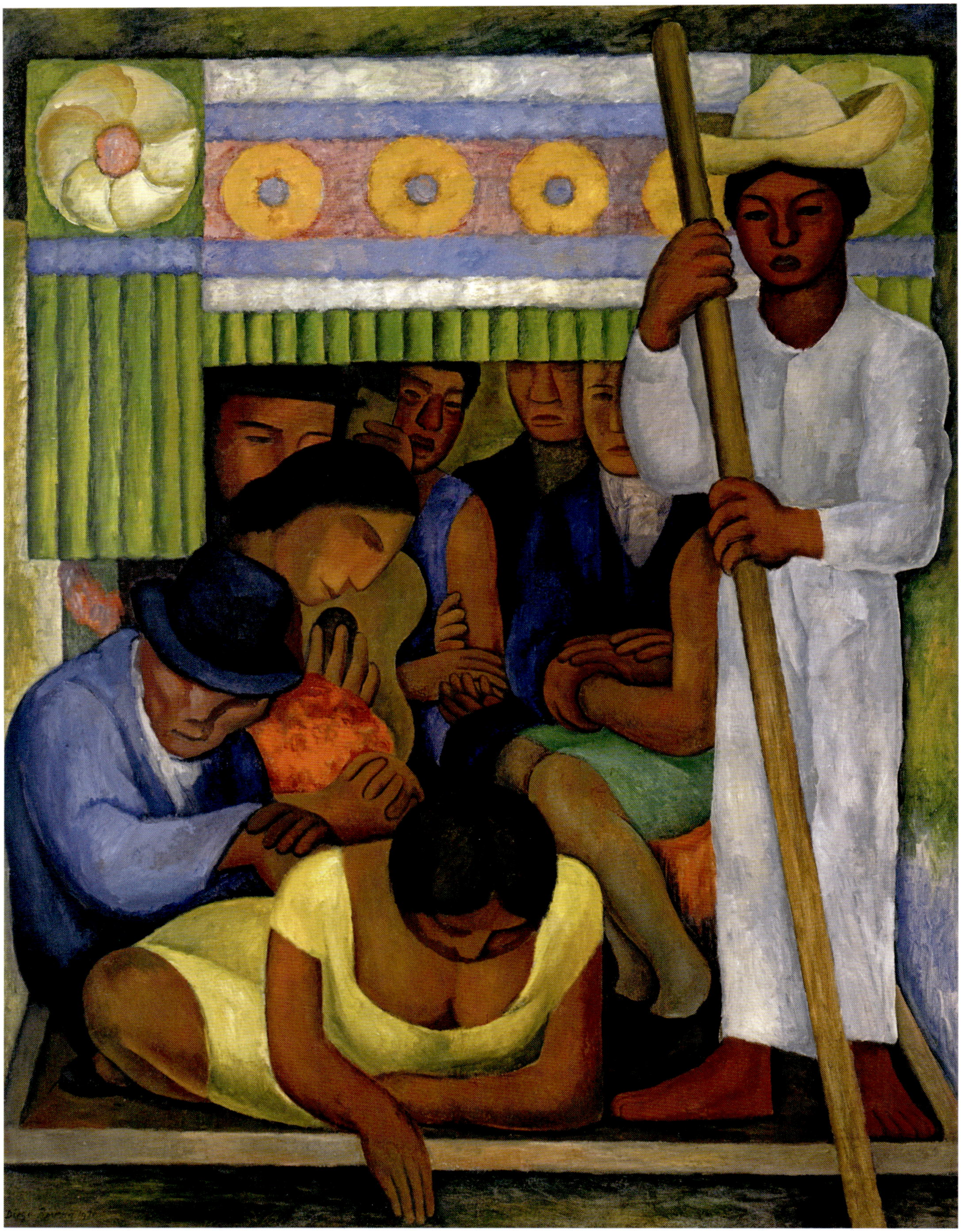

Diego Rivera, *Flowered Canoe*, 1931

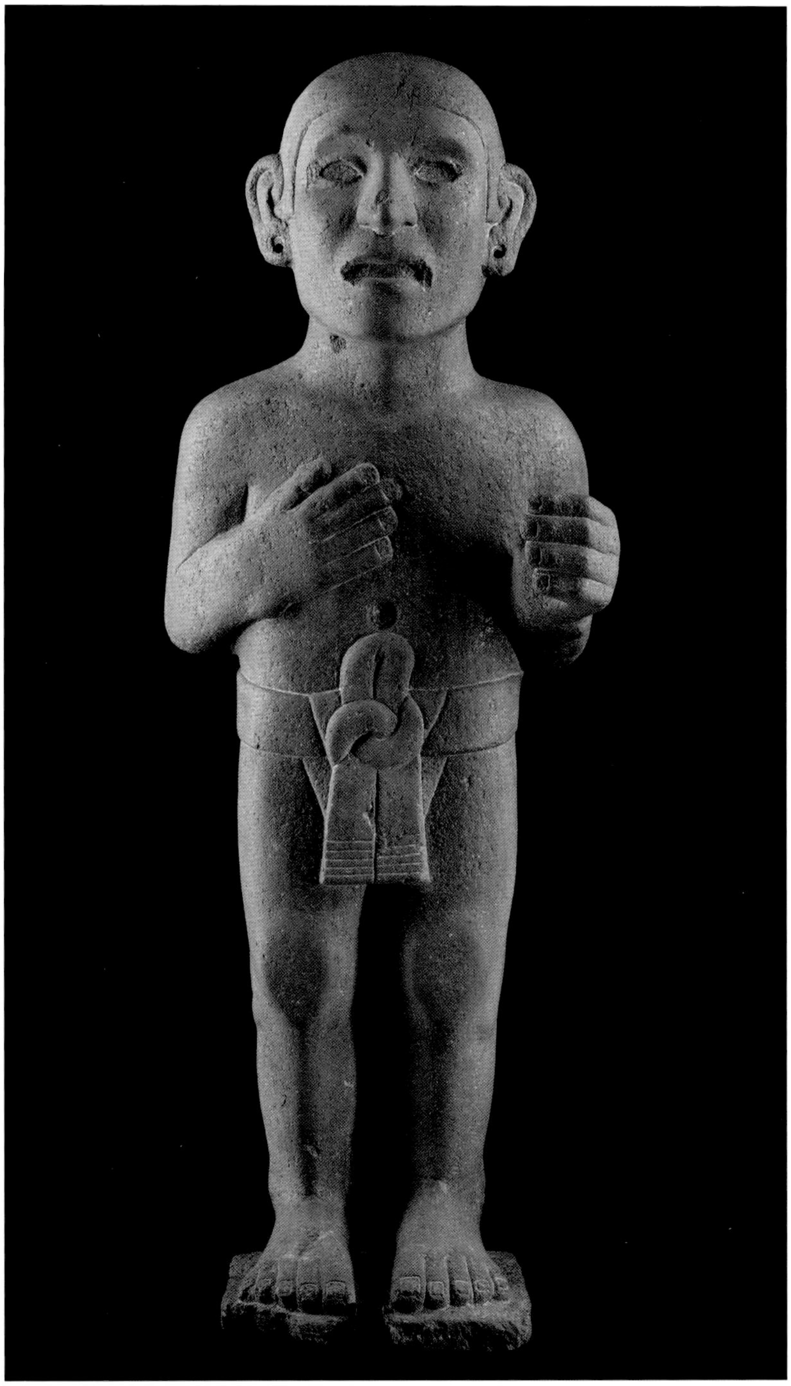

Macehual (*Commoner*), Mexico, Aztec, 1250–1521

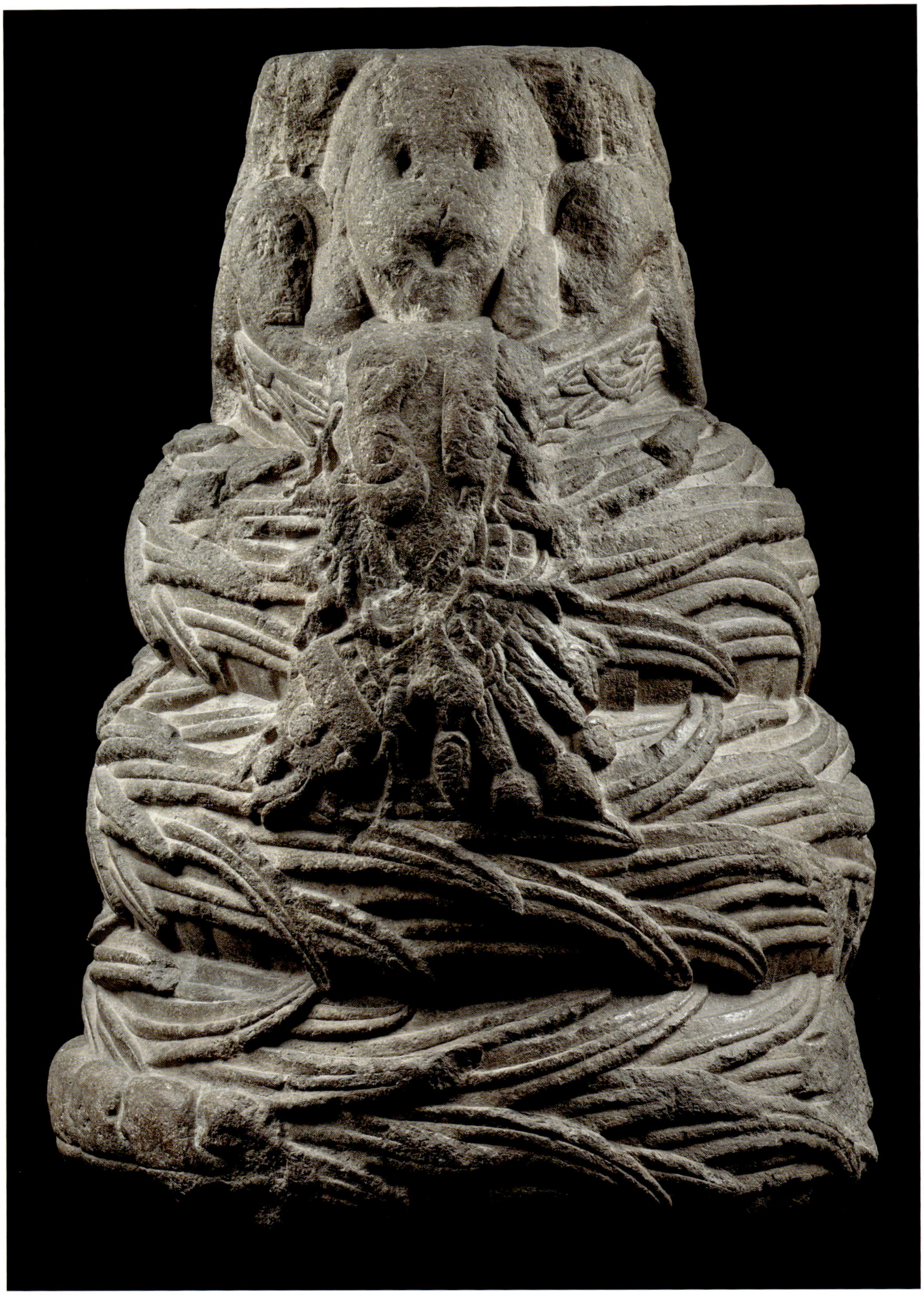

Quetzalcóatl (*Feathered Serpent*), Mexico, Aztec, 1250–1521

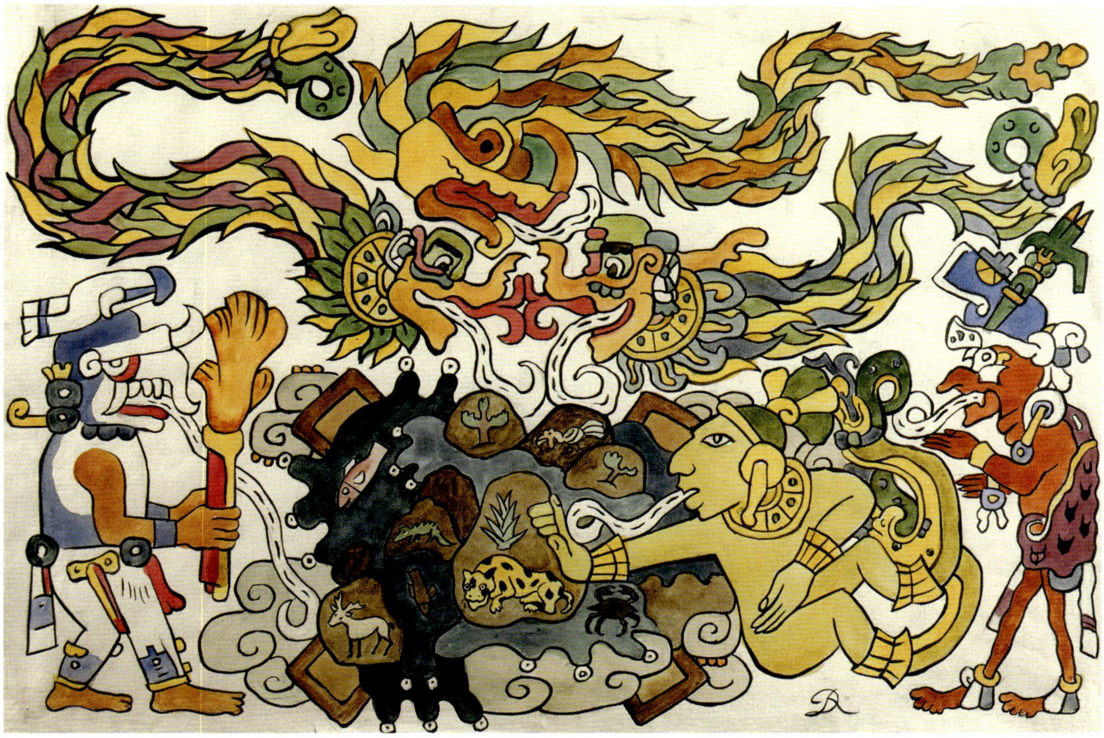

Diego Rivera, *Creation of the Universe*, 1931

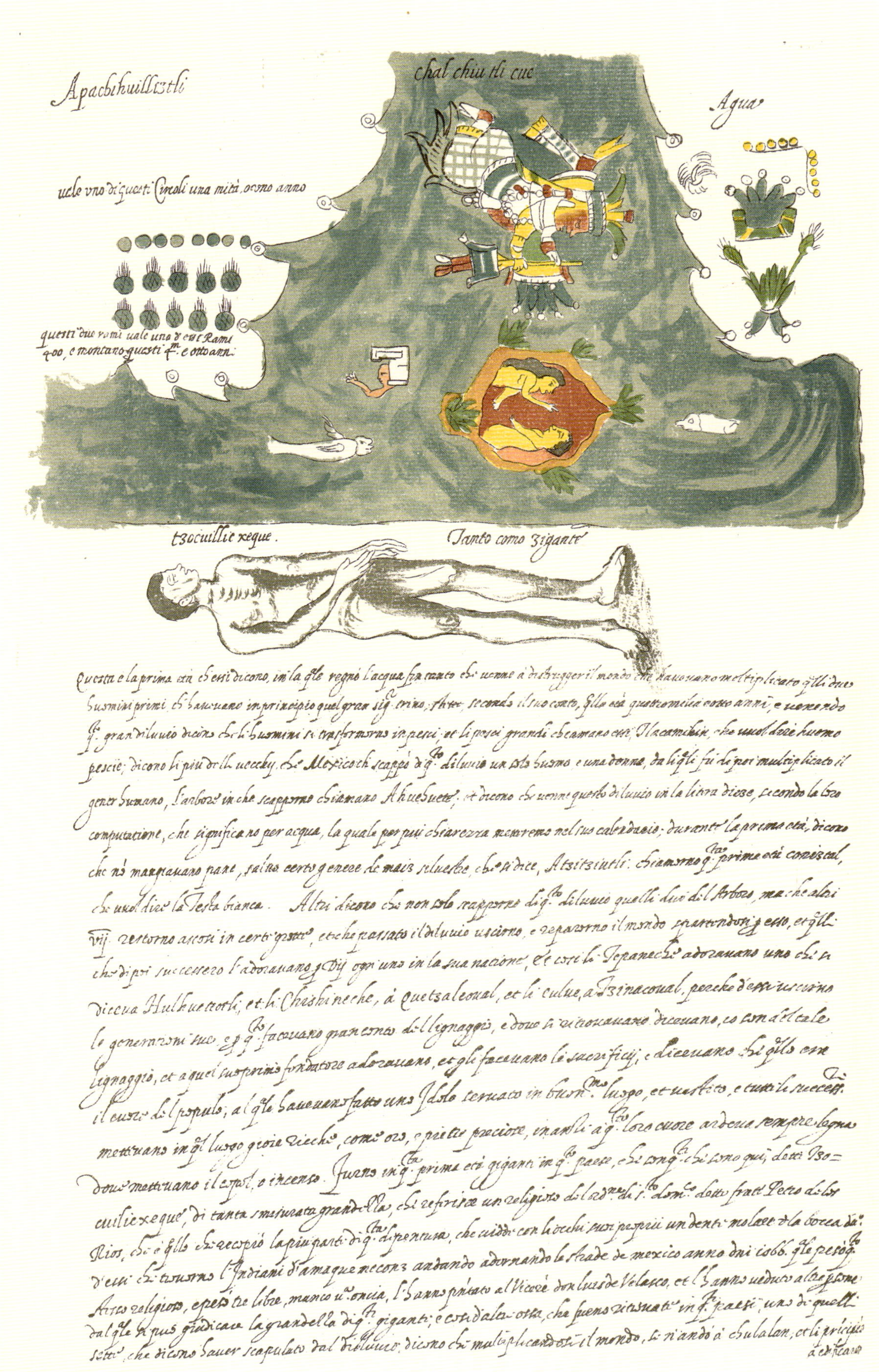

Codex Vaticanus 3738 (Codex Ríos), 1566; color reproduction (1979)

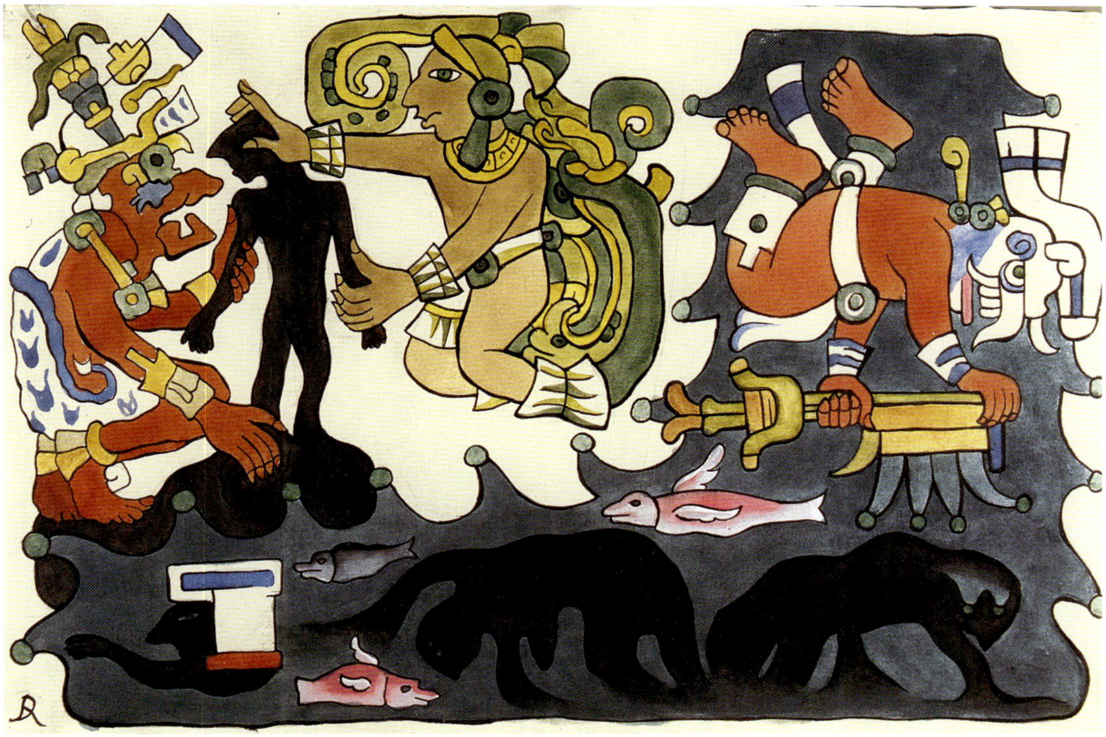

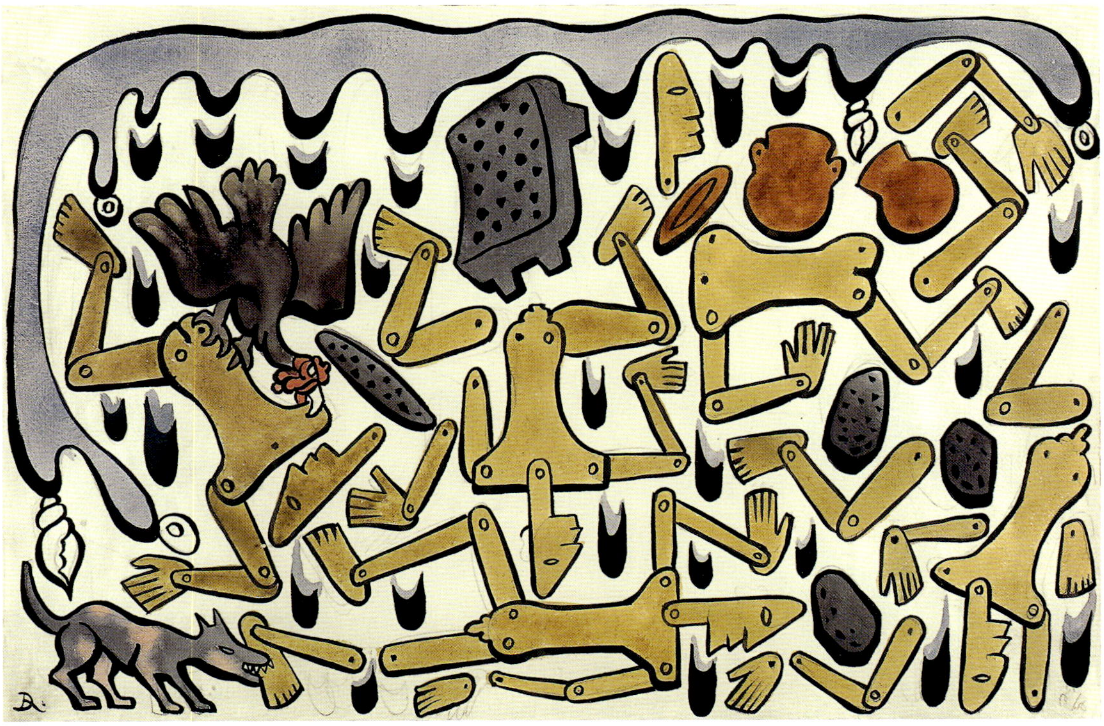

Diego Rivera, *The Creation of Man*, 1931

Diego Rivera, *The Flood and Destruction of the Wooden Men*, 1931

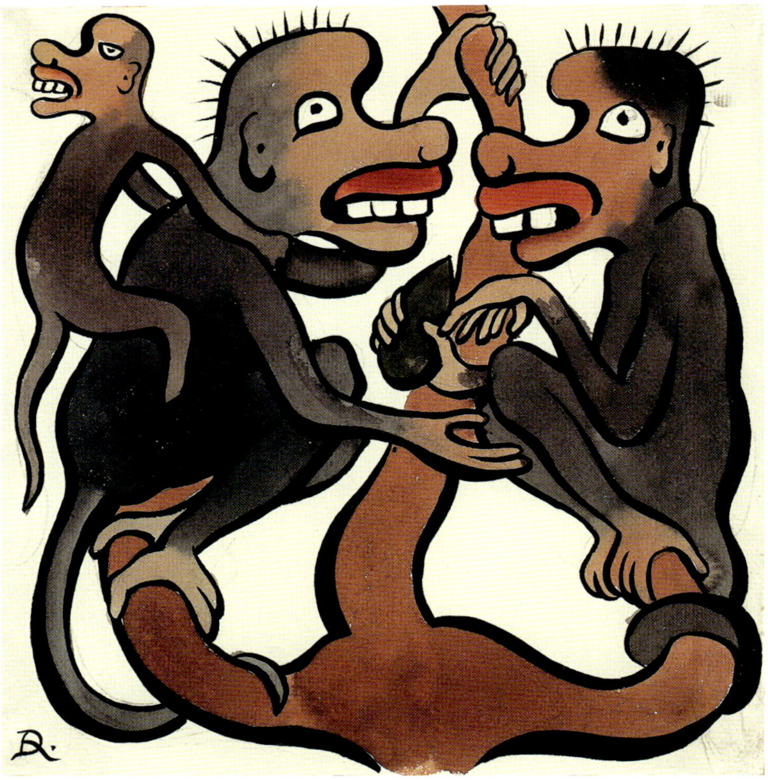

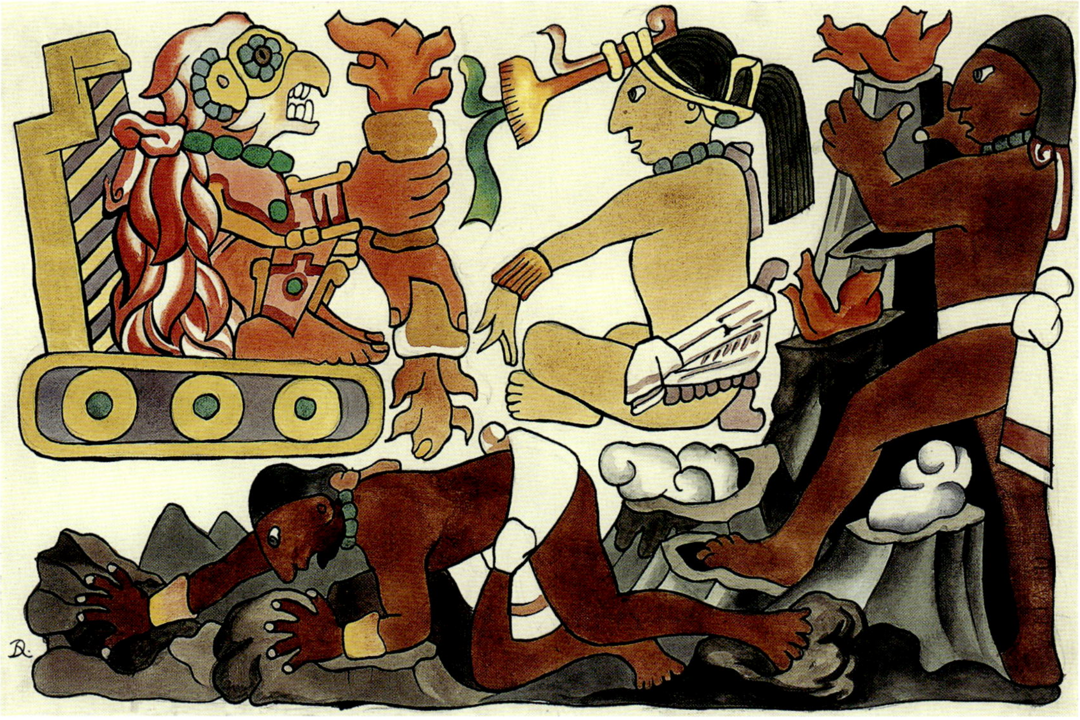

Diego Rivera, ***The Monkeys who Descended from the Wooden Men***, 1931

Diego Rivera, ***The Creation of Mountains***, 1931

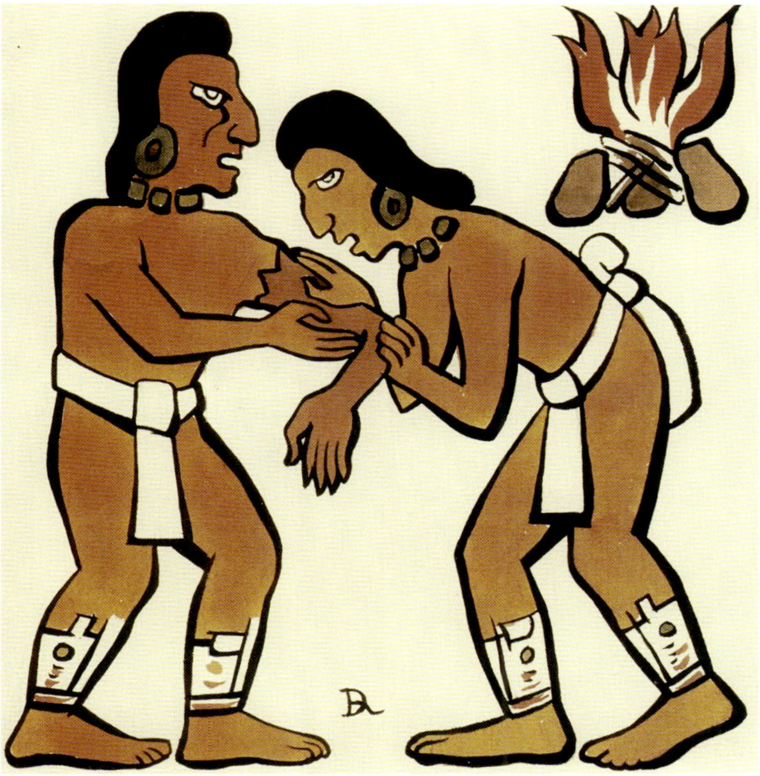

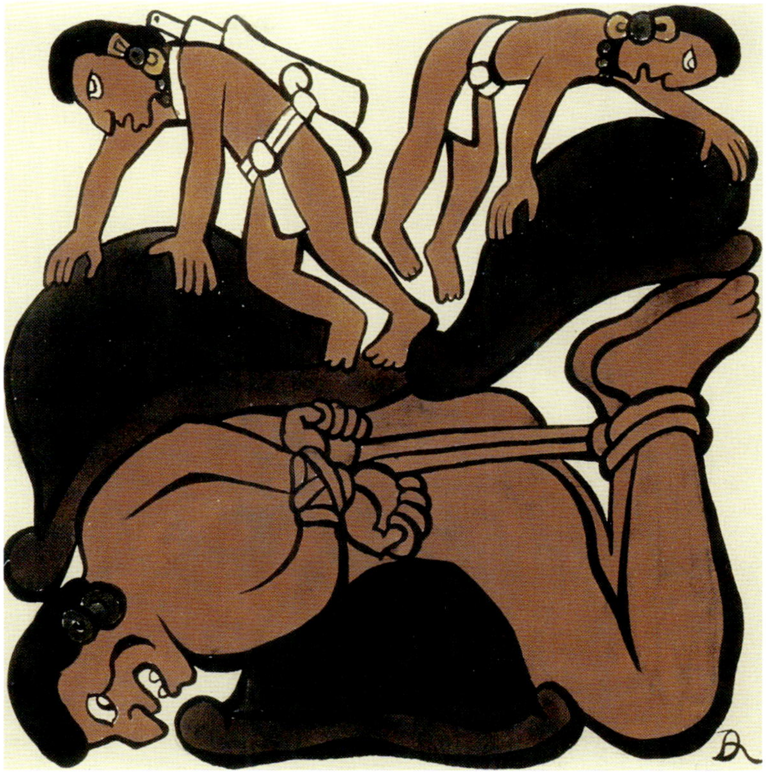

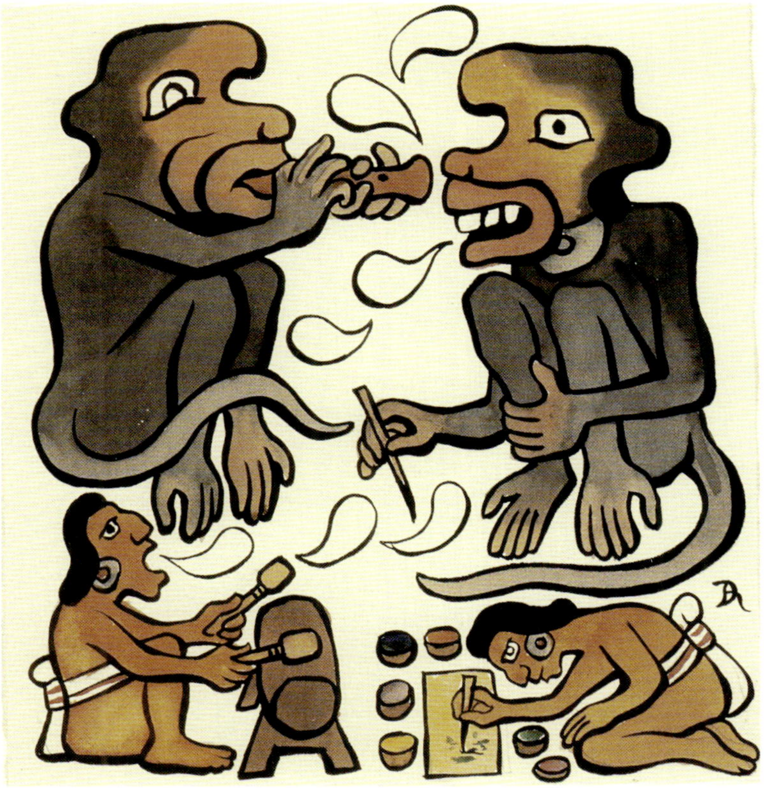

CLOCKWISE FROM TOP LEFT

Diego Rivera, *Hunahpú Recovers His Arm*, 1931

Diego Rivera, *The Death of Cabracan*, 1931

Diego Rivera, *Birth of Hunahpú and Ixbalanqué*, 1931

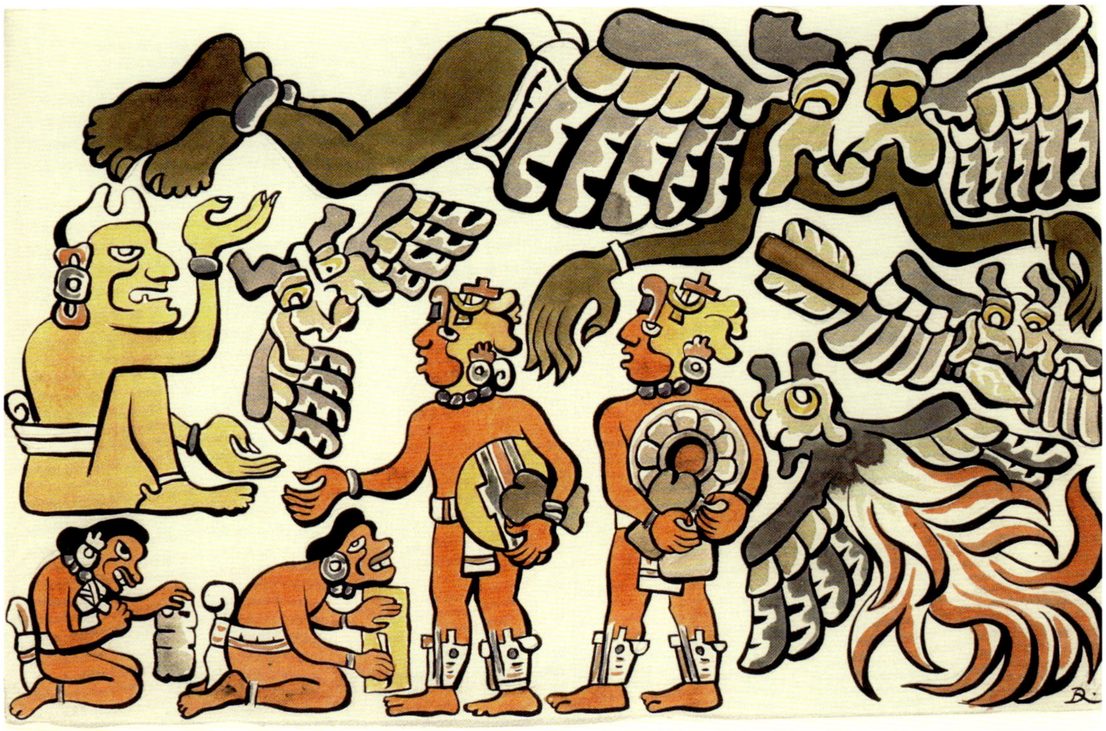

Diego Rivera, *Xibalba's Messengers Invite the Ball Players*, 1931

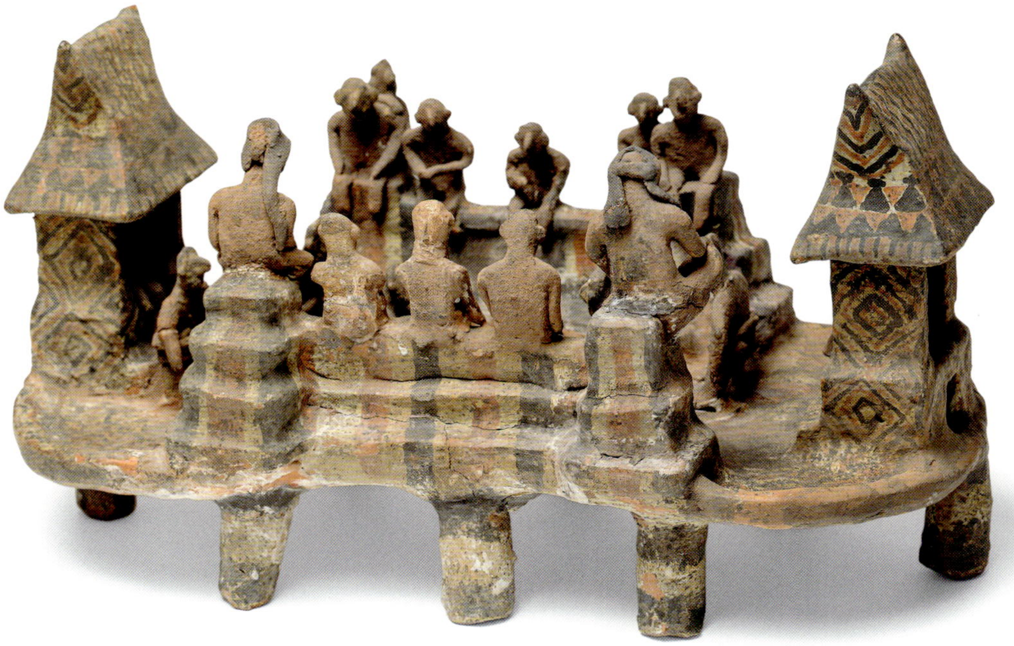

Ball Court Model, Mexico, Nayarit, 200–500

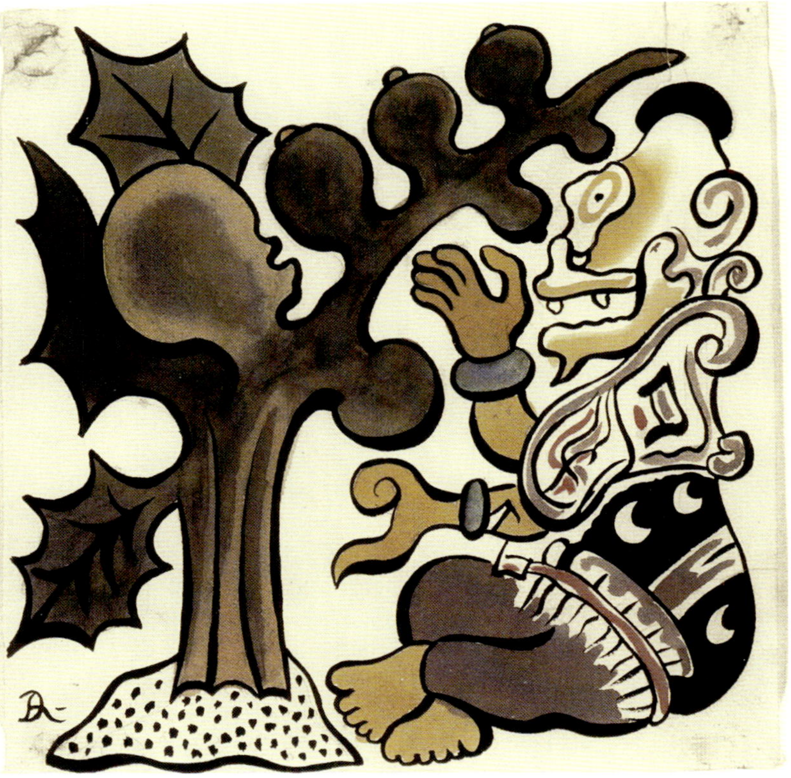

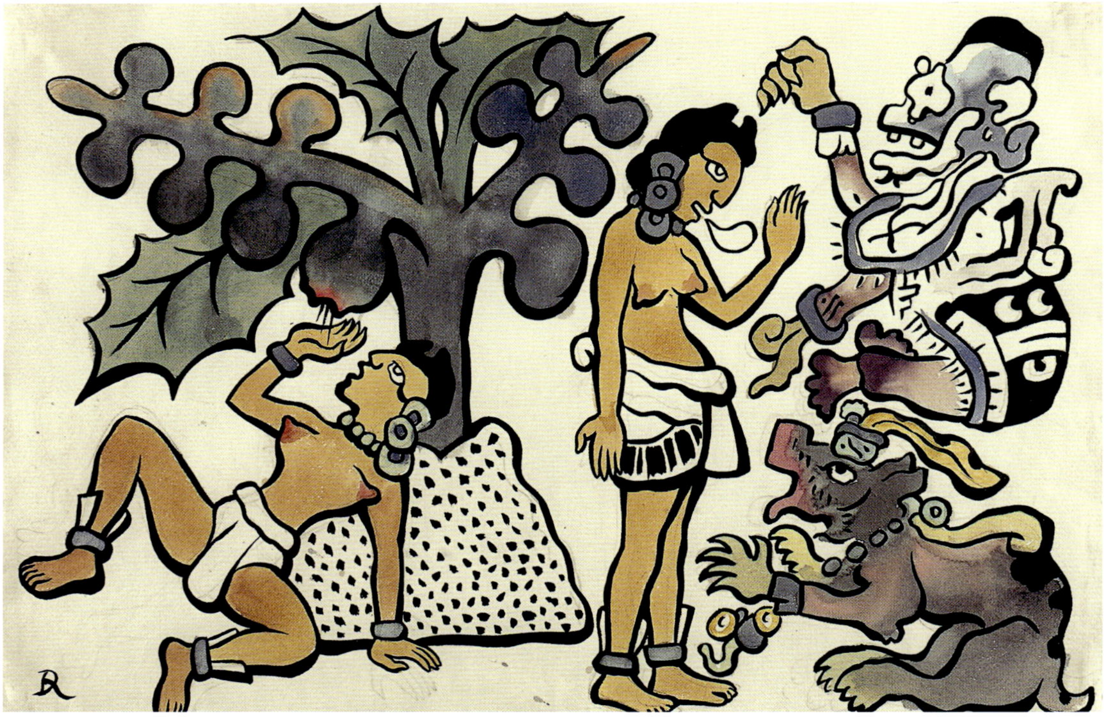

Diego Rivera, *The Head of Hun-Hunahpú Grows on a Tree*, 1931

Diego Rivera, *The Saliva of Hun-Hunahpú Impregnates the Maiden*, 1931

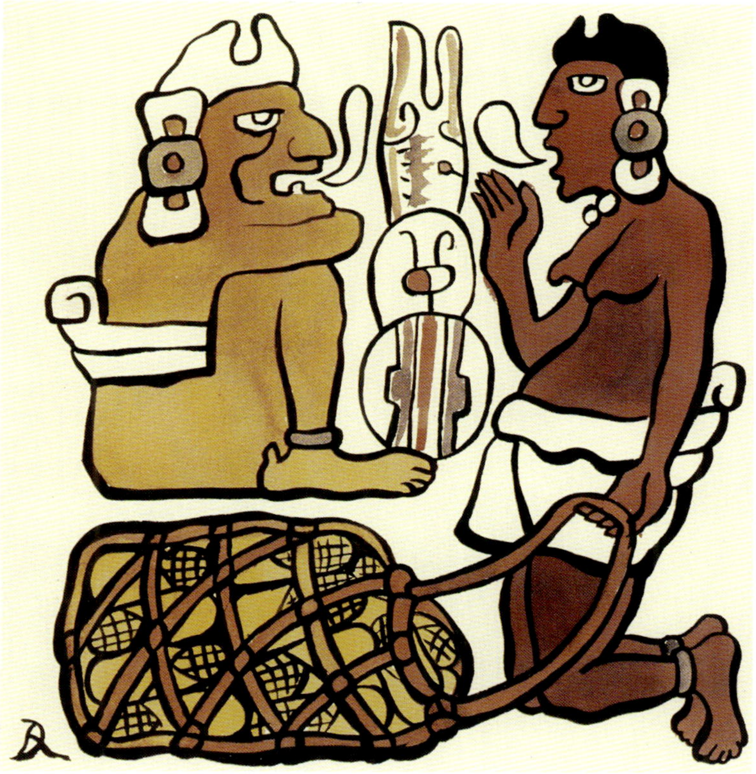

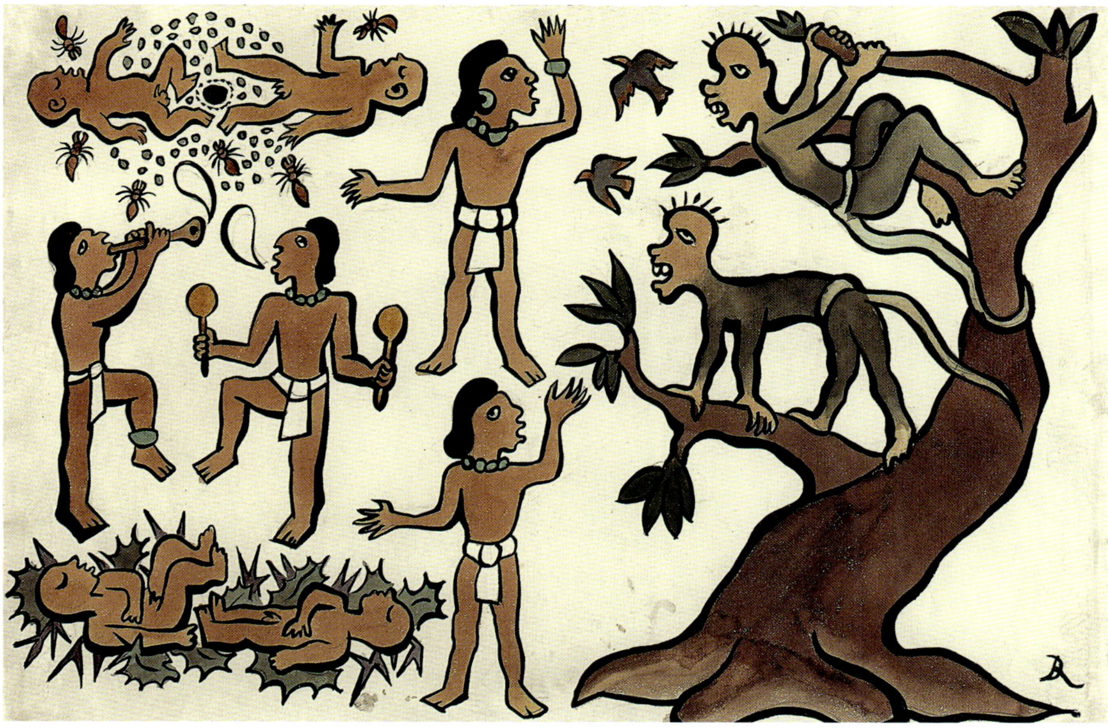

Diego Rivera, *The Old Woman's Amazement before the Collected Corn*, 1931

Diego Rivera, *How They Taught the Arts to Hunbatz and Hunchoven*, 1931

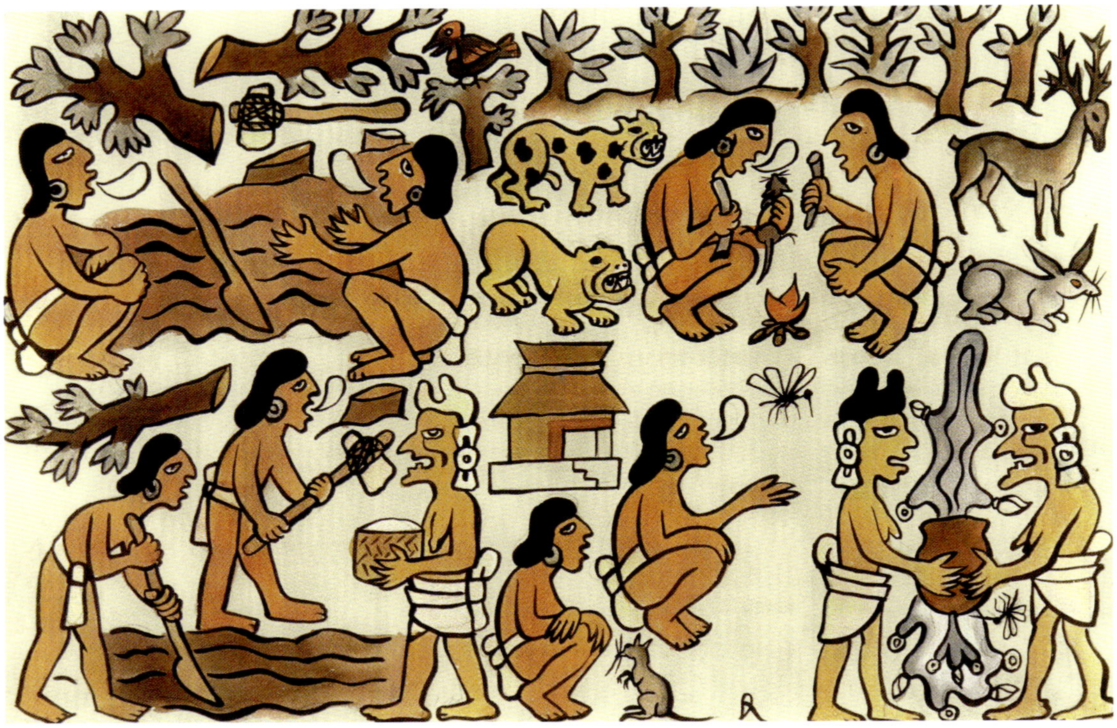

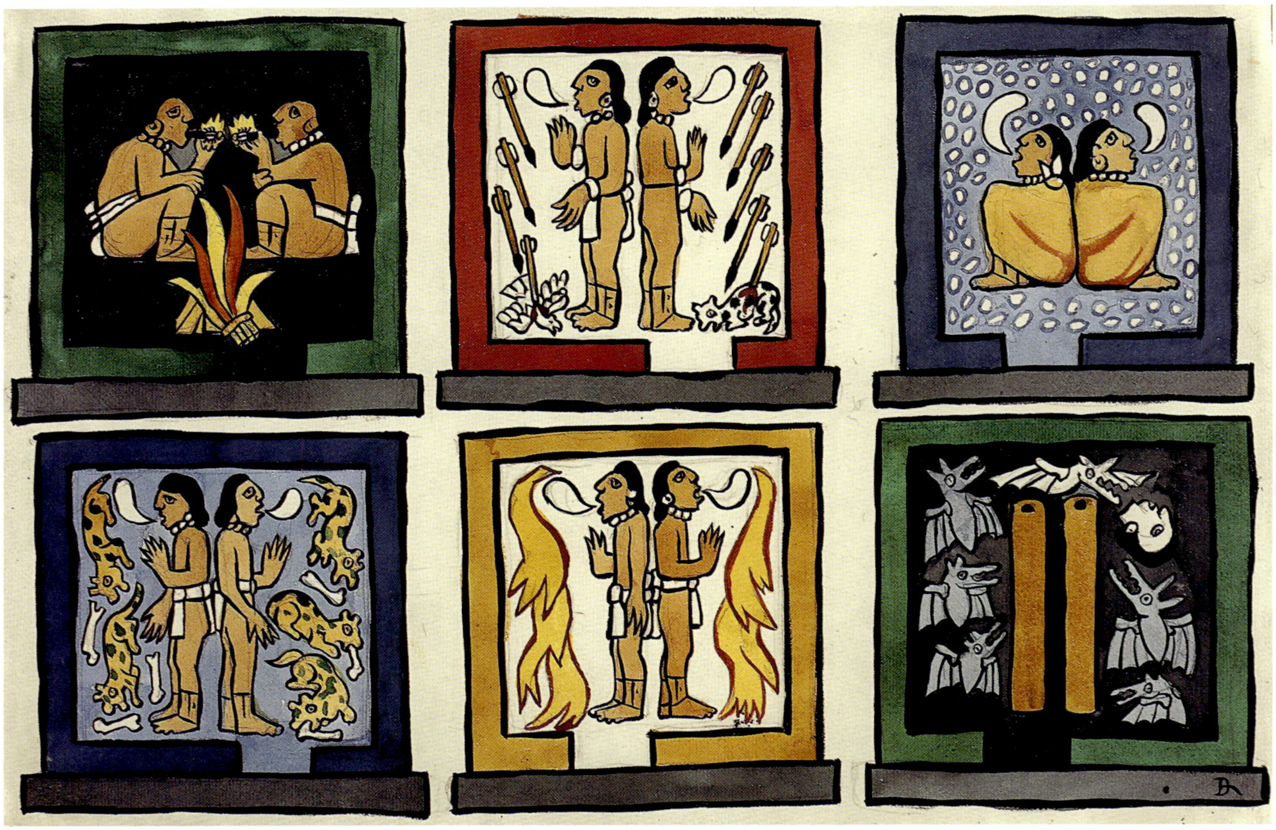

Diego Rivera, *Protecting the Corn Field*, 1931

Diego Rivera, *The Mansions of Xibalba*, 1931

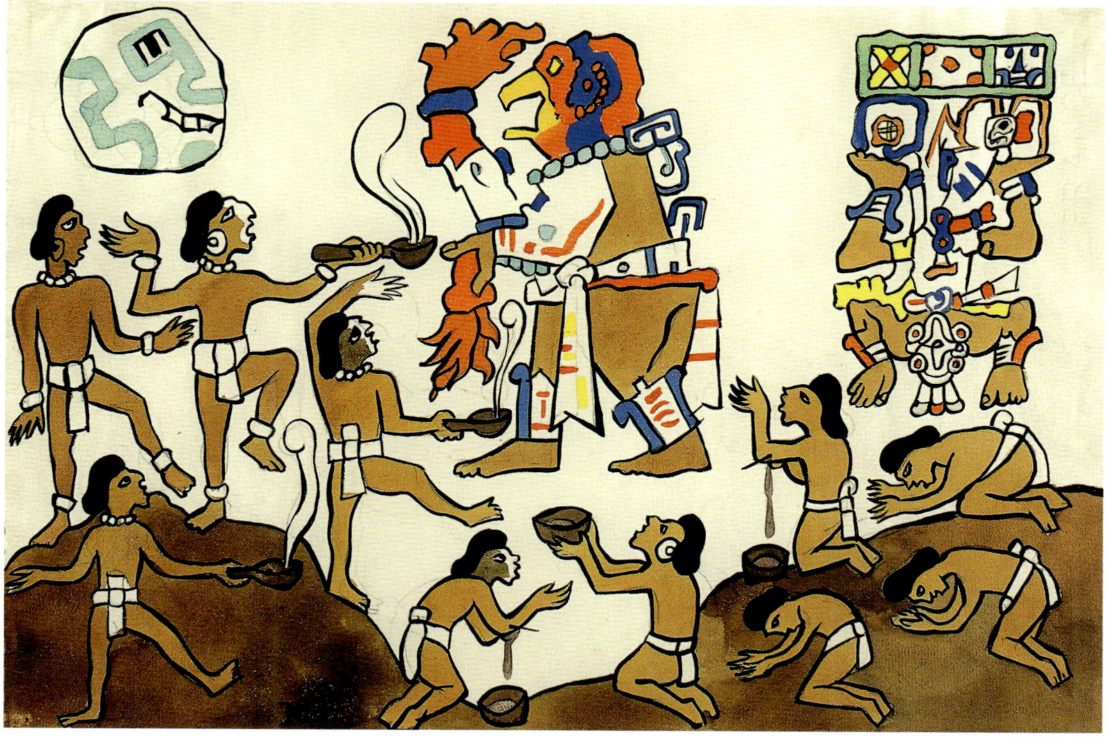

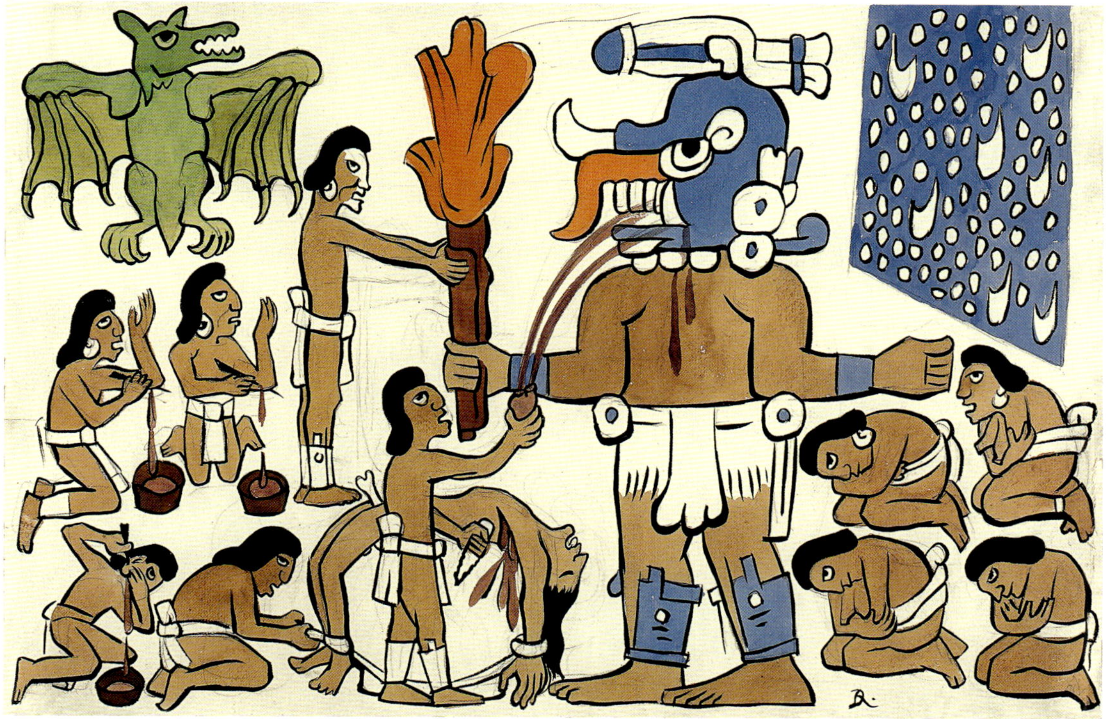

Diego Rivera, ***Man's Adoration of the Gods***, 1931

Diego Rivera, ***The Human Sacrifice and Self Human Sacrifice before the God Tohil***, 1931

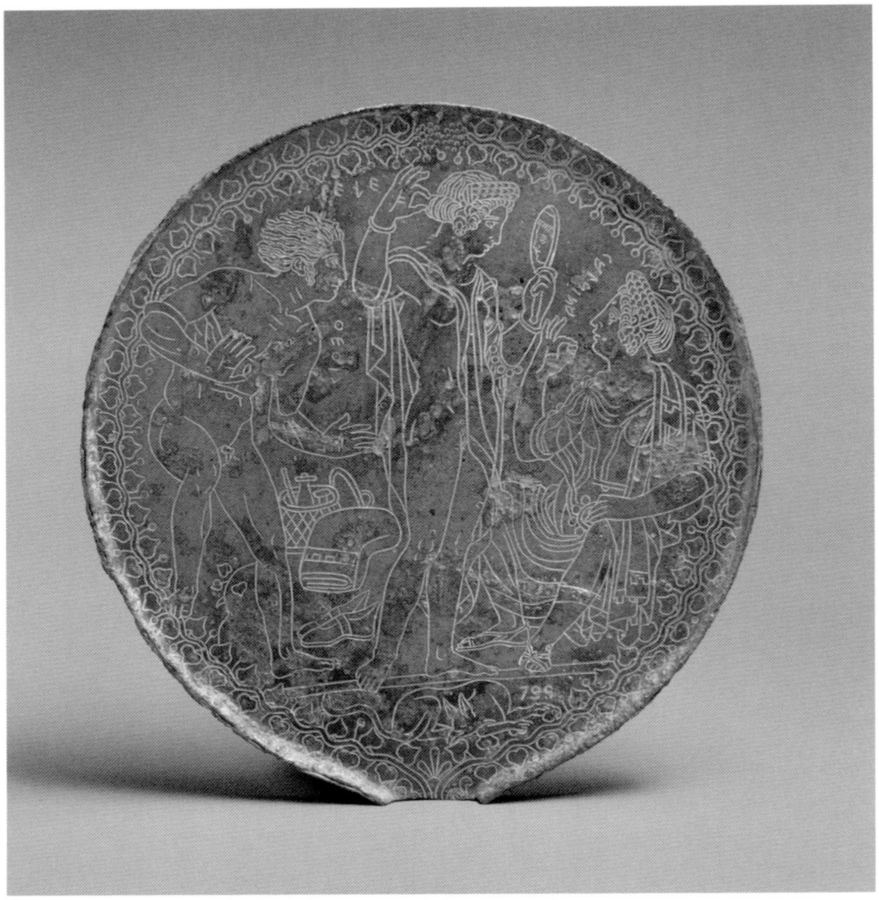

Bronze Mirror, Etruscan, Late Classical, c. 350 BCE

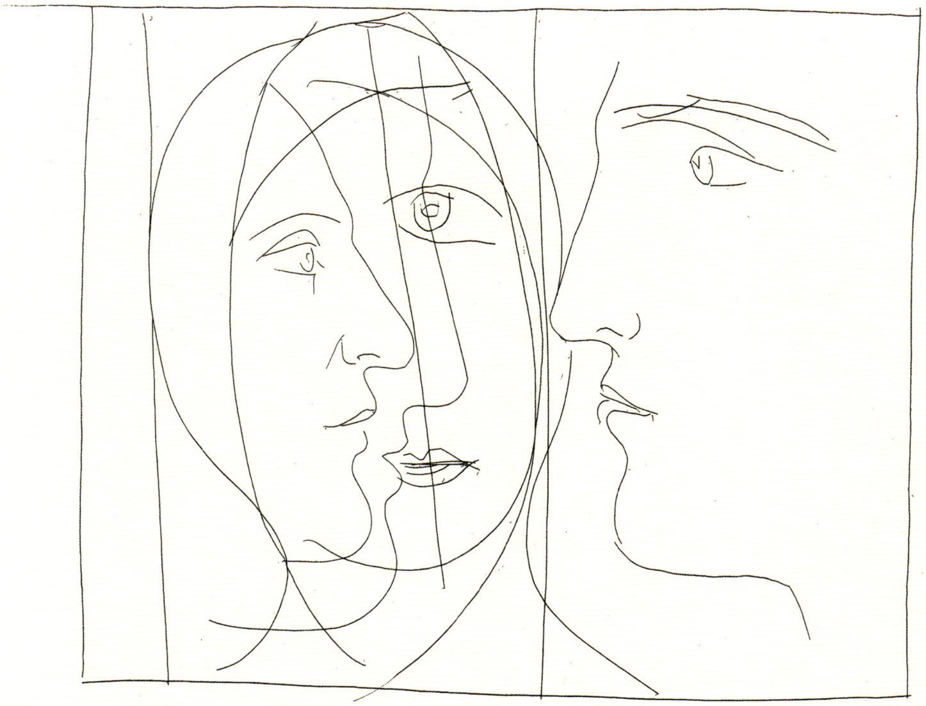

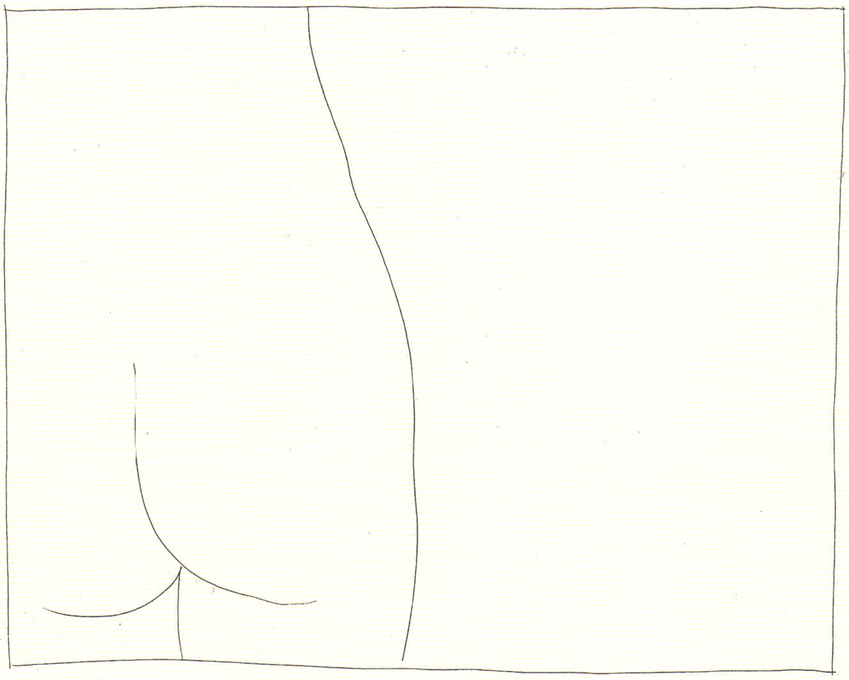

Pablo Picasso, *Heads*, 1931

Pablo Picasso, *Partial Female Figure*, 1931

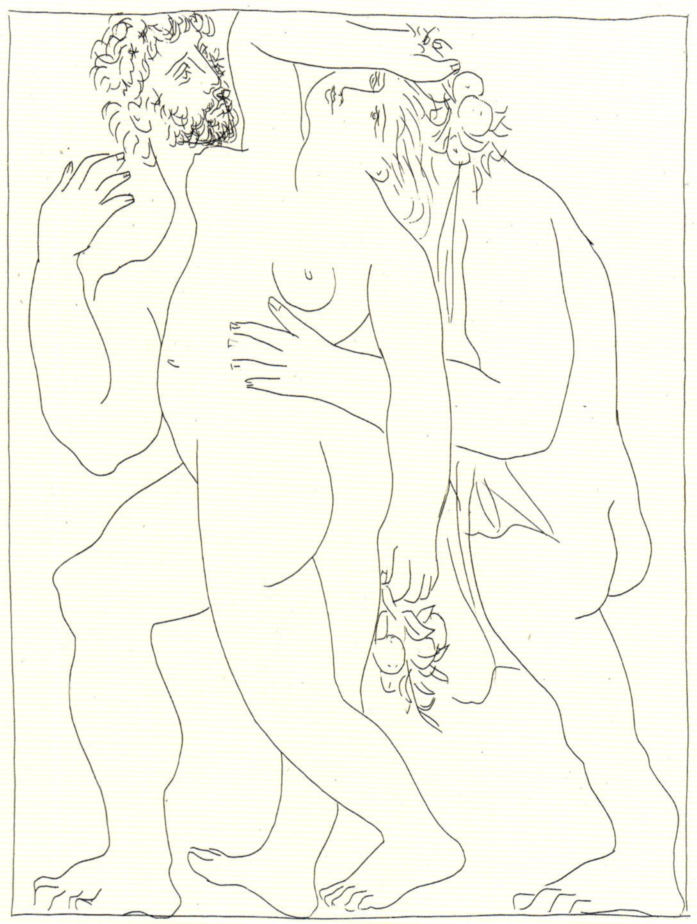

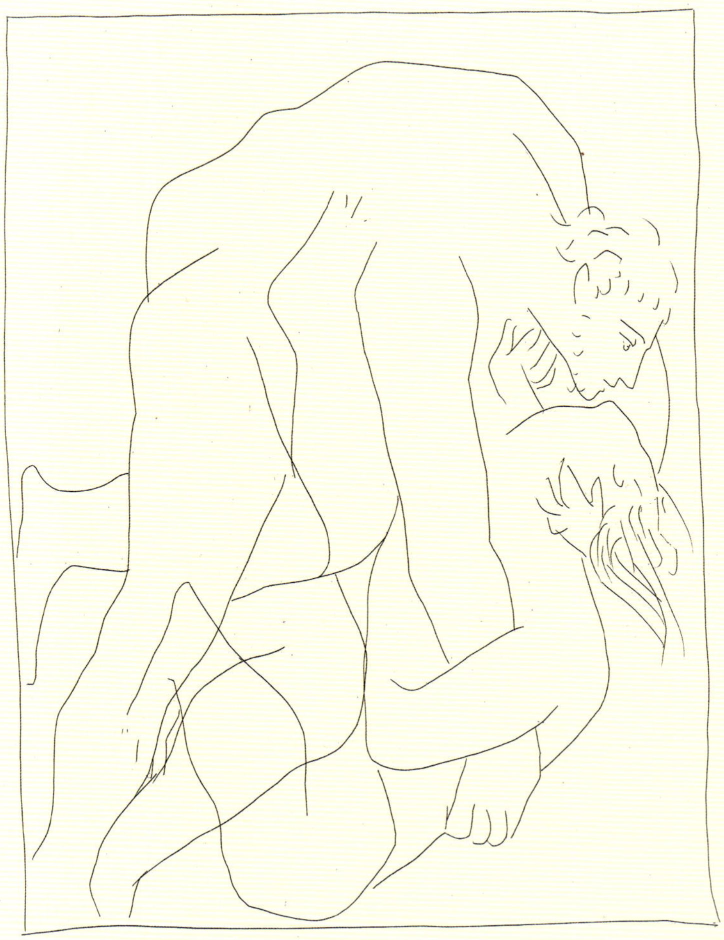

Pablo Picasso, ***Vertume Pursues Pomona for Her Love***, 1931

Pablo Picasso, ***Struggle between Tereus and His Sister-in-Law Philomela***, 1931

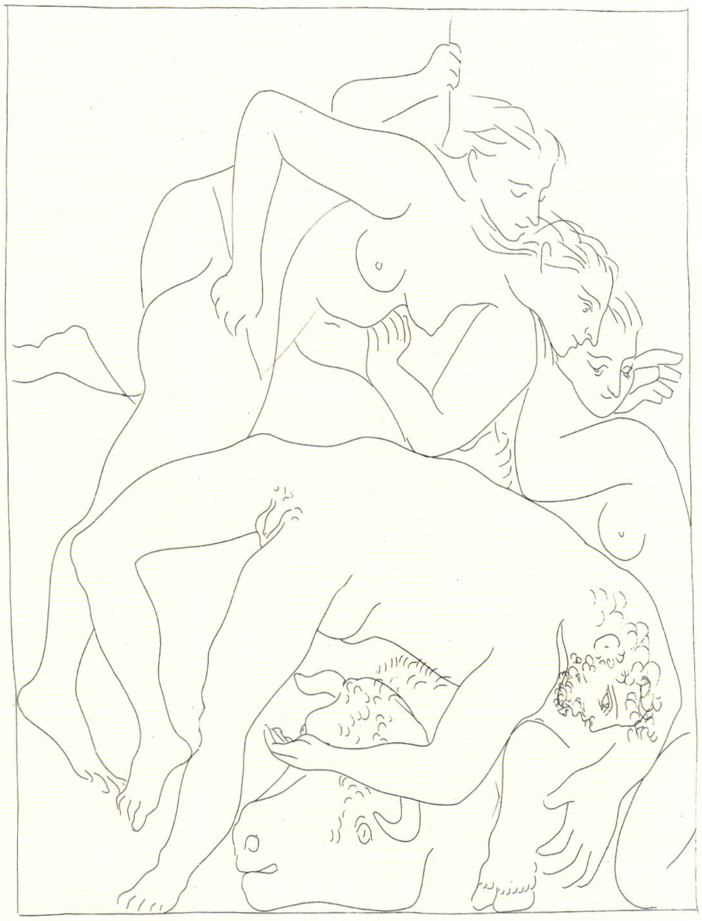

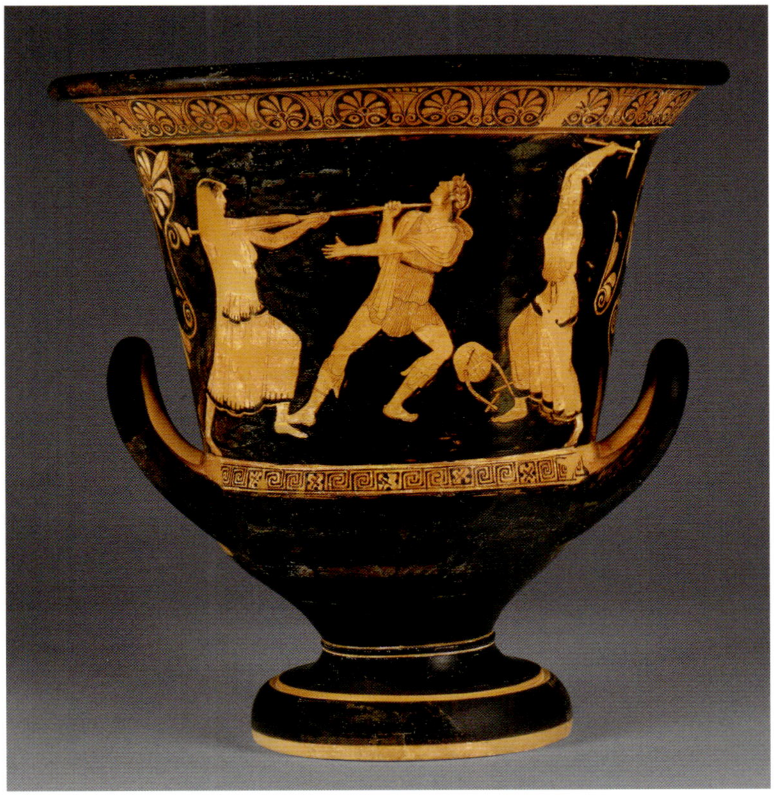

Pablo Picasso, ***Death of Orpheus***, 1931

Attic Red-Figure Calyx Krater, Greek, Athens, 460–450 BCE

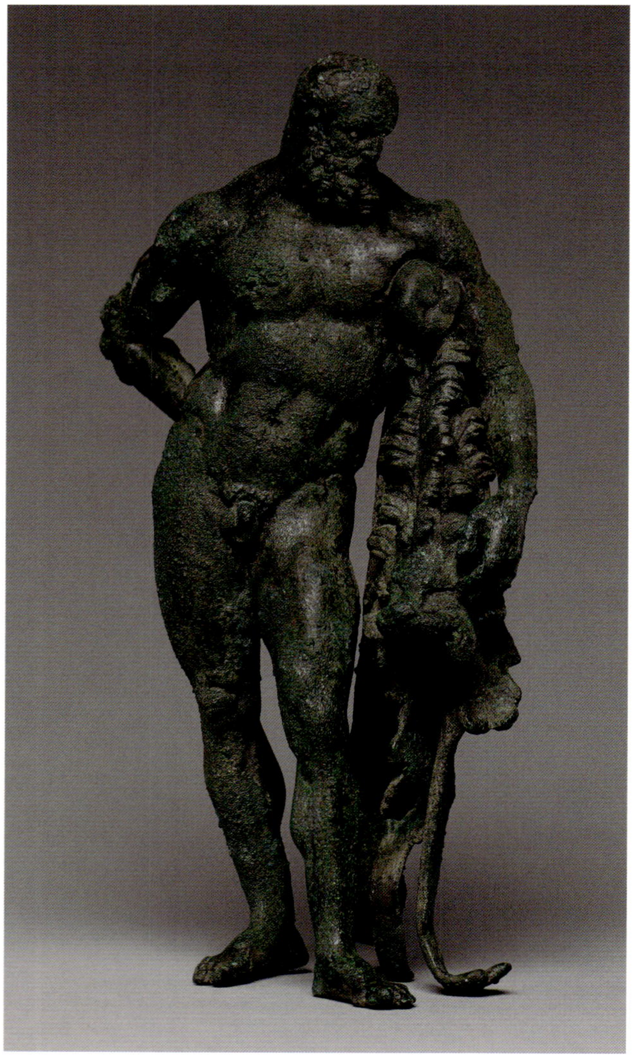

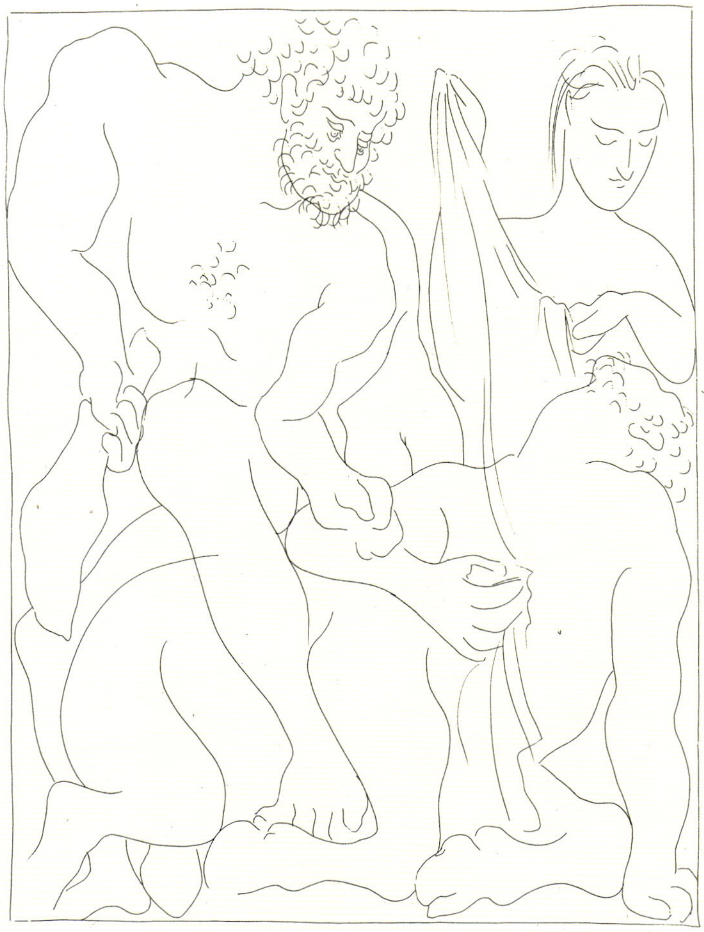

Statuette of Herakles, Roman, Roman Empire, 40–70 CE

Pablo Picasso, ***Hercules Kills the Centaur Nessus***, 1931

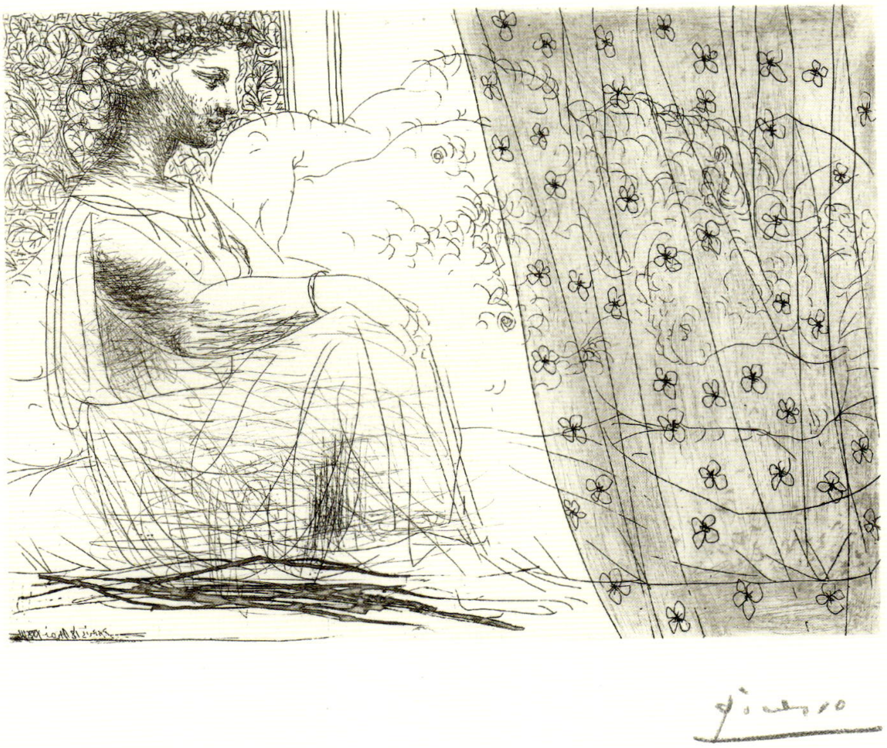

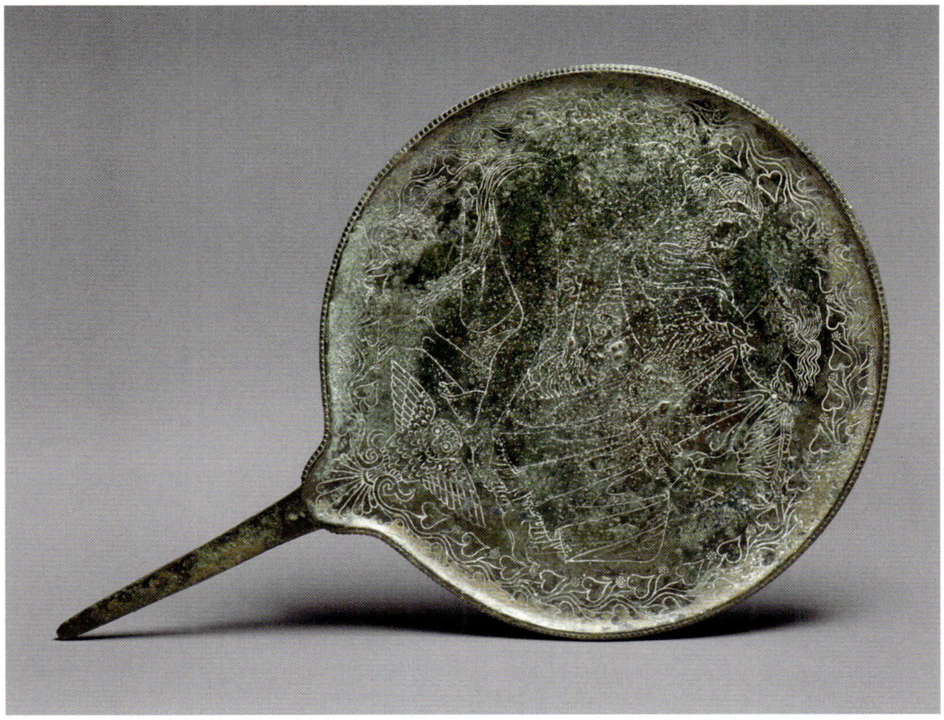

Pablo Picasso, ***Woman Contemplating Sleeping Minotaur***, May 18, 1933

Bronze Mirror, Etruscan, Classical, c. 425–400 BCE

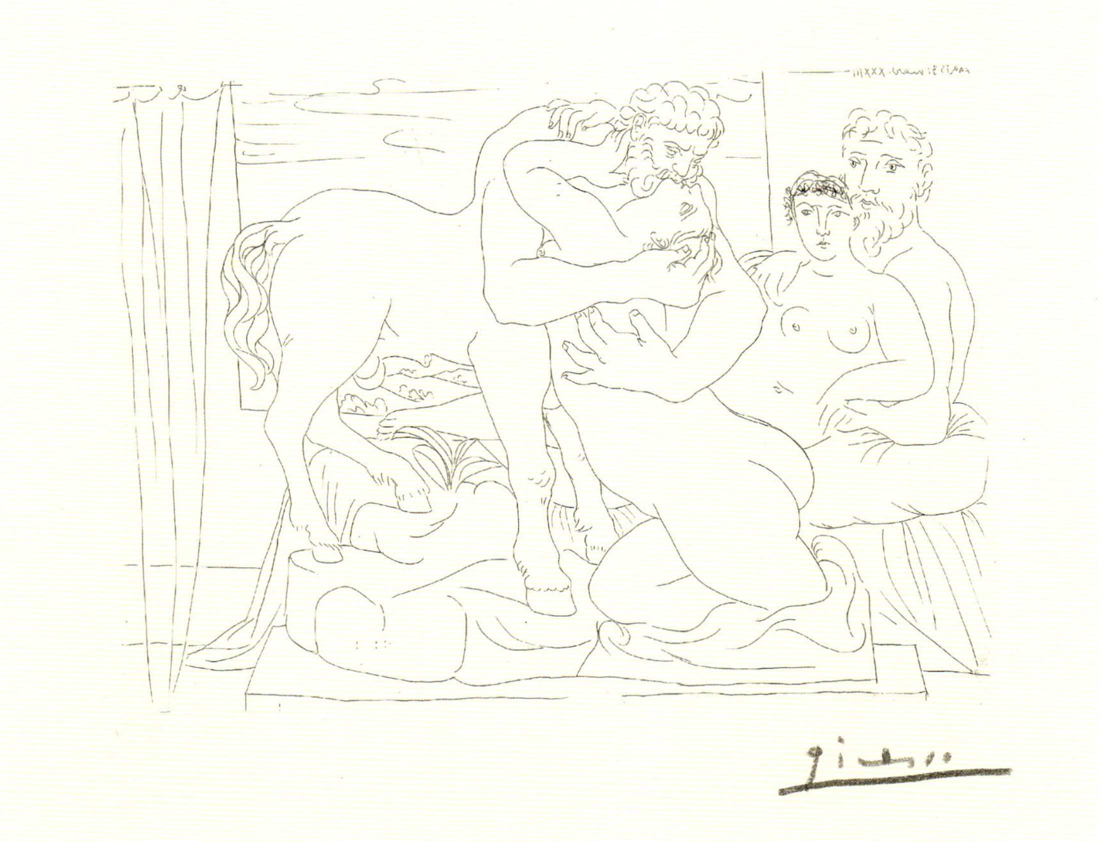

Pablo Picasso, *Sculptor at Rest before a Centaur and a Woman,*
May 31, 1933

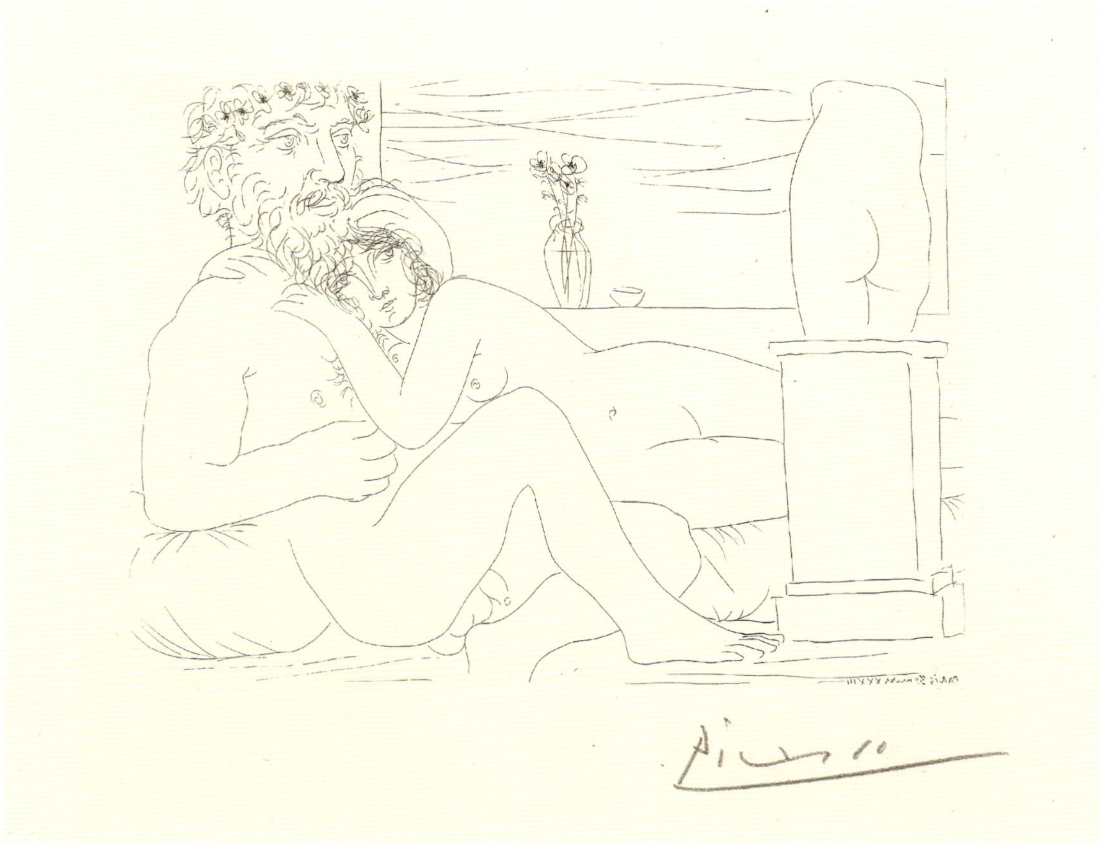

Pablo Picasso, ***Sculptor Reclining before Small Torso***, March 30, 1933

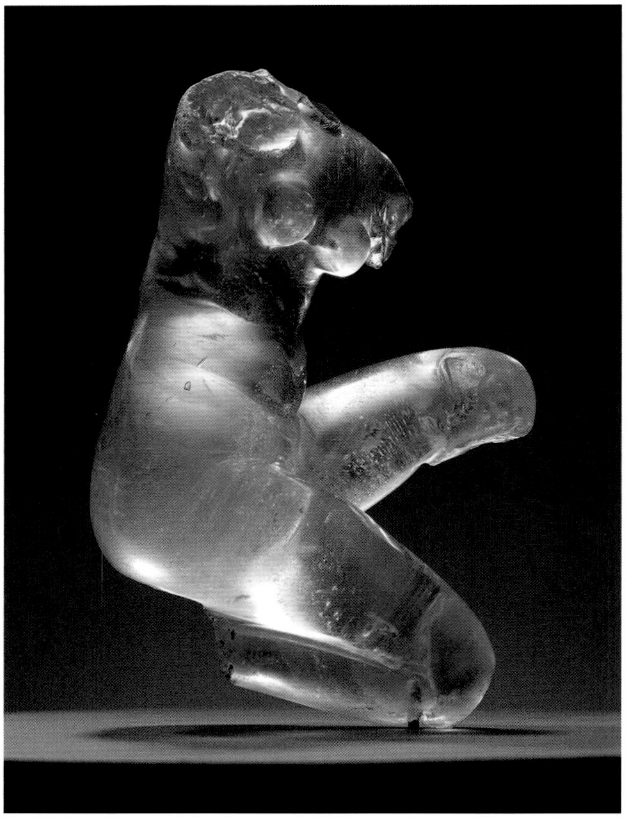

Statuette of Venus, Crouching Aphrodite, Greek, Ptolemaic, or Roman, Egypt, 1st century BCE

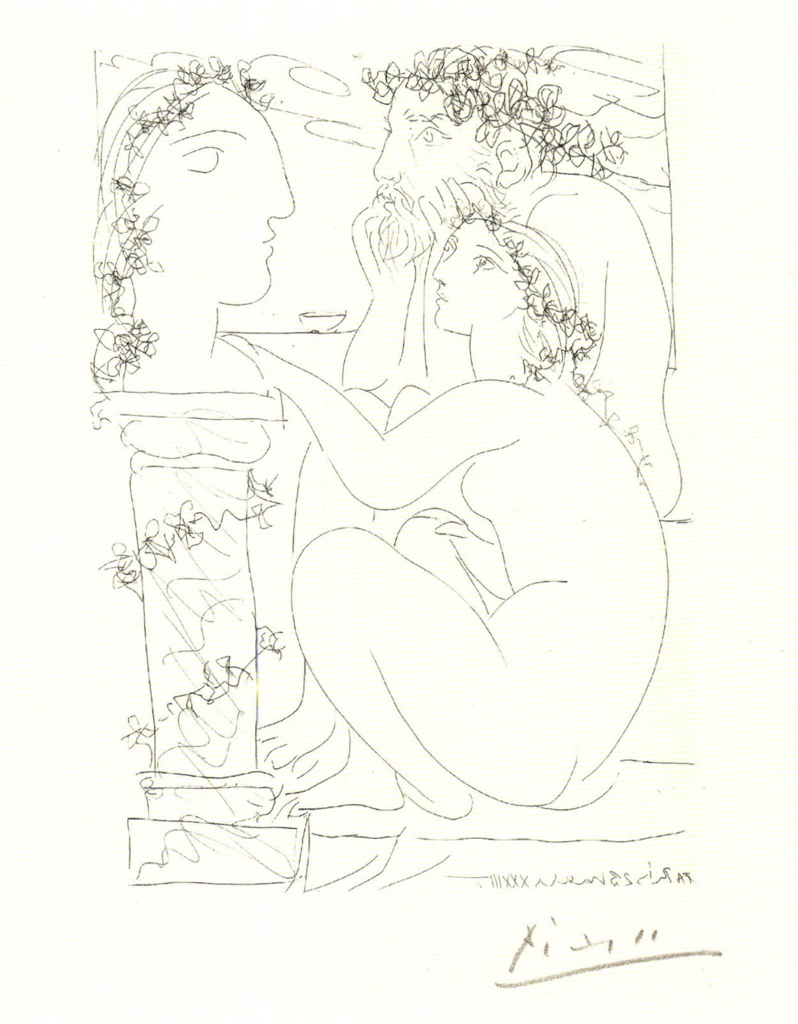

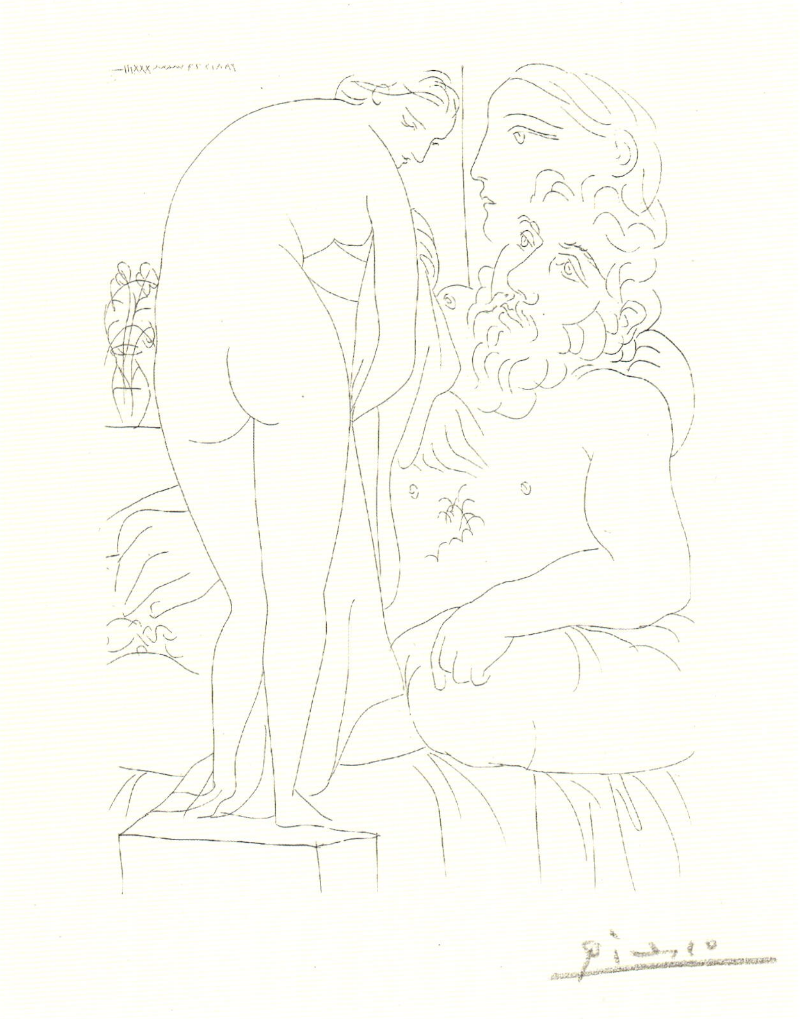

Pablo Picasso, ***Sculptor and Model Admiring a Sculpted Head***, March 31, 1933

Pablo Picasso, ***Sculptor Reclining before Nude***, March 27, 1933

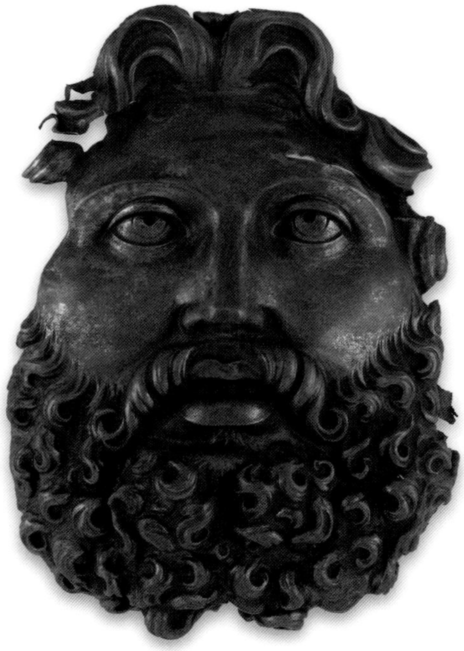

Relief of Jupiter, Roman, Asia Minor, 1–150 CE

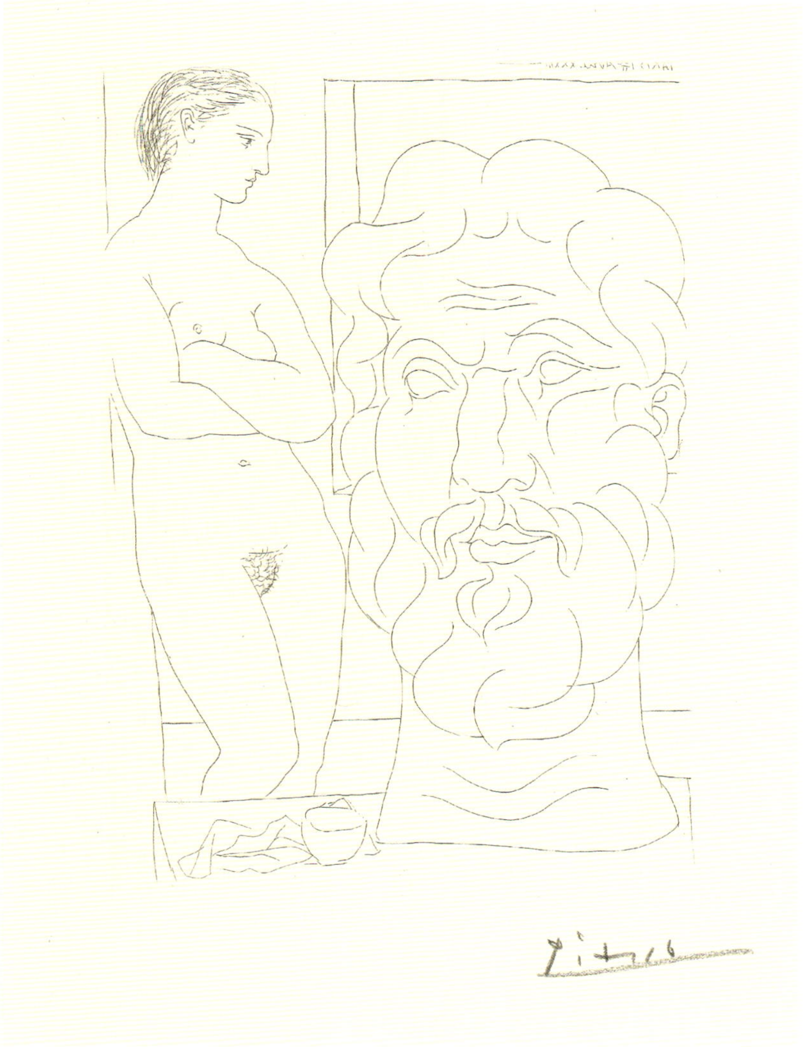

Pablo Picasso, ***Model and Large Sculpted Head***, April 1, 1933

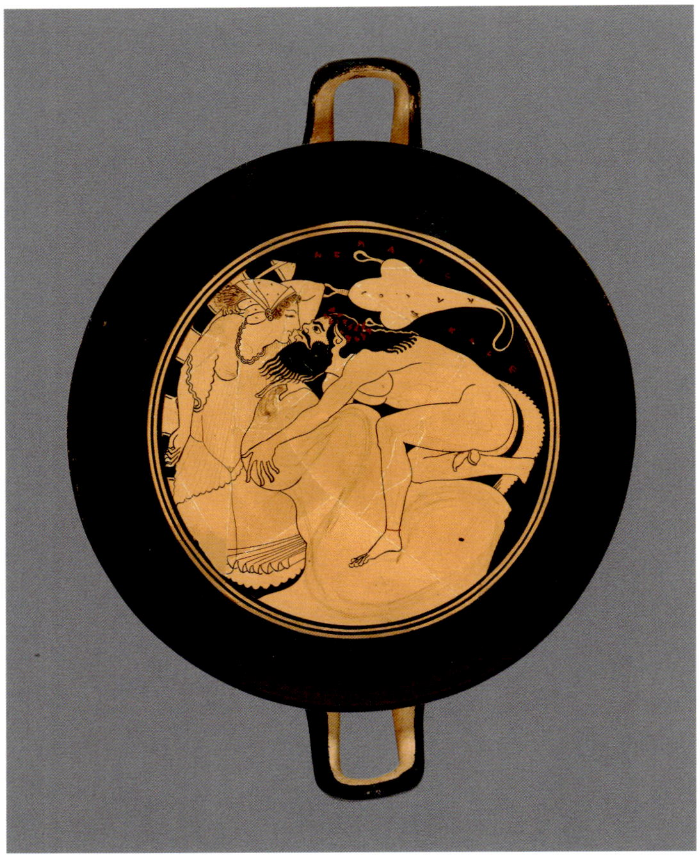

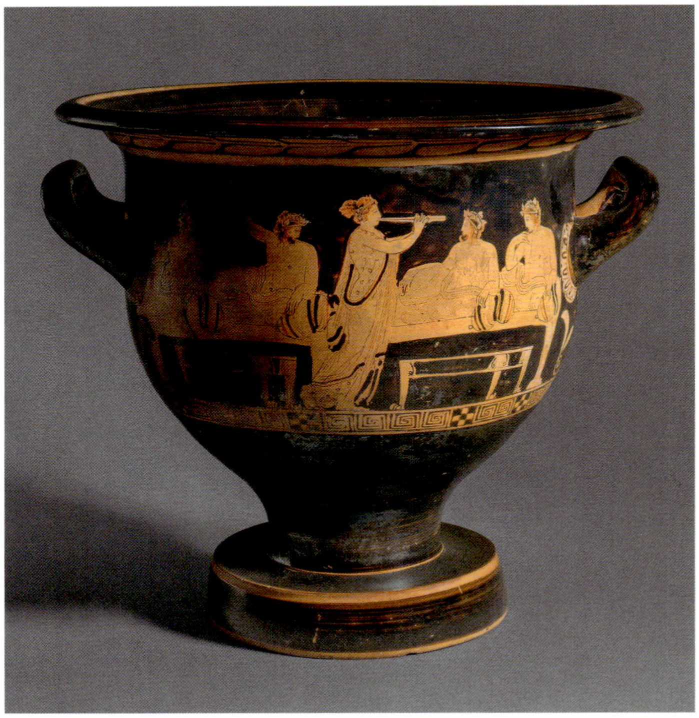

Attic Red-Figure Kylix, Greek, Athens, 500–490 BCE

Red-Figure Bell-Krater with a Symposium, Greek, Athens, c. 400–380 BCE

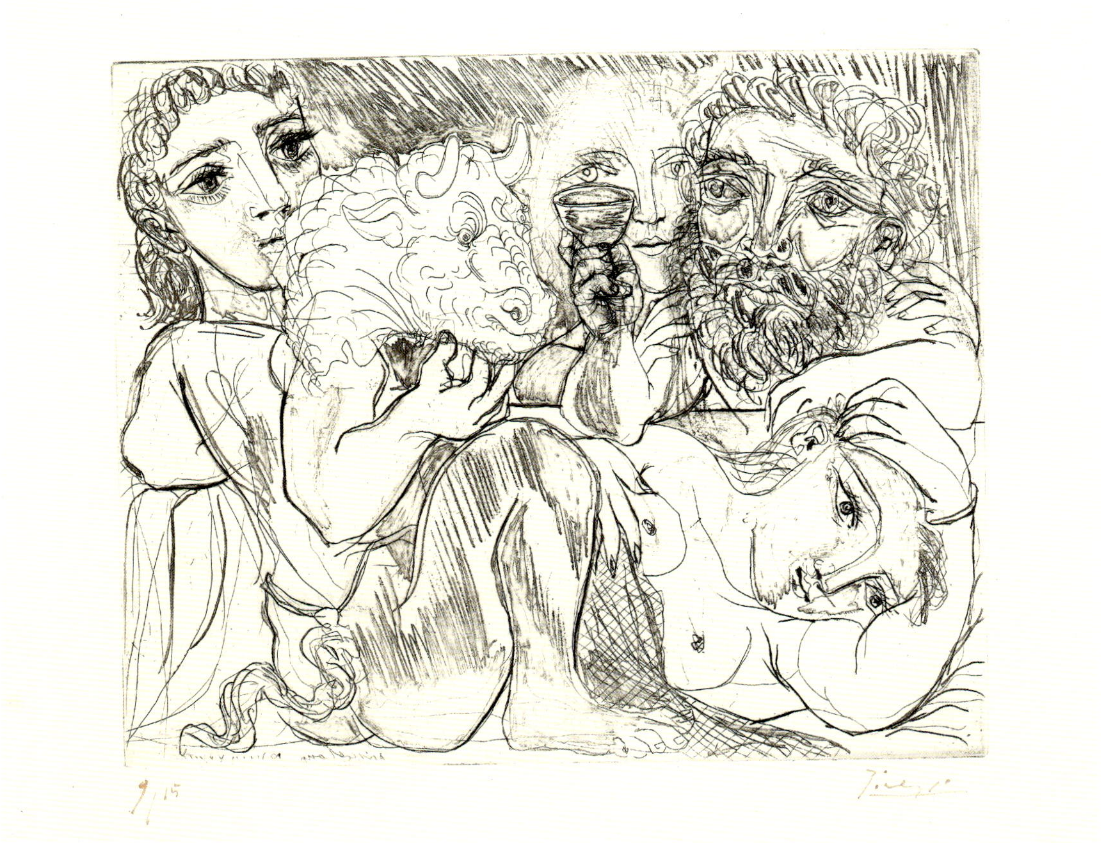

Pablo Picasso, ***Minotaur, Drinker, and Women***, June 18, 1933

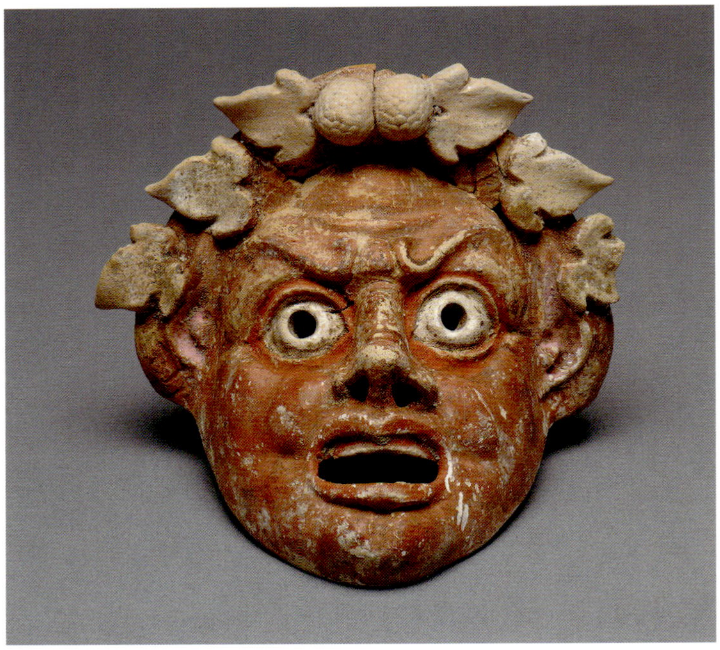

Mask of a Satyr, Greek, Sicily, 200–100 BCE

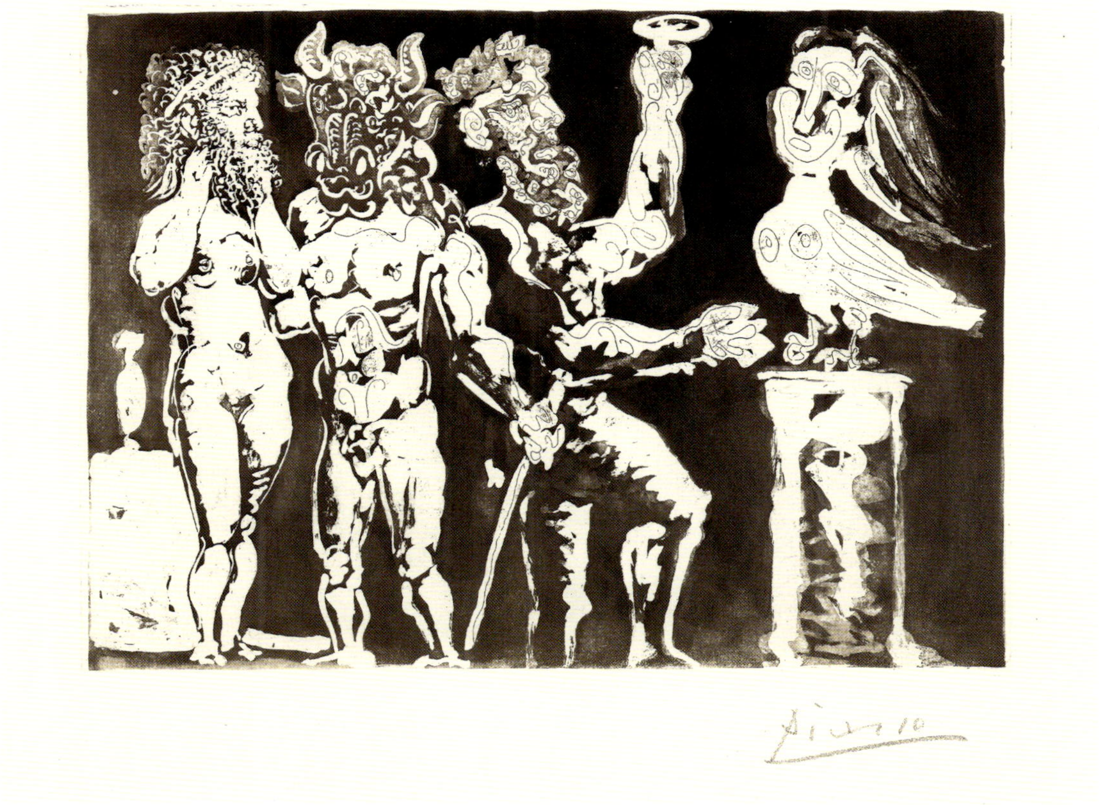

Pablo Picasso, ***Masked Characters and Bird-Woman***, November 19, 1934

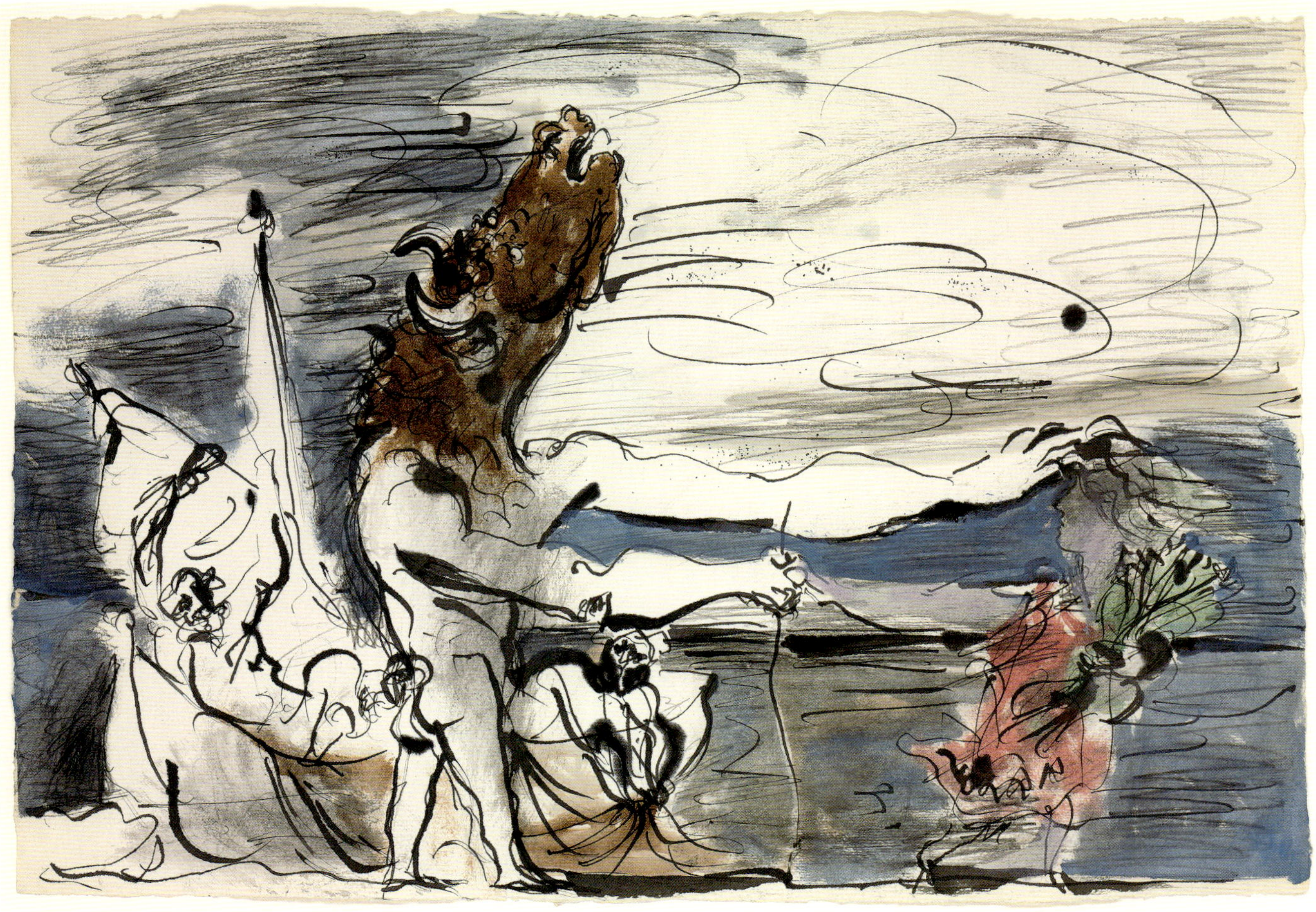

Pablo Picasso, ***Blind Minotaur Led by a Young Girl***, 1934

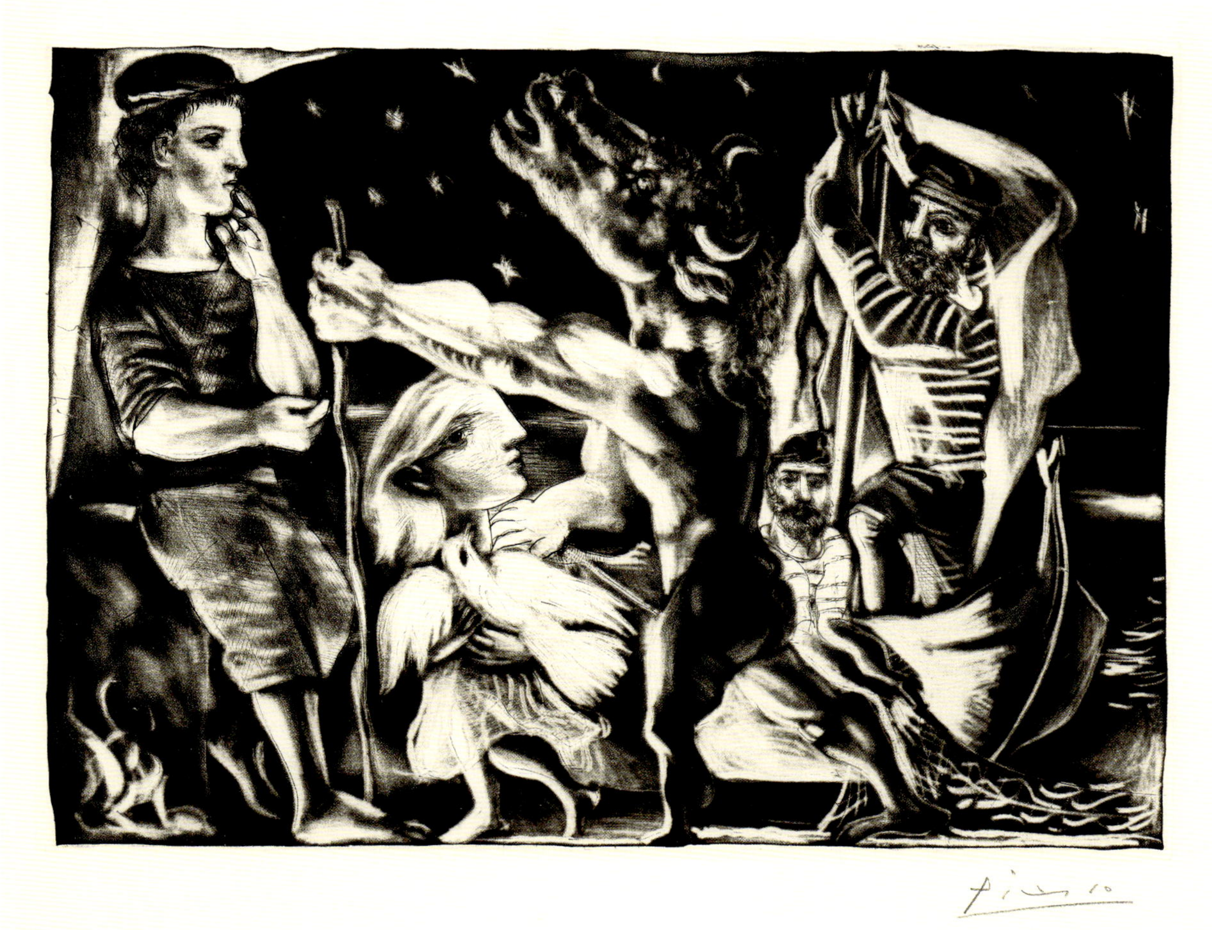

Pablo Picasso, *Blind Minotaur Led by a Young Girl at Night,*
November 1934

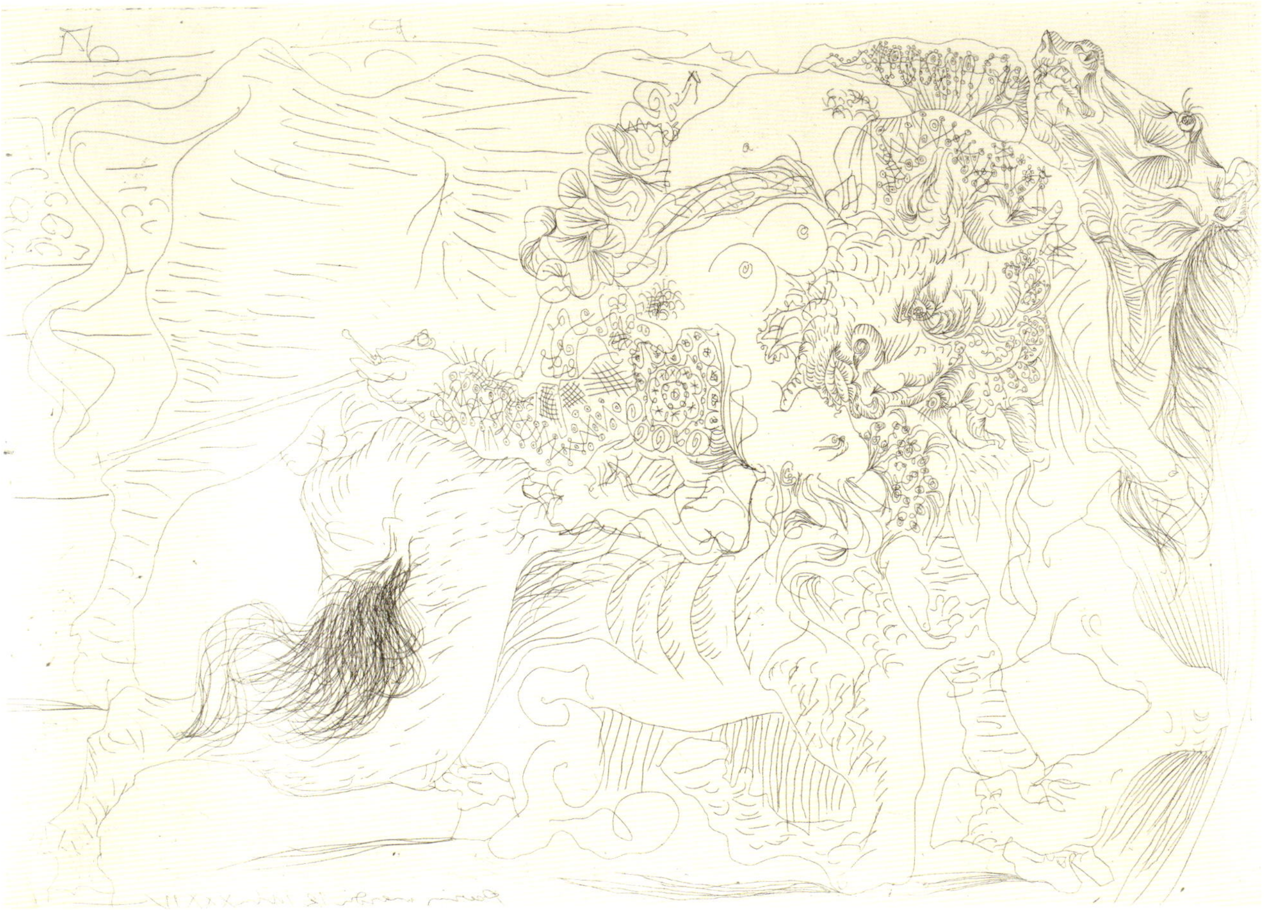

Pablo Picasso, ***Woman Bullfighter: Last Kiss***, 1934

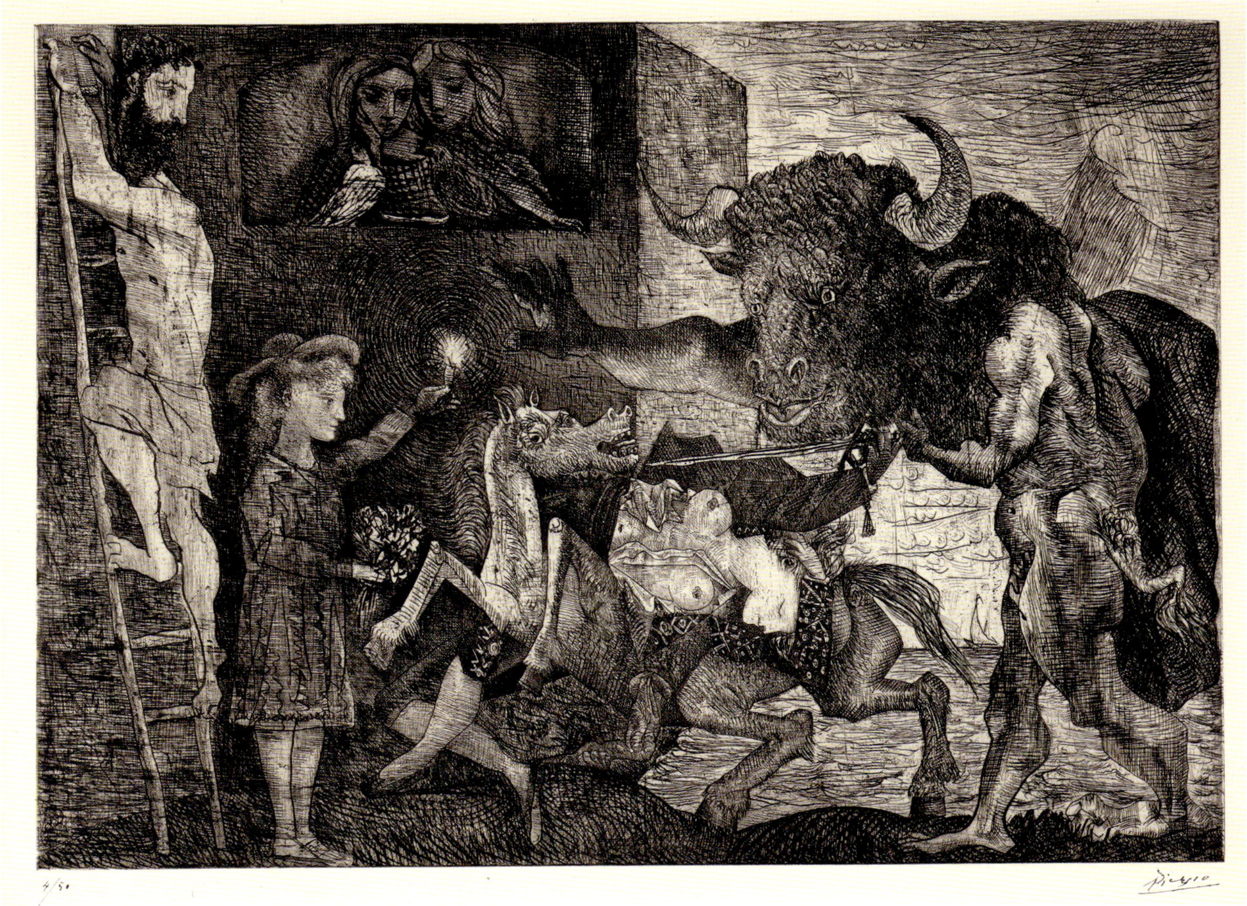

Pablo Picasso, ***Minotauromachy***, 1935

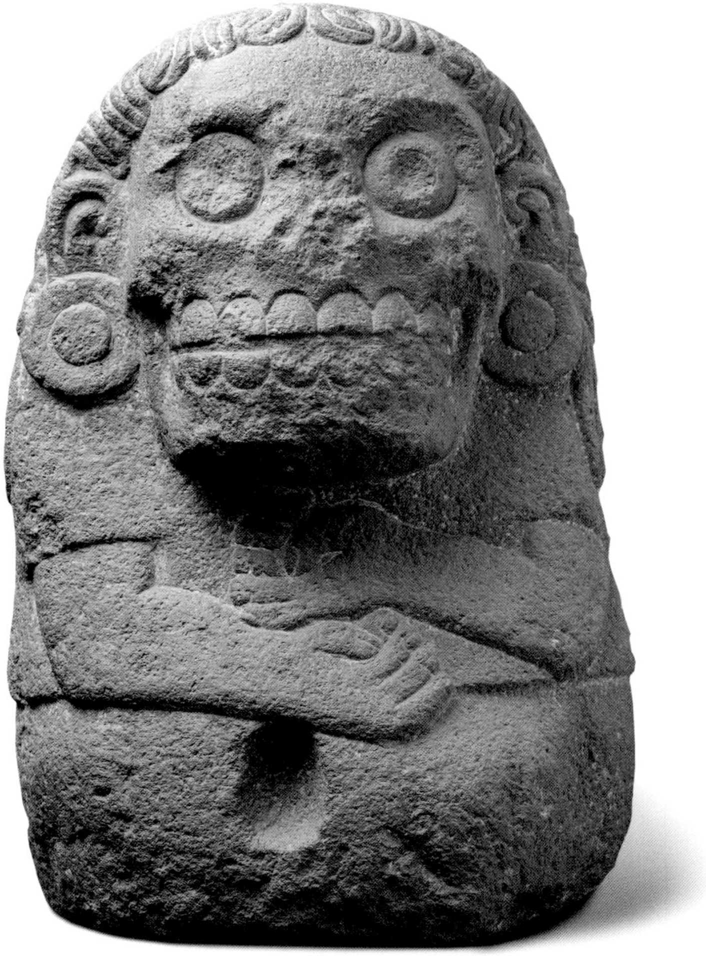

Tzitzimitl (*Death Goddess of Childbirth*), Mexico, Aztec, 1250–1521

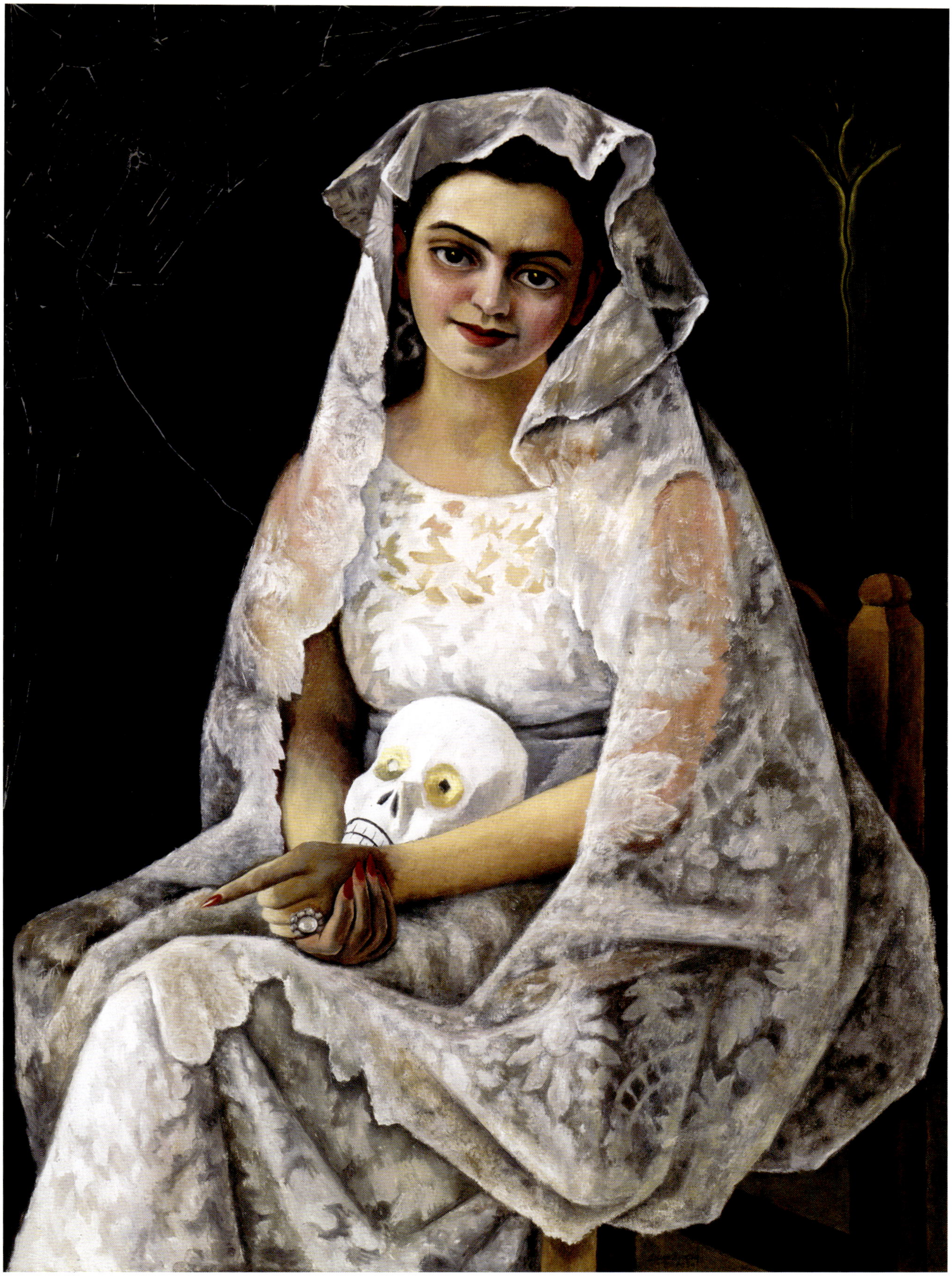

Diego Rivera, ***Mandrake***, 1939

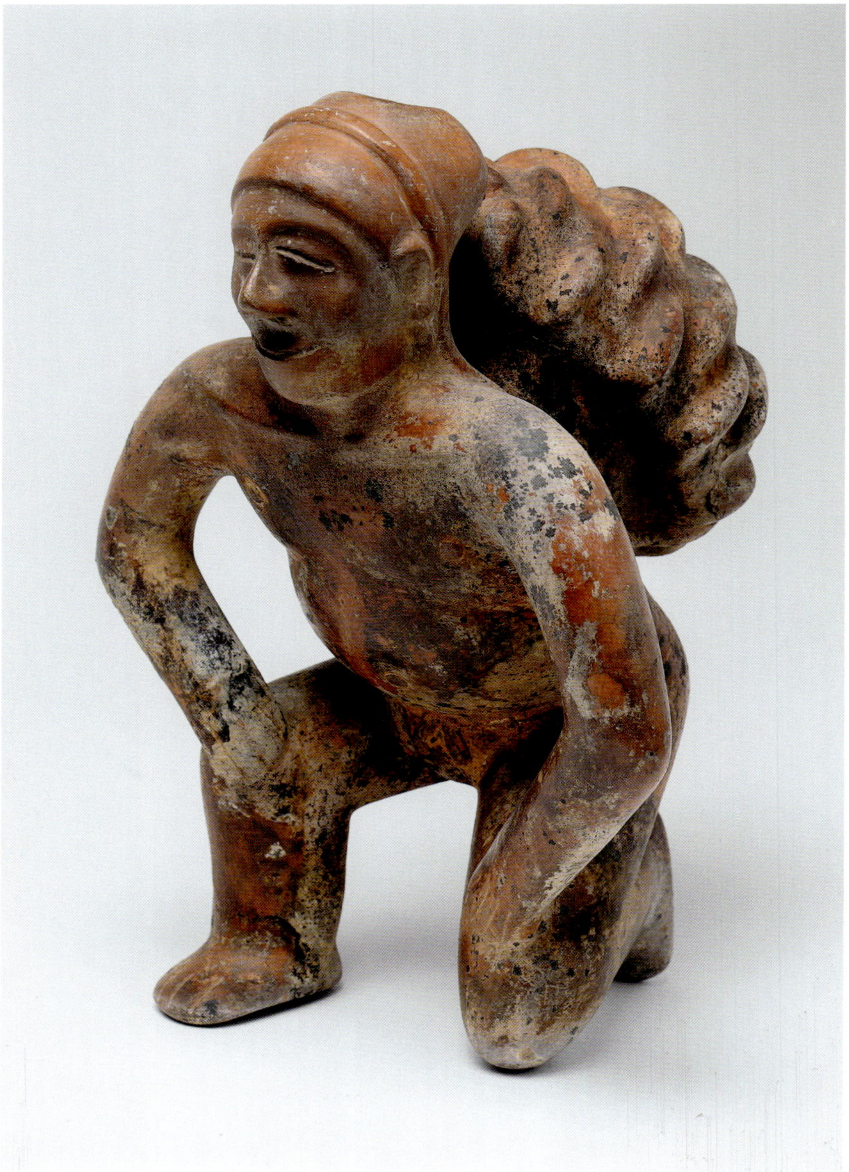

Cargador (*Carrier*), Mexico, Nayarit, 600–900

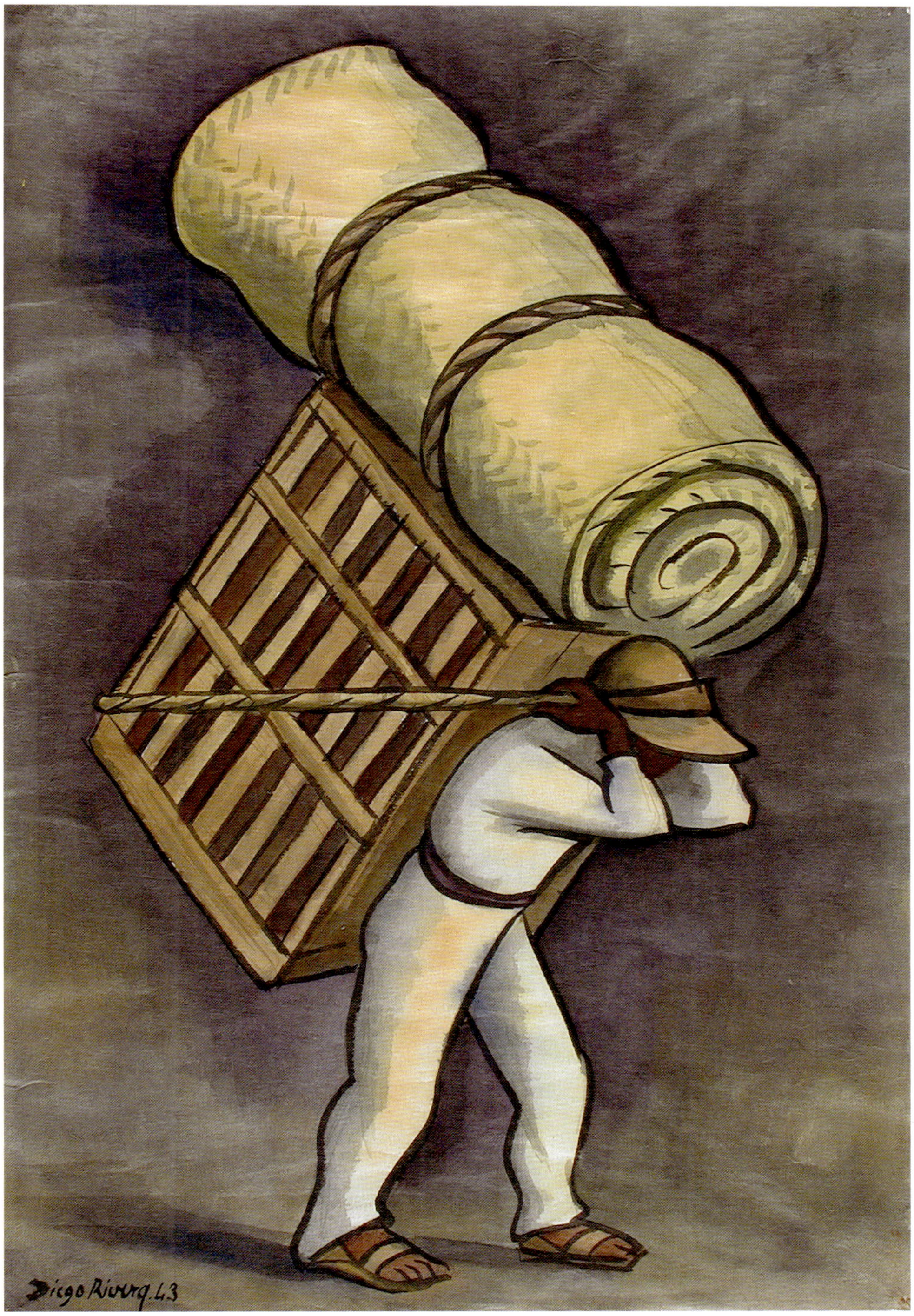

Diego Rivera, *Petate Bearer*, 1943

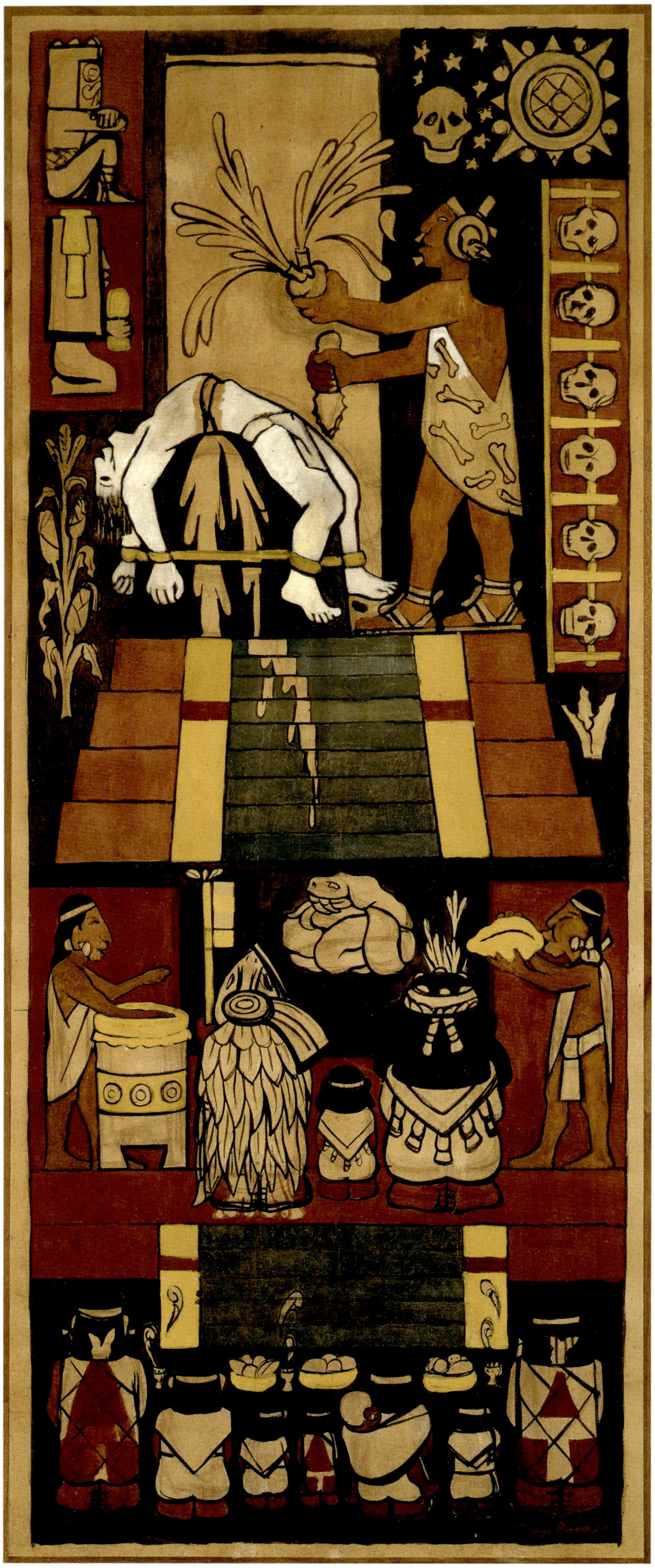

Diego Rivera, *History of Religion V*, 1956

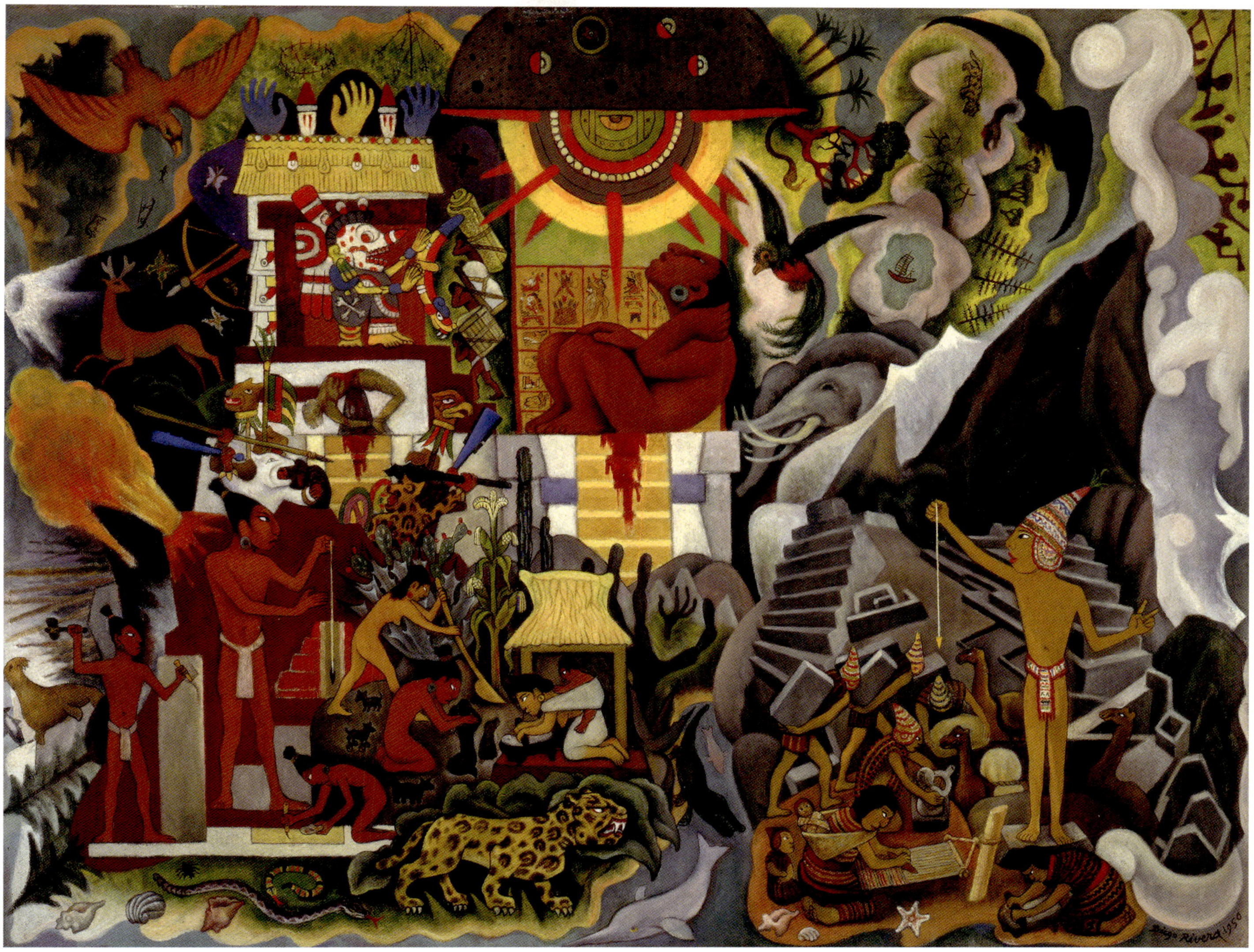

Diego Rivera, ***Pre-Columbian America***, 1950

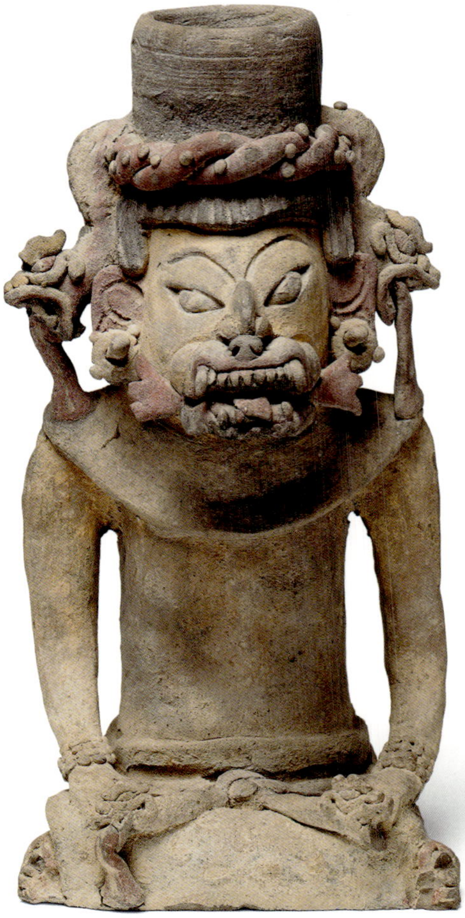

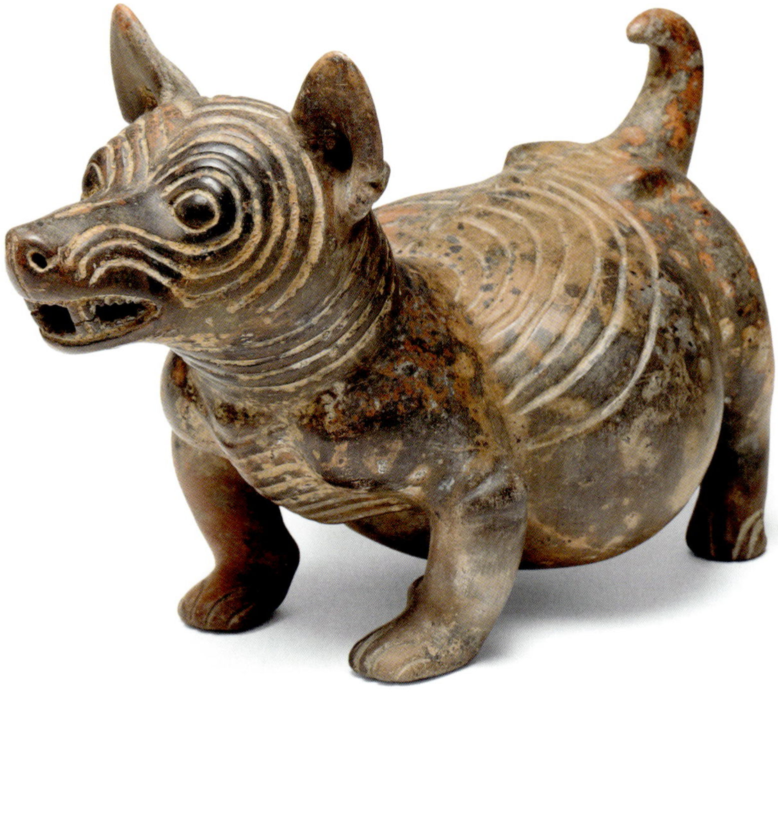

Zapotec Deity, Mexico, Zapotec, Oaxaca, 600–900

Hairless Dog with Wrinkles, Mexico, Colima, 200–500

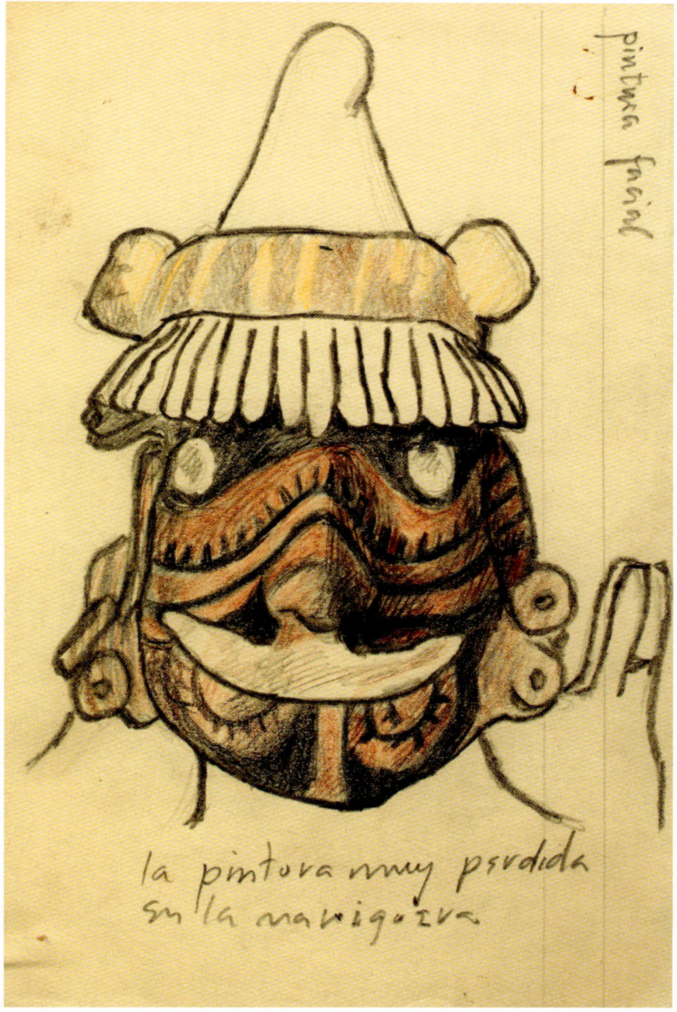

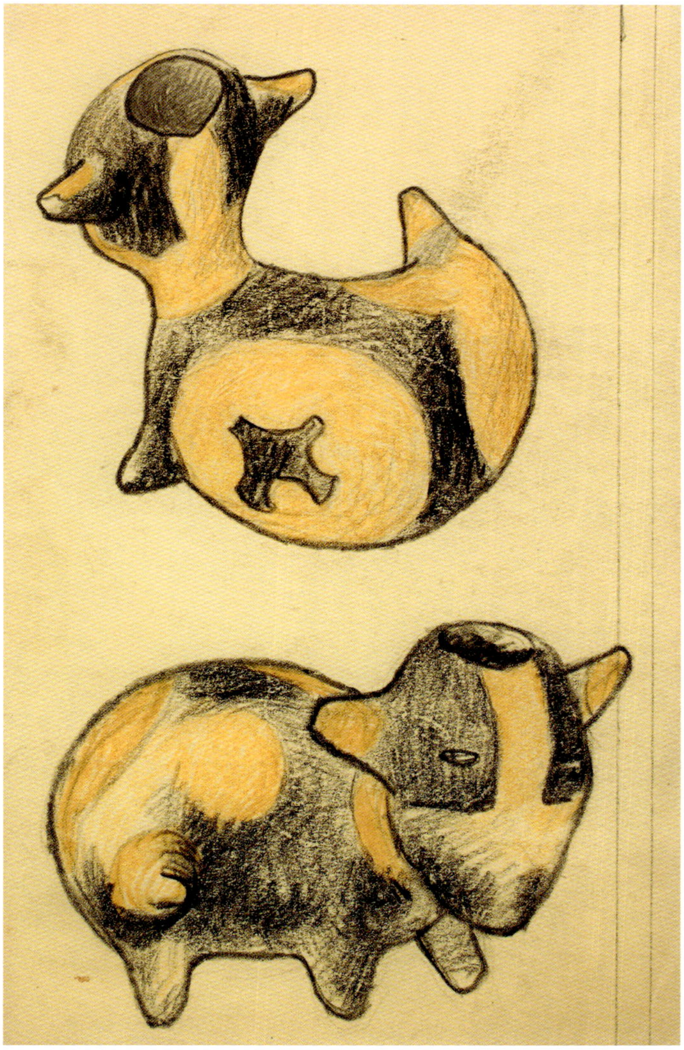

Diego Rivera, **Studies of Pre-Columbian Figurines**, c. 1955–56

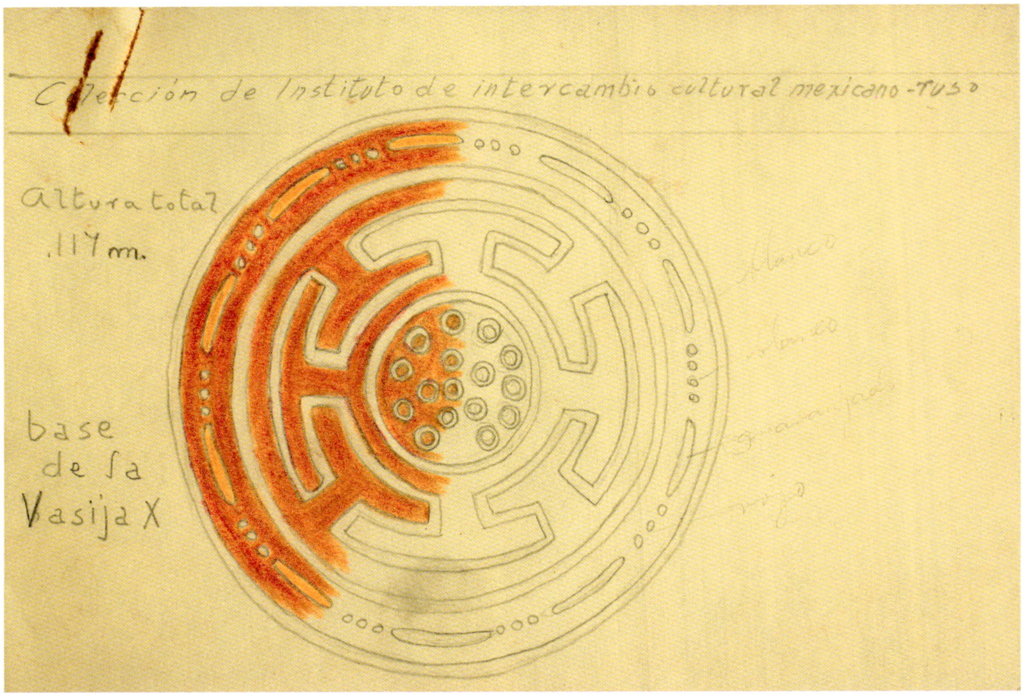

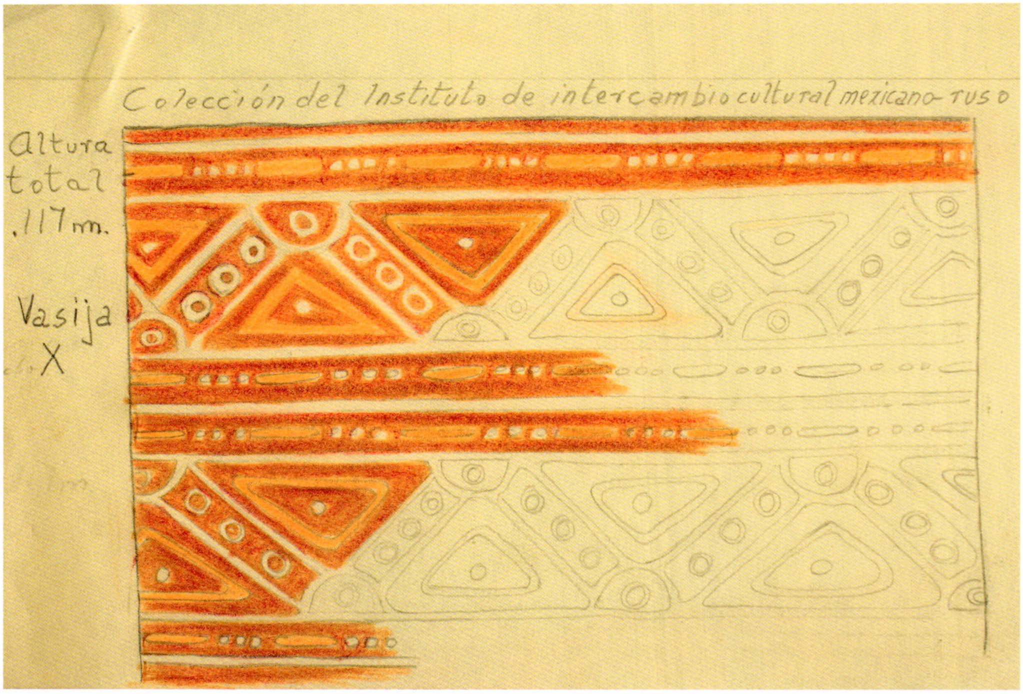

Diego Rivera, **Studies of Pre-Columbian Figurines**, c. 1955–56

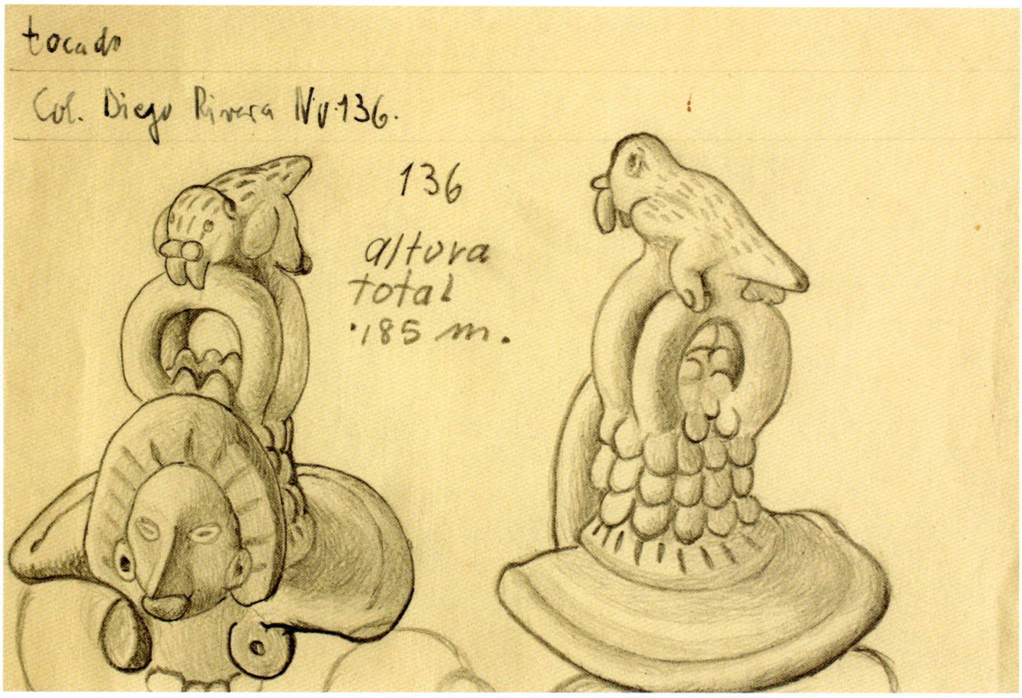

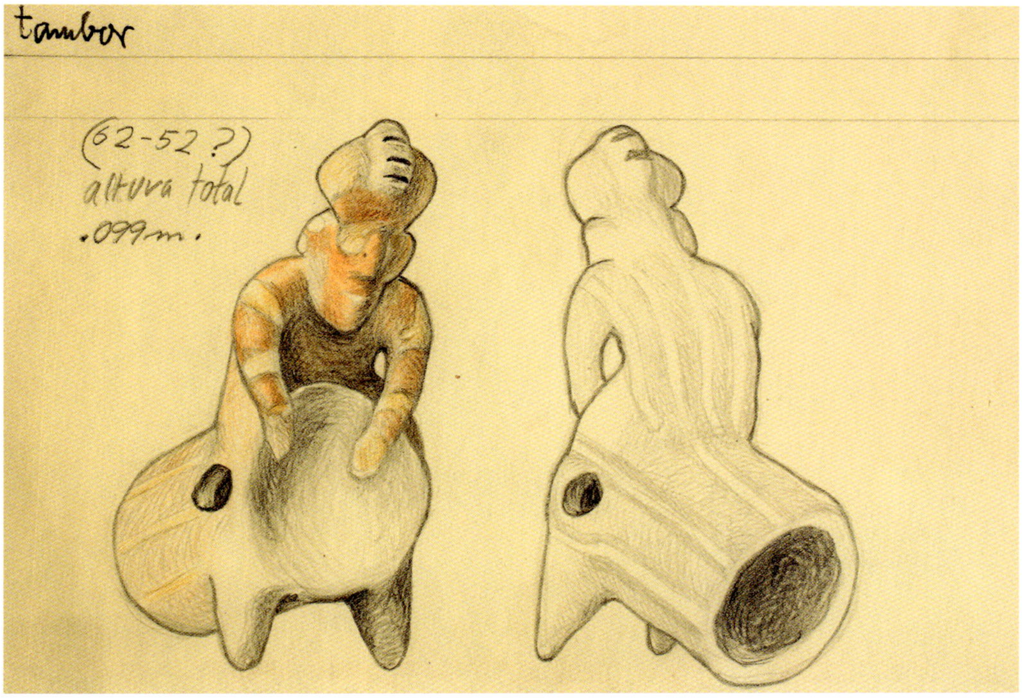

Diego Rivera, **Studies of Pre-Columbian Figurines**, c. 1955–56

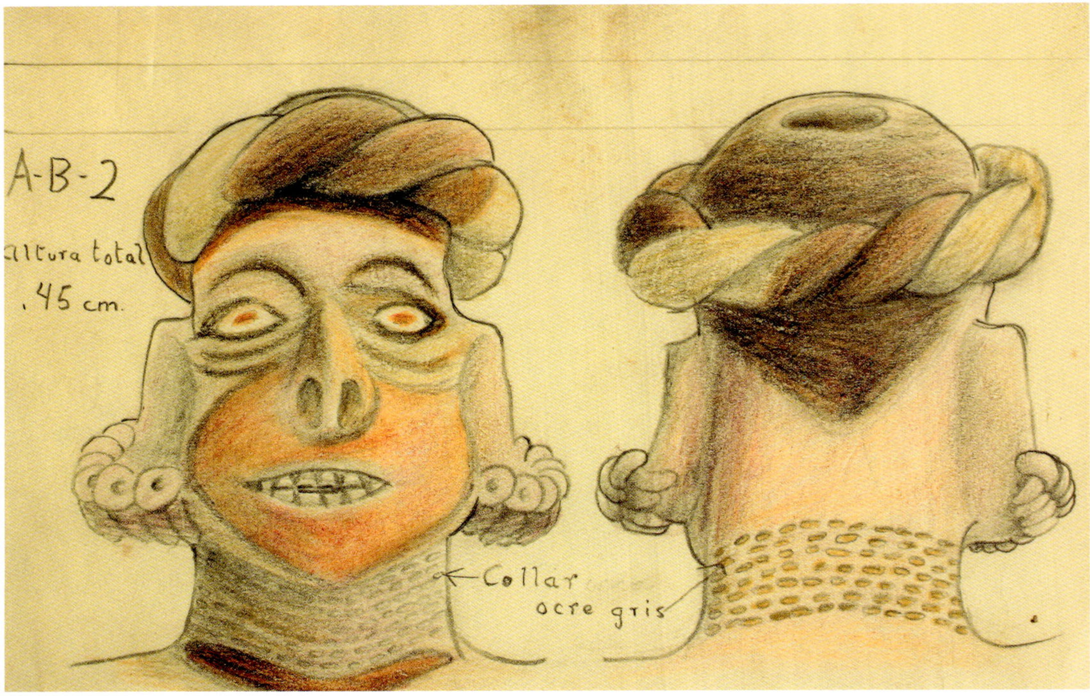

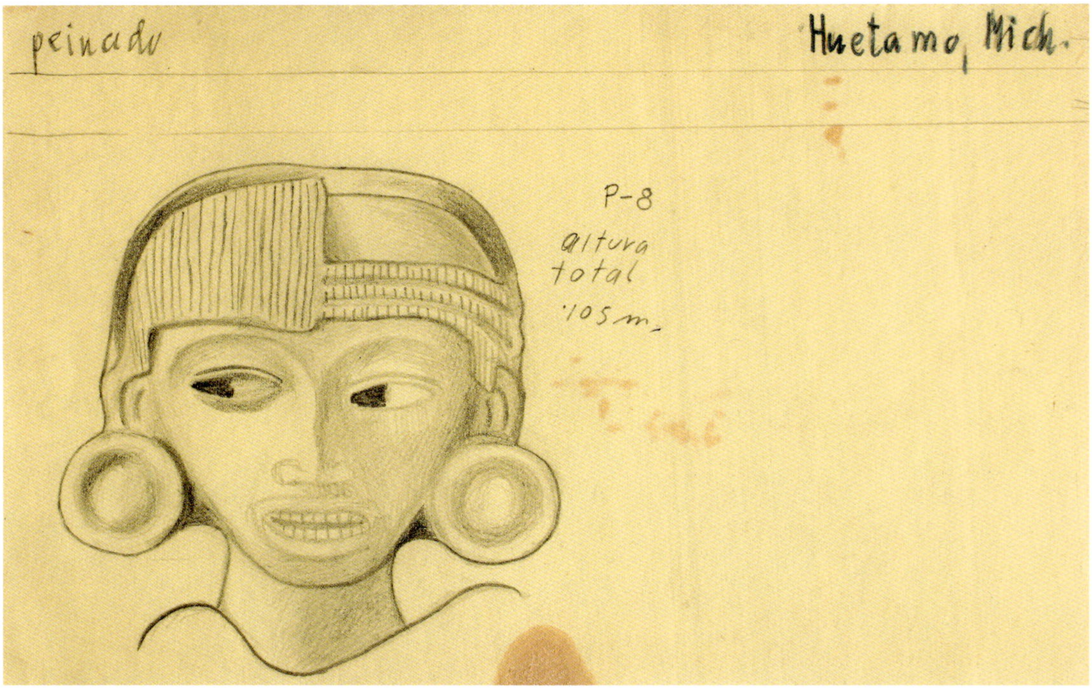

Diego Rivera, **Studies of Pre-Columbian Figurines**, c. 1955–56

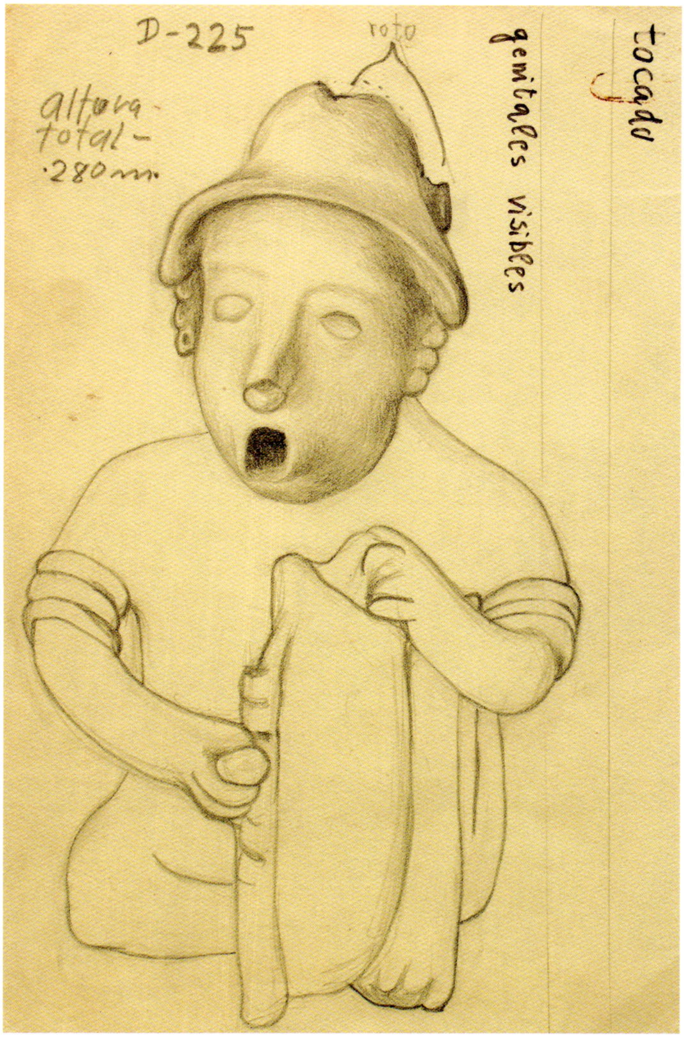

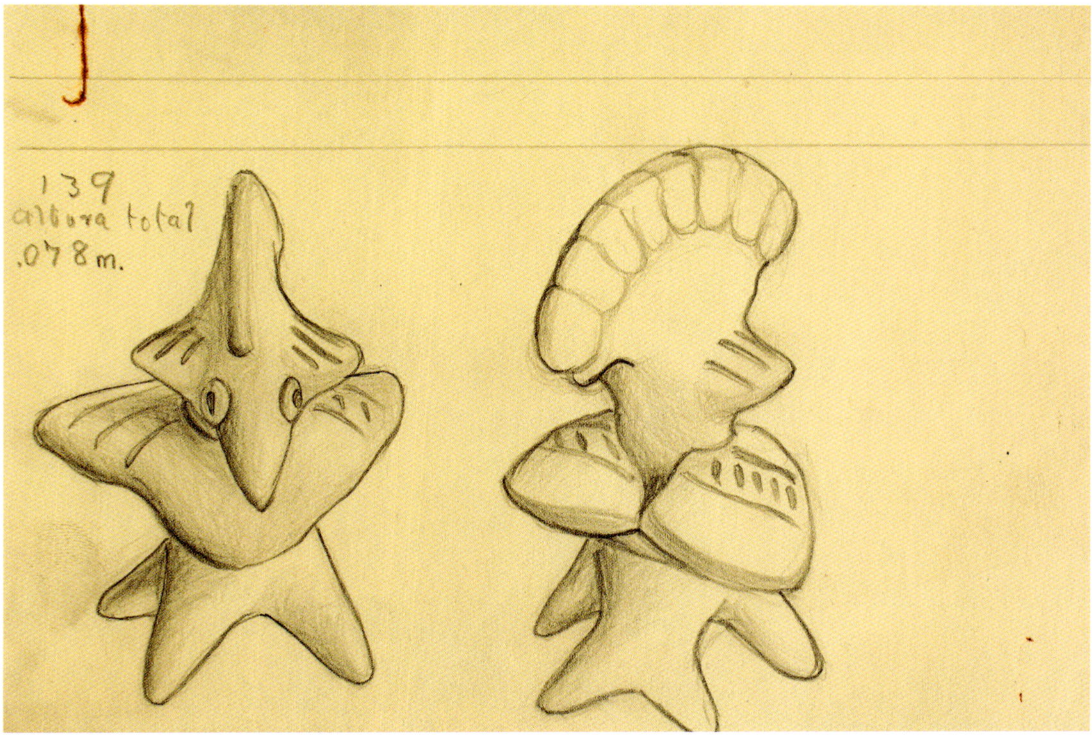

Diego Rivera, **Studies of Pre-Columbian Figurines**, c. 1955–56

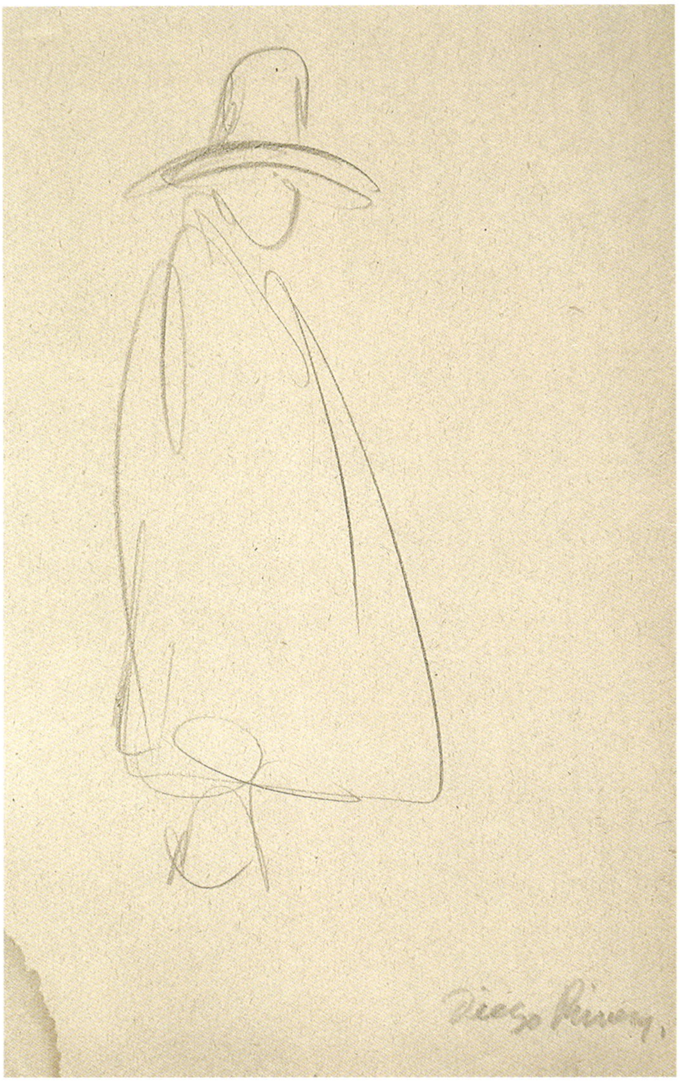

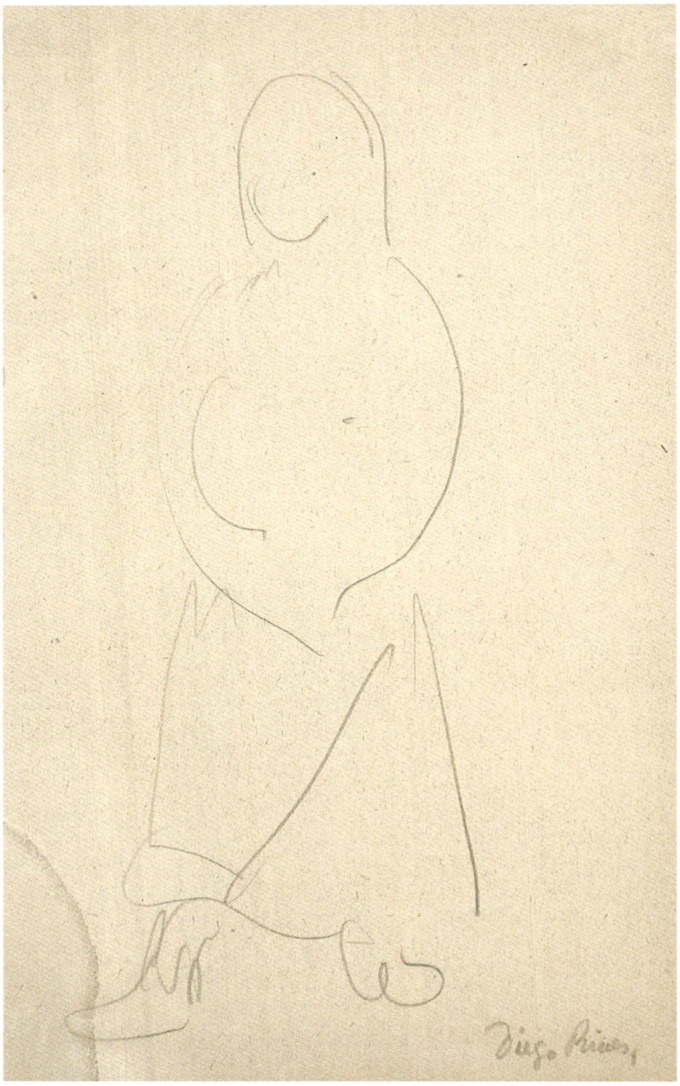

Diego Rivera, ***Untitled*** (***Man with Cloak and Hat***), 1923–25

Diego Rivera, ***Untitled*** (***Female Figure***), 1923–25

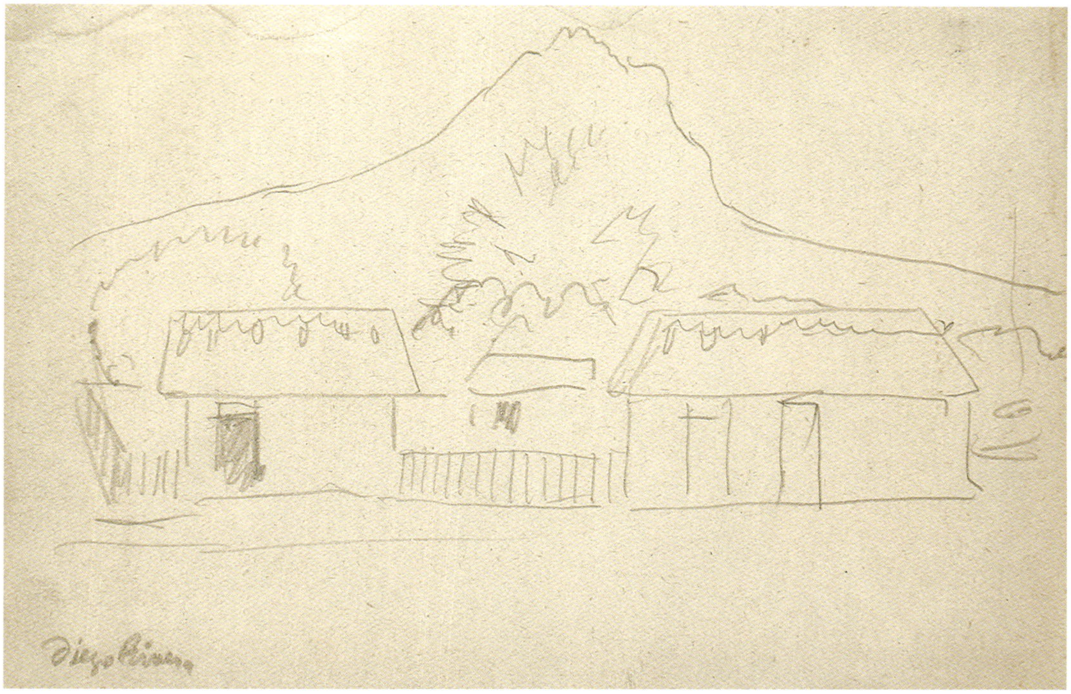

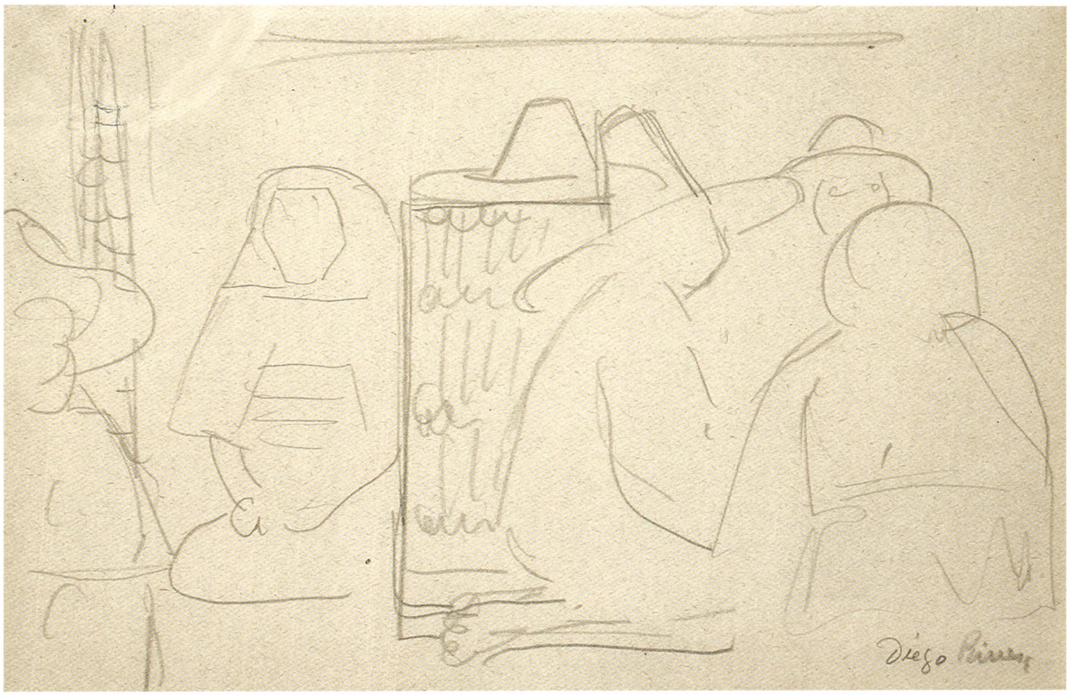

Diego Rivera, ***Untitled** (**Mountain with Huts**)*, 1923–25

Diego Rivera, ***Untitled** (**Group of Seated Figures**)*, 1923–25

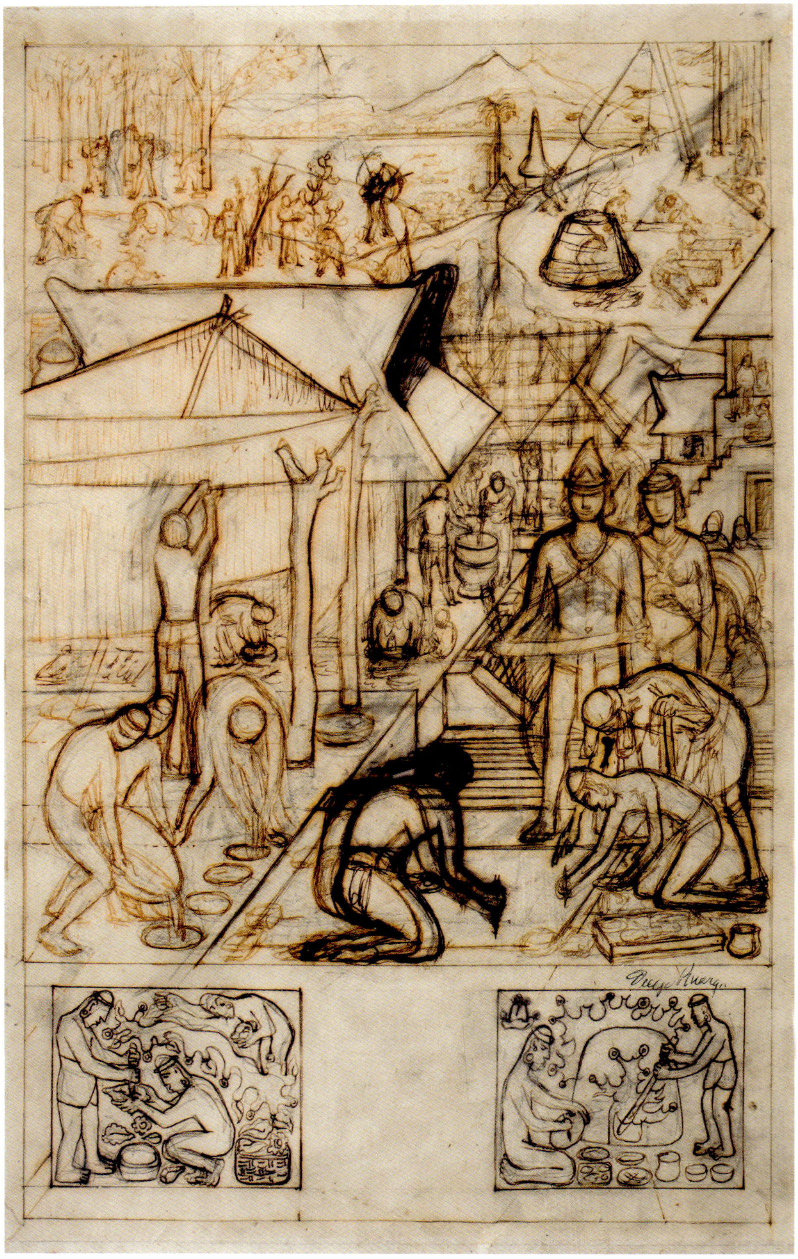

Diego Rivera, Sketch for *Tarasca Culture* mural, *Painters and Dyers*, 1942

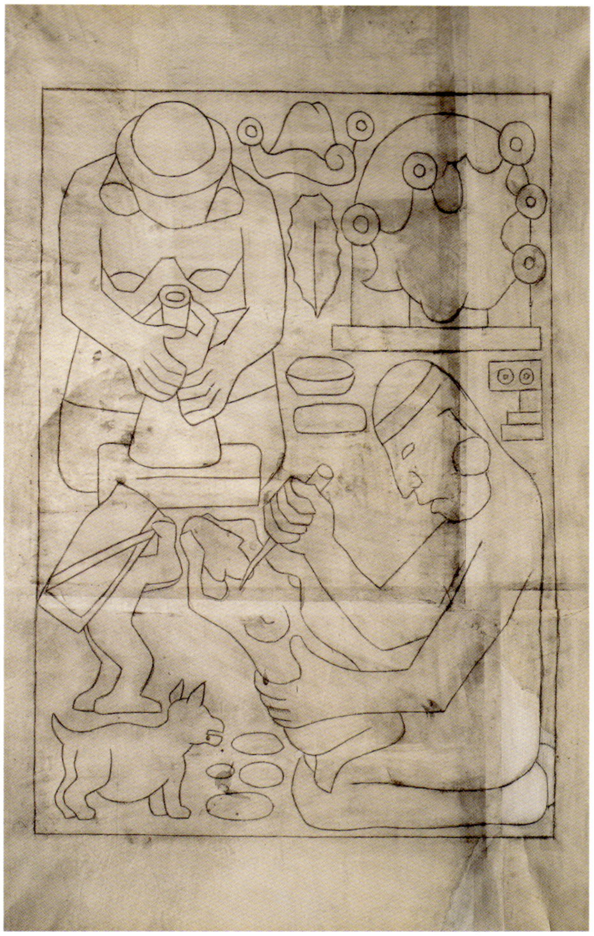

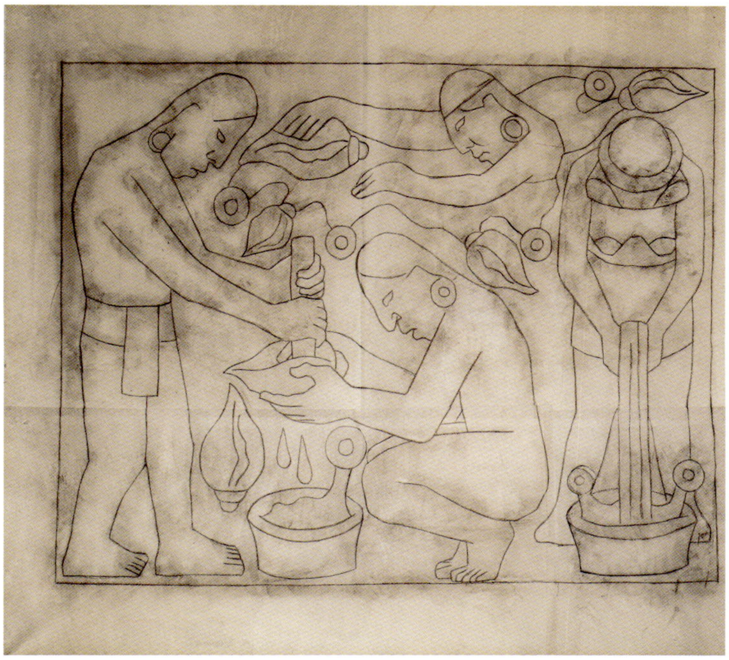

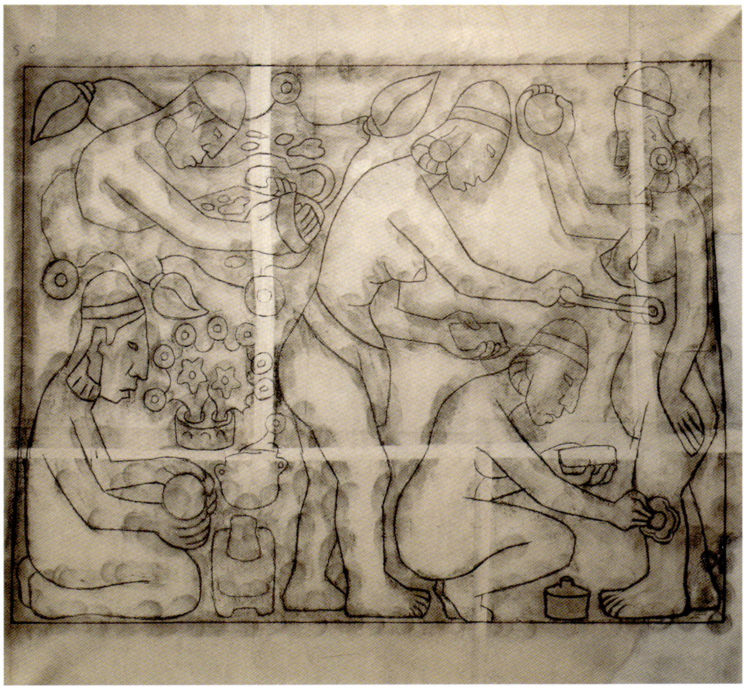

CLOCKWISE FROM TOP LEFT

Diego Rivera, ***Sculpture and Pottery***, 1942

Diego Rivera, Sketch for grisaille of ***Purépecha Culture*** mural, ***Pigment Preparation***, 1942

Diego Rivera, Sketch for grisaille of ***Purépecha Culture*** mural, ***Body Paint Application***, 1942

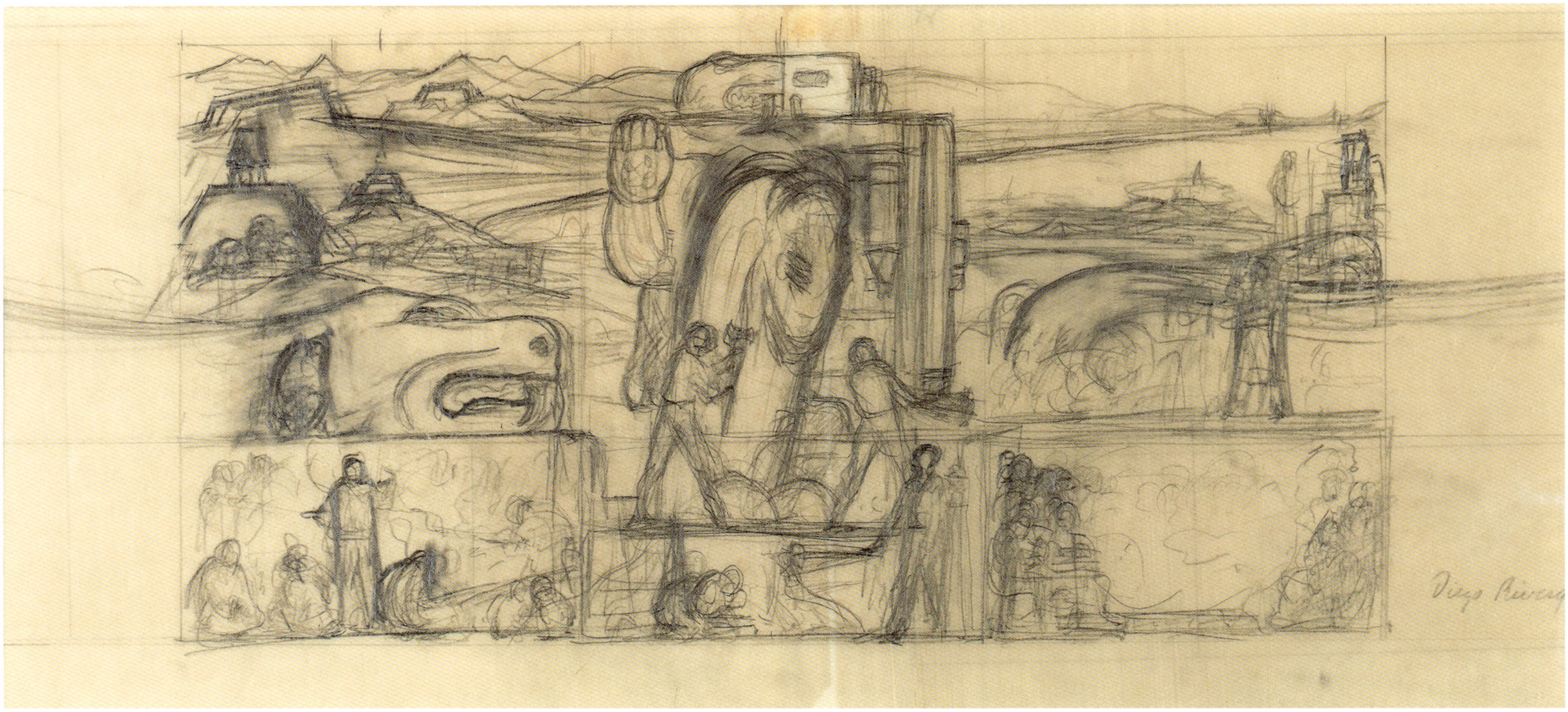

Diego Rivera, First sketch for ***Pan American Unity*** mural, 1940

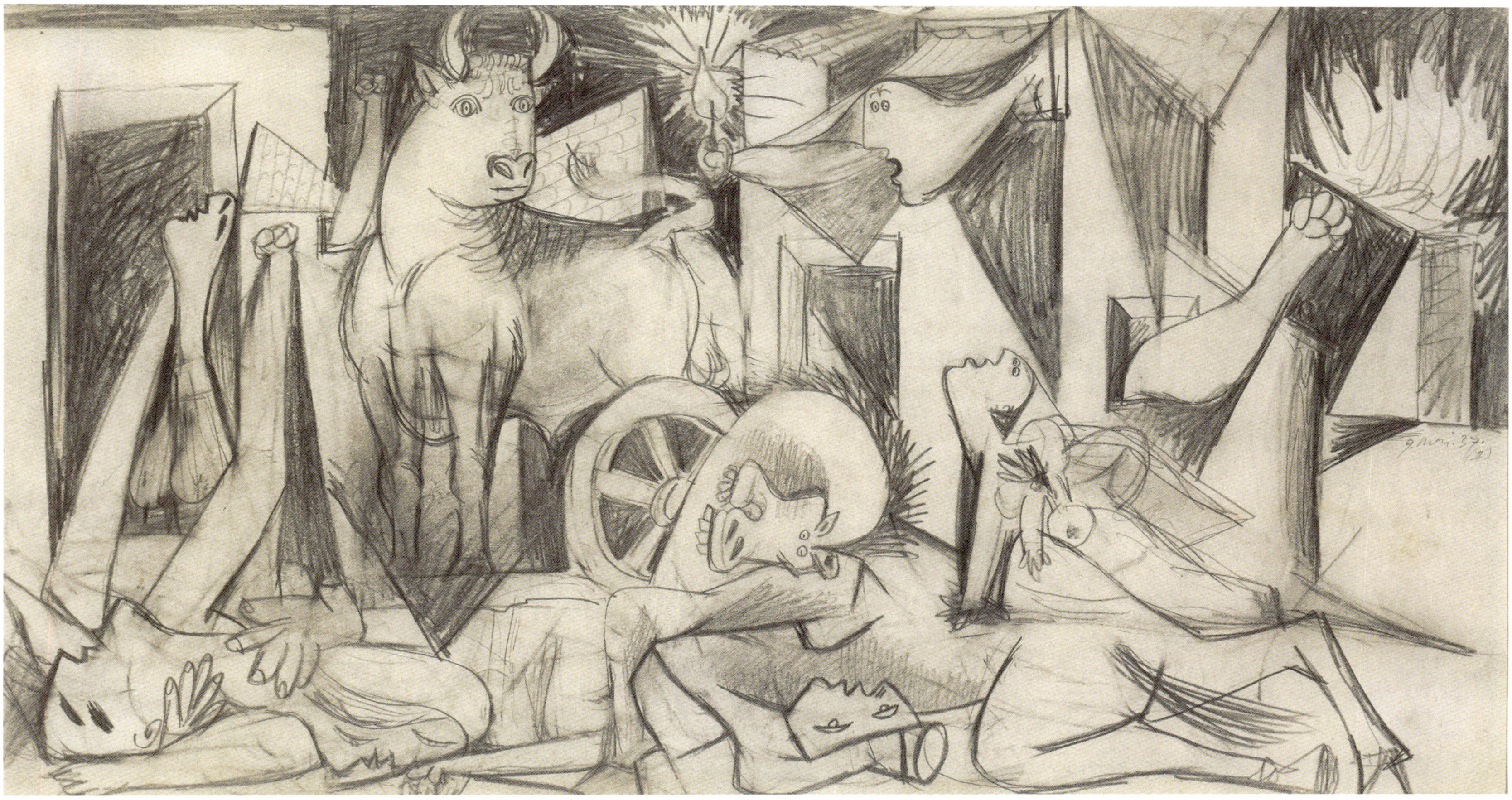

Pablo Picasso, ***Guernica Composition Study VII***, May 9, 1937

RIVERA AND THE LANGUAGE OF CLASSICISM

MICHELE GREET

In the somber, circumspect climate following World War I, a new classicism permeated the visual arts. This "return to order," as it would come to be known, eclipsed the emphasis on the more radical aesthetic experiments—distorted flattened figures, bold non-natural color, and abstracted or entirely nonobjective compositions—that were the hallmark of avant-garde art before 1914.[1] Artists such as Pablo Picasso and Georges Braque turned to painting monumental nudes, idyllic peasants, and images of maternity and tradition, which conveyed the postwar desire for order and stability.[2] These paintings expressed a yearning to return to the land, nature, and traditional values after the chaos of war.[3] According to Kenneth E. Silver, "Picasso was the first, strongest, and most prolific practitioner of a wartime revival of traditional draftsmanship, brilliantly aping Ingres in portraits of his friends and colleagues. After the war, he was the best and most unabashed neoclassicist (while continuing to make Cubist art)."[4] These images were not a wholesale reversion to the past and traditional modes of painting, however; postwar artists were seeking an aesthetic model that emphasized continuity over rupture while still expressing their modernity. Their notion of classicism was broad and their sources varied, including classical Greek and Roman, Italian Renaissance, and French neoclassical art, which they reinterpreted to express new ideas. For many artists, selectively incorporating signifiers of classicism—monumentality, visual clarity, harmony, humanism—was a way to revitalize modern art at a moment when many felt that artistic production was headed in the wrong direction, and that the prewar experiments of the avant-garde were devoid of human sentiment and lacked social purpose.

This new classicism held an appeal beyond postwar Europe. Many Latin American artists, especially those who studied and exhibited in Paris in the late 1910s and 1920s, coopted the return-to-order aesthetic, transforming it to suit the purposes and environments of their home countries. Indeed, one of the first of these artists to deliberately and systematically explore classicizing tendencies was Diego Rivera, for whom Picasso's classical imagery served as a point of departure. Even when the two artists were no longer living on the same continent, the press brought news of Picasso to Mexico and of Rivera to France, circulating ideas as well as perpetuating dialogue across the Atlantic. This essay explores Rivera's path toward classicism, his affinity with and divergence from Picasso, and the implications of his embrace of a classicizing aesthetic in Mexico.

REJECTING CUBISM

Prior to and during World War I, Diego Rivera, like Picasso, worked predominantly in a Cubist mode. In 1916, after returning to Paris from Spain, he signed with French art dealer Léonce Rosenberg, who was becoming a dominant force in the contemporary art market and a leading champion of Cubism. With virtually no competition, Rosenberg signed Juan Gris, Jacques Lipchitz, Henri Laurens, and Braque that same year (and Fernand Léger as soon as he returned from the front in December 1917), gaining unprecedented control over the presentation and sale of their work.[5] Indeed, Rosenberg may very well have taken advantage of artists whose sources of support had disappeared during the war in order to build up his stock of paintings.[6] While Picasso never signed an exclusive contract with Léonce Rosenberg, he did work with him briefly before leaving Léonce to be represented by the latter's brother Paul in 1918.[7] But it was French artist André Lhote, whom Rivera had first met in 1913, who had the most impact on Rivera when he joined Rosenberg's gallery.

Lhote and Rivera shared a desire to maintain readability in their Cubist compositions.[8] Both envisioned

1
For more on the return to order, also known as the call to order, see Kenneth E. Silver, *Esprit de Corps: The Art of the Parisian Avant-Garde and the First World War, 1914–1925* (Princeton: Princeton University Press, 1989).

2
Romy Golan discusses the importance of images of peasants to the return to order in "Rusticizing the Modern," chap. 2 in *Modernity and Nostalgia: Art and Politics in France Between the Wars* (New Haven: Yale University Press, 1995).

3
Ibid., 19–21.

4
Kenneth E. Silver, "A More Durable Self," in *Chaos and Classicism: Art in France, Italy, and Germany 1918–1936*, ed. Kenneth E. Silver (New York: Guggenheim Museum, 2010), 23.

5
The original contracts are in the Fonds Léonce Rosenberg, Bibliothèque Kandinsky, Paris.

6
My thanks to James Oles for this observation.

7
For more information, see Michael C. FitzGerald, *Making Modernism: Picasso and the Creation of the Market for Twentieth-Century Art* (Berkeley: University of California Press, 1996), 48.

8
Lhote describes his process in Maurice Raynal, *Modern French Painters* (New York: Brentano's, 1928), 117.

Cubism as an outgrowth of traditional pictorial conventions rather than a radical break with the past, and it was most likely this outlook that led to their subsequent exploration of classicizing tendencies. In a letter from Lhote to his friend G. Pauli dated July 26, 1917, Lhote asserts: "I've made some sensational discoveries with my friend Rivera concerning the laws of construction of a picture. They have been the same ever since the Greeks and up to Cézanne (who zealously kept the secret) via Rembrandt, El Greco, Velázquez...."[9] What Lhote describes here is a trajectory that links the past to the present via the crucial figure of Paul Cézanne.

While Rivera renewed his contract with Rosenberg on November 15, 1917, tensions had begun to mount between the artist and his dealer over the new direction Rivera's art was taking, the limitations of Cubism, and artistic freedom. The following summer, Rivera and his wife, Angelina Beloff, traveled with Danish artists Adam and Ellen Fischer to the Bay of Arcachon on France's Atlantic coast. Lhote and French writer Jean Cocteau were staying nearby, and the group often spent afternoons together.[10] There, Rivera made a pencil portrait of Cocteau that evidences an almost Ingres-like classicism in explicit defiance of Rosenberg's continued advocacy of a narrowly defined Cubist approach. While Rivera did not intend the portrait for Rosenberg's gallery, his contract was so binding that he had to write to his dealer to request permission to offer the drawing to Cocteau.[11] This degree of control over artistic output did not sit well with Rivera.

During the summer of 1918 Rivera continued exploring new aesthetic directions, chafing more and more under Rosenberg's oversight. Together Rivera and Lhote embarked on a rediscovery of Cézanne as a means to redeploy the lessons of Cubism as the foundation for a more traditionally readable composition.[12] One of his paintings of that period was *Landscape at Arcachon*, which clearly indicates Rivera's close study of Cézanne in its structuring of the surface with patches of pigment, its areas of passage, and its muted palette of greens and warm earth tones. Lhote, too, partook of an exploration of Cézanne with works such as *Village by the Sea*. Together with Adam Fischer, Rivera and Lhote began preparing a group exhibition of their work (along with younger artists Eugène Corneau, André Favory, and Gabriel Fournier) to be held at the Galerie Blot in Paris.[13] Fischer would later employ the term *modern classicism* to describe the work created for the show, thereby framing these artists' explorations of Cézanne as the link between the classical past, a grand French tradition, and modern ideas.[14] Their plans to exhibit non-Cubist paintings based on the precepts of Cézanne heightened the rift between them and Rosenberg, instigating what French critic André Salmon deemed *l'affaire Rivera*.[15]

To express his discontent, Rosenberg published a letter in art critic Louis Vauxcelles's column "Carnet des ateliers" in the journal *Carnet de la semaine*, calling Rivera and Lhote to task for straying from the Cubist

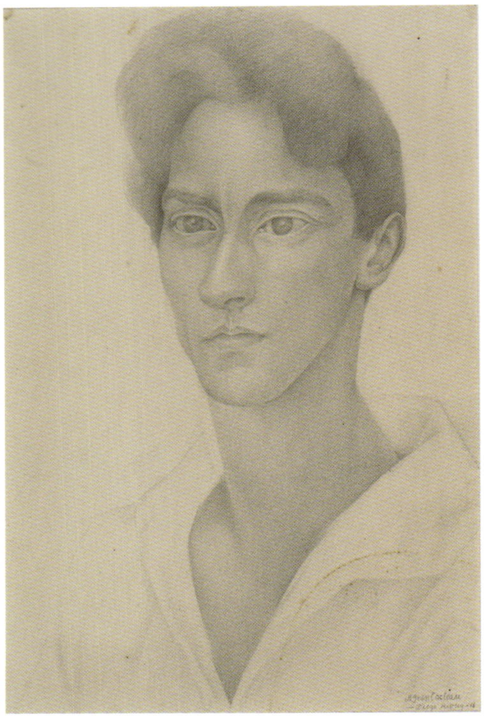

Diego Rivera, ***Portrait of Jean Cocteau***, 1918; pencil, 18⅛ × 11¾ in. (46 × 30 cm); Carlton Lake Collection, Harry Ransom Humanities Research Center, The University of Texas at Austin

9
Letter from André Lhote to G. Pauli, July 26, 1917, reprinted in *Diego Rivera: les années cubistes*, ed. Françoise Garcia (Musée des Beaux-Arts Bordeaux, 2011), 142.

10
Patrick Marnham, *Dreaming with His Eyes Open: A Life of Diego Rivera* (Berkeley: University of California Press, 2000), 136.

11
Françoise Garcia, "Diego Rivera: Cubism as the Initial Concept of Mural Art," in *Diego Rivera: les années cubistes*, 144.

12
Lhote would later write about the importance of Cézanne: "It is this orderly, intelligible and visual fusion of forms, this overlap of lively planes, this loving entanglement of objects that henceforth could never live without one another and that we cannot cut out with the brush, or separate without killing them, it is this sensitive fusion that Cézanne reconstituted in his paintings, in which it matters little that they represent a glass container filled with potatoes, a landscape from here or elsewhere, or a figure. The material object, here, no longer counts, or rather there is no longer one object on view: it is emotion born of sensation." André Lhote, "L'enseignement de Cézanne," *Nouvelle revue francaise* 15, no. 86 (November 1920): 663. All translations are mine unless otherwise noted. In 1920, there was also an important Cézanne retrospective at the Galerie Bernheim-Jeune (*Exposition Cézanne*, December 1–18, 1920). Rivera's turn to Cézanne may also have stemmed from his friendship with art theorist Élie Faure, who wrote *Les constructeurs* (Paris: G. Cres, 1914). For more on Faure and Rivera, see Lynda Klich, "Revolution and Utopia: Estridentismo and the Visual Arts, 1921–27" (PhD diss., New York University, 2008), 340–41.

13
Galerie Blot, *Exposition de peinture, aquarelles et dessins de Eugène Corneau, André Favory, Gabriel Fournier, André Lhote et Diego Rivera*, October 28–November 19, 1918.

14
Adam Fischer, "Moderne Klassisk Kunst I Paris," *Klingen* 2, no. 3 (1919): n.p. Cited in Klich, "Revolution and Utopia," 391.

15
Salmon coined the term in his editorials of August and September 1918. In Marnham, *Dreaming with His Eyes Open*, 137.

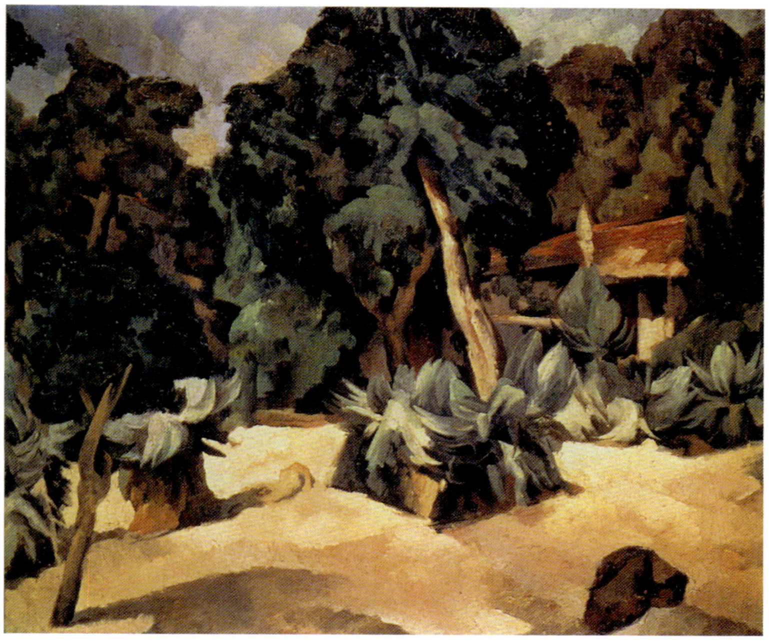

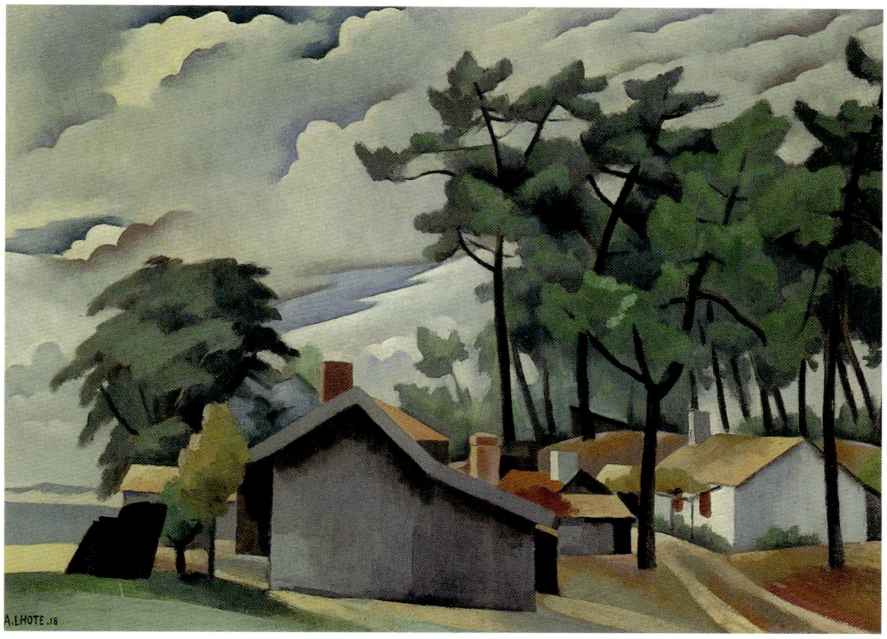

framework. Vauxcelles, who felt the movement was too restrictive and was actively encouraging artists to leave Rosenberg, was all too happy to print Lhote's and Rivera's responses in the next issue.[16] Indeed, his introduction practically revels in Lhote's and Rivera's vehement defense of their right to evolve as artists and move beyond Cubism.[17] Lhote begins:

> I noted in the letter that M. Léonce Rosenberg asked you to print in the last *Carnet des ateliers* a passage that concerns me since the content could be misinterpreted by the reader. Mr. Léonce Rosenberg speaks of "the Cubist aspect that my paintings possessed during a certain period." One might think that he was tricked into being interested in my efforts when this "Cubist aspect" appeared and that he was right to lose interest in them the day that my paintings possessed less of a "modern effort," and represented forbidden subjects such as nudes and portraits. While during the year that M.L.R bought my paintings, I was brought fatally close…to working parallel to the so-called Cubists.… During that same year, never did I hide the fact that I distanced myself from all formulas that allow logic to encroach on sensitivity, or my taste to be guided by instinct.[18]

Rivera followed up with a defense of his own, asserting:

> My most essential endeavor was always to follow Cézanne's teachings. Instinct directed me to search for a foundation, a structure. Once that base was established, that same instinct pushed me to decorate the structure, which cannot be humanized if it remains a scaffolding. Hence, the necessity to paint fully.… And if because of this we are no longer Cubists, oh well, all the better.[19]

Rivera's nonchalant dismissal of Cubism suggests that his choice to abandon the movement's precepts was definitive and that he would not attempt a compromise with his dealer. For both artists, Cubism had become formulaic and they would not comply with Rosenberg's desire to establish a set of norms for what constituted modern art. Whereas Rosenberg felt he was within his

16
For views on Vauxcelles, see Marie-Claude Chaudonneret, *Les Artistes étrangers à Paris: de la fin du Moyen Âge aux années 1920* (Bern: Peter Lang, 2007), 248.

17
In his column, Vauxcelles writes, "André Lhote and Diego Rivera, who were taken to task by Mr. Léonce Rosenberg and reproached for not being Cubists anymore, have addressed two letters to us. They replied with a blinding clarity that they can paint however they please, and that their evolution as artists depends only on themselves." Louis Vauxcelles, "Carnet des ateliers: Au pays du Cube," *Le carnet de la semaine*, October 6 and October 27, 1918.

18
Ibid.

19
Ibid.

LEFT Diego Rivera, ***Landscape at Arcachon***, 1918; oil on canvas, 21¼ × 25⅝ in. (54 × 65 cm); private collection

RIGHT André Lhote, ***Village by the Sea***, 1918; oil on canvas, 17⅞ × 25⅝ in. (45.5 × 65 cm); private collection

rights to demand a certain aesthetic from his artists, Lhote and Rivera believed that he should accept their evolution as artists without shaping it.

Unfortunately for Rivera, in his efforts to control and define the market, Rosenberg turned out to be quite vindictive, essentially hoarding Rivera's works and keeping them from circulation in the months prior to and after canceling his contract. As Fischer related: "For the past half year a powerful press campaign has been carried on against a certain art dealer who is sitting on a large stock of Cubist art, and who, in order not to damage his business, has made use of a contract he had with a young painter to take his entire production in order to, by hiding his pictures, conceal the fact that he was on the point of abandoning Cubism."[20] Rosenberg finally relented and released Rivera from his contract just in time for him to open his show at the Galerie Blot, which Vauxcelles conveniently stepped in to coorganize.

The Galerie Blot exhibition marked Rivera's ultimate departure from Rosenberg and Cubism. In his review of the exhibition, however, André Salmon suggested that Rivera's outright rejection of Cubism was a ploy to position himself as a leader rather than a follower of the likes of Braque and Picasso. By positing Cubism as a means rather than an end in itself, he argued, Rivera constructed Cubism as a "blocked passageway" that could be escaped only through renunciation.[21] In renouncing it he would be moving modern art in a new direction. But Rosenberg remained a significant controlling force in the Parisian art market, impeding Rivera from making the mark he had hoped. He continued to hold all of Rivera's paintings in his possession for nearly three years, until finally putting them up for sale at public auction in 1921 along with works by Lhote, Lipchitz, María Gutiérrez Blanchard, and Ángel Zárraga, all of whom were no longer working with the dealer.[22]

After leaving Rosenberg's gallery, Rivera and Lhote remained in contact and began a more concerted exploration of classicism. Lhote often verbalized ideas that only appear in visual form in Rivera's work. Beginning in 1919, Lhote's essays were frequently published in French and British journals.[23] In his writings, Lhote downplayed his engagement with Cubism by relegating it to a previous historical moment, deeming the approach useful in the present only as a formal exercise. For him, Cubist techniques were a means to structure the pictorial surface, not an end in themselves. Instead, Lhote advanced the idea of a great French tradition that highlighted artists such as Jacques-Louis David, Georges Seurat, Jean-Auguste-Dominique Ingres, and especially Cézanne.

In an essay about the reopening of the Louvre after World War I, Lhote explained the impulse toward classicism that overtook so many artists:

> The reopening of the Louvre was for us artists of the younger generation…a serious event. It seemed indispensable to us all to form a decisive opinion on traditional art, and at the same time to take our bearings in the troubled ocean of painting at last. At the first instant of contact with our masters, the skilled captains who made such splendid voyages without shipwreck, we realized the distance our vessel was out of its course. To discover the direction of the current, which had thus diverted us, and to regain by the shortest possible route a traditional harbor, was the resolution which the most clear-sighted of us brought away from our visit.[24]

For Lhote, studying the great masters was the way back from the diversion Cubism had created. Indeed, several Latin American artists who studied with Lhote in the 1920s remarked on the emphasis on classicism in his teachings. Brazilian artist Tarsila do Amaral wrote about her time studying with Lhote: "I can still see the Michelangelo reproductions glued to the walls as examples of good drawing: Lhote became the link

20
Ramón Favela, *Diego Rivera: The Cubist Years* (Phoenix, AZ: Phoenix Art Museum, 1984), 151. Favela cites Fischer, "Moderne Klassisk Kunst I Paris."

21
André Salmon, "La Semaine artistique: Selon Cézanne (Galerie Blot)," *L'Europe nouvelle* 4, no. 43 (November 2, 1918): 2069–70. See also the discussion of Rivera's views in Salmon, "La Semaine artistique: Exposition André Lhote," *L'Europe nouvelle* 4, no. 48 (December 7, 1918): 2309–10.

22
The sale took place on April 28, 1921. A letter from Rosenberg advising Rivera that his works were put up for auction is dated February 14, 1921, but the letter was returned to sender. Fonds Léonce Rosenberg, Bibliothèque Kandinsky, Paris.

23
For additional examples of some of Lhote's theoretical writings, see André Lhote, "A First Visit to the Louvre," *Athenaeum* (August 22, 1919): 787–88; "The Paris Salon," *Athenaeum* (July 16, 1920): 87–88, 117–18; "Peinture d'un cubisme 'sensible,'" *La Vie des Lettres et des Arts* 15 (April 2, 1924): 1–6; and "De l'utilisation plastique du coup de foudre," *Nouvelle revue française* (March 1924): 289–302.

24
Lhote, "First Visit to the Louvre," 787.

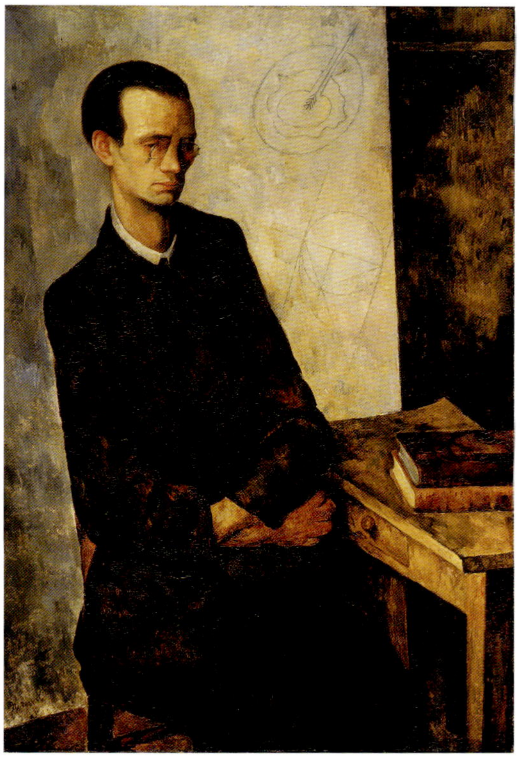

Diego Rivera, *The Mathematician*, 1918

between classicism and modernism.... He explained in his southern accent how we could adapt the technique and compositional methods of the old masters to the demands of contemporary art."[25] And Argentine artist Héctor Basaldúa recalled that Lhote "invoked the great deformers: Tintoretto, Ingres, Greco, Rodin."[26] Rivera's turn to classicism stemmed from a dialogue between innovators, as seen in *The Mathematician* (1918). Rivera and Lhote were friends and colleagues during a period of transition and exploration, and while Lhote wrote much more prolifically about his ideas during this period than Rivera, his writings reveal the impetus behind Rivera's new direction. It was this impulse toward classicism that led Rivera to Italy before returning to Mexico in 1921.

AN ITALIAN TOUR

In 1920 Mexican Secretary of Education José Vasconcelos invited Rivera to return to Mexico to paint public murals. One of the stipulations of Rivera's agreement to leave Paris was that the Mexican government would first sponsor a trip to Italy in the tradition of the Grand Tour: an extended voyage around Europe whose primary objective was exposure to classical Greek and Roman antiquities and the works of the Italian Renaissance. For Rivera, the trip lasted from January 1920 until July 1921.[27] His friend Élie Faure, an art historian, designed the itinerary, from Ravenna in the north to the southern tip of Italy and back up the east coast. During his travels Rivera paid special attention to the relationship between painting and architecture in Renaissance murals, establishing the groundwork for his mural production upon his return home. He also made numerous drawings of classical antiquities and Renaissance paintings and took extensive handwritten notes in French, often directly on the surface of the drawings.[28]

In Italy, Rivera made sketches after Tintoretto, Francesco Bonsignori, Giovanni Francesco Caroto, Stefano di Zevio, Andrea Mantegna, and Titian. Significantly, in his Italian notebooks there is a marked absence of drawings of the High Renaissance masters Michelangelo, Leonardo da Vinci, and Raphael. Instead, Rivera seemed to have a noticeable preference for the quattrocento and the later works of Tintoretto, which most likely stemmed from his artistic discussions and explorations with Lhote. This focus on less-known figures rather than on iconic Renaissance artists indicates Rivera's fascination with the oddities of pictorial construction instead of the "perfect" expressions of classical values. Indeed, the Italian notebooks reveal that the artist was much more interested in the underlying structure of a composition than in surface detail, chiaroscuro, or narrative. In his sketch after Bonsignori's *La Madonna con il Bambino* (1481), for example, he breaks the composition into three horizontal segments, with the

25
Tarsila do Amaral, "Memories of Paris" (1952), *Tarsila do Amaral* (Madrid: Fundación Juan March, 2009), 48–49.

26
Letter from Basaldúa to his friends, 1923, quoted in Guillermo Whitelow, *Héctor Basaldúa* (Buenos Aires: Academia Nacional de Bellas Artes/Fondo Nacional de las Artes, 1980), 46.

27
Diego Rivera (with Gladys March), *My Art, My Life: An Autobiography* (New York: Dover, 1991), 71.

28
Ibid.

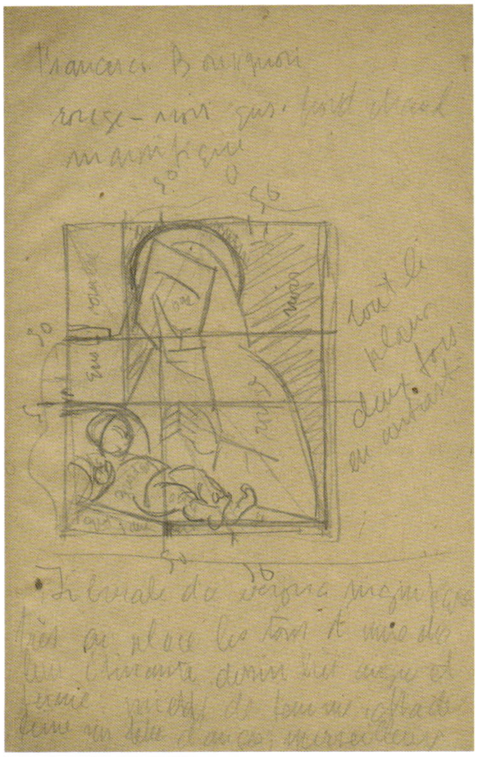

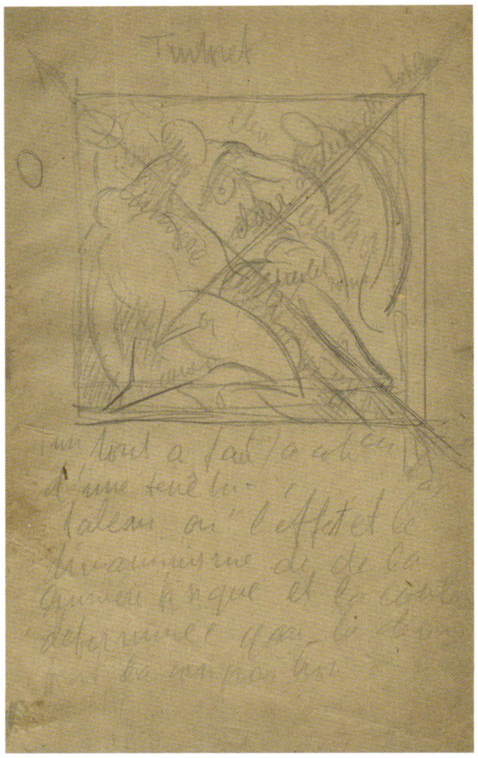

middle segment, which encompasses the Madonna's neck and shoulders, narrower than the upper and lower sections. He further divides the composition with two vertical lines, creating a rectangle that links the mother's gaze to the sleeping child. The veil and halo around the Madonna's head have been simplified to basic geometries, revealing the framework Bonsignori used to construct and organize his composition. This exploration of structure relates directly to Rivera's investigation of Cézanne over the previous three years in collaboration with Lhote. By applying the lessons of Cézanne to Renaissance paintings, Rivera established a trajectory from the classical to the modern and positioned his own work as the confluence of the two.

In a second example, a sketch after Tintoretto's *Three Graces and Mercury* (1578), Rivera again identifies the underlying rhythms and structure of the composition. He divides the composition with two intersecting diagonal lines to discover how Tintoretto situated the three bodies in space. His representation of the bodies is entirely schematic, with simple ovals for heads and arabesques for limbs. The curved outer arms of the upper and lower figures form a set of parentheses encircling the composition. By identifying how the composition was structured, Rivera was able to derive the lessons of the great Italian masters.

Following his extended stay in Italy, Rivera finally returned to Mexico in 1921 after having spent fourteen years abroad. This departure in no way extricated him from the milieu of European modernism, however. Not only did Rivera maintain contact with his European acquaintances and follow European developments, but Parisian circles also continued to watch him, with various articles on the artist appearing in the Parisian press in the late 1920s. Similarly, the Mexican press kept tabs on European trends and printed various reviews and assessments of Picasso's work. For both Rivera and Picasso, this period marked a moment of intensified exploration of notions of the classical, often along very similar aesthetic lines but with different ideological implications.

LEFT Diego Rivera, ***Sketch after Bonsignori, "La Madonna con il Bambino,"*** 1920–21; pencil on paper, 8 × 5 in. (20.3 × 12.7 cm); Martin Charlot Collection

RIGHT Diego Rivera, ***Sketch after Tintoretto, "Three Graces and Mercury,"*** 1920–21; pencil on paper, 8 × 5 in. (20.3 × 12.7 cm); Martin Charlot Collection

DEPLOYING CLASSICISM IN MEXICO

Despite Rivera's friendship and interchange with Lhote in Paris, it was Picasso who remained a foil for Rivera upon his return to Mexico in 1921. The Mexican press celebrated Rivera's return, publishing several articles about his time abroad and plans for the future. These articles emphasized his break with Cubism and embrace of classicism, and specifically aligned him with Picasso, stressing the similarities between the two and the comparable caliber of their work. Writing for *Azulejos*, for example, Pedro Henríquez Ureña asserted:

> The important question is whether Diego Rivera is still making Cubist works in Mexico. And the answer is easy, perhaps even superficial: no, what Rivera is doing now can be called classical...or something else. The same thing has happened with Picasso, with Zárraga, with María Gutiérrez Blanchard, with Brune, with Bissière, with so many of the other formerly militant Cubists. But Rivera, and Picasso, and all of them, assure us that they are still as Cubist as they were before, even though their works now look like Goyas or Titians. They have changed in appearance; but the means of approaching the problem, of studying the lines and tones, has not changed.[29]

There are several interesting points that can be derived from this passage. First, Henríquez Ureña reiterates Rivera's recent assertion that Cubism is useful as an approach or a method but not as a style in and of itself. In other words, Cubist structure still informs picture-making, but the final products look entirely different, "like Goyas or Titians." Second, he asserts that Rivera's work can "now be called classical." This articulation of the label "classical" in relation to Rivera's artistic production became a specific strategy on the part of the artist to distinguish himself from his predecessors and to carve out a space for himself as the new voice of Mexican modernism. As Lynda Klich has argued, Rivera's advancement of a style that was "strong and constructive" was a means of both displacing the sinuous art nouveau aesthetic that dominated Mexican art in the 1910s and situating himself as a leader of "a new era in Mexican painting."[30] Finally, the pairing of Rivera with Picasso twice in this short passage serves to establish Rivera as an artist of equal stature to the renowned Spanish artist. Even though Rivera's relationship with Picasso in Paris was tenuous at best (and he had a much more direct link to Lhote), comparison to Picasso served as a benchmark of success that elevated him in the eyes of his compatriots. Indeed, Rivera's assessment of Picasso fluctuated according to his agenda of the moment. At times, he expressed great admiration for the artist, whereas other times he positioned himself as Picasso's rival and competitor.

Immediately upon his return, however, Rivera emphasized his alignment with Picasso in an interview for *El Universal Ilustrado*, as a means to validate his new vision for Mexican art and distinguish it from the decorative sensibilities of his Mexican contemporaries. The interview took place in the courtyard of the Escuela Nacional de Bellas Artes among the plaster casts of classical statues used for artistic instruction. In this context, Rivera presented his aesthetic as contiguous with classicism because it was informed by Picasso's emphasis on an object's "internal makeup":

> Picasso, he tells us, is now the greatest genius. Why? For the simple reason that, forgetting the surfaces of objects, he has understood that their life resides not only in their decorative qualities, but also in their amazing internal makeup, that is to say, in the very substance that gives them beauty, life, powerful tremors.... And consequently in everything that he paints, the internal strength of the forms present themselves.[31]

29 Pedro Henríquez Ureña, "En la orilla: notas sobre Diego Rivera," *Azulejos* 1, no. 2 (September 1921): 22–23.

30 Klich, "Revolution and Utopia," 339.

31 Roberto Barrios, "Diego Rivera pintor," *El Universal Ilustrado* 5, no. 221 (July 1921): 23.

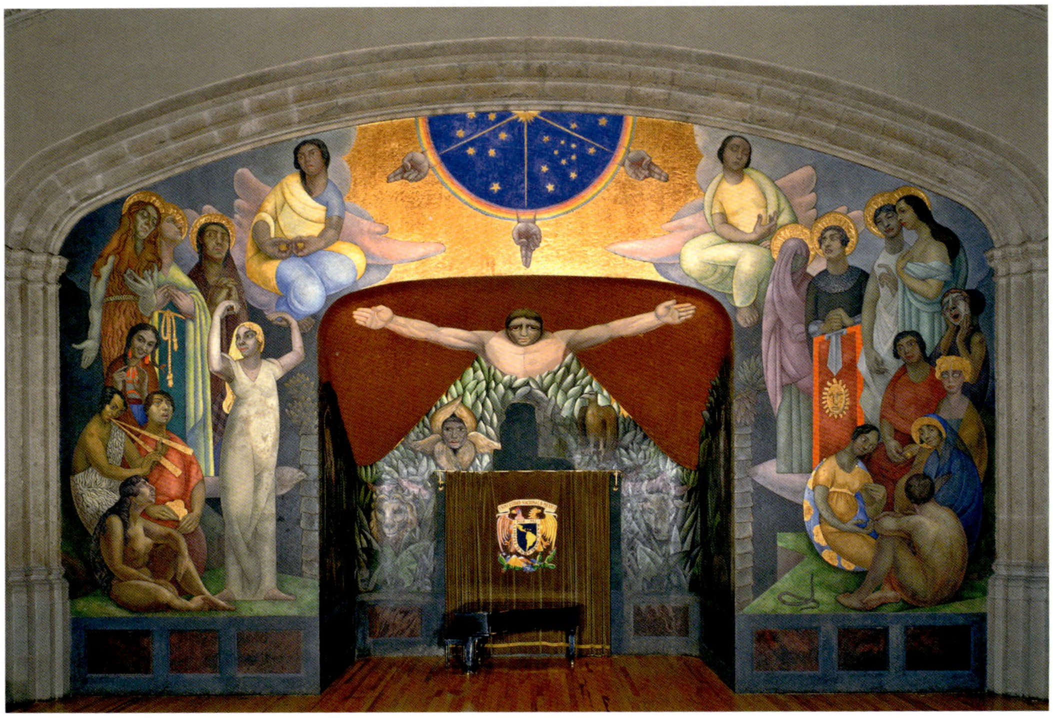

Significantly, Rivera's description of Picasso's genius parallels almost exactly his own approach to art making. For Rivera, "construction" was the most important element of painting, and his goal was to find the union between "pure sensitivity and the laws of physics."[32] During the interview, Rivera also declared that the artist should be understood as "a constructor and a worker."[33] While this language stems directly from the rhetoric surrounding the Mexican Revolution, Rivera contends that "construction" is the link between the artist and the worker: whereas the worker constructs a building or a commodity, the artist builds a composition based on the perceived internal geometries of figures and objects.

The interview also touched on another interesting point that Rivera would continue to elaborate as he delved into future mural projects, that of Pre-Columbian art and architecture as a form of Latin American classicism. Rivera asserts that he returned to Mexico in order to "study manifestations of popular art, the ruins of our astonishing past."[34] While he was certainly not the first Mexican artist to take note of Mexico's Pre-Columbian heritage as a source of national pride and renewal—other examples include Dr. Atl (Gerardo Murillo) and Adolfo Best Maugard—the combination of a Mediterranean classicizing aesthetic and his new interest in Pre-Columbian motifs and indigenous subjects served as a visual proclamation of Pre-Columbian history as the pan-American equivalent of the Greco-Roman tradition. This concept can be traced back to the writings of celebrated Cuban journalist and author José Martí, who asserted that "the history of America, from the Incas to the present, should be taught in perfect detail, even if it means not teaching the history of the archons of Greece. Our Greece is preferable to the Greece that is not ours. It is more necessary for us."[35] Rivera's visual articulation of the idea served to undermine further the notion of Europe's historical and cultural hegemony and to redefine his vision of classicism as specific to the Americas.

Markers of classicism manifest in the structure, style, and composition of *Creation*, the first official mural Rivera painted for Mexico's Escuela Nacional Preparatoria (ENP) between 1922 and 1923. Its classical symmetry, monumental figures, and allegorical content are a synthesis of the lessons Rivera learned in France and Italy. Whereas the weighty monumentality of the figures relates to Picasso's recent paintings of

32
Ibid., 22.

33
Ibid.

34
Ibid.

35
José Marti, *Nuestra América* (1891; repr. Havana: Centro de Estudios Martianos/Casa de las Américas, 1991), 18. Quoted in Mark Thurner, "Peruvian Genealogies of History and Nation," in *After Spanish Rule: Postcolonial Predicaments of the Americas*, ed. Mark Thurner and Andrés Guerrero (Durham, NC: Duke University Press, 2003), 145.

Diego Rivera, ***Creation***, 1922–23; mural, Escuela Nacional Preparatoria San Ildefonso, Mexico City

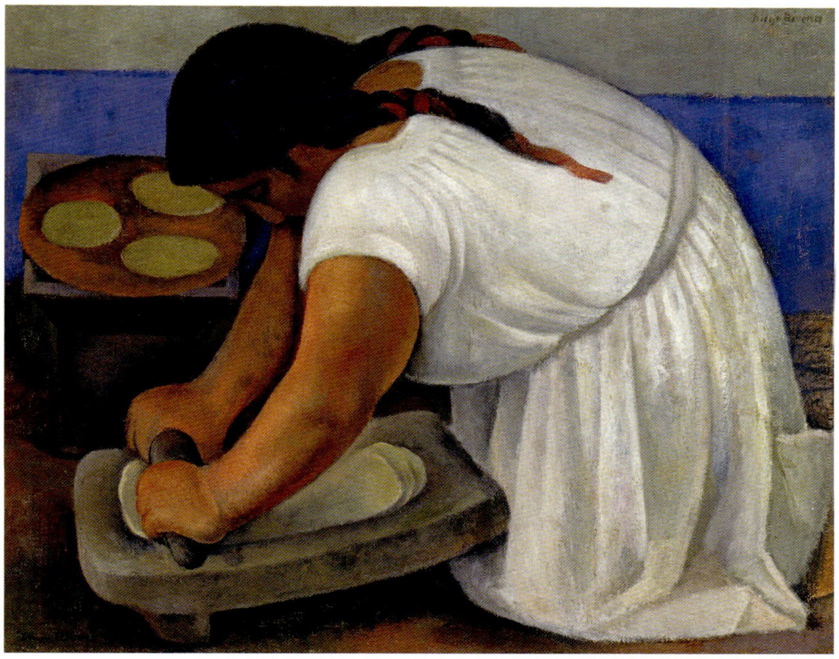

Diego Rivera, ***Woman Making Tortillas* (*The Grinder*)**, 1926; oil on canvas, 35 7/16 × 46 1/16 in. (90 × 117 cm); Museo Nacional de Arte Moderno

massive sculptural bodies, the gold background, allegorical theme, and symmetrical organization all draw on the religious murals Rivera observed in Italy.[36] But the superimposition of indigenous and mestizo characteristics onto several of the monumental bodies in the mural moves Rivera's conception of classicism in a new direction, one that would align muralism with critical issues in Mexico.

Rivera's paintings of the period echo the aesthetic he developed in *Creation* and consequently continue to demonstrate a strong affinity with Picasso's works of this period. Rivera's *Flower Day* (p. 89) of 1925, for example, is similar in many ways to Picasso's famous painting *Three Women at the Spring* of 1921 (p. 115). Both paintings depict a group of three figures that allude to the Three Graces in Greek mythology. Both artists simplified and schematized their figures, reducing their visages and bodies to geometric shapes and planes. And both artists paid acute attention to the arrangement of forms and linear rhythms on the surface of the canvas. In Picasso's painting, the three women converge around a pinwheel-like formation formed by their hands as they reach toward one another without actually touching. The striated drapery recalls the flutes on Doric columns, and the color palette—cool grays and warm earth tones—suggests stone or terracotta sculpture.[37]

Rivera's composition is more geometric and controlled. The kneeling figure's two straight braids echo the rigid body of the central figure, a circular basket creates a counterpoint to a bowed head, and the bright white-and-yellow calla lilies fill but remain contained by the top of the frame. Like Picasso's, Rivera's figures have a stone-like solidity and monumentality that recall classical Greek and Roman sculpture. Despite these stylistic similarities, however, there are some distinct differences that indicate just how Rivera transformed Picasso's classicizing aesthetic. In Rivera's hands, the subject changes. Rather than depicting timeless allegorical figures, Rivera grafts indigenous traits onto classical Mediterranean bodies and situates them at a traditional festival. Although the title suggests celebration, the heavy load of calla lilies on the central figure's back alludes to labor and the land, themes that Rivera developed much more explicitly in paintings such as *Woman Making Tortillas*.

In *Woman Making Tortillas*, Rivera transforms the monumental female figure that was characteristic of the French return to order into an indigenous laborer. The woman's simple white tunic drapes loosely over her body, and her hunched form fills the pictorial space. Her powerful arms roll out a tortilla on a heavy stone *metate*, whose weight and solidity match that of the woman. While the compositional structure and geometric shapes—the horizontal pattern on the wall, the circular tortillas, the mirrored forms of two braids and two extended arms—reflect the lessons of Cézanne, the sculptural quality of the figure remains in direct dialogue with Picasso. The figure is no longer a languorous seminude in a timeless Arcadian landscape, but rather a laborer from the peasant class. Rivera has redeployed the visual language of classicism as a signifier of heritage and tradition, but a tradition that is specific to Mexico.

36
For a discussion of Rivera's "modern classicism," see Klich, "Revolution and Utopia," 337–38.

37
Silver, *Esprit de Corps*, 274.

Rivera was not the only Mexican artist to embrace a classicizing aesthetic, however, and certain artists resented his claims of leadership in this regard. Upon the inauguration of *Creation* in 1923, muralists Jean Charlot and David Alfaro Siqueiros (writing under the pseudonym Juan Hernández Araujo) published "Comparative Aspects of Modern European and Mexican Paintings' Orientation toward Classicism: The First Graphic Work by the Engineer Juan Hernández Araujo" in *El Demócrata*.[38] In a reprise of French critic André Salmon's accusations (but from a different vantage point), the muralists situated Rivera as a follower of Picasso's classicism rather than an innovator in his own right. They then went on to chronicle the evolution of classicism, beginning with Egyptian art and ending with two works by Picasso: a monumental classicized head and a female figure in the same style. By comparing Picasso's paintings to Rivera's study for a monumental head in the *Creation* mural, they emphasized the parity between the two. Their objective was not so much to denounce Rivera's embrace of a classicizing aesthetic, but rather to situate his work in a broader trend that had been initiated in European modernist circles. In doing so, they argued that Rivera was one among many (themselves included) to coopt classicizing tendencies for new ends in Mexico.[39]

The ideological implications of promoting this new classicism in Mexico differentiated Rivera and his contemporaries from Picasso. Whereas Picasso continued to produce Cubist works simultaneously with his classicizing paintings, Rivera's classicism marked a new phase in his artistic development. Indeed, rejecting Cubism was essential to Rivera's philosophical outlook. As Kenneth E. Silver has pointed out, after World War I many artists deemed Cubism too individualistic "in its failure of collectivity."[40] While the artists who had exhibited at the Galerie Blot had contemplated the idea of collective production,[41] with Rivera's public embrace of communism upon his return to Mexico, collectivity became central to his artistic philosophy: art must be of and for the people, not esoteric and impenetrable. For Picasso, there were no such political constrictions on style. Over the next decade, modern Latin American artists increasingly equated Cubism with "pure art" and instead called for art that was collective, humanist, and accessible. Classicism, with its ties to Renaissance humanism, was the appropriate visual language with which to express these ideas.

As Vicky Unruh has noted, "*human* and *humanized* became veritable buzzwords in Latin American vanguardist discourse" in the 1920s and 1930s.[42] Latin American intellectuals questioned the pertinence of formal experimentation in a society where poverty and corruption dominated everyday existence. Furthermore, many felt that such art could not contribute to the project of national self-definition. Others, Rivera in particular, viewed the spread of "pure art," art that disavowed context, as a form of European cultural imperialism. Quoted in the Peruvian journal *Amauta*, Rivera proclaimed that those who create "pure art" are not just passive and neutral but reinforce existing bourgeois values.[43]

By denigrating "pure art," with which Cubism was equated, and embracing humanized art, Rivera asserted his modern classicism as a visual expression of pan-American values. Evaluation of Picasso's impact on this aesthetic therefore required some rhetorical maneuvering. A 1936 article in *Frente a frente*, "What Do We Owe to Cubism: The Negation of Bourgeois Art," states that Cubism is "incomprehensible for the masses, and seems to respond to the same totalitarian sensibility as imperialism."[44] Although Picasso developed Cubism and continued to paint in a Cubist mode alongside his classicizing production into the 1930s, artists and intellectuals could not deny his importance as a trailblazer. The author therefore describes Picasso's evolution as an artist, but edits out his continued adherence to Cubism,

38
Juan Hernández Araujo [Jean Chariot and David Alfaro Siqueiros], "Aspectos comparativos de la orientación al clasicismo de la moderna pintura europea y mexicana: primer cuadro grafico por el Ingeniero Juan Hernández Araujo," *El Demócrata*, July 29, 1923. My summary here derives from Lynda Klich's astute analysis of this article ("Revolution and Utopia," 390–94).

39
Klich, "Revolution and Utopia," 391–92.

40
Silver, *Esprit de Corps*, 199.

41
Klich, "Revolution and Utopia," 345.

42
These arguments were made in response to Spanish philosopher José Ortega y Gassett's 1925 essay "The Dehumanization of Art." Vicky Unruh, *Latin American Vanguards: The Art of Contentious Encounters* (Berkeley: University of California Press, 1994), 23. See Michele Greet, *Beyond National Identity: Pictorial Indigenism as a Modernist Strategy in Andean Art, 1920–1960* (University Park: Pennsylvania State University Press, 2009), 73.

43
Esteban Pavletich, "Diego Rivera: El artista de una clase," *Amauta* 1, no. 5 (1927): 8.

44
"Qué debemos al cubismo: La negación del arte burgués," *Frente a frente: Órgano central de la liga de escritores y artistas revolucionarios*, no. 2 (April 1936): 14.

choosing instead to illustrate the article with Picasso's neoclassical *Bather* of 1922. To justify how Picasso could remain a useful example, he asserts: "A knowledge and study of Picasso's technique should be accompanied by a revolutionary class consciousness to make the art of the proletariat painter what it should be: a weapon in the agrarian and anti-imperialist fight."[45] What we see here, therefore, is a selective appropriation of Picasso's classicizing aesthetic. Many Mexican artists had completely rejected Cubism, but still envisioned Picasso as a useful prototype as long as the resulting works conveyed revolutionary intent. Rivera and his contemporaries thus coopted the classicizing aesthetic that Picasso propagated in Europe between the wars, but transformed it to serve Mexico's revolutionary aims.

THE MEXICAN RENAISSANCE IN THE FRENCH PRESS

The new vision of modernism that Mexican artists forged in the 1920s soon grabbed the attention of the press in Paris. Rivera, as a known and respected entity, was the focus of these inquiries, and European critics were quick to praise his particular neoclassicism. The first article to feature Rivera's accomplishments in Mexico appeared in 1928 in the French journal *La Renaissance de l'art français et des industries de luxe*: a French translation of Mexican-born Latvian American historian and art critic Anita Brenner's "Une Renaissance Mexicaine," which had originally been published in the United States in 1925.[46] Brenner's essay featured photographs of murals (including Rivera's *Market Day* at the Ministry of Public Education, José Clemente Orozco's *Franciscan and the Indian* at the ENP, and an untitled mural by Siqueiros) that had never circulated in France. Significantly, this article was most likely the means by which many Latin American artists living in Paris became acquainted with Mexican muralism.[47]

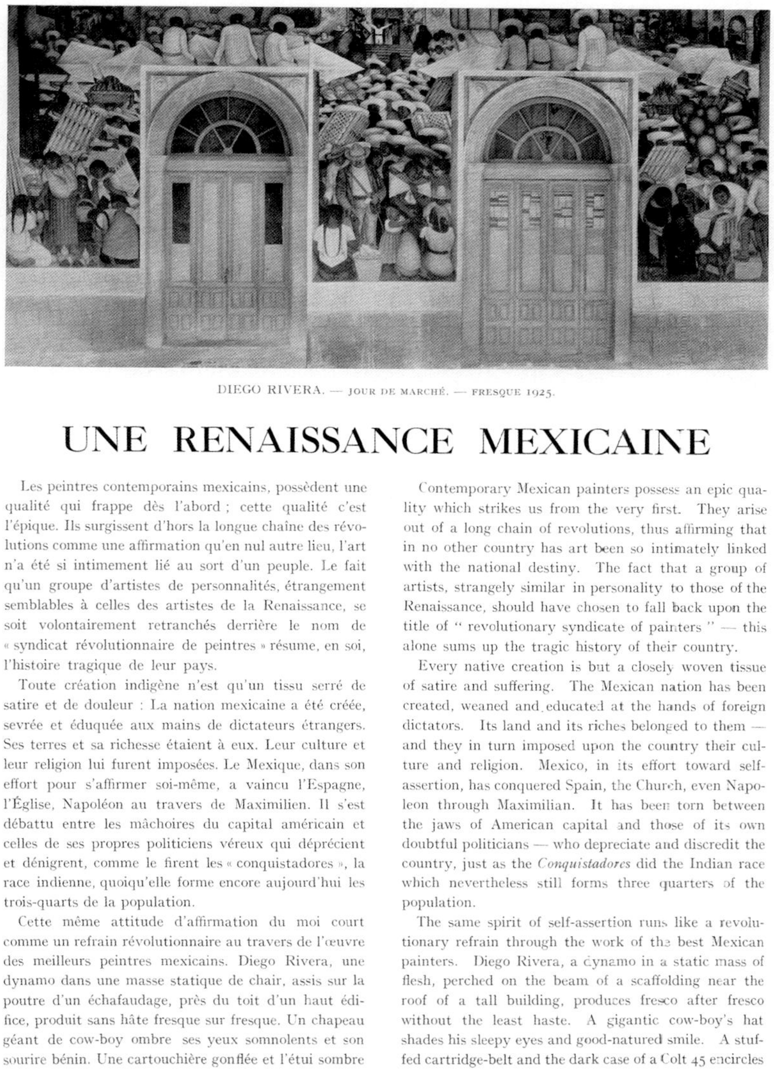

DIEGO RIVERA. — JOUR DE MARCHÉ. — FRESQUE 1925.

UNE RENAISSANCE MEXICAINE

Les peintres contemporains mexicains, possèdent une qualité qui frappe dès l'abord ; cette qualité c'est l'épique. Ils surgissent d'hors la longue chaîne des révolutions comme une affirmation qu'en nul autre lieu, l'art n'a été si intimement lié au sort d'un peuple. Le fait qu'un groupe d'artistes de personnalités, étrangement semblables à celles des artistes de la Renaissance, se soit volontairement retranchés derrière le nom de « syndicat révolutionnaire de peintres » résume, en soi, l'histoire tragique de leur pays.

Toute création indigène n'est qu'un tissu serré de satire et de douleur : La nation mexicaine a été créée, sevrée et éduquée aux mains de dictateurs étrangers. Ses terres et sa richesse étaient à eux. Leur culture et leur religion lui furent imposées. Le Mexique, dans son effort pour s'affirmer soi-même, a vaincu l'Espagne, l'Église, Napoléon au travers de Maximilien. Il s'est débattu entre les mâchoires du capital américain et celles de ses propres politiciens véreux qui déprécient et dénigrent, comme le firent les « conquistadores », la race indienne, quoiqu'elle forme encore aujourd'hui les trois-quarts de la population.

Cette même attitude d'affirmation du moi court comme un refrain révolutionnaire au travers de l'œuvre des meilleurs peintres mexicains. Diego Rivera, une dynamo dans une masse statique de chair, assis sur la poutre d'un échafaudage, près du toit d'un haut édifice, produit sans hâte fresque sur fresque. Un chapeau géant de cow-boy ombre ses yeux somnolents et son sourire bénin. Une cartouchière gonflée et l'étui sombre

Contemporary Mexican painters possess an epic quality which strikes us from the very first. They arise out of a long chain of revolutions, thus affirming that in no other country has art been so intimately linked with the national destiny. The fact that a group of artists, strangely similar in personality to those of the Renaissance, should have chosen to fall back upon the title of " revolutionary syndicate of painters " — this alone sums up the tragic history of their country.

Every native creation is but a closely woven tissue of satire and suffering. The Mexican nation has been created, weaned and educated at the hands of foreign dictators. Its land and its riches belonged to them — and they in turn imposed upon the country their culture and religion. Mexico, in its effort toward self-assertion, has conquered Spain, the Church, even Napoleon through Maximilian. It has been torn between the jaws of American capital and those of its own doubtful politicians — who depreciate and discredit the country, just as the *Conquistadores* did the Indian race which nevertheless still forms three quarters of the population.

The same spirit of self-assertion runs like a revolutionary refrain through the work of the best Mexican painters. Diego Rivera, a dynamo in a static mass of flesh, perched on the beam of a scaffolding near the roof of a tall building, produces fresco after fresco without the least haste. A gigantic cow-boy's hat shades his sleepy eyes and good-natured smile. A stuffed cartridge-belt and the dark case of a Colt 45 encircles

Anita Brenner, "Une Renaissance Mexicaine," *La Renaissance de l'art francais et des industries de luxe* (February 1928)

45
Ibid., 15.

46
Anita Brenner, "Une Renaissance Mexicaine," *La Renaissance de l'art français et des industries de luxe* 11: 2 (February 1928): 60–68. Published in the United States as "A Mexican Renascence," *The Arts* 8, no. 3 (September 1925): 127–50.

47
Brenner, "Une Renaissance Mexicaine."

Brenner's essay introduced the notion of a "Mexican Renaissance" to French readers, suggesting that artistic innovation could take place outside of the confines of Europe and offering a different approach to the notion of classicism in the Americas. Here the term *renaissance* refers to a moment of aesthetic innovation and to the rebirth of Mexican art through an embrace of Pre-Columbian and indigenous heritage. While the comparison of Mexico's burgeoning art scene to the Italian Renaissance dates back to at least 1922 in the writings of Mexican intellectuals,[48] the inclusion of Brenner's essay in a French journal initiated a shift in the perception of Latin American art, or at the very least Mexican art, in the French press. This marked the first time that contemporary Latin American art not produced in Europe and not made for exhibition there received critical attention in an important European art magazine.

Following Brenner's lead, in 1929 Jean Cassou wrote "The Renaissance of Mexican Art" for *L'Art vivant*, which was accompanied by reproductions of several works by Carlos Mérida and Agustín Lazo and highlighted the importance of Rivera, Orozco, and Rufino Tamayo.[49] In writing of Mexico's recent "awakening" to "strong ancestral forces,"[50] Cassou describes a parallel process to Italy's reevaluation of the classical past during the Renaissance or France's periods of neoclassicism. About Rivera, he writes: "Rivera, having returned to his country, realized there a body of work that, through its dimensions, its broad and voluntary unity, its strong popular conception, does not have an equal in contemporary European art."[51] Thus, like Brenner, Cassou sees the so-called Mexican Renaissance as based on both an espousal of Pre-Columbian motifs and indigenous themes, and a moment of aesthetic innovation distinct from European developments.

The following year, the entire January issue of *L'Art vivant* was dedicated to *Le Mexique*, with articles on Pre-Columbian civilizations; archaeology; Zapotec art; reproductions of objects from the Museo Nacional de México; photographs of landscapes, colonial churches, and volcanoes; popular art; an article by Dr. Atl titled "The Ultra Baroque"; an essay titled "The Open Air School"; a section on contemporary art by E. Gomez Maillefert; and an article titled "Mexican Aesthetic" by José Guadalupe Zuno. In "Mexican Contemporary Painting: Its Characteristics," Maillefert followed Brenner's example, proclaiming that Mexico was undergoing an artistic renaissance. But whereas Brenner suggested that the innovative character of Mexican art, which paralleled the experimental ethos of the Italian Renaissance, stemmed from the country's revolutionary context, Maillefert argues that this renaissance was inspired by artists' travels to Europe and their exposure to Impressionism, Divisionism, and the art of the Italian Renaissance in European museums. While both factors were most likely at play, the difference here is one of agency: Brenner credits context, whereas Maillefert still traces the root of all innovation back to Europe. Maillefert nevertheless concludes that Mexican art is "one of the strongest visual expressions of our time."[52] In his discussion, Maillefert highlights the work of Dr. Atl, Rivera, Siqueiros, and Orozco, as well as Fermín Revueltas and Fernando Leal.[53]

L'Art vivant's Mexique issue was particularly noteworthy because it included an extensive spread of photographs by Tina Modotti of Orozco's ENP murals and Rivera's Ministry of Public Education and Chapingo murals, thereby significantly expanding on the imagery made available by Brenner to the French public. For Maillefert, the profound influence of the Italian Renaissance on Rivera's oeuvre comes through most explicitly in the Chapingo murals.[54] Indeed, in their location in a former chapel, their virtuoso foreshortening of the human form, and their incorporation of monumental classicizing nudes, these murals serve to posit Rivera as a Michelangelo of the Americas. In the European press, Rivera's work (and that of his Mexican contemporaries)

48 See Silvestre Arqueles Vela, "Nuestras Encuestas ¿Existe un renacimiento literario en México?," *El Universal Ilustrado* 5, no. 249 (February 9, 1922): 24; Arqueles Vela, "La Influencia francesa en el renacimiento de nuestra literaria," *El Universal Ilustrado* 6, no. 277 (August 24, 1922): 2; José Juan Tablada, "Mexican Painting of To-Day," *International Studio* 76, no. 308 (January 1923): 267–76; Dr. Atl, "Colaboración Artística—u—¿Renacimiento Artístico?," *El Universal*, July 13, 1923, sec. 1, 3. Thank you to Lynda Klich for providing these sources.

49 Jean Cassou, "La Renaissance de l'art mexicain," *L'Art vivant* 5 (1929): 758–60. Although *L'Art vivant* reviewed many individual Latin American artists (including Angel Zárraga, Pedro Figari, Manuel Rendón Seminario, Pablo Curatella Manes, Tarsila do Amaral, Domingos Toledo-Piza, Carlos Alberto Castellanos, Joaquín Torres García, Manuel Ortiz de Zarate, and Vicente do Rego Monteiro), Cassou's was the first article to examine the artistic production of a specific country. Another review of Mexican art appeared in *Le Monde* magazine in 1929: "Artistes et poetes mexicains," *Le Monde*, no. 50 (May 18, 1929): 8–9.

50 Cassou, "La Renaissance de l'art mexicain," 758.

51 Ibid.

52 E. Gomez Maillefert, "La Peinture mexicaine contemporaine," *L'Art vivant* 6 (June 15, 1930): 83.

53 Ibid.

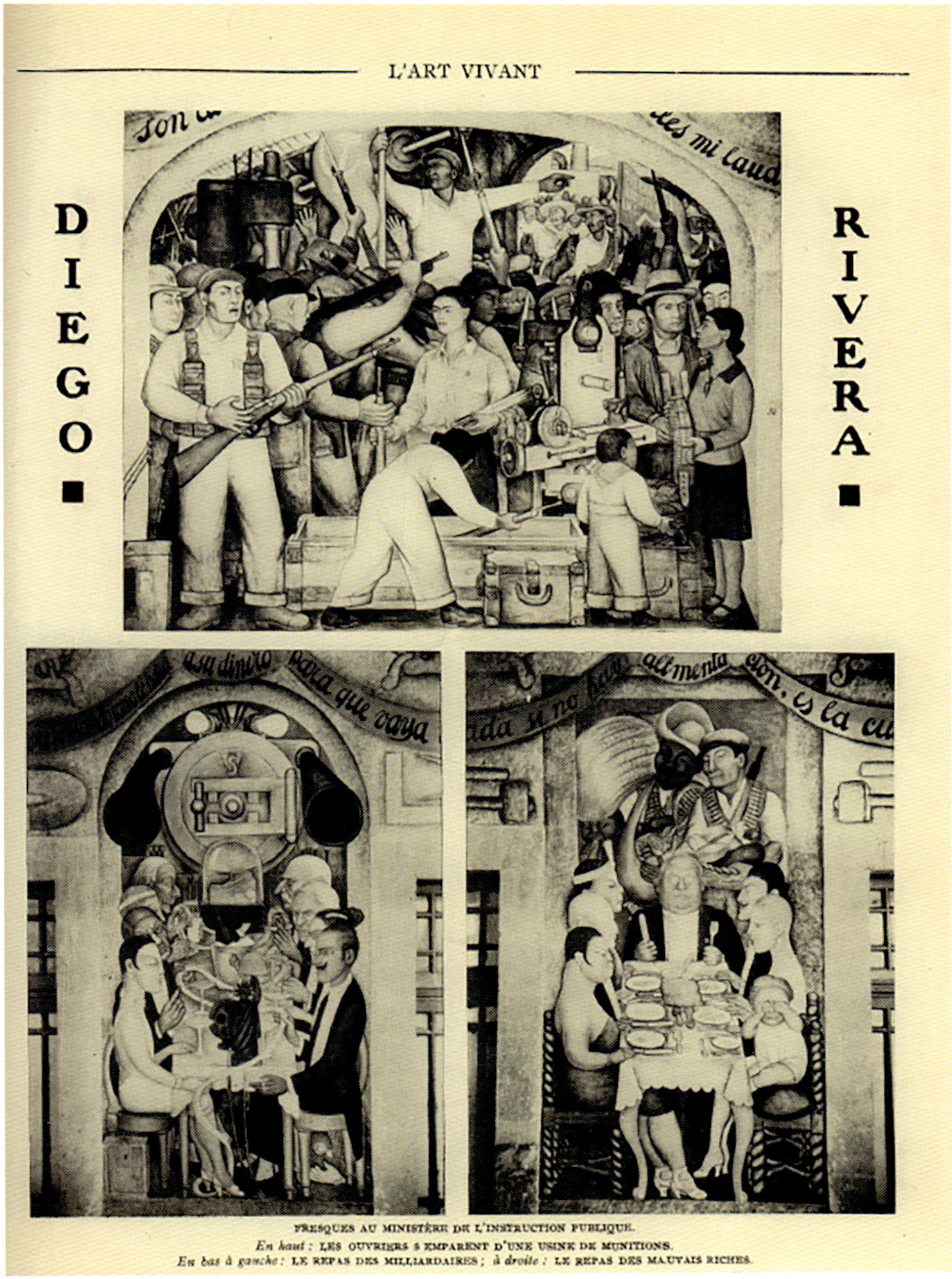

L'ART VIVANT

DIEGO ■ RIVERA ■

FRESQUES AU MINISTÈRE DE L'INSTRUCTION PUBLIQUE.
En haut : LES OUVRIERS S'EMPARENT D'UNE USINE DE MUNITIONS.
En bas à gauche : LE REPAS DES MILLIARDAIRES ; *à droite :* LE REPAS DES MAUVAIS RICHES.

Diego Rivera's Ministry of Public Education murals reproduced in *L'Art vivant* (June 15, 1930)

fulfilled a demand for expressions of cultural authenticity. Consequently, none of these articles mention a connection to Picasso; rather, they laud Mexican artists for achieving artistic independence and leading the way to a New World aesthetic.

Rivera's classicism, while stemming from the return to order in postwar Paris, came to signify something different in post-revolutionary Mexico. In Paris, Rivera's relationship to Picasso had fluctuated from admiration to rivalry. The two artists were dominant figures in the Cubist movement, and both started to experiment with classicizing motifs in the years immediately following World War I. This parity created competition, however, and Rivera took pains to differentiate his objectives and methods from those of Picasso. Rivera's exploration of Cézanne and subsequent Italian tour shaped his approach to the classical, marking his work as distinct from his rival. Classicism, for Rivera, served several purposes: as an alternative to Cubism, a connection to the past, and, upon his return home, a means of asserting a strong constructive approach to art making as a way forward for Mexican artists.

In Mexico, classicism soon came to embody different ideological implications than it did in Europe. When employed to represent Pre-Columbian civilizations and indigenous subjects, it signaled the legitimacy of Mexico's ancient past as a counterpoint to ancient Greece and Rome. Moreover, Rivera promoted his strong and constructive aesthetic as the appropriate visual language with which to represent the Mexican laborer and the fight to overturn bourgeois values. By the late 1920s, Rivera's accomplishments in Mexico had come to the attention of the French press, and critics lauded him as a leader in the Mexican Renaissance. The transatlantic circulation of ideas had therefore come full circle.

54 Ibid.

INDIGENOUS ANTIQUITY IN THE WORK OF DIEGO RIVERA

ITZEL A. RODRÍGUEZ MORTELLARO

On my arrival in Mexico I was overcome by the indescribable beauty of this country that is at once rich and austere, wretched and bursting with energy. And it was Mexico, with its splendid folk art and its ancient art that is so current in the life of the country, like the frescos of the old masters in revolutionary Italy, that gave me, suddenly, as if in a revelation, the fully formed style of my painting.[1]

After almost a decade of living in Europe, Diego Rivera returned to his country with the mission of contributing to the national reconstruction launched by the government that emerged from the Mexican Revolution. His new encounter with indigenous antiquity would be instrumental in the development of his nationalistic work. This essay presents a panorama of the forms in which the artist interpreted and integrated the legacy of the Mesoamerican past in murals, graphics, architecture, and wall mosaics.

The year was 1921: returning to his homeland, Rivera began to elaborate a Mexican style that would soon establish him as a national hero. He had left Mexico in 1906, his political, social, and artistic background rooted in the cultural confines of the Porfiriato (the regime of Porfirio Díaz, 1876–1911). Evolutionism, positivism and its faith in science, liberalism as a political credo, the academic tradition, pride in the indigenous past, and symbolism were all part of the baggage with which the young artist traveled to Europe. There he would incorporate Cubism, avant-garde primitivism, and Marxist socialism. But in many ways he remained faithful to his roots. He would always speak of his mentors, such as educator and liberal politician Justo Sierra and academic painters José María Velasco, Santiago Rebull, and Félix Parra, with devotion. Rivera's education in the culture of the old regime would form the basis of his modern and revolutionary persona.

The great mobilization of indigenous and mestizo peasants during the civil war shed public light on the inescapable reality of a complex social situation to which the political and cultural elite needed to respond.[2] Thus, during the revolutionary decade, the paradigm of the mestizo nation, originally posited in late nineteenth-century evolutionism, gained impetus, offering a future of unity and progress. In the new version of this ideology, the category of race remained in force, but now racial integration was seen as a means to achieve cultural homogeneity.[3] Revolutionary nationalism aspired to the expression of *mestizaje*—the blending of cultures—in different areas of social life, including art.

In Mexico, the father of the modern theory of *mestizaje* was archaeologist and anthropologist Manuel Gamio, who held an official position in the first revolutionary government and exerted influence on the state plan for social reform as well as the reevaluation of Pre-Columbian art.[4] For Gamio, the study of the material and intellectual manifestations of the indigenous past was key to understanding the current population, because ancestral cultural expressions persisted in various forms in the present, whether synthesized in forms such as folk art, or in essence as a more intangible presence. This concept of cultural continuity dissolved the notion of biological "inferiority" because it based national standards on cultural values. Thus, unlike the Porfiriato, in which the exemplary indigenous presence remained exclusively in the past, revolutionary nationalism ascribed virtues to the contemporary indigenous population that enabled it to be integrated in the new

1
Diego Rivera, "La obra del pintor Diego Rivera," in *Obras*, vol. 1, *Textos de arte*, ed. Xavier Moyssén Echeverría (Mexico City: El Colegio Nacional, 1996), 118. Unless otherwise noted, all quotations are translated by Rose Vekony.

2
Renato González Mello, "Estilos, historias, comunidades," in *El Anahuacalli de Diego*, ed. Federico Rubli Kaiser (Mexico City: Chapa Ediciones, Banco de México, 2008), 76.

3
Alan Knight, "Racism, Revolution and Indigenism: Mexico 1910–1940," in *The Idea of Race in Latin America, 1870–1940*, ed. Richard Graham (Austin: University of Texas Press, 1990), 71–113.

4
Marie-Areti Hers, "Manuel Gamio y los estudios sobre arte prehispánico: contradicciones nacionalistas," in *El arte en México: autores, temas, problemas*, ed. Rita Eder, Biblioteca mexicana, serie arte (Mexico City: Consejo Nacional para la Cultura y las Artes/Lotería Nacional para la Asistencia Pública/Fondo de Cultura Económica, 2001), 29–63.

project of the nation. In the cultural realm, the qualities said to belong to the indigenous race—spirituality and aesthetic sensitivity—were extolled; these were considered the contribution of that social group to national and mestizo culture.[5]

In general terms, Rivera subscribed to this anthropological perspective and in the early 1920s made indigenism one of the pillars of his nationalistic thought.[6] In terms of his own artistic identity, he recognized in ancient Mesoamerican art the universal and classical principle of his revolutionary creations.

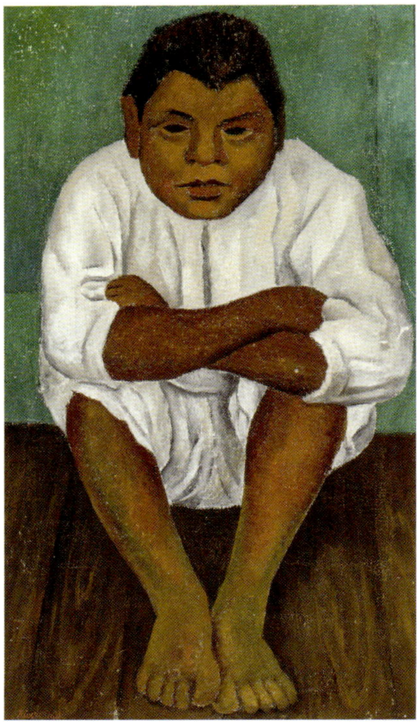

THE CLASSICAL AND UNIVERSAL FOUNDATION

In a manifesto published in Barcelona in 1921, David Alfaro Siqueiros proposed expanding avant-garde classicism (also known as "the return to order") to encompass the perspective of the Americas through the modern use of the great arts of indigenous civilizations, idealized for their constructional and monumental qualities as well as their economy of expressive means.[7]

For Rivera as well, the modern art of the Americas needed to build on "classical values" determined by the structural and volumetric relations found in Pre-Columbian art. "In contemplating the great masterpieces, and above all the ancient sculpture and architecture of my own country," Rivera wrote, "I began to delve deeply to discover their essence, the true framework of things."[8] For the artist, a national art had to be based on the "purity and artistic solidity" of Pre-Columbian art,[9] which expressed, like all great art, an atemporal beauty and internal life, described by the painter as "the dynamic of forces...seeking balance, in harmony with the laws of the visible universe and the secret soul of man."[10] Rivera understood classical art as one produced in harmony with an internal spiritual rhythm, which in the case of Mexico was "cosmic mysticism."[11]

Rivera knew the architectural and constructional aspect of art from his studies at the Academy of San Carlos and integrated it in his work around 1917 through his painstaking study of Paul Cézanne. In Mexico he discovered these artistic values in indigenous aesthetics. One need only observe his paintings to intuit, beneath the faces and bodies, the compact masses of ancestral art. See, for instance, *Flower Day* (p. 89), *Flower Day, Xochimilco* (p. 119), and *Frida's Friend*, in which the volumes and the sculptural aspect of the indigenous figures allude to Pre-Columbian pieces.

5
Alicia Azuela, "Lo que la grandeza mexicana debe al arte indígena," in *Arte popular mexicano: Cinco siglos*, ed. Olga Sáenz (Mexico City: Antiguo Colegio de San Ildefonso, 1996), 97–103.

6
González Mello, "Manuel Gamio, Diego Rivera, and the Politics of Mexican Anthropology," *Res: Anthropology and Aesthetics* 45 (Spring 2004): 161–85.

7
"Tres llamamientos de orientación actual a los pintores y escultores de la nueva generación americana" [Three appeals for the current guidance of the new generation of American painters and sculptors] was published in the sole issue of the magazine *Vida americana* in May 1921 in Barcelona. Siqueiros was the magazine's editor-in-chief and art director. The magazine contained illustrations by Mexican artists Rivera, Marius de Zayas, and Siqueiros himself, as well as Uruguayan artists Joaquín Torres García and Rafael P. Barradas. This manifesto is included in the anthology of documents collected in *Palabras de Siqueiros*, ed. Raquel Tibol (Mexico City: Fondo de Cultura Económica, 1996), 17–20.

8
Rivera, "De la libreta de apuntes de un pintor mexicano," in *Obras*, 1:65.

9
Rivera, "La exposición de la Escuela Nacional de Bellas Artes," in *Obras*, 1:27.

10
Rivera, "De la libreta de apuntes," in *Obras*, 1:65.

11
Ibid., 67.

Diego Rivera, ***Frida's Friend***, 1931

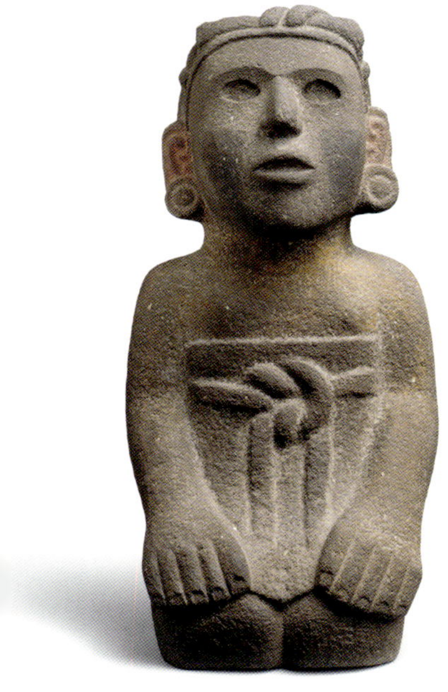

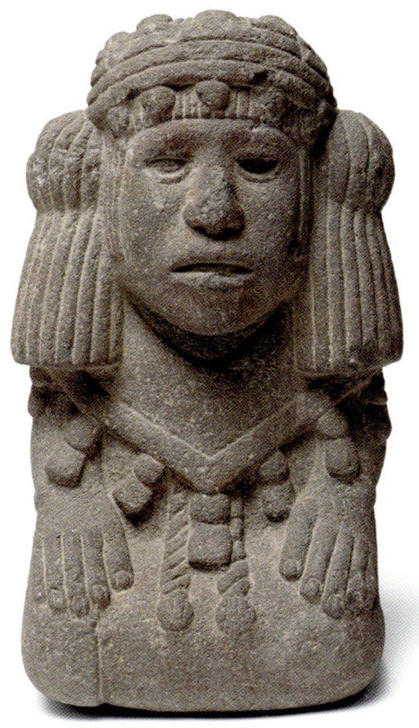

LEFT *Kneeling Female Figure*, Mexico, Aztec, 15th–early 16th century

RIGHT *Chalchiuhtlicue (Water Deity)*, Mexico, Aztec, 1200–1521

ARTISTIC RENAISSANCE

Toward the end of 1923, the artists participating in the Sindicato de Obreros Técnicos, Pintores y Escultores (Union of Technical Workers, Painters, and Sculptors), to which Rivera belonged, issued a statement on the indigenous and mestizo origin of Mexican greatness that integrated art and aesthetics with the proper political evolution not only of Mexico but also of the world. Thus we read in the manifesto sentences such as these: "All that is virtue is a gift from our people (from our Indians especially).... The art of the people of Mexico is the greatest and most worthy spiritual manifestation in the world, and its indigenous tradition is the best of all."[12]

The muralist movement was conceived as an "artistic renaissance," since it reconciled notions of continuity and, simultaneously, renewal.[13] This movement identified itself with the Renaissance of fifteenth-century Italy and, like the Europeans, the Mexicans broke with the preceding period, particularly academic neoclassicism, taking a modern and humanistic stance and proclaiming the "true" classical tradition of the Americas, one from which they extracted aesthetic models and spiritual essences. As the artist Jean Charlot wrote, summing up this attitude: "Indian archaeological remains stand in relation to Mexican art as Greco-Roman ruins and fragments did to Renaissance Italy."[14]

The artistic force of ancient indigenous art served as a symbolic banner of renewal in the first period of muralism. Each artist gave his appropriation of indigenous antiquity a personal character; Rivera's modern perspective was defined in the course of the 1920s particularly through his mural programs, in which he reflected on origin, race, and culture. From that point on, he spoke frequently of a single cultural essence expressed in Pre-Columbian art, folk art, and nationalist art.[15] Rivera cultivated the notion of the existence of an "aesthetic force of the [indigenous] race" and liked to boast that his drawings and indigenous codices resembled each other "like one prickly pear does another, because they are the fruit of the same Mexican nopal."[16] For him, as for much of the intellectual elite, *arte mexicano* expressed the cultural substance that emerged in the Origin.

ARCHAEOLOGY OF THE ORIGIN

The first time that Rivera portrayed an archaeological piece in a mural was in 1928, in the building of the Secretaría de Educación Pública (SEP). It was the famous stone sculpture of Xochipilli—the Aztec god of flowers, games, and pleasure—that was on exhibit at the Museo Nacional (p. 254 right). This scene is part of a group of murals on the subject of the evolution of Mexico from the origin of life to the revolution and reconstruction. Lush tropical vegetation frames a ritual: a man in a state of trance, attired as Xochipilli, is worshipped by a group of naked women, some in hieratic poses. It is the representation of a primordial paradise, of a state of "original innocence"—with connotations of fertility,

12
"Manifiesto del Sindicato de Obreros Técnicos, Pintores y Escultores," in *Palabras de Siqueiros*, 24.

13
Teresa del Conde, "El Renacimiento mexicano," in *Tiempo y arte: XIII Coloquio Internacional de Historia del Arte*, Estudios de arte y estética 33 (Mexico City: Universidad Nacional Autónoma de México, Instituto de Investigaciones Estéticas, 1991), 389–407. Conde indicates that painter Jean Charlot, art historian and critic Walter Pach, writer Anita Brenner, and historian Laurence E. Schmeckebier were the first to use the term *renaissance* in reference to muralism.

14
Jean Charlot, *The Mexican Mural Renaissance, 1920–1925* (New Haven: Yale University Press, 1963), 1.

15
Alfredo Cardona Peña, *El monstruo en su laberinto: conversaciones con Diego Rivera, 1949–1950* (Mexico City: Costa-Amic, 1965), 139–42.

16
Ibid., 38.

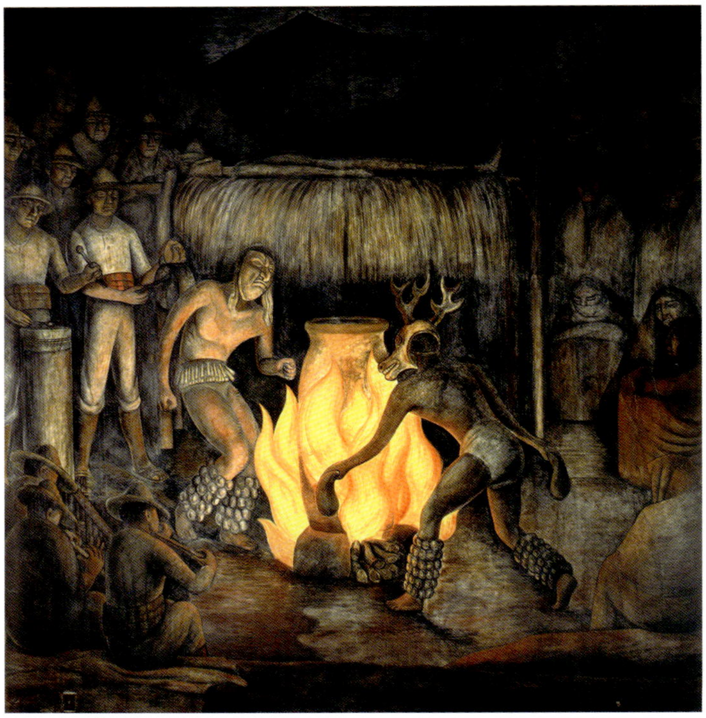

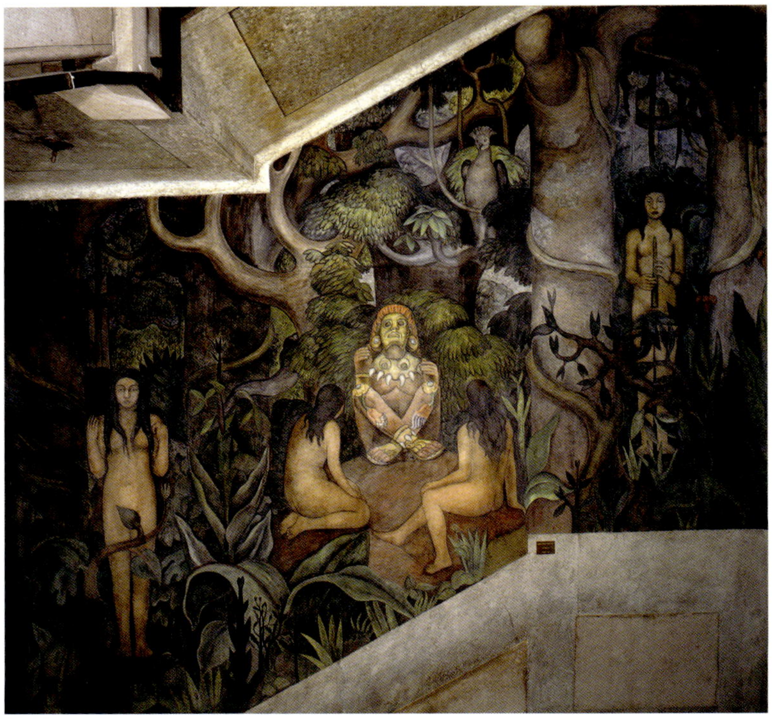

abundance, and sensuality—that powerfully recalls the exoticist primitivism of Paul Gauguin and Henri Rousseau. In the visual narrative, Xochipilli establishes the spiritual foundation of the progress toward rational modernity in Mexico.

The first murals that Rivera painted in the SEP present the beginnings of the nation's cultural uniqueness from an anthropological perspective. In them we see forms of community life: work, traditional festivals, and political meetings in urban and rural settings from various regions of the country. At the end of the 1920s, he conveyed his agrarianist and socialist convictions in a series of frescoes set in different historical moments, from the recent past to the revolutionary present and the socialist utopia of the future. The mural program as a whole aims to reveal "eternal Mexico," as reflected in discrete allusions to the indigenous past found here and there—a poem by King Nezahualcóyotl (1402–1472) in a lintel; a pair of serpents and an effigy of the rain god Tlaloc above the *Ballad of the Agrarian Revolution* (1928); rattlesnakes associated with the watery landscape of Tehuantepec.[17] Although less forceful than the archaeological monument, these icons signal the existence of deep strata in the contemporary culture in Mexico. So, too, do the panels in which Rivera emphasizes the connection between the past and the present through traditional festivals and rituals—for example, the Deer Dance, the maize harvest, and the rural celebration of the Day of the Dead.

Rivera was the first muralist to represent the ancient indigenous past as an autonomous universe. He did so in one of the murals of his triptych *The History of Mexico,* painted between 1929 and 1935 in the Palacio Nacional, the building that symbolizes political power in Mexico. During this period, Rivera maintained close relations with the revolutionary state and was an intellectual active in public debate. Faithful to the liberal credo, he saw nation as the keystone of collective identity, national history as the source of political teaching, and indigenous antiquity as the "origin myth" of nationality. The mural *Ancient Mexico* in the Palacio Nacional differs from the other two segments of the large mural because it is the only scene from the past that interweaves history and myth. Rivera's representation of the Pre-Columbian world is divided into two parts: on one side, harmony and social concord reign, with indigenous people engaged in creative and productive activities, such as fine arts,

17 Antonio Rodríguez also points out stylized profiles "typical of a codex" in a fresco depicting seated women. Rodríguez, *El hombre en llamas: historia de la pintura mural en México* (London: Thames and Hudson, 1970), 203.

LEFT Diego Rivera, ***Deer Dance***, 1923–24; Court of Fiestas, Ministry of Public Education, Mexico City

RIGHT Diego Rivera, ***Tropical Mexico and Xochipilli and His Votaries***, 1928; North Wall Stairwell, Ministry of Public Education, Mexico City

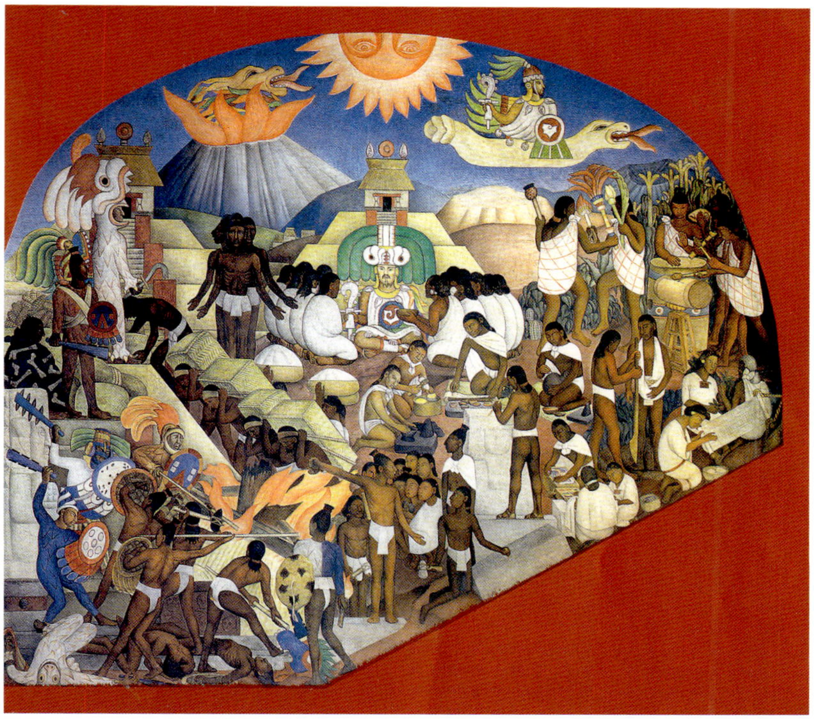

industrial arts, music, dance, and agriculture; on the other, we see conflict and war, with subjugated Indians handing over tributes and fighting among themselves. Each of these parts is protected by a god: Huitzilopochtli, the lord of war, and Quetzalcóatl, the civilizer. The tension between Huitzilopochtli and Quetzalcóatl epitomizes the opposition between barbarianism—in the dual sense of backwardness and violence—and civilization, understood as the triumph of reason and progress. This dialectic projects the perception of Mexico abroad in the decades following the devastating civil war of 1910 to 1921.

The idyllic part of the mural, where the people are engaged in artistic tasks, create textiles, perform rituals, and cultivate the land, can be understood as a "constructive" space that synthesizes the reformist aspiration of the revolutionary state, while at the same time establishing the origin of the populace's cultural identity. In this scene Quetzalcóatl plays a leading role. That figure, with his long trajectory in Mesoamerican myths and legends, was Westernized in later reelaborations of his story. In the first decades of the twentieth century, writers and philosophers characterized him as a modern leader: a good governor, legislator, educator, and promoter of the arts. Quetzalcóatl was an ethical model, and his presence at the origin of the nation suggested the possibility of emulating in the present the exemplary acts of that cultural hero. In this way, the Pre-Columbian god of Rivera's mural is the product of an interpretation based on Western values; we might even say that he belongs more to the world of the "whites" than to the indigenous realm.

But on the other hand, on another level of meaning, Quetzalcóatl, the "god-man," held an ulterior message to which only certain initiates had access.[18] During the 1920s, Rivera, along with other intellectuals and politicians of the power elite, were members of the Rosicrucian Order that met at the Grand Lodge Quetzalcóatl, for which he painted *Feathered Serpent* (p. 113), an enigmatic picture with roses and the emblem of the lodge.[19] This secret society shared the hermetic philosophy and alchemy of the Freemasons, with all the associated symbols. The mural *Ancient Mexico*, the first part of the triptych in the Palacio Nacional, can be read using the Rosicrucian esoteric code. The three symbols that stand out, because they condense the hidden meaning of the mural, are Sun, Temple, and Master. In the mural they appear as Tzontemoc (the setting sun), a pyramid, and Quetzalcóatl, who presides over a meeting of initiates. These fundamental symbols of the hermetic tradition project moral, spiritual, and rational elevation over the indigenous world. Rivera made use of symbolic language to reinforce the nationalistic need to establish the starting point for the spiritual ascent and rational consciousness of the nation in the Pre-Columbian past. In the dominant scheme of cultural continuity, spirituality was seen as one of the essential goods that indigenous antiquity bequeathed to the mestizo nation. Rationality, on the other hand, had a fundamental figure as its protagonist: Quetzalcóatl, a founding master of the Mexican lineage of initiates.[20]

18
Alfredo López Austin presents an in-depth study of the history and significance of this figure in *Hombre-dios: religión y política en el mundo náhuatl* (Mexico City: Universidad Nacional Autónoma de México, Instituto de Investigaciones Históricas, 1989).

19
Raquel Tibol, "¡Apareció la serpiente! Diego Rivera y los Rosa-Cruces," *Proceso*, April 9, 1990, www.proseco.com.mx/154789/aparecio-la-serpiente-diego-rivera-y-los-rosacruces. Tibol made this painting public; it is undated and unsigned. For an examination of the esoteric language in Rivera's work see Renato González Mello, *La máquina de pintar: Rivera, Orozco y la invención de un lenguaje emblemas, trofeos y cadáveres* (Mexico City: Universidad Nacional Autónoma de México, Instituto de Investigaciones Estéticas, 2008).

20
Itzel Rodríguez Mortellaro, "La espiral del poder: Diego Rivera y la representación del pasado indígena en el Palacio Nacional," *Historia y Grafía* 23 (2004): 159–91.

Diego Rivera, ***The Legend of Quetzalcoatl***, 1929–30; North Wall, ***The History of Mexico***, Palacio Nacional, Mexico City

In parallel with the first phase of work at the Palacio Nacional, Rivera undertook a mural program at the Palacio de Cortés, in Cuernavaca, commissioned by Dwight Morrow, the U.S. ambassador to Mexico from 1927 to 1930. Here he depicted the Spanish conquest of the territory that is now the state of Morelos, creating battle scenes between the Nahuas and the Spaniards that he would develop, with variations, in his portrayal of the conquest in his mural at the Palacio Nacional. To configure both mural paintings, which bear similarities to the Renaissance mural triptych *The Battle of San Romano* (c. 1438–40) by Paolo Uccello, Rivera drew on a rich variety of historical documents and archaeological objects.[21] An enormous array of iconographic sources informed his representations of the indigenous past. Among the codices, he preferred the graphic records produced during the viceroyalty—such as the Florentine Codex, the Durán Codex, and Codex Mendoza—to those from the Pre-Columbian period, partly because the former offered more "naturalistic" and "realistic" images than the latter, and particularly because those manuscripts passed down their visual testimony of Nahua daily life and the events of the conquest. He also turned to pieces conserved in the Museo Nacional—such as Aztec sculptures of coiled serpents and the famous statue of the Eagle Warrior; percussion instruments such as the *panhuehuetl* from Malinalco and the *teponaxtle* from Tlaxcala; the Teocalli of the Sacred War and Coatlicue monoliths—and to a lesser extent used images inspired by Pre-Columbian architectural elements that can still be seen at archaeological sites, such as the serpent-shaped pilasters from the Temple of the Jaguars at Chichén Itzá. Certain nineteenth-century images might also be counted among Rivera's iconographic sources, such as José Obregón's *The Discovery of Pulque* (1869) and Félix Parra's *Fray Bartolomé de las Casas* (1875), as well as book illustrations such as those in Alfredo Chavero's *Historia antigua y de la Conquista*.[22]

Pieces from Rivera's collection of Pre-Columbian art began to appear in his murals and paintings in the 1940s—for example, in the paintings he did for the Palacio Nacional between 1942 and 1951, where he developed the subject of Pre-Columbian "production methods" based on selected cultures. As Roberto Velasco has pointed out in his detailed analysis of the Palacio Nacional murals, Rivera relied predominantly on "institutionalized" images belonging to the collections of the Academy of San Carlos and the Museo Nacional.[23] This strategy of legitimation endowed his works with a sense of reality and truth, in spite of the interpretive license he took in composing his scenes of the past.

In 1930 Rivera instituted a model for the artistic and ideological reelaboration of archaeological objects that gave rise to a school. The principal image of the central segment of his *History of Mexico* is an ancient icon that synthesizes the meaning of this great mural: an eagle that holds in its beak the symbol of Sacred War—the creative conflagration at the inception of every cosmic era, according to the Aztecs, that unites contrary forces, water and fire. This representation is found in the relief on the reverse side of the Aztec monument known as Teocalli of the Sacred War, unearthed by Alfonso Caso from the foundations of the Palacio Nacional in 1926. The archaeologist proposed that the monument was dedicated to Sacred War, the aim of which was to obtain prisoners for sacrifice in order to maintain the movement of the Sun.[24] Rivera applied the dialectic of the symbol *atl-tlalchinolli*—from Nahuatl, *atl* 'water' and *tlalchinolli* 'something burned'—the metaphorical expression that refers to Sacred War among the Nahuas, to establish the symbolic underpinning of the historical confrontation and its transcendence in the evolution of the nation.[25] The dualistic scheme of the history of Mexico as presented by Rivera can be summed up as the constant confrontation of two essences, one positive and the other negative.

21
Stanton L. Catlin, "Political Iconography in the Diego Rivera Frescoes at Cuernavaca, Mexico," in *Art and Architecture in the Service of Politics*, ed. Henry A. Millon and Linda Nochlin (Cambridge, MA: MIT Press, 1978), 194–215; Itzel Rodríguez Mortellaro, "El pasado indígena en el nacionalismo revolucionario: El mural *México antiguo* (1929) de Diego Rivera en el Palacio Nacional" (master's thesis, Universidad Nacional Autónoma de México, Facultad de Filosofía y Letras, 2005).

22
Alfredo Chavero's *Historia antigua y de la Conquista* is the first volume of *México a través de los siglos*, ed. Vicente Riva Palacio, 5 vols. (Barcelona, 1884–89).

23
Roberto Velasco Alonso, "A raíz expuesta: Fuentes historiográficas, arqueológicas y artísticas del Códice Rivera," in *Epopeya del pueblo mexicano: los murales de Palacio Nacional*, ed. Arturo Chapa (Mexico City: Chapa Ediciones/Banco de México, 2010), 112–335.

24
Alfonso Caso, *El teocalli de la guerra sagrada: descripción y estudio del monolito encontrado en los cimientos del Palacio Nacional* (Mexico City: Talleres Gráficos de la Nación, 1927). Caso associates the eagle with the Sun and the prickly pears with the hearts of the victims of sacrifice. He writes: "To move, the Sun requires sacrifice, which provides its food of blood and human hearts, and sacrifice in turn requires war," 62.

25
Barbara Braun, "Diego Rivera: Heritage and Politics," in *Pre-Columbian Art and the Post-Columbian World: Ancient American Sources of Modern Art* (New York: Harry N. Abrams, 1993), 185–249; Rodríguez, "El pasado indígena."

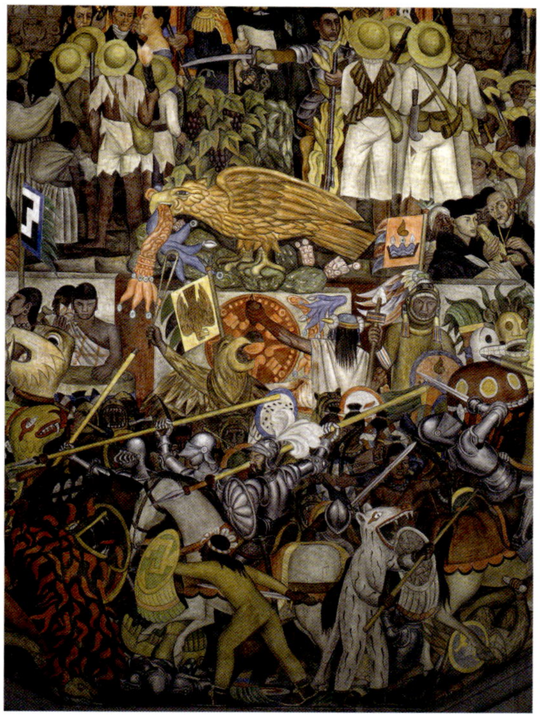

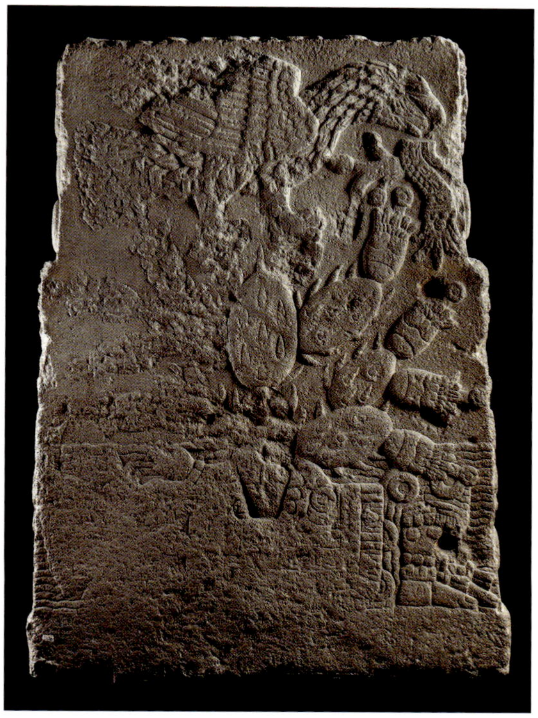

After this allusion to Teocalli of the Sacred War, Rivera turned to other ancient icons to express his ideological positions. As part of this strategy, he incorporated in his repertoire the ancient monolith that, more than any other, intrigued and fascinated Mexican writers, artists, and intellectuals from all periods: the monumental statue of Coatlicue, the Aztec goddess of life and death. In the frescos that Rivera painted at the Detroit Institute of Arts (1932–33) by commission of Henry Ford, the artist interpreted the Detroit automobile industry as a "golden age" that integrates, in a rhythm of progress and harmony, workers of different races, science, technology, and the industrial processes of the transformation of raw material.[26] In the murals, the cadence produced by workers and machines re-creates scenes of great dynamism that perfectly express Rivera's industrialist utopia. On the south wall of the artistic complex, we see Coatlicue transfigured into a stamping press (p. 70). Her imposing form presents the meeting of spirit and technology, of past and present.

Rivera takes this thesis even farther in his mural *Pan American Unity*, in San Francisco, which expounds his idea of American solidarity with historical roots in the culture of Mexico and the United States (p. 71). In his visual argument, the Americas have two complementary parts: one humanistic, rooted in the spiritual values contained in the art that is understood to be of indigenous origin (folk and Pre-Columbian art) from Latin American countries; the other progress-oriented, obtained through the science and technology developed in North America. In the mural, Coatlicue encapsulates the integration to which Rivera aspires in her very body, composed of human flesh, stone, and machine. Stone represents the cultural and archaeological legacy of the past; flesh, humanity; and metal, technological modernity. The images of this mural show the Mexican indigenous past as the primordial source of art and spirituality; for that reason Quetzalcóatl and the plumed serpent appear as well. The corollary of the mural program is that the creative powers of the Americas—both spiritual and progressive—serve as a counterweight to the warlike impulse of European totalitarianism.

Beginning with his modern resignification of the Nahua numens Quetzalcóatl, Huitzilopochtli, and Coatlicue, Rivera participated actively in twentieth-century history of thought.[27] The artist also had a predilection for water deities—the god Tlaloc

26
Linda Bank Downs, *Diego Rivera: The Detroit Industry Murals* (New York: W.W. Norton, 1999), 165–71.

27
After portraying Huitzilopochtli in the Palacio Nacional, Rivera returned to the god's warlike essence in the panel *Danza de los Huichilobos*, part of the mural *Carnaval de la vida mexicana* (1936). For a closer look at the critical relation established in the 1940s between Coatlicue and Rivera's work, see Itzel Rodríguez Mortellaro, "Coatlicue asiste al homenaje a Diego Rivera: creación de significados culturales en el discurso museográfico de Fernando Gamboa," *Discurso visual* n.s. 5 (January–April 2006), http://discursovisual.net/dvweb05/entorno/entitzel.htm.

LEFT Diego Rivera, ***Conquest*** (detail), 1931; West Wall, ***The History of Mexico***, Palacio Nacional, Mexico City

RIGHT ***Teocalli of the Sacred War*** (back view), c. 1507; basalt, HEIGHT 48⅜ in. (123 cm); Museo Nacional de Antropología, Mexico City

RIVERA'S
Pre-Columbian Collection

LILLY CASILLAS AND DIANA MAGALONI

Over the course of his life, Diego Rivera amassed a remarkable collection of some 59,400 Pre-Columbian ceramics and stone sculptures, believing that such objects were carriers of a mystical, cultural energy that was essential to his own life and the life of the Mexican nation.[1] Rivera recounted that his interest in collecting Pre-Columbian works started when his family moved from Guanajuato to Mexico City and he started buying small pieces at El Volador, a famous flea market today known as La Lagunilla.[2] His interest was serious enough by the 1920s to have seemingly become a point of contention in his marriage; Guadalupe Marín, his second wife, is said to have served Rivera a soup of *ídolos* for his dinner, for despite his meager earnings he spent generously on his collection.[3] He continued to acquire Pre-Columbian art until his death in 1957, with the intention of preserving Mexico's ancient heritage.

Rivera studied his collection in great detail, creating flash cards for each object with his own detailed drawings and archaeological notes by his assistant, Ana Teresa Ordiales (pp. 225–29). He directly incorporated or loosely adapted many of these pieces in his easel and mural paintings, and he used his knowledge of the shapes and structures of these objects starting with his murals at the Ministry of Public Education (SEP), painted between 1923 and 1928 and featuring historic subjects and scenes from ancient Mexico.

Despite Rivera's passion for Pre-Columbian Mexican art, very few exhibitions have shown his work alongside ancient Mexican sculptures. In 1916, Marius de Zayas, a Mexican-born artist and owner of the influential Modern Gallery in New York, showed Rivera's works alongside Pre-Columbian sculptures from De Zayas's own collection. Although at this time Rivera's Cubist work would have been considered more French than Mexican (which it was), the Modern Gallery exhibition, *Paintings by Diego M. Rivera and Mexican Pre-Conquest Art*, implied that Rivera was part of an American artistic lineage dating to ancient Mesoamerican times, separate from the Western classical tradition.

It would not be until 1940 that Rivera's work would be shown again side by side with Pre-Columbian art. That year, for the Fourth International Surrealist Exhibition at the Galería de Arte Mexicano in Mexico City, Rivera loaned a selection of ceramics from Colima and masks from Guerrero, whose shapes and designs had the uncanny qualities that Surrealists searched for to confirm the universal application of their (mainly Breton's) theories. A vessel in the form of a torso with two spread legs at the base and an abstracted face carved in serpentine with eyes, mouth, nose, and ears in stylized geometric forms were among the objects from Rivera's collection on display; he also created two paintings for the exhibition, including *Mandrake* (p. 219), which features a woman holding a large papier-mâché or sugar skull in her lap of the same type as those used in traditional Day of the Dead celebrations. (Rivera had previously depicted the Day of the Dead in one of the SEP murals.)

Rivera spent about twenty years of his life planning and building the Museo Anahuacalli (a word meaning "house of Anahuac," in reference to the territory of the Aztecs), where he would house his collection of Pre-Columbian art.[4] During that time, numerous Mexican archaeologists, architects, businessmen, and even poets supported his vision of creating a sort of museum-temple where the objects' primal energy—their *mana*—would be as important as their archaeological data.[5] The Anahuacalli, like many ancient cities and temples, was built with four main galleries facing the cardinal directions, with each dedicated to a deity: Centéotl (earth), Ehécatl (wind), Tlaloc (water), and Huehueteótl (fire). The exterior and interior walls were constructed from locally excavated volcanic rock (deposited by an eruption of the nearby volcano Xitle), while the structure's door openings and building profiles were derived from Maya and central Mexican buildings (combining the two cultures, as in his Popol Vuh drawings). A stone mosaic of Coatlicue, the earth goddess and mother of all gods, greets visitors at the entrance; on the roof, sculptures of serpents resembling Quetzalcóatl mark the four directions. Ultimately, Rivera bequeathed both his collection and the Museo Anahuacalli to the Mexican nation. In his own words: "I return to the people the artistic heritage I was able to redeem from their ancestors." This phrase is inscribed in the stone slab at the entrance of the museum.[6]

1 Juan Coronel Rivera, "Diego Rivera: Idólatra," in *Diego Rivera: Coleccionista* (Mexico City: Instituto Nacional de Bellas Artes, 2007), 18–40.

2 Alfredo Cardona Peña, "El Negocio del Arte Prehispánico," in *Diego Rivera: Coleccionista*, 79.

3 Coronel Rivera, "Diego Rivera: Idólatra," 35.

4 The Anahuacalli was conceived as part of a larger complex of buildings, like an acropolis, that was never completed. See James Oles, *Art and Architecture in Mexico* (New York: Thames & Hudson, 2013), 219–20.

5 Coronel Rivera, "Diego Rivera: Idólatra," 38.

6 Diego Rivera, *Museum Anahuacalli* (Mexico City: Committee of the Games of the 19th Olympiad, 1968), 18.

and the goddess Chalchiuhtlicue—whom he represented in works from the 1940s and 1950s: Tlaloc in the Anahuacalli (1942–63) and the *Tlaloc Fountain* (1951); Chalchiuhtlicue evoked by her insignia in the mural *Huastec Civilization* (1950) at the Palacio Nacional and portrayed as the primordial woman in the mural *Water, the Origin of Life* (1951) at Chapultepec Park.[28] Goddesses of agriculture, sexuality, and the protection of human life also inhabit his paintings, such as Chicomecóatl, the guardian of sustenance, particularly corn, in *Huastec Civilization*; and Tlazoltéotl-Ixcuina the patron of doctors and midwives, associated with lust and moral transgression as well as with purification and healing, who appears—based on her effigy in the Codex Borbonicus—as the protagonist of *Medicine Yesterday and Today* (1953–54) in the Centro Médico Nacional La Raza. In the latter mural Rivera portrays Pre-Columbian medicine, based on botanical knowledge, as being on a par with modern medical science.[29] Rivera invariably presents antiquity in a positive and exemplary light, as seen in the paradises he depicted in the second phase of his mural painting at the Palacio Nacional—even in works with polemical subjects, such as human sacrifice. In the easel painting *Pre-Hispanic America* (1950) ritual sacrifice establishes the cosmic axis vital to the American indigenous world, while in the unfinished series *History of Religion* (1950), the offerings of human hearts maintain the movement of the cosmos, assuring natural and social order as well as the unity of the gods with humanity.[30]

MODERN CODICES

In 1921, Rivera designed a cover for the government publication *El Maestro: Revista de cultura nacional* that typifies his ideological eclecticism, bringing together images as disparate as a hammer and sickle, a mystic eye in a Star of David, the word *México*, ancient glyphs, and typography inspired by the volumes of Pre-Columbian sculpture.[31] This drawing, which combines a variety of Rivera's interests—occultism, indigenism, and socialism—exhibits one of the main strategies he used to configure meaning in his works. Thus, we find drawings in which he relates ancient icons with contemporary images, as in the cover of the book *México en pensamiento y acción* (1926) by Rosendo Salazar, where a stone sculpture of the plumed serpent that Rivera so often portrayed is flanked by hands clutching spikes of grain; the famous cover of *Mexican Folkways* in 1926, in which workers rendered as Aztec sculptures flank a feathered serpent that carries a wheat stalk in its jaws; or another cover of *Mexican Folkways*, in 1928, that shows two serpents, one with feathers on its body and the other adorned with ears of maize, just as he would paint in the SEP murals that same year.

By bringing the indigenous past into the present, Rivera sought to penetrate the indigenous visual language expressed in Pre-Columbian or colonial codices and ancient reliefs and frescoes. This form of appropriation is evident in his drawings for the book *Cuauhtémoc* (1925), by Joaquín Méndez Rivas; their aesthetics and narrative plan are firmly based on codices from the viceroyal period, such as the Durán Codex and the Lienzo de Tlaxcala. In 1935, Rivera illustrated *The Land of the Pheasant and the Deer,* the English-language translation, by Enid Eder Perkins, of *La tierra del faisán y el venado,* originally published in 1922 by Antonio Mediz Bolio, the writer, politician, and Mayanist who translated the sacred books of the Chilam Balam into Spanish. Rivera sought to reflect Maya culture in his interpretation of Mediz Bolio's story, including the concept of dualism and the rattlesnake, *tzáab kaan*; he also drew a plumed serpent, an image that had spread throughout the Maya area from the period of Chichén Itzá (800–1200).[32] We should also mention the novel *El Indio* (1937), by Gregorio López y Fuentes, in which Rivera alluded to the survival of the past in indigenous

28 Betty Ann Brown, "The Past Idealized: Diego Rivera's Use of Pre-Columbian Imagery," in *Diego Rivera: A Retrospective* (New York: Founders Society, Detroit Institute of Arts, in association with W.W. Norton, 1986), 141; Velasco, "A raíz expuesta," 259.

29 Also depicted in this mural is the famous sculptural mask of life and death from the Preclassic civilization of Tlatilco.

30 Cecilia Delgado Masse, "La imagen sacrificial," in *Los pinceles de la historia: la arqueología del régimen, 1910–1955*, ed. Jaime Soler Frost (Mexico City: Museo Nacional de Arte, Instituto Nacional de Bellas Artes, 2003), 96–100.

31 The central symbol, of the eye within the star, was also present in one of Rivera's first murals, in the now-demolished Estadio Nacional.

32 I am grateful to Dr. Erik Velásquez for information on Maya iconography.

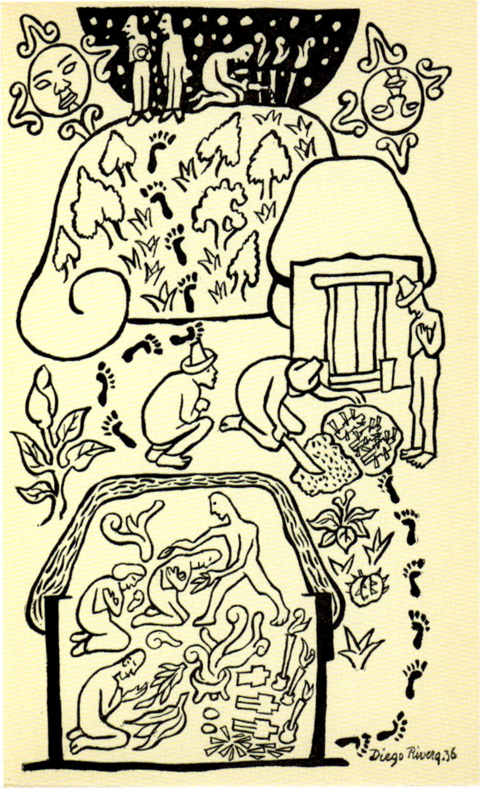

communities with icons of the Pre-Columbian world, such as the footprints that stand for human migration and the *altepetl* 'water mountain', a fundamental concept in the Mesoamerican worldview that designates an ethnic and territorial entity.

Rivera's most ambitious graphic work was the series of watercolors and ink drawings that he produced for the English translation of the Popol Vuh, or "Book of Counsel," a compendium of stories and legends from the Guatemalan Maya-K'iche' people that recounts the creation of the world, man, and food, as well as stories of notable figures. The history of these illustrations goes back to 1930, when Rivera painted *Allegory of California* at the Luncheon Club of the San Francisco Pacific Stock Exchange and prepared his retrospective exhibition at the Museum of Modern Art in New York. It was then that writer John Weatherwax sought out Rivera to propose that he illustrate his English translation of the Popol Vuh.[33] According to Lucretia Hoover Giese, the close collaboration between the translator and the artist, which took place during long nights in which one read while the other drew, was formalized in a contract whereby Rivera agreed to produce drawings within the text as well as vignettes that were to appear at the beginning and end of each chapter.[34] When Weatherwax had three watercolors and two drawings, he began to look for a North American publisher for the work, but various circumstances impeded its publication. The artist continued to paint watercolors—currently we know of twenty-four—but apparently did not complete the number of illustrations originally proposed.[35]

Rivera held this graphic work in high regard, and for years he tried to arrange for a Mexican edition of the Popol Vuh, but he never succeeded.[36] The consensus among those who have studied this material is that the first watercolor Rivera painted was *The Creation*, a composite labyrinth that contains numerous figures—both human and animal—drawn with an attractive simplicity. Each plate displays narrative autonomy, and together they offer a rich variety of formal ideas. But *The Creation* set the pattern for the distorted space seen in all the illustrations, which Rivera would also export to other projects, such as the cover of the Surrealist journal *Minotaure* in 1939.

As for the iconographic sources used in the Popol Vuh series, elements from two Maya texts have been identified—the Dresden Codex and the Madrid Codex—as well as one from the central area of the Maya territory—Codex Borgia—and Codex Ríos, also known as Codex Vatican A.[37] The stylistic influence of Pre-Columbian codices in the watercolors is evident in the fusion of different time frames in the two-dimensional plane as well as the absence of volume in the figures, which are shown as flat, whether in profile or facing forward, and "float" on the white page, with no perspective and minimal spatial references.[38] With regard to the visual representation of an oral tradition, Rodrigo Ruiz explains that the translator and artist worked in a manner that approached the traditional custom

33
Lucretia Hoover Giese, "A Collaboration: Diego Rivera, John Weatherwax, and the Popol Vuh," *Archives of American Art Journal* 39, nos. 3–4 (1999): 2–10. Weatherwax met Rivera through American author Upton Sinclair and Russian director Sergei Eisenstein. In 1931, the first English translation of the Popol Vuh was completed; it was done by Weatherwax, assisted by Clara and Gerald Strang, his sister and brother-in-law. This translation was titled "Seven-Times-The-Colour-of-Fire: Ancient American Mythology of the Popol Vuh."

34
Ibid., 4.

35
Manuel Rodrigo Ruiz Díaz, "Un laberinto maya: Diego Rivera y las ilustraciones del Popol Vuh" (bachelor's thesis, Universidad Nacional Autónoma de México, Facultad de Filosofía y Letras, 2013), 7. Of the known illustrations, twenty-two are watercolors and two are drawings in black ink. According to Ruiz Díaz, three of these illustrations are variations on previous ones.

36
Raquel Tibol, *Diego Rivera: gran ilustrador* (Mexico City: Editorial RM, 2008), 38. The first edition of the Popol Vuh with illustrations by Rivera was published in Japan in 1961.

37
Ruiz Díaz, "Un laberinto maya," 13, 43. Diana Magaloni suggests that Rivera was also inspired by Codex Vatican A or Codex Ríos.

38
Hoover Giese, "A Collaboration," 8.

Diego Rivera, illustration for Gregorio López y Fuentes's ***El Indio*** (1937)

in which these stories were recorded—namely, they were recited while the *tlacuilo* created the images.[39] In antiquity the *tlacuilo*—the painter or scribe—was an initiate of the secrets of his language, a master in the art of spatial treatment and graphic narrative, who had full knowledge of the colors, materials, and manufacturing technique for the codices.[40] One of Rivera's great aspirations was to become a modern *tlacuilo*.

GODS AND STONES

Rivera compiled an immense collection of Pre-Columbian art—almost 59,400 pieces.[41] A renowned archaeologist noted that this private collection is nearly half the size of the Museo Nacional de Antropología's collection, which consists of 126,000 archaeological and ethnographic pieces.[42] Anecdotes and legends about Rivera's "treasure" abound, thanks to which it has been possible to reconstruct the story of its origin and formation, the social diversity of his suppliers, who his main advisers were—Alfonso Caso, Eulalia Guzmán, Miguel Covarrubias, and Carlos Pellicer—which places he frequented to acquire the pieces, and the difficulties he encountered in obtaining and conserving his "idols."[43] Rivera formed his collection with the same didactic, antiquarian spirit evident in his murals in the corridor of the Palacio Nacional, where his aesthetic and mystical appreciation, as well as his desire to recreate a past way of life in the greatest possible detail, prevailed over the archaeological and historical parameters.[44] The objects that Rivera accumulated during more than three decades enriched his imagery of the ancient past and influenced the way that he represented the cultures of this period. The artist studied his objects, carefully classified them, and created "stagings" of distant times.[45] Recent studies, such as those by Roberto Velasco and Daniel Vargas, have shown which pieces intrigued Rivera and which ones he used to produce interpretations of the past.[46] He was passionate about gods, symbolic animals—serpents, dogs, jaguars—and representations that enabled him to picture both daily and ritual life as experienced by the common people through accessories, clothing, hairstyles, postures, and gestures. His collection also included a section on erotic art.

In general, Rivera acquired small or medium-sized objects made of clay and stone. The majority of his collection was made up of Aztec art and pieces from western Mexico—the present states of Guanajuato, Guerrero, Michoacán, Colima, Nayarit, Jalisco, and Sinaloa. He also had some objects from the other cultures in the Valley of Mexico, as well as from the Gulf Coast and Oaxaca. Most notable is the absence of Mayan art.[47] Rivera deeply admired the delicate female figurines found in Tlatilco, a Preclassic settlement in the Valley of Mexico (dating between 1500 BCE and 500 BCE), with their evident Olmec influence. He took great pride in having contributed to the widespread recognition of

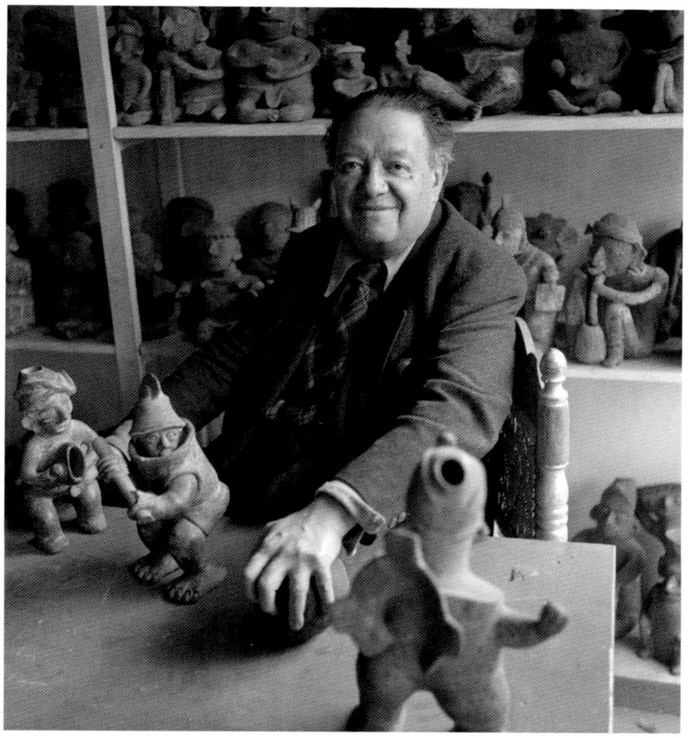

Diego Rivera with his collection of Pre-Columbian works in his studio in San Ángel, c. 1955. Photo: Juan Guzmán (Juan Guzmán Fund, Televisa Foundation)

39
Ruiz Díaz, "Un laberinto maya," 63.

40
Perla Valle, "Memorias en imágenes de los pueblos indios," *Arqueología mexicana: Códices coloniales* 7, no. 38 (1999): 9.

41
Juan Coronel Rivera, "Diego Rivera: Idólatra," in *Diego Rivera Coleccionista* (Mexico City: Instituto Nacional de Bellas Artes, 2007), 18–41. Coronel notes that Rivera dated his first acquisitions of Pre-Columbian art to 1894, when he was eight years old. Documentary evidence indicates that he began to form his collection in 1921.

42
This comparison was made by Felipe Solís Olguín, the director of the Museo Nacional de Antropología from 2000 to 2009.

43
Details of these stories are found in the books *Diego Rivera: Coleccionista* and *El Anahuacalli de Diego*.

44
Braun, "Diego Rivera," 235.

45
With the help of Ana Teresa Ordiales, Rivera produced illustrated cards cataloguing and classifying the pieces from western Mexico.

46
Velasco, "A raíz expuesta"; Daniel Vargas, "Juegos de basalto: De la integración plástica y su resistencia en el Estadio Universitario" (master's thesis, Universidad Nacional Autónoma de México, Facultad de Filosofía y Letras, 2010).

47
Felipe Solís, "Testimonio de una gran pasión: La colección arqueológica de Diego Rivera," in *El Anahuacalli de Diego*, 146–215.

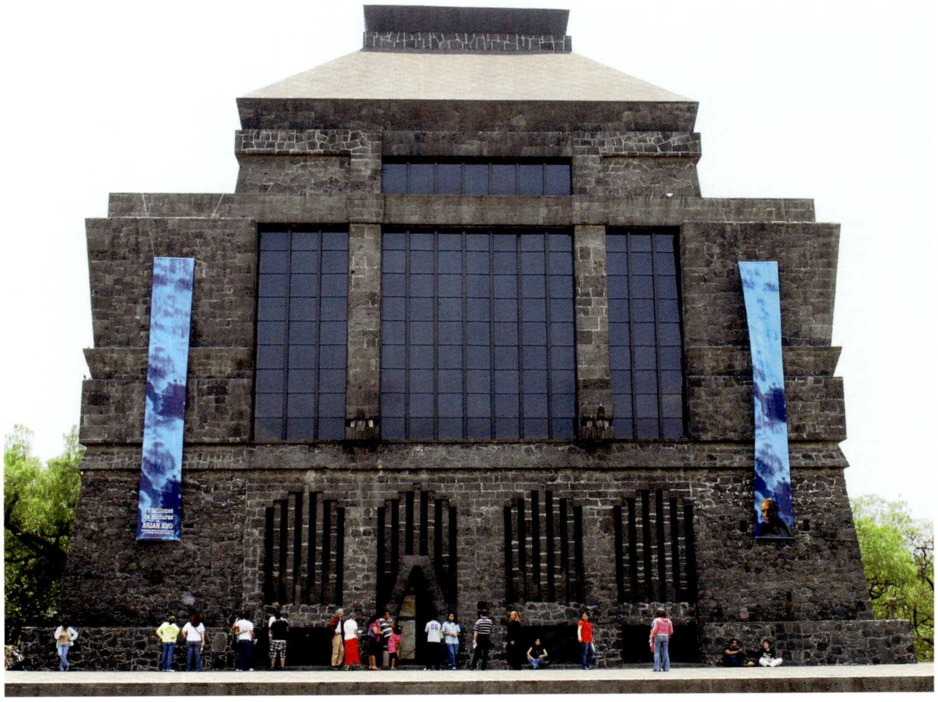

the ancient art of western Mexico, which up to then had been little known, through an exhibition based on his pieces that took place in 1946 in the Palacio de Bellas Artes. Rivera described his collecting ethic as a nationalistic act, dedicated to defending the ancestral heritage against traffickers who pillaged ancient sites and took the pieces out of the country.[48] In this spirit, he built a space to house his collection.

In 1942, Rivera placed the first stone of the Anahuacalli (from *atl* 'agua', *náhuac* 'close by', and *calli* 'house'), a neoindigenist building that combines various Pre-Columbian styles, made entirely of basaltic rock and designed and constructed under the artist's continual supervision (or that of his daughter, after his death). This enterprise, to which Rivera applied all his mental energy and economic resources, relied on the technical support and collaboration of the architect and painter Juan O'Gorman, who concluded the work several years after Rivera's death in 1957. As a long-term project it underwent changes in direction, but from the beginning Rivera considered this space the realization of his mysticism; thus he called it a temple or pyramid. In term of the social goals it was to fulfill, Rivera thought of the structure as a City of the Arts, with a theater, artisan workshops, a museum, concert halls, and spaces for exhibitions and cinema.[49]

Today the Anahuacalli is a museum that conserves Rivera's Pre-Columbian collection, respecting the organization and layout chosen by the artist and executed by Carlos Pellicer, following formal and mystical criteria. From its conception, Rivera envisioned the building as a sacred space, a temple that would house the gods. Felipe Solís explained the complex floor plan as a re-creation of the Mesoamerican cosmic plane, integrated by the four corners of the universe.[50] Four "chambers" aligned along the cardinal points are dedicated to the deities Centéotl, Ehécatl, Tlaloc, and Huehueteótl, which in turn are linked to the four elements: earth, wind, water, and fire.[51] The imposing Coatlicue presides over the entrance of the temple from a ceiling mosaic of natural stone. The mask of Tlaloc, the rain god, governs one of the chambers, which has a staircase that descends to a body of water fed by an ancient spring; there Rivera portrayed a toad, alluding to his own nickname, *sapo-rana* (toad-frog). In the rest of the building, meanings are encoded in the stone mosaics that cover most of the interior spaces and in

48
Alfredo Cardona Peña, "El negocio del arte prehispánico," in *Diego Rivera: Coleccionista*, 77–99.

49
Xavier Guzmán Urbiola, "Un espacio para la vida: El Anahuacalli, edificio neoindígena y wrightiano," in *El Anahuacalli de Diego*, 113, 123. In the beginning Rivera also considered building a farm or ranch on the land.

50
Solís, "Testimonio de una gran pasión," 159.

51
Coronel, "Diego Rivera," 38.

Museo Diego Rivera Anahuacalli, Mexico City

which we see mythological beings, cosmogonic signs, and certain contemporary images and Western symbols, such as the dove of peace and the hammer and sickle. In Juan Coronel Rivera's interpretation, the iconography of the mosaics expresses a metaphor of spiritual ascent. On the ground floor, where darkness and labyrinthine spaces predominate, the mosaics are monochromatic, because it is the kingdom of Coatlicue in the bowels of the Earth. But as one ascends to the upper part of the pyramid or sacred mountain, which contains the artist's spacious and well-lit studio, the colorful mosaics announce entry to a higher dimension of knowledge.[52]

The mosaic technique of natural stones on reinforced concrete slabs was invented by Rivera and evokes the polychrome mosaics of indigenous antiquity—made with shells, turquoise, obsidian, and other precious materials—used to decorate sacred and ceremonial objects. The stones in most of the mosaics, as well as those used to construct the building, come from the site where the Anahuacalli is located, in the community of San Pablo Tepetlapa in southern Mexico City. This zone is part of a vast area called Pedregal de San Ángel (lava field of San Ángel), covered by petrified lava from the eruption of the Xitle Volcano a little more than 1,600 years ago.[53] The eruption radically changed the landscape of this part of the valley, destroying lakes and forests and forming a large island of basaltic rock some thirty-three feet thick, with fanciful shapes, crags, ravines, crevices, caves, tunnels, and walls of volcanic stone. As centuries passed, a rich ecosystem flourished in this formerly inhospitable and desolate place.[54] Today in Pedregal de San Ángel, very ancient structures—such as the archaeological site of Cuicuilco, from the Preclassic period—coexist with modern neighborhoods developed at the same time as the Anahuacalli, such as the Ciudad Universitaria and the residential development El Pedregal, a project by architect Luis Barragán.

In the shapes, textures, and materials of this special place, as well as the temporal dimension captured within them, Rivera and O'Gorman found the raw material to solve the problem of artistic integration—the indissoluble union between architecture, painting, and sculpture—from a wholly Mexican perspective. In the development of this conception, Frank Lloyd Wright's notion of organic architecture, which calls for the harmonious relation between architecture and its natural surroundings, came into play. Xavier Guzmán has shown that one of the inspirations for the Anahuacalli was Wright's famous Fallingwater, or Kaufmann Residence (1935–39), which Rivera saw in photographs sent to him by the son of Edgar Kaufmann, whom he met between 1937 and 1938.[55] Moreover, O'Gorman visited the Kaufmann Residence and was impressed by the beauty he found in the coexistence of architecture and nature. Guzmán has remarked on the similarities between the Anahuacalli and Wright's architecture, as has Barbara Braun, for whom the Mexican building recalls works such as the Ennis House (1923) in Los Angeles, as well as Taliesin West (1937), Wright's home and office in Scottsdale, Arizona.[56] We should emphasize, however, that unlike Wright's work, Rivera's building is set in a landscape that bore nationalistic and metaphysical connotations.[57]

As a result of the construction of the Anahuacalli, Rivera renovated part of the Casa Azul, where he lived with Frida Kahlo, with certain architectural elements of the house (for example, the fireplace) inspired by Pre-Columbian forms and utilizing volcanic stone; he also added a step pyramid to hold pieces from his collection and mosaics of natural stone. In the early 1950s he began another work made of mosaics using stone and broken tiles: the Tlaloc Fountain in Mexico City's Chapultepec Park. This work is part of an ensemble of architecture, artwork, and sculpture in which Rivera accepted the technical challenge of painting an underwater mural (*Water, the Origin of Life*), located in an enormous water tank known as the Cárcamo del Río

52
Juan Coronel Rivera, "Los mosaicos del Museo Anahuacalli," in *El Anahuacalli de Diego*, 251.

53
Antonio Lot Helgueras, "El Anahuacalli, fragmento de lava, relicto de vida," in *El Anahuacalli de Diego*, 323. Pedregal de San Ángel covers an area of about thirty-one square miles.

54
Ibid., 334.

55
Guzmán, "Un espacio para la vida," 95–98. The younger Kaufmann sent Rivera the photographs to propose that the artist design tapestries for the house, though ultimately Rivera did not do so.

56
Braun, "Diego Rivera," 239–40.

57
Coronel, "Los mosaicos del Museo Anahuacalli," 248. Coronel thinks that for Rivera the lava represented the bowels of the Earth, and as such it lent a metaphysical character to Templo-Anahuacalli. His essay develops the transcendent aspect of the Anahuacalli in relation to Western and Pre-Columbian metaphysical ideas, especially Nahua cosmogony.

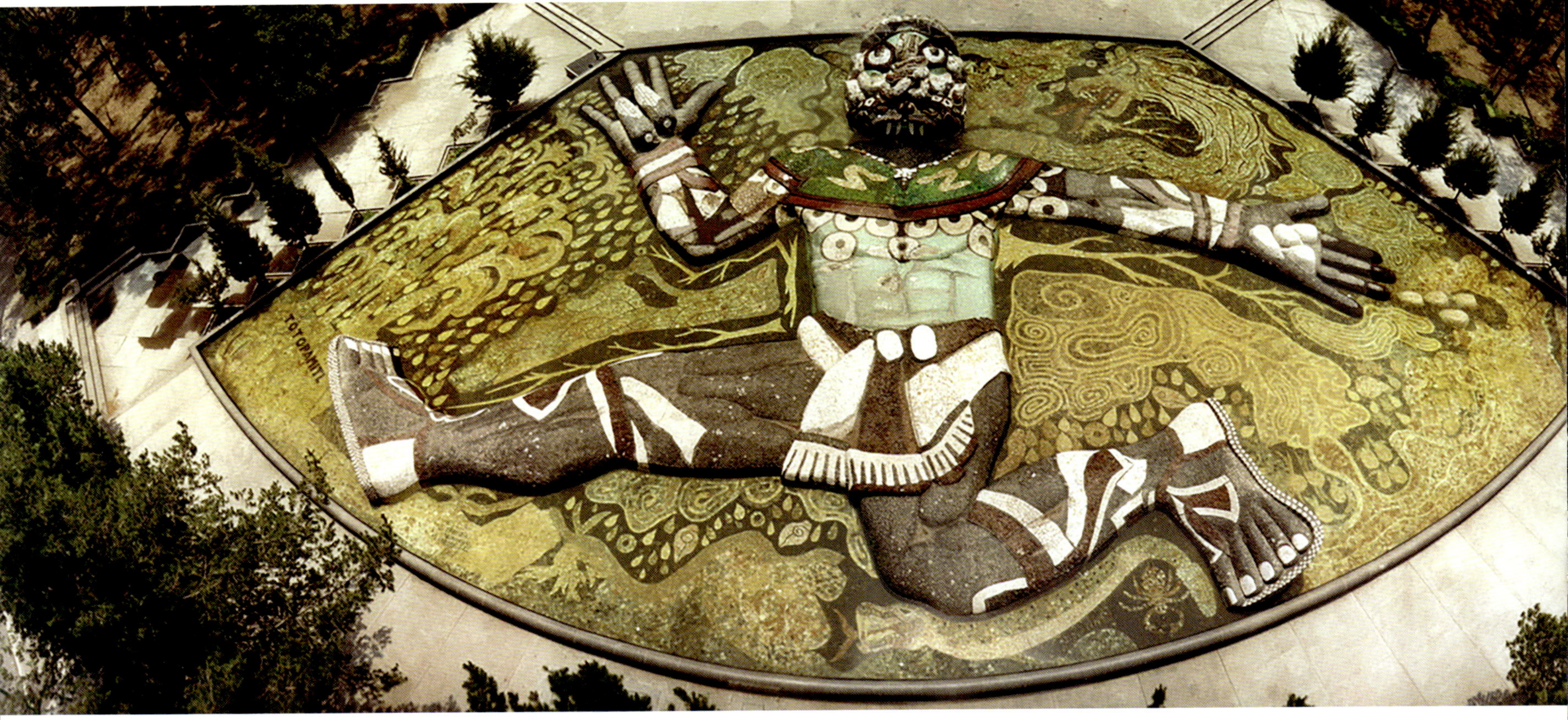

Lerma. The Tlaloc Fountain shows the whole figure of the god in a dynamic position. Rivera conceived this work to be appreciated from a great height; he calculated that Tlaloc would greet those who flew over the work by airplane. To realize this "aerial" composition, he invoked the tradition of North American mound builders.[58] In this way, he paid homage to the early indigenous cultures of North America while also adapting their tradition for a new and modern "visibility."

Another work that reflects Rivera's desire to integrate the arts with their natural and social environment on the basis of a native tradition was the monumental sculptural mosaic that he constructed on an exterior wall of the Estadio Olímpico in the Ciudad Universitaria, a stadium in the form of a volcanic crater. The development of this urban architectural complex intensified the debate on how to integrate the international, essentially geometric, architectural style with realist painting, such as muralism. Among the various positions taken in this discussion, Rivera and O'Gorman rejected internationalism and assumed a Mexicanist stance that demanded coherence between the works and "the national soil," recognizing the Pre-Columbian architecture of Mexico—for example, Teotihuacán, Tula, and Chichén Itzá—as a model of absolute artistic integration.[59] Rivera asserted that in the buildings of the indigenous past,"one couldn't tell where the sculpture and painting began or ended; they formed part, along with the building itself, of a harmonious whole that was totally integrated with the art."[60] The sculptural mosaics that were to cover the extensive stadium wall would develop the subject of the history of sports in Mexico.[61] However, due to lack of funding, Rivera was able to realize only a tiny part of the mural program: an allegory of *mestizaje* supported by a serpent whose body is spotted with ears of maize, which Rivera had first drawn for the magazine *Mexican Folkways*. The preliminary project alluded to the Mexica, Maya, and western Mexican cultures. These images included an archaeological interpretation of a ball game using a stick and references to the flower

58
Diego Rivera, "Integración plástica en la cámara de distribución del agua del Lerma. Tema medular: El agua, origen de la vida en la Tierra," in *Obras*, 1:339–40.

59
Diego Rivera, "El Estadio Olímpico Universitario," in *Obras*, vol. 2, pt. 2, *Textos polémicos (1950–1957)*, ed. Esther Acevedo et al. (Mexico City: El Colegio Nacional, 1999), 694.

60
Diego Rivera, "Un pintor opina," in *Obras* 1:360.

61
Ibid., 695. The architect of the stadium was Augusto Pérez Palacios.

Aerial view of Diego Rivera's **Tlaloc Fountain**, 1950–52, Chapultepec Park, Mexico City

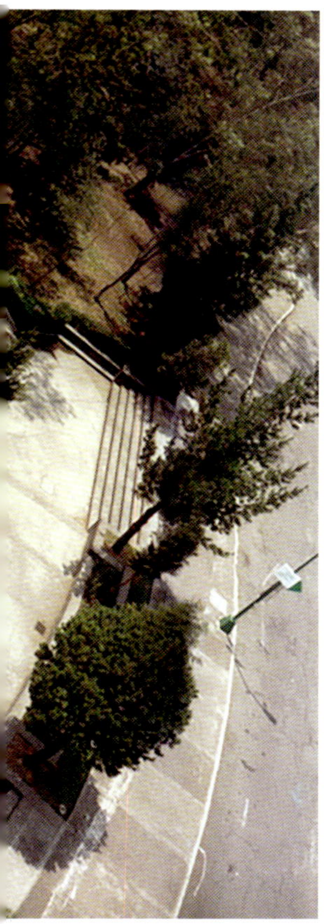

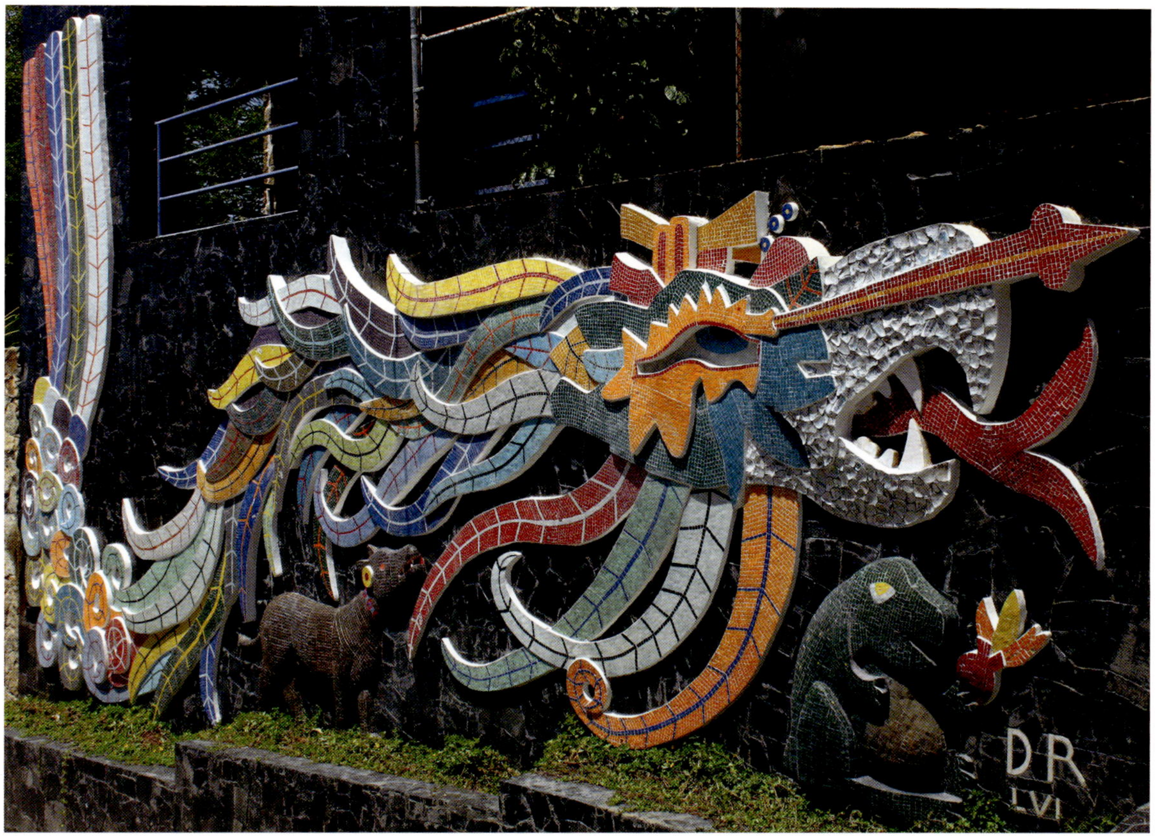

wars of the Postclassic period—battles in which the prisoners were captured for ritual sacrifices.[62]

Following his work at the Ciudad Universitaria, Rivera continued to create mosaics, some in mixed media, for private residences, such as the interior decorations and enormous serpents (Ehécatl Quetzalcóatl and Tlaloc) that crisscross the outside walls of Dolores Olmedo's house in Acapulco; zoomorphic figures designed for the provincial properties of Emma Hurtado; and representations of the Pre-Columbian cosmogony in the former Quinta Ofelia, now the public park El Batán. He also worked with Venetian mosaic in *Tlatilco Dancer* and *Juchitán River*, for houses in Cuernavaca, and *History of the Theater in Mexico*, with his beloved figures of Tlatilco, on the facade of the Teatro de los Insurgentes.

Rivera's artistic and ideological identity is marked by his commitment to the indigenous past, intimately linked with the value placed on "the indigenous" in his day as a source of national identity as well as of universality. This angle of Rivera's thought has yet to be fully explored. His best Mexican works are characterized by an eclectic conceptual richness, and attempting to understand them in terms of one of his interests—be it nationalism, esotericism, Marxism, or any other perspective—would prove limiting. Rivera's artistic impulse responded to a variety of passions. Among them, indigenous antiquity was perhaps his deepest and most abiding.

Translated by ROSE VEKONY

62
Vargas, "Juegos de basalto," 70–76.

Diego Rivera, ***Ehécatl Tlalocan Calli***, 1956; natural stone mosaic inlaid with mother-of-pearl shell, Dolores Olmedo House, Acapulco, Mexico

DIEGO RIVERA'S POPOL VUH

DIANA MAGALONI *and* LILLY CASILLAS

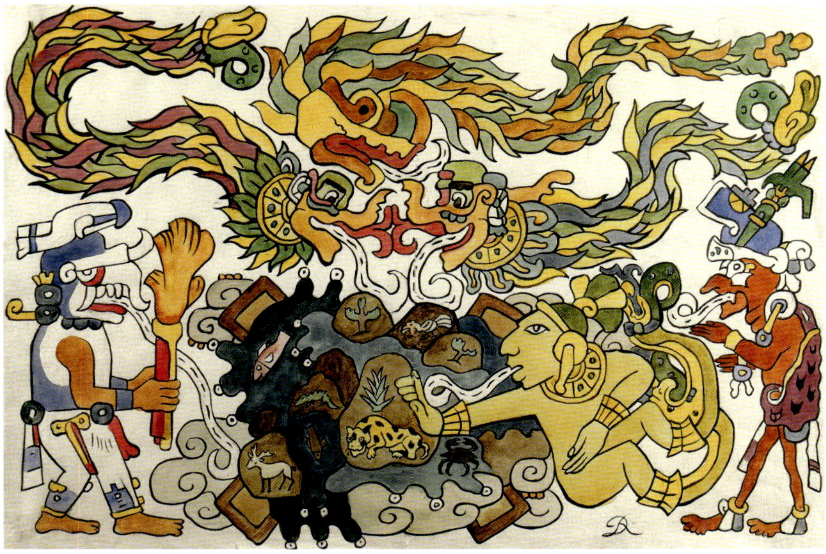

According to his daughter Guadalupe Rivera, Diego Rivera kept the Spanish version of the Popol Vuh on his nightstand and could recite entire verses from memory, enjoying the visual and poetic beauty as well as the moral teachings of the creation myth written by the ancient K'iche' Maya of Guatemala.[1] The Popol Vuh, one of the most important Mesoamerican narratives, was recorded in the sixteenth century in the K'iche' language as a way to preserve the words of their ancestors from the destruction that followed the Spanish conquest. The myth tells the story of the creation of the current world and of the four previous worlds, when the gods had failed to create human beings who would respect their makers. More specifically, it explains the formation of the K'iche' Maya from maize dough, and the adventures of two heroic twins named Hunahpú and Ixbalanqué. The twins were to maintain the cosmic order by vanquishing the false and conceited Sun god, and by surviving the tests set by the trickster gods of the underworld through their sharp judgment, cunning problem-solving skills, and great hunting abilities.

Rivera made at least twenty-four watercolors illustrating scenes from the Popol Vuh for two different projects, though scholars have located only twenty-one. In 1930, while Rivera was painting the *Allegory of California* mural at the Pacific Stock Exchange in San Francisco, writer John Weatherwax commissioned Rivera to illustrate his English version of the Popol Vuh, titled *Seven-Times-the-Colour-of-Fire*. (The book was never published.)[2] Three watercolors from this first series are held in the Kislak Collection at the Library of Congress: *Creation*, *Human Sacrifice before Tohil*, and *Trials of the Hero*, all dated 1931. Two others, *Hero Twins in the Ballgame* and *Death of Zipacná*, are in private collections and were published for the first time in 2008, to accompany a new translation of the original text by Adrian I. Chavez, the first translator who is also a native K'iche' Maya speaker. The second series consists of seventeen watercolors that are today part of the collection at the Museo Casa Diego Rivera in Guanajuato. According to Guadalupe Rivera, these works were commissioned to illustrate a Japanese translation of the Popol Vuh, and were probably completed between 1934 and 1940.[3]

The watercolors that illustrate the creation myth and the adventures of Hunahpú and Ixbalanqué clearly show that Rivera carefully considered how best to represent these multilayered stories, particularly as the narrative of the Popol Vuh presents events that occur in nonlinear time. The creation story is filled with poetic imagery and allegories that can best be compared to dreams or kaleidoscopic visions. To create these mythic narratives of creation, Rivera borrowed Mesoamerican artistic conventions of different ancient traditions and combined them to create a panindigenous mode of expression. This is evident in the first illustration, *Creation of the Universe*, which depicts figures and forms from different times and cosmic spaces in a single plane, much like a Cubist painting. A scene with a mountain surrounded by water and contained within a mountain range is positioned at the center, in a smaller size than the principal figures. The central mountain is drawn as the central Mexican emblem of *altepetl* (Nahuatl, 'water mountain'), a common symbol of an established, bountiful town that was frequently used in many indigenous maps and sacred books in the

1 Guadalupe Rivera Marín, "Diego Rivera y el Popol Wuj," in *Pop Wuj*, trans. Adrián I. Chávez (Mexico City: Centro de Investigaciones y Estudios Superiores en Antropología Social; Consejo Nacional para la cultura y las Artes; Instituto Nacional de Antropología e Historia; Fundación Diego Rivera, 2008), 37–39.

2 For more on the collaboration between Weatherwax and Rivera, see Lucretia Hoover Giese, "A Collaboration: Diego Rivera, John Weatherwax, and the Popol Vuh," *Archives of American Art Journal* 39, nos. 3–4 (1999): 2–10.

3 The only known edition of this Japanese version of the Popol Vuh is its translation into Spanish dated much later in 1961: *Popol Vuh, Las Antiguas historias del Quiché* (Tokyo: Chuo-Koron Sha, 1961), an edition based on the 1947 Spanish translation from Fondo de Cultura Económica. See Laura Cortés Gutiérrez, *Diego Rivera: Catálogo general de obra mural y fotografía personal* (Mexico City: SEP/Instituto Nacional de Bellas Artes, 1988), 384.

Diego Rivera, ***Creation of the Universe***, 1931

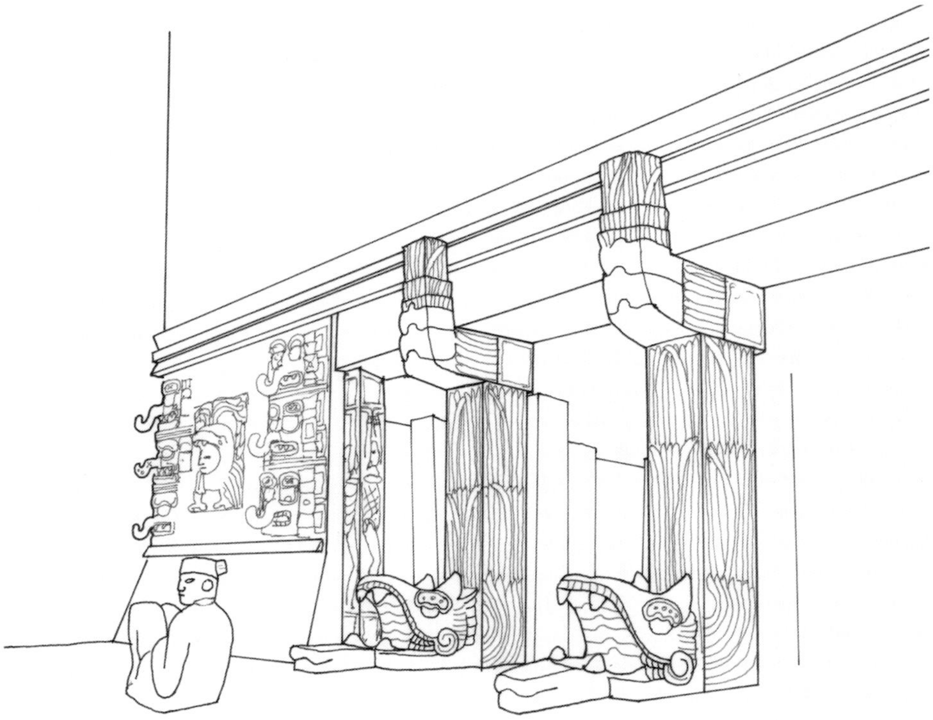

sixteenth century. Rivera uses the symbol of *altepetl* here to describe the primeval earth emerging from the still waters of the ocean before time and the sun were created. Atop the mountains, Rivera placed the first animals, trees, and plants. Encircling this scene are six creator gods, whose size and placement in the composition suggest that they are forces larger than the land and the sea themselves.

The Popol Vuh narrates that two great forces of nature, thought of as supreme gods, combined their powers to create the earth: the Sovereign Plumed Serpent, glittering in the depths of the ocean, and Hurricane, the Heart of the Sky, who took the form of three different types of thunderbolts. In *Creation of the Universe*, Rivera painted these two Maya gods of creation as three plumed serpents in the upper section of the watercolor and as three different gods inspired by ancient Mayan deities. To create these deities Rivera drew upon the art and architecture of the ancient Maya city of Chichén Itzá, which he had visited in November 1921.[4] The Sovereign Plumed Serpent is rendered as three multicolored serpents, which are a combination of the bodies of the feather serpent columns

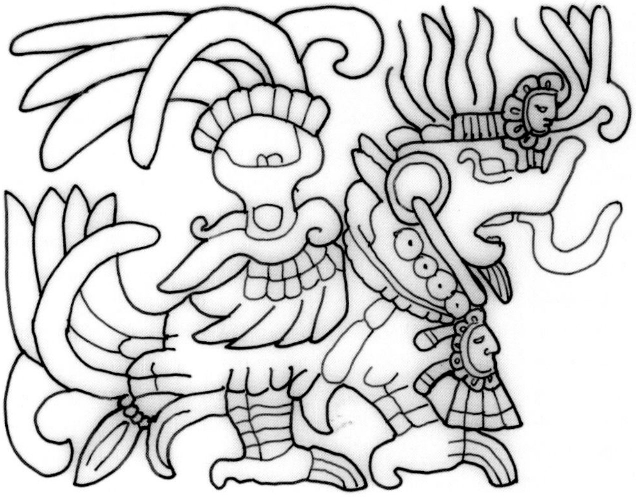

4 In 1931, Earl H. Morris and Ann Morris published the results of their archaeological project in their seminal book, *The Temple of the Warriors at Chichen Itzá, Yucatán* (Washington, DC: Carnegie Institution of Washington, 1931), coauthored with muralist Jean Charlot. Ann Morris and Charlot copied the impressive mural paintings of the Chacmool Temple and the Jaguar Temples. As a friend of Charlot, Rivera would have been familiar with this publication. The style he employs in his Popol Vuh series is reminiscent of the drawings of the murals.

Temple of the Warriors Facade with Chacmool in the foreground, Chichén Itzá (drawing by Linda Schele)

Itzamna, Chichén Itzá (drawing by Linda Schele)

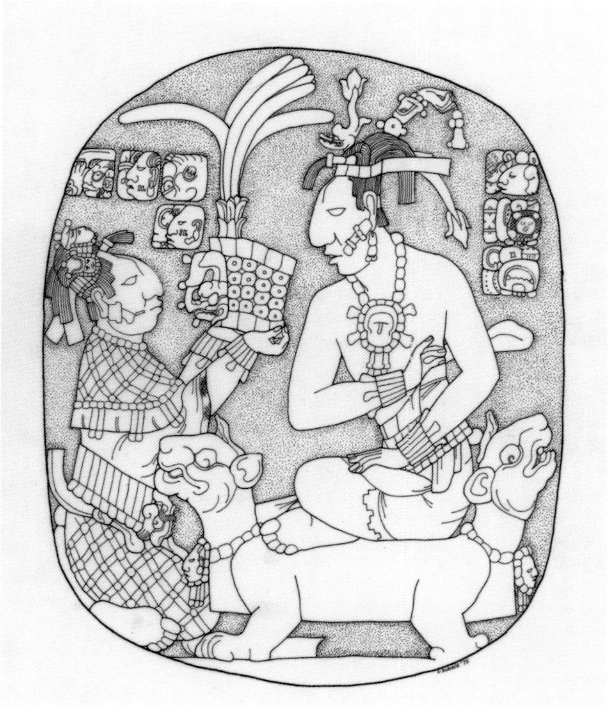

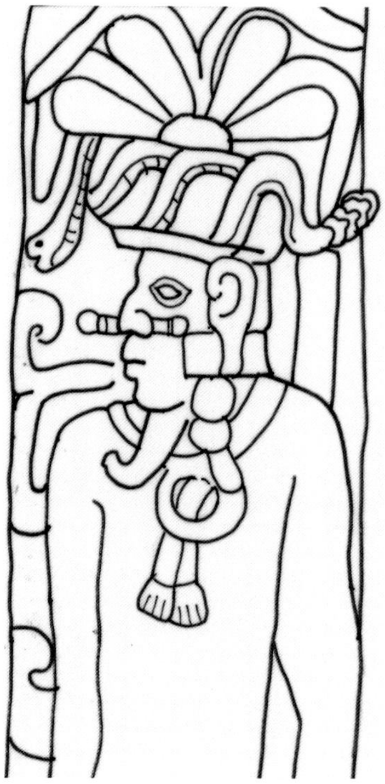

of the recently restored Temple of the Warriors and the elaborate profile of the supreme Maya god Itzamna, both from Chichén Itzá (opposite). Rivera's combination of the two makes perfect sense, given that the Popol Vuh refers to the Sovereign Plumed Serpent as "the maker and modeler, mother-father of life, of humankind, giver of breath, giver of heart, who is supreme god."[5]

Hurricane, who in the narrative takes the form of three lightning bolts, is shown by Rivera as three Maya gods of different ages. The young god at the center of the representation of great physical beauty appears in profile with yellow skin, covered in fine jewelry and adornments including the sprouting headdress that evokes the maize god. The ancient Maya conceived the young maize god in this manner, as seen in the relief of lord Pakal dressed as the maize god on the Oval Palace Tablet in Palenque, Chiapas (above left), which Rivera must have known from both the famous drawings of Palenque's monuments published by Jean Frédéric Waldeck in 1866 and from Frans Blom's 1923 publication.[6] Following his method of uniting fragments from different sources, Rivera draws the headdress of his creator god as the four-lobed headdress worn by the young warriors carved in the columns of the North Temple at Chichén Itzá (above right). The figure of the elderly god at the right side of the watercolor, wearing a prominent blue hat and an animal pelt, corresponds to representations of the Maya god of commerce, God L, who was thought to be an elderly man, as seen in the relief from the eastern jamb of the Temple of the Cross in Palenque (p. 270 top right). The deity at the extreme left of the watercolor wears a blue-and-white mask with prominent fangs and a downturned snout with big red and white circular eyes, and seems to be inspired by the Maya god Chaac, according to the representations of this god in the almanac of Chaac in the Madrid Codex (p. 270 left).[7] In recasting ancient Mesoamerican images from different traditions and periods in this way, Rivera followed the same process he had learned during his academic training—namely, to copy the art of antiquity, only this time he replaced ancient Greek and Roman sculptures with ancient Maya sculptures and paintings, thus granting them an equivalent status as high art.

5
Popol Vuh: The Definitive Edition of the Mayan Book of the Dawn of Life and the Glories of Gods and Kings, trans. Dennis Tedlock (New York: Simon and Schuster, 1986), 72.

6
Danish archaeologist Frans Blom was commissioned by anthropologist Manuel Gamio, a close friend of Rivera, to explore Palenque. He published his study in *Las Ruinas de Palenque, Xupá y Finca Encanto* (Mexico City: Instituto Nacional de Antropología e Historia, 1982 [1923]). See "Return to the Great Forests: Frans Blom's Letters from Palenque, December 1922–March 1923," trans. Jesper Nielsen and Tore Leifer, *The PARI Journal* 4, no. 3 (2004): 7–10 and no. 4 (2004): 13–16, www.mesoweb.com/pari/publications/journal/403/Blom-Palenque.pdf, and *Jean Frédéric Waldeck, Peintre: Le premier explorateur des ruines mayas* (Paris: Hazan, 1993).

7
A Chaac with the same mask and fangs appears in the Codex Madrid, folios 27b–28b; see Gabrielle Vail and Anthony Aveni, *The Madrid Codex: New Approaches to Understanding an Ancient Maya Manuscript* (Boulder: University Press of Colorado, 2004), 280.

LEFT Oval Palace Tablet, Palenque (drawing by Linda Schele)

RIGHT Warrior Figure on East and West doorjambs from the Upper Temple of the Jaguars, Chichén Itzá (drawing by Linda Schele)

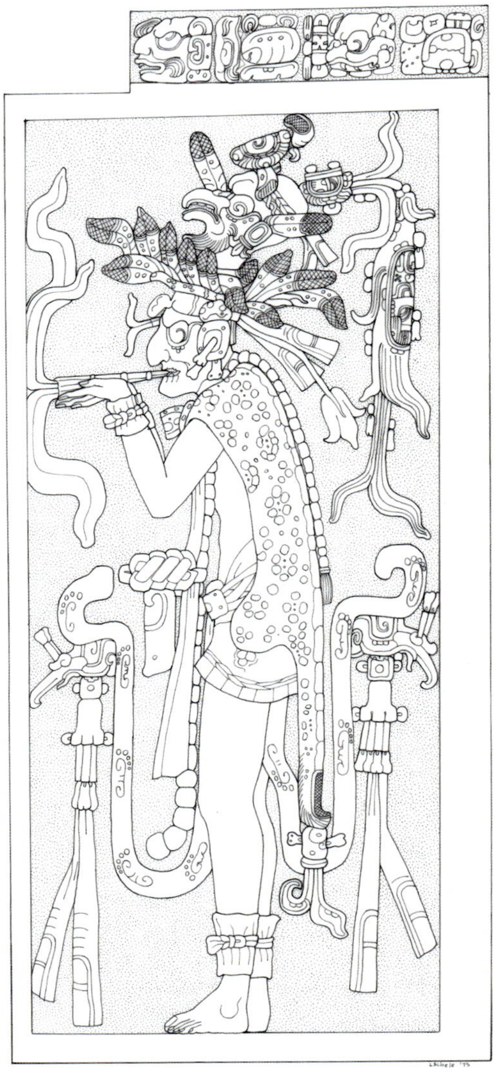

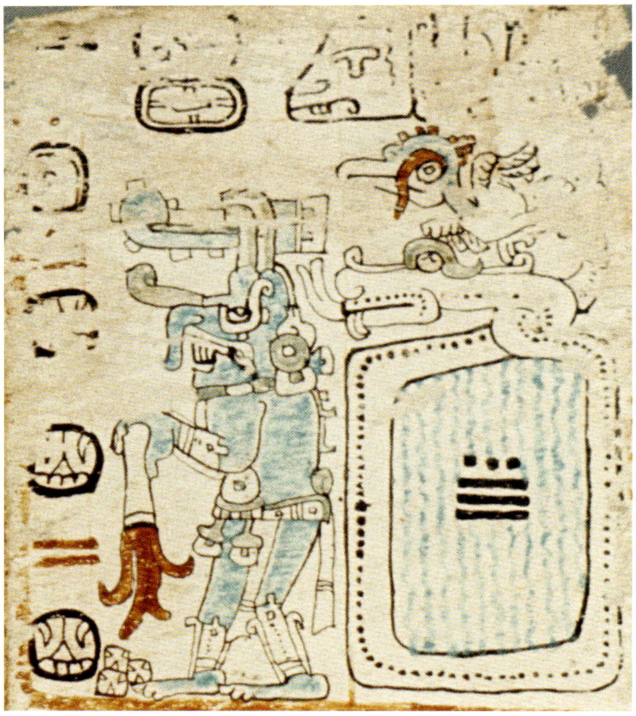

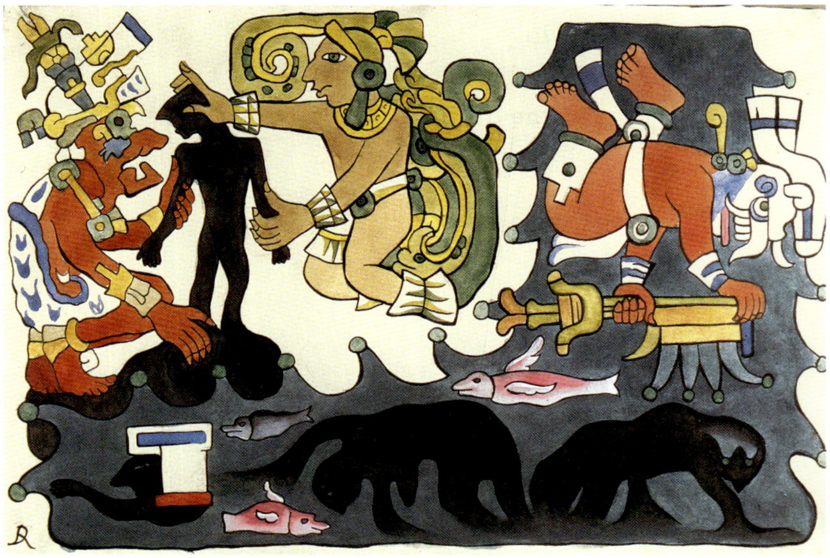

LEFT Chaac (Maya rain god), Madrid Codex, 1250–1450; Museo de América, Madrid, Spain

TOP RIGHT Temple of the Cross, East Jamb, Palenque (drawing by Linda Schele)

BOTTOM RIGHT Diego Rivera, ***The Creation of Man***, 1931

Another watercolor, known as *Creation of Man* (opposite), chronicles the gods' failed attempt to create humankind by modeling men of clay. Here Rivera sets the scene against the backdrop of another ancient painted story of creation, that of the Central Mexican Nahua people, which was preserved in the indigenous sixteenth-century document known as the Codex Ríos or Codex Vaticanus (p. 188). As in the codex image, Rivera's *Creation of Man* shows a large stream of water gushing from the sky. Beneath this torrent, men of clay are destroyed as they dissolve into the dark waters. As can be seen by comparing both images, Rivera also painted the fish, the house, and the descending deity in his composition. These are ancient Central Mexican symbols (not Maya) that refer to the destruction of a previous world era. Rivera borrowed from the Codex Ríos because there is no other indigenous painted manuscript that addresses the creation and destruction of world eras; in this manner, he gives precedence to the indigenous painting tradition and introduces a historic depth to his representation of the Popol Vuh.

The Popol Vuh would have been originally preserved through paintings and hieroglyphic writing. Following the Spanish conquest, Maya histories were deemed heretical and all but a very few Maya books were burned; countless images of the ancient gods and the creation of the world were lost in these fires. Rivera's watercolors bring those lost manuscripts back to life. Using original Mesoamerican sources to bring the ancient K'iche' Maya creation story to the modern era, Rivera thereby added himself to a Mesoamerican artistic lineage.

DIEGO RIVERA

ASSERTING THE AMERICAS

JUAN RAFAEL CORONEL RIVERA

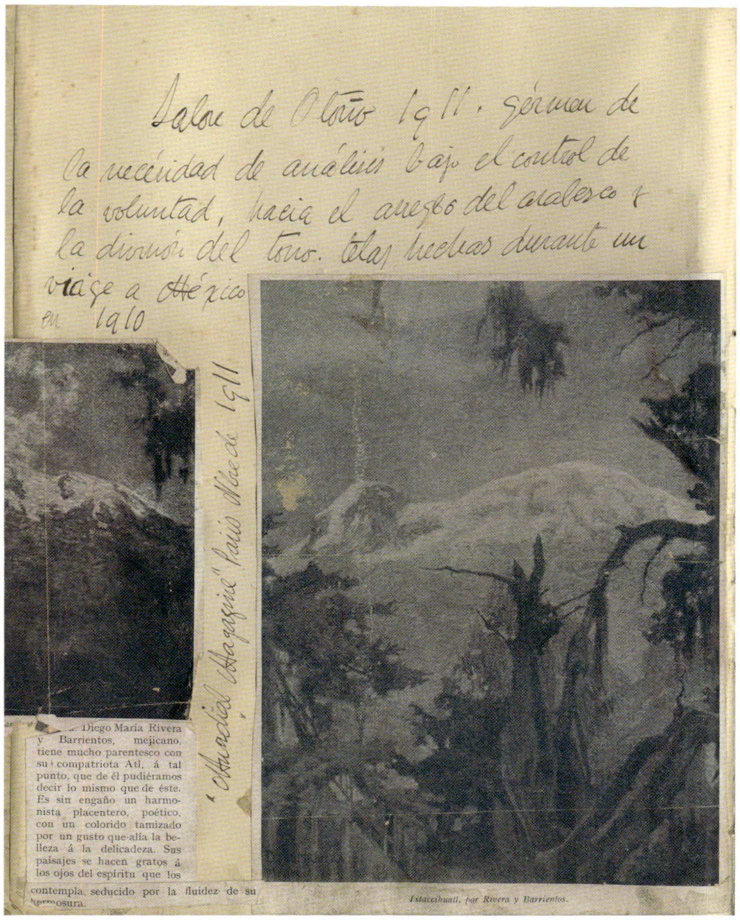

Page from Diego Rivera's notebook, with a reproduction of his painting ***Iztaccíhuatl*** (1901); Diego Rivera and Frida Kahlo Archive

RIVERA'S CHALLENGE TO THE MODERN

Diego Rivera's enduring relationship with modern artists from the United States began in Europe between 1911 and 1913, when he was absorbing the styles of the Parisian avant-garde and making them his own. It was during these years that he met Stanton Macdonald-Wright, Morgan Russell, and José Moya del Pino. These relationships prefigure one of Rivera's most important contributions to art history: muralism. Moreover, they mark the inception of the pan-American position that Rivera would uphold in his art, and which not only erased the borders between Latin America and the United States but also helped promote an understanding of modernism through cultural plurality, positing a far more complex and interesting modernity than that proposed in Paris or New York.

It's important to review the precepts on which Rivera's tradition as a muralist was based, as well as to ask what it meant to be modern in Mexico during the last decade of the nineteenth century and the first decade of the twentieth—the period when Rivera took classes at the Escuela Nacional de Bellas Artes (ENBA), which emerged from the Academy of San Carlos.[1] First we need to know that the word *modern* does not in itself imply a state of invention or discovery, nor does it even refer to fashion (*moda*). *Modern* comes from Latin *modernus*, meaning "of or pertaining to present or recent times."[2] It describes temporariness, without entailing any conceptual advance or regression; it simply marks a transitory origin.

The Western notion of the modern goes back to eighteenth-century Europe and was built on the principles of the Industrial Revolution, its philosophy tailored to the needs of that economic and social phenomenon. Thus almost all the cultures of humanity lay outside its parameters and interests, as well as its acceptance of the Renaissance reinterpretation of ancient Greek and Roman art as the origin and apogee of culture. Developed civilizations in foundational cities—such as Benin City (Nigeria), Uxmal (Mexico), or Kanchipuram (India)—and their cultural output were not taken into account; the aesthetics and philosophy of those exceptional societies were excluded from Western thought.

During the nineteenth and twentieth centuries, a substantial number of artists, intellectuals, and historians whom we will call "eccentric" (*excéntrico*), in the etymological sense of being outside the center, began to question this omission and introduced a series of inclusive ideas intended to modify the chauvinistic European postulate. One of these artists was the visionary Miguel Covarrubias, who identified Olmec culture as the matrix of Mesoamerican civilization and also produced a study on the island of Bali. Rivera was another great eccentric in this sense, due to his incorporation of ancient Mexican art into modern European art, thus according it the same esteem given to classical

1
The Real Academia de San Carlos de las Nobles Artes de la Nueva España (Royal Academy of San Carlos of the Noble Arts of New Spain) was the first art school in the Americas, opened in 1785. It was renamed the Escuela Nacional de Bellas Artes (National School of Fine Arts) in 1867.

2
Etymologies quoted in this essay are from etymonline.com.

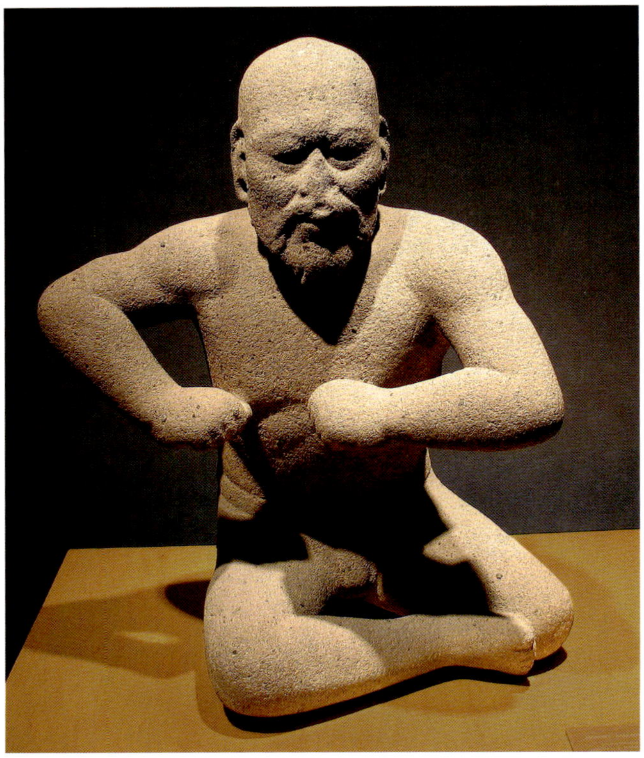

Greco-Roman art. Covarrubias and Rivera, among other Latin Americans, made clear the ideological and cultural plurality of the modern, illuminating the different possibilities surrounding it as a concept.

At the dawn of the twentieth century, this formulation of a modernity with different intellectual foundations was happening not only in Mexico but also in other peripheral countries in parts of the Americas, Asia, and Africa. In Mexico, this gave rise to muralism, and the sixty-eight fundamental original cultures—including Wixárika (Huichol), Otomí, and Rarámuri—were incorporated into universal art. When Rivera arrived in Mexico City and enrolled at the ENBA, he entered into the modern current then in vogue in his country. Contemporary Mexican culture was under the influence of pro-independence, secular, and antimonarchical ideologies, which generated an approach to modernity with unique critical and creative qualities. The most important of these in the visual arts consisted of an inward cultural exploration whereby "the European" ceased to predominate, in an effort to bring about a revision—an invention—of "the national," with an inclusive tone that had been prohibited during the viceroyalty.

In the New Spanish period very few works of indigenous origin were included in the daily life of the Spaniards. Tonalá ceramics were one exception, as seen in Francisco de Zurbarán's paintings. Mexican featherwork was adopted as a model of esteemed work with indigenous origins, but its themes were completely changed. But following Mexican independence in 1821, liberalism had a great impact on the visual arts due to its promotion of equality among races and individuals. As a result, the aesthetic and social panorama of culture was definitively transformed over the following two decades. The ordinances that regulated artisan guilds were repealed, and as the guilds lost power, they gave way to a singular aesthetic revelation: the creative impulse made it possible for any individual to produce a masterwork. And I deliberately stress "masterwork," since many of the pieces created had a thousand-year-old tradition—untouched during Spanish rule—belonging to an original culture. Nahuas, Zapotecs, and Tzotzils could now position their works as art without threat of imprisonment or excommunication; in the twentieth century these works were called "folk art." There was no longer a ruling academy, and creative pluralism emerged.

The modern in the art of Mexico during this period—originating in the aesthetic principles that sprung from the new creative freedom and that were combined with ideas put forth in nineteenth-century academic art—opened a very interesting cultural chapter: that of *mestizaje* (the intermingling of cultures) in art. This was doubtless the most important philosophical subject for understanding Rivera's relation to "his" historical past and the fundamental difference between his idea of antiquity and that articulated by Pablo Picasso. The European (but by no means universal) concept of art arose from the classical Greco-Roman tradition. The Aristotelian philosophical model through which it was implemented shaped the academic tradition of Picasso; thus, the driving force behind Picasso's creativity and Rivera's had different origins. The Greeks considered

Antonio Plaza Monument 1, Olmec, 1500–400 BCE; basalt, 26 in. (66 cm); Museo Nacional de Antropología, Mexico City

artistic manifestations to be the mimesis of nature, so that creators were seen as imitators of the perceptible world. However, nothing could be further from the mestizo approach; the "eccentric" creators and their aesthetic project, whose conceptualization harks back to the antiquity of the Americas, were never actually interested in representing reality, as conceived in the notion of mimesis, but rather in establishing metaphors with regard to it. Their aesthetic vision was metaphysical and allegorical.

In terms of the Western canons, and especially the Greek treatises on art recovered during the two centuries of academicism, the indigenous American cultures did not fit into the Eurocentric aesthetic approach. But Rivera rejected that premise, and beginning in 1911, he put forward a series of arguments in each of his works to show clearly how philosophy, metaphysics, and aesthetics had other viewpoints, of equal importance to those proposed by the Greeks and embraced by Western culture. That is the Americas' discovery: the incorporation of mestizo ideas into world art.

At this point, we need to make another conceptual distinction. To be sure, from the time of the Fauves to the return of neo-academic figurative art around 1917, European artists incorporated a great many objects from African and Asian Pacific cultures into their works, including Pre-Columbian objects some years later, with artists such as Henry Moore. Picasso came into contact with African art between 1906 and 1907, and it figured in his paintings during those years. But such pieces were not part of these artists' cultural tradition; rather, they were, as Rivera called them, "war booty":[3] their arrival in Europe was framed by colonialism and slavery. By contrast, Nahua culture (for example) came from a civilization with enormous influence in Mexico, with which there were daily social interactions, particularly during Rivera's lifetime. A great number of Mexicans—perhaps even a quarter of the population—are of Nahua descent. In the local environment, the Nahuas were not a distant, idealized society but an active (albeit subjugated) part of the country's population.

Following the War of Independence (1810–21) and the Mexican-American War (1846–47), Mexico remained connected with the formative and economic processes of the northern continent. Porfirio Díaz, who served seven terms as president of Mexico beween 1876 and 1911, saw in the historical past a foundational process indispensable to shaping the nation's viability. Within this framework, he promoted the spread of archaeology, implementing a reassessment of Pre-Columbian civilizations; to that end, he also created the Museo Nacional in Calle Moneda, which housed the largest collection of pre-conquest art in the Americas at that time, and sponsored the *Anales de Antropología*. In short, Díaz saw culture as a useful political instrument. Thus he launched a program in support of the arts, focusing especially on the applied arts, painting, and sculpture, which he presented at various world's fairs held in the United States and Europe.

The Mexican pavilions at the world's fairs during the last decades of the nineteenth century were also of great importance in establishing an approach to modernism, particularly the so-called "neo-Maya" Art Deco style. Mexican visual arts were lavishly promoted, and the works of a good number of teachers from the ENBA were presented at the fairs, where artists from several Mexican states won prestigious prizes. These events initiated a fertile exchange of ideas among North American artists, which solidified when Alfred Stieglitz and Marius de Zayas brought modernism to New York.[4]

Rivera studied under two directors during his time at the ENBA. The first was painter Santiago Rebull, who had trained at the Accademia di San Luca in Rome, and whose directorship ran from 1860 to 1902, the period in which the most pioneering modern works in Mexico were produced, marked by the liberal ideology that had deep roots within the school. I would go so far as to call these the most exceptional artistic expressions of pictorial *mestizaje* on the international art scene,

3
See *Diego Rivera: Palabras ilustres*, Vol. 1, 1886–1921, ed. Juan Rafael Coronel Rivera (Mexico City: Instituto Nacional de Bellas Artes, Museo Estudio Diego Rivera / Editorial RM, 2007), 324–26.

4
As de Zayas wrote to Alfred H. Barr Jr. in the late 1940s: "Modern art, to become, let us say, popular in New York took eleven years of hard labor, from 1908 to 1918. These years can be divided into three periods: the first under the name of Photo-Secession; the middle period, when '291,' instead of meaning only the number of a building, became a symbol, the symbol of something in which each individual person believed; and finally the period of the Modern Gallery." Marius de Zayas, *How, When, and Why Modern Art Came to New York* (Cambridge, MA: MIT Press, 1996), 1.

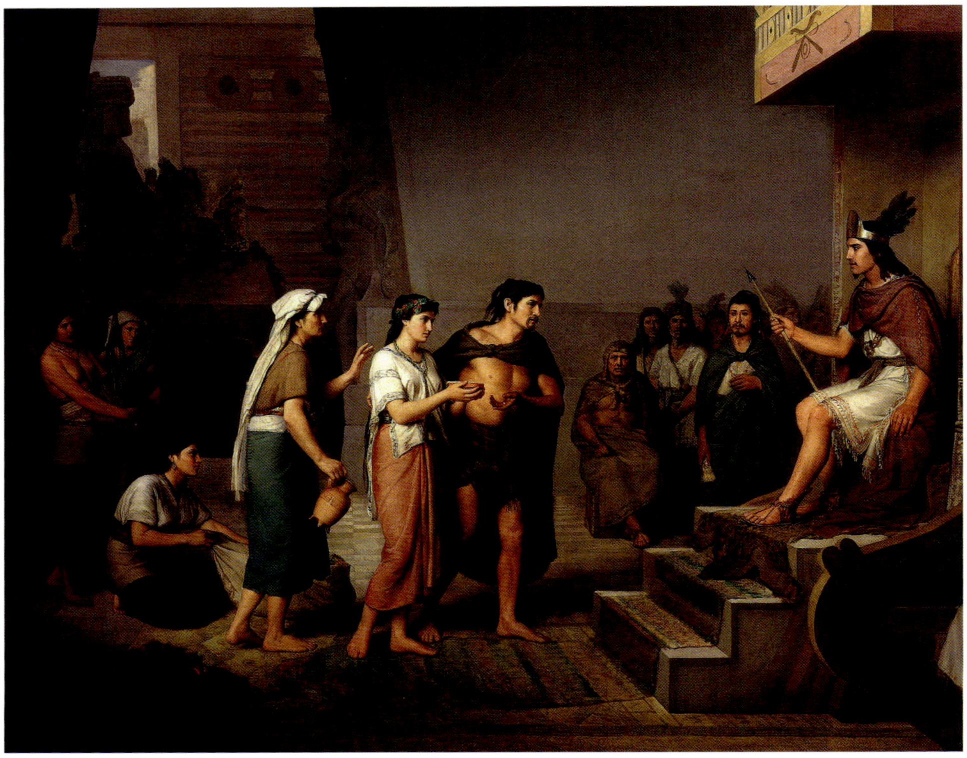

José María Obregór, ***The Discovery of Pulque***, 1869; oil on canvas, 74⅜ × 90½ in. (189 × 230 cm); Museo Nacional de Arte, INBA

ruled as it was by Western art schools. Here a group of paintings presented in the context of the academic style, and following neoclassical principles, invent the first vignettes with scenes in which the protagonists are neither Greek nor Roman but rather Nahua, Maya, and Zapotec. And I use the word *invent* (from Latin *in* + *ventus*, past participle of "to come") intentionally, to indicate something new arising from the origin—in this case, from the mestizo interior. José María Obregón's 1869 painting *The Discovery of Pulque*, which Rivera not only saw but also carefully studied, is doubtless his first modern visual source with content relating to the Pre-Columbian past. This narrative work should be associated with the "recounting" of historical episodes that Rivera proposed in his murals, beginning with those he created for the Secretaría de Educación Pública. And in 1940, in his portable fresco titled *Pan American Unity*, he poses an ideological comparison akin to Obregón's, in his nineteenth-century painting, by producing a mestizo synthesis in the figure of a mechanized Coatlicue (p. 71).

Following Rebull's death, the Catalan painter Antonio Fabrés, a Barcelona native who had studied in 1867 at the Escola de la Llotja (officially, the Escola d'Arts i Oficis de Barcelona), arrived as the new director of the ENBA. Among the many important developments under his tenure was the introduction of the Pillet drawing system,[5] learned during his studies at La Llotja—the same school where Picasso enrolled in 1895 shortly after his father, José Ruiz y Blasco, was appointed professor of figure drawing there. Interestingly, then, in spite of their five-year age difference, Picasso and Rivera both participated in the educational system proposed by La Llotja, which contributed to the similarity between their work made during their training. Though they had no firsthand contact yet, they were nevertheless already connected through their mode of education.

With his mestizo baggage, Rivera departed from Mexico for Spain; it was his first trip abroad. He arrived on February 2, 1907, and was soon following the style of realists Eduardo Chicharro y Agüera and Ignacio Zuloaga. At that time Rivera wanted to be a "correct" artist (from Latin *correctus*, past participle of *corrigere* "to put straight, reduce to order, set right"), a desire stemming from his upbringing in Mexico. Rivera's parents, in spite of their politically liberal leanings, upheld the conservative customs of the provincial middle class. Diego was raised Catholic, having been baptized (along with his twin brother, Carlos, who died in infancy), and later receiving his First Communion. At the age of ten, the young Rivera began taking night classes in drawing at the ENBA, where he excelled in producing work in the neoclassical vein. His early works show an artist who has certain personal ideas, reflected in creations such as his *Venus de Milo* (p. 77), who nevertheless executes them in conformity with the canon in a demonstration of his academic rigor. The value of this training was that it gave him a virtuosic understanding of anatomy that he would later transform into a personal vision as he incorporated his historical truth. That is what defined his style: he made

5
The first system of art in New Spain was governed by the guilds; bylaws dictated artistic production, which was viewed as a mechanically repetitive act. Following the establishment of the Academy of San Carlos, the three branches of fine art were considered as part of the liberal arts, and a teacher was free to instruct students according to his own artistic criteria. The Pillet system put an end to this freedom. As a manual that students were required to follow, it precluded the possibility of students creating their own work or cultivating a personal style, since the instructional drawings were to be copied faithfully.

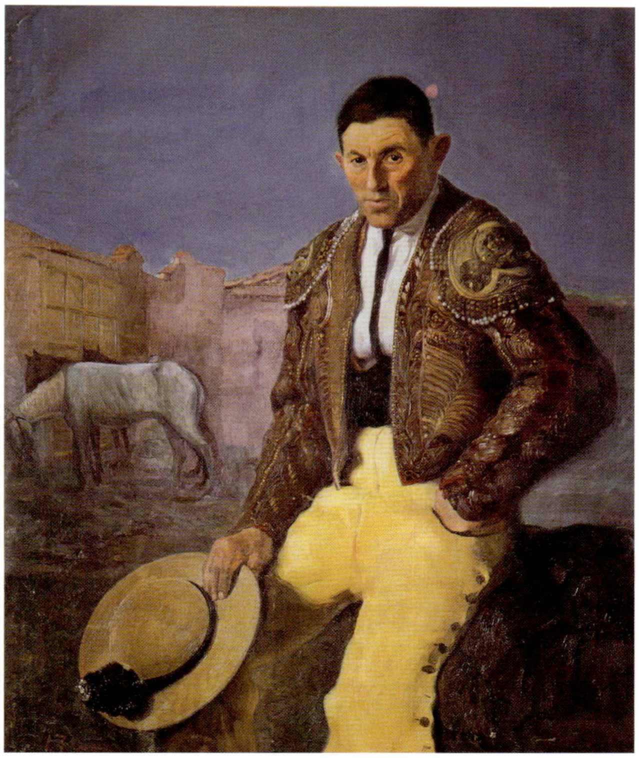

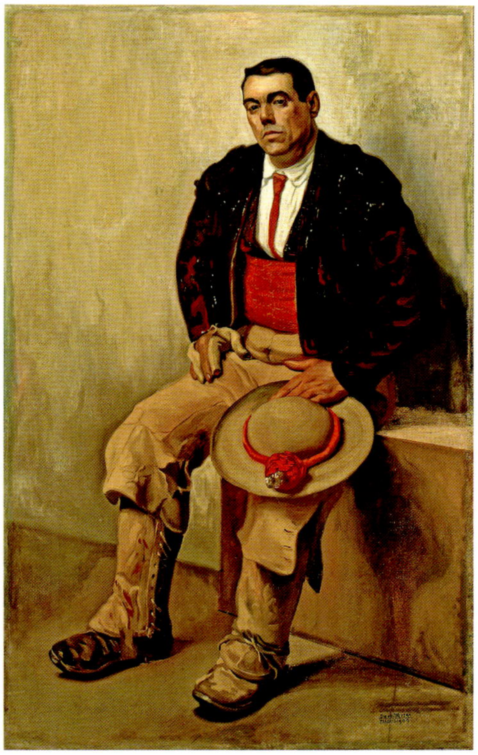

use of those resources by placing them within modern art—for example, in his 1931 drawing *Reclining Nude*, which he made in San Francisco. Without his academic verism, he would not have attained his modern reality.

Around 1908, however, having settled in Europe, the twenty-two-year-old painter suffered a crisis: he needed to divorce himself from Spanish bourgeois realist art and prove himself within the contemporary context. Painter José Moya del Pino, who was born in Spain and later became a U.S. citizen, recounted meeting Rivera (along with another Mexican artist, Ángel Záraga, in Madrid): "He was enthusiastic about the Impressionists and was a friend of Renoir.... We used to go to our cafe all the time and discuss art, and Diego appeared at that cafe, and we all had much discussion because some of the Spanish painters had been in Paris. They didn't like Cézanne at that time."[6] The group of artists who were not fond of Cézanne included Chicharro and Zuloaga.

The foregoing shows that, however unconsciously, Rivera was still trying to honor his origins; indeed, he would acknowledge this years later:

> My contact with Spanish art, however, affected me in the most unfortunate way. The qualities inherent in my first works in Mexico were gradually strangled by the pedestrian Spanish skill in painting. Surely the most insipid and trivial of my paintings were those that I did in Spain in 1907 and 1908.... I have often tried to find an explanation for the incongruence between my understanding of life and my manner of responding to it in this period of my painting. Probably the timidity that is natural in youth was one factor. But more powerful, although I barely realized it at the time, was my Mexican–Latin American inferiority complex, my reverence toward European history and culture.[7]

Here we clearly see the distinction between the culture of the Americas and their historical position, on the one hand, and European culture and its origins in classical antiquity, on the other.

In the first months of 1909, Rivera set out for France and settled in Paris, where he would live for the next two years. Between 1907 and 1921, he traveled only once to his homeland, from September 1910 to April

6
José Moya del Pino, interview by Mary Fuller McChesney, September 10, 1964, Smithsonian Institution Archives of American Art. Consulted online: www.aaa.si.edu/files/resources/OHProgram/PDF/moyade64.pdf.

7
Diego Rivera: Palabras ilustres, 212, 234.

LEFT Ignacio Zuloaga, ***Chiribiqui***, n.d.; oil on canvas, 51⅛ × 43¼ in. (130 × 110 cm); private collection

RIGHT Diego Rivera, ***The Bullfighter***, 1909; oil on canvas, 46 × 44½ in. (177 × 113 cm); Collection Museo Dolores Olmedo, Mexico City

1911, during which he was confronted with an explosive social and cultural setting. On November 20, 1910, the Mexican Revolution was declared. Rivera did not get involved, since his revolution was personal and internal; he was focused on his self-transformation. What sustained him at that moment was difference, the Other—the original history of Mexico that had no links to the West, as we shall see.

Two of Mexico's social characteristics during the first half of the twentieth century were the physical displacement of the native peoples and the enthronement of indigenous cultures as the great source of the mestizo paradigm—contradictory acts that dispossessed native peoples of their land while recognizing these same peoples for their cultural significance in the constitution of Mexican identity. War dislodged entire communities from their ancestral lands, and many indigenous people sought refuge in the outskirts of cities. For the first time, these hundreds of thousands of individuals—with their different languages, clothing, and gods—made themselves known in an emphatic way. Their presence in the modern cities was as unequivocal as the circularity of the enigmatic Sun Stone—that petrified universe that strikes us with its mysterious words.

Since his adolescence, Rivera had a clear notion of what would eventually be called *indigenismo* (indigenism) in the 1940s. As he wrote in 1911 from Amecameca to his then wife, Russian painter Angelina Beloff, shortly before he returned to Europe:

> When I was assembling the *chassis* [stretchers] and preparing the canvases here, I took a short walk in these mountains, which are the highest in my country [Iztaccíhuatl and Popocatépetl]. There are many enormous trees, very old, covered with parasitic plants that flower in balls of thorns or hang in bundles like old fathers' beards: pagan trees. I don't remember whether I've already told you about this place, but it contains a sanctuary with a recumbent figure of Jesus called "el Señor del Sacromonte" (*du montsacré* [of the Holy Mount]); here you can see the mixture of extreme Catholicism and Indian paganism that I mentioned in describing the people of my country.[8]

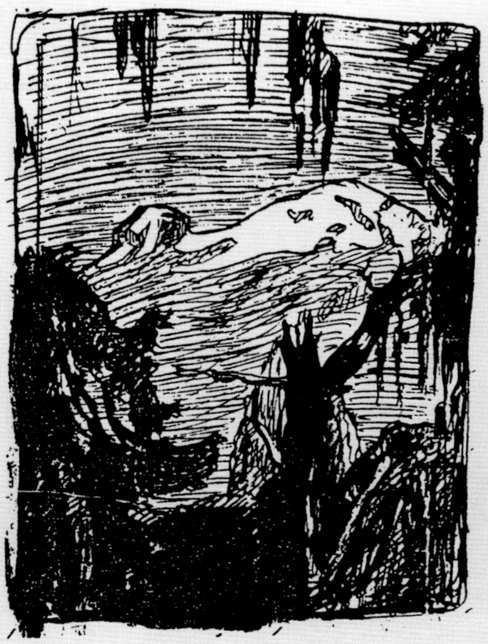

Boceto enviado por Diego Rivera a Angelina Beloff en esta carta. Paradero desconocido, foto cortesia de *Excélsior/Plural*.

Notice that he twice uses the term *pagan* (from Latin *paganus*, "villager," from *pagus*, "country people; province, rural district"). Following the decriminalization of Christianity under the Roman emperor Constantine, "pagan" gradually took on the meaning of those who continued to practice old religions and were therefore outside the bounds of the Christian community. Rivera, in referring to "pagan trees," alludes to the *ahuehuetes* (Montezuma cypress) endemic to the zone of Amecameca, and which the *tlatoani* (king) and poet Nezahualcóyotl referred to in his verses. By referring to them this way, the painter associates them with their Pre-Columbian origins, turning them into metaphor. In this context, his allusion to the rites performed at the Sacromonte illustrates that he was perfectly aware of the cultural syncretism that situates Mexicans as mestizos.

Rivera was at a creative crossroads; his dilemma was whether to follow the figurative norms of Spanish art at

8
Rivera (March 1, 1911) to Beloff, in *Encuentros con Diego Rivera*, ed. Guadalupe Rivera Marín and Juan Rafael Coronel Rivera (Mexico City: Siglo XXI, 1993), 80.

Diego Rivera, sketch sent to Angelina Beloff from Amecameca, March 1, 1911

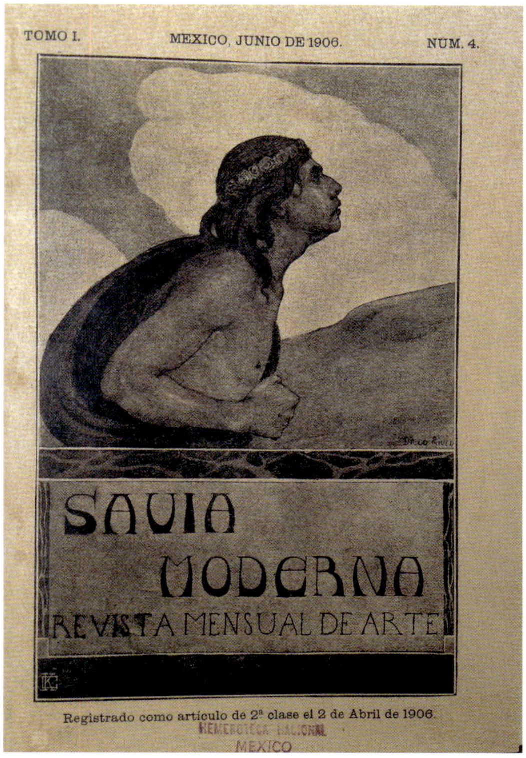

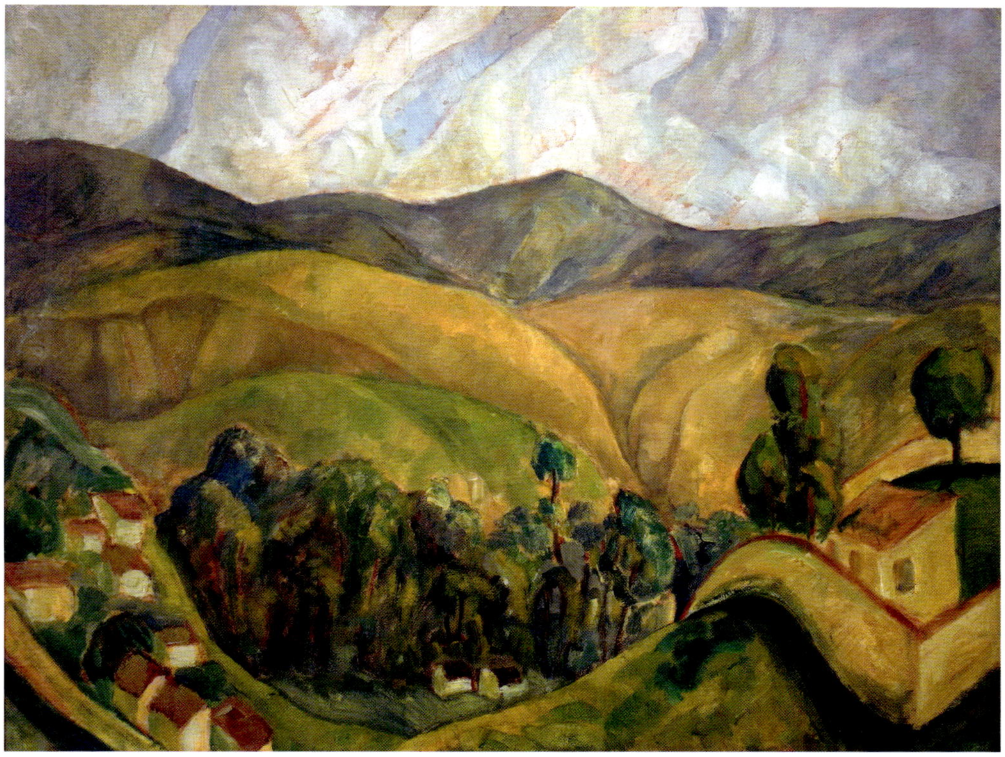

the beginning of the century—for example, the realism of Zuloaga and Chicharro—or to fully embrace the modern tendencies dictated by the avant-garde of Montparnasse. To resolve this question, which had concerned him since 1908, he went to Amecameca, outside of Mexico City. As a community made up of mestizos and indigenous people with no connection to the Eurocentric cultural trends of the period, no place could be more "eccentric." Was Rivera hiding out there? Returning to his origins? Was his stay akin to the forty days and forty nights that Jesus spent in the desert? No doubt he came up against the mestizo devil—so tame, at least in appearance.

Having recently started studying Cézanne and incorporating his aesthetics into his own work, Rivera produced a series of at least four paintings over three weeks in the countryside. He described one of them to Beloff in a sketch that captures the old *ahuehuetes* framing Iztaccíhuatl. The drawing is rendered in a Symbolist manner, which by then was outmoded; the final, painted version is unfortunately unknown. Significantly, the sketch recovers Pre-Columbian allegories and the indigenous landscape to incorporate them in modern art via an intelligent pictorial metaphor. The "pagan trees" that he idolizes—as a pagan himself—serve here as a reference to Popocatépetl;[9] thus Rivera incorporated him in modern art, with his very personal point of view. In this work he suddenly and unequivocally returns to the mythology he had abandoned since 1906 (when he designed the cover of the magazine *Savia Moderna*) but kept up his sleeve. Rivera awakens. His ideas rise up.

Only one painting from the Amecameca series is presently known: *Contreras Canyon Landscape*, which came to light in 2006, was painted between 1910 and 1911 and is housed in the collection of the Frida Kahlo Museum in Coyoacán. Rivera stipulated that the boxes holding his and Kahlo's private collections remain unopened for fifteen years following his death, which occurred in 1957; in fact, they were not opened for forty-nine years. This oil on canvas is the crucial piece for understanding how Rivera integrated his work into the program of the Parisian avant-garde, as well as for clarifying his historical premises, which proved extraordinary owing to their symbolic ideology. He produced his first modern attestation in a mestizo region that in those days still maintained indigenous customs; indeed, some of its residents still

9
For more on the legend of Popocatépetl and Iztaccíhuatl, see en.wikipedia.org/wiki/ Popocatépetl_and_Iztaccíhuatl.

LEFT Diego Rivera, cover illustration for ***Savia Moderna***, July 1906

RIGHT Diego Rivera, ***Contreras Canyon Landscape***, 1910–11; oil on canvas, dimensions unknown; Frida Kahlo Museum, Coyoacán, Mexico

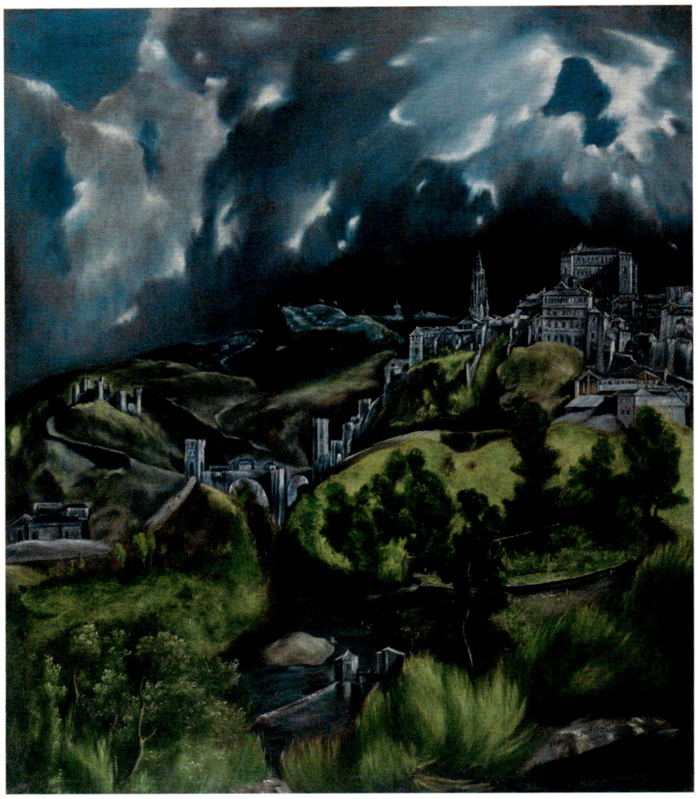

spoke Nahuatl. Clearly, Contreras was not part of Western modernity. Might Rivera have chosen this approach as an artistic postulate against the grain, intentionally challenging Western precepts?

In *Contreras Canyon Landscape*, Rivera demonstrated his ideological course; he then spent the next six years glossing each of the ideas elaborated there, manifesting the clarity of his ideas. His writings contain many examples, the first observation being a paraphrase from El Greco. Rivera wrote to Beloff from Madrid on September 18, 1910, shortly before returning to Mexico:

> I sat on a bench beside the door [outside the Velázquez gallery at the Prado].... Across from the bench hung the El Greco paintings *The Ascension of Jesus, The Crucifixion, Pentecost,* and *The Baptism of Christ*.... I was somewhat crushed [French: *anéanti*] by my experience with Velázquez [who had ceased to be surprising] and looked forward with my eyes, and inward with my spirit, and little by little I was seeing ahead as well,... and then my spirit saw beyond, to where one can see through the symphonies of colors and emotions, and through those depths that are lace woven with mysteries,... the paintings of El Greco.[10]

As this makes clear, Rivera always asserted that his foray into the Parisian avant-garde came about through El Greco. Before those works, Rivera not only experienced an aesthetic epiphany but also found the key to his own pictorial path at that moment. Most striking here is his allusion to the "symphonies of colors," a Platonic idea that he would use in his first mural, *Creation* (1921–1923). In comparing Rivera's *Contreras Canyon Landscapes* and El Greco's *View of Toledo*, we can see how Rivera echoes the manner of painting the sky in his work. (It is worth noting that Zuloaga reintroduced El Greco–style firmaments during his so-called black Spain period, between 1898 and 1914.)

But Rivera went far beyond that. The painting reveals a strong influence of Cézanne, which immediately links it to the initial investigations of Cubism that took place between 1907 and 1909; Rivera thereby defied both his teacher Chicharro as well as Zuloaga, relinquishing that adolescent academic "correctness," the link to his father, and in doing so continued to discover his own conviction as an artist. There is nothing like watching an artist gird his loins: it is a lesson in ethics. The cultural creations that have changed the course of art have not been bound to academia or to the trends set by museums and their patrons or, of course, by the market. Rather, they emerge from the internal search for a philosophical-artistic presentation of that moment of human life. In *Contreras Canyon Landscapes* we observe Rivera breaking through and even experimenting, albeit somewhat timidly, with analytical Cubism. This experimentation is evident by comparison to his works that are formally Cubist beginning in 1913, where he likewise presents a cultural counterproposal, as in *Still Life with Gray Bowl* (p. 111) or *Zapatista Landscape* (p. 153), whose trees are the *ahuehuetes* of Contreras and Amecameca.

10 *Encuentros con Diego Rivera*, 69.

El Greco (Doménikos Theotokopoulos), ***View of Toledo***, 1607; oil on canvas, 47⅝ × 42⅞ in. (121 × 109 cm); The Metropolitan Museum of Art, H. O. Havemeyer Collection, Bequest of Mrs. H. O. Havemeyer, 1929

Visiting museums during his trip to Mexico, Rivera saw his country's works with fresh eyes. Imagine his shock upon entering the Museo Nacional and its gallery of monoliths, after having lived for three years in Europe and visiting some of its greatest institutions, including the Musée d'Ethnographie du Trocadéro. During this time, he recovered his ancestral past. Moreover, now that he was aware of the influence of sub-Saharan African art on modern art, the association must have been immediate. Here was something that had not yet been taken into account: some hundred non-Western civilizations, erudite cultures as important as any other that needed to be included in modern art. Herein resides the great philosophical difference between Rivera and Picasso: the Mexican painter's works were not conceptions executed from a Western stance, as was the case with the Spaniard. Rivera was a mestizo and included, in each canvas, the blood that ran through his veins: the "exotic." This sudden realization befell him like a hailstorm to the unconscious. As Rivera wrote to Beloff after visiting the Museo Nacional with architect Jesús T. Acevedo:

> I think Acevedo was right, although I don't know why it seems so sad to me. He said...that when an artist of today turns to the source of primitive art to create nationalisms, he restricts his means and in the end remains outside his time and produces a work that is artificial, even though it can be very interesting. I believe that the important thing is for me to be sincere with myself and not be afraid of my own feelings, whatever they may be; of course, this path is the most uncomfortable of all, but for me, it's the one I want to make my own, as long as I have the strength to follow it.[11]

And he followed that path until his death.

[11] Ibid., 82.

ANTIQUITY AND THE AVANT-GARDE IN THE UNITED STATES

Rivera returned to Paris in the summer of 1911. Beloff recalled him opening his suitcases to pull out a series of Mexican "artifacts": colorful serapes, whimsically woven grass mats, and some Tehuana blouses, one of which he incorporated into his 1914 painting *The Alarm Clock*. In opening these suitcases full of souvenirs, Rivera was unpacking his idiosyncrasy, his identity. He brought with him what he had not dared to present to the world until then. The act of merging these objects with his work signaled the Parisian avant-garde's recognition of the cultural manifestations of the ancient Amerindian peoples. I specify "the Parisian avant-garde" because other artists in Mexico, such as Saturnino Herrán, were tackling this subject. Thus we see how the recovery of aboriginal aesthetics took place in two different modern contexts, which underlines the existence of different modern periods and the fallacy of considering European thought alone to be the norm. This was Rivera's great proposal and his essential contribution to the theory of art. The focus on a single modern vision has stymied any true study of the processes of international art, not just the aesthetic causes put forth in Montparnasse. In this regard, it is worth noting that for many years the modern art of postrevolutionary Mexico was called "the Mexican school"; in a certain sense the name is apt, because the philosophy that it proposed was not Western but mestizo, which constitutes a vast difference.

During this same period (1912–13), Rivera struck up a friendship with the group of U.S. artists based in Paris, including Stanton Macdonald-Wright and Morgan Russell, the developers of the color theory known as Synchromism. Synchromist works were among the first abstract paintings produced by U.S. artists. The theory was related to Cubism as well as to Robert and Sonia Delaunay's Orphism. Macdonald-Wright and Russell visited Rivera's studio a few times, after he had already garnered a certain prestige and was forming his friendships with Modigliani and Picasso. On one of their visits, they brought painter Thomas Hart Benton, whom Rivera did not like because he found him too opinionated. Nevertheless, Rivera would become a central presence in the lives of all these artists. In the 1930s Macdonald-Wright moved to California and produced a series of murals for the Santa Monica Public Library that was greatly influenced by Rivera; in fact, he continued his career in this vein, abandoning abstraction. The antagonism between Rivera and Benton has been discussed elsewhere,[12] and while their enmity persisted, Rivera's influence on Benton was definitive. The same was true of his influence on Stuart Davis, who produced a portable mural titled *New York Mural* (1932), in which a giant serpent symbolizes Chinese culture, in a Riveran manner. Each of these artists tapped into Rivera's historical vision—that is, the modern model of recasting ancient culture to incorporate into their works as Rivera had done—thereby establishing a pan-American artistic canon.

The *ahuehuete* trees in Rivera's paintings, mentioned above, are well known within Cubism, as they initiated the break with Picasso. As Beloff wrote:

> Picasso and Diego were good friends for a long time. He would come visit us, and we would also go to his studio, where he'd show us his paintings. He was starting to become famous, and once when we met him at a cafe, his girlfriend (Eva Gouel) told us, with admiration and a touch of pride, "You know, Pablo has sold paintings to the Russian millionaire [Sergei] Shchukin's museum, and he is already getting to be known."... Diego had a falling out with Picasso as a result of an incident around painting. At that time [1915], Diego was painting Cubist landscapes and interpreting trees through a procedure that he had invented. One day he went to see Picasso, and looking at the canvases turned against the wall he saw a landscape painted using the same procedure. Picasso told him that it was a painting he had done some time ago. Diego then mischievously ran a finger over the painting, which left it smeared. The paint was fresh. Picasso took offense, and that was how their friendship ended.[13]

The split with Picasso was the prelude to Rivera's return to the Americas. His first solo show there had been in Mexico City, at his former academy, the ENBA, on November 20, 1910. On that occasion, he exhibited figurative and postimpressionist works, displaying his "correct" side. Rivera's second show, however, was presented in New York, from October 2 to October 21, 1916. His friend Marius de Zayas, from Veracruz, had visited him in Paris in 1915 and invited him to exhibit individually the following year at the Modern Gallery in New York. The importance of this show, *Exhibition of Paintings by Diego M. Rivera and Mexican Pre-Conquest Art*, has not been sufficiently recognized; it marks the beginning of the relocation of the modern art hegemony from Paris to New York, accepting the diaspora of the modern while simultaneously opening the door to the conceptualization of the murals that Rivera would create in the United States beginning in 1930. The artist introduced at this exhibition was not a European surrounded by African art—although such shows were also held at the Modern Gallery—but rather a mestizo, alongside the pieces that situated him as such. As Antonio Saborit relates:

> [The Modern Gallery] announced an exhibition of "Mexican art before the Conquest," and Zayas published his essay on the black art of Africa and its influence on modern art. Who in New York was interested in buying Amerindian art? We know with all certainty, for example, that Walter Conrad Arensberg [an art critic, poet, and collector] began his own collection of pre-Hispanic pieces (today as impressive as it is forgotten) in 1915, thanks to Zayas's mediation, and that the lawyer John Quinn, in addition to buying *Le Samaritain*, by Diego

12 See, for example, Justin Wolff, *Thomas Hart Benton: A Life* (New York: Farrar, Straus and Giroux, 2012), 237–38.

13 Angelina Beloff, *Memorias* (Mexico City: Universidad Nacional Autónoma de México, 2000), 47–48.

Rivera, for $200, later acquired an onyx mask from Cholula for $250 and an Aztec idol made of volcanic rock for $130.[14]

At this time Rivera had already begun incorporating pieces of folk art into his Cubist works, such as *Portrait of Jacques Lipchitz* (1914), and also made references to Pre-Columbian art in paintings such as *Young Man with a Pen* (1915). Western modernism—beginning with the Fauves, who presented their first works in 1905, up to the Surrealist exile spurred by World War II—was dominated by the Parisian avant-garde, as well as those in Central European cities such as Vienna and Berlin. However, in 1921 a group of artists, the majority of them Mexican, imposed the first modern directive generated outside the European circuit: muralism. That occurrence marked the globalization of art and the regionalization of trends in art. Several of these artists—such as José Clemente Orozco and Diego Rivera—produced some of their most visible works in the United States, planting the seeds that would sprout into a pluralistic art and lay the foundations for today's globalization of contemporary art. That global phenomenon began precisely in this artistic landscape, as these mestizos painted walls in the United States.

Rivera began his murals in Detroit on April 2, 1932. There he created *Detroit Industry* (pp. 70 and 94), a pictorial ensemble that constitutes an artistic event of the same significance as Picasso's groundbreaking *Les Demoiselles d'Avignon* in 1907 (p. 131). For the first time, this continental region succeeded in deploying a mestizo theory of universal art. The frescoes were the most important artwork of their day. In Rivera's painting, we can see a mechanized Coatlicue; a comic strip hero, Dick Tracy;[15] and the workers building the capitalism of that time, preparing to take command: the new American wonder.

Translated by ROSE VEKONY

14
Antonio Saborit, *Una visita a Marius de Zayas* (Xalapa, Mexico: Instituto Veracruzano de la Cultura, Universidad Veracruzana, 2009), 69, 70.

15
Dick Tracy makes cameo appearance in a crowd scene on the South Wall.

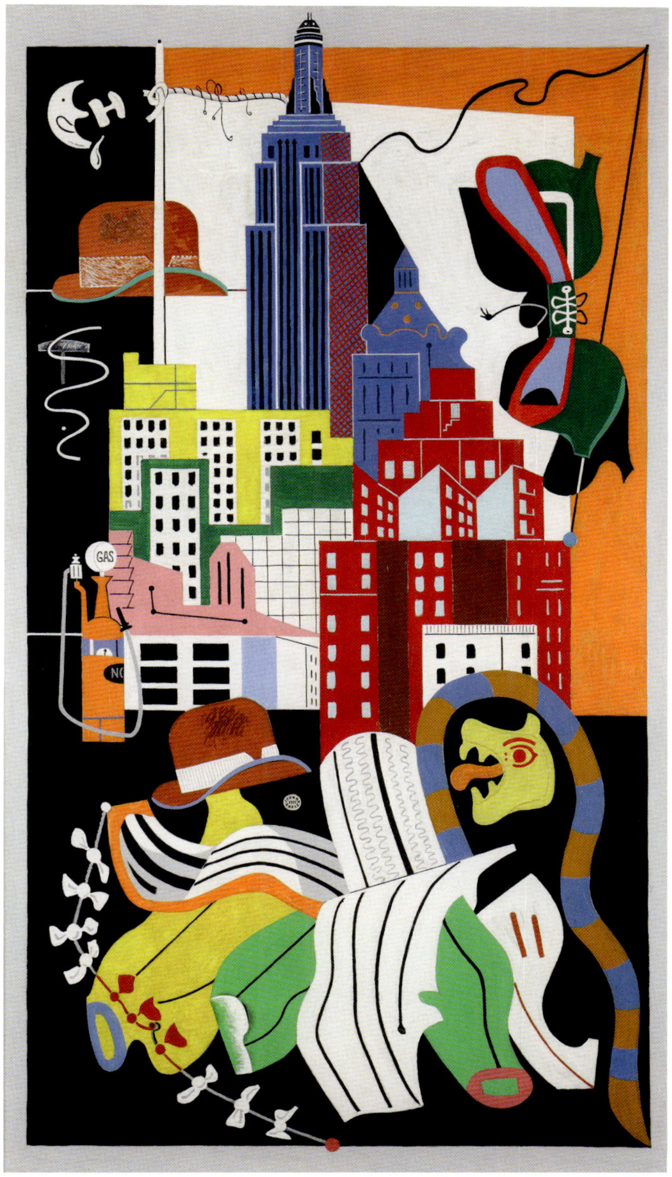

Stuart Davis, ***New York Mural***, 1932; oil on canvas, 84 x 48 in.; Norton Museum of Art, West Palm Beach, Florida, Purchase, the R.H. Norton Trust, 64.17

CHECKLIST OF THE EXHIBITION

NOTE TO THE READER

Dates for works by Picasso include month (and day) when this information is available. Titles of works by Picasso and Rivera have been given in English, with original French or Spanish titles following; descriptive titles such as *Study*, *Self-Portrait*, etc., have for the most part been given in English only. For dimensions, height precedes width precedes depth. Checklist for the Los Angeles County Museum of Art exhibition is final as of July 2016; for a complete list of works exhibited at the Museo del Palacio de Bellas Artes, Mexico City, please consult their forthcoming publication, *Picasso y Rivera: Conversaciones a través del tiempo.*

PABLO PICASSO

(Spanish, active France, 1881–1973)

Academic Study: Torso, 1892–93
Charcoal and Conté crayon on paper
20½ × 14½ in. (52.1 × 36.7 cm)
Museu Picasso Barcelona,
gift of Pablo Ruiz-Picasso, 1970
P. 75

Academic Study: Foot, 1894
Charcoal and Conté crayon on paper
13⅛ × 19⅝ in. (33.2 × 49.7 cm)
Museu Picasso Barcelona,
gift of Pablo Ruiz-Picasso, 1970
P. 97

Venus de Milo, 1895–96
Charcoal and traces of black pencil on paper
24⅜ × 18¾ in. (61.8 × 47.7 cm)
Museu Picasso Barcelona,
gift of Pablo Ruiz-Picasso, 1970
P. 76

Portrait of Sebastià Junyer Vidal, June 1903
Oil on canvas
Overall: 49¾ × 37 in. (126.7 × 94 cm);
FRAME: 63 × 49½ (160 × 125.7 cm)
Los Angeles County Museum of Art,
David E. Bright Bequest
P. 101

Self-Portrait, 1906
Oil on canvas
25⅝ × 21¼ in. (65 × 54 cm)
Musée Picasso Paris
P. 83

Self-Portrait with a Palette
(Autoportrait à la palette), 1906
Oil on canvas
36³⁄₁₆ × 28⅞ in. (91.9 × 73.3 cm)
Philadelphia Museum of Art,
A. E. Gallatin Collection, 1950
P. 29

Study for *Self-Portrait with a Palette*
(Autoportrait à la palette), Fall 1906
Graphite pencil on white laid paper
12½ × 19 in. (31.5 × 47.5 cm)
Musée Picasso Paris
[MPBA ONLY]
P. 294

Landscape at Céret (Paysage de Céret), Summer 1911
Oil on canvas
25¾ × 19⅞ in. (65.4 × 50.5 cm)
Solomon R. Guggenheim Museum, Solomon R. Guggenheim
Founding Collection, by gift 37.538
P. 103

The Poet (Le poète), 1912
Oil on canvas
23⅝ × 18⅞ in. (60 × 48 cm)
Kunstmuseum Basel, gift of Maja Sacher-Stehlin,
deposited by the commune of inhabitants
of the canton Basel-Stadt, 1967
P. 106

Student with Newspaper (L'etudiant au journal), 1913–14
Oil and sand on canvas
28¾ × 23⅜ in. (73 × 59.5 cm)
The Metropolitan Museum of Art,
promised gift from the Leonard A. Lauder Collection
P. 105

Man Leaning on a Table (Homme accoudé à une table), 1914
Watercolor and ink wash on paper
SHEET: 12¼ × 9¼ in. (31.1 × 23.5 cm)
Patricia Phelps de Cisneros Collection
P. 110

Man with a Pipe (Homme au chapeau
melon assis dans un fauteuil), 1915
Oil on canvas
51¼ × 35¼ in. (130.2 × 89.5 cm)
Art Institute of Chicago, gift of Mr. Leigh B. Block
in memory of Albert D. Lasker
P. 108

Études, 1920
Oil on canvas
39⅜ × 31⅞ in. (100 × 81 cm)
Musée Picasso Paris
P. 59

Three Women at the Spring
(Trois femmes à la fontaine), Summer 1921
Oil on canvas
80¼ × 68½ in. (203.9 × 174 cm)
The Museum of Modern Art, New York,
gift of Mr. and Mrs. Allan D. Emil
P. 115

The Source (La Source), Summer 1921
Crayon on canvas
60⅜ × 79⅛ in. (153.5 × 201 cm)
Musée Picasso Paris
P. 121

The Pipes of Pan (La Flûte de Pan), Summer 1923
Oil on canvas
80 3/4 × 68 1/2 in. (205 × 174 cm)
Musée Picasso Paris
P. 116

Woman in Blue Veil (La femme au voile bleu), Fall 1923
Oil on canvas
39 1/2 × 32 in. (100.3 × 81.3 cm)
Los Angeles County Museum of Art,
Mr. and Mrs. George Gard De Sylva Collection
P. 123

Studio with Plaster Head
(Atelier avec tête et bras de plâtre), June 1925
Oil on canvas
38 5/8 × 51 5/8 in. (97.9 × 131.1 cm)
Museum of Modern Art, New York, Purchase
P. 183

Running Minotaur (Minotaure courant), 1928
Oil on canvas
64 × 51 1/8 in. (162.5 × 130 cm)
Musée Picasso Paris
P. 125

Death of Orpheus (Mort d'Orphée), 1931
From *Les Métamorphoses*, published by Albert Skira,
Lausanne, 1931 (INSERTED BETWEEN PP. 273–74)
Etching
SHEET: 12 1/4 × 8 3/4 in. (31.2 × 22.3 cm)
Museum of Fine Arts, Boston,
Bequest of W. G. Russell Allen
P. 201

Heads (Têtes), 1931
From *Les Métamorphoses*, published by Albert Skira,
Lausanne, 1931 (PP. 61–62)
Folded leaf with etching and text
SHEET (FOLDED): 8 3/4 × 12 5/16 in (22.3 × 31.2 cm)
Museum of Fine Arts Boston,
Bequest of W. G. Russell Allen, 1963
P. 199

Partial Female Figure (Fragment de corps de femme), 1931
From *Les Métamorphoses*, published by Albert Skira,
Lausanne, 1931 (PP. 343–44)
Folded leaf with etching and text
SHEET (FOLDED): 8 3/4 × 12 5/16 in (22.3 × 31.2 cm)
Museum of Fine Arts Boston, Bequest of W. G. Russell Allen
P. 199

Struggle between Tereus and His Sister-in-Law Philomela
(Lutte entre Térée et sa belle-soeur Philomèle), 1931
From *Les Métamorphoses*, published by Albert Skira,
Lausanne, 1931
(INSERTED BETWEEN PP. 144–45)
Etching
SHEET: 12 5/16 × 8 3/4 in. (31.3 × 22.1 cm)
Museum of Fine Arts Boston, Bequest of W. G. Russell Allen
P. 200

Vertume Pursues Pomona for Her Love
(Vertumne poursuit Pomone de son amour), 1931
From *Les Métamorphoses*, published by Albert Skira,
Lausanne, 1931 (INSERTED BETWEEN PP. 356–57)
Etching
SHEET: 12 5/16 × 8 3/4 in. (31.2 × 22.3 cm)
Museum of Fine Arts Boston, Bequest of W. G. Russell Allen
P. 200

Hercules Kills the Centaur Nessus
(Hercule tue la Centaure Nessus), 1931
From *Les Métamorphoses*, published by Albert Skira,
Lausanne, 1931 (INSERTED BETWEEN PP. 224–25)
Etching
SHEET: 12 5/16 × 8 3/4 in. (31.2 × 22.3 cm)
Museum of Fine Arts Boston, Bequest of W. G. Russell Allen
P. 202

Minotaur Caressing the Hand of a Sleeping Woman
with His Muzzle (Minotaure caressant une dormeuse),
June 18, 1933
From the **Vollard Suite**
Copper etching on Montval laid paper
SHEET: 13 3/8 × 17 1/2 in. (34 × 44.5 cm);
PLATE: 11 3/4 × 14 5/8 in. (30 × 37 cm)
Private collection, Aspen, CO
P. 53

Minotaur, Drinker, and Women
(Minotaure, buveur et femmes), June 18, 1933
From the **Vollard Suite**
Copper etching on Montval laid paper
SHEET: 13 3/8 × 17 1/2 in. (34 × 44.5 cm);
PLATE: 11 3/4 × 14 3/8 in. (29.8 × 36.5 cm)
Private collection, Aspen, CO
P. 211

Minotaur Holding Goblet and a Young Woman
(Minotaure, une coupe à la main, et jeune femme),
May 17, 1933
From the **Vollard Suite**
Copper etching on Montval laid paper
SHEET: 13 3/8 × 17 3/8 in. (34 × 44 cm);
PLATE: 7 5/8 × 10 1/4 in. (19.4 × 26 cm)
Private collection, Aspen, CO
P. 47

Sculptor Reclining before Nude
(Sculpteur au repos avec Marie-Thérèse et sa
représentation en Venus pudique), March 27, 1933
From the **Vollard Suite**
Copper etching on Montval laid paper
SHEET: 17 1/2 × 13 3/8 in. (44.5 × 34 cm);
PLATE: 10 1/2 × 7 5/8 in. (26.7 × 19.3 cm)
Private collection, Aspen, CO
P. 207

Woman Contemplating Sleeping Minotaur
(Minotaure endormi contemplé par une femme), May 18, 1933
From the **Vollard Suite**
Copper etching on Montval laid paper
SHEET: 13 3/8 × 17 1/2 in. (34 × 44.5 cm);
PLATE: 7 5/8 × 10 1/2 in. (19.4 × 26.8 cm)
Private collection, Aspen, CO
P. 203

Model, Sculpture Viewed from the Rear,
and Bearded Head (Modèle accroupi, sculpture de dos
et tête barbue), May 5, 1933
From the **Vollard Suite**
Copper etching on Montval laid paper
SHEET: 17 1/2 × 13 3/8 in. (44.5 × 34 cm);
PLATE: 10 1/2 × 7 5/8 in. (26.7 × 19.3 cm)
Private collection, Aspen, CO
NOT ILLUSTRATED

Sculptor Reclining before Small Torso
(Le repos du sculpteur devant le petit torse), March 30, 1933
From the **Vollard Suite**
Copper etching on Montval laid paper
SHEET: 13 3/8 × 17 1/2 in. (34 × 44.5 cm);
PLATE: 7 11/16 × 10 1/2 in. (19.6 × 26.7 cm)
Private collection, Aspen, CO
P. 205

Sculptor and Model Admiring a Sculpted Head
(Sculpteur et modèle admirant une tête sculptée),
March 31, 1933
Copper etching on Montval laid paper
SHEET: 17 1/2 × 13 3/8 in. (44.5 × 34 cm)
PLATE: 10 1/2 × 7 3/4 in. (26.7 × 19.7 cm)
Private collection, Aspen, CO
P. 207

Model and Large Sculpted Head
(Modèle et grande tête sculptée), April 1, 1933
From the **Vollard Suite**
Copper etching on Montval laid paper
SHEET: 17 5/16 × 13 3/8 in. (44 × 34 cm);
PLATE: 10 1/2 × 7 5/8 in. (26.7 × 19.3 cm)
Private collection, Aspen, CO
P. 209

Vanquished Minotaur (Minotaure vaincu), May 29, 1933
From the Vollard Suite
Copper etching on Montval laid paper
SHEET: 13 3/8 × 17 1/2 in. (34 × 44.5 cm);
PLATE: 7 5/8 × 10 9/16 in. (19.3 × 26.9 cm)
Private collection, Aspen, CO
P. 39

Dying Minotaur (Minotaure mourant), May 30, 1933
From the Vollard Suite
Copper etching on Montval laid paper
SHEET: 13 3/8 × 17 1/2 in. (34 × 44.5 cm);
PLATE: 7 11/16 × 10 9/16 in. (19.6 × 26.8 cm)
Private collection, Aspen, CO
P. 39

Sculptor at Rest before a Centaur and a Woman (Le repos du sculpteur), May 31, 1933
From the Vollard Suite
Copper etching on Montval laid paper
SHEET: 13 3/8 × 17 1/2 in. (34 × 44.5 cm);
PLATE: 7 5/8 × 10 9/16 in. (19.4 × 26.8 cm)
Private collection, Aspen, CO
P. 204

Blind Minotaur Led by a Young Girl (Minotaure aveugle guide par une fille aux fleurs), September 22, 1934
From the Vollard Suite
Copper etching on Montval laid paper
SHEET: 13 3/8 × 17 11/16 in. (34 × 45 cm);
PLATE: 9 15/16 × 13 11/16 in. (25.2 × 34.8 cm)
Private collection, Aspen, CO
P. 42

Blind Minotaur Led by a Young Girl at Night (Minotaure aveugle guide par une fillette dans une nuit étoilée), November 1934
From the Vollard Suite
Copper etching on Montval laid paper
SHEET: 13 3/8 × 17 11/16 in. (34 × 45 cm);
PLATE: 9 3/4 × 13 11/16 in. (24.7 × 34.7 cm)
Private collection, Aspen, CO
P. 215

Masked Characters and Bird-Woman (Homme au masque de Minotaure et femme au masque de sculpteur), November 19, 1934
From the Vollard Suite
Copper etching and aquatint on Montval laid paper
SHEET: 13 3/8 × 17 11/16 in. (34 × 45 cm);
PLATE: 9 13/16 × 13 11/16 in. (24.9 × 34.8 cm)
Private collection, Aspen, CO
P. 213

Faun Uncovering a Woman (Faune dévoilant une dormeuse), June 12, 1936
From the Vollard Suite
Copper etching and aquatint on Montval laid paper
SHEET: 13 3/8 × 17 5/16 in. (34 × 44 cm);
PLATE: 12 1/2 × 16 7/16 in. (31.7 × 41.7 cm)
Private collection, Aspen, CO
P. 46

Blind Minotaur Led by a Young Girl (Minotaure aveugle conduit par une petite fille), 1934
Gouache, watercolor, brush, and ink
PLATE: 13 3/4 × 20 1/8 in. (35 × 51 cm)
Private collection, Aspen, CO
P. 214

Woman Bullfighter: Last Kiss (Femme Torero: Dernier Baiser), 1934
Etching
PLATE: 19 3/8 × 27 1/2 in. (49.1 × 69.7 cm);
SHEET: 22 1/4 × 30 in. (56.5 × 76.2 cm)
Los Angeles County Museum of Art,
purchased with funds provided by Dr. Richard E. Brandes
P. 216

Minotauromachy (La minotauromachie), 1935
Etching with scraper and engraving on Montval laid paper, seventh (final) state
PLATE: 19 1/2 × 27 3/8 in. (49.5 × 69.5);
MAT: 21 1/2 × 28 3/4 in. (54.6 × 73 cm)
Private collection, Aspen, CO
P. 217

Guernica Composition Study VII, May 9, 1937
Graphite on paper
9 1/2 × 17 7/8 in. (24 × 45.3 cm)
Museo Nacional Centro de Arte Reina Sofia
P. 235

DIEGO RIVERA

(Mexican, 1886–1957)

Classical Head (Cabeza clásica), 1898
Oil on canvas
19 1/4 × 15 1/2 in. (49 × 39.5 cm)
Museo Casa Diego Rivera, Guanajuato, Instituto Nacional de Bellas Artes, Mexico
P. 98

Classical Head (Cabeza clásica), 1898
Pencil on paper
5 1/4 × 6 1/4 in. (13.5 × 16 cm)
Juan Coronel Rivera Collection, Mexico
P. 99

Classical Standing Figure (Figura clásica de pie), 1899
Pencil on paper
20 × 13 7/8 in. (50.7 × 35.2 cm)
Facultad de Artes y Diseño, Universidad Nacional Autónoma de México
P. 96

Venus de Milo, 1903
Pencil on paper
13 3/8 × 17 3/4 in. (34 × 45 cm)
Facultad de Artes y Diseño, Universidad Nacional Autónoma de México
P. 77

The Era (La Era), 1904
Oil on canvas
39 3/8 × 45 1/8 in. (100 × 114.5 cm)
Museo Casa Diego Rivera, Guanajuato, Marta R. Gómez Collection, Instituto Nacional de Bellas Artes, Mexico
P. 100

Self-Portrait, 1906
Oil on canvas
22 × 21 1/4 in. (56 × 54 cm)
Museo de Arte de Sinaloa, Gobierno del Estado de Sinaloa Collection
P. 28

Sun Breaking through the Fog (El sol rompiendo la bruma), 1913
Oil on canvas
32 7/8 × 23 1/4 in. (83.5 × 59 cm)
Museo Dolores Olmedo
P. 102

Portrait of Sculptor Elie Indenbaum (Retrato del escultor Elie Indenbaum, hombre del cigarillo), 1913
Oil on canvas
31 1/2 × 27 1/2 in. (80 × 70 cm)
Modern Art International Foundation
P. 107

Sailor at Lunch (*Marinero almorzando*), 1914
Oil on canvas
44⅞ × 27½ in. (114 × 70 cm)
Museo Casa Diego Rivera, Guanajuato,
Marte R. Gómez Collection,
Instituto Nacional de Bellas Artes, Mexico
P. 104

Cubist Composition (*Still Life with Bottle of Anis and Inkwell*)
(*Composition cubiste [nature morte à la bouteille d'anis et encrier]*), 1914–15
Oil, charcoal, and sand on canvas
18½ × 10⅝ in. (47 × 27 cm)
Almine and Bernard Ruiz-Picasso Foundation
P. 137

The Architect (*Portrait of Jesús T. Acevedo*)
(*El arquitecto, retrato de Jesús T. Acevedo*), 1915
Oil on canvas
56¾ × 44¾ in. (144 × 113.5 cm)
Museo de Arte Carrillo Gil,
Instituto Nacional de Bellas Artes, Mexico
P. 109

Still Life with Gray Bowl
(*Naturaleza muerta con tazon gris*), 1915
Oil on canvas
31¼ × 25⅛ in. (79.4 × 63.8 cm)
Lyndon Baines Johnson Presidential Library
P. 111

Zapatista Landscape (*Paisaje zapatista*), 1915
Oil on canvas
57 × 49 in. (145 × 125 cm)
Museo Nacional de Arte, Mexico
P. 24

The Mathematician (*El matemático*), 1918
Oil on canvas
46½ × 33⁷⁄₁₆ in. (118 × 85 cm)
Museo Dolores Olmedo
[MPBA ONLY]
P. 57

Sketch for *The Mathematician* (*El matemático*), 1918
Ink on paper
11 × 8 in. (27.8 × 20 cm)
Museo Dolores Olmedo
[MPBA ONLY]
P. 56

Bather in Tehuantepec (*Bañista de Tehuantepec*), 1923
Oil on canvas
24¾ × 21⅝ in. (63 × 55 cm)
Museo Casa de Diego Rivera, Guanajuato,
Marta R. Gómez Collection,
Instituto Nacional de Bellas Artes, Mexico
P. 120

Untitled (*Head of an Indian Woman*)
(*Cabeza de mujer indigena*), 1923–25
Pencil on paper
4¾ × 7¼ in. (12.1 × 18.4 cm)
Los Angeles County Museum of Art,
the Bernard and Edith Lewin Collection of Mexican Art
P. 93

Untitled (*Face*) (*Rostro*), 1923–25
Pencil on paper
7¼ × 4¾ in. (18.4 × 12.1 cm)
Los Angeles County Museum of Art,
the Bernard and Edith Lewin Collection of Mexican Art
P. 93

Untitled (*Head of Devil*) (*Cabeza de diablo*), 1923–25
Pencil on paper
7¼ × 4¾ in. (18.4 × 12.1 cm)
Los Angeles County Museum of Art,
the Bernard and Edith Lewin Collection of Mexican Art
P. 304

Untitled (*Figure with Mask*) (*Figura con máscara*), 1923–25
Pencil on paper
7¼ × 4¾ in. (18.4 × 12.1 cm)
Los Angeles County Museum of Art,
the Bernard and Edith Lewin Collection of Mexican Art
NOT ILLUSTRATED

Untitled (*Man with Cloak and Hat*)
(*Hombre con capa y sombrero*), 1923–25
Pencil on paper
7¼ × 4¾ in. (18.4 × 12 cm)
Los Angeles County Museum of Art,
the Bernard and Edith Lewin Collection of Mexican Art
P. 230

Untitled (*Female Figure*) (*Figura de mujer*), 1923–25
Pencil on paper
7¼ × 4¾ in. (18.4 × 12.1 cm)
Los Angeles County Museum of Art,
the Bernard and Edith Lewin Collection of Mexican Art
P. 230

Untitled (*Mountain with Huts*)
(*Montaña con cabañas*), 1923–25
Pencil on paper
4¾ × 7¾ in. (12.1 × 19.7 cm)
Los Angeles County Museum of Art,
the Bernard and Edith Lewin Collection of Mexican Art
P. 231

Untitled (*Group of Seated Figures*)
(*Grupo con figuras sentadas*), 1923–25
Pencil on paper
4¾ × 7¼ in. (12.1 × 18.4 cm)
Los Angeles County Museum of Art,
the Bernard and Edith Lewin Collection of Mexican Art
P. 231

Flower Day (*Día de Flores*), 1925
Oil on canvas
58 × 47½ in. (147.3 × 120.7 cm)
Los Angeles County Museum of Art,
Los Angeles County Fund
P. 89

Flower Day, Xochimilco
(*El día de las flores, Xochimilco*), 1926
Oil on canvas
25¼ × 31 in. (64.1 × 78.7 cm);
FRAME: 28¾ × 34½ in. (73 × 87.6 cm)
Fresno Art Museum,
gift of Mr. and Mrs. W. Clarence Harris
P. 119

Feathered Serpent
(*Quetzalcóatl, la serpiente emplumada*), 1926
Oil on canvas
39¾ × 48 in. (101 × 122 cm)
Centro Cultural Rosacruz AMORC
P. 113

Frida's Friend (*El Amigo de Frida*), 1931
Oil on canvas
31¾ × 26 in. (80.7 × 66 cm)
Nader Latin American Art Museum, Gary Nader Bequest
P. 127

Flowered Canoe (*La canoa enflorada*), 1931
Oil on canvas
78¾ × 63 in. (200 × 160 cm)
Museo Dolores Olmedo
P. 184

Creation of the Universe (*La creación del universo*), 1931
Illustration for the **Popol Vuh**
Watercolor on paper
SHEET: 12¼ × 18⅞ in. (31 × 48 cm)
Museo Casa Diego Rivera, Guanajuato,
Marta R. Gómez Collection,
Instituto Nacional de Bellas Artes, Mexico
P. 187

The Creation of Man (*La creación del hombre*), 1931
Illustration for the **Popol Vuh**
Watercolor on paper
SHEET: 12³⁄₁₆ × 19⅛ in. (31 × 48.5 cm)
Museo Casa Diego Rivera, Guanajuato,
Marta R. Gómez Collection,
Instituto Nacional de Bellas Artes, Mexico
P. 189

The Flood and Destruction of the Wooden Men (El diluvio y la destrucción de los hombres de palo), 1931
Illustration for the *Popol Vuh*
Watercolor on paper
SHEET: 12 1/4 × 19 1/8 in. (31 × 48.5 cm)
Museo Casa Diego Rivera, Guanajuato,
Marta R. Gómez Collection,
Instituto Nacional de Bellas Artes, Mexico
P. 189

The Monkeys who Descended from the Wooden Men (Los monos descendientes de los hombres de palo), 1931
Illustration for the *Popol Vuh*
Watercolor on paper
SHEET: 9 7/16 × 9 7/16 in. (24 × 24 cm)
Museo Casa Diego Rivera, Guanajuato,
Marta R. Gómez Collection,
Instituto Nacional de Bellas Artes, Mexico
P. 190

The Creation of Mountains (La creación de los montes), 1931
Illustration for the *Popol Vuh*
Watercolor on paper
SHEET: 12 3/16 × 18 7/8 in. (31 × 48 cm)
Museo Casa Diego Rivera,
Guanajuato, Marta R. Gómez Collection,
Instituto Nacional de Bellas Artes, Mexico
P. 190

Hunahpú Recovers His Arm (Hunahpú recupera su brazo), 1931
Illustration for the *Popol Vuh*
Watercolor on paper
SHEET: 9 7/16 × 9 7/16 in. (24 × 24 cm)
Museo Casa Diego Rivera, Guanajuato,
Marta R. Gómez Collection,
Instituto Nacional de Bellas Artes, Mexico
P. 191

The Death of Cabracan (La muerte de Cabracan), 1931
Illustration for the *Popol Vuh*
Watercolor on paper
SHEET: 9 7/16 × 9 7/16 in. (24 × 24 cm)
Museo Casa Diego Rivera, Guanajuato,
Marta R. Gómez Collection,
Instituto Nacional de Bellas Artes, Mexico
P. 191

Birth of Hunahpú and Ixbalanqué (Nacimiento de Hunahpú e Ixbalanque), 1931
Illustration for the *Popol Vuh*
Watercolor on paper
SHEET: 9 7/16 × 9 7/16 in. (24 × 24 cm)
Museo Casa Diego Rivera, Guanajuato,
Marta R. Gómez Collection,
Instituto Nacional de Bellas Artes, Mexico
P. 191

Xibalba's Messengers Invite the Ball Players (Los mensajeros de Xibalba invitan a los jugadores de pelota), 1931
Illustration for the *Popol Vuh*
Watercolor on paper
SHEET: 12 3/16 × 18 7/8 in. (31 × 48 cm)
Museo Casa Diego Rivera, Guanajuato,
Marta R. Gómez Collection,
Instituto Nacional de Bellas Artes, Mexico
P. 192

The Head of Hun-Hunahpú Grows on a Tree (La cabeza de Hun-Hunahpú fructifica en árbol), 1931
Illustration for the *Popol Vuh*
Watercolor on paper
SHEET: 9 1/2 × 9 1/2 in. (24 × 24 cm)
Museo Casa Diego Rivera, Guanajuato,
Marta R. Gómez Collection,
Instituto Nacional de Bellas Artes, Mexico
P. 194

The Saliva of Hun-Hunahpú Impregnates the Maiden (La saliva de Hun-Hunahpú fecunda a la doncella), 1931
Illustration for the *Popol Vuh*
Watercolor on paper
SHEET: 12 3/16 × 18 7/8 in. (31 × 48 cm)
Museo Casa Diego Rivera, Guanajuato,
Marta R. Gómez Collection,
Instituto Nacional de Bellas Artes, Mexico
P. 194

The Old Woman's Amazement before the Collected Corn (El asombro de la vieja ante el maíz recolectado), 1931
Illustration for the *Popol Vuh*
Watercolor on paper
SHEET: 9 7/16 × 9 7/16 in. (24 × 24 cm)
Museo Casa Diego Rivera, Guanajuato,
Marta R. Gómez Collection,
Instituto Nacional de Bellas Artes, Mexico
P. 195

How They Taught the Arts to Hunbatz and Hunchoven (Como les enseñaron las artes a Hunbatz y Hunchoven), 1931
Illustration for the *Popol Vuh*
Watercolor on paper
SHEET: 12 3/16 × 18 7/8 in. (31 × 48 cm)
Museo Casa Diego Rivera, Guanajuato,
Marta R. Gómez Collection,
Instituto Nacional de Bellas Artes, Mexico
P. 195

Protecting the Corn Field (La custodia de la milpa), 1931
Illustration for the *Popol Vuh*
Watercolor on paper
SHEET: 12 3/16 × 18 1/2 in. (31 × 47 cm)
Museo Casa Diego Rivera, Guanajuato,
Marta R. Gómez Collection,
Instituto Nacional de Bellas Artes, Mexico
P. 196

The Mansions of Xibalba (Las mansiones de Xibalba), 1931
Illustration for the *Popol Vuh*
Watercolor on paper
SHEET: 12 3/16 × 18 7/8 in. (31 × 48 cm)
Museo Casa Diego Rivera, Guanajuato,
Marta R. Gómez Collection,
Instituto Nacional de Bellas Artes, Mexico
P. 196

Man's Adoration of the Gods (La adoración de los dioses por los hombres), 1931
Illustration for the *Popol Vuh*
Watercolor on paper
SHEET: 12 3/16 × 18 1/2 in. (31 × 47 cm)
Museo Casa Diego Rivera, Guanajuato,
Marta R. Gómez Collection,
Instituto Nacional de Bellas Artes, Mexico
P. 197

The Human Sacrifice and Self Human Sacrifice before the God Tohil (El sacrificio y el auto sacrificio humano ante el dios Tohil), 1931
Illustration for the *Popol Vuh*
Watercolor on paper
SHEET: 12 3/16 × 19 1/8 in. (31 × 48.5 cm)
Museo Casa Diego Rivera, Guanajuato,
Marta R. Gómez Collection,
Instituto Nacional de Bellas Artes, Mexico
P. 197

Mandrake (Mandrágora), 1939
Oil on canvas
47 1/2 × 36 in. (120.7 cm × 91.4 cm)
San Diego Museum of Art, gift of Mrs. Irving T. Snyder
P. 219

First sketch for *Pan American Unity* mural, 1940
Pencil on paper
7 7/8 × 22 7/8 in. (20 × 58 cm)
Private collection, Mexico
P. 234

Sketch for *Tarasca Culture (Cultura Tarasca)* mural, *Painters and Dyers (Pintores y tintoreros)*, 1942
Pencil and charcoal on paper
20 1/8 × 9 1/2 in. (51 × 24 cm)
Juan Coronel Rivera Collection, Mexico
P. 232

Sculpture and Pottery (Escultura y cerámica), 1942
Pencil on paper
45 5/8 × 35 3/8 in. (116 × 90 cm)
Juan Coronel Rivera Collection, Mexico
P. 233

Sketch for grisaille of *Purépecha Culture (Cultura Purépecha)* mural, *Pigment Preparation (Preparación de pigmentos)*, 1942
Pencil on paper
27½ × 42½ in. (70 × 108 cm)
Juan Coronel Rivera Collection, Mexico
P. 233

Sketch for grisaille of *Purépecha Culture (Cultura Purépecha)* mural, *Body Paint Application, (Aplicación de pintura corporal)*, 1942
Pencil on paper
27½ × 42½ in. (70 × 108 cm)
Juan Coronel Rivera Collection, Mexico
P. 233

Petate Bearer (Cargador de Petate), 1943
Watercolor on paper
15 × 10¾ in. (38.1 × 27.3 cm)
Los Angeles County Museum of Art, Bernard and Edith Lewin Collection of Mexican Art
P. 221

Pre-Columbian America (América prehispánica), 1950
Oil on canvas
27½ × 36¼ in. (70 × 92 cm)
Private collection, Mexico
P. 223

History of Religion III (Historía de la religion III), 1950
Oil on canvas
76¾ × 29⅛ in. (195 × 74 cm)
Rafael Coronel Collection
NOT ILLUSTRATED

Studies of Pre-Columbian Figurines from Diego Rivera's Collection, c. 1955–56
12 drawings, pencil on paper
Each: 4 × 5⅞ in. (10 × 15 cm)
Juan Coronel Rivera Collection, Mexico
PP. 225–29

History of Religion V (Historia de la religión V), 1956
Tempera on paper on wood
78¾ × 31⅞ in. (200 × 81 cm)
Juan Coronel Rivera Collection, Mexico
P. 222

ANTIQUITIES

Greek and Roman

Attic Black-Figure Amphora
Attributed to Lydos (active 565–535 BCE) or a painter close to Lydos
Greek, Athens, 550–540 BCE
Terracotta
17$\frac{5}{16}$ × 12$\frac{13}{16}$ in. (45.6 × 32.5 cm)
J. Paul Getty Museum
P. 124

Attic Red-Figure Kylix
Attributed to Onesimos (active 500–480 BCE)
Greek, Athens, 500–490 BCE
Terracotta
3¼ × 12 × 9¼ in. (8.3 × 30.4 × 23.5 cm)
J. Paul Getty Museum
P. 210

Attic Red-Figure Calyx Krater
Villa Giulia Painter (active c. 470–440 BCE)
Greek, Athens, 460–450 BCE
Terracotta
16$\frac{13}{16}$ × 17$\frac{1}{16}$ in (42.7 × 43.3 cm)
J. Paul Getty Villa, gift of Dr. Paul Flanagan
P. 201

Fragment of a Head
Greek, Tarentum (Taras), 440–430 BCE
Terracotta with clay slip
5$\frac{9}{16}$ × 5½ in. (14.2 × 14 cm)
J. Paul Getty Museum, Purchase 1982
P. 58

Bronze Mirror
Etruscan, Classical, c. 425–400 BCE
Bronze
9$\frac{9}{16}$ × 6 in. (24.3 × 15.3 cm)
The Metropolitan Museum of Art, Rogers Fund, 1920
P. 203

Red-Figure Bell-Krater with a Symposium
Attributed to the Nostell Painter
Greek, Athens, c. 400–380 BCE
Red-figure ceramic with added red and white
H: 13½ in. (34.3 cm)
Los Angeles County Museum of Art, William Randolph Hearst Collection
P. 210

Foot
Reduced copy, plaster cast, 2016
Original: unknown, possibly Greek, c. 400–100 BCE
13¾ × 7½ × 13¾ in. (35 × 19 × 35 cm)
Facultad de Artes y Diseño, Universidad Nacional Autónoma de México
P. 97

Bronze Mirror
Etruscan, Late Classical, c. 350 BCE
Bronze
Diameter: 6⅜ in. (16.2 cm)
The Metropolitan Museum of Art, Rogers Fund, 1909
P. 198

Grave Naiskos of a Seated Woman with Two Standing Women
Greek, Athens, c. 340 BCE
Marble
43$\frac{5}{16}$ × 39⅜ × 9$\frac{15}{16}$ in. (110 × 100 × 25.2 cm)
J. Paul Getty Museum
P. 122

Mask of a Satyr
Greek, Sicily, 200–100 BCE
Terracotta with polychromy (brownish red, orange red, white, black, pink, sky blue)
4¾ × 3$\frac{15}{16}$ × 6⅛ in. (12 × 10 × 15.5 cm)
J. Paul Getty Museum, gift of Barbara and Lawrence Fleischman
P. 212

Venus de Milo (Aphrodite of Milos)
Reduced copy, plaster cast, 2016
Original: Greek, c. 130–100 BCE
31⅞ × 11¾ × 11⅜ in. (81 × 30 × 29 cm)
Facultad de Artes y Diseño, Universidad Nacional Autónoma de México
P. 76

Statuette of Venus (Crouching Aphrodite)
Unknown sculptor, after Doidalsas of Bithynia
Greek, Ptolemaic, or Roman, Egypt, 1st century BCE
Rock crystal
3⅜ × 1$\frac{9}{16}$ × 2⅜ in. (8.5 × 4 × 6 cm)
J. Paul Getty Museum
P. 206

Belvedere Torso
Reduced copy, plaster cast, 2016
Original: Roman, 1st century BCE or CE
22½ × 13¾ × 17 ¾ in. (57 × 35 × 45 cm)
Museo Nacional de las Culturas
P. 74

Lansdowne Artemis
Roman, 1st century BCE or 1st century CE
Marble
70 × 26 × 17 in. (177.8 × 66 × 43.2 cm)
Los Angeles County Museum of Art, William Randolph Hearst Collection
P. 114

Relief of Jupiter
Roman, Asia Minor, 1–150 CE
Silver
$7\frac{1}{16} \times 5\frac{1}{8} \times 1\frac{15}{16}$ in. (18 × 13 × 5 cm)
J. Paul Getty Museum
P. 208

Statuette of Herakles
Roman, Roman Empire, 40–70 CE
Bronze with silver-inlaid eyes
H: 6 in. (15.2 cm)
J. Paul Getty Museum,
gift of Barbara and Lawrence Fleischman
P. 202

Male Torso
Roman, 100 CE
Marble
$40\frac{9}{16} \times 24 \times 11\frac{7}{16}$ in. (103 × 61 × 29.1 cm)
J. Paul Getty Museum
P. 117

Mithraic Sacrifice Scene
Roman, 2nd century CE
Marble
$27\frac{1}{2} \times 39\frac{3}{8}$ in. (70 × 100 cm)
Musée du Louvre
P. 38

Iberian

Man Attacked by a Lion
Iberian, Osuna, 6th–5th century BCE
Limestone, bas-relief
$16\frac{1}{8} \times 11\frac{3}{4} \times 15$ in. (41 × 30 × 38 cm)
Museo Arqueológico Nacional, Madrid
P. 82

Pre-Columbian

Roof Ornament with Tlaloc Emblem
Mexico, Teotihuacán, 250–650
Stone
$50\frac{3}{8} \times 41$ in. (128 × 104 cm)
Museo Nacional de Antropología, INAH
P. 112

Ball Court Model
Mexico, Nayarit, 200–500
Ceramic
$9\frac{7}{8} \times 16\frac{7}{8}$ in. (25 × 43 cm)
Museo Diego Rivera-Anahuacalli
P. 193

Hairless Dog with Wrinkles
Mexico, Colima, 200–500
Ceramic
$9\frac{7}{8} \times 13$ in. (25 × 33 cm)
Museo Diego Rivera-Anahuacalli
P. 224

Mask
Mexico, Teotihuacán, 200–650
Green alabaster
$5\frac{7}{8} \times 2\frac{3}{8}$ in. (15 × 6 cm)
Museo Diego Rivera-Anahuacalli
P. 92 (RIGHT)

Mask
Mexico, Teotihuacán, 200–650
Greenstone
$5\frac{7}{8} \times 2\frac{3}{8}$ in. (15 × 6 cm)
Museo Diego Rivera-Anahuacalli
P. 92 (LEFT)

Zapotec Deity
Mexico, Zapotec, Oaxaca, 600–900
Ceramic
$7\frac{7}{8} \times 3\frac{1}{2}$ in. (20 × 9 cm)
Museo Diego Rivera-Anahuacalli
P. 224

Cargador (Carrier)
Mexico, Nayarit, 600–900
Ceramic
$11 \times 7\frac{7}{8}$ in. (28 × 20 cm)
Museo Diego Rivera-Anahuacalli
P. 220

Goddess from Tlalmanalco
Mexico, Aztec, Tlalmanalco, 1250–1521
Basalt and shell or bone
42 × 16 in. (107 × 41 cm)
Museo Nacional de Antropología, INAH
P. 118

Tzitzimitl (Death Goddess of Childbirth)
Mexico, Aztec, 1250–1521
Basalt
$31\frac{1}{2} \times 11 \times 7\frac{1}{2}$ in. (80 × 28 × 19 cm)
Museo Diego Rivera-Anahuacalli
P. 218

Macehual (Commoner)
Mexico, Aztec, 1250–1521
Stone
$31\frac{1}{2} \times 11 \times 7\frac{1}{2}$ in. (80 × 28 × 19 cm)
Museo Nacional de Antropología, INAH
P. 185

Chalchiuhtlicue (Water Deity)
Mexico, Aztec, 1200–1521
Basalt
$10\frac{1}{4} \times 5\frac{7}{8}$ in. (26 × 15 cm)
Museo Diego Rivera-Anahuacalli
P. 88 (LEFT)

Chalchiuhtlicue (Water Deity)
Mexico, Aztec, 1200–1521
Basalt
$7\frac{7}{8} \times 4\frac{3}{8}$ in. (20 × 11 cm)
Museo Diego Rivera-Anahuacalli
P. 22

Chalchiuhtlicue (Water Deity)
Mexico, Aztec, 1200–1521
Green stone
$5\frac{1}{8} \times 3\frac{3}{4}$ in. (13 × 9.5 cm)
Museo Diego Rivera-Anahuacalli
P. 88 (RIGHT)

Quetzalcóatl (Feathered Serpent)
Mexico, Aztec, 1250–1521
Stone
H: $45\frac{1}{4}$ in. (115 cm)
Museo Nacional de Antropología, INAH
P. 186

Seated Standard Bearer
Mexico, Aztec, Veracruz, 1250–1521
Sandstone, laminated
OVERALL: $31\frac{3}{4} \times 13\frac{3}{8} \times 13$ in. (80.5 × 34.1 × 33.1 cm)
The Metropolitan Museum of Art,
Harris Brisbane Dick Fund, 1962
P. 126

LENDERS TO THE EXHIBITION

Almine and Bernard Ruiz-Picasso Foundation
Art Institute of Chicago
Centro Cultural Rosacruz AMORC, Mexico City
Colección Patricia Phelps de Cisneros
Facultad de Artes y Diseño, Universidad Nacional Autónoma de México
Fresno Art Museum
Fundación Diego Rivera
Getty Research Institute
The Getty Villa, J. Paul Getty Museum
Institut Amatller d'Art Hispànic
Juan Coronel Rivera Collection
Kunstmuseum Basel
Leonard A. Lauder Collection
Lyndon Baines Johnson Presidential Library and Museum
The Metropolitan Museum of Art
Modern Art International Foundation
Musée du Louvre
Musée Picasso, Paris
Museo Arqueológico Nacional, Madrid, Spain
Museo de Arte Carrillo Gil
Museo Casa Diego Rivera, Guanajuato
Museo de Arte de Sinaloa
Museo Dolores Olmedo
Museo Nacional Centro de Arte Reina Sofía
Museo Nacional de Antropología, Mexico City
Museo Nacional de las Culturas
Museos Diego Rivera–Anahuacalli y Frida Kahlo
Museu Picasso Barcelona
Museum of Fine Arts, Boston
Museum of Modern Art, New York
Nader Latin American Art Museum
Rafael Coronel Collection
Rivera Collection, City College of San Francisco Library
San Diego Museum of Art
Solomon R. Guggenheim Museum

And those who wish to remain anonymous

SELECTED BIBLIOGRAPHY

PICASSO

Ashton, Dore, ed. *Picasso on Art: A Selection of Views*. Boston: Da Capo Press, 1988.

Baldassari, Anne. *Picasso and Photography: The Dark Mirror*. Translated by Deke Dusinberre. Paris: Flammarion, 1997.

Bloch, Georges. *Pablo Picasso*. Vol. 1, *Catalogue de l'oeuvre gravé et lithographié, 1904–1967*. Bern: Editions Kornfeld et Kipstein, 1968.

Chipp, Herschel, and Alan Wofsy, eds. *Picasso's Paintings, Watercolors, Drawings and Sculpture: A Comprehensive Illustrated Catalogue, 1885–1973*. San Francisco: Alan Wofsy Fine Arts, 1995.

Clair, Jean, and Odie Michel, eds. *Picasso: The Italian Journey, 1917–1924*. New York: Rizzoli, 1998.

Clark, T. J. *Picasso and Truth: From Cubism to Guernica*. Princeton, NJ: Princeton University Press, 2013.

Conzen, Ina, Guido Messling, and Anke Spötter. *Picasso: Bathers*. Ostfildern-Ruit, Germany: Hatje Cantz, 2005.

Cowling, Elizabeth. *Picasso: Style and Meaning*. London: Phaidon, 2002.

Daix, Pierre. *Picasso: Life and Art*. Translated by Olivia Emmet. New York: Icon Editions, 1991.

Daix, Pierre, Georges Boudaille, and Joan Rosselet. *Picasso, the Blue and Rose Periods: A Catalogue Raisonné of the Paintings, 1900–1906*. Translated by Phoebe Pool. Greenwich, CT: New York Graphic Society, 1967.

Daix, Pierre, and Joan Rosselet. *Picasso, the Cubist Years, 1907–1916: A Catalogue Raisonné of the Paintings and Related Works*. Translated by Dorothy S. Blair. Boston: New York Graphic Society, 1979.

Florman, Lisa. *Myth and Metamorphosis, Picasso's Prints of the 1930s*. Cambridge, MA: MIT Press, 2000.

Galassi, Susan Grace, and Marilyn McCully. *Picasso's Drawings, 1890–1921: Reinventing Tradition*. New Haven, CT: Yale University Press, 2011.

Green, Christopher, ed. *Picasso's "Les Demoiselles d'Avignon."* Cambridge: Cambridge University Press, 2001.

Govan, Michael. *The Minotaur & the Light: Sources for Picasso c. 1935*. Williamstown, MA: Williams College Museum of Art, 1985.

Mallen, Enrique, ed. "Online Picasso Project." Sam Houston State University, 1997–2015. https://picasso.shsu.edu/

McCully, Marilyn. *Picasso in Paris, 1900–1907*. Edited by Michael Raeburn. New York: Vendome Press, 2011.

——, ed. *Picasso: The Early Years, 1892–1906*. Washington, DC: National Gallery of Art, 1997.

Ocaña, Maria Teresa, ed. *Picasso: The Development of a Genius, 1890–1904*. Barcelona: Lunwerg Editore, 1997.

Palau i Fabre, Josep. *Picasso Cubism (1907–1917)*. Translated by Susan Branyas, Richard-Lewis Rees, and Patrick Zabalbeascoa. New York: Rizzoli, 1990.

——. *Picasso: The Early Years, 1881–1907*. New York: Rizzoli, 1981.

Penrose, Roland, and John Golding, eds. *Picasso in Retrospect*. New York: Praeger, 1973.

Rabinow, Rebecca A., ed. *Cézanne to Picasso: Ambroise Vollard, Patron of the Avant-Garde*. New York: The Metropolitan Museum of Art, 2006.

Richardson, John. *A Life of Picasso*. 3 vols. New York: Alfred A. Knopf, 2007.

——, ed. *Picasso & the Camera*. New York: Gagosian Gallery, 2014.

Rose-de Viejo, Isadora, and Janie Cohen. *Etched on the Memory: The Presence of Rembrandt in the Prints of Goya and Picasso*. Translated by Lynne Richards. London: Lund Humphries, 2000.

Rubin, William. *Picasso and Braque: Pioneering Cubism*. New York: Museum of Modern Art, 1989.

——, ed. *Pablo Picasso: A Retrospective*. New York: Museum of Modern Art, 1980.

——, ed. *Picasso and Portraiture: Representation and Transformation*. New York: Museum of Modern Art, 1996.

Staller, Natasha Elena. *A Sum of Destructions: Picasso's Cultures and the Creation of Cubism*. New Haven: Yale University Press, 2001.

Stein, Gertrude. *Gertrude Stein on Picasso*. Edited by Edward Burns. New York: Liveright, 1970.

Stepan, Peter. *Picasso's Collection of African & Oceanic Art: Masters of Metamorphosis*. New York: Prestel, 2006.

Sweeney, James Johnson. "Picasso and Iberian Sculpture." *The Art Bulletin* 23, no. 3 (September 1941): 191–98.

Tinterow, Gary, and Carmen Jimenez. *Picasso Clásico*. Málaga: Junta de Andalucía, 1992.

RIVERA

Arquin, Florence. *Diego Rivera: The Shaping of an Artist, 1889–1921*. Norman: University of Oklahoma Press, 1971.

Coronel Rivera, Juan. "Diego Rivera: Idólatra." In *Diego Rivera: Coleccionista*, edited by Marte Rodolfo Gómez Segura. Mexico City: Instituto Nacional de Bellas Artes, 2007.

Cortés Gutiérrez, Laura, ed. *Diego Rivera: catálogo general de obra de caballete*. Mexico City: Consejo Nacional para la Cultura y las Artes, Dirección General de Publicaciones: Instituto Nacional de Bellas Artes, 1989.

——. *Diego Rivera: catálogo general de obra mural y fotografía personal*. 1st ed. Mexico City: SEP, Dirección General de Publicaciones y Medios: Instituto Nacional de Bellas Artes, 1988.

Craven, David. *Diego Rivera: As Epic Modernist*. New York: G. K. Hall, 1997.

Debroise, Olivier. *Diego de Montparnasse*. Mexico City: Fondo de Cultura Económica, 1979.

Diego Rivera: A Retrospective. New York: Founders Society, Detroit Institute of Arts, in association with W. W. Norton, 1986.

Downs, Linda Bank. *Diego Rivera: The Detroit Industry Murals*. New York: W. W. Norton, 1999.

Favela, Ramón. *Diego Rivera: The Cubist Years*. Phoenix, AZ: Phoenix Art Museum, 1984.

Hamill, Pete. *Diego Rivera*. New York: Harry N. Abrams, 1999.

Lozano, Luis-Martín, Agustín Arteaga, and William Robinson, eds. *Diego Rivera: Art and Revolution*. Mexico City: Instituto Nacional de Bellas Artes: Landucci Editores, 1999.

Lozano, Luis-Martín, and Juan Coronel Rivera. *Diego Rivera: The Complete Murals*. Los Angeles: Taschen, 2008.

Marnham, Patrick. *Dreaming with His Eyes Open: A Life of Diego Rivera*. New York: Knopf, 1998.

Navarrete, Sylvia, et al. *Diego Rivera: The Cubist Portraits 1913–1917*. London: Philip Wilson, 2009.

Oles, James. *Diego Rivera, David Alfaro Siqueiros, José Clemente Orozco*. New York: Museum of Modern Art, 2011.

Rivera, Diego. *Diego Rivera: Illustrious Words*. Vol. 1, *1886–1921*. Mexico City: Instituto Nacional de Bellas Artes, 2007.

——. *Diego Rivera: Illustrious Words*. Vol. 2, *1921–1957*. Mexico City: Instituto Nacional de Bellas Artes, 2007.

——. *My Art, My Life: An Autobiography*. With Gladys March. New York: Dover Publications, 1991. First published in 1960 by Citadel Press.

Rochfort, Desmond. *The Murals of Diego Rivera*. London: South Bank Board in collaboration with Journeyman, 1987.

Tibol, Raquel. *Diego Rivera: Great Illustrator*. Translated by Gregory Dechant. Mexico City: Editorial RM, 2008.

Torriente, Loló de la. *Memoria y Razón de Diego Rivera*. Mexico City: Editorial Renacimiento, 1959.

Wolfe, Bertram David. *The Fabulous Life of Diego Rivera*. New York: Stein and Day, 1963.

GENERAL WORKS

Antliff, Mark, and Patricia Leighten. *Cubism and Culture*. New York: Thames and Hudson, 2001.

Bargellini, Clara, and Elizabeth Fuentes Rojas. *Guía que permite captar lo bello: yesos y dibujos de la Academia de San Carlos, 1778–1916*. Mexico City: UNAM, Instituto de Investigaciones Estéticas: Escuela Nacional de Artes Plásticas, 1989.

Boehm, Gottfried, Ulrich Mosch, and Katharina Schmidt, eds. *Canto d'Amore: Classicism in Modern Art and Music, 1914–1935*. Basel: Öffentliche Kunstsammlung Basel/Kunstmuseum: Paul Sacher Foundation in association with Merrell Holberton Publishers, 1996.

Boone, Elizabeth Hill, ed. *Collecting the Pre-Columbian Past: A Symposium at Dumbarton Oaks, 6th and 7th October 1990*. Washington, DC: Dumbarton Oaks Research Library and Collection, 1993.

Braun, Barbara. *Pre-Columbian Art and the Post-Columbian World: Ancient American Sources of Modern Art*. New York: Harry N. Abrams, 1993.

Braun, Emily, and Rebecca Rabinow, eds. *Cubism: The Leonard A. Lauder Collection*. New York: The Metropolitan Museum of Art, 2014.

Cowling, Elizabeth, and Jennifer Mundy, eds. *On Classic Ground: Picasso, Léger, De Chirico, and the New Classicism, 1910–1930*. London: Tate Gallery, 1990.

FitzGerald, Michael C. *Making Modernism: Picasso and the Creation of the Market for Twentieth Century Art*. New York: Farrar, Straus and Giroux, 1995.

Golding, John. *Cubism: A History and an Analysis, 1907–1914*. Boston: Boston Book & Art Shop, 1968.

Greet, Michele. *Beyond National Identity: Pictorial Indigenism as a Modernist Strategy in Andean Art, 1920–1960*. University Park: Pennsylvania State University Press, 2009.

Leighten, Patricia. *The Liberation of Painting: Modernism and Anarchism in Avant-Guerre Paris*. Chicago: University of Chicago Press, 2013.

Matos Moctezuma, Eduardo. *Las piedras negadas: De la Coatlicue al Templo Mayor*. Mexico City: Consejo Nacional para la Cultura y las Artes, 1998.

Naumann, Francis M., ed. *How, When, and Why Modern Art Came to New York*. Cambridge, MA: MIT Press, 1996.

Navarrete Linares, Federico. *Las relaciones interétnicas en México*. Mexico City: UNAM, 2004.

Pollitt, J. J. *Art and Experience in Classical Greece*. Cambridge: Cambridge University Press, 1972.

Prettejohn, Elizabeth. *The Modernity of Ancient Sculpture: Greek Sculpture and Modern Art from Winckelmann to Picasso*. London and New York: I. B. Tauris, 2012.

Silver, Kenneth E. *Esprit de Corps: The Art of the Parisian Avant-Garde and the First World War, 1914–1925*. Princeton, NJ: Princeton University Press, 1989.

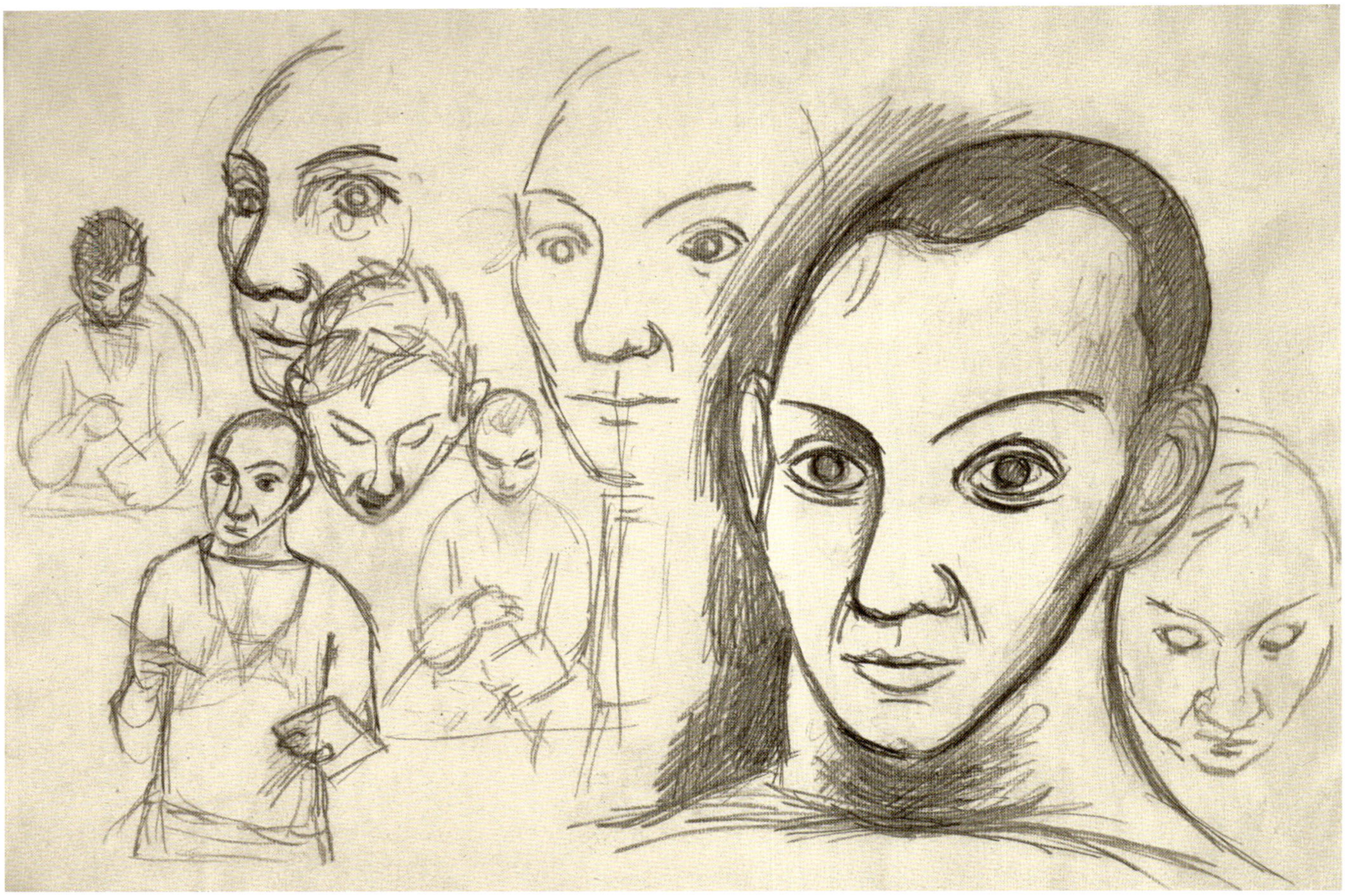

Pablo Picasso, Stucy for ***Self-Portrait with a Palette***, Fall 1906

ACKNOWLEDGMENTS

The honor of organizing this exhibition has brought with it a great debt of gratitude to countless people, whose knowledge, hard work, and generosity we have relied upon for every aspect of this project. First, we would like to thank Miguel Fernández Félix, Director of the Museo del Palacio de Bellas Artes in Mexico City for joining us on this ambitious undertaking.

From the outset of this exhibition we had the great fortune to meet with Laurent Le Bon, Director of the Musée National Picasso Paris, who was immediately and immensely supportive; Picasso loans are among the most difficult to secure and due to his support and encouragement we were able to build a strong foundation for the exhibition. Mr. and Mrs. Bernard Ruiz-Picasso at the Fundacíon Almine y Bernard Ruiz-Picasso offered not only loans but also knowledgeable advice, and their great gift to the exhibition opened a new path of research on Picasso and Rivera's friendship. Absolutely essential loans from many more institutions in Europe contributed to the success of the project. We are especially grateful to the following individuals for their invaluable support in securing these exquisite loans: Andrés Carretero Pérez and Carmen Marcos Alonso, Museo Arqueológico Nacional, Madrid; Jean-Luc Martinez, Musée du Louvre; Bernardo Laniado-Romero, Museu Picasso, Barcelona; Manuel Borja-Villel, Museo Nacional Centro de Arte Reina Sofía; Bernhard Medes Bürgi, Kunstmuseum Basel; and Santiago Alcolea and Núria Peiris Pujolar, Institut Amatller d'Art Hispànic.

We owe the great honor of bringing loans from Diego Rivera's Museo Anahuacalli to the United States for the first time to Carlos Phillips Olmedo, Director of the Museos Dolores Olmedo, Frida Kahlo, and Diego Rivera–Anahuacalli, and to the generous support of Teresa Franco, Director General of the Instituto Nacional de Antropología e Historia. An exhibition of this complexity would not be possible without the generosity of museums and private collectors in Mexico. We are grateful to the following: Hilda Trujillo, Museo Anahuacalli and Museo Frida Kahlo; Vania Rojas Solis, Museo de Arte Carrillo Gil; Antonio Saborit, Museo Nacional de Antropología, Mexico City; Josefina García, Museo Dolores Olmedo; Minerva Solano Moreno, Mario López Valdez, María Luisa Miranda Monrreal, and Ricardo De Rueda, Museo de Arte de Sinaloa; Soror Jacqueline Zepeda Fernandez, Centro Cultural Rosacruz AMORC, Mexico City; Juan Rafael Coronel Rivera, Juan Coronel Rivera Collection; Elizabeth Fuentes Rojas and José de Santiago Silva, Facultad de Artes y Diseño, Universidad Nacional Autónoma de México; Juan Alcocer Flores and Martín Antonio Aguirre Huerta, Museo Casa Estudio Diego Rivera, Guanajuato; Gloria Artis Mercadet and Luis Felipe Crespo, Museo Nacional de las Culturas, Mexico City; and Guadalupe Rivera Marín and Diego López Rivera, Fundación Diego Rivera.

We knew that no better case for Picasso's use of classicism could be made than his *Three Women at the Spring*, and we are greatly appreciative of Glenn D. Lowry and his curatorial staff at the Museum of Modern Art in New York for its loan. From the Metropolitan Museum of Art, thanks to Thomas P. Campbell and his curatorial staff, Joanne Pillsbury and Carlos A. Picón, for the loans of classical and Pre-Columbian objects, as well as their newly promised gift of Picasso's *Student with Newspaper*. Many thanks as well to donor Leonard A. Lauder for his great generosity, and to curators Rebecca Rabinow and Emily Braun for all their help.

All of the lending museums in the United States were incredibly generous. We extend our deep appreciation to Richard Armstrong and Nancy Spector, Solomon R. Guggenheim Museum; Douglas Druick and Stephanie D'Alessandro, Art Institute of Chicago; Matthew Teitelbaum and Helen Burnham, Museum of Fine Arts, Boston; Gabriel Pérez-Barreiro, Colección Patricia Phelps de Cisneros; Thomas W. Gaehtgens and Marcia Reed, Getty Research Institute; Gary Nader, Nader Latin American Art Museum; Michele Ellis Pracy and Kristina Hornback, Fresno Art Museum; Roxana Velásquez, Anita Feldman, and Ariel Plotek, San Diego Museum of Art; Michael MacDonald, Lyndon Baines Johnson Library and Museum; Julia Bergman, City College of San Francisco Library, Diego Rivera Collection; and Manuel Reyero, Modern Art International Foundation. Most touching to us was the support we received from the J. Paul Getty Museum at the Getty Villa, and we are grateful to Jeffrey Spier and Timothy Potts for their effusive collaboration and numerous loans as well as advice. We also thank those anonymous lenders who lent so many key works to our exhibition for the Los Angeles and Mexico City venues. Truly, this project would be hard to imagine without each of these remarkable loans.

We are grateful to the leaders of cultural institutions in Mexico and France without whom this show would not be possible. In Mexico: Rafael Tovar y de Teresa, Minister of Culture; José Luis Martínez Hernández, Director General for International Affairs, Secretaría de Cultura; María Cristina García Cepeda, Director, Instituto Nacional de Bellas Artes; Magdalena Zavala Bonachea, National Coordinator, Coordinación Nacional de Artes Visuales; Teresa Franco, Director General, and José Enrique Ortiz Lanz, National Coordinator of Museums and Exhibitions, Instituto Nacional de Antropología e Historia. In France: Marie-Christine Labourdette, Director, Musées de France.

Over the course of the exhibition many key individuals helped facilitate loans and research from lending institutions and private collections in Europe, Mexico, and the United States, as well as providing special insight and access regarding works in our own collection at the Los Angeles County Museum of Art. Our warm thanks to Stephanie Barron, Ilona Katzew, J. Patrice Marandel, Ilene Fort, Britt Salvesen, Naoko Takahatake, Carol Eliel, Susan Power, Leah Lehmbeck, Wendy Kaplan, Megan O'Neil, Jennifer King, Rachel Kaplan, Stéphanie Molins, Sarah Lagrevol, Sophie Annoepel-Cabrignac, Marie Brisson, Iro Biehler, Thomas Chaineux, Christine Pinault, Isabelle Vignon, Anna Fabregas Sauret, Carmen Cabrera, Victoria Fernández, Christina Guldaguer, Karla Niño de Rivera Tórres, Veronica Rincon, Angélica Valentino, Eva Ayala, Inna Alvarez, Julian Martinez, Marilyn Castillo, América Juárez, Cora Rosevear, Anna Simonovic, Janet Moore, Jordan Agamie, Conrado de la Torre, Paige-Marie Ketner, Irene Phillips, Cory Woodall, Janet Moore, Patrick Murphy, Jacob Coley, David Rhoads, Skye Amelia Monson, Ruth Goerger, Matt Heffernan, Irene Martin, and Bill Jordan. We also thank Tely Duarte for her thoughtful role in tracking down loans of important works by Diego Rivera.

An exhibition of this kind would not be possible without the collective efforts of our many colleagues at LACMA, who were exceptionally professional and generous. We especially thank Zoe Kahr, deputy director for exhibitions and planning; Sabrina Lovett, senior exhibition coordinator; and Victoria Behner, assistant director of exhibition design and production. Additionally, we are grateful to Emily Saccenti and Errin Copple in Registration and Collections; Erika Franek, Maia November, and Delfin Magpantay in Risk Management; Amy Crum and Michelle Rich in Art of the Ancient Americas; John Hirx, Soko Furuhata, and Silviu Boariu in the Conservation Center; Melissa Bomes, Kris Lewis, Jennifer Holmes, Celia Yang, and Jennifer Snow in

Development; Miranda Carroll, Stephanie Sykes, and Chi-Young Kim in Communications; Jane Burrell and Amber Smith in Education and Public Programs; David Karwan in Graphic Design; Peter Brenner, Steve Oliver, and Laura Cherry in Photographic Services; Tracy Kerr, Douglas Cordell, and Kristi Yuzuki in the Research Library; and Bill Stahl, Jeff Haskin, and their respective teams in Gallery Construction and Art Preparation and Installation.

Very special thanks to a great artist and filmmaker, Rodrigo García, who created for the exhibition a montage of Picasso's *Guernica* and Rivera's *Pan American Unity*. The film was expertly produced by Erin Wright, LACMA's director of artist initiatives. We are grateful to her and her team, including Christopher Hall, Elizabeth Gray, and Patrick Heilman.

The preparation of the exhibition catalogue could not have been accomplished without the great dedication demonstrated by the Publications department, in particular LACMA's publisher, Lisa Mark; Sara Cody, senior editor; and Piper Severance, senior associate of Rights and Reproductions. Many thanks as well to Mary DelMonico, of DelMonico Books/Prestel. We owe the elegant design of this catalogue to Lorraine Wild and Xiaoqing Wang from Green Dragon Office.

Additional thanks to Émilie Bouvard, Lilly Casillas, Juan Rafael Coronel Rivera, Michele Greet, Patricia Leighten, Camille Mathieu, Itzel A. Rodríguez Mortellaro, James Oles, and Jennifer Stager, our colleague authors of this publication. In addressing the thematic sections of the exhibition, their thought-provoking essays greatly enhance not only our understanding of Picasso and Rivera's relationship and artistic trajectories, but also their original ways of recasting the arts of antiquity.

We are very grateful to our colleagues at the Museo del Palacio de Bellas Artes in Mexico City, who provided extraordinary support for this undertaking: Arturo López Rodríguez, Adriana López Álvarez, Andrea Villalba Camacho, Antonieta Bautista Ruíz, Daniela Rojas Ramírez, Edith Sánchez Moctezuma, Óscar Pastor Plascencia, Ingrid González Díaz, Roxana Romero Muñoz, Marie Krystel Sánchez Riot, Evelyn Useda Miranda, and Víctor Hugo González Guadarrama.

We shared the joys and difficulties of creating a complex and eloquent dialogue between two great artists and two ancient cultural traditions with a team of dedicated curators on this project, and we are delighted to acknowledge their essential contributions. Juan Rafael Coronel Rivera led the project at the Museo del Palacio de Bellas Artes; he was an incredible facilitator in securing loans in Mexico and conceiving the dialogues between Picasso and Rivera through their works, and we would not have been able to accomplish this exhibition without his knowledge and guidance. Jennifer Stager's expertise on the arts of classical antiquity greatly contributed to the success of the show. We are grateful to her for always offering herself as a resource. James Oles's incisive advice and expertise on Mexican modernism provided a secure foundation and a standard for excellence. We must additionally thank Patricia Leighten for her expertise on Picasso and her generous support of the project. We are especially grateful to curatorial assistant Lilly Casillas for her professionalism, joyous disposition, and deep understanding of the exhibition.

MICHAEL GOVAN
CEO and Wallis Annenberg Director
Los Angeles County Museum of Art

DIANA MAGALONI
Deputy Director and Director of the Program for Art of the Ancient Americas
Los Angeles County Museum of Art

INDEX

Page numbers in *italics* denote illustrations.

P

Q

R

PHOTO CREDITS

5 top, 7 top left, 9, 11 right, 13, 15 left, 17, 29, 39, 42, 43, 46, 47, 53, 59, 75, 76 right, 83, 84, 97 bottom, 101, 103, 105, 106, 108, 110, 115, 116, 121, 123, 125, 131, 132, 137 left, 138, 139, 140, 147 left, 148 right, 163, 164, 165, 167, 168, 169, 173, 174, 175, 179, 183, 199, 200, 201 left, 202 right, 203 top, 204, 205, 207, 209, 211, 213, 214, 215, 216, 217, 235, 294: © 2016 Estate of Pablo Picasso/Artists Rights Society (ARS), New York

11 left, 19, 24, 28, 56, 57, 68, 70, 71, 77, 79, 85, 86, 89, 90, 91, 93, 94, 96, 98, 99, 100, 102, 104, 107, 109, 111, 113, 119, 120, 127, 134, 137 right, 141 right, 142, 148 left, 153, 155, 158, 184, 187, 189, 190, 191, 192, 194, 195, 196, 197, 219, 221, 222, 223, 225, 226, 227, 228, 229, 230, 231, 232, 233, 234, 238, 239 left, 241, 242, 244, 245, 249, 252, 254, 255, 257 left, 260, 264, 265, 273, 277 right, 278, 279, 304: © 2016 Banco de México Diego Rivera Frida Kahlo Museum Trust, Mexico, D.F./Artists Rights Society (ARS), New York

5 top: Photo © Leemage/Bridgeman Image; 5 bottom, 98, 100, 104, 189 bottom, 190, 191, 192, 194, 195, 196, 197: Photo courtesy Museo Casa Estudio Diego Rivera y Frida Kahlo, Guanajuato; 7 top left, 9, 11 right, 59: Photo © RMN-Grand Palais/Art Resource, NY; 7 top right: Photo courtesy of Museos Diego Rivera–Anahuacalli y Frida Kahlo, digital photo by Agustin Estrada; 7 bottom: Photo © Fundació Institut Amatller d'Art Hispànic, Arxiu Mas; 11 left: Photo © Colección Fundación Diego Rivera, A.C.; 13: Digital Image © Pushkin Museum of Fine Arts; 15 left, 15 top right, 17 top, 43, 115, 131, 139, 141 right, 164, 167, 183, 217: Digital Image © The Museum of Modern Art/Licensed by SCALA/Art Resource, NY; 17 bottom left: © Dora Maar Estate/Artists Rights Society (ARS), New York. Photo © RMN-Grand Palais/Art Resource, NY/Franck Raux; 17 bottom right: © 2016 Calder Foundation, New York/Artists Rights Society (ARS), New York. Photo Credit: The New York Public Library/Art Resource, NY; 19 top: Photo courtesy of the Historical Archive of the Galeria de Arte Mexicano; 19 bottom: Photo courtesy City College of San Francisco Library; 21: Photo courtesy of Museos Diego Rivera–Anahuacalli y Frida Kahlo; 22: Photo courtesy of Museos Diego Rivera–Anahuacalli y Frida Kahlo, by Javier Hinojosa; 28: Photo courtesy Museo de Arte de Sinaloa, Colección ISIC-MASIN, by Agustin Estrada; 29, 84 right: Photo credit: Philadelphia Museum of Art/Art Resource; 38: Photo © RMN-Grand Palais/Art Resource, NY, by Stephane Marechall; 39, 42, 46, 47, 159, 203 top, 204, 205, 207, 209, 210 top, 213: Photo © The Norton Simon Foundation; 40: Photo © The Morgan Library & Museum; 49, 89, 93, 101, 114, 123, 210 bottom, 216, 221, 230, 231, 304: Photo © Museum Associates/LACMA; 53: San Diego Museum of Art, USA/Bequest of Earle W. Grant/Bridgeman Images; 56, 57, 85, 86, 91, 102, 184, 241, 277 right: Photo © Schalkwijk/Art Resource, NY; 58, 117, 122, 124, 202 left, 206, 208, 211 top, 212: Photo courtesy J. Paul Getty Museum, Villa Collection, Malibu, California; 60 left: Photo credit: Werner Forman/Art Resource, NY; 60 right, 187, 267: Photo credit: Album/Art Resource, NY; 61: Photo © Dorothy Sloan-Rare Books; 62: Photo courtesy Medicea Laurenziana Library, Florence; 63: Photo courtesy Library of Congress Prints and Photographs Division Washington, D.C. 20540 USA (LC-USZC4-6810); 66: Photo courtesy Museo de Aguascalientes, Conaculta–INAH; 68, 99, 222, 225, 226, 227, 228, 229, 232, 233: Photo © Museum Associates/LACMA, by Francisco Kochen; 70: Photo © Detroit Institute of Arts; 71: Photo © City College of San Francisco, California; 74: Photo by Francisco Kochen; 75, 76 right: Photo © Museu Picasso, Barcelona, by Gasull Fotografia; 76 left, 97 top: Photo © UNAM/dGPU/National School of Plastic Arts/Maestro. José Luis Aguirre Guevara; 77, 96: Photo © UNAM/dGPU/National School of Plastic Arts/MSc. Sergio Carlos Rey; 79, 111: Photo courtesy LBJ Library Photo, by Lauren Gerson; 81: Photo © RMN-Grand Palais/Art Resource, NY, by Daniel Arnaudet; back cover (detail), 82: Photo: Fernando Velasco Mora. Museo Arqueológico Nacional, Spain (N.I. 38426); back cover (detail), 83, 138 right, 173: Photo © RMN-Grand Palais/Art Resource, NY, by René-Gabriel Ojéda; 84 left: Photo © Cleveland Museum of Art/Bridgeman Images; 88, 92, 193, 218, 220, 224, 253 right: Photo © Museum Associates/LACMA, by Javier Hinojosa; 90: Photo © Evgeny Zhivago; 94: Photo credit: Detroit Institute of Arts, USA/Bridgeman Images; 97 bottom: Photo © Museu Picasso, Barcelona; 103: Photo © Solomon R. Guggenheim Foundation/Art Resource, NY, by Kristopher McKay; back cover (detail), 105, 126, 198, 203 bottom, 253 left, 280: Photo courtesy The Metropolitan Museum of Art; 106: Photo credit: Kunstmuseum, Basel, Switzerland/De Agostini Picture Library/Bridgeman Images; 107: Photo © Modern Art International Foundation; 108: Photo © Art Institute of Chicago; 109: Photo credit: Museo de Arte Alvar, Mexico City, Mexico/Index, Barcelona/Bridgeman Images; 112, 118, 185, 186, 257 right: Photo © Museo Nacional de Antropología; 113: Photo © Centro Cultural Rosacruz Quetzalcóatl, A.C.; 116, 121, 294: Photo © RMN-Grand Palais/Art Resource, NY, by Jean-Gilles Berizzi; 119: Photo courtesy Fresno Museum of Art, by Randy Vaughn-Dotta; 120, 276: Photo © Gianni Dagli Orti/The Art Archive at Art Resource, NY; 125: Photo credit: Musée Picasso, Paris, France/Peter Willi/Bridgeman Images; back cover (detail), 127, 252: Photo © Nader Latin American Art Museum; 132: Photo © Mildred Lane Kemper Art Museum; 134: Photo credit: Visual Arts Library/Art Resource, NY; 137 left, 273: Digital photo © Diego Rivera and Frida Kahlo Archive, Mexico City; 137 right: Photo © FABA Photo: Marc Domage; 138 left, 141 left: Image © The Metropolitan Museum of Art/Art Resource, NY; 140: Photo © Pinacoteca Giovanni e Marella Agnelli, Turin, Italy; 141 middle: Photo © Phillips Collection, Washington, DC; 142, 261: Photo © Fundación Televisa Collection and Archive; 143: Photo: Snark/Art Resource, NY; 147 right: © Alexandre Zinoviev, photo courtesy of Sotheby's; 24, 153: Photo © Bridgeman-Giraudon/Art Resource, NY; 155: Photo © Meadows Museum, by Michael Bodycomb; 157: Photo by WH Horne Company, digital photo by Interim Archives/Getty Images; 160: Photo © Victoria and Albert Museum, London; 161: Photo courtesy dioscorides.ucm.es via Wikimedia Commons; 163: Photo © RMN-Grand Palais/Art Resource, NY, by Thierry Le Mage; 165, 169: Photo © RMN-Grand Palais/Art Resource, NY, by Franck Raux; 168, 201 right: Photo © Fine Arts Museums of San Francisco; 174, 214, 215: Photo © Christie's Images/Bridgeman Images; 175: Photograph by Ellen Page Wilson, courtesy Pace Gallery; 179 left: © Dora Maar Estate/Artists Rights Society (ARS), New York/ADAGP, Paris. Photo © CNAC/MNAM/Dist. RMN-Grand Palais/Art Resource, NY; 170 right: © Calder Foundation, New York/Artists Rights Society (ARS), New York. Photo © Baranger–RMN, Ministère de la Culture/Médiathèque du Patrimoine, Dist. RMN-Grand Palais/Art Resource, NY; 180: Photo Credit: Getty Images/Stringer; 181 left: © James de la Vega. Photo courtesy CUNY/student projects/2005; 181 right: © Ron English, photo courtesy of the artist; 189 top, 270 right: Photo credit: Museo Casa Diego Rivera (INBA), Guanajuato, Mexico/Index/Bridgeman Images; 199, 200 left, 201 left, 202 right: Photography © Museum of Fine Arts, Boston. All Rights Reserved; 201 right: Digital image © 2009 J. Paul Getty Trust; 219: Photo © San Diego Museum of Art; 223, 254, 257 left: Photo © Rafael Doniz; 234: Photo © Javier Hinajosa; 238: Photo credit: Harry Ransom Center, The University of Texas at Austin; 239 right: © André Lhote Estate; 242: Photo © Mary-Anne Martin Fine Art; 244, 245: Photo credit: Schalkwijk/Art Resource, NY; 247: © Anita Brenner Estate; 260: Photo courtesy Lilly Library, Indiana University, Bloomington, Indiana; 262: Photo © Alejandro Linares Garcia; 265: Photo by Prayitno, Los Angeles; 268, 269, 270 top: Drawing by Linda Schele © David Schele; 270 left: Photo © Bettmann/CORBIS; 274: Photo by Luidger; 277 left: Photo by Pedro Feria; 278: Photo courtesy Excélsior/Plural, 283: Art © Estate of Stuart Davis/Licensed by VAGA, New York, NY. Photo © Norton Museum of Art, by Jacek Gancarz

CONTRIBUTORS

ÉMILIE BOUVARD is a heritage curator and officer for cultural development and digital technologies at the Musée National Picasso in Paris.

LILLY CASILLAS is a curatorial assistant at the Los Angeles County Museum of Art. She holds her MA in curatorial practice from Central Saint Martins and her BA in art history from the University of California–Berkeley. She specializes in modern and contemporary art, focusing on Latin America.

JUAN RAFAEL CORONEL RIVERA is a poet, fiction writer, and photographer, as well as critic and art historian. He has written or contributed to 114 books and catalogues.

MICHAEL GOVAN is CEO and Wallis Annenberg Director of the Los Angeles County Museum of Art. At LACMA, he has pursued his vision of contemporary artists and architects interacting with the museum's historic collections. He was previously president and director of Dia Art Foundation and deputy director of the Solomon R. Guggenheim Museum.

MICHELE GREET is an associate professor of modern Latin American and European art at George Mason University and director of the Art History program. Her book *Transatlantic Encounters: Latin American Artists in Paris between the Wars, 1918–1939* is forthcoming from Yale University Press. She is also the author of *Beyond National Identity: Pictorial Indigenism as a Modernist Strategy in Andean Art, 1920–1960* (2009).

PATRICIA LEIGHTEN is a professor emerita of art history and visual studies at Duke University. She is the author of *Re-Ordering the Universe: Picasso and Anarchism, 1897–1914* (1989) and *The Liberation of Painting: Modernism and Anarchism in Avant-Guerre Paris* (2013), and the coauthor of *Cubism and Culture* (2001) and *A Cubism Reader: Documents and Criticism, 1906–1914* (2008). Her current project is on photography, modernism, and anarchism.

DIANA MAGALONI is the director of the Art of the Ancient Americas program at the Los Angeles County Museum of Art, where she is also a deputy director. She was previously director of Mexico's Museo Nacional de Antropología and is a professor of art history at the Institute of Aesthetic Research at the National Autonomous University of Mexico (UNAM). She is the author of *The Colors of the New World: Artists, Materials, and the Creation of the Florentine Codex* (2014).

CAMILLE MATHIEU is a visiting assistant professor of art history and visual studies at the University of Manchester.

ITZEL A. RODRÍGUEZ MORTELLARO is an art historian with the Faculty of Philosophy and Letters at the National Autonomous University of Mexico (UNAM). Her research and writing focuses on modern art and cultural history in Mexico during the first half of the twentieth century.

JAMES OLES divides his time between Wellesley College, where he is a senior lecturer in art, and Mexico City, where he works as an independent curator. He is also adjunct curator of Latin American art at Wellesley's Davis Museum. His most recent book is the comprehensive survey *Art and Architecture in Mexico* (2013).

JENNIFER STAGER is a writer, curator, and art historian based in San Francisco.

LOS ANGELES COUNTY MUSEUM OF ART BOARD OF TRUSTEES, 2015–16

LOS ANGELES COUNTY BOARD OF SUPERVISORS, 2015–16

This exhibition is sponsored by Christie's.

Support is provided by The Kenneth T. and Eileen L. Norris Foundation with additional funding from the Robert Lehman Foundation.

This exhibition is supported by an indemnity from the Federal Council on the Arts and Humanities.

The publication is supported in part by The Ahmanson Foundation and The Andrew W. Mellon Foundation.

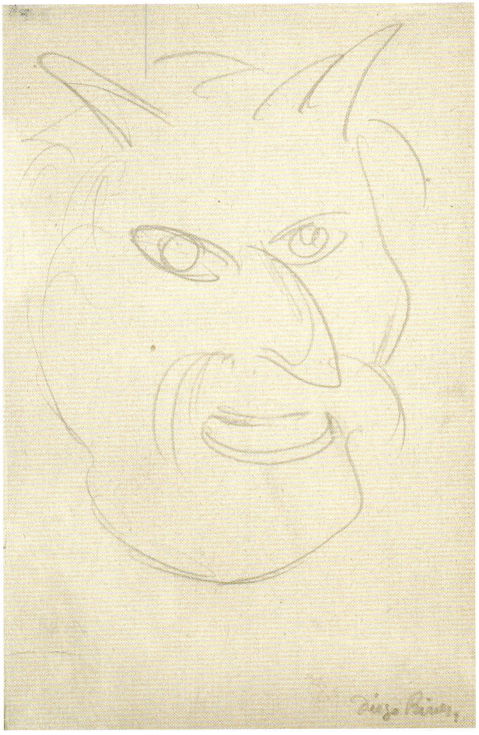

EXHIBITION ITINERARY
Los Angeles County Museum of Art
December 4, 2016–April 30, 2017

Museo del Palacio de Bellas Artes, Mexico City
May 31–September 10, 2017

PUBLISHED IN CONJUNCTION WITH THE EXHIBITION

PICASSO & RIVERA: CONVERSATIONS ACROSS TIME

ORGANIZED BY THE LOS ANGELES COUNTY MUSEUM OF ART AND THE MUSEO DEL PALACIO DE BELLAS ARTES.

Copublished by Los Angeles County Museum of Art and DelMonico Books, an imprint of Prestel Publishing

Los Angeles County Museum of Art
5905 Wilshire Boulevard
Los Angeles, California 90036
lacma.org

Prestel, a member of Verlagsgruppe Random House GmbH
Prestel Verlag
Neumarkter Strasse 28
81673 Munich

Prestel Publishing Ltd.
14–17 Wells Street
London W1T 3PD

Prestel Publishing
900 Broadway, Suite 603
New York, NY 10003
prestel.com

PICASSO & RIVERA: CONVERSATIONS ACROSS TIME
PUBLISHER Lisa Gabrielle Mark
SENIOR EDITOR Sara Cody
PHOTO EDITOR Piper Severance
DESIGNERS Lorraine Wild and Xiaoqing Wang for Green Dragon Office
INDEXER Kathleen Preciado
PRODUCTION MANAGER Karen Farquhar for Prestel
COLOR SEPARATIONS Echelon Color, Santa Monica, California

ISBN: 978-3-7913-5555-9

ABOVE Diego Rivera, *Untitled (Head of Devil)*, 1923–25
BACK COVER (CLOCKWISE) Pablo Picasso, *Self-Portrait* (detail), 1906; *Man Attacked by Lion* (detail), Iberian, Osuna, 6th–5th century BCE; Diego Rivera, *Frida's Friend* (detail), 1931; *Seated Standard Bearer* (detail), Mexico, Aztec, Veracruz, 1250–1521

Printed and bound in China

Library of Congress Cataloging-in-Publication Data

Names: Magaloni Kerpel, Diana. | Govan, Michael. | Los Angeles County Museum of Art, organizer, host institution. | Museo del Palacio de Bellas Artes (Mexico), organizer, host institution.
Title: Picasso and Rivera : conversations across time / Curated by Juan Rafael Coronel Rivera, Michael Govan, Diana Magaloni, James Oles, and Jennifer Stager ; with assistance by Lilly Casillas ; edited by Diana Magaloni and Michael Govan ; with contributions by Émilie Bouvard, Lilly Casillas, Juan Rafael Coronel Rivera, Michael Govan, Michele Greet, Patricia Leighten, Diana Magaloni, Camille Mathieu, Itzel A. Rodríguez Mortellaro, James Oles, and Jennifer Stager.
Description: Los Angeles : Los Angeles County Museum of Art : DelMonico Books/Prestel, 2016. | Includes bibliographical references.
Identifiers: LCCN 2016030800 | ISBN 9783791355559 (hardback)
Subjects: LCSH: Picasso, Pablo, 1881-1973—Exhibitions. | Rivera, Diego, 1886-1957—Exhibitions. | BISAC: ART / Individual Artists / Monographs. | ART / Collections, Catalogs, Exhibitions / Group Shows.
Classification: LCC N6853.P5 A4 2016 | DDC 709.2/2--dc23
LC record available at https://lccn.loc.gov/2016030800